Managing Breast Cancer Risk

Managing Breast Cancer Risk

MONICA MORROW, MD
Professor of Surgery
Director, Lynn Sage Breast Center

V. CRAIG JORDAN, OBE, PhD, DSc
Diana, Princess of Wales Professor of Cancer Research
Director, Lynn Sage Breast Cancer Research Program

both of

Northwestern University
Feinberg School of Medicine
Chicago, Illinois

2003
BC Decker Inc
Hamilton • London

BC Decker Inc
P.O. Box 620, L.C.D. 1
Hamilton, Ontario L8N 3K7
Tel: 905-522-7017; 800-568-7281
Fax: 905-522-7839; 888-311-4987
E-mail: info@bcdecker.com
www.bcdecker.com

03 04 05 06/WPC/9 8 7 6 5 4 3 2 1

ISBN 1-55009-260-X

Printed in The United States of America

Sales and Distribution

United States
BC Decker Inc
P.O. Box 785
Lewiston, NY 14092-0785
Tel: 905-522-7017; 800-568-7281
Fax: 905-522-7839; 888-311-4987
E-mail: info@bcdecker.com
www.bcdecker.com

Canada
BC Decker Inc
20 Hughson Street South
P.O. Box 620, LCD 1
Hamilton, Ontario L8N 3K7
Tel: 905-522-7017; 800-568-7281
Fax: 905-522-7839; 888-311-4987
E-mail: info@bcdecker.com
www.bcdecker.com

Foreign Rights
John Scott & Company
International Publishers' Agency
P.O. Box 878
Kimberton, PA 19442
Tel: 610-827-1640
Fax: 610-827-1671
E-mail: jsco@voicenet.com

Japan
Igaku-Shoin Ltd.
Foreign Publications Department
3-24-17 Hongo
Bunkyo-ku, Tokyo, Japan 113-8719
Tel: 3 3817 5680
Fax: 3 3815 6776
E-mail: fd@igaku-shoin.co.jp

UK, Europe, Scandinavia, Middle East
Elsevier Science
Customer Service Department
Foots Cray High Street
Sidcup, Kent
DA14 5HP, UK
Tel: 44 (0) 208 308 5760
Fax: 44 (0) 181 308 5702
E-mail: cservice@harcourt.com

Singapore, Malaysia, Thailand, Philippines, Indonesia, Vietnam, Pacific Rim, Korea
Elsevier Science Asia
583 Orchard Road
#09/01, Forum
Singapore 238884
Tel: 65-737-3593
Fax: 65-753-2145

Australia, New Zealand
Elsevier Science Australia
Customer Service Department
STM Division
Locked Bag 16
St. Peters, New South Wales, 2044
Australia
Tel: 61 02 9517-8999
Fax: 61 02 9517-2249
E-mail: stmp@harcourt.com.au
www.harcourt.com.au

Mexico and Central America
ETM SA de CV
Calle de Tula 59
Colonia Condesa
06140 Mexico DF, Mexico
Tel: 52-5-5553-6657
Fax: 52-5-5211-8468
E-mail: editoresdetextosmex@prodigy.net.mx

Argentina
CLM (Cuspide Libros Medicos)
Av. Córdoba 2067 - (1120)
Buenos Aires, Argentina
Tel: (5411) 4961-0042/(5411) 4964-0848
Fax: (5411) 4963-7988
E-mail: clm@cuspide.com

Brazil
Tecmedd
Av. Maurílio Biagi, 2850
City Ribeirão Preto – SP – CEP: 14021-000
Tel: 0800 992236
Fax: (16) 3993-9000
E-mail: tecmedd@tecmedd.com.br

To our parents, Maxine and J. Robert Morrow, and Cynthia Jordan,
for teaching us what is important in life

PREFACE

Ten years ago there was no need for this book. The emphasis in cancer was on early treatment, and prophylactic mastectomy was the only option to reduce risk for the high-risk woman. In the past decade, breast cancer genetics has become a reality, tamoxifen is clinically available to reduce breast cancer risk, and risk assessment is an active area of clinical research. Breast cancer risk assessment and management is a true multidisciplinary endeavor. It requires an understanding of epidemiology, genetics, imaging, and drugs traditionally associated with cancer treatment, as well as surgery and psychology. Even in major cancer centers, multidisciplinary teams devoted to risk management are uncommon. The purpose of this book is to bring together a multidisciplinary group of experts to address breast cancer risk in a clinically meaningful way. Chapters providing detailed information on individual risk factors are accompanied by a discussion of models that integrate multiple factors for a more complete assessment of risk. Traditional strategies for risk management, including surveillance and prophylactic surgery, are reviewed, and the data on newer techniques such as ductal lavage and screening with magnetic resonance are presented. The rationale for chemoprevention with selective estrogen receptor modulators (SERMs) is discussed, and the evidence for tamoxifen as a chemopreventive is updated. The potential for chemoprevention with newer SERMs and the aromatase inhibitors is reviewed. Finally, the critical (and often ignored) areas of quality of life and symptom management are addressed.

This book is a single source for information needed by primary care physicians, nurses, and gynecologists, as well as oncologic specialists who deal with women who are concerned about breast cancer.

Monica Morrow, MD and V. Craig Jordan, OBE, PhD, DSc
July 2003

CONTENTS

Section One: Evaluation of Risk

Section Two: Risk Management Strategies

Surveillance

Chemoprevention

Surgical Prevention

Section Three: Practical Management Guidelines

Acknowledgments

The authors acknowledge the invaluable assistance of Burton Korman, who helped make this book a reality.

CONTRIBUTORS

LESLIE BERNSTEIN, PhD
Professor and AFLAC Inc.,
Chair in Cancer Research
Preventive Medicine
Keck School of Medicine
University of Southern California
Los Angeles, California

JOSEPH P. CONSTANTINO, DrPH
Professor, Biostatistics
Graduate School of Public Health
Pittsburgh, Pennsylvania

AARATI DIDWANIA, MD
Clinical Instructor, Internal Medicine
Feinberg School of Medicine
Northwestern University
Chicago, Illinois

NEIL A. FINE, MD, FACS
Assistant Professor, Plastic Surgery
Feinberg School of Medicine
Northwestern University
Chicago, Illinois

PATRICIA A. GANZ, MD
Professor, Hematology / Oncology
Director, Cancer Prevention and Control Research
UCLA Schools of Medicine and Public Health
Jonsson Comprehensive Cancer Center at UCLA
Los Angeles, California

SUSAN M. GAPSTUR, PhD, MPH
Associate Professor, Preventive Medicine
Feinberg School of Medicine
Northwestern University
Chicago, Illinois

MEHRA GOLSHAN, MD
Fellow, Breast Surgery
Feinberg School of Medicine
Northwestern University
Chicago, Illinois

PAUL E. GOSS, MD, PhD, FRCPC, FRCP (UK)
Professor, Medicine
Director, Breast Cancer Prevention Program
Princess Margaret Hospital
University Health Network
University of Toronto
Toronto, Ontario

WILLIAM J. GRADISHAR, MD, FACP
Associate Professor, Medicine
Director, Breast Medicine Oncology
Feinberg School of Medicine
Northwestern University
Chicago, Illinois

R. EDWARD HENDRICK, PhD, FACR
Research Professor, Radiology
Director, Breast Imaging Research
Lynn Sage Breast Center
Feinberg School of Medicine
Northwestern University
Chicago, Illinois

CLAUDINE ISAACS, MD, FRCPC
Associate Professor of Medicine and Oncology
Georgetown University Medical Center
Washington, District of Columbia

V. CRAIG JORDAN, OBE, PhD, DSc
Diana, Princess of Wales Professor of Cancer Research
Director, Lynn Sage Breast Cancer Research Program
Feinberg School of Medicine
Northwestern University
Chicago, Illinois

SEEMA A. KHAN, MD
Associate Professor, Surgery
Feinberg School of Medicine
Northwestern University
Chicago, Illinois

STEPHANIE R. LAND, PhD
Research Assistant Professor, Biostatistics
University of Pittsburgh
Pittsburgh, Pennsylvania

CHARLES LOPRINZI, MD
Professor and Chair, Medical Oncology
Mayo Clinic
Rochester, Minnesota

ELLEN B. MENDELSON, MD, FACR
Professor, Radiology
Director, Breast Imaging
Lynn Sage Breast Center
Feinberg School of Medicine
Northwestern University
Chicago, Illinois

MONICA MORROW, MD
Professor, Surgery
Director, Lynn Sage Breast Center
Feinberg School of Medicine
Northwestern University
Chicago, Illinois

FAINA NAKHLIS, MD
Fellow, Breast Surgery
Feinberg School of Medicine
Northwestern University
Chicago, Illinois

RUTH M. O'REGAN, MD
Assistant Professor, Medicine
Feinberg School of Medicine
Northwestern University
Chicago, Illinois

JEAN R. PAQUELET, MD, FACR
Director, Breast Imaging
Department of Radiology
Grant Medical Center
Columbus, Ohio

BETH N. PESHKIN, MS, CGC
Senior Certified Genetic Counselor
Research Assistant Professor of Oncology and Medicine
Georgetown University Medical Center
Washington, District of Columbia

APARNA PRIYANATH, MD, MPH
Clinical Instructor, Internal Medicine
Feinberg School of Medicine
Northwestern University
Chicago, Illinois

ROBERT M. SALTZMANN, BA
Feinberg School of Medicine
Northwestern University
Chicago, Illinois

MARC SCHWARTZ, PhD
Associate Professor of Oncology
Co-Director, Cancer Control
Lombardi Cancer Center
Georgetown University Medical Center
Washington, District of Columbia

TAIT D. SHANAFELT, MD
Clinical Instructor, Oncology
Mayo Clinic
Rochester, Minnesota

KATHRIN STRASSER-WEIPPL, MD
Medical Oncology
Wilhelminen Hospital
Vienna, Austria

VALERIE L. STARADUB, MD
Assistant Professor, Surgical Oncology
Lynn Sage Breast Center
Feinberg School of Medicine
Northwestern University
Chicago, Illinois

JULIA TCHOU, MD, PhD
Fellow, Breast Surgery
Lynn Sage Breast Center
Feinberg School of Medicine
Northwestern University
Chicago, Illinois

D. LAWRENCE WICKERHAM, MD
Associate Professor, Human Oncology
Associate Chairman, NSABP
Drexal University School of Medicine
Allegheny General Hospital
Pittsburgh, Pennsylvania

ELIZABETH L. WILEY, MD
Associate Professor, Surgical Pathology
Feinberg School of Medicine
Northwestern University
Chicago, Illinois

Evaluation
of Risk

CHAPTER 1

OVERVIEW OF CLINICAL RISK ASSESSMENT

Julia Tchou, MD, PhD
Monica Morrow, MD

Risk factors for breast cancer have traditionally been categorized according to their magnitude. Risks are reported as relative risks or odds ratios depending on whether the data came from prospective cohort or retrospective case-control studies, respectively.[1] When the relative risk or odds ratio of a specific characteristic defined as a risk factor is greater than 1.0, for instance 1.7, a group of women with the specific characteristic is 1.7 times more likely to develop breast cancer than a group of women who do not have the specific risk factor. Conversely, when the relative risk is less than 1.0, for instance 0.5, then a group of women who have the specific characteristic will be half as likely to develop breast cancer as a group of women who do not have the characteristic. For the general public, the concept of relative risk is abstract, because it requires an understanding of the magnitude of the absolute risk of developing breast cancer in women with and without the specific risk factor. A woman is much more interested in knowing whether she is going to have breast cancer and the actual chance of developing breast cancer.[2] A more concrete and meaningful way to explain the risk of developing breast cancer is to tell the woman about her chances of developing breast cancer within a finite period of time, for example, her percent chances of developing breast cancer in the next 10 years. However, most epidemiologic studies focus on a single risk factor of interest and fail to consider the effects of various combinations of risk factors that may both increase and decrease risk and which characterize the risk profiles of most women.

Increasing age and female gender are the most common breast cancer risk factors. A large number of other factors that increase risk have been described. These are discussed in detail in Chapters 2 through 5 and will be briefly reviewed here.

The mounting evidence to support tamoxifen as a chemoprevention agent for breast cancer has emphasized the need to find better ways of assessing a woman's risk of developing breast cancer.[3,4] The available risk assessment tools, such as the Gail Model[5] used in the National Surgical Adjuvant Breast and Bowel Project (NSABP) P-1 trial and the model proposed by Claus and colleagues,[6] will be reviewed with a focus on the applicability of these models in the individual patient. The Gail Model is a mathematical model which incorporates several risk factors to give a woman an absolute risk of developing breast cancer in the next 5 years and in her lifetime.[5] The Claus Model incorporates the patient's age and the number of affected first-degree and second-degree relatives together with the age of breast cancer diagnosis in the affected relatives to derive the absolute risk of developing breast cancer.

Finally, an approach to a high-risk patient in the clinical setting will be discussed with the emphasis on how to assimilate available risk assessment data for the individual patient. The roles of surveillance and chemoprevention will also be discussed.

IDENTIFICATION OF THE WOMAN AT RISK

It is estimated that 212,600 newly diagnosed breast cancers will occur in the year 2003 in the United States.[7] Breast cancer, which accounts for 32% of all new cancer cases, is the most common cancer

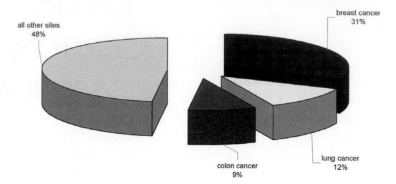

Figure 1-1 Leading causes of cancer in women in the United States in 1999. The incidence of newly diagnosed cancers in women in 1999 as reported by the Surveillance, Epidemiology and End Results (SEER) program is depicted in the pie chart. Breast cancer is the most commonly diagnosed cancer in women, comprising 31% of all new cancer cases.

diagnosed in women, followed by lung cancer (12%) and colon cancer (9%) (Figure 1-1).

Although breast cancer is the most commonly diagnosed cancer in women, it is not the number one cause of cancer death. As shown in Figure 1-2, lung cancer is the most common cause of cancer death, accounting for 65,700 deaths or 6% of deaths from all causes. Breast cancer, the second leading cause of cancer death in women, accounted for 39,600 deaths or 3% of deaths from all causes in 1999.

Data from the Surveillance, Epidemiology and End Results (SEER) program have shown that breast cancer incidence has been increasing since the early 1980s. The lifetime risk (to age 90) of being diagnosed with invasive breast cancer is 13.33%, better known to the public as the "one in

eight" statistic.[8] This astounding statistical fact, however, deserves clarification. As Phillips and colleagues have noted, the "one in eight" chance refers to the cumulative lifetime risk of breast cancer if a woman lives past the age of 85.[8] However, a more practical way of interpreting the lifetime risk is by assessing the absolute risk of developing breast cancer in 10-, 20-, and 30-year intervals as depicted in Table 1-1. The absolute risk of a woman being diagnosed with breast cancer in the next 10, 20, or even 30 years never reaches the astounding number of one in eight (see Table 1-1). However, women are increasingly aware of the one in eight lifetime risk of developing breast cancer, and more and more women will present to healthcare professionals in either the primary or specialty care setting to have their risk assessed.

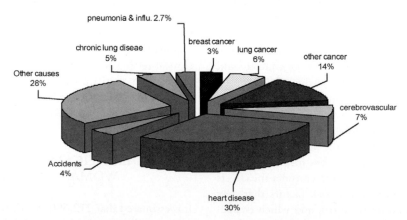

Figure 1-2 Leading causes of death in women in the United States in 1999. As reported by the SEER, the major known cause of death in women is heart disease (30%) followed by cancer other than breast or lung (14%). Lung cancer (6%) surpasses breast cancer (3%) in the cause of death in women by 3%.

TABLE 1-1 Absolute Risk of Being Diagnosed with Invasive Breast Cancer,
Given Cancer Free at Current Age

Current Age (years)	+10 yrs (%)	+20 yrs (%)	+30 yrs (%)	Eventually (%)*
0	0	0	0.05 (1 in 2,000)	13.33
10	0	0.05 (1 in 2,000)	0.44 (1 in 227)	13.43
20	0.05 (1 in 2,000)	0.44 (1 in 227)	1.89 (1 in 53)	13.47
30	0.40 (1 in 250)	1.85 (1 in 54)	4.56 (1 in 22)	13.48
40	1.47 (1 in 68)	4.21 (1 in 24)	7.53 (1 in 13)	13.24
50	2.84 (1 in 35)	6.25 (1 in 15)	9.68 (1 in 10)	12.16
60	3.67 (1 in 27)	7.35 (1 in 14)	9.54 (1 in 10)	10.00

*Lifetime risk of being diagnosed with invasive breast cancer = 13.33% or 1 in 7.5.
Lifetime risk of dying of breast cancer = 3.12%.

WHAT DEFINES HIGH RISK?

Epidemiologic studies have identified multiple characteristics, both intrinsic and extrinsic, that are associated with increased risk of breast cancer development. Intrinsic risk factors include endogenous hormonal factors, familial and genetic predisposition, and benign breast lesions confirmed pathologically to confer high risk.[9] Extrinsic risk factors include exogenous hormonal factors, geographic location, environmental exposure, and diet. The risk factors that confer relative risks > 4 are arbitrarily categorized as risk factors associated with high risk of developing breast cancer. Those risk factors with relative risks 2 through 4 and < 2 are those that confer moderately and slightly increased risk of developing breast cancer, respectively. These risk factors are tabulated in their order of magnitude in Table 1-2. However, it is important to recognize that although risk factors are characterized as high and low, there is no consensus on what level of risk in an individual is sufficient to classify her as high risk. There is also no consensus on what level of risk is sufficient to warrant increased surveillance or consideration of chemoprevention or prophylactic surgery.

RISK FACTORS ASSOCIATED WITH SLIGHTLY INCREASED RISKS OF DEVELOPING BREAST CANCER

Early Menarche, Late Menopause, and Nulliparity

Most of the risk factors listed in Table 1-2 with a relative risk of less than 2 are related to the level of endogenous hormone exposure in various settings. Breast cancer is clearly related to endogenous hormones, and numerous studies have linked breast

TABLE 1-2 Magnitude of Known Breast Cancer Risk Factors

Relative Risk < 2	Relative Risk 2–4	Relative Risk > 4
Early menarche	One 1st degree relative with breast cancer	Two 1st degree relatives with breast cancer
Late menopause	Radiation exposure	Gene mutations
Nulliparity	Prior breast cancer	Lobular carcinoma in situ
Age > 35 first birth	Dense breast	Ductal carcinoma in situ
Hormone replacement		Atypical hyperplasia
Obesity		
Alcohol use		
Proliferative benign breast disease		

cancer to the age at menarche, menopause, and first pregnancy. The absolute risk of being diagnosed with breast cancer increases with age and is higher in postmenopausal than premenopausal women (see Table 1-1). The lifetime risk of developing breast cancer, however, decreases from 13.33% to 10% after age 60 (see Table 1-1), suggesting that ovarian activity plays a major part in the causation of breast cancer.[10] Further support for the promotional role of estrogen in breast cancer development comes from the observations that early menarche,[11] late menopause,[12] nulliparity, and late age at first birth[13] all increase the risk of breast cancer development. An increased number of ovulatory cycles is suggested to be the common mechanism of increased risk.

Although the hormonal risk factors described in the preceding paragraph are well established, others are more speculative. Intrauterine exposure to high levels of estrogen has been suggested to increase risk, but further studies are needed to confirm this observation.[14] Abortion, whether spontaneous or induced, has been reported by some authors to increase risk,[15,16] whereas other studies have found no relationship between abortion and breast cancer risk.[17,18] Studies of the effect of lactation on breast cancer risk have also been inconclusive,[19,20] but recent studies have suggested that a long duration of lactation reduces breast cancer risk in premenopausal women.[21] Physical activity in adolescence is reported to decrease risk, perhaps due to a higher rate of anovulatory cycles,[22,23] but an increased level of physical activity later in life has not been shown to reduce breast cancer risk.[24]

Hormone Replacement

Although observational data suggested a putative benefit of hormone replacement therapy (HRT) in protecting against coronary heart disease in postmenopausal women, the results of a recent randomized control trial coordinated by the Women's Health Initiative show unequivocally that HRT, in the form of estrogen plus progestin, confers no cardiovascular protection for postmenopausal women.[25] The trial was stopped early after a mean follow-up of 5.2 years because the global index statistics indicated risks exceeding benefits. The number of adverse effects, including the number of invasive breast cancers, had exceeded the stopping boundary before the proposed follow-up of 8.5

years. The relative risk of postmenopausal women taking estrogen and progestin versus placebo in developing breast cancer was 1.26 (95% confidence interval [CI] 1.00–1.59). Hormonal risk factors are reviewed in detail in Chapter 2.

Obesity

Postmenopausal obesity has also been shown to increase risk, perhaps due to increased peripheral estrogen production.[26] This relationship between weight and risk is not observed in premenopausal women. In fact, some studies have reported an inverse relationship between weight and risk at younger ages.[27]

Alcohol Use

Alcohol consumption has been linked to increased risk of breast cancer. A metaanalysis of 12 case control studies demonstrated a relative risk of 1.4 for each 24 grams of alcohol consumed daily.[28] Defining a relationship between the duration of alcohol consumption and breast cancer risk is more difficult, with conflicting data on the importance of drinking early in life.[29,30]

Proliferative Benign Breast Disease

The College of American Pathologists has divided benign breast disease into three categories as shown in Table 1-3.[31] Nonproliferative lesions, which are associated with no increase in risk, accounted for 85% of the lesions in Dupont and Page's series of 10,542 women who had a median follow-up of 17 years.[32] Atypical lesions constitute only 4% of clinical lesions, but make up 12 to 17% of mammographic abnormalities.[33,34]

RISK FACTORS ASSOCIATED WITH A MODERATELY INCREASED RELATIVE RISK OF DEVELOPING BREAST CANCER

One First-Degree Relative With Breast Cancer

The relative risk of a woman with one first-degree relative diagnosed with breast cancer is estimated to be between 2.6 and 2.8 depending on the parity and the age of first birth of the woman.[5] The Claus Model for estimating risk for women with a significant family history in first- and second-degree relatives and the influence of family history on risk in

TABLE 1-3 Benign Breast Disease Categorized by Relative Risks

No Increased Risk	Slightly Increased Risk (1.5 to 2 times)	Moderately Increased Risk (5 times)
Adenosis, sclerosing or florid	Hyperplasia, moderate or florid, solid or papillary	Atypical hyperplasia (borderline lesion) Ductal Lobular
Apocrine metaplasia	Papilloma with fibrovascular core	
Cysts, macro and/or micro		
Duct ectasia		
Fibroadenoma		
Fibrosis		
Hyperplasia, mild		
Mastitis (inflammation)		
Periductal mastitis		
Squamous metaplasia		

women with a diagnosis of proliferative breast lesion, for example, atypical hyperplasia or lobular carcinoma in situ, is discussed in later sections.[6]

Radiation Exposure

Exposure to ionizing radiation, whether secondary to nuclear explosion or to medical procedures, has been clearly demonstrated to increase breast cancer risk.[35–38] The level of risk varies with the age at exposure with a minimal increase in risk observed for exposures in women older than 40 years.

Prior Breast Cancer

The risk of subsequent contralateral breast carcinomas in a woman with unilateral carcinoma had been reported to range from 0.53 to 0.80% per year.[39–41]

Most of these data were obtained from retrospective studies. One such study reviewed records from 644 patients who were treated at Memorial Sloan-Kettering Cancer Center from 1964 through 1970 and reported subsequent contralateral breast cancer in a 20-year follow-up.[41] These 644 patients had either Stage I or Stage II primary breast carcinoma. Women with concurrent contralateral invasive cancer were excluded, whereas those with concurrent contralateral in situ carcinoma were included. The contralateral carcinomas were characterized by size, histologic type, and lymph node involvement.

Overall, the risk of contralateral breast cancer appears to be unaffected by the tumor pathology, that is, infiltrating ductal, lobular, or mixed carcinoma,[42] and remains essentially constant throughout a 20-year follow-up period.[41] However, the rate of development of contralateral carcinoma appears to be inversely related to age at diagnosis of ipsilateral carcinoma. There was no significant difference in the rate of development of contralateral breast cancer between patients who had adjuvant chemotherapy or radiation and those who did not. The authors concluded that surveillance of the contralateral breast must continue throughout the patient's lifetime.

Ipsilateral breast radiation in breast-conserving therapy has been investigated as a possible carcinogen for the contralateral breast. Zucali and colleagues showed that scattered radiation from breast irradiation as part of breast-conserving therapy is not carcinogenic to the contralateral breast.[43] This is confirmed by the 20-year follow-up data from two prospective randomized trials, the NSABP B-06 and Milan-1, that compared the rate of contralateral breast cancer occurrence in patients after breast-conserving surgery with or without radiation and patients after radical or modified radical mastectomy.[44,45]

In the Milan study, of the 349 women who were randomized to the radical mastectomy group, 34 developed contralateral breast cancer, whereas 29 out of 352 women who were randomized to quadrantectomy with axillary node dissection and ipsilateral breast radiation developed contralateral breast cancer. The crude 20-year cumulative rate was 9.7% and 8.2%, respectively. The adjusted rate was 0.66% per woman-year.[45] In the NSABP B-06 study, the crude 20-year cumulative rate of contralateral breast cancer was 8.5%, 9.4%, and 8.8% after modified radical mastectomy, lumpectomy with axillary node dissection and radiation, or lumpectomy with axillary node dissection alone.

In summary, the annual risk of developing contralateral breast cancer in a woman with ipsilateral breast cancer ranges from 0.6 to 0.8% per year, or about 6 to 8% in 10 years. This translates to about a 2- or 4-fold increase in relative risk for an average 50- or 40-year-old woman, respectively.[7]

Breast Density

The mammographic appearance of breast tissues can vary depending on the amount of adipose tissue relative to connective and epithelial tissue in the breast. Fat is radiolucent and, therefore, appears less dense on mammograms. However, when the parenchyma of the breast is comprised mainly of fibrous and/or ductal tissue, the mammogram of the breast will appear dense.[46] Wolfe was the first to describe a correlation of breast cancer risk to breast density.[47,48] Wolfe described and classified mammograms into four parenchymal patterns: N1, P1, P2, and DY.[47] N1 describes the appearance of breast parenchyma composed primarily of fat. P1 describes the mammographic appearance of a breast that is mainly fat but has up to 25% volume of prominent ducts, whereas P2 is a parenchyma that is composed of greater than 25% volume of prominent ducts. DY, or dysplasia, is used to describe parenchyma that appears homogeneously dense. Wolfe reported in his first prospective cohort study that women with the DY pattern were 37 times more likely to develop breast cancer than women with the N1 pattern.[47,48] When women with the P2 and DY patterns (high-risk group) were compared to women with the N1 and P1 (low-risk group), Wolfe noted a 7- to 9-fold increase in risk in women with the high-risk pattern.

There have been many reports supporting Wolfe's finding of an increase in risk in women with denser breasts, but the majority reported relative risks or odds ratios in the 2 through 4 range.

Most of the earlier studies were prospective cohort studies that used Wolfe's classification, which is qualitative and prone to reviewer's bias. When the concordance between interobserver and intraobserver classification of mammograms was examined, the concordance was reported to range from 52 to 84%.[49–51] The subjective aspect of Wolfe's classificiation has led to more objective evaluations of breast density using the planimeter[52–54] or the digitized mammogram.[55]

The large differences in relative risk reported in different studies are partially attributable to differences in study design. One source of variation is differences in the study population, that is, women from screening populations who are mainly asymptomatic versus women from a referred population who often have specific breast symptoms. Another factor is whether the cancer cases are prevalent or incident. Prevalent cases are cancer cases diagnosed at the time of the initial screening mammogram, whereas incident cases refer to cancer cases that are diagnosed at least 6 months after a negative screening mammogram.

In Wolfe's studies,[47,48] the women were mainly from a screening population, whereas in Egan and Mosteller's study,[56] which showed no difference in risk between Wolfe's high-risk and low-risk patterns, the population consisted of a cohort of women who were all referred due to breast symptoms. The differences between screened and referred populations were addressed in the case-control study by Boyd and colleagues.[50] In this study, two control groups were used. The first control group was selected from a screening population and the second from women who were referred to mammography due to the presence of a breast complaint. An increase in breast cancer risk on the basis of density was not observed when symptomatic women were used as a control group.

When prevalent cases were considered, Egan and Mosteller reported no difference in risk between the high-density and low-density groups.[56] However, when only incident cases were considered in their study, there was a 3.7-fold increase in relative risk for women who had P2 and DY mammograms. An increase in breast cancer risk in incident, but not in prevalent, cases was observed in other studies.[57–60] One reason for the difference in the significance of density between prevalent and incident cases is that breast cancers are harder to diagnose in dense breasts, and therefore more cancers are diagnosed in subsequent screenings in women with dense breasts, resulting in a higher number of incident breast cancer cases in this group.[46,61] The "masking" effects of dense breasts should, therefore, be minimal in case-control studies such as the one reported by Saftlas and colleagues.[51] In this study, case subjects were women who were diagnosed with unilateral breast cancer during the fifth year of screening while participating in the Breast Cancer Detection and Demonstration Project (BCDDP). The initial ipsilateral mammograms were compared to those of women without cancer who were matched in age, race, and length of participation in the BCDDP. The odds ratios of other risk factors such as family history, age at first birth, body weight, and history of breast biopsy were also analyzed. The age- and weight-adjusted odds ratio of women with the P2 or DY parenchymal pattern was 2.8. The odds ratios reported in this study are very similar to other well-conducted studies.[54,62-64] In the largest case-control study comparing 1,880 cases to 2,152 controls, the weight-adjusted odds ratios of women with P2 and DY parenchymal patterns were 3.2 and 2.9, respectively.[54]

In summary, a woman with dense breasts on mammogram has approximately a 2- to 4-fold increased risk of developing breast cancer. Breast density appears to be inversely associated with age and body weight.[56,59,62,63,65] The association of breast density with family history, and other risk factors such as height, age at first birth, and history of biopsy, is less clear. In the largest series reported, Byrne and colleagues were able to show an association between breast density and family history by demonstrating that there were more women diagnosed with breast cancer who have dense breasts and a positive first-degree family history compared to those who do not have a positive family history (40% vs 31%).[54] Saftlas and colleagues also observed that the presence of a positive family history in a first-degree relative further increased the odds ratio from 2.8 to 5.5 for women with dense breasts.[53] A recent study comparing mammographic density of monozygotic and dizygotic twins showed that mammographic density is heritable, because the correlation coefficient for the percentage of dense tissue for monozygotic twins was 0.61 in Australia and 0.67 in America versus 0.25 and 0.27 for dizygotic twins, respectively.[66] Further study on the ge-

netics of breast density may help elucidate more breast cancer susceptiblity genes.

RISK FACTORS ASSOCIATED WITH HIGHLY INCREASED RELATIVE RISK OF DEVELOPING BREAST CANCER

Gene Mutations

Genetic-linkage studies of large families with multiple members with a history of breast cancer or ovarian cancer or both have led to the discovery of two breast cancer susceptibility genes, BRCA1 and BRCA2, in 1994 and 1995.[67,68] The BRCA1 and BRCA2 genes reside in the long arms of chromosome 17 (17q) and 13 (13q), respectively.[67-69] Women who have BRCA1 or BRCA2 mutations have a 35 to 85% cumulative risk to age 70 of developing invasive breast cancer and a 9 to 65% cumulative lifetime risk of developing invasive epithelial ovarian cancer.[70-73] A family history of male breast cancer is strongly linked to the BRCA2 mutation. About 5 to 10% of all breast cancers are attributable to breast cancer susceptibility genes.[74] However, only about 15% of all familial breast cancers are attributable to BRCA1 and BRCA2 mutations, indicating that other breast cancer susceptibility genes may exist.[73,75] The prevalence of BRCA1 and BRCA2 mutations in the general population is unknown, but it is thought to be less than 0.12% and 0.044%, respectively.[76-79] The prevalence of three common BRCA1 and BRCA2 mutations in the Ashkenazi Jewish population, however, is reported to range from 0.1 to 2%.[70,77,78]

The incidence of germ-line mutations in BRCA1 and BRCA2 in women with early age onset of breast cancer has also been studied.[80,81] Germ-line mutations in BRCA1 were identified in 9 of 73 women (12%, 95% CI 5.8–22%) who developed breast cancer before age 32. The proportion of women with germ-line mutations in BRCA2 was significantly smaller (2.8%, 95% CI 0.4–9.6%).[81] When mutations testing was done in 39 Ashkenazi women with breast cancer diagnosed at or before age 40, 8 of 39 women (21%) harbored the 185delAG mutation. A less common mutation, 5382insC, which occurs in 0.1% of the Ashkenazi population, was found in 1 of the 39 women (2.6%). The BRCA2 mutation, 6174delT, which was found in 1.3% of the Ashkenazi population overall, was detected in 1 of 39 women (2.6%). The authors concluded that germ-line mutations in *BRCA2* contribute to fewer cases of early age onset breast cancer than mutations in *BRCA1*.

Genetic-linkage analyses of families from earlier studies suggest that almost half (45%) of all hereditary cases of breast cancer and 80 to 90% of hereditary cases of combined breast and ovarian cancer are associated with *BRCA1* mutations.[82,83] These analyses were based on selected large families with several cases of ovarian cancer. To ascertain if this reported incidence of *BRCA1* mutation is applicable in women who have a personal and family history of breast cancer commonly seen in a specialized-care setting, Couch and coworkers studied 263 such subjects.[84] Of the 169 women with breast cancer and a familial risk factor, 27 (16%) had a *BRCA1* mutation. In 45 families with members with breast and ovarian cancer, 18 (40%) carried a *BRCA1* mutation. Ten of 57 (18%) families with members with bilateral breast cancer had *BRCA1* mutations. The incidence of *BRCA1* mutations among Ashkenazi Jewish women was 26%.

In summary, *BRCA1* and *BRCA2* mutations are rare in the general population but may be found in as many as 2% of the general Ashkenazi Jewish population. About 16% of women with a diagnosis of breast cancer and a family history of breast cancer will likely carry a *BRCA1* mutation.[84] In women with early onset of breast cancer, that is, diagnosis before age 32, the incidence of *BRCA1* or *BRCA2* mutation is around 12%. However, in women with breast cancer and a family history of breast and ovarian cancers, the incidence of *BRCA1* mutation can range from 40 to 80 or 90%. Therefore, the following criteria are used at our institution for referral to breast cancer genetic counseling:

- Age of diagnosis < 40
- Male breast cancer at any age
- Any family history of breast cancer
- Family/personal history of ovarian cancer
- Bilateral or multiple primary breast cancers
- Any age of diagnosis if of Ashkenazi ancestry

Lobular Carcinoma In Situ

In 1941, Foote and Stewart described a noninvasive form of mammary carcinoma arising from the lobules and terminal ducts which they called lobular carcinoma in situ (LCIS).[85] Their initial report identified three important features of LCIS: (1)

The lesion is an incidental microscopic finding and cannot be identified clinically or by gross pathologic examination; (2) invasive cancers that develop following LCIS may be either infiltrating ductal or infiltrating lobular neoplasms; and (3) the lesion is multifocal in the breast. These observations led Foote and Stewart to conclude that LCIS was a premalignant lesion best treated by simple mastectomy. Additional information accrued since the report of Foote and Stewart suggests that LCIS is a risk factor for breast cancer rather than a premalignant lesion.

The true incidence of LCIS is difficult to determine because it lacks mammographic or clinical features. The histologic changes of LCIS are noted in from 0.8 to 8% of breast biopsies, with an incidence of 2.5% thought to reflect the frequency of the lesion when all breast biopsies are considered.[86–88] LCIS is noted to be more frequent in premenopausal women with a mean age of 44 to 46 reported in several series.[87,88] The frequency with which LCIS is diagnosed appears to be increasing, with a 15% rise in the number of cases seen from 1973 to 1988 reported in one series.[89] This apparent increase in the incidence of LCIS might simply be due to the increased number of breast biopsies done for mammographic abnormalities, because although LCIS lacks mammographic signs,[90] it accounted for 14% of mammographically detected lesions in one large series,[91] or it might reflect increased awareness of the histologic features of LCIS.

The major issue in the management of LCIS is whether the LCIS is a premalignant lesion or a marker of increased risk for the development of carcinoma.[85] Mastectomy was the treatment Foote and Stewart recommended for LCIS, based on the belief that the lesion was a precursor of invasive carcinoma.[85] A significant body of data exists supporting the idea that LCIS is a risk factor rather than a precancerous lesion. The major finding that supports this assertion is the bilaterality of the breast cancer risk after a diagnosis of LCIS, even if the LCIS is present in only one breast.[86,92] The data on laterality of cancer after a diagnosis of LCIS is summarized in Table 1-4.[92–95] Although McDivitt and colleagues found ipsilateral cancers to be somewhat more frequent, most studies show no difference in incidence between the ipsilateral and the contralateral breast.[93] The interval to the development of carcinoma after a diagnosis of LCIS can be quite

TABLE 1-4 Cumulative Risk of Development of Invasive Breast Carcinoma in the Ipsilateral and
Contralateral Breast after Diagnosis of Lobular Carcinoma in Situ

| Authors | n | Mean Follow-up (years) | Cumulative Risk (%) | |
			Ipsilateral Breast Cancer	Contralateral Breast Cancer
Haagensen et al[92]	211	14	10	10
McDivitt et al[93]	40	15	30	15
Rosen et al[94]	99	24	18	14
Andersen[95]	52	15.9	20	17

protracted. Rosen and colleagues noted that the majority of subsequent carcinomas in their series occurred 15 or more years after the diagnosis of LCIS, and 38% presented 20 or more years after the initial biopsy.[94] In contrast to the data presented for atypical hyperplasia (see below), the increased risk of breast cancer seen with LCIS does not diminish with follow-up through 25 years. Estimates of relative risks of breast cancer in women with LCIS range from 6.9 to 12.[92,94,95]

Efforts to identify features of LCIS associated with a higher likelihood of the development of malignancy have been largely unsuccessful. However, the immunohistochemistry and molecular analysis of infiltrating pleomorphic lobular carcinoma (PLC), an aggressive variant of infiltrating lobular carcinoma, may provide clues in the understanding of potential significant prognostic markers for LCIS. Immunohistochemical analysis of infiltrating pleomorphic lobular carcinoma showed that *Her2/neu* overexpression (81% vs 0 to 1%) and *p*53 mutation (48% vs 3%) are more commonly detected in PLC than the typical form of infiltrating lobular carcinoma (ILC).[96] The identification of these markers might help identify those women with LCIS who have a higher propensity of developing invasive cancer.

Haagensen and colleagues noted that the relative risk of breast cancer increased from 5.7 for women with LCIS alone to 8.5 in women with both a family history and LCIS,[92] an association similar to that observed for atypical hyperplasia and a family history of breast carcinoma.[32] Histologic features, including the amount of LCIS present, have not been predictive of the subsequent development of invasive carcinoma.[94]

Based on the preceding information, a logical management option for the woman with LCIS is

careful observation, as would be carried out for any woman known to be at increased risk for the development of breast cancer due to a personal history of breast cancer or a positive family history. For the majority of women, this will be an acceptable option. In women unwilling to accept the 20 to 30% risk of the development of breast cancer, surgical therapy must be directed toward both breasts. Bilateral total (simple) mastectomy, usually with immediate breast reconstruction, is the treatment of choice if prophylactic therapy is elected. Axillary dissection is not indicated. Radiotherapy has no role in the management of LCIS, and if observation is carried out, it is unnecessary to obtain histologically negative margins, because LCIS is known to be a diffuse lesion. Treatment strategies that address one breast would seem to be illogical, because the risk of LCIS is bilateral regardless of the findings of the contralateral biopsy. Women with LCIS are excellent candidates for breast cancer prevention trials due to their high-risk status and persistence of this risk over time.

Ductal Carcinoma In Situ

Ductal carcinoma in situ (DCIS) has traditionally been considered to be a precursor of invasive breast carcinoma rather than a risk factor for the disease, and in the past, most patients with DCIS were treated with mastectomy. As a result, little information is available on the natural history of DCIS. In addition, most of the earlier series[97–99] consisted of patients with palpable DCIS. Gross or palpable DCIS is a relatively uncommon lesion, accounting for only 2% of 10,054 breast cancers in an American College of Surgeons Survey in 1980.[100] The incidence of DCIS appears to be increasing, and much of the DCIS seen since 1992 is detected as a result of screening mammography and is clinically occult.[89] Whether the malignant potential of microscopic DCIS is equivalent to that of gross DCIS is unknown.

The data supporting the idea that DCIS could be considered a risk factor for invasive carcinoma came from several small series that included women who were found to have DCIS on review of biopsies that were originally classified as benign. Page and colleagues reported 25 cases of untreated DCIS, with a mean follow-up of 16 years. Seven women subsequently developed invasive carcinoma (28%). This represented a relative risk of 11 compared to age-matched controls from the Third National Cancer Survey for White Women in Atlanta.[101] Rosen and colleagues reported 30 women with untreated DCIS, with complete follow-up available for only 15.[102] Seven invasive cancers occurred at a mean of 9.7 years after the diagnosis of DCIS, an incidence of 27% if all cases are included or 53% if only patients with complete follow-up are considered. In the reports of both Page and Rosen, all carcinomas were in the index breast, usually in the vicinity of the biopsy site. In a similar report, Eusebi and colleagues described 28 cases of DCIS with an 11% incidence of invasive carcinoma at a median follow-up of 16.7 years.[103] One of the three subsequent carcinomas in this study was in the contralateral breast.

Not all DCIS will progress to clinically significant disease, that is, invasive carcinoma, but being diagnosed with DCIS certainly increases a woman's risk of developing subsequent carcinoma in the index breast as well as the contralateral breast.[104,105] Solin and colleagues reported that the risk of contralateral breast tumor occurrence was 6% at 10 years in women who were treated for DCIS with lumpectomy and radiation therapy in the index breast.[104] Similar results were reported in the NSABP B-17 trial.[105] The cumulative incidence of contralateral breast tumors in women treated for DCIS and followed for a median of 7.5 years was 5.7%. This absolute risk of development of contralateral breast cancer in a woman with a diagnosis of DCIS can be translated into a relative risk of 2 to 3.

Treatment options for DCIS remain controversial. Breast-conserving surgery has been shown to be effective and safe.[104–106] Local recurrence rates after lumpectomy and breast irradiation range from 12 to 17% after 7.5 to 10 years of follow-up, and local recurrence rates after excision alone range from 15 to 27%. About half of these recurrences (36 to 53%) are invasive breast tumors.[104–106] Because DCIS itself is not life threatening, the goal of management should be prevention of the development of invasive carcinoma. In this sense, women with DCIS are at increased risk, even though the treatments employed are the same as those used for invasive carcinoma.

Atypical Hyperplasia

Atypical hyperplasia, ductal or lobular, falls into the category of benign proliferative breast disease. As mentioned earlier in the section under proliferative benign breast disease, atypical lesions constitute only 4% of clinical lesions, but make up 12 to 17% of mammographic abnormalities.[33,34]

The relative risk of breast cancer development for atypical hyperplasia is reported to range from 4.0 to 5.0.[32] A marked interaction between atypia and a family history of a first-degree relative with breast cancer was noted by Dupont and Page, and Page and colleagues.[32,101] This subgroup of women had a risk 11 times that of women with nonproliferative disease. The absolute risk of breast cancer development in women with a positive family history and atypical hyperplasia was 20% at 15 years compared to 8% in women with atypical hyperplasia and a negative family history of breast carcinoma.

The interval from the diagnosis of atypical ductal hyperplasia to the development of carcinoma was 8.2 years, and only 56% of the carcinomas occurred in the index breast.[101] In contrast, in women with atypical lobular hyperplasia, the interval to cancer development was 11.9 years, and 69% of the carcinomas occurred in the same breast as the index biopsy. The overall incidence of carcinoma did not differ between women with atypical ductal and atypical lobular hyperplasia, and the presence of a first-degree relative with breast carcinoma doubled the relative risk of cancer development for either category of atypical hyperplasia.

RISK ASSESSMENT TOOLS

Gail Model

Public awareness of breast cancer risk has increased greatly in the past decade, and the availability of tamoxifen for breast cancer chemoprevention has made accurate risk assessment a practical clinical problem. As a result of the need for better counseling of patients on the subject of breast cancer risk and prevention, investigators have developed models to estimate the absolute risk of developing breast cancer, taking into consideration various risk factors. One such model, commonly referred to as the Gail Model, was developed from data from the BCDDP, a study to examine the effects of screening mammography in 284,780 women.[5] Cases were defined as women with incident breast cancer (invasive and noninvasive) between 1973 and 1980 at 28 participating centers. There were a total of 2,852 detected cancers in women in this group, and about 10% of these were in situ. The 3,146 controls were women who did not receive a recommendation for biopsy during the same screening period. The matching variables were age at entry, race, and location and length of participation. The analysis was restricted to white women, and age was dichotomized as < 50 and ≥ 50 for the variable of number of breast biopsies.

A number of medications were found to have no effect on risk of breast cancer development, including oral contraceptives. Cigarette smoking and methylxanthine (caffeine) consumption were also found to have no relation to the risk of breast cancer development. Alcohol consumption, long-term HRT, and height were found to increase risk, but the number of women with these specific risk factors was limited, so these variables were not included in the evaluation. The variables found to be major predictors of risk include age of menarche, number of breast biopsies, age at first live birth, and number of first-degree relatives with breast cancer. Of note, inclusion of information on age of onset of breast cancer among relatives and bilateral breast cancers did not improve the estimate of relative risk by the variable of number of first-degree relatives.

Based on the four risk factors, the authors were able to derive, by a series of calculations, the relative risk for a subject with constellations of these risk factors at any specific age range in increments of 10 years. The two risk factors that are associated with relative risk greater than 2 are two breast biopsies prior to age 50 and having at least one first-degree relative with breast cancer. The associated relative risks determined by the four risk factors in this study are summarized in Table 1-5.

TABLE 1-5 Summary of Gail Risk Factors with Associated Relative Risks Greater Than 1.5

Risk Factors	Relative Risks	
No. of Breast Biopsies at Age	< 50	≥ 50
1	1.698	1.273
≥ 2	2.882	1.620

Age at First Live Birth (years) with No. of First-Degree Relatives with Breast Cancer	< 20	20–24	25–29	> 30
0	1.00	1.244	1.548	1.927
1	2.607	2.681	2.756	2.834
2	6.798	5.775	4.907	4.169

Adapted from Gail MH et al[5]

The Gail Model, or Model 1, which predicts risks of developing both noninvasive and invasive breast cancer, has been modifed to Model 2, which projects the absolute risk of developing invasive breast cancer.[107] The other major modification is the incorporation of the risk factor of breast biopsies with or without atypical hyperplasia. This modified model, Model 2, was used to define the eligibility criteria for the Breast Cancer Prevention Trial (BCPT).[3] By incorporating data from the age-specific breast cancer rates from the SEER (1983-1987),[7] the model was also used to predict breast cancer incidence in black women.[107]

Both Models 1 and 2 have been validated in various studies.[107–110] In the study by Costantino and colleagues, Model 2 was validated using prospective data from 5,969 women in the placebo arm of the BCPT who were older than 35 years and had a projected 5-year risk of developing invasive breast cancer of at least 1.66%.[107] This study also summarized and compared the risk factor–specific relative risks of developing breast cancer in three other independent studies that used data from the BCDDP,[5] the Cancer and Steroid Hormone (CASH) Study,[111] and the Nurses' Health Study (NHS)[109] in addition to the BCPT.[107] The risk factors were those described in Gail Model 1 and they included age at menarche, number of breast biopsies before and after age 50, number of first-degree relatives with breast cancer, and age at first live birth (age less than 20, age 20–24, age 25–29, or nulliparous or age greater than

30). In general, the relative risks were comparable across the four data sets.

In summary, age of menarche less than 12 is associated with a relative risk of 1.20 to 1.29. As the number of breast biopsies increases to 2 or greater, the relative risk of developing breast cancer also increases from 1.23 to 3.89 for biopsies done before age 50 and 1.62 to 3.13 for those done after age 50. The risk factor associated with the highest relative risk was a family history of two or more first-degree relatives affected with breast cancer, ranging from 3.17 to 6.80. The relative risk appeared to decrease in women with two or more affected first-degree relatives as the age of first live birth increased from age 20 to age 30 or greater, indicating a negative interaction between increased age of first live birth and the number of affected first-degree relatives. Costantino and colleagues further stratified the 5,969 women in the placebo arm of the BCPT by age and the predicted 5-year risk (%) by the Gail Model divided into five quintiles (< 2.32, 2.32–2.65, 2.66–3.28, 3.29–4.73, and > 4.73).[107] The expected number of breast cancers was then calculated using the Gail Models 1 and 2, compared to the observed number of breast cancers in this group of 5,969 women, and expressed as an expected to observed ratio (E/O ratio).

The findings of this study are summarized in Table 1-6. An ideal model will theoretically yield an E/O ratio as close to unity as possible. When the E/O ratio is less than 1, the model of interest is underestimating the number of cases and vice versa. In general, when Gail Model 1 was used to predict

the number of expected cases in the study group, it resulted in an underestimate of the absolute risk of women greater than 60 years of age. The E/O ratio was 0.66. For ages 49 or less and ages 50 to 59, Model 1 does better, yielding E/O ratios of 0.91 and 0.96, respectively. Overall, Model 1 predicted 171 cancers in the study group, but there were 204 observed breast cancers (invasive and in situ), yielding an E/O ratio of 0.84. When the Gail Model 2 was used to predict the number of cases for the same study group, the overall E/O ratio was 1.03. The overall number of predicted cases was 159 compared to the 155 observed breast cancer cases. Among the three stratified age groups, Model 2 also performed well, predicting an E/O ratio close to 1 in all three age groups (0.93 for ages 49 or less, 1.13 for ages 50–59, and 1.05 for ages greater than 60). However, Model 2 did not perform as well within the three age groups who were further stratified into five quintiles of predicted 5-year risk. Model 2 tends to underestimate at the lower quintiles, especially among women with a 5-year predicted risk between 1.94 and 2.41%. The E/O ratio ranges from 0.58 to 0.62 among women less than age 49 and women between ages 50 to 59, respectively. When the study group was further stratified by individual Gail risk factors, Model 2 performed well but was inconsistent when predicting the number of breast cancers in younger women (less than age 50) who had biopsies with or without atypia. In women with one biopsy without atypia, the E/O was 0.67, whereas in women with two biopsies without atypia, the E/O was 1.76. In women with one biopsy with atypia, the E/O was 0.51, whereas the E/O was 2.99 in women with two biopsies with a history of atypia.

Based on this study, the National Cancer Institute has developed a personal computer software package from Model 2 and distributed it to healthcare providers in the United States.[112] The tool is also available on the Internet at <http://bcra.nci.nih.gov>. An example of Gail risk calculation for a 50-year-old white woman with age of menarche between 12 and 13, who is nulliparous and has one affected first-degree relative and one breast biopsy with atypia, using this Web site is shown in Figure 1-3. Her calculated 5-year and lifetime risks are 4.3% and 34.3%, respectively.

Even though Model 2 does well in predicting the absolute risk of developing breast cancer for women

TABLE 1-6 Ratio of Expected to Observed Number of Breast Cancers Using Two Versions of the Gail Model

Age	Gail Model 1 E/O Ratio	Gail Model 2 E/O Ratio
< 49	0.91	0.93
1 biopsy no atypia	-	0.67
2 biopsies no atypia	-	1.76
2 biopsies with atypia	-	2.99
50–59	0.96	1.13
> 60	0.66	1.05
Overall	0.84	1.03

E/O = Expected to observed.

Questions:

For a brief explanation of the following questions click the **?**

- What is the age of your patient?
  The program calculates risk for patients 35 or older. **?**
  [50 ⬍]

- What was the patient's age at time of first menstrual period? **?**
  [12 to 13 ⬍]

- What was patient's age at first live birth of a child? **?**
  [No births ⬍]

- How many of patient's first-degree relatives—mother and/or sister(s)—have had breast cancer? **?**
  [1 ⬍]

- Has the patient ever had a breast biopsy? **?**
  [Yes ⬍]

  - How many previous breast biopsies (positive or negative) has patient had? **?**
    [1 ⬍]

  - Has patient had at least one biopsy with atypical hyperplasia? **?**
    [Yes ⬍]

- If known, please indicate the race/ethnicity of your patient. **?**
  [White ⬍]

Figure 1-3 Sample Gail risk calculation using the Internet address <http://brca.nci.nih.gov>. Using the breast cancer risk assessment tool available from the Internet, a sample calculation of the 5-year and lifetime risk of developing breast cancer of a Caucasian 50-year-old woman is shown. The Gail risk parameters are age of menarche between 12 and 13 years of age, nulliparous, one first-degree relative with breast cancer, and one breast biopsy with atypia.

as a group, the model does not address the issue of individual risk prediction. This question was addressed in a study by Rockhill and colleagues in which the discriminatory accuracy, that is, the ability to separate individuals who will develop breast cancer or not, was examined.[110] The authors concluded that Gail Model 2 does well in predicting the risk of breast cancer development in groups stratified by various risk factors. However, the discriminatory accuracy is only 0.58 (0.56–0.60), meaning that the model is only slightly better than pure chance in predicting the 5-year risk of developing breast cancer in an individual.[113]

The Rockhill study was done by prospectively following a cohort of women from the NHS.[110] The NHS prospective cohort study began in 1976 when 121,700 married women who were registered nurses aged 30 to 55 returned a detailed questionnaire on medical history and lifestyle factors. Subsequent questionnaires were mailed every 2 years. More than 98% of the participants were white. The study of Rockhill and colleagues was restricted to a 5-year period from 1992 to 1997 corresponding to the BCPT study.[110] Of 104,064 who returned the 1992 survey, 95,743 were followed disease-free through the 1998 survey. Of these 95,743 women, 81,209 women between the ages of 46 to 71 were eligible, because these women had complete data on the required risk factors in 1992 and were white. Results from this study showed that when women were grouped according to risk factors as defined by Gail Model 2, the ratio of expected and observed numbers of breast cancer cases as predicted by Gail Model 2 was near unity. The biggest deviation was in the E/O ratio of 0.55 in women with no affected first-degree relatives who had their first live birth before age 20.

As mentioned earlier, the discriminatory accuracy of the 5-year risk prediction of Model 2 was found to be 0.58. This means that, for a predetermined level of risk, for instance 5-year risk greater than 1.67%, there is a 58% chance that a woman who developed breast cancer has a risk level greater than the predefined level. On the other hand, there is also a 42% chance for a woman who developed breast cancer to have a risk lower than the predetermined level. Ideally, a model should have a discriminatory accuracy as close to unity as possible. When the 5-year risk of 1.67% was used as the cutoff point for the definition of high risk, only 44% of the 1,354 women who developed breast cancer had a 5-year estimated risk 1.67% or greater. In other words, 54%, the majority of women who developed breast cancer, had a 5-year estimated risk less than 1.67%.

It is noteworthy that the Gail Model is not appropriate for risk assessment for women who are younger than age 35, with a history suspicious of hereditary breast cancer, a history of prior breast cancer, LCIS, or DCIS, or women not undergoing annual screening mammograms. The clinician should also bear in mind that the Gail Model might not have the discriminatory accuracy to identify the individual woman at increased risk.[113]

Claus Model

Using data from the CASH Study, which is a multicenter, population-based, case-control study conducted by the Centers for Disease Control, the authors of the Claus Model applied various genetic models to fit the age-specific occurrence data of breast cancer among first-degree relatives of breast cancer patients and control subjects.[6] The study population included 4,730 patients with histologically confirmed breast cancer between ages 20 and 54 years and 4,688 control subjects. Control subjects were frequency-matched to patients according to geographic region and 5-year categories of age. Patients and control subjects were interviewed about breast cancer history in relatives. Only the mothers and sisters of Caucasian patients and control subjects were included for the entire analyses in the study. Daughters as well as second-degree relatives and nonwhites were excluded due to underreporting of the disease for these groups.

Goodness-of-fit tests were used to determine the best-fitting genetic models. The model that best fit the observed age-specific breast cancer rates was the autosomal dominant major gene model. An assumption was made that the genes that regulate breast cancer susceptibility and age of onset are at the same single diallelic major locus.

The Claus Model takes into consideration the woman's age and the age of onset of breast cancer in the affected first- or second-degree relative. Other variables that were shown to be important in the Gail Model, such as age of menarche, number of biopsies, history of atypical hyperplasia, and age at first live birth, were not taken into consideration in risk prediction in the Claus Model. The authors found that the number and type of relatives with breast cancer and the age of onset of breast cancer in the affected relatives were strong predictors of the risk of breast cancer development in a woman with a positive family history. The risks of breast cancer development in women with one or two first-degree or second-degree relatives were then calculated and listed in life tables according to the age of onset (in increments of 10 years) of cancer in these relatives starting at age 29. A sample of the cumulative probabilities of developing breast cancer calculated by Claus and colleagues is listed in Table 1-7.[6] For the sake of simplicity, only the cumulative probabilities for a woman with one first-degree relative affected at ages 30 to 39 or ages 40 to 49 and another woman with two first-degree relatives affected at the two above age ranges are shown.

The Claus Model predicts the cumulative probability of breast cancer development in a woman with a family history of breast cancer in first-degree and/or second-degree relatives up to age 79. For example, a woman who has two first-degree relatives affected with breast cancer at ages 20 to 29 will have a predicted cumulative probability of breast cancer development of 48%.

In order to compare the differences in risk prediction between the Gail and Claus Models, a sample calculation is used as shown in Gail and col-

TABLE 1-7　Cumulative Probabilities of Breast Cancer in White Women as Predicted by the Claus Model

Age of Woman (years) with:	Age of Onset of Affected Relative 30–39			Age of Onset of Affected Relative 40–49		
	One First-Degree Relative	Two First- or Second-Degree Relatives	Two First-Degree Relatives	One First-Degree Relative	Two First- or Second-Degree Relatives	Two First-Degree Relatives
29	.005	.017	.018	.003	.013	.014
39	.017	.058	.062	.012	.046	.048
49	.044	.139	.148	.032	.110	.117
59	.086	.249	.265	.064	.199	.210
69	.130	.350	.371	.101	.282	.298
79	.165	.414	.437	.132	.338	.354

Adapted from Claus EB et al.[6]

TABLE 1-8 Comparison of Breast Cancer Risks Calculated by the Gail and Claus Models

Age Interval (years)	SEER Probability (%)	Gail Model Probability (%)[#]	Claus Model		
			Probability (%) (40–49)*	Probability (%) (30–39)*	Probability (%) (20–29)*
30–40	0.40	6.1	3.4	4.5	4.9
40–50	1.48	16.0	7.2	9.2	10.4
50–60	2.92	15.2	10.5	13.7	15.5
30–60	4.66	32.7	19.9	25.2	28.0
40–70	7.83	39.8	26.3	32.9	36.8
50–80	10.17	36.8	26.8	33.9	38.1

Adapted from Gail MH et al.[5]

[#]Risks are those of a white woman with menarche at age 12, one prior breast biopsy, age less than 20 at first live birth, and two affected first-degree relatives.

*Age of onset of both affected first-degree relatives.

SEER = Surveillance, Epidemiology and End Results.

leagues for Subject 2 in their original paper.[5] Results are shown in Table 1-8. Subject 2 had the following risk factors: history of one breast biopsy, age of menarche < 12, age at first live birth < 20, two affected first-degree relatives, and age < 50.[5] The Claus Model was then applied toward this woman's scenario. Her risks of developing breast cancer are calculated acknowledging the fact that the Claus Model includes only the woman's age and the age of onset of the affected relatives as its variables. The cumulative probabilities of breast cancer development between ages x and y are then calculated using life tables for two affected first-degree relatives and the following equation:

$$RC(y/x) = R(y) - R(x)/(1-R(x))$$

where x is the current disease-free age of the woman to be counseled and y is the age to which risks are to be calculated.[6] RC(y/x) is the cumulative probability of developing breast cancer from age x to y. Because the affected relatives' ages may vary, our calculations are based on two relatives with similar affected age at several age ranges, that is, 20 to 29, 30 to 39, and 40 to 49.

As shown in Table 1-8, the risks calculated using the Claus Model are, in general, lower than those calculated by the Gail Model. The risk of this woman as calculated by the Gail Model exceeds that of a woman with two first-degree relatives affected at ages 20 to 29. For comparison, the risks of devel-

oping breast cancer in an average white woman from the SEER Cancer Statistics Review Results are also listed.[7] The calculations done here are for the sole purpose of illustrating the differences in risk prediction between the Gail and Claus Models.

Two studies have been done to compare the concordance of risk prediction in both the Gail and Claus Models.[113,114] In the study by McTiernan and colleagues, women with a family history of breast cancer in one or more first- or second-degree relatives were recruited as part of a larger randomized trial of breast cancer risk counseling methods.[114] Women who were likely to have a highly penetrant inherited gene such as BRCA1 or BRCA2 were excluded. Women with a daughter or half-sister with breast cancer were also excluded. There were 491 women included in the study. The study showed that the Gail estimates of risk were found to be higher than the Claus estimates, a finding similar to an earlier study comparing these models.[114] The study population, age, age at menarche, age at first live birth, history of breast cancer in a second-degree relative, and history of one or more breast biopsies were found by McTiernan and colleagues to contribute to the differences between the two models. In contrast, nulliparity and a history of breast biopsy were the factors most responsible for the difference in risk estimates in another study.[113] The average lifetime risks (to age 79) for all groups combined as calculated by the Gail and Claus Models were 13.2% and 11.2%, respectively.[114] Of note, African-Americans were found to have a higher lifetime risk estimated by the Claus Model: 10.3% as opposed to 6.1% when the Gail Model was used.[114]

In summary, both the Gail and Claus Models provide an important foundation for the initial discussion with a woman who is concerned about her risk of developing breast cancer. The Claus Model is particularly useful when assessing the risk of a woman who is between the ages of 29 and 35 and has a family history of breast cancer. Because more validation studies have been done for the Gail Model, and the Gail Model calculator is easily accessible via the Internet, the Gail Model is most widely used to estimate breast cancer risk in the clinical setting.

APPROACHING THE WOMAN AT RISK IN THE CLINICAL SETTING

As discussed in previous sections, risk factors vary in terms of the magnitude of relative risk. The relative risk applies only to the individual woman with the risk factor. In addition, some risk factors occur more frequently than others. Therefore, in order to assess the proportion of breast cancer cases that can be attributed to a risk factor, the risk factor has to be evaluated in a group of women (population). An additional variable, therefore, is needed which is the prevalence of the risk factor, or how commonly the risk factor occurs in the population. The interaction of the prevalence and the magnitude of the relative risk of a certain risk factor is defined as the population attributable risk (PAR).[1] For example, the PAR of women with two affected first-degree relatives (relative risk = 5.0) is 0.14, which means that 14% of all breast cancer cases can be attributed to this risk factor. More than half of the breast cancers that develop cannot be attributed to any known risk factors.[1] When a woman presents herself for evaluation of risk, the following steps are recommended in the consultation:

1. A detailed history focusing on the woman's reproductive and gynecologic history, family history of breast, ovarian, and other malignancies, and personal history of breast biopsies and cancer. A history of radiation exposure should be sought, and lifestyle factors such as diet and alcohol evaluated. The detailed history taking can

be facilitated by using a risk assessment form. Information on the woman's overall health status should be obtained to evaluate competing causes of mortality.

2. A careful clinical breast examination should be performed to exclude the presence of any pathology and to determine the degree of nodularity of the breasts.

3. Breast imaging studies should be reviewed to assess the density of the breasts, both as a risk factor for breast cancer development and to provide a rough estimate of the utility of mammographic screening as a surveillance approach.

4. In women at risk on the basis of a histologic lesion such as atypia, LCIS, or DCIS, the pathology slides should be reviewed by a pathologist experienced in the evaluation of breast lesions. These borderline lesions, including epithelial hyperplasia with or without atypia and carcinoma in situ (CIS), represent a continuum of histologic features with an increasing propensity for the development of invasive carcinoma.[115] The diagnosis of these borderline epithelial lesions, however, is not always clear-cut. In the study by Rosai, five pathologists with special interest in breast pathology were asked to review 17 breast lesions, including 10 ductal and 7 lobular lesions.[115] The lesions were categorized into hyperplasia, atypical hyperplasia, or CIS. There was not a single lesion for which all five pathologists agreed on the same diagnosis. Four of the five pathologists agreed on a diagnosis in two lesions (11%). There were seven lesions (41%) in which there was disagreement spanning from hyperplasia to CIS. In a similar study, six pathologists with extensive experience in breast pathology were asked to evaluate 24 cases of proliferative ductal lesions and were provided with diagnostic criteria for lesion categories.[116] Complete agreement was achieved in 14 cases (58%). Five or more pathologists agreed on the same diagnosis in 17 cases (71%), and four or more pathologists agreed on the same diagnosis in 22 of 24 cases (92%), indicating that when guidelines are provided for evaluation of proliferative lesions, the interobserver concordance in diagnosis is improved. The magnitude of the interobserver variability observed in this study[116] is similar to that reported in a recent study analyzing the response of 2,952 pathologists who

diagnosed a case as part of the 1995 Performance Improvement Program.[117] About 58% of the pathologists agreed upon the established diagnosis of atypical lobular hyperplasia, while 17% upgraded the diagnosis to LCIS. Due to the potential for a diagnosis of atypia or CIS to significantly elevate a woman's level of risk, and the interobserver variability in diagnosis of these borderline lesions, a second opinion on the pathology is crucial in the counseling of women with a diagnosis of a borderline epithelial lesion.

This information obtained in steps 1 through 4 will allow women to be separated into two groups; those at risk on the basis of factors other than a strong family history of breast cancer, and those with a history suggestive of a predisposition mutation. The approach to these two groups of women, as well as the management options, differ slightly, so this is a clinically useful distinction.

Risk Assessment Counseling for Women With a Family History Suggestive of Hereditary Breast Cancer

The criteria for referral to genetic counseling at our institution have been discussed previously. However, there are no uniform criteria for genetic testing. Several published models may help an individual estimate her risk of having a predisposition mutation.[84,118–120] A computer program, BRCA-program (*BRCA*-PRO), is available to estimate the probability of carrying a deleterious *BRCA1* or *BRCA2* mutation in an individual.[121,122] This program is available free of charge in a Web-based format at the Internet address <http://www.swmed.edu/home_pages/cancergene/>. The model has been validated in both Ashkenazi (AJ) and non-Ashkenazi (non-AJ) women using retrospective data from five genetic counseling centers obtained between 1992 and 1998.[119] The authors found that the *BRCA*-PRO program is particularly good at predicting the risk of testing positive when the carrier probability is less than 70%. The program tends to overestimate risk when the carrier probability is high and underestimate risk when the carrier probability is low, for both AJ and non-AJ women. The *BRCA*-PRO is a good starting point in the discussion of the probability of being the carrier of a deleterious gene. The computer model is especially helpful to assess genetic risk in families that have 1 to 5 affected family members. It would be reason-

able to refer a woman to genetic counseling if the woman's carrier probability is greater than 5%, a level of risk that is 50-fold higher than that of the general population, assuming the prevalence of a deleterious mutation is 0.1%. As there are no set criteria for genetic testing, the clinician and the woman at risk should have a discussion regarding the ramifications of a positive or negative test result. Options for management of the woman suspected or proven to have a deleterious mutation include surveillance, prophylactic oophorectomy, prophylactic mastectomy, and tamoxifen.

The current recommendations for surveillance and follow-up of women suspected or proven to have a genetic mutation include breast self-examination, semiannual clinical breast examination, and annual mammography beginning between the ages of 25 and 35.[123] These recommendations were developed by a task force of the Cancer Genetics Studies Consortium (CGSC) for follow-up of carriers of *BRCA1* and *BRCA2* mutations.

In women at genetic risk, data is accumulating to suggest that a significant number of cancers are detected during the interval between annual mammograms. This has resulted in a number of studies evaluating the use of breast magnetic resonance imaging or ultrasound for surveillance in high-risk women. This is discussed in Chapter 8. At the present time, the high number of false positive results with these modalities is a significant drawback to their use as screening tools outside of centers with special expertise.

At present, the role of ductal lavage in the gene mutation carrier is unclear. Studies of prophylactic mastectomy specimens from these women demonstrate high rates of clinically unsuspected histologic risk lesions[124] which are more frequent in women over age 40 than in their younger counterparts. This information suggests that the identification of atypia could indicate progression toward malignancy, but this remains to be proven. Women should be counseled regarding these uncertainties. If they believe that lavage would be helpful in the decision-making process, it is reasonable to perform the procedure.

The benefit of tamoxifen in mutation carriers is controversial. The number of women who developed cancer in the NSAPB-P1 trial who were mutation carriers was too small to allow a meaningful evaluation. However, in a case-control study of women with known *BRCA1* or *BRCA2* mutation, Narod and colleagues demonstrated that the use of tamoxifen reduced the risk of contralateral cancer by 75%.[125] Oophorectomy is another strategy, proven to reduce risk in gene carriers, which is appropriate to consider once childbearing is complete. Because of their high level of risk, mutation carriers are the group most often considered for prophylactic mastectomy. However, as discussed in Chapter 15, this option is unacceptable to a significant number of mutation carriers. It is worthy of discussion, particularly for the woman who has carcinoma in one breast. Studies have shown that while the risk of true local recurrence after lumpectomy and radiation is not increased in gene carriers, there is a high risk of new second primary cancers in both the treated and the untreated breasts.[126]

Risk Assessment Counseling for Women Without a Strong Family History Suggestive of Hereditary Breast Cancer

Before discussing the estimate of a woman's risk, it is important to assess the woman's self-perception of risk. Most women in good health tend to underestimate their risk, whereas women with affected relatives often perceive their risk to be higher than it actually is.[2,127] The Gail Model risk assessment tool is a good starting point in the conversation about risk assessment.[5] The 5-year and lifetime risk of breast cancer development should be calculated and presented. It is important to discuss risk in absolute terms such as those calculated by the Gail Model rather than in relative terms such as relative risks or odds ratios.

Options for management of the woman at increased risk on the basis of nongenetic factors include surveillance, tamoxifen chemoprevention, prophylactic mastectomy, or participation in ongoing studies of newer chemopreventive agents. Each of these is discussed in detail in subsequent chapters. For the woman at risk on the basis of factors other than histologic atypia, LCIS, or DCIS, epithelial sampling may provide additional information for risk stratification. Cytologic atypia can be identified by ductal lavage or random fine-needle aspiration in approximately 25% of high-risk women without clinical or mammographic abnormalities.[128,129] Data from our institution indicate that women at risk on the basis of LCIS or atypia are significantly more likely to opt for tamoxifen

chemoprevention than women with a similar level of risk due to other factors.[130] In this study, 219 women seeking risk evaluation between the publication date of the NSABP-P1 Breast Cancer Prevention Trial (September 1998) and October 2002 were seen at the Lynn Sage Breast Center. Patients underwent risk assessment and neutral counseling on the risks and benefits of tamoxifen. Factors influencing the offering and acceptance of tamoxifen were analyzed. The median age was 47 (range 22 to 76), and the median 5-year Gail risk was 2.25 (range 0.3 to 9.1). Thirty patients were at risk due to LCIS. Of the entire group, 60% were offered tamoxifen and 41% of those offered accepted (25% of the entire group). Of the women with LCIS/atypia, 91% of the women were offered tamoxifen and 53% accepted ($p = .008$). LCIS/atypia were the major predictors of women being offered and accepting tamoxifen.[130]

After an assessment of the level of risk, women should be advised about what is entailed in each of the risk management approaches and the risks and benefits of each. We find it useful to emphasize the fact that risk estimates are for the occurrence of breast cancer, not for breast cancer death. The risk of breast cancer death is approximately one-third of the risk estimate. When discussing surveillance, it is useful to mention that strict adherence to a surveillance regimen does nothing to prevent the development of breast cancer. It is merely an attempt to detect the disease at an early stage. However, as discussed in detail in Chapter 7, only about one-third of high-risk women undergoing conventional surveillance (clinical breast exam and mammography) are diagnosed with DCIS, and approximately 40% will have metastases to the axillary nodes. Close surveillance is not a guarantee that cancer will be diagnosed at an early and favorable stage, although it improves the odds that this will occur.

There are many misconceptions about the side effects of tamoxifen and which women are at risk. The discussion of the risks and benefits of tamoxifen will differ considerably between premenopausal and postmenopausal women. The incidence of the potentially life-threatening side effects of tamoxifen (thromboembolism, endometrial carcinoma) is not increased in premenopausal women. Many premenopausal women believe that tamoxifen causes menopause, because side effects such as menstrual irregularity and hot flashes mimic the symptoms of menopause. In fact, tamoxifen induces ovulation and, in the past, was used as a fertility drug in other countries. However, the drug is not known to be safe for use during pregnancy, so women attempting to have children should not use this for chemoprevention. Postmenopausal women often greatly overestimate the risk of the serious toxicities of tamoxifen, and the absolute risk of these events should be discussed (see Chapter 11). Finally, a considerable amount of information on quality of life issues in women taking tamoxifen is now available and provides reassurance that this is a well-tolerated agent for chemoprevention. This is discussed in detail in Chapter 14.

Prophylactic mastectomy is an aggressive approach to risk reduction, which is unacceptable to many women. It is important to emphasize that prophylactic mastectomy does not provide 100% protection against subsequent breast cancer development (see Chapter 16). In addition, approximately 90% of women with Stage I cancer and 70% of those with DCIS and Stage II disease are candidates for treatment with breast-conserving therapy should cancer develop.[131]

Finally, chemoprevention remains an active area of investigation, and there are many studies ongoing in an attempt to identify agents that are more effective or have less toxicity than tamoxifen. Participation in research provides the benefits of surveillance coupled with the potential for risk reduction. Decisions regarding an approach to risk management should not be made in haste, and often several consultations are needed to fully discuss the risks and benefits of the different approaches. Psychological counseling may be useful in the decision-making process.

For the woman who is found to be at average or minimally increased risk of breast cancer development after a thorough risk evaluation, reassurance is the initial step in the consultation. Breast cancer screening should be reviewed, and lifestyle modifications that appear to be beneficial, such as weight reduction for obese postmenopausal women and limiting alcohol intake, should be discussed. Drugs such as raloxifene, which provide protection against osteoporosis and appear to reduce breast cancer incidence in postmenopausal women at average or below-average risk of breast cancer, may also be appropriate in this group.[132] Finally, this is an ideal opportunity to review other, potentially more significant, health risks and encourage appropriate preventive behaviors as discussed in Chapters 5 and 6.

CONCLUSION

It is conceivable that we may accurately predict an individual woman's true risk of developing breast cancer if we completely understand the pathogenesis of breast cancer. As we increase our understanding of the human genome, we may one day reach the goal of analyzing our genomic data to predict the likelihood of the development of various disease processes including breast cancer. Until the development of this ultimate customized risk assessment tool, we must continue to rely on our current knowledge of the various breast cancer risk factors and available risk assessment tools to make our best educated guess of the level of risk in an individual woman. In the subsequent chapters of this book, the risk factors overviewed in this chapter, as well as surveillance and management strategies, are discussed in greater detail.

REFERENCES

1. Vogel VG. Assessing women's potential risk of developing breast cancer. Oncology (Huntingt) 1996; 10:1451–8, 1461–3.
2. Stefanek ME. Counseling women at high risk for breast cancer. Oncology (Huntingt) 1990;4:27–34, 37–8.
3. Fisher B, Costantino JP, Wickerham DL, et al. Tamoxifen for prevention of breast cancer: report of the National Surgical Adjuvant Breast and Bowel Project P-1 Study. J Natl Cancer Inst 1998;90: 1371–88.
4. First results from the International Breast Cancer Intervention Study (IBIS-I): a randomised prevention trial. Lancet 2002;360(9336):817–24.
5. Gail MH, Brinton LA, Byar DP, et al. Projecting individualized probabilities of developing breast cancer for white females who are being examined annually. J Natl Cancer Inst 1989;81:1879–86.
6. Claus EB, Risch N, Thompson WD. Autosomal dominant inheritance of early-onset breast cancer. Implications for risk prediction. Cancer 1994;73:643–51.
7. Ries L, Eisner M, Kosary C, et al. SEER cancer statistics review, 1973–1999. Bethesda (MD): National Cancer Institute; 2002.
8. Phillips KA, Glendon G, Knight JA. Putting the risk of breast cancer in perspective. N Engl J Med 1999;340:141–4.

9. Morrow M. Identification of the woman at risk for breast cancer: problem solved? Recent Results Cancer Res 1999;151:85–95.

10. Henderson BE, Ross R, Bernstein L. Estrogens as a cause of human cancer: the Richard and Hinda Rosenthal Foundation award lecture. Cancer Res 1988;48:246–53.

11. MacMahon B, Trichopoulos D, Brown J, et al. Age at menarche, probability of ovulation and breast cancer risk. Int J Cancer 1982;29:13–6.

12. Trichopoulos D, MacMahon B, Cole P. Menopause and breast cancer risk. J Natl Cancer Inst 1972; 48:605–13.

13. MacMahon B, Cole P, Lin TM, et al. Age at first birth and breast cancer risk. Bull World Health Organ 1970;43:209–21.

14. Ekbom A, Trichopoulos D, Adami HO, et al. Evidence of prenatal influences on breast cancer risk. Lancet 1992;340(8826):1015–8.

15. Daling JR, Malone KE, Voigt LF, et al. Risk of breast cancer among young women: relationship to induced abortion. J Natl Cancer Inst 1994;86: 1584–92.

16. Newcomb PA, Storer BE, Longnecker MP, et al. Pregnancy termination in relation to risk of breast cancer. JAMA 1996;275:283–7.

17. Harris BM, Eklund G, Meirik O, et al. Risk of cancer of the breast after legal abortion during first trimester: a Swedish register study. BMJ 1989;299 (6713):1430–2.

18. Melbye M, Wohlfahrt J, Olsen JH, et al. Induced abortion and the risk of breast cancer. N Engl J Med 1997;336:81–5.

19. Layde PM, Webster LA, Baughman AL, et al. The independent associations of parity, age at first full term pregnancy, and duration of breastfeeding with the risk of breast cancer. Cancer and Steroid Hormone Study Group. J Clin Epidemiol 1989; 42:963–73.

20. Kvale G, Heuch I. Lactation and cancer risk: is there a relation specific to breast cancer? J Epidemiol Community Health 1988;42:30–7.

21. Newcomb PA, Storer BE, Longnecker MP, et al. Lactation and a reduced risk of premenopausal breast cancer. N Engl J Med 1994;330:81–7.

22. Frisch RE, Gotz-Welbergen AV, McArthur JW, et al. Delayed menarche and amenorrhea of college athletes in relation to age of onset of training. JAMA 1981;246:1559–63.

23. Bernstein L, Henderson BE, Hanisch R, et al. Physical exercise and reduced risk of breast cancer in young women. J Natl Cancer Inst 1994;86:1403–8.

24. Dorgan JF, Brown C, Barrett M, et al. Physical activity and risk of breast cancer in the Framingham Heart Study. Am J Epidemiol 1994;139:662–9.

25. Rossouw JE, Anderson GL, Prentice RL, et al. Risks and benefits of estrogen plus progestin in healthy postmenopausal women: principal results from the Women's Health Initiative randomized controlled trial. JAMA 2002;288:321–33.

26. de Waard F, Baanders-van Halewijn EA. A prospective study in general practice on breast-cancer risk in postmenopausal women. Int J Cancer 1974;14: 153–60.

27. London SJ, Colditz GA, Stampfer MJ, et al. Prospective study of relative weight, height, and risk of breast cancer. JAMA 1989;262:2853–8.

28. Longnecker MP, Berlin JA, Orza MJ, Chalmers TC. A meta-analysis of alcohol consumption in relation to risk of breast cancer. JAMA 1988;260:652–6.

29. Young TB. A case-control study of breast cancer and alcohol consumption habits. Cancer 1989;64:552–8.

30. Gapstur SM, Potter JD, Sellers TA, Folsom AR. Increased risk of breast cancer with alcohol consumption in postmenopausal women. Am J Epidemiol 1992;136:1221–31.

31. Is 'fibrocystic disease' of the breast precancerous? Arch Pathol Lab Med 1986;110:171–3.

32. Dupont WD, Page DL. Risk factors for breast cancer in women with proliferative breast disease. N Engl J Med 1985;312:146–51.

33. Owings DV, Hann L, Schnitt SJ. How thoroughly should needle localization breast biopsies be sampled for microscopic examination? A prospective mammographic/pathologic correlative study. Am J Surg Pathol 1990;14:578–83.

34. Rubin E, Visscher DW, Alexander RW, et al. Proliferative disease and atypia in biopsies performed for nonpalpable lesions detected mammographically. Cancer 1988;61:2077–82.

35. Land CE, McGregor DH. Breast cancer incidence among atomic bomb survivors: implications for radiobiologic risk at low doses. J Natl Cancer Inst 1979;62:17–21.

36. Hildreth NG, Shore RE, Dvoretsky PM. The risk of breast cancer after irradiation of the thymus in infancy. N Engl J Med 1989;321:1281–4.

37. Miller AB, Howe GR, Sherman GJ, et al. Mortality from breast cancer after irradiation during fluoroscopic examinations in patients being treated for tuberculosis. N Engl J Med 1989;321:1285–9.

38. Hancock SL, Tucker MA, Hoppe RT. Breast cancer after treatment of Hodgkin's disease. J Natl Cancer Inst 1993;85:25–31.

39. Schell SR, Montague ED, Spanos WJ Jr, et al. Bilateral breast cancer in patients with initial stage I and II disease. Cancer 1982;50:1191–4.

40. Storm HH, Jensen OM. Risk of contralateral breast cancer in Denmark 1943–80. Br J Cancer 1986; 54:483–92.

41. Rosen PP, Groshen S, Kinne DW, Hellman S. Contralateral breast carcinoma: an assessment of risk and prognosis in stage I (T1N0M0) and stage II (T1N1M0) patients with 20-year follow-up. Surgery 1989;106:904–10.

42. Sastre-Garau X, Jouve M, Asselain B, et al. Infiltrating lobular carcinoma of the breast. Clinicopathologic analysis of 975 cases with reference to data on conservative therapy and metastatic patterns. Cancer 1996;77:113–20.

43. Zucali R, Luini A, Del Vecchio M, et al. Contralateral breast cancer after limited surgery plus radiotherapy of early mammary tumors. Eur J Surg Oncol 1987;13:413–7.

44. Fisher B, Anderson S, Bryant J, et al. Twenty-year follow-up of a randomized trial comparing total mastectomy, lumpectomy, and lumpectomy plus irradiation for the treatment of invasive breast cancer. N Engl J Med 2002;347:1233–41.

45. Veronesi U, Cascinelli N, Mariani L, et al. Twenty-year follow-up of a randomized study comparing breast-conserving surgery with radical mastectomy for early breast cancer. N Engl J Med 2002;347:1227–32.

46. Thurfjell E. Breast density and the risk of breast cancer. N Engl J Med 2002;347:866.

47. Wolfe JN. Breast patterns as an index of risk for developing breast cancer. AJR Am J Roentgenol 1976;126:1130–7.

48. Wolfe JN. Risk for breast cancer development determined by mammographic parenchymal pattern. Cancer 1976;37:2486–92.

49. Moskowitz M, Gartside P, McLaughlin C. Mammographic patterns as markers for high-risk benign breast disease and incident cancers. Radiology 1980;134:293–5.

50. Boyd NF, O'Sullivan B, Campbell JE, et al. Bias and the association of mammographic parenchymal patterns with breast cancer. Br J Cancer 1982;45:179–84.

51. Saftlas AF, Wolfe JN, Hoover RN, et al. Mammographic parenchymal patterns as indicators of breast cancer risk. Am J Epidemiol 1989;129:518–26.

52. Wolfe JN, Saftlas AF, Salane M. Mammographic parenchymal patterns and quantitative evaluation of mammographic densities: a case-control study. AJR Am J Roentgenol 1987;148:1087–92.

53. Saftlas AF, Hoover RN, Brinton LA, et al. Mammographic densities and risk of breast cancer. Cancer 1991;67:2833–8.

54. Byrne C, Schairer C, Wolfe J, et al. Mammographic features and breast cancer risk: effects with time, age, and menopause status. J Natl Cancer Inst 1995;87:1622–9.

55. Boyd NF, Byng JW, Jong RA, et al. Quantitative classification of mammographic densities and breast cancer risk: results from the Canadian National Breast Screening Study. J Natl Cancer Inst 1995;87:670–5.

56. Egan RL, Mosteller RC. Breast cancer mammography patterns. Cancer 1977;40:2087–90.

57. Krook PM, Carlile T, Bush W, Hall MH. Mammographic parenchymal patterns as a risk indicator for prevalent and incident cancer. Cancer 1978;41:1093–7.

58. Egan RL, McSweeney MB. Mammographic parenchymal patterns and risk of breast cancer. Radiology 1979;133:65–70.

59. Tabar L, Dean PB. Mammographic parenchymal patterns. Risk indicator for breast cancer? JAMA 1982;247:185–9.

60. de Stavola BL, Gravelle IH, Wang DY, et al. Relationship of mammographic parenchymal patterns with breast cancer risk factors and risk of breast cancer in a prospective study. Int J Epidemiol 1990;19:247–54.

61. Krook PM. Mammographic parenchymal patterns as risk indicators for incident cancer in a screening program: an extended analysis. AJR Am J Roentgenol 1978;131:1031–5.

62. Brisson J, Merletti F, Sadowsky NL, et al. Mammographic features of the breast and breast cancer risk. Am J Epidemiol 1982;115:428–37.

63. Brisson J, Morrison AS, Kopans DB, et al. Height and weight, mammographic features of breast tissue, and breast cancer risk. Am J Epidemiol 1984;119:371–81.

64. Carlile T, Kopecky KJ, Thompson DJ, et al. Breast cancer prediction and the Wolfe classification of mammograms. JAMA 1985;254:1050–3.

65. Gravelle IH, Bulstrode JC, Bulbrook RD, et al. The relation between radiological patterns of the breast and body weight and height. Br J Radiol 1982;55(649):23–5.

66. Boyd NF, Dite GS, Stone J, et al. Heritability of mammographic density, a risk factor for breast cancer. N Engl J Med 2002;347:886–94.

67. Miki Y, Swensen J, Shattuck-Eidens D, et al. A strong candidate for the breast and ovarian cancer susceptibility gene BRCA1. Science 1994;266(5182):66–71.

68. Wooster R, Bignell G, Lancaster J, et al. Identification of the breast cancer susceptibility gene BRCA2. Nature 1995;378(6559):789–92.

69. Hall JM, Lee MK, Newman B, et al. Linkage of early-onset familial breast cancer to chromosome 17q21. Science 1990;250(4988):1684–9.

70. Struewing JP, Hartge P, Wacholder S, et al. The risk of cancer associated with specific mutations of BRCA1 and BRCA2 among Ashkenazi Jews. N Engl J Med 1997;336:1401–8.

71. Ford D, Easton DF, Stratton M, et al. Genetic heterogeneity and penetrance analysis of the BRCA1 and BRCA2 genes in breast cancer families. The Breast Cancer Linkage Consortium. Am J Hum Genet 1998;62:676–89.

72. Satagopan JM, Offit K, Foulkes W, et al. The lifetime risks of breast cancer in Ashkenazi Jewish carriers of BRCA1 and BRCA2 mutations. Cancer Epidemiol Biomarkers Prev 2001;10:467–73.

73. Antoniou AC, Pharoah PD, McMullan G, et al. A comprehensive model for familial breast cancer incorporating BRCA1, BRCA2 and other genes. Br J Cancer 2002;86:76–83.

74. Claus EB, Schildkraut JM, Thompson WD, Risch NJ. The genetic attributable risk of breast and ovarian cancer. Cancer 1996;77:2318–24.

75. Antoniou AC, Pharoah PD, McMullan G, et al. Evidence for further breast cancer susceptibility genes in addition to BRCA1 and BRCA2 in a population-based study. Genet Epidemiol 2001;21:1–18.

76. Couch FJ, Weber BL. Mutations and polymorphisms in the familial early-onset breast cancer (BRCA1) gene. Breast Cancer Information Core. Hum Mutat 1996;8:8–18.

77. Struewing JP, Abeliovich D, Peretz T, et al. The carrier frequency of the BRCA1 185delAG mutation is approximately 1 percent in Ashkenazi Jewish individuals. Nat Genet 1995;11:198–200.

78. Roa BB, Boyd AA, Volcik K, Richards CS. Ashkenazi Jewish population frequencies for common mutations in BRCA1 and BRCA2. Nat Genet 1996;14: 185–7.

79. Oddoux C, Struewing JP, Clayton CM, et al. The carrier frequency of the BRCA2 6174delT mutation among Ashkenazi Jewish individuals is approximately 1%. Nat Genet 1996;14:188–90.

80. Langston AA, Malone KE, Thompson JD, et al. BRCA1 mutations in a population-based sample of young women with breast cancer. N Engl J Med 1996;334:137–42.

81. Krainer M, Silva-Arrieta S, FitzGerald MG, et al. Differential contributions of BRCA1 and BRCA2 to early-onset breast cancer. N Engl J Med 1997;336: 1416–21.

82. Easton DF, Bishop DT, Ford D, Crockford GP. Genetic linkage analysis in familial breast and ovarian cancer: results from 214 families. The Breast Cancer Linkage Consortium. Am J Hum Genet 1993; 52:678–701.

83. Easton DF, Ford D, Bishop DT. Breast and ovarian cancer incidence in BRCA1-mutation carriers. Breast Cancer Linkage Consortium. Am J Hum Genet 1995;56:265–71.

84. Couch FJ, DeShano ML, Blackwood MA, et al. BRCA1 mutations in women attending clinics that evaluate the risk of breast cancer. N Engl J Med 1997;336:1409–15.

85. Foote FJ, Stewart F. Lobular carcinoma in situ: a rare form of mammary carcinoma. Am J Pathol 1941; 17:491–6.

86. Frykberg ER, Santiago F, Betsill WL Jr, O'Brien PH. Lobular carcinoma in situ of the breast. Surg Gynecol Obstet 1987;164:285–301.

87. Schwartz GF, Feig SA, Rosenberg AL, et al. Staging and treatment of clinically occult breast cancer. Cancer 1984;53:1379–84.

88. Wheeler JE, Enterline HT, Roseman JM, et al. Lobular carcinoma in situ of the breast. Long-term followup. Cancer 1974;34:554–63.

89. Simon MS, Schwartz AG, Martino S, Swanson GM. Trends in the diagnosis of in situ breast cancer in the Detroit metropolitan area, 1973 to 1987. Cancer 1992;69:466–9.

90. Pope TL Jr, Fechner RE, Wilhelm MC, et al. Lobular carcinoma in situ of the breast: mammographic features. Radiology 1988;168:63–6.

91. Silverstein MJ, Gamagami P, Colburn WJ, et al. Nonpalpable breast lesions: diagnosis with slightly overpenetrated screen-film mammography and hook wire-directed biopsy in 1,014 cases. Radiology 1989;171:633–8.

92. Haagensen CD, Lane N, Lattes R, Bodian C. Lobular neoplasia (so-called lobular carcinoma in situ) of the breast. Cancer 1978;42:737–69.

93. McDivitt RW, Hutter RV, Foote FW Jr, Stewart FW. In situ lobular carcinoma. A prospective follow-up study indicating cumulative patient risks. JAMA 1967;201:82–6.

94. Rosen PP, Kosloff C, Lieberman PH, et al. Lobular carcinoma in situ of the breast. Detailed analysis of 99 patients with average follow-up of 24 years. Am J Surg Pathol 1978;2:225–51.

95. Andersen JA. Lobular carcinoma in situ of the breast. An approach to rational treatment. Cancer 1977; 39:2597–602.

96. Middleton LP, Palacios DM, Bryant BR, et al. Pleomorphic lobular carcinoma: morphology, immunohistochemistry, and molecular analysis. Am J Surg Pathol 2000;24:1650–6.

97. Kinne DW, Petrek JA, Osborne MP, et al. Breast carcinoma in situ. Arch Surg 1989;124:33–6.

98. von Rueden DG, Wilson RE. Intraductal carcinoma of the breast. Surg Gynecol Obstet 1984;158: 105–11.

99. Westbrook KC, Gallager HS. Intraductal carcinoma of the breast. A comparative study. Am J Surg 1975;130:667–70.

100. Rosen PP, Senie R, Schottenfeld D, Ashikari R. Noninvasive breast carcinoma: frequency of unsuspected invasion and implications for treatment. Ann Surg 1979;189:377–82.

101. Page DL, Dupont WD, Rogers LW, Rados MS. Atypical hyperplastic lesions of the female breast. A long-term follow-up study. Cancer 1985;55: 2698–708.

102. Rosen PP, Braun DW Jr, Kinne DE. The clinical significance of pre-invasive breast carcinoma. Cancer 1980;46(4 Suppl):919–25.

103. Eusebi V, Foschini MP, Cook MG, et al. Long-term follow-up of in situ carcinoma of the breast with special emphasis on clinging carcinoma. Semin Diagn Pathol 1989;6:165–73.

104. Solin LJ, Kurtz J, Fourquet A, et al. Fifteen-year results of breast-conserving surgery and definitive breast irradiation for the treatment of ductal carcinoma in situ of the breast. J Clin Oncol 1996; 14:754–63.

105. Fisher B, Dignam J, Wolmark N, et al. Lumpectomy and radiation therapy for the treatment of intraductal breast cancer: findings from National Surgical Adjuvant Breast and Bowel Project B-17. J Clin Oncol 1998;16:441–52.

106. Silverstein MJ, Lagios MD, Groshen S, et al. The influence of margin width on local control of ductal carcinoma in situ of the breast. N Engl J Med 1999;340:1455–61.

107. Costantino JP, Gail MH, Pee D, et al. Validation studies for models projecting the risk of invasive

and total breast cancer incidence. J Natl Cancer Inst 1999;91:1541–8.

108. Bondy ML, Lustbader ED, Halabi S, et al. Validation of a breast cancer risk assessment model in women with a positive family history. J Natl Cancer Inst 1994;86:620 5.

109. Spiegelman D, Colditz GA, Hunter D, Hertzmark E. Validation of the Gail et al. model for predicting individual breast cancer risk. J Natl Cancer Inst 1994;86:600–7.

110. Rockhill B, Spiegelman D, Byrne C, et al. Validation of the Gail et al. model of breast cancer risk prediction and implications for chemoprevention. J Natl Cancer Inst 2001;93:358–66.

111. Gail MH, Benichou J. Assessing the risk of breast cancer in individuals. In: DeVita VJ, Hellman S, Rosenberg S, editors. Cancer prevention. Philadelphia (PA): Lippincott; 1992. p. 1–15.

112. Breast cancer risk assessment tool for health care providers. Bethesda (MD): National Cancer Institute; 1998.

113. McGuigan KA, Ganz PA, Breant C. Agreement between breast cancer risk estimation methods. J Natl Cancer Inst 1996;88:1315–7.

114. McTiernan A, Kuniyuki A, Yasui Y, et al. Comparisons of two breast cancer risk estimates in women with a family history of breast cancer. Cancer Epidemiol Biomarkers Prev 2001;10:333–8.

115. Rosai J. Borderline epithelial lesions of the breast. Am J Surg Pathol 1991;15:209–21.

116. Schnitt SJ, Connolly JL, Tavassoli FA, et al. Interobserver reproducibility in the diagnosis of ductal proliferative breast lesions using standardized criteria. Am J Surg Pathol 1992;16:1133–43.

117. Fitzgibbons PL. Atypical lobular hyperplasia of the breast: a study of pathologists' responses in the College of American Pathologists Performance Improvement Program in Surgical Pathology. Arch Pathol Lab Med 2000;124:463–4.

118. Berry DA, Iversen ES Jr, Gudbjartsson DF, et al. BRCAPRO validation, sensitivity of genetic testing of BRCA1/BRCA2, and prevalence of other breast cancer susceptibility genes. J Clin Oncol 2002;20: 2701–12.

119. Shattuck-Eidens D, Oliphant A, McClure M, et al. BRCA1 sequence analysis in women at high risk for susceptibility mutations. Risk factor analysis and implications for genetic testing. JAMA 1997; 278:1242–50.

120. FitzGerald MG, MacDonald DJ, Krainer M, et al. Germ-line BRCA1 mutations in Jewish and non-Jewish women with early-onset breast cancer. N Engl J Med 1996;334:143 9.

121. Parmigiani G, Berry D, Aguilar O. Determining carrier probabilities for breast cancer-susceptibility genes BRCA1 and BRCA2. Am J Hum Genet 1998;62:145–58.

122. Berry DA, Parmigiani G, Sanchez J, et al. Probability of carrying a mutation of breast-ovarian cancer gene BRCA1 based on family history. J Natl Cancer Inst 1997;89:227–38.

123. Burke W, Daly M, Garber J, et al. Recommendations for follow-up care of individuals with an inherited predisposition to cancer. II. BRCA1 and BRCA2. Cancer Genetics Studies Consortium. JAMA 1997; 277:997–1003.

124. Hoogerbrugge N, Bult P, de Widt-Levert LM, et al. High prevalence of premalignant lesions in prophylactically removed breasts from women at hereditary risk for breast cancer. J Clin Oncol 2003;21:41–5.

125. Narod SA, Brunet JS, Ghadirian P, et al. Tamoxifen and risk of contralateral breast cancer in BRCA1 and BRCA2 mutation carriers: a case-control study. Hereditary Breast Cancer Clinical Study Group. Lancet 2000;356(9245):1876–81.

126. Pierce LJ, Strawderman M, Narod SA, et al. Effect of radiotherapy after breast-conserving treatment in women with breast cancer and germline BRCA1/2 mutations. J Clin Oncol 2000;18:3360–9.

127. Lipkus IM, Klein WM, Rimer BK. Communicating breast cancer risks to women using different formats. Cancer Epidemiol Biomarkers Prev 2001;10:895–8.

128. Dooley WC. Ductal lavage, nipple aspiration, and ductoscopy for breast cancer diagnosis. Curr Oncol Rep 2003;5:63–5.

129. Fabian CJ, Kimler BF. Breast cancer risk prediction: should nipple aspiration fluid cytology be incorporated into clinical practice? J Natl Cancer Inst 2001;93:1762–3.

130. Tchou J, Hou N, Rademaker A, et al. Patient acceptance of tamoxifen as chemoprevention. Proc Am Soc Clin Oncol 2003;22:551.

131. Morrow M, Strom EA, Bassett LW, et al. Standard for breast conservation therapy in the management of invasive breast carcinoma. CA Cancer J Clin 2002; 52:277–300.

132. Cummings SR, Eckert S, Krueger KA, et al. The effect of raloxifene on risk of breast cancer in postmenopausal women: results from the MORE randomized trial. Multiple Outcomes of Raloxifene Evaluation. JAMA 1999;281:2189–97.

FAMILIAL AND GENETIC RISK

Claudine Isaacs, MD,
Beth N. Peshkin, MS, CGC,
Marc Schwartz, PhD

Many factors are known to influence the risk of breast cancer. Among the most significant are family history and increasing age. Approximately 20 to 30% of women with breast cancer have at least one relative with the disease; however, only 5 to 10% may have inherited predisposition attributable to mutations in the *BRCA1* and *BRCA2* genes.[1–3] Three hallmark signs of hereditary breast cancer include (1) the presence of several female relatives affected with breast and/or ovarian cancer, usually with predominantly early onset (eg, breast cancer diagnosed at < 50 years of age), (2) women with double primary cancers of the breast and ovary, and (3) vertical transmission in two or more generations, including transmission through male relatives (consistent with autosomal dominant inheritance).

Genetic counseling and testing are integral parts of the management of women who face an increased risk of breast cancer. In addition, heightened surveillance and the use of risk-reducing strategies can potentially decrease morbidity and mortality for such high-risk women. Furthermore, persistent worry may be relieved for women who test negative for a predisposing familial mutation.

Despite these potential benefits associated with genetic testing, critical questions remain regarding cancer risks in gene carriers, the efficacy of management options, and the extent to which genetic testing may pose psychological and social risks. Patients who face the decision to undergo genetic testing and the providers who counsel them are challenged by these uncertainties. This chapter provides an overview of the medical and psychological issues relevant to the process of genetic counseling.

ASSESSING THE PROBABILITY OF INHERITED SUSCEPTIBILITY: AN OVERVIEW

The most critical tool in cancer risk assessment is a review of the pedigree to determine whether a family history is consistent with an inherited cancer predisposition syndrome. Although many high-risk families have histories suggestive of *BRCA1/2* mutations, a qualitative review of the pedigree may also reveal the presence of other syndromes such as Li-Fraumeni syndrome (LFS) or Cowden disease (which are described in detail later in this chapter). The probability that a specific individual harbors a gene mutation and the associated cancer risks may be derived from Mendelian analysis and estimates of gene penetrance. If hereditary breast cancer is not suggested by a patient's history, her cancer risk can be determined by using empiric models, which are discussed in Chapter 1.

As discussed, alterations in a single gene account for only 5 to 10% of breast cancers.[3] The Breast Cancer Linkage Consortium (BCLC) studied 237 families containing at least four cases of female breast cancer (and no ovarian cancer) and estimated that 28% of the family histories were attributable to *BRCA1* mutations, 37% to *BRCA2* mutations, and 35% to unidentified gene mutations.[4] In families containing cases of both breast and ovarian cancers, a much higher proportion (80%) were due to *BRCA1* mutations, whereas only 15% were attributable to *BRCA2* mutations, and 5% were due to unidentified mutations.[4] In clinical risk evaluation settings, the proportion of individuals who test positive will likely be lower than the numbers derived from these highly enriched families.[5-7]

Founder Mutations

Ascertaining the patient's ethnic background is another important aspect of an accurate risk assessment. Three founder mutations, two in *BRCA1* (187delAG and 5385insC) and one in *BRCA2* (6174delT), occur with a background frequency of approximately 1 in 40 (2.3%) in individuals of central or eastern European (Ashkenazi) Jewish descent.[8] In contrast, the carrier frequency for *BRCA1* mutations in the general population is estimated to be between 1 in 500 and 1 in 800[9] and lower for *BRCA2*. Therefore, patients with Ashkenazi Jewish ancestry on both sides of their family, who also have a relative who carries one of these mutations, should be tested for all three founder mutations.[10]

The following studies highlight the effect of ancestry on the likelihood of identifying a *BRCA1* or *BRCA2* mutation. Peto and colleagues tested 617 British women diagnosed with breast cancer ≤ 45 years, who were unselected for family history, of whom 5% tested positive for *BRCA1* or *BRCA2* mutations.[11] By comparison, in 275 unselected Jewish breast cancer patients diagnosed by age 49, Satagopan and colleagues found that 16% tested positive for *BRCA1* or *BRCA2* founder mutations.[12] More striking still are the findings with respect to ovarian cancer. For example, Risch and colleagues conducted a population-based series in Ontario among 515 women with invasive ovarian cancer, finding that 12% had a *BRCA1* or *BRCA2* mutation.[13] Moslehi and colleagues conducted a multicenter population-based study, in which a founder mutation was identified in 41% of the 213 Jewish women with ovarian cancer.[14] It is important then to consider *BRCA1* and *BRCA2* testing for Jewish patients with early-onset breast cancer or ovarian cancer, even in the absence of a family history of these cancers.

Although the three founder mutations are prevalent in high-risk Jewish families, it is important to counsel patients about the likelihood that another mutation may be present if these are ruled out. Frank and colleagues reported that 74 of 737 (10%) Jewish individuals tested positive for deleterious mutations, 16 of which were nonfounder mutations (although 5 of these individuals also had

non-Jewish ancestry).[6] In a smaller study, Kauff and colleagues observed that only 3 of 70 (4%) Jewish women with personal and possibly family histories of ovarian and breast cancers tested positive for a deleterious nonfounder mutation.[15] Although it is not clear what factors predict the presence of a nonfounder mutation, it is reasonable to consider full sequencing of *BRCA1/2* if women have a high prior probability of testing positive based on models such as BRCAPRO, and/or whose family history strongly suggests the presence of a mutation (eg, owing to multiple cases of ovarian and breast cancers, male breast cancer, or pancreatic cancer).

Founder mutations have been observed, albeit with less frequency, in other groups, most notably in Icelanders, in whom it is estimated that 0.6% of the population carries a single *BRCA2* mutation (999del5).[16] This mutation is also present in approximately 8% of females with breast cancer and 40% of males with breast cancer.[16] Founder effects have been observed in many other populations including (but not limited to) Belgians, Finns, French-Canadians, Germans, Latvians, Norwegians, Russians, and Swedes.[17,18] Information is also emerging about the presence of founder mutations in Asians[19] and African-Americans,[20-22] although in the latter, many of the sequence variants are novel or missense mutations of uncertain significance.[23-25]

Another finding that has important clinical implications is the observation that large rearrangements in the *BRCA1* gene which are not identifiable by routine sequencing have been found with increased frequency in individuals of mainly European, particularly English and Dutch, extraction. These mutations include a large (6 kb) duplication of exon 13, and three large deletions, the latter accounting for over one-third of all *BRCA1* mutations in Dutch patients.[26,27] Unger and colleagues showed that large *BRCA1* rearrangements were identified in 5 of 42 (12%) American families with breast and ovarian cancers that tested negative for *BRCA1/2* coding-region mutations.[28] Thus, the presence of these rearrangements contributes to the rate of false-negative results for high-risk individuals who may undergo sequencing only. As a result, a commercial laboratory now includes testing for specific *BRCA1* rearrangements as part of routine full gene analysis (BRACAnalysis® Technical Specifications, Myriad Genetic Laboratories, Salt Lake

City, Utah, USA, updated 7 February 2003). In general, full *BRCA1/2* gene testing is warranted for patients other than those of Ashkenazi Jewish or Icelandic descent where founder effects are marked.

Quantitative Models of Estimating *BRCA1/2* Carrier Probabilities

Once a family history is recorded, quantitative models may be used to estimate the probability that an individual carries a *BRCA1* or *BRCA2* mutation. Some models estimate probability based on data from clinical populations. For example, the updated "Couch" Model, available in tabular form (with software to be available), is based on 615 tested families from the United Kingdom and the United States, containing at least two cases of breast or ovarian cancer per family.[29–31] Logistic regression analysis was used to determine the likelihood of a *BRCA1* or *BRCA2* mutation. As expected, the presence of early-onset breast cancer, ovarian or fallopian tube cancers, and Ashkenazi Jewish ancestry were the strongest predictors of finding a *BRCA1* or *BRCA2* mutation.

Another empirically based tool, available in tabular form, is derived from actual rates of *BRCA1/2* mutation prevalence in 10,000 consecutive gene analyses performed by a commercial laboratory.[6] Probabilities were determined based on the family history (at least one first- or second-degree relative) and age of diagnosis of breast or ovarian cancer, as well as the presence or absence of Ashkenazi Jewish ancestry. Again, the occurrence of breast and ovarian cancer within a family, especially in conjunction with Jewish ancestry, was associated with a higher probability of testing positive for a *BRCA1* or *BRCA2* mutation.[6] However, Jewish ancestry appears to have a less significant impact on carrier probabilities in families with multiple cases of breast and ovarian cancers.[6] An important limitation of these data is that family history information may have been incomplete and/or not verified with medical records. Updated tables for this study are posted on the Myriad Genetic Laboratories Web site at <http://www.myriadtests.com/provider/mutprev.htm> (accessed August 6, 2003), and are downloadable to personal digital assistants (PDAs).

BRCAPRO is another quantitative method of determining carrier probabilities. This is a computerized model that uses Bayesian theory and family history information, as well as *BRCA1/2* mutation frequency and a range of mutation penetrance fig-

ures, to estimate *BRCA1/2* carrier probabilities.[32,33] A validation study showed that the model predicted the rates of positive results reasonably well for both high- and low-risk groups.[34] As probabilities vary depending on which person is chosen for analysis, the clinician may wish to run the model on the person most likely to harbor a mutation, and then calculate Mendelian probabilities for other relatives.

Several of these models can be run concurrently through the *CancerGene* software program package, available at <http://www3.utsouthwestern.edu/cancergene> (accessed August 6, 2003). Excellent reviews of these models have recently been published.[30,35]

It is important to bear in mind that although pedigree analysis is central to the risk assessment process, several factors may affect the clinician's ability to discern a pattern of hereditary breast cancer within a specific family. For example, *BRCA1/2* mutations are associated with variable expressivity and incomplete penetrance. In addition, an individual may have limited knowledge of her family history; next of kin may be few in number, or may contain more at-risk males than females; or, female relatives may be too young to exhibit the phenotype.

CLINICAL CHARACTERISTICS OF HEREDITARY BREAST CANCER

As previously stated, mutations in *BRCA1* and *BRCA2* account for the majority of cases of hereditary breast cancer. However, a very small proportion of hereditary breast cancer is attributable to mutations in genes associated with rare conditions such as LFS, Cowden disease, Peutz-Jeghers syndrome, and ataxia-telangiectasia heterozygosity. The cancer risks associated with an inherited predisposition to hereditary breast cancer are summarized below. Management strategies are addressed in Section Two.

BRCA1 and *BRCA2*

Cancer Risks

Breast Cancer. Studies have demonstrated a significant variation in the risk of breast and ovarian cancer in *BRCA1* and *BRCA2* mutation carriers (Table 2-1). International studies conducted by the BCLC, performed in very highly selected families with multiple cases of breast and ovarian cancers, ascertained that the lifetime risk of breast cancer in

TABLE 2-1 Estimated Cancer Risks Associated with *BRCA1* and *BRCA2* Mutations

Cancer Type	Risk in BRCA1/2 Carriers to Age 70 Years	General Population Risk to Age 70 Years	Comments	References
Breast	40–85%	8%	The incidence of breast cancer diagnosed < 50 years is higher in *BRCA1* carriers compared to *BRCA2* carriers, but both groups have an increased risk of premenopausal breast cancer	4,8,12,13,36–43,46
Contralateral breast	40–65%	0.5–1% per year of follow-up	Over long follow-up periods, the risk of ipsilateral breast cancer is also elevated	36,37,39,46–49
Ovarian	25–65% *BRCA1*; 15–25% *BRCA2*	1%	The incidence of ovarian cancer diagnosed at < 50 years is higher in *BRCA1* carriers, and overall rare in all carriers less than age 40. Risk of fallopian tube cancer is also substantially elevated	4,8,36–39,43–45
Colon	Unclear	2%		8,36,38,39,47,50, 53–55
Prostate	Probably elevated; absolute risk not well defined	8%		8,36,38,39,47,50
Male breast	? < 10%	0.1%		6,39,51,52
Pancreatic	? < 10%	0.4%		38,39,47,50,152
Other sites	To be determined	Varied		39,47,50

Reproduced with permission from Isaacs C, Peshkin B, Schwartz M. Evaluation and Management of Women with a Strong Family History. In: Harris JR, Lippman ME, Morrow M, Osborne CK, editors. Diseases of the Breast. 3rd edition. Philadelphia: Lippincott, Williams and Wilkins; [In Press].

Lifetime risks of cancer are approximate, and are generally from birth to age 70 years.

General population risks for most sites are derived from SEER data.[38]

BRCA1 carriers was 87% (95% CI 72–95%)[36] and in *BRCA2* carriers (95% CI 43–95%) was 84%.[4] In addition, it has been noted that these women have significantly elevated risks of premenopausal breast cancer, with a risk of breast cancer by age 50 years of approximately 50% in *BRCA1* carriers[37] and 28% in *BRCA2* carriers.[4] These risks are substantially higher than those observed in the general population, which is 2% by age 50 and 7% by age 70.[38]

A study performed by Brose and colleagues in a less highly selected group of individuals ascertained through academic-based high-risk clinics, estimated a lifetime penetrance of 73% for breast cancer in *BRCA1* carriers (95% CI 68–78%), a finding very similar to that originally observed in BCLC families.[39] However, because these penetrance risks may not apply to individuals with less suggestive

family histories, several investigators have undertaken studies to examine this issue. For example, among Ashkenazi Jewish breast cancer patients unselected for family history, studies have demonstrated the lifetime risk to be between 36 and 60%.[8,12,40,41] A population-based study in Iceland found that female carriers of the *BRCA2* founder mutation 999del5 had a 37% lifetime risk of developing breast cancer (95% CI 22–54%).[42] More recently, Antoniou and colleagues pooled pedigree data from 22 studies for a metaanalysis involving 8,139 index case patients who were unselected for family history.[43] Of 6,965 women and 176 men with breast cancer and 998 women with ovarian cancer, 289 were *BRCA1* carriers and 221 were *BRCA2* carriers.[43] The average cumulative breast cancer risk to 70 years in *BRCA1* carriers was 65%

(95% CI 51–75%), versus 45% (95% CI 33–54%) in *BRCA2* carriers.[43] Also, these analyses indicated that breast cancer incidence in *BRCA1* carriers increased with age, but starting at 50 years, the incidence remained somewhat constant.[43] On the other hand, the incidence in *BRCA2* carriers continued to rise.[43]

Ovarian and Fallopian Tube Cancers. The lifetime risk for ovarian cancer was also found to vary substantially among studies. The BCLC studies of highly selected families estimated that the risk of ovarian cancer for *BRCA1* carriers was roughly between 30–60% by age 70 years[36,37] and up to 27% for *BRCA2* carriers (95% CI 0–47%).[4] Again, similar risks were found in the study of Brose and colleagues, where *BRCA1* carriers had an ovarian risk of about 40% (95% CI 36–46%).[39]

Interestingly, a case-control study of unselected Jewish patients with ovarian cancer showed that lifetime ovarian cancer risk was comparable to that observed by the BCLC: 37% (95% CI 25–71%) in *BRCA1* carriers and 21% (95% CI 13–41%) in *BRCA2* carriers.[44] In the metaanalysis by Antoniou and colleagues, the pooled data indicated that the lifetime risk of ovarian cancer was 39% (95% CI 22–51%) in *BRCA1* carriers and 11% (95 % CI 4.1–18%) for *BRCA2* carriers.[43] These data also confirmed that the risk of ovarian cancer in carriers under age 30 is low, but after that, the risk rises more dramatically, especially for *BRCA1* carriers. Taken together, all studies demonstrate that carriers face a significantly elevated risk of ovarian cancer relative to the general population, in which the risk is about 1.5%.[38] Although a rare occurrence, *BRCA1* and *BRCA2* mutations are also associated with an excess risk for primary fallopian tube cancer.[39,45]

Second Malignancies. The predisposition toward multiple primary cancers is a hallmark of hereditary cancer. It is estimated that *BRCA1* carriers affected with breast cancer have a 40 to 65% cumulative risk of contralateral breast cancer.[37,39,46] For *BRCA2* carriers, the risk is comparable at 52% (95% CI 42–61%).[47] Individuals with sporadic breast cancer have a 0.5 to 1% annual risk of contralateral breast cancer. After long follow-up periods, elevated rates of ipsilateral breast cancer are also apparent, although it is difficult to quantify specific risks.[48,49] Factors affecting surgical decisions should be based upon the recognition that *BRCA1/2* carriers face elevated risks for second primary breast cancers.

The lifetime risk of ovarian cancer in *BRCA1* carriers affected with breast cancer ranges from 19% (95% CI 14–24%)[39] and 44% (95% CI 28–56%) by age 70 years.[36] In *BRCA2* carriers, the risk is approximately 15% (95% CI 8–23%) by age 70. [47] The risk in patients with sporadic breast cancer is comparably 2 to 3%.

Other Cancers. Many studies have suggested that prostate cancer is likely to be part of the tumor spectrum associated with *BRCA1* and *BRCA2* mutations, although the absolute risk remains unclear. In 699 high-risk families studied by the BCLC, the overall relative risk in *BRCA1* carriers was 1.07 (95% CI 0.75–1.54), although interestingly, most of this risk was accounted for in men under age 65.[50] The clinic-based study by Brose and colleagues found no excess risk of prostate cancer in *BRCA1* carriers.[39] By contrast, the BCLC study of 173 *BRCA2* families found an overall relative risk of 4.6 (95% CI 3.5–6.2), which translated to a cumulative risk of 19.8% (95% CI 15.2–24.2%) by age 80 years.[47]

Recent data have shown that the risk of male breast cancer appears to be roughly equivalent in both *BRCA1* and *BRCA2* carriers, with a cumulative risk of under 10%.[39,51,52] The median age at diagnosis is between 52 and 59 years, respectively, which is younger than the average 69 years in the general population.[6,39]

Pancreatic cancer has also been noted more frequently in both *BRCA2* and *BRCA1* carriers. Although based on a relatively small number of cases, the BCLC estimated the cumulative lifetime risk to be 3.5% in *BRCA2* carriers, (95% CI 1.87–6.58%) with the highest risk found in individuals younger than age 65.[47] Brose and colleagues estimated the risk to be 3.6% (95% CI 1.9–5.3%) in *BRCA1* carriers compared to the general population risk of 1.3%.[39]

Conflicting data make it unclear if the risk of colon cancer is elevated in *BRCA1* and *BRCA2* carriers. While some studies have supported this notion, [36,39,50] others have not.[8,47,53–55] Increased relative risks for other cancer sites (eg, melanoma, stomach) have been reported for carriers.[39,47,50] Additional studies are needed to verify these findings.

To summarize, when performing a qualitative assessment of a pedigree containing cases of (female) breast and/or ovarian cancer, the presence of male breast cancer or pancreatic cancer, for example, may contribute to the likelihood that an inherited predisposition exists due to *BRCA1/2* mutations. Although the risks of these other cancers are low, they are significantly higher than in the general population. It is difficult to provide carriers with precise cancer risk estimates, given the wide confidence intervals that have been reported in most studies. In addition, most studies have been performed in Caucasians, and it is not clear whether these risks extrapolate to other populations.[18] Also, it is uncertain whether genotype-phenotype correlations exist, and if so, how they translate into provision of risk estimates (see p. 32). Furthermore, it is unclear whether characteristics of a patient's family history can place these risks into context, given the aforementioned limitations such as small family size, lack of family history information, and the inability to verify some diagnoses for affected relatives. Despite these constraints, it remains clear that *BRCA1* and *BRCA2* mutations substantially elevate a woman's risk of breast and ovarian cancers, with increased risks that persist throughout her lifetime.

BRCA1- *and* BRCA2-*Associated Breast Cancer: Phenotype and Prognosis*

BRCA1-associated breast cancers are noted to be more frequently high grade,[56] have higher mitotic counts,[46,56,57] and are more often estrogen and progesterone receptor negative.[58,59] These tumors also exhibit more lymphocytic infiltration and continuous pushing margins than is seen typically in sporadic breast cancer[57] and have more frequent medullary or atypical features.[56,60] Studies have demonstrated that up to 41% of *BRCA1* carriers with breast cancer had ductal carcinoma in situ (DCIS) around areas of invasive disease as compared to 51% in sporadic disease.[56] *BRCA1*-associated breast cancers showed an increased incidence of *p53* mutations[58,61] on molecular analysis, but a decreased incidence of overexpression of *erb*B-2.[58,62–64]

BRCA2-associated breast cancer studies demonstrate more variable findings for both mitotic indices and for tubule formation.[56,57] Two studies observed excess numbers of tubulolobular or pleomorphic lobular carcinomas in *BRCA2* carriers.[65,66] A third study did not confirm this finding.[67] With respect to mitotic indices, one study detected higher scores,[57] and another noted no differences

compared with sporadic cancers.[56] Some studies report that *BRCA2*-associated cancers are more frequently positive than sporadic disease with regard to hormone receptor status,[67] whereas others do not report any differences between sporadic and mutation carriers.[58,68] Finally, in contrast to *BRCA1*, *BRCA2*-associated breast cancers did not exhibit any differences in expression of *p53* or *erb*B-2.[58]

The observed phenotypic differences between sporadic and *BRCA1*- or *BRCA2*-associated breast cancers have been the focus of many studies investigating prognostic implications. Methodologic limitations such as the retrospective nature of these studies and the inclusion of only small numbers of patients have resulted in widely variable findings, making it difficult to draw clear conclusions.[59,63,69–74] At present, the mutation status of the patient is not an independent predictor of clinical outcome, and should not, therefore, be used to influence systemic therapy decisions.

Cancer Risk Modifiers

Individuals within the same family carrying the same mutation may have significant differences in the age of onset and type of cancer they develop. In light of these differences, investigators have been led to examine the role of genetic and environmental risk modifiers.

Reproductive Factors. Reproductive factors such as the effect of age at menarche, pregnancy, and breastfeeding have been central questions in the few studies examining whether these risk factors, which affect women in the general population, are applicable to *BRCA1/2* carriers. In one study of 333 women with *BRCA1* mutations, a slightly elevated risk of breast cancer was noted in association with early menarche and low parity, whereas age at first full term pregnancy was not found to be an influence.[75] Two other studies provide contrasting results over the question of whether pregnancy may be associated with early onset of breast cancers in carriers.[76,77] The impact of parity on risk of ovarian cancer is controversial. Similar to what is seen in the general population, one study observed a 12% (95% CI 2.3–21%) reduction in risk of ovarian cancer with each additional birth.[78] However, a second study found that each additional birth resulted in an increased relative risk of 1.4. This same study offered the consolation that a protective effect was found for women whose last birth was at age 30 years or over, with a 48% reduction in risk, in contrast to those who were 29 years old or less at last birth.[75] In summary, too few studies with very limited data preclude drawing any definitive conclusions with respect to reproductive factors. Thus, the information has generally not been used to refine risk estimates or alter management strategies.

Oral Contraceptives. The impact of oral contraceptives on the risk of ovarian cancer remains unclear. One case-control study of 232 *BRCA1* and *BRCA2* carriers with ovarian cancer and 232 unaffected carriers reported that the use of oral contraceptives reduced ovarian cancer risk by more than half (odds ratio 0.44%, 95% CI 0.28–0.68).[79] However, a second study found that oral contraceptive use did not reduce the risk of ovarian cancer in carriers.[78]

The impact of oral contraceptives on the risk of breast cancer has been examined in a multinational study involving 1,311 pairs of women with *BRCA1/2* mutations.[80] *BRCA1* carriers using the pill before 1975, before age 30 years, or who used it for 5 years or more, appeared to have an increased risk of early-onset breast cancer (relative risks approximately 1.3 to 1.4), although the lower boundary of the confidence interval hovered around 1.0. No elevations in risk were noted for *BRCA2* carriers.

Based on the limited nature of these data, further research is needed to validate the true impact of oral contraceptives on breast and ovarian cancer risk.

Tubal Ligation and Bilateral Salpingo-Oophorectomy. In the general population, tubal ligation has been demonstrated to reduce the incidence of ovarian cancer.[81] In a case-control study of mutation carriers affected and unaffected with ovarian cancer, tubal ligation was found to exert an independent protective effect in *BRCA1* carriers (odds ratio 0.39, 95% CI 0.22–0.70), but not in *BRCA2* carriers (odds ratio 1.19, 95% CI 0.38–3.68).[80] In addition, bilateral salpingo-oophorectomy significantly reduces the risk of ovarian cancer among *BRCA1/2* carriers.[82,83] This is discussed in Chapter 16, "Prophylactic Surgery."

Genotype–Phenotype Correlations Within BRCA1 *and* BRCA2. Patients often ask whether cancer risks can be tailored to the specific mutation that has been identified in their family. Although emerging studies have demonstrated that some genotype–phenotype correlations do exist, the data are too preliminary to be translated into the clinic. For example, a study of 164 families reported that mutations within the central region of the *BRCA2* gene, called the ovarian cancer cluster region (OCCR), were associated with a lower risk of breast cancer (RR 0.63, 95% CI 0.46–0.84) and a higher risk of ovarian cancer (RR 1.88, 95% CI 1.08–3.33).[51] Another study focused on unselected *BRCA2* carriers with ovarian cancer. Their first-degree relatives had ovarian, colon, stomach, pancreatic, or prostate cancer only when the proband's mutation was in the OCCR, suggesting that mutations in this region may be associated with a broader tumor spectrum altogether.[13] Together, these studies suggest that mutations within the OCCR may be associated with a diminished risk of breast cancer, but not necessarily higher risk of ovarian cancer.[51] With respect to the *BRCA1* gene, findings are not consistent, although some genotype–phenotype correlations may exist.[84] Further research may also reveal that some variants of uncertain significance could be associated with modified risks for breast and/or ovarian cancer. In addition, some population-based, case-control studies have revealed that specific polymorphisms within the *BRCA1/2* genes may also be associated with elevated risks of breast and ovarian cancers, although at rates much lower than those seen with other deleterious mutations.[85–87] These polymorphisms may also function as risk modifiers when occurring in conjunction with germline deleterious *BRCA* mutations.[88] Before data can be used to refine risk estimates in the clinic, further studies are needed in *BRCA1* and *BRCA2* carriers, including population-based cases.

Modifier Genes. Modifier genes also may affect gene penetrance. A single nucleotide polymorphism in the *RAD51* gene has been found to be associated with increased breast cancer risk in *BRCA2*, but not in *BRCA1* carriers.[89,90] Phelan and colleagues found, in regard to ovarian cancer risk, that *BRCA1* carriers with two rare *HRSA1* alleles were approximately twice as likely to develop ovarian cancer than were carriers with only common *HRSA1* alleles.[91] Interestingly, Rebbeck and colleagues found that *BRCA1/2* carriers with certain alleles of the *A1B1* gene (amplified in breast cancer 1), coupled with reproductive risk factors such as nulliparity and late age at first birth, had an over 4-fold risk of developing breast cancer in comparison to carriers without any of these risk factors.[92] However preliminary, these important results indicate that in the future, data may become available to allow individualized risk assessments for carriers based on multiple genetic and environmental parameters.

Other Syndromes

In clinical practice, the proportion of familial breast cancers attributable to *BRCA1* and *BRCA2* mutations is often less than that predicted by linkage studies.[5–7] This finding suggests that other highly penetrant, though rarely occurring, mutations or sequence variants in so-called low-penetrance genes may account for a significant proportion of familial breast cancers.

An interesting study of unselected breast cancer patients in Helsinki, Finland showed that those with a positive family history of breast cancer were more likely to harbor a specific alteration (1100delC) in the *CHEK2* gene (OR 2.27, 95% CI 1.11–4.63).[93] It has been estimated that the resulting increase in breast cancer is about 2-fold in women and about 10-fold in men.[94] *CHEK2* gene modifications have also been identified in a small number of families with LFS (see below). The proportion of familial breast cancers attributable to other low-penetrance genes, for example, *CYP1A1*, *CYP17* (involved in estrogen metabolism), glutathione S-transferases (involved in detoxification of hydrocarbons), and the estrogen and progesterone receptor genes, is unknown, but could be sizable.[95] On the other hand, less than 1% of all breast cancers are caused by other highly penetrant mutations associated with the conditions described below.

Li-Fraumeni Syndrome

Soft tissue sarcomas, osteosarcomas, leukemias, brain tumors, adrenocortical malignancies, and early-onset breast cancer are characteristic of LFS, a rare autosomal dominant condition.[96,97] Other early-onset malignancies such as cancers of the lung, gastrointestinal tract (stomach, colon, pancreas), and ovary, as well as lymphomas and melanoma, may be part of this tumor spectrum, according to the findings from a study of 738 evaluable cancers in LFS kindreds.[98]

In up to 70% of families with LFS, mutations in the tumor suppresser gene, *p53*, have been documented, although rates vary depending on the ascer-

tainment criteria used and the extent of the testing.[99] De novo mutations have also been reported.[100] More recently, mutations in the *CHEK2* gene have been found in a few families with LFS.[101,102]

LFS is a highly penetrant syndrome. Half of the carriers of LFS will develop some form of cancer by age 30 years and 90% by age 70 years.[103] In a report including 200 individuals from 24 LFS families, approximately 30 out of 45 women who developed breast cancer were diagnosed by age 45 years.[104] Of these women, 25% were diagnosed with multiple breast cancers and over 25% had additional primary tumors. Of note, many of these cancers occurred within previously irradiated areas.[104,105] One potential implication of this information is that treatment options may be different for women with LFS and a diagnosis of breast cancer (eg, they may wish to avoid breast conservation and radiation therapy).

For individuals at risk for LFS, it is recommended that breast cancer surveillance in women begin at age 20 to 25 years, or on a case-by-case basis depending on the age of onset of cancers within the family.[106,107] As radiation sensitivity is a concern, magnetic resonance imaging (MRI) or ultrasound might be the diagnostic tools of choice rather than an annual mammogram (see Chapter 8). Also, beginning at age 20 to 25 years, annual comprehensive physical examinations focusing on rare cancers are recommended.[106] Surveillance may be tailored according to family history, and prompt follow-up is urged for suggestive symptoms.[108]

Testing for *p53* mutations is available clinically. Thus, when a *p53* mutation is identified, predictive testing is available for at-risk family members. However, proven screening strategies are not currently available for most of the components of these cancers, particularly for childhood cancers. In addition, ethical issues surrounding the testing of minors should be carefully explored before testing children.

Cowden Disease

Multiple hamartomatous lesions, early-onset breast cancer, and thyroid cancer are characteristic of Cowden disease, a rare autosomal dominant condition.[109] Hamartomas may occur in the skin, oral mucosa, breasts, and intestines. Mucocutaneous hamartomas, which are pathognomonic for the condition, include papillomas of the lips and mucous membranes, acral keratosis of the skin, and rough surfaced facial papules called trichilemmomas.[109] Skin lesions in individuals affected with Cowden disease usually develop by age 20 years.[110] In females affected with Cowden disease, the risk of breast cancer is between 25 and 50%, with a high risk for premenopausal cancer.[110] These cancers are usually ductal in origin and often surrounded by densely collagenized hamartomatous lesions.[111] Interestingly, many women with Cowden disease and breast cancer have no known family history of breast cancer.[111] A number of benign breast conditions affect up to 70% of women with Cowden disease, including ductal hyperplasia, intraductal papillomas, adenosis, lobular atrophy, fibroadenomas, and fibrocystic changes.[110,111] The breast conditions, both benign and malignant, are also more likely to be identified bilaterally.[111] Thyroid tumors, both benign and malignant, are also commonly observed. Up to 10% of individuals affected with Cowden disease have follicular carcinomas, and over 50% have follicular adenomas or multinodular goiters.[110] Recently, endometrial and renal cancers were added to this tumor spectrum.[109]

Germline mutations in the *PTEN* (phosphatase and tensin homologue) gene have been identified in individuals with Cowden disease, for which clinical testing is available.[112,113] A multidisciplinary team of surgeons, gynecologists, and dermatologists will usually manage patients presenting with this disorder. Mammography at age 30 to 35, or 5 to 10 years earlier than the youngest age of breast cancer onset in the family, monthly self-examination, and annual breast examinations are the recommended methods of managing breast cancer risk in these individuals.[106] Management of the other cancer risks includes comprehensive annual physical examination beginning at age 18 or 5 years younger than the youngest age of onset in the family, annual urinary analysis with cytology, baseline thyroid ultrasound at age 20 years with annual ultrasound thereafter if indicated, and annual endometrial biopsies beginning at age 35 to 40 years for premenopausal women or 5 years earlier than the youngest age at onset.[106] Annual endometrial ultrasounds are also recommended for postmenopausal women.[106]

Peutz-Jeghers Syndrome

Peutz-Jeghers syndrome is an autosomal dominant condition characterized by hamartomatous polyps in the gastrointestinal tract and by mucocutaneous melanin deposits in the buccal mucosa, lips, fingers, and toes.[114] This syndrome is associated with marked increases in risk for both intestinal and extraintestinal malignancies, with studies demonstrating a cumulative risk of cancer of 93% by age 65.[115] With respect to extraintestinal cancers, the most significant risk is for breast cancer, with a lifetime risk estimated at 55%, which approaches that observed in *BRCA1/2* carriers.[115] Although few cases have been reported overall, onset prior to age 50 years and bilateral disease are not uncommon.[115,116] The risk of ovarian cancer, estimated at about 20%, is significant, and of note, many of these are nonepithelial sex cord tumors.[115,116] Women also face elevated risks for uterine cancer.[115] Therefore, women should consider heightened surveillance for breast, uterine, and ovarian cancers.[114,115,117] Clinical testing for mutations in the *STK11* gene is available, although other susceptibility genes are likely to be implicated in this syndrome.[118–121]

Ataxia Telangiectasia

Immunodeficiency, cerebellar degeneration, oculocutaneous telangiectasia, and a markedly elevated risk of solid tumors, leukemia, and lymphoma characterize the autosomal recessive condition of ataxia telangiectasia. Several studies of obligate carriers suggest an excess risk of breast cancer, ranging from about a 4-fold to a 16-fold elevation in risk.[122,123] Concern has also been raised about the effect of ionizing radiation in carriers, which may have implications for both screening and breast cancer treatment.[124,125] Further research is needed, however, to establish the optimal means of mutation screening, carrier identification, and clinical implications in *ATM* carriers.

Hereditary Nonpolyposis Colon Cancer

Hereditary nonpolyposis colon cancer (HNPCC) is characterized by early onset of often predominantly proximal colorectal cancer, as well as endometrial, ovarian, small bowel, stomach, and genitourinary system cancers.[126] Germline mutations in the mismatch repair genes *hMLH1* and *hMLH2* have been identified in many high-risk families,[127] and clinical testing is available. There is debate as to whether breast cancer is part of the tumor spectrum in HNPCC. Microsatellite instability (MSI) has been identified in some HNPCC patients with breast cancers, but the association has not been universally confirmed.[128,129] These findings have led to the suggestion that while there may not be an elevation in risk of breast cancer in women with HNPCC, defects in the DNA mismatch repair system may contribute to tumor progression, which results in early age at diagnosis.[128] There is not yet enough evidence, however, to determine if women with HNPCC kindreds should pursue aggressive surveillance for early detection of breast cancer.

THE GENETIC COUNSELING PROCESS

Genetic counseling, both before and after genetic testing, is critical given the complex issues surrounding risk assessment, test result interpretation, medical management options, and potential psychological, social, and familial implications. The first step in this process is the collection of a comprehensive family history, which may be recorded and continually updated in the form of a pedigree, which should include information about ethnic background and medical history for maternal and paternal relatives over at least three generations, if possible. It is important to document (and verify with medical records, when possible) cancer or precancerous diagnoses, age at diagnosis, laterality, treatment, and surgical history (prophylactic or otherwise). Relevant exposure history should also be recorded. Pedigree analysis based on hallmark features provides the basis for accurate risk assessment.

For patients who are deemed to be at high risk, a simplified discussion of empiric and modeled data and principles of autosomal dominant inheritance (if appropriate) can be used to frame the risk of carrying a gene mutation and the risk of developing cancer. Quantitative information about carrier probabilities may be especially important as individuals weigh the financial costs of testing. These costs can be very expensive, although in the United States, many insurance companies will reimburse all or part of the costs, such as for *BRCA1/2* testing, although a letter of medical necessity may be required (personal communication, Myriad Genetic Laboratories, January 9, 2003).

The possible benefits, risks, and limitations of genetic testing should also be reviewed. Potential benefits include reduction of uncertainty due to increased knowledge, and informed decision-making about medical options including prophylactic surgery. For instance, some high-risk women who are candidates for breast conservation therapy or unilateral mastectomy may choose to learn their *BRCA1/2* status before making a definitive decision regarding breast cancer surgery, in the event that they may opt to undergo bilateral mastectomies instead.[130] Another major benefit of testing is that it may provide valuable risk information to family members.

In contrast, genetic testing may be declined for fear of genetic discrimination in areas of employment and health and life insurance, although few cases have been documented.[131–133] Patients should be aware of federal and state laws which do provide some, but not complete, protection against genetic discrimination.

Individuals who learn that they are carriers of mutated cancer genes may experience feelings of depression, anxiety, or sadness. In addition, individuals may feel overwhelmed at being the gatekeeper of information for other family members. The issue of "survivor guilt," a phenomenon experienced by some individuals who do not inherit a familial mutation, may also need to be acknowledged and addressed, in both the pre- and post-test genetic counseling sessions. In certain instances, referrals for psychological counseling may be appropriate. Educational materials and individualized letters are valuable tools for summarizing information about test result interpretation and management issues, and providing information about support and informational resources for patients. Written materials should also address specifically which family members are at risk of carrying a gene mutation, and may also provide guidance about ways that relatives can communicate information to these relatives.

In summary, the process of genetic counseling is designed to facilitate informed decision-making, thereby aiming to maximize the benefits of, and reduce the potential adverse effects from, genetic testing.[134,135] Specially trained genetic counselors and nurses often function within a multidisciplinary health-care team comprised of oncologists, surgeons, geneticists, and psychologists to attain these goals.

ISSUES IN *BRCA1/2* TEST RESULT INTERPRETATION

The most unambiguous results of testing are either true positives or true negatives. *True positive* refers to a gene change that is deleterious (ie, associated with heightened cancer risks). These are usually nonsense or frameshift mutations (eg, deletions or insertions) that result in protein truncation, or they may be genomic rearrangements such as large duplications or deletions. Specific missense mutations may also be classified as deleterious based on the outcome of functional assays or RNA studies.[136,137] Whereas some mutations have been identified in numerous high-risk families, others are "private" mutations that have been reported only once. A catalogue of reported mutations in the BRCA1 and BRCA2 genes is available online at <http://research.nhgri.nih.gov/bic/> (accessed Aug 6, 2003). *True negative* results apply when an individual tests negative for the specific mutation identified in a close relative. In BRCA families, the standard practice is to test relatives only for the presence or absence of the familial mutation, except for Ashkenazi Jewish individuals, who should be tested for all founder mutations given the frequency with which these mutations occur in this population. A true negative result can reassure an individual that his or her risk is equivalent to that of the general population.

As discussed, genetic testing should always be initiated, if possible, in an individual most likely to yield a positive result. For example, Susan, a healthy 30-year-old woman, approaches her genetic counselor about pursuing BRCA1/2 testing. She reports that she has two living relatives with cancer: her mother, who was diagnosed with breast cancer at age 48, and her maternal aunt, who had ovarian cancer at age 50. She also reports that her maternal grandmother and another maternal aunt had breast cancer, both of whom were diagnosed in their late 50s and are now deceased. In this case, the counselor should recommend that the aunt with ovarian cancer be approached about genetic counseling and testing. Although Susan could be tested first, if she tests negative for a BRCA1/2 mutation, the interpretation will be unclear unless it can be determined whether a mutation is even present in the family. If her aunt undergoes testing and is positive, then Susan can be tested for the identified mutation and receive either a true positive or a true negative result. However, if her aunt tests negative (or, in general, if a high-risk proband tests negative), this *uninformative (or indeterminate) result* could be attributable to the presence of a gene mutation that was not detected by a specific method of analysis

(eg, sequencing may not detect large genomic rearrangements). Another possible explanation is that a mutation could be implicated in another gene (eg, that is not yet isolated or is associated with a rare syndrome). It is also possible that the individual tested developed sporadic cancer (ie, the cancer is a phenocopy). However, ovarian cancer is less likely than breast cancer to be a phenocopy in high-risk families. In families with a history of breast cancer only (ie, no ovarian cancer), it may be appropriate to offer testing to more than one affected individual, particularly if the proband was diagnosed postmenopausally. Again, in such families, it is optimal to test a woman with breast cancer diagnosed at the youngest age.

Another type of indeterminate result that may be obtained is one in which a sequence variant is identified. Such alterations, which have been reported in 10 to 20% of individuals tested for BRCA1/2 mutations, are usually missense mutations (single base pair changes) which may not overtly affect the gene's protein product.[6,130,138-140] In some instances, the significance of specific variants may be clarified based on functional studies, observations of its frequency within population samples, or cosegregation with deleterious mutations or with the cancer phenotype within families.[138,139,141]

It is difficult to distinguish what explanation accounts for indeterminate test results in high-risk families whose histories are consistent with hereditary breast cancer. Because an unidentified mutation could be present with associated elevated risks of breast and ovarian cancers, management plans for the proband and her relatives need to be developed and reviewed in counseling.

PSYCHOSOCIAL ISSUES

Patients must be educated about benefits, limitations, and risks of testing so that they may make an informed decision about testing. Reported rates of uptake have varied depending on the setting in which testing has occurred (eg, research versus clinical) and other factors including patients' ethnicity, whether they were insured, their perceived risk of cancer, and whether they were at risk for a previously identified familial mutation.[131,142-147]

With respect to the psychological impact of test result disclosure, within our own clinical research program, at 6 months post-disclosure, we found no evidence of increased distress among women who received positive or uninformative test results, a finding which is consistent with previous research.[148] As anticipated, women who received definitive (true) negative results reported significantly decreased psychological distress.[148] Wide variability, however, exists in response to testing. Women from hereditary breast cancer families, who decline counseling despite the presence of significant cancer-related stress, appear to be at increased risk for subsequent depression.[149] Women who initially underestimated the short-term adverse emotional effects of receiving mutation testing results reported psychological distress 6 months following disclosure of BRCA or p53 results.[150] Such individuals, as well as those who find it difficult to share positive results with family members, could be targeted for enhanced psychosocial support during and after the counseling and testing process.

It is interesting to note that many testing programs have studied women who were predominantly white, well educated, and of high socioeconomic status. The studies were designed specifically to assess the effects of counseling and testing, and therefore, might not generalize to the community setting where clinicians may not have had extensive training in genetic counseling or might not provide comprehensive pre- and post-test genetic counseling.[151] Social outcomes must also be reevaluated as testing becomes increasingly available to individuals in the general population who are of diverse ethnic, racial, and socioeconomic backgrounds.

SUMMARY

Most individuals with a family history of breast cancer have a familial rather than hereditary risk of developing this disease. For women with hereditary breast cancer, BRCA1 and BRCA2 mutations account for the majority of cases. Mutations in these genes are associated with a significantly elevated risk of early-onset breast cancer and ovarian cancer. In addition, other cancers may be seen with an increased frequency in mutation carriers. Models based on personal cancer history, family history, and ethnic background are available to guide clinicians in estimating the likelihood that an individual harbors a risk-conferring mutation. Data are

emerging regarding the benefits of various cancer screening and prevention options. Due to the complexities involved in decision-making about genetic testing and medical management, genetic counseling is critical prior to and after undergoing genetic testing. Further studies on genetic and environmental cancer risk modifiers, genotype–phenotype correlations, and the impact of cancer screening and prevention options are underway and will continue to provide greater insight into the features and management of high-risk individuals.

REFERENCES

1. Slattery ML, Kerber RA. A comprehensive evaluation of family history and breast cancer risk. The Utah Population Database. JAMA 1993;270:1563–8.
2. Claus EB, Risch NJ, Thompson WD. Age at onset as an indicator of familial risk of breast cancer. Am J Epidemiol 1990;131:961–72.
3. Claus EB, Schildkraut JM, Thompson WD, et al. The genetic attributable risk of breast and ovarian cancer. Cancer 1996;77:2318–24.
4. Ford D, Easton DF, Stratton M, et al. Genetic heterogeneity and penetrance analysis of the BRCA1 and BRCA2 genes in breast cancer families. The Breast Cancer Linkage Consortium. Am J Hum Genet 1998;62:676–89.
5. Martin AM, Blackwood MA, Antin-Ozerkis D, et al. Germline mutations in BRCA1 and BRCA2 in breast-ovarian families from a breast cancer risk evaluation clinic. J Clin Oncol 2001;19:2247–53.
6. Frank TS, Deffenbaugh AM, Reid JE, et al. Clinical characteristics of individuals with germline mutations in BRCA1 and BRCA2: analysis of 10,000 individuals. J Clin Oncol 2002;20:1480–90.
7. Shih HA, Couch FJ, Nathanson KL, et al. BRCA1 and BRCA2 mutation frequency in women evaluated in a breast cancer risk evaluation clinic. J Clin Oncol 2002;20:994–9.
8. Struewing J, Hartge P, Wacholder S, et al. The risk of cancer associated with specific mutations of BRCA1 and BRCA2 among Ashkenazi Jews. N Engl J Med 1997;336:1401–8.
9. Ford D, Easton DF, Peto J. Estimates of the gene frequency of BRCA1 and its contribution to breast and ovarian cancer incidence. Am J Hum Genet 1995;57:1457–62.
10. Friedman E, Bar-Sade Bruchim R, Kruglikova A, et al. Double heterozygotes for the Ashkenazi founder mutations in BRCA1 and BRCA2 genes. Am J Hum Genet 1998;63:1224–7.
11. Peto J, Collins N, Barfoot R, et al. Prevalence of BRCA1 and BRCA2 gene mutations in patients with early-onset breast cancer. J Natl Cancer Inst 1999;91:943–9.

12. Satagopan JM, Offit K, Foulkes W, et al. The lifetime risks of breast cancer in Ashkenazi Jewish carriers of *BRCA1* and *BRCA2* mutations. Cancer Epidemiol Biomarkers Prev 2001;10:467–73.

13. Risch HA, McLaughlin JR, Cole DE, et al. Prevalence and penetrance of germline *BRCA1* and *BRCA2* mutations in a population series of 649 women with ovarian cancer. Am J Hum Genet 2001;68:700–10.

14. Moslehi R, Chu W, Karlan B, et al. *BRCA1* and *BRCA2* mutation analysis of 208 Ashkenazi Jewish women with ovarian cancer. Am J Hum Genet 2000;66:1259–72.

15. Kauff ND, Perez-Segura P, Robson ME, et al. Incidence of non-founder *BRCA1* and *BRCA2* mutations in high risk Ashkenazi breast and ovarian cancer families. J Med Genet 2002;39:611–4.

16. Thorlacius S, Sigurdsson S, Bjarnadottir H, et al. Study of a single *BRCA2* mutation with high carrier frequency in a small population. Am J Hum Genet 1997;60:1079–84.

17. Tonin PN, Mes-Masson AM, Futreal PA, et al. Founder *BRCA1* and *BRCA2* mutations in French Canadian breast and ovarian cancer families. Am J Hum Genet 1998;63:1341–51.

18. Neuhausen SL. Founder populations and their uses for breast cancer genetics. Breast Cancer Res 2000; 2:77–81.

19. Liede A, Narod SA. Hereditary breast and ovarian cancer in Asia: genetic epidemiology of *BRCA1* and *BRCA2*. Hum Mutat 2002;20:413–24.

20. Gao Q, Tomlinson G, Das S, et al. Prevalence of *BRCA1* and *BRCA2* mutations among clinic-based African American families with breast cancer. Hum Genet 2000;107:186–91.

21. Mefford HC, Baumbach L, Panguluri RC, et al. Evidence for a *BRCA1* founder mutation in families of West African ancestry. Am J Hum Genet 1999; 65:575–8.

22. Gao Q, Neuhausen S, Cummings S, et al. Recurrent germ-line *BRCA1* mutations in extended African American families with early-onset breast cancer. Am J Hum Genet 1997;60:1233–6.

23. Panguluri RC, Brody LC, Modali R, et al. *BRCA1* mutations in African Americans. Hum Genet 1999; 105:28–31.

24. Olopade OI, Fackenthal JD, Dunston G, et al. Breast cancer genetics in African Americans. Cancer 2003;97:236–45.

25. Shen D, Wu Y, Subbarao M, et al. Mutation analysis of *BRCA1* gene in African-American patients with breast cancer. J Natl Med Assoc 2000;92:29–35.

26. Petrij-Bosch A, Peelen T, van Vliet M, et al. *BRCA1* genomic deletions are major founder mutations in Dutch breast cancer patients. Nat Genet 1997;17: 341–5.

27. The exon 13 duplication in the *BRCA1* gene is a founder mutation present in geographically diverse populations. The *BRCA1* Exon 13 Duplication Screening Group. Am J Hum Genet 2000;67:207–12.

28. Unger MA, Nathanson KL, Calzone K, et al. Screening for genomic rearrangements in families with breast and ovarian cancer identifies *BRCA1* mutations previously missed by conformation-sensitive gel electrophoresis or sequencing. Am J Hum Genet 2000;67:841–50.

29. Couch FJ, DeShano ML, Blackwood MA, et al. *BRCA1* mutations in women attending clinics that evaluate the risk of breast cancer. N Engl J Med 1997;336:1409–15.

30. Domchek SM, Eisen A, Calzone K, et al. Application of breast cancer risk prediction models in clinical practice. J Clin Oncol 2003;21:593–601.

31. Blackwood A, Yang H, Nathanson KL, et al. Predicted probability of breast cancer susceptibility gene mutations. Breast Cancer Res Treat 2001;69: 127a.

32. Parmigiani G, Berry D, Aguilar O. Determining carrier probabilities for breast cancer-susceptibility genes *BRCA1* and *BRCA2*. Am J Hum Genet 1998;62:145–58.

33. Berry DA, Parmigiani G, Sanchez J, et al. Probability of carrying a mutation of breast-ovarian cancer gene *BRCA1* based on family history. J Natl Cancer Inst 1997;89:227–38.

34. Berry DA, Iversen ES Jr, Gudbjartsson DF, et al. BRCAPRO validation, sensitivity of genetic testing of *BRCA1/BRCA2*, and prevalence of other breast cancer susceptibility genes. J Clin Oncol 2002;20: 2701–12.

35. Rubinstein WS, O'Neill SM, Peters JA, et al. Mathematical modeling for breast cancer risk assessment. State of the art and role in medicine. Oncology (Huntingt) 2002;16:1082–94; discussion 1094, 1097–9.

36. Ford D, Easton DF, Bishop DT, et al. Risks of cancer in *BRCA1*-mutation carriers. Breast Cancer Linkage Consortium. Lancet 1994;343:692–5.

37. Easton DF, Ford D, Bishop DT. Breast and ovarian cancer incidence in *BRCA1*-mutation carriers. Breast Cancer Linkage Consortium. Am J Hum Genet 1995;56:265–71.

38. Ries LAG, Eisner MP, Kosary CL, et al. SEER cancer statistics review, 1975–2000. Bethesda (MD): National Cancer Institute. Available at: http://seer.cancer.gov/csr/1975_2000 (accessed May 12, 2003).

39. Brose MS, Rebbeck TR, Calzone KA, et al. Cancer risk estimates for *BRCA1* mutation carriers identified in a risk evaluation program. J Natl Cancer Inst 2002;94:1365–72.

40. Warner E, Foulkes W, Goodwin P, et al. Prevalence and penetrance of *BRCA1* and *BRCA2* gene mutations in unselected Ashkenazi Jewish women with breast cancer. J Natl Cancer Inst 1999;91:1241–7.

41. Fodor FH, Weston A, Bleiweiss IJ, et al. Frequency and carrier risk associated with common *BRCA1* and *BRCA2* mutations in Ashkenazi Jewish breast cancer patients. Am J Hum Genet 1998;63:45–51.

42. Thorlacius S, Struewing JP, Hartge P, et al. Population-based study of risk of breast cancer in carriers of *BRCA2* mutation [see comments]. Lancet 1998;352:1337–9.

43. Antoniou A, Pharoah PD, Narod S, et al. Average risks of breast and ovarian cancer associated with *BRCA1* or *BRCA2* mutations detected in case series unselected for family history: a combined analysis of 22 studies. Am J Hum Genet 2003; 72:1117–30.

44. Satagopan JM, Boyd J, Kauff ND, et al. Ovarian cancer risk in Ashkenazi Jewish carriers of *BRCA1* and *BRCA2* mutations. Clin Cancer Res 2002;8: 3776–81.

45. Aziz S, Kuperstein G, Rosen B, et al. A genetic epidemiological study of carcinoma of the fallopian tube. Gynecol Oncol 2001;80:341–5.

46. Marcus JN, Watson P, Page DL, et al. Hereditary breast cancer: pathobiology, prognosis, and *BRCA1* and *BRCA2* gene linkage [see comments]. Cancer 1996;77:697–709.

47. Cancer risks in *BRCA2* mutation carriers. The Breast Cancer Linkage Consortium. J Natl Cancer Inst 1999;91:1310–6.

48. Turner BC, Harrold E, Matloff E, et al. *BRCA1/ BRCA2* germline mutations in locally recurrent breast cancer patients after lumpectomy and radiation therapy: implications for breast-conserving management in patients with *BRCA1/BRCA2* mutations. J Clin Oncol 1999;17:3017–24.

49. Haffty BG, Harrold E, Khan AJ, et al. Outcome of conservatively managed early-onset breast cancer by *BRCA1/2* status. Lancet 2002;359:1471–7.

50. Thompson D, Easton DF. Cancer incidence in *BRCA1* mutation carriers. J Natl Cancer Inst 2002; 94:1358–65.

51. Thompson D, Easton D. Variation in cancer risks, by mutation position, in *BRCA2* mutation carriers. Am J Hum Genet 2001;68:410–9.

52. Easton DF, Steele L, Fields P, et al. Cancer risks in two large breast cancer families linked to *BRCA2* on chromosome 13q12-13. Am J Hum Genet 1997;61:120–8.

53. Peelen T, de Leeuw W, van Lent K, et al. Genetic analysis of a breast-ovarian cancer family, with 7 cases of colorectal cancer linked to *BRCA1*, fails to support a role for *BRCA1* in colorectal tumorigenesis. Int J Cancer 2000;88:778–82.

54. Lin KM, Ternent CA, Adams DR, et al. Colorectal cancer in hereditary breast cancer kindreds. Dis Colon Rectum 1999;42:1041–5.

55. Johannsson O, Loman N, Moller T, et al. Incidence of malignant tumours in relatives of *BRCA1* and *BRCA2* germline mutation carriers. Eur J Cancer 1999;35:1248–57.

56. Pathology of familial breast cancer: differences between breast cancers in carriers of *BRCA1* or *BRCA2* mutations and sporadic cases. Breast Cancer Linkage Consortium. Lancet 1997;349:1505–10.

57. Lakhani SR, Jacquemier J, Sloane JP, et al. Multifactorial analysis of differences between sporadic breast cancers and cancers involving *BRCA1* and *BRCA2* mutations. J Natl Cancer Inst 1998;90: 1138–45.

58. Lakhani SR, Van De Vijver MJ, Jacquemier J, et al. The pathology of familial breast cancer: predictive value of immunohistochemical markers estrogen receptor, progesterone receptor, *HER-2*, and *p53* in patients with mutations in *BRCA1* and *BRCA2*. J Clin Oncol 2002;20:2310–8.

59. Verhoog LC, Brekelmans CT, Seynaeve C, et al. Survival and tumour characteristics of breast-cancer patients with germline mutations of *BRCA1*. Lancet 1998;351:316–21.

60. Eisinger F, Jacquemier J, Charpin C, et al. Mutations at *BRCA1*: the medullary breast carcinoma revisited. Cancer Res 1998;58:1588–92.

61. Phillips KA, Nichol K, Ozcelik H, et al. Frequency of *p53* mutations in breast carcinomas from Ashkenazi Jewish carriers of *BRCA1* mutations. J Natl Cancer Inst 1999;91:469–73.

62. Quenneville LA, Phillips KA, Ozcelik H, et al. *HER-2/neu* status and tumor morphology of invasive breast carcinomas in Ashkenazi women with known *BRCA1* mutation status in the Ontario Familial Breast Cancer Registry. Cancer 2002;95: 2068–75.

63. Phillips KA, Andrulis IL, Goodwin PJ. Breast carcinomas arising in carriers of mutations in *BRCA1* or *BRCA2*: are they prognostically different? J Clin Oncol 1999;17:3653–63.

64. Johannsson OT, Idvall I, Anderson C, et al. Tumour biological features of *BRCA1*-induced breast and ovarian cancer. Eur J Cancer 1997;33:362–71.

65. Marcus JN, Watson P, Page DL, et al. *BRCA2* hereditary breast cancer pathophenotype. Breast Cancer Res Treat 1997;44:275–7.

66. Armes JE, Egan AJ, Southey MC, et al. The histologic phenotypes of breast carcinoma occurring before age 40 years in women with and without *BRCA1* or *BRCA2* germline mutations: a population-based study. Cancer 1998;83:2335–45.

67. Agnarsson BA, Jonasson JG, Bjornsdottir IB, et al. Inherited *BRCA2* mutation associated with high grade breast cancer. Breast Cancer Res Treat 1998; 47:121–7.

68. Loman N, Johannsson O, Bendahl PO, et al. Steroid receptors in hereditary breast carcinomas associated with *BRCA1* or *BRCA2* mutations or unknown susceptibility genes. 1998;83:310–9.

69. Stoppa-Lyonnet D, Ansquer Y, Dreyfus H, et al. Familial invasive breast cancers: worse outcome related to *BRCA1* mutations. J Clin Oncol 2000; 18:4053–9.

70. Chappuis PO, Kapusta L, Begin LR, et al. Germline *BRCA1/2* mutations and p27(Kip1) protein levels independently predict outcome after breast cancer. J Clin Oncol 2000;18:4045–52.

71. Robson M, Gilewski T, Haas B, et al. *BRCA*-associated breast cancer in young women. J Clin Oncol 1998;16:1642–9.

72. Eerola H, Vahteristo P, Sarantaus L, et al. Survival of breast cancer patients in *BRCA1*, *BRCA2*, and non-*BRCA1/2* breast cancer families: a relative survival analysis from Finland. Int J Cancer 2001; 93:368–72.

73. Lee JS, Wacholder S, Struewing JP, et al. Survival after breast cancer in Ashkenazi Jewish *BRCA1* and *BRCA2* mutation carriers. J Natl Cancer Inst 1999; 91:259–63.

74. Verhoog LC, Brekelmans CT, Seynaeve C, et al. Survival in hereditary breast cancer associated with germline mutations of *BRCA2*. J Clin Oncol 1999; 17:3396–402.

75. Narod SA, Goldgar D, Cannon-Albright L, et al. Risk modifiers in carriers of *BRCA1* mutations. Int J Cancer 1995;64:394–8.

76. Johannsson O, Loman N, Borg A, et al. Pregnancy-associated breast cancer in *BRCA1* and *BRCA2* germline mutation carriers. Lancet 1998;352: 1359–60.

77. Jernstrom H, Lerman C, Ghadirian P, et al. Pregnancy and risk of early breast cancer in carriers of *BRCA1* and *BRCA2*. Lancet 1999;354:1846–50.

78. Modan B, Hartge P, Hirsh-Yechezkel G, et al. Parity, oral contraceptives, and the risk of ovarian cancer among carriers and noncarriers of a *BRCA1* or *BRCA2* mutation. N Engl J Med 2001;345: 235–40.

79. Narod SA, Sun P, Ghadirian P, et al. Tubal ligation and risk of ovarian cancer in carriers of *BRCA1* or *BRCA2* mutations: a case-control study. Lancet 2001;357:1467–70.

80. Narod SA, Dube MP, Klijn J, et al. Oral contraceptives and the risk of breast cancer in *BRCA1* and *BRCA2* mutation carriers. J Natl Cancer Inst 2002;94:1773–9.

81. Hankinson SE, Hunter DJ, Colditz GA, et al. Tubal ligation, hysterectomy, and risk of ovarian cancer. A prospective study. JAMA 1993;270:2813–8.

82. Rebbeck TR, Lynch HT, Neuhausen SL, et al. Prophylactic oophorectomy in carriers of *BRCA1* or *BRCA2* mutations. N Engl J Med 2002;346: 1616–22.

83. Kauff ND, Satagopan JM, Robson ME, et al. Risk-reducing salpingo-oophorectomy in women with a *BRCA1* or *BRCA2* mutation. N Engl J Med 2002; 346:1609–15.

84. Thompson D, Easton D. Variation in *BRCA1* cancer risks by mutation position. Cancer Epidemiol Biomarkers Prev 2002;11:329–36.

85. Spurdle AB, Hopper JL, Chen X, et al. The *BRCA2* 372 HH genotype is associated with risk of breast cancer in Australian women under age 60 years. Cancer Epidemiol Biomarkers Prev 2002;11:413–6.

86. Auranen A, Spurdle AB, Chen X, et al. *BRCA2* Arg372His polymorphism and epithelial ovarian cancer risk. Int J Cancer 2003;103:427–30.

87. Ishitobi M, Miyoshi Y, Ando A, et al. Association of *BRCA2* polymorphism at codon 784 (met/val) with breast cancer risk and prognosis. Clin Cancer Res 2003;9:1376–80.

88. Ginolhac SM, Gad S, Corbex M, et al. *BRCA1* wild-type allele modifies risk of ovarian cancer in carriers of *BRCA1* germ-line mutations. Cancer Epidemiol Biomarkers Prev 2003;12:90–5.

89. Levy-Lahad E, Lahad A, Eisenberg S, et al. A single nucleotide polymorphism in the *RAD51* gene modifies cancer risk in *BRCA2* but not *BRCA1* carriers. Proc Natl Acad Sci U S A 2001;98: 3232–6.

90. Wang WW, Spurdle AB, Kolachana P, et al. A single nucleotide polymorphism in the 5′ untranslated region of *RAD51* and risk of cancer among *BRCA1/2* mutation carriers. Cancer Epidemiol Biomarkers Prev 2001;10:955–60.

91. Phelan CM, Rebbeck TR, Weber BL, et al. Ovarian cancer risk in *BRCA1* carriers is modified by the *HRAS1* variable number of tandem repeat (VNTR) locus. Nat Genet 1996;12:309–11.

92. Rebbeck TR, Wang Y, Kantoff PW, et al. Modification of *BRCA1*- and *BRCA2*-associated breast cancer risk by *AIB1* genotype and reproductive history. Cancer Res 2001;61:5420–4.

93. Vahteristo P, Bartkova J, Eerola H, et al. A *CHEK2* genetic variant contributing to a substantial fraction of familial breast cancer. Am J Hum Genet 2002;71:432–8.

94. Meijers-Heijboer H, van den Ouweland A, Klijn J, et al. Low-penetrance susceptibility to breast cancer due to *CHEK2*(*)1100delC in noncarriers of *BRCA1* or *BRCA2* mutations. Nat Genet 2002; 31:55–9.

95. Nathanson KL, Weber B. Breast cancer. In: King RA, Rotter JI, Motvisky AG, editors. The genetic basis of common diseases. 2nd ed. New York: Oxford University Press; 2002. p. 670–99.

96. Li FP, Fraumeni JF Jr. Soft-tissue sarcomas, breast cancer, and other neoplasms. A familial syndrome? Ann Intern Med 1969;71:747–52.

97. Li FP, Fraumeni JF Jr, Mulvihill JJ, et al. A cancer family syndrome in twenty-four kindreds. Cancer Res 1988;48:5358–62.

98. Nichols KE, Malkin D, Garber JE, et al. Germ-line *p53* mutations predispose to a wide spectrum of early-onset cancers. Cancer Epidemiol Biomarkers Prev 2001;10:83–7.

99. Varley JM, McGown G, Thorncroft M, et al. Germline mutations of *TP53* in Li-Fraumeni families: an extended study of 39 families. Cancer Res 1997; 57:3245–52.

100. Chompret A, Brugieres L, Ronsin M, et al. *p53* germline mutations in childhood cancers and cancer risk for carrier individuals. Br J Cancer 2000; 82:1932–7.

101. Bell DW, Varley JM, Szydlo TE, et al. Heterozygous germ line *hCHK2* mutations in Li-Fraumeni syndrome. Science 1999;286:2528–31.

102. Vahteristo P, Tamminen A, Karvinen P, et al. *p53, CHK2*, and *CHK1* genes in Finnish families with Li-Fraumeni syndrome: further evidence of *CHK2* in inherited cancer predisposition. Cancer Res 2001;61:5718–22.

103. Malkin D. The Li-Fraumeni syndrome. Cancer: Principles and Practice of Oncology Updates 1993;7:1–14.

104. Hisada M, Garber JE, Fung CY, et al. Multiple primary cancers in families with Li-Fraumeni syndrome. J Natl Cancer Inst 1998;90:606–11.

105. Limacher JM, Frebourg T, Natarajan-Ame S, et al. Two metachronous tumors in the radiotherapy fields of a patient with Li-Fraumeni syndrome. Int J Cancer 2001;96:238–42.

106. NCCN: clinical practice guidelines in oncology: genetic/familial high-risk assessment: breast. Vol 1. 2002. Available at: http://www.nccn.org/physician _gls/f_guidelines.html (accessed May 12, 2003).

107. Eng C, Hampel H, de la Chapelle A. Genetic testing for cancer predisposition. Annu Rev Med 2001; 52:371–400.

108. Schneider KA, Li FP. Li-Fraumeni syndrome (GeneReviews). Updated December 30, 2002. Available at: http://www.geneclinics.com/et (accessed May 12, 2003).

109. Eng C. Will the real Cowden syndrome please stand up: revised diagnostic criteria. J Med Genet 2000; 37:828–30.

110. Eng C. Genetics of Cowden syndrome: through the looking glass of oncology. Int J Oncol 1998;12:701–10.

111. Schrager CA, Schneider D, Gruener AC, et al. Clinical and pathological features of breast disease in Cowden's syndrome: an underrecognized syndrome with an increased risk of breast cancer. Hum Pathol 1998;29:47–53.

112. Nelen MR, van Staveren WC, Peeters EA, et al. Germline mutations in the *PTEN/MMAC1* gene in patients with Cowden disease. Hum Mol Genet 1997;6:1383–7.

113. Marsh DJ, Coulon V, Lunetta KL, et al. Mutation spectrum and genotype-phenotype analyses in Cowden disease and Bannayan-Zonana syndrome, two hamartoma syndromes with germline *PTEN* mutation. Hum Mol Genet 1998;7:507–15.

114. Tomlinson IP, Houlston RS. Peutz-Jeghers syndrome. J Med Genet 1997;34:1007–11.

115. Giardiello FM, Brensinger JD, Tersmette AC, et al. Very high risk of cancer in familial Peutz-Jeghers syndrome. Gastroenterology 2000;119:1447–53.

116. Trau H, Schewach-Millet M, Fisher BK, et al. Peutz-Jeghers syndrome and bilateral breast carcinoma. Cancer 1982;50:788–92.

117. McGrath DR, Spigelman AD. Preventive measures in Peutz-Jeghers syndrome. Familial Cancer 2001;1:121–5.

118. Olschwang S, Markie D, Seal S, et al. Peutz-Jeghers disease: most, but not all, families are compatible with linkage to 19p13.3. J Med Genet 1998;35:42–4.

119. Jenne DE, Reimann H, Nezu J, et al. Peutz-Jeghers syndrome is caused by mutations in a novel serine threonine kinase. Nat Genet 1998;18:38–43.

120. Wang ZJ, Churchman M, Avizienyte E, et al. Germline mutations of the *LKB1* (*STK11*) gene in Peutz-Jeghers patients. J Med Genet 1999;36:365–8.

121. Yoon KA, Ku JL, Choi HS, et al. Germline mutations of the *STK11* gene in Korean Peutz-Jeghers syndrome patients. Br J Cancer 2000;82:1403–6.

122. Athma P, Rappaport R, Swift M. Molecular genotyping shows that ataxia-telangiectasia heterozygotes are predisposed to breast cancer. Cancer Genet Cytogenet 1996;92:130–4.

123. Chenevix-Trench G, Spurdle AB, Gatei M, et al. Dominant negative *ATM* mutations in breast cancer families. J Natl Cancer Inst 2002;94:205–15.

124. Swift M, Morrell D, Massey RB, et al. Incidence of cancer in 161 families affected by ataxia-telangiectasia. N Engl J Med 1991;325:1831–6.

125. Su Y, Swift M. Outcomes of adjuvant radiation therapy for breast cancer in women with ataxia-telangiectasia mutations. JAMA 2001;286:2233–4.

126. Lynch HT, de la Chapelle A. Genetic susceptibility to non-polyposis colorectal cancer. J Med Genet 1999;36:801–18.

127. Lynch HT, de la Chapelle A. Hereditary colorectal cancer. N Engl J Med 2003;348:919–32.

128. de Leeuw WJ, van Puijenbroek M, Tollenaar RA, et al. Correspondence re: A. Muller et al., Exclusion of breast cancer as an integral tumor of hereditary nonpolyposis colorectal cancer. Cancer Res., 62:1014-1019, 2002. Cancer Res 2003;63:1148–9.

129. Risinger JI, Barrett JC, Watson P, et al. Molecular genetic evidence of the occurrence of breast cancer as an integral tumor in patients with the hereditary nonpolyposis colorectal carcinoma syndrome. Cancer 1996;77:1836–43.

130. Peshkin BN, DeMarco TA, Brogan BM, et al. *BRCA1/2* testing: complex themes in result interpretation. J Clin Oncol 2001;19:2555–65.

131. Lerman C, Narod S, Schulman K, et al. *BRCA1* testing in families with hereditary breast-ovarian cancer. A prospective study of patient decision making and outcomes. JAMA 1996;275:1885–92.

132. Peterson EA, Milliron KJ, Lewis KE, et al. Health insurance and discrimination concerns and *BRCA1/2* testing in a clinic population. Cancer Epidemiol Biomarkers Prev 2002;11:79–87.

133. Shinaman A, Bain LJ, Shoulson I. Preempting genetic discrimination and assaults on privacy: report of a symposium. Am J Med Genet 2003; 120A:589–93.

134. McKinnon WC, Baty BJ, Bennett RL, et al. Predisposition genetic testing for late-onset disorders in adults. A position paper of the National Society of Genetic Counselors. JAMA 1997;278:1217–20.

135. Peshkin BN, Lerman C. Genetic counselling for hereditary breast cancer. Lancet 1999;353:2176–7.

136. Wu LC, Wang ZW, Tsan JT, et al. Identification of a RING protein that can interact in vivo with the *BRCA1* gene product. Nat Genet 1996;14:430–40.

137. Maquat LE. Defects in RNA splicing and the consequence of shortened translational reading frames. Am J Hum Genet 1996;59:279–86.

138. Frank TS, Manley SA, Olopade OI, et al. Sequence analysis of *BRCA1* and *BRCA2*: correlation of mutations with family history and ovarian cancer risk. J Clin Oncol 1998;16:2417–25.

139. Petrucelli N, Lazebnik N, Huelsman KM, et al. Clinical interpretation and recommendations for patients with a variant of uncertain significance in *BRCA1* or *BRCA2*: a survey of genetic counseling practice. Genet Test 2002;6:107–13.

140. Shen D, Vadgama JV. *BRCA1* and *BRCA2* gene mutation analysis: visit to the Breast Cancer Information Core (BIC). Oncol Res 1999;11:63–9.

141. Petersen GM, Parmigiani G, Thomas D. Missense mutations in disease genes: a Bayesian approach to evaluate causality. Am J Hum Genet 1998;62:1516–24.

142. Meijers-Heijboer EJ, Verhoog LC, Brekelmans CT, et al. Presymptomatic DNA testing and prophylactic surgery in families with a *BRCA1* or *BRCA2* mutation. Lancet 2000;355:2015–20.

143. Biesecker BB, Ishibe N, Hadley DW, et al. Psychosocial factors predicting *BRCA1/BRCA2* testing decisions in members of hereditary breast and ovarian cancer families. Am J Med Genet 2000;93:257–63.

144. Schwartz MD, Hughes C, Roth J, et al. Spiritual faith and genetic testing decisions among high-risk breast cancer probands. Cancer Epidemiol Biomarkers Prev 2000;9:381–5.

145. Thompson HS, Valdimarsdottir HB, Duteau-Buck C, et al. Psychosocial predictors of *BRCA* counseling and testing decisions among urban African-American women. Cancer Epidemiol Biomarkers Prev 2002;11:1579–85.

146. Armstrong K, Calzone K, Stopfer J, et al. Factors associated with decisions about clinical *BRCA1/2* testing. Cancer Epidemiol Biomarkers Prev 2000;9:1251–4.

147. Lee SC, Bernhardt BA, Helzlsouer KJ. Utilization of *BRCA1/2* genetic testing in the clinical setting: report from a single institution. Cancer 2002;94:1876–85.

148. Schwartz MD, Peshkin BN, Hughes C, et al. Impact of *BRCA1/BRCA2* mutation testing on psychologic distress in a clinic-based sample. J Clin Oncol 2002;20:514–20.

149. Lerman C, Hughes C, Lemon SJ, et al. What you don't know can hurt you: adverse psychologic effects in members of *BRCA1*-linked and *BRCA2*-linked families who decline genetic testing. J Clin Oncol 1998;16:1650–4.

150. Dorval M, Patenaude AF, Schneider KA, et al. Anticipated versus actual emotional reactions to disclosure of results of genetic tests for cancer susceptibility: findings from *p53* and *BRCA1* testing programs. J Clin Oncol 2000;18:2135–42.

151. Chen WY, Garber JE, Higham S, et al. *BRCA1/2* genetic testing in the community setting. J Clin Oncol 2002;20:4485–92.

152. Ozcelik H, Schmocker B, Di Nicola N, et al. Germline *BRCA2* 6174delT mutations in Ashkenazi Jewish pancreatic cancer patients. Nat Genet 1997;16:17–8.

CHAPTER 3

ENDOCRINE RISK FACTORS

Leslie Bernstein, PhD

Breast cancer is the most common cancer among women worldwide and continues to be a major cause of cancer deaths.[1] Both epidemiologic and experimental studies point to the importance of reproductive variables in the development of breast cancer.[2–5] This evidence, as well as that from clinical studies, implicates the ovarian hormones, estradiol and progesterone, in the etiology and promotion of this disease. These hormones influence normal breast cell growth and development. Endogenous estrogens and progesterone, as well as exogenous formulations of these hormones, drive cellular proliferation in the breast; this increased proliferation provides greater opportunity for the accumulation of random errors, which may lead to tumor development.[6] A number of relatively well-established breast cancer risk factors can be understood in light of their potential effects on a woman's lifetime exposure to these ovarian hormones. These include reproductive factors, physical activity, postmenopausal obesity, and use of exogenous hormones. In developing new hypotheses regarding novel risk factors, epidemiologists seek to find other factors that may alter exposure to these hormones.

The first hint that reproductive factors might be important predictors for breast cancer risk was derived from inspection of breast cancer incidence patterns. This chapter describes these patterns of risk in populations, discusses the role of endogenous hormones in the etiology of breast cancer, and then briefly reviews breast cancer risk factors, describing how they support an endocrinologic basis for breast cancer.

INCIDENCE PATTERNS

Women have breast cancer incidence rates that are, on average, 100 times greater than those of men.[7]

Female breast cancer incidence rates vary substantially worldwide, with women in North America and northern Europe at highest risk, women in southern Europe and Central and South America at intermediate risk, and women in Asia and Africa at lowest risk.[7] Despite this range of risk, the largest increases in incidence rates in recent years have occurred among women at lowest risk.[7–9] Typically, women from low-risk populations (eg, Japan and China) who migrate to areas of higher risk (eg, the United States) have higher breast cancer incidence rates within one to two generations.[10,11] These observations have stimulated research into factors that might account for these changes, particularly changes in reproductive patterns and lifestyle habits.

Invasive breast cancer incidence rates vary by racial ethnic group within the United States (Table 3-1)[12]; non-Hispanic white women have the highest rates, followed by black women. Rates are lower for Asian/Pacific Island women and Hispanic white women. Although US black women have lower breast cancer incidence relative to non-Hispanic white women, their breast cancer mortality rates are the highest of any US population subgroup.[12] Recent data from one Surveillance, Epidemiology and End Results (SEER) registry, Los Angeles County, suggest that rates for Japanese women, who have lived in the United States, on average, longer than other Asian women, will soon overtake those for non-Hispanic white women.[10]

Age is a major predictor of breast cancer risk. Among women in the United States (Figure 3-1) and other high-risk countries, incidence rates increase with age, but the upward slope of the age-specific incidence curve is not constant throughout life and declines after about 45 to 50 years of age.[12] The age pattern in countries with historically low breast cancer risk shows this even more dramati-

TABLE 3-1 Average Annual Age-adjusted Incidence Rates of Invasive Breast Cancer

Race/Ethnicity	Rate/100,000 women
Non-Hispanic white	144.5
All women	132.1
Black	120.7
Asian/Pacific islander	93.4
Hispanic white	87.1

Women in 12 Surveillance, Epidemiology and End Results (SEER) Regions of the United States by Race/Ethnicity, 1992–1999.[12] Rates are standardized to the age distribution of the 2000 US population.

cally as the curve flattens out and even declines somewhat after the peak at 45 to 50 years of age (see Figure 3-1).[7] This change in the slope of the age-specific incidence rates at the time of menopause and the fact that breast cancer is not diagnosed until late adolescence or early adulthood have stimulated research on reproductive and hormonal risk factors in relation to breast cancer risk.

Mathematical models devised to predict age-specific incidence rates on the basis of reproductive risk factors clearly show that risk accumulates most rapidly from menarche to a woman's first birth and that the first birth is associated with an immediate but transient increase in risk and a later, long-term reduction in risk, and that multiparity and early menopause also reduce the risk of breast cancer.[13,14]

ROLE OF ENDOGENOUS HORMONES

Estrogen, Sex-Hormone Binding Globulin, and Progesterone

The age-incidence relationship, demonstrating the rapid increase in breast cancer incidence during a woman's reproductive years, and epidemiologic evidence indicating that factors related to reproductive function are critical to risk, led to the proposal that a woman's cumulative exposure to estradiol, the most biologically active of the circulating estrogens, and progesterone during ovulatory menstrual cycles are key exposures related to breast cancer risk.[15] During ovulatory menstrual cycles, estradiol is low in the early follicular phase, peaks midcycle

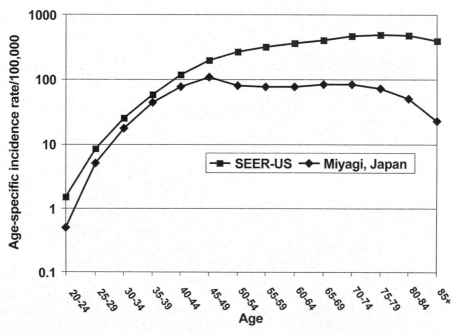

Figure 3-1 Age-specific incidence rates of invasive breast cancer per 100,000 women in 11 Surveillance, Epidemiology and End Results (SEER) regions of the United States, 1995–1999[12] and in Miyagi, Japan, 1988–1992.[7]

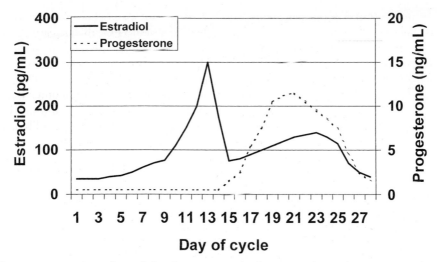

Figure 3-2 Serum concentrations of estradiol and progesterone by day in a 28-day ovulatory menstrual cycle (based on data from Goebelsmann U and Mishell D[16] and reproduced with permission from Bernstein L. Epidemiology of endocrine risk factors for breast cancer. J Mammary Gland Biol Neoplasia 2002;7:3–15).

at about the time of ovulation, and then, although it declines somewhat in the luteal phase (which represents, approximately, the last half of the cycle), it remains elevated until the beginning of the next cycle (Figure 3-2).[16] Progesterone levels are low during the follicular phase of the menstrual cycle and peak in the luteal phase, signifying that ovulation has occurred.

Studies of breast epithelial cell division rates show that proliferation rates vary across the menstrual cycle; they are low during the follicular phase, when estradiol and progesterone levels are low, and are some 2-fold higher during the luteal phase of the cycle when levels of these ovarian hormones are substantially higher.[17] Breast cell proliferation is quite low after menopause when estradiol levels are low and progesterone is absent.

Well-designed seroepidemiologic studies comparing hormone levels of women at high and low risk of breast cancer, as well as studies comparing hormone levels of breast cancer patients and controls, show that differences in estrogen levels can account for differences in risk.[18] Studies of premenopausal women are difficult to conduct and are complicated by the need to study all women at the same time during the menstrual cycle. Because the follicular and luteal phases of the menstrual cycle vary in length (as does the length of the menstrual cycle) within the same woman, these studies must take particular care in timing blood collection. When comparing luteal phase hormone levels, the appropriate day to collect biologic specimens can be determined only retrospectively by counting backward from the first day of the next menstrual cycle (ie, the first day of menstrual bleeding). All seroepidemiologic studies suffer from the practical necessity of using only one or a few spot samples from each woman to represent the overall hormonal milieu to which she is exposed. Because of these factors, study results have been more consistent for postmenopausal than for premenopausal women.

Comparisons of postmenopausal breast cancer patients and controls from both retrospective and prospective studies demonstrate that women who develop breast cancer have higher levels of circulating estrogens than those who do not.[18,19] The combined worldwide data from nine prospective studies of the relationship of endogenous hormones to breast cancer risk found that breast cancer risk of postmenopausal women increased with increasing estradiol.[20] Each of these studies collected blood samples and then followed women over time for the development of breast cancer. The breast cancer risk of postmenopausal women in the quintile of highest estradiol concentration was two times greater than that of women in the lowest quintile.

Studies have been conducted to determine whether differences in estrogen levels explain the wide variation in breast cancer incidence rates by race/ethnicity. Substantial evidence exists to show that serum estradiol levels are markedly lower among both premenopausal and postmenopausal women in low-risk Asian countries than in high-risk countries like the United States or Great Britain.[18,19] Among premenopausal women, differences in estradiol levels may be partially explained by a reduced frequency of ovulatory cycles in the lower-risk populations and less effective corpus luteum formation in those cycles when ovulation does occur. Differences in diet or energy expenditure may be responsible for these ovulatory differences. Much of the difference in estradiol levels by race/ethnicity for postmenopausal women may be due to differences in body mass index between the populations despite attempts to control for this factor in well-designed studies. The impact of body mass on hormones is described below.

The amount of estradiol that is available to enter breast epithelial cells (that which is "bioavailable") is governed by the amount and binding affinity of circulating sex-hormone binding globulin (SHBG), which binds about 98% of plasma estradiol.[21] Yet the amount of bioavailable (non–SHBG-bound) estradiol is highly correlated with the total concentration of estradiol.[22] The combined analysis of nine prospective studies reported even greater differences in postmenopausal breast cancer risk for estradiol not bound to SHBG than for total estradiol, with a 2.4-fold higher risk among women in the highest quintile relative to those in the lowest quintile.[20] Although one would hypothesize that high circulating levels of SHBG should be associated with lower breast cancer risk, studies have been mixed, with some showing lower levels among women with breast cancer and others showing higher levels.[6,19] The combined analysis does show a 34% reduced breast cancer risk among postmenopausal women with SHBG levels in the highest quintile relative to the lowest quintile, but no reduction for women in intermediate quintiles.[20] Circulating SHBG levels are strongly related to level of obesity, with heavier women having lower levels of this protein[23]; levels also increase among women taking conjugated equine estrogen as estrogen replacement therapy.[24] SHBG has greater binding affinity for testosterone than for estradiol; hence SHBG binding capacity is also related to the amount of circulating testosterone.[25]

Progestins used in hormone replacement therapy are breast mitogens[26]; this suggests that endogenous progesterone levels may also be related to risk. Yet the literature regarding the effects of endogenous progesterone on breast cancer risk is confusing and inconsistent, as the effects of this hormone can be studied only during ovulatory menstrual cycles. Most studies that have evaluated progesterone levels in premenopausal women do not report whether measurement was restricted to ovulatory cycles. During anovulatory menstrual cycles, progesterone levels remain low throughout the cycle. Furthermore, it is impractical in most epidemiologic studies to make certain that the progesterone measurement occurs on the day of the progesterone peak; this requires daily measurements throughout the luteal phase of the cycle. With strong evidence that breast cancer risk is increased among women taking combined hormone therapy (estrogen plus a progestin, described below), the seroepidemiology of progesterone is of great interest.[27–29]

Androgens

The androgens, testosterone and androstenedione, which are derived directly from ovarian and adrenal secretion,[30] are also of interest in the development of breast cancer, as they increase the growth and proliferation of breast cancer cells.[31] Both can be aromatized into estrogens, either in the granulosa cells of the ovarian follicle or in fat and other tissues. Testosterone is biologically the most potent androgen among women. In the combined analyses of nine prospective studies, testosterone was positively associated with postmenopausal breast cancer risk, with a 2.2-fold greater risk among women with levels in the highest versus the lowest quintile.[20] Substantially lower testosterone levels have been reported among Asian women compared with whites,[32–34] which may be due to the lower body weight of Asian women[34] and their concomitant lower estrogen levels.[35]

Androstenedione has received less attention in the literature, and, thus, its role in the development of breast cancer is not clear. Nevertheless, the combined analysis of prospective studies, referred to previously, found a 2-fold difference in breast cancer risk comparing postmenopausal women with levels in the highest quintile to those with levels in the lowest quintile.[20] Dehydroepiandrosterone (DHEA) and DHEA sulfate (DHEAS), two adrenal androgens, have been hypothesized to act like estrogen in stimulating cell growth.[36] Yet, data from experimental studies support the possibility of a protective role for DHEA and DHEAS.[37,38] Prospective studies show postmenopausal breast cancer risk increasing with increasing levels of both DHEA and DHEAS, with results somewhat stronger for DHEAS, where women with levels in the highest quintile had a nearly 1.8-fold higher risk than women with levels in the lowest quintile.[20]

Prolactin

Prolactin is considered as possibly important in the development of breast cancer, because it is essential for mammary gland development and lactation[39]; it stimulates the growth of human breast cancer cells in culture, and most breast cancers have prolactin receptors.[40] Although a relationship between increased prolactin levels and increased breast cancer risk is well supported by animal data, it has been difficult to study in seroepidemiologic studies.[41] The measurement of prolactin is complicated by several factors, including the effects of cyclic and diurnal variation, menopausal status, age, and, in the past, nonspecific assay techniques.[18] With newer assay techniques, the ability to study prolactin in seroepidemiologic studies has improved. Few studies have shown any relationship between prolactin levels and breast cancer risk.[18] However, results from the prospective Nurses' Health Study indicated substantial differences between postmenopausal women who later developed breast cancer and those who remained unaffected by breast cancer.[42]

RISK FACTORS

Age at Menarche

Age at menarche is an established risk factor for breast cancer, with modest elevations in breast cancer risk associated with younger ages at first menstrual period.[43] In general, breast cancer risk declines 10 to 20% with each year that menarche is delayed. Age is not the only aspect of menarche that is important in determining breast cancer risk; risk has also been associated with the time when "regular" or predictable menstrual cycles are first established. Henderson and colleagues have shown a 2-fold greater breast cancer risk among women whose menstrual cycles became regular within 1 year of their first menstrual period than for women with a 5-year or longer delay in the onset of regular cycles.[44] Furthermore, among women with early menarche (age 12 years or younger) who had regular cycles within their first menstrual year, breast cancer risk was more than four times greater than among women with late menarche (age 13 years or older) and a long duration of irregular cycles.

These observations support the hypothesis that regular ovulatory menstrual cycles increase women's risk of breast cancer.[15] Studies have documented that the frequency of ovulatory menstrual cycles is related both to age at menarche and years since first menstrual period (gynecologic age). Apter and Vihko followed a cohort of Finnish schoolgirls through menarche and into adulthood, and showed that girls with early menarche established ovulatory cycles more quickly than girls with later onset of menstruation.[45] Among girls with menarche prior to age 12 years, 80% of menstrual cycles were ovulatory within 2.5 years of menarche, whereas among girls with menarche at age 13 years or older, only about 25% of menstrual cycles were ovulatory within that time frame. In fact, at a time point 6.5 years after first menstrual period, only 60% of menstrual cycles of girls with menarche at age 13 years or older were ovulatory. Thus, frequency of ovulation during adolescence, which is dependent on age at menarche, may explain the protective effect of late age at menarche on breast cancer risk.

A persistent effect of age at menarche on estrogen concentrations may also partially explain the higher breast cancer risk of women with early menarche. Later reports on the hormonal patterns of the Finnish cohort indicate that early menarche (before age 12 years) is associated with significantly higher estradiol levels in the adolescent period[46] and with higher follicular (but not luteal) phase estradiol levels in women 20 to 31 years of age.[47] Furthermore, at ages 20 to 31 years, women with menarche before age 12 years had 30% lower SHBG concentrations than those with menarche after age 13 years.[47]

Age at Menopause

As described above and in Figure 3-1, breast cancer incidence rates increase more slowly or plateau after menopause. A consistent finding in epidemiologic studies is that women who are older at menopause have higher breast cancer risk than women who are younger when their menstrual periods stop. Earlier menopause represents a shorter time period of exposure to ovulatory menstrual cycles. Among women whose menstrual periods stop naturally, breast cancer risk is about two times greater for those with a last menstrual period at age 55 years or later than for those whose last period occurred at age 45 years or younger.[48] The effect on breast cancer risk of artificial menopause, by either bilateral oophorectomy or pelvic irradiation, is somewhat greater than that for natural menopause,[48,49] but a hysterectomy without bilateral oophorectomy has no apparent effect.[49] The greater impact of oophorectomy or pelvic irradiation on breast cancer risk is due to the immediate cessation of ovarian function following these procedures, whereas for women with natural menopause, ovarian function declines gradually over a period of months to several years following the last menstrual period.

Parity and Age at First Full-Term Pregnancy

Two of the earliest known and most reproducible features of breast cancer epidemiology are the decreased risks associated with parity and early age at first term pregnancy. MacMahon and colleagues first showed that the breast cancer risks of single women and nulliparous married women were similar and were approximately 40% greater than that of parous married women, and that the overall protective effect of parity was due to the protective effect of a young age at first birth.[2] Women whose first birth was at age 20 years or earlier had about half the breast cancer risk of women whose first birth was at age 30 years or older. Although their study showed no additional effects of subsequent births on breast cancer risk, after considering age at first full-term pregnancy, more recent studies in other populations have observed a small additional protective effect of an increasing number of births, suggesting that, under certain circumstances, multiparity offers further protection.[50] A late first-term pregnancy (generally considered to be after the age of 35 years) is associated with a higher breast cancer risk than is observed among nulliparous women.[2] This paradoxical effect of a late first-term pregnancy has been confirmed repeatedly.

Pregnancy appears to have a dual effect on breast cancer risk, with a transient increase immediately after childbirth and a longer-term reduction in risk. Looking backward, women who have had a birth within the past 3 years have greater risk than women of equivalent age whose most recent birth was at least 10 years earlier.[51] Other investigators have attempted to determine whether this increase is restricted to women with one versus two term pregnancies[52] and to define the time window of increased risk.[53] Breast cancer risk is greater immediately following a woman's first pregnancy than following the second pregnancy.[52] The increase in risk associated with a recent pregnancy appears to decline 5 years following the delivery, although the longer-term reduction in risk is not apparent for several more years.[53] A study of pregnancy estrogens comparing a woman's estradiol level in the first trimester of her first pregnancy to that in her second pregnancy has shown that estradiol levels are lower in the second pregnancy.[54] At a molecular level, it is likely that the hormonal changes during pregnancy induce irreversible differentiation and apoptosis in some cells that have already accumulated one or more of the relevant somatic mutations necessary for breast cancer development.

Although early studies heightened concern that breast cancer risk was elevated among women who had incomplete pregnancies, particularly in those who had induced abortions, a careful evaluation of the published literature on this topic revealed inconsistent findings across studies and concluded that breast cancer risk does not appear to be associated with an increased number of either spontaneous or induced abortions.[55] Two large studies conducted in Sweden and Denmark using data on induced abortions collected prior to the onset of breast cancer found no increase in risk associated with induced abortion.[56,57]

Lactation

Breastfeeding is a behavior that can be modified, and, thus, its impact on breast cancer risk is extremely important. Lifetime duration of breastfeeding is obviously related to the number of children a woman has and the number she breastfeeds. Sorting out the reduction in risk associated with larger family size from that associated with lactation is complex. A pooled analysis of 47 epidemiologic studies conducted throughout the world has carefully evaluated these relationships and found that breast cancer risk decreases by 4.3% for every 12 months of breastfeeding after taking into account a reduction in risk of 7% for each birth.[3] Lactation would be expected to reduce breast cancer risk by reducing the cumulative number of ovulatory menstrual cycles a woman experiences, because breastfeeding results in a substantial delay in reestablishing ovulation following a completed pregnancy.

Body Weight

Obesity, ratio of waist-to-hip circumferences, and weight gain as an adult, all aspects of body mass, are associated with higher breast cancer risk among postmenopausal women.[58-60] Most studies report relative risks of 1.5 to 2.5 for comparisons of the most obese (or those with the largest waist-to-hip ratio or largest weight gain) to the thinnest women (or those with smallest waist-to-hip ratio or little or no weight gain). This increase in risk associated with high body mass is restricted to those postmenopausal women with no history of prior use of hormone therapies (estrogen alone or combined estrogen and progestin).[60,61]

The increased risk in heavy postmenopausal women can be attributed to higher levels of circulating estrogen in these women, because the main source of endogenous estrogen after menopause is the conversion of the androgen precursor androstenedione to estrone in adipose tissue.[62] The lack of an effect among users of hormone therapy is explained by the fact that the increase in estrogen levels associated with obesity is negligible among hormone therapy users relative to the exposure received from the therapy itself. Obesity is also strongly associated with lower SHBG production and, thus, with increased non–SHBG-bound estradiol.[23,63] Key and Pike have estimated that doubling the weight of a postmenopausal woman from 54 kg to 108 kg would reduce her SHBG levels by 85% and increase her total, free, and non–SHBG-bound estradiol levels by 60%.[64] Other mediators of the obesity–breast cancer relationship include insulin, insulin-like growth factors, and androgens.[65]

In contrast to the effects of obesity on the breast cancer risk of postmenopausal women, obesity is associated with a 10 to 30% reduction in breast cancer risk in premenopausal women.[66] Among premenopausal women, the effect of obesity on nonovarian estrogen production is likely the same as among postmenopausal women, but this production adds only a small increment to the high blood levels produced by the ovary during ovulatory menstrual cycles. In addition, obese premenopausal women frequently experience anovulatory menstrual cycles, so that the slightly lower breast cancer risk of obese premenopausal women may be the result of their experiencing fewer ovulatory cycles.[67]

Physical Activity

Physical activity is an important predictor of breast cancer risk, in part because of its potential effects on hormone profiles and weight gain. Strenuous physical activity may delay menarche and cause secondary amenorrhea [68] and oligomenorrhea among women athletes.[69-71] Three studies comparing the prevalence of anovulation in female athletes and sedentary control subjects found substantially increased frequency of anovulation among the athletes.[72-74] Moderate physical activity during adolescence can also lead to anovulatory menstrual cycles. In a study of high school girls, those who engaged in regular, moderate physical activity (averaging at least 600 kcal of energy expended per week over the school year) were 2.9 times more likely to experience anovulatory cycles than were girls who engaged in lesser amounts of physical activity.[75] Two studies of the relationship between exercise activity and serum estradiol levels during ovulatory menstrual cycles showed that athletes had substantially lower estradiol levels over the menstrual cycle than did sedentary women.[74,76]

Early epidemiologic studies of the relationship between physical activity and breast cancer risk used surrogate measures of activity, such as occupation or participation in college sports.[77,78] Despite this indirect approach, many of these studies showed lower breast cancer risk among more active women. A case-control study conducted among women 40 years of age or younger demonstrated that adolescent and adult participation in physical exercise activities significantly reduces breast cancer risk.[79] The risk of women who averaged four or more hours of exercise activity per week during their reproductive years was nearly 60% lower than that of inactive women. These same methods were used to study the breast cancer risk of postmenopausal women aged 55 to 64 years.[80] This study also demonstrated an inverse relationship between breast cancer risk and lifetime history of exercise activity and found measures of lifetime activity to be stronger risk predictors than activity during any particular age period. The International Agency for Research on Cancer recently reviewed all of the existing epidemiologic evidence linking physical activity to breast cancer risk and concluded that regular physical activity reduces the risk of breast cancer.[81] Questions remain, however, regarding which subgroups of women benefit the most, whether specific activities are more protective than others, and whether lifetime or more recent activity provides the greatest protection.

Exogenous Hormones

Oral Contraceptives

Oral contraceptives have been available to women as a birth control method since the 1960s. Most oral contraceptive formulations are a combination of ethinyl estradiol or mestranol (which is metabolized to ethinyl estradiol) and a progestin. High estrogen doses (100 μg) were typical when oral contraceptives were first introduced in the 1960s, but low doses (20–30 μg) are typical of today's formulations. Oral contraceptives inhibit gonadotropin secretion, thus reducing ovarian hormone production to very low levels. Studies of the potential effects of oral contraceptives on breast cancer risk began in the 1970s. The possibility that these preparations provided higher levels of estrogen and progestin during an oral contraceptive cycle than the woman would have produced during a normal ovulatory cycle heightened concern that these agents might increase breast cancer risk, particularly if a woman first used them at a young age. Based on this theory, one would predict that, as the concentrations of estrogens in oral contraceptives became lower, the effects on breast cancer risk would become less apparent.

Several early studies suggested that the long-term use of oral contraceptives increased the risk for breast cancer diagnosed before age 35 and possibly up to age 45, ages at which breast cancer is relatively uncommon.[82] Two case-control studies conducted in Los Angeles County at different time points suggest that the effects observed for the relationship between oral contraceptives and breast cancer risk have changed over time, possibly reflecting changes in pill formulation. The first study, conducted among women aged 37 years or younger, was completed in 1983; it showed that breast cancer risk was strongly related to a woman's duration of oral contraceptive use.[83] Yet, in the second study of women diagnosed with breast cancer more recently (1983–1987), oral contraceptive use did not affect breast cancer risk.[84] In 1996, the Collaborative Group on Hormonal Factors in Breast Cancer published a reanalysis of data collected from 54 breast cancer studies conducted in 25 countries which specifically collected detailed information on oral contraceptive use.[85] In this pooled analysis, only a history of recent oral contraceptive use was predictive of breast cancer risk. The effect of recent oral contraceptive use was strongest among those women who first used oral contraceptives before age 20 years. The greatest increase in breast cancer risk was observed among women who were youngest at the time of their diagnoses. Of importance, the breast cancers diagnosed among oral contraceptive users were less advanced clinically than those diagnosed among women who had never used oral contraceptives.

The most recent large study of oral contraceptives and breast cancer risk, the Women's Contraceptive and Reproductive Experiences (CARE) Study conducted in the mid- to late 1990s in five areas of the United States recruited 4,575 African-American and white women with newly diagnosed breast cancer and 4,682 control subjects.[86] This study focused on the breast cancer risk of women 35 to 64 years of age, as earlier studies had insufficient data on the effects of oral contraceptive use throughout a woman's reproductive years.[82] The results of this study were negative; current or former oral contraceptive use did not increase breast cancer risk overall, by race, or among women with a family history of breast cancer or those who began oral contraceptive use at a young age. This study also showed no increase in risk among older women.

Similarly, progestin-only oral contraceptives and the long-acting injectable progestogen contraceptive depot-medroxyprogesterone acetate, do not appear to affect breast cancer risk.[87]

Hormone Replacement Therapy

Meta-analyses and combined analyses of the relationship between estrogen therapy and breast cancer risk find an approximately 10% increase in breast cancer risk per 5 years of use.[88–90] Consistent with this estimated increase in risk, a large case-control study of postmenopausal women conducted in the late 1980s and early 1990s found a 6% increase in breast cancer risk per 5 years of use of estrogen therapy.[28] Unlike current oral contraceptives that provide lower levels of estrogen and progestin than a woman would produce during an ovulatory menstrual cycle, estrogen therapy provides dosages of estrogen that exceed that which women produce following the menopause (and combined hormone therapy, which adds progestin to the estrogen therapy, provides progestins when no progesterone is produced). The reason that risk is not increased to a greater extent by estrogen therapy regimens is that relatively low doses of estrogen are used.[91]

Combined hormone therapy regimens are designed to reduce the risk of endometrial cancer associated with estrogen therapy. This progestin may be added at the end of each cycle for 10 to 12 days or may be given continuously with the estrogen. In these combined regimens, progestins may enhance the proliferative effects of estrogen and further increase breast cancer risk. Three large-scale population-based epidemiologic studies of combined therapy show that adding a progestin to the estrogen regimen changes the increase in breast cancer risk after 5 years of use from approximately 10% (on estrogen alone) to approximately 30% (for estrogen plus a progestin).[27,28,92]

Clinical trials have also assessed breast cancer risk in relation to the use of combined hormone therapy. In considering the results of such trials, it is important to pay attention to the characteristics of participants and the treatment regimen used as they impact the generalizability of the findings. The Heart and Estrogen/progestin Replacement Study (also know as HERS), a randomized trial of combined hormone therapy (0.625 mg/d of conjugated estrogen plus 2.5 mg of medroxyprogesterone acetate versus placebo, average duration of treatment, 6.8 years), was designed to examine the effects of hormone therapy on coronary heart disease among postmenopausal women with documented evidence of coronary heart disease.[93] The average age of participants at their enrollment into the trial was 67 years. Women in this trial had high body mass index relative to the general population. Results have been published for cancer and other outcomes among the 93% of the original participants who were alive and agreed to continue in a follow-up study, HERS II; for breast cancer, the relative hazard comparing women in the hormone therapy group to those receiving a placebo was 1.27, and confidence intervals included 1.0.

The Women's Health Initiative randomized postmenopausal women aged 50 to 79 years (mean age 63 years) to receive one of three regimens; those with an intact uterus were randomized to receive 0.625 mg/d of conjugated estrogen plus 2.5 mg of medroxyprogesterone acetate or a placebo, whereas those who had previously had a hysterectomy were randomized to receive estrogen therapy or a placebo.[29] The combined hormone therapy arm was halted after an average 5.2 years of follow-up based on the facts that (1) the risk of invasive breast cancer was substantially elevated among the women treated with hormone therapy, and (2) the overall calculated risk (based on all adverse outcomes) of taking combined hormone therapy exceeded the calculated benefits of the therapy. The hazard rate ratio for invasive breast cancer comparing women treated with combined hormone therapy to those receiving a placebo was 1.26 (95% confidence interval, 1.00–1.59). These results are consistent with those observed in the HERS II trial[93] and in observational epidemiologic studies.[28,90] Important questions remain, such as whether results differ for women with and without menopausal symptoms, which may reflect different endogenous hormonal milieus, and whether other combination formulations (or differing dosages) or estrogen-only regimens affect breast cancer risk. The Women's Health Initiative estrogen-only trial is continuing and will finish in 2005.

Several observational studies have shown that combined hormone therapy may particularly increase risk of breast cancers with a lobular histology, which have better prognoses overall than ductal tumors.[94,95] However, it may be that women who develop breast cancer during or after hormone therapy use have a better prognosis irrespective of histologic subtype as they appear less likely to have metastatic disease than those who do not use hormone therapy.[90]

Diethylstilbestrol

Diethylstilbestrol (DES) is a synthetic estrogen that was widely prescribed to pregnant women during the 1950s and 1960s to prevent spontaneous abortion and other pregnancy complications. The offspring of these pregnancies were exposed to high levels of this estrogen while in utero. DES was later linked to risk of clear-cell carcinoma of the vagina and cervix in female offspring of those treated pregnancies and concern exists regarding breast cancer risk as the cohort of female offspring ages.[96] Recent results from a cohort of 4,821 women exposed to DES in utero and 2,095 unexposed women followed for an average of 19 years demonstrates an overall rate ratio of 1.4 comparing exposed versus unexposed women. This estimate of risk had a wide confidence interval that included 1.0. DES exposure was associated with a marked increase in risk for women aged 40 years or older (rate ratio = 2.5; 95% confidence interval [CI] 1.0–6.3) and no increase in risk among younger women (rate ratio = 0.5; 95% CI 0.3–1.7). The mothers themselves face a modest increase in their risk of breast cancer in association with DES use. The long-term follow-up study of two cohorts of women exposed to DES during pregnancy indicates that exposed women had a 27% greater breast cancer risk than comparable unexposed women (relative risk = 1.27; 95% CI 1.07–1.52).[97]

Gonadotropin-Releasing Hormone

Gonadotropin-Releasing Hormone (GnRH) agonists and antagonists are drugs that have been used in the management of ovulation induction and assisted reproductive techniques as well as in the treatment of several conditions such as precocious puberty, prostate cancer, endometriosis, and uterine leiomyoma. Pike and Spicer have proposed using a GnRH agonist to impede ovulation (while adding a small amount of estrogen and progestin to counteract the adverse effects of hypoestrogenism), thereby reducing a woman's exposure to endogenous estradiol and progesterone and, ultimately, her breast cancer risk.[98] A GnRH agonist has been shown to reduce the incidence of contralateral breast cancer among premenopausal breast cancer patients.[99] A small randomized trial of GnRH administration to women at high risk of breast cancer shows dramatic decreases in mammographic densities (which are strongly related to breast cancer risk) of women on the regimen relative to those who were not treated.[100]

Infertility Treatment

Few studies have examined the effects of ovarian stimulation on breast cancer risk. One report described 16 cases of relatively young women who developed breast cancer after prolonged periods of ovulation induction.[101] Two studies have examined

risk among cohorts of women who had ovarian stimulation as treatment for infertility.[102,103] Neither had substantial statistical power to discern small increases in breast cancer risk. The first compared the incidence of breast cancer in a group of 5,564 women who had ovarian stimulation to induce multiple folliculogenesis to a group of 4,794 women referred for in vitro fertilization (IVF), but who were untreated or had "natural cycle" treatment.[102] After a follow-up period ranging from 1 to 15 years, no increase in risk was noted among IVF-treated women in this study. The second study followed 39,837 women evaluated for infertility between 1974 and 1985.[103] Only 27 women developed in situ or invasive breast cancer (vs 28.8 expected within the cohort). The Women's CARE Study asked extensive questions regarding specific infertility treatments received by the participants and found little evidence of an overall increase in breast cancer risk among treated women relative to all women or to those reporting infertility problems but who were not treated for their infertility.[104] This study did suggest, however, that among the small number of women who had been treated with human menopausal gonadotropins (hMG) for 6 months or more (or who used hMG for six or more treatment cycles), the risk of breast cancer was two to three times greater than that of other women.

Prenatal Factors

A relatively recent area of epidemiologic interest for breast cancer has been the potential effect of the intrauterine environment on later breast cancer risk. The early phases of mammary gland development, growth, and cell differentiation occur during gestation.[105] It has been proposed that intrauterine exposure to high concentrations of pregnancy estrogens during gestation will influence a fetus's breast cancer risk as an adult, perhaps by influencing the number and degree of differentiation of breast stem cells.[106] Fetal estrogen exposure could also increase the probability of gene mutations relevant to cancer development or alter the breast's sensitivity to hormones.[107] Data regarding the effects of in utero DES exposure on breast cancer risk are reviewed above. Some data exist suggesting that preeclampsia, a condition associated with impaired placental function, and low birth weight are related to low pregnancy estrogen levels,[108,109] and, thus, women who experienced these conditions in utero might be expected to have lower breast cancer risk. Although not entirely consistent, some studies show that low birth weight translates into a lower breast cancer risk[109–111] as does experiencing preeclampsia in utero.[109,111] Also of interest is the effect of preeclampsia or pregnancy-induced hypertension on the breast cancer risk of the mother herself. A cohort study that compared parous women who experienced preeclampsia or pregnancy-induced hypertension during their first pregnancy with those who did not showed that these conditions were associated with a 19% reduced risk of breast cancer (95% CI 9–29%) with adjustments made for age, calendar period of diagnosis, age at first birth, and parity.[112] Although this association had been reported previously in case-control studies, this is the first prospective study to report on this relationship.

SUMMARY

Evidence from descriptive epidemiology, analytic epidemiologic studies, seroepidemiologic studies, and clinical trials strongly supports the role of hormones, particularly estrogen and progesterone, in the development of breast cancer risk. Ages at menarche and menopause define the period when substantial breast cancer risk accrues and the period in a women's life when she experiences the greatest exposure to estrogen and progesterone. Having a full-term pregnancy may provide a transitory increase in breast cancer risk, but the long-term result of such a pregnancy is a reduction in breast cancer risk. Age at the first full-term pregnancy is important as is the number of full-term pregnancies, with women who are younger at their first pregnancy and those who have a greater number of term pregnancies at lower risk. Breastfeeding is associated with a reduced breast cancer risk, which is likely due to the lactation-induced delayed onset of ovulatory menstrual cycles following childbirth. Postmenopausal women who are obese are at greater breast cancer risk owing to the conversion of an adrenal androgen to an estrogen by an enzyme in body fat; thus an obese postmenopausal woman has higher estrogen levels than a woman who is of normal weight. Physical activity also reduces breast cancer risk, and this reduction is probably due to the effects of activity on hormone profiles. With regard to exogenous hormones, oral contraceptives as currently formulated do not increase breast cancer risk as they provide lower levels of estrogen and progestin than a woman would experience during an ovulatory menstrual cycle. Hormone therapy increases breast cancer risk; the increase in risk among women using estrogen therapy is substantially lower than that of women using combined hormone therapy (an estrogen plus a progestin). Evidence is accumulating that in utero exposures may be important determinants of breast cancer risk.

REFERENCES

1. Parkin D, Bray F, Devesa S. Cancer burden in the year 2000. The global picture. Eur J Cancer 2001;37 Suppl 8:S4–S66.
2. MacMahon B, Cole P, Lin MT, et al. Age at first birth and cancer of the breast. A summary of an international study. Bull WHO 1970;43:209–21.
3. Collaborative Group on Hormonal Factors in Breast Cancer. Breast cancer and breastfeeding: collaborative reanalysis of individual data from 47 epidemiological studies in 30 countries, including 50,302 women with breast cancer and 96,973 women without the disease. Lancet 2002;360: 187–95.
4. Russo IH, Koszalka M, Russo J. Comparative study of the influence of pregnancy and hormonal treatment on mammary carcinogenesis. Br J Cancer 1991;64:481–4.
5. Russo IH, Russo J. Mammary gland neoplasia in long-term rodent studies. Environ Health Perspect 1996;104:938–67.
6. Henderson BE, Feigelson HS. Hormonal carcinogenesis. Carcinogenesis 2000;21:427–33.
7. Parkin DM, Whelan SL, Ferlay J, et al. Cancer incidence in five continents. Vol. VII. IARC Scientific Publications No: 143. Lyon, France: International Agency for Research on Cancer; 1997.
8. Parkin DM, Muir CS, Whelan SL, et al. Cancer incidence in five continents. IARC Scientific Publications No: 120. Lyon, France: International Agency for Research on Cancer; 1992.
9. Waterhouse J, Muir C, Shanmugaratnam K, Powell JE. Cancer incidence in five continents, Vol. IV, IARC Scientific Publications No: 42. Lyon, France: International Agency for Research on Cancer; 1982.
10. Deapen D, Liu L, Perkins C, et al. Rapidly rising breast cancer incidence rates among Asian-American women. Int J Cancer 2002;99:747–50.
11. Ziegler RG, Hoover RN, Pike MC, et al. Migration patterns and breast cancer risk in Asian-American women. J Natl Cancer Inst 1993;85:1819–27.

12. Ries LAG, Eisner MP, Kosary CL, et al. SEER Cancer Statistics Review, Bethesda, MD, 1973–1999. National Cancer Institute; 2002.

13. Pike MC, Krailo MD, Henderson BE, et al. "Hormonal" risk factors, "breast tissue age" and the age-incidence of breast cancer. Nature 1983;303:767–70.

14. Rosner B, Colditz G. Extended mathematical model of breast cancer incidence in the Nurses' Health Study. J Natl Cancer Inst 1996;88:359–64.

15. Henderson BE, Ross RK, Judd HL, et al. Do regular ovulatory cycles increase breast cancer risk? Cancer 1985;56:1206–8.

16. Goebelsmann U, Mishell D. The menstrual cycle. In: Mishell D, Davajan V, editors. Reproductive endocrinology, infertility and contraception. Philadelphia (PA): FA Davis Co; 1979. p. 67–89.

17. Pike MC, Spicer DV, Dahmoush L, Press MF. Estrogens, progestogens, normal breast cell proliferation, and breast cancer risk. Epidemiol Rev 1993; 15:17–35.

18. Bernstein L, Ross RK. Hormones and breast cancer. Epidemiol Rev 1993;15:48–65.

19. Key T. Serum estradiol and breast cancer risk. Endocr Relat Cancer 1999;6:175–80.

20. The Endogenous Hormones and Breast Cancer Collaborative Group. Endogenous sex hormones and breast cancer in postmenopausal women: reanalysis of nine prospective studies. J Natl Cancer Inst 2001;93:606–16.

21. Zeginiadou T, Kortsaris AH, Koliais S, Antonoglou O. Sex hormone binding globulin inhibits strongly the uptake of estradiol by human breast carcinoma cells via a deprivative mechanism. Cancer Biochem Biophys 1998;16:253–63.

22. Dorgan JF, Longcope C, Stephenson HE, et al. Relation of prediagnostic serum estrogen and androgen levels to breast cancer risk. Cancer Epidemiol Biomarkers Prev 1996;5:533–9.

23. Anderson DC. Sex-hormone-binding globulin. Clin Endocrinol 1974;3:69–96.

24. Nachtigall LE, Raju U, Banerjee S, et al. Serum estradiol-binding profiles in postmenopausal women undergoing three common estrogen replacement therapies: associations with sex hormone-binding globulin, estradiol, and estrone levels. Menopause 2000;7:243–50.

25. Knochenhauer ES, Boots LR, Potter HD, Azziz R. Differential binding of estradiol and testosterone to SHBG. Relation to circulating estradiol levels. J Reprod Med 1998;43:665–70.

26. Cline JM, Soderqvist G, von Schoultz E, et al. Effects of hormone replacement therapy on the mammary gland of surgically postmenopausal macaques. Am J Obstet Gynecol 1996;174:93–100.

27. Schairer C, Lubin J, Troisi R, et al. Menopausal estrogen and estrogen-progestin replacement therapy and breast cancer risk. JAMA 2000;283:485–91.

28. Ross RK, Paganini-Hill A, Wan PC, Pike MC. Effect of hormone replacement therapy on breast cancer risk: estrogen versus estrogen plus progestin. J Natl Cancer Inst 2000;92:328–32.

29. Writing Group for the Women's Health Initiative Investigators. Risks and benefits of estrogen plus progestin in healthy postmenopausal women: principal results from the Women's Health Initiative Randomized Controlled Trial. JAMA 2002; 288:321–33.

30. Grodin JM, Siiteri PK, MacDonald PC. Source of estrogen production in postmenopausal women. J Clin Endocrinol Metab 1973;36:207–14.

31. Lippman M, Bolan G, Huff K. The effects of androgens and antiandrogens on hormone-responsive human breast cancer in long-term tissue culture. Cancer Res 1976;36:4610–8.

32. Hill P, Garbaczewski L, Kasumi F. Plasma testosterone and breast cancer. Eur J Clin Oncol 1985;21: 1265–6.

33. Goldin BR, Adlercreutz H, Gorbach SL, et al. The relationship between estrogen levels and diets of Caucasian American and Oriental immigrant women. Am J Clin Nutr 1986;44:945–53.

34. Key TJA, Chen J, Wang DY, et al. Sex hormones in women in rural China and in Britain. Br J Cancer 1990;62:631–6.

35. Shimizu H, Ross RK, Bernstein L, et al. Serum estrogen levels in postmenopausal women: comparison of US whites and Japanese in Japan. Br J Cancer 1990;62:451–4.

36. Ebeling P, Koivisto VA. Physiological importance of dehydroepiandrosterone. Lancet 1994;343:1479–81.

37. Schwartz AG. Inhibition of spontaneous breast cancer formation in female C3H (Avy/a) mice by long-term treatment with dehydroepiandrosterone. Cancer Res 1979;39:1129–32.

38. Thijssen JHH, Poortman J, Schwarz F. Androgens in postmenopausal breast cancer: excretion, production and interaction with estrogens. J Steroid Biochem 1975;6:729–34.

39. Vonderhaar BK. Prolactin transport, function, and receptors in mammary gland development and differentiation. In: Neville M, Daniels C, editors. The mammary gland development, regulation and function. New York: Plenum Press; 1987. p. 383–438.

40. Vonderhaar BK. Prolactin involvement in breast cancer. Endocr Relat Cancer 1999;6:389–404.

41. Welsch CW, Nagasawa H. Prolactin and murine mammary tumorigenesis: a review. Cancer Res 1977;37:951–63.

42. Hankinson SE, Willett WC, Michaud DS, et al. Plasma prolactin levels and subsequent risk of breast cancer in postmenopausal women. J Natl Cancer Inst 1999;91:629–34.

43. Henderson BE, Pike MC, Bernstein L, Ross RK. Breast cancer. In: Schottenfeld D, Fraumeni J Jr, editors. Cancer epidemiology and prevention. New York: WB Saunders Co; 1996. p. 1022–39.

44. Henderson BE, Pike MC, Casagrande JT. Breast cancer and the oestrogen window hypothesis. Lancet 1981;2:363–4.

45. Apter D, Vihko R. Early menarche, a risk factor for breast cancer, indicates early onset of ovulatory cycles. J Clin Endocrinol Metab 1983;57:82–6.

46. Vihko R, Apter DJ. Endocrine characteristics of adolescent menstrual cycles: impact of early menarche. Steroid Biochem 1984;20:231–6.

47. Apter D, Reinila M, Vihko R. Some endocrine characteristics of early menarche, a risk factor for breast cancer are preserved into adulthood. Int J Cancer 1989;44:783–7.

48. Trichopoulos D, MacMahon B, Cole P. The menopause and breast cancer risk. J Natl Cancer Inst 1972;48:605–13.

49. Brinton LA, Schairer C, Hoover RN, Fraumeni JF. Menstrual factors and risk of breast cancer. Cancer Invest 1988;6:245–54.

50. Yuan JM, Yu MC, Ross RK, et al. Risk factors for breast cancer in Chinese women in Shanghai. Cancer Res 1988;48:1949–53.

51. Bruzzi P, Negri E, La Vecchia C, et al. Short term increase in risk of breast cancer after full term pregnancy. BMJ 1988;297:1096–8.

52. Lambe M, Hsieh CC, Trichopoulos D, et al. Transient increase in the risk of breast cancer after giving birth. New Engl J Med 1994;331:5–9.

53. Liu Q, Wuu J, Lambe M, et al. Transient increase in breast cancer risk after giving birth: postpartum period with the highest risk. Cancer Causes Control 2002;13:299–305.

54. Bernstein L, Depue RH, Ross RK, et al. Higher maternal levels of free estradiol in first compared to second pregnancy: a study of early gestational differences. J Natl Cancer Inst 1986;75:1035–9.

55. Wingo PA, Newsome K, Marks JS, et al. The risk of breast cancer following spontaneous and induced abortion. Cancer Causes Control 1997;8:93–108.

56. Harris BML, Eklund G, Meirik O, et al. Risk of cancer of the breast after legal abortion during the first trimester: a Swedish register study. BMJ 1989;299:1430–2.

57. Melbye M, Wohlfahrt J, Olsen JH, et al. Induced abortion and the risk of breast cancer. New Engl J Med 1997;366:81–5.

58. Hunter DJ, Willett WC. Diet, body size, and breast cancer. Epidemiol Rev 1993;15:110–32.

59. Kaaks R, Van Noord PAH, Den Tonkelaar I, et al. Breast-cancer incidence in relation to height, weight and body-fat distribution in the Dutch "DOM" cohort. Int J Cancer 1998;76:647–51.

60. Huang Z, Hankinson SE, Colditz GA, et al. Dual effects of weight and weight gain on breast cancer risk. JAMA 1997;278:1407–11.

61. Morimoto LM, White E, Chen Z, et al. Obesity, body size, and risk of postmenopausal breast cancer: the Women's Health Initiative (United States). Cancer Causes Control 2002;13:741–51.

62. Siiteri PK, MacDonald PC. Role of extraglandular estrogen in human endocrinology. In: Geiger SR, Astwood EB, Greep RO, editors. Handbook of physiology. Washington (DC): American Physiological Society; 1973. p. 615–29.

63. Moore JW, Key TJA, Bulbrook RD, et al. Sex hormone binding globulin and risk factors for breast cancer in a population of normal women who had

64. Key TJA, Pike MC. The dose-effect relationship between "unopposed" oestrogens and endometrial mitotic rate: its central role in explaining and predicting endometrial cancer risk. Br J Cancer 1988; 57:205–12.

65. Kaaks R, Lukanova A. Effects of weight control and physical activity in cancer prevention: role of endogenous hormone metabolism. Ann NY Acad Med 2002;963:268–81.

66. Ursin G, Longnecker MP, Haile RW, Greenland S. A meta-analysis of body mass index and risk of premenopausal breast cancer. Epidemiology 1995; 6:137–41.

67. Pike MC. Reducing cancer risk in women through lifestyle-mediated changes in hormone levels. Cancer Detect Prev 1990;14:595–607.

68. Frisch RE, Gotz-Welbergen AV, McArthur JW, et al. Delayed menarche and amenorrhea of college athletes in relation to age of onset of training. JAMA 1981;246:1559–63.

69. Schwartz B, Cumming DC, Riordan E, et al. Exercise-associated amenorrhea: a distinct entity? Am J Obstet Gynecol 1981;141:662–70.

70. Shangold MM, Levine HA. The effect of marathon training upon menstrual function. Am J Obstet Gynecol 1982;143:862–9.

71. Shangold MM. Exercise and amenorrhea. Sem Reprod Endocrinol 1985;3:35–43.

72. Dale E, Gerlach D, Wilhite AL. Menstrual dysfunction in distance runners. Obstet Gynecol 1979; 54:47–53.

73. Pirke KM, Schweiger U, Broocks A, et al. Luteinizing hormone and follicle stimulating hormone secretion patterns in female athletes with and without menstrual disturbances. Clin Endocrinol 1990;33: 345–53.

74. Broocks A, Pirke KM, Schweiger U, et al. Cyclic ovarian function in recreational athletes. J Appl Physiol 1990;68:2083–6.

75. Bernstein L, Ross RK, Lobo RA, et al. The effects of moderate physical activity on menstrual cycle patterns in adolescence: implications for breast cancer prevention. Br J Cancer 1987;55:681–5.

76. Russell JB, Mitchell D, Musey PI, Collins DC. The relationship of exercise to anovulatory cycles in female athletes: hormonal and physical characteristics. Obstet Gynecol 1984;63:452–6.

77. Friedenreich CM, Rohan TE. A review of physical activity and breast cancer. Epidemiology 1995;6:311–7.

78. McTiernan A, Ulrich C, Slate S, Potter J. Physical activity and cancer etiology: associations and mechanisms. Cancer Causes Control 1998;9:487–509.

79. Bernstein L, Henderson BE, Hanisch R, et al. Physical exercise and reduced risk of breast cancer in young women. J Natl Cancer Inst 1994;86:1403–8.

80. Carpenter CL, Ross RK, Paganini-Hill A, Bernstein L. Lifetime exercise activity and breast cancer risk among post-menopausal women. Br J Cancer 1999; 80:1852–8.

never used exogenous sex hormones. Br J Cancer 1987;56:661–6.

81. International Agency for Research on Cancer (IARC). Weight control and physical activity. Lyon, France: IARC Press; 2002.

82. Bernstein L, Henderson BE. Exogenous hormones. In: Schottenfeld D, Fraumeni JF Jr, editors. Cancer epidemiology and prevention. 2nd ed. New York: WB Saunders, Co; 1996. p. 462–88.

83. Bernstein L, Pike MC, Krailo M, Henderson BE. Update of the Los Angeles Study of oral contraceptives and breast cancer: 1981 and 1983. In: Mann R, editor. Oral contraceptives and breast cancer. Park Ridge (NJ): Parthenon Publishing; 1990. p. 169–80.

84. Ursin G, Ross RK, Sullivan-Halley J, et al. Use of oral contraceptives and risk of breast cancer in young women. Breast Cancer Res Treat 1998;50:175–84.

85. Collaborative Group on Hormonal Factors in Breast Cancer. Breast cancer and hormonal contraceptives. Lancet 1996;347:1713–27.

86. Marchbanks PA, McDonald JA, Wilson GH, et al. Oral contraceptives and the risk of breast cancer. New Engl J Med 2002;346:2025–32.

87. Stanford JL, Thomas DB. Exogenous progestins and breast cancer. Epidemiol Rev 1993;15:98–107.

88. Steinberg KK, Thacker SB, Smith SJ, et al. A meta-analysis of the effect of estrogen replacement therapy on the risk of breast cancer. JAMA 1991;265:1985–90.

89. Pike MC, Bernstein L, Spicer DV. The relationship of exogenous hormones to breast cancer risk. In: Niederhuber J, editor. Current therapy in oncology. St. Louis (MO): Mosby; 1993. p. 292–303.

90. Collaborative Group on Hormonal Factors in Breast Cancer. Breast cancer and hormone replacement therapy: collaborative reanalysis of data from 51 epidemiological studies of 52,705 women with breast cancer and 108,411 women without breast cancer. Lancet 1997;350:1047–59.

91. Key TJ, Pike MC. The role of oestrogens and progestagens in the epidemiology and prevention of breast cancer. Eur J Cancer Clin Oncol 1988;13:29–43.

92. Magnusson C, Baron JA, Correia N, et al. Breast-cancer risk following long-term oestrogen- and oestrogen-progestin-replacement therapy. Int J Cancer 1999;81:339–44.

93. Hulley S, Furberg C, Barrett-Connor E, et al. Noncardiovascular disease outcomes during 6.8 years of hormone therapy: Heart and Estrogen/progestin Replacement Study follow-up (HERS II). JAMA 2002;288:58–66.

94. Chen CL, Weiss NS, Newcomb P, et al. Hormone replacement therapy in relation to breast cancer. JAMA 2002;287:734–41.

95. Daling JR, Malone KE, Doody DR, et al. Relation of regimens of combined hormone replacement therapy to lobular, ductal, and other histologic types of breast carcinoma. Cancer 2002;95:2455–64.

96. Herbst AL, Ulfelder H, Poskanzer DC. Adenocarcinoma of the vagina. Association of maternal stilbestrol therapy with tumor appearance in young women. New Engl J Med 1971;248:878–81.

97. Titus-Ernstoff L, Hatch EE, Hoover RN, et al. Long-term cancer risk in women given diethylstilbestrol (DES) during pregnancy. Br J Cancer 2001;84:126–33.

98. Pike M, Spicer D. Hormonal contraception and chemoprevention of female cancers. Endocr Relat Cancer 2000;7:73–83.

99. Baum M. Adjuvant treatment of premenopausal breast cancer with zoladex and tamoxifen: results from the ZIPP trial organized by the Cancer Research Campaign (CRC) Breast Cancer Trials Group [abstract]. Breast Cancer Res Treat 1999;57:30.

100. Spicer DV, Ursin G, Parisky YR, et al. Changes in mammographic densities induced by a hormonal contraceptive designed to reduce breast cancer risk. J Natl Cancer Inst 1994;86:431–6.

101. Brzezinski A, Peretz T, Mor-Yosef S, Schenker JG. Ovarian stimulation and breast cancer: is there a link? Gynecol Oncol 1994;52:292–5.

102. Venn A, Watson L, Lumley J, et al. Breast and ovarian cancer incidence after infertility and *in vitro* fertilisation. Lancet 1995;346:995–1000.

103. Rossing MA, Daling JR, Weiss NS, et al. Risk of breast cancer in a cohort of infertile women. Gynecol Oncol 1996;60:3–7.

104. Burkman RT, Tang MTC, Malone KE, et al. Infertility drugs and the risk of breast cancer: findings from the National Institute of Child Health and Human Development Women's Contraceptive and Reproductive Experiences Study. Fertil Steril 2003;79:844–51.

105. Russo J, Russo IH. Development of the human mammary gland. In: Neville M, Daniel C, editors. The mammary gland. New York: Plenum Publishing Co; 1987. p. 67–93.

106. Trichopoulos D. Hypothesis: does breast cancer originate *in utero*? Lancet 1990;335:939–40.

107. Anbazhagan R, Gusterson BA. Prenatal factors may influence predisposition to breast cancer. Eur J Cancer 1994;30A:1–3.

108. Petridou E, Panagiotopoulou K, Katsouyanni K, et al. Tobacco smoking, pregnancy estrogens, and birth weight. Epidemiology 1990;1:247–50.

109. Ekbom A, Trichopoulos D, Adami HO, et al. Evidence of prenatal influences on breast cancer risk. Lancet 1992;340:1015–8.

110. Michels KB, Trichopoulos D, Robins JB, et al. Birthweight as a risk factor for breast cancer. Lancet 1996;348:1542–6.

111. Ekbom A, Hsieh CC, Lipworth L, et al. Intrauterine environment and breast cancer risk in women: a population-based study. J Natl Cancer Inst 1997;89:71–6.

112. Vatten LJ, Romundstad PR, Trichopoulos D, Skjærven R. Pre-eclampsia in pregnancy and subsequent risk for breast cancer. Br J Cancer 2002;87:971–3.

BENIGN BREAST DISEASE AND BREAST CANCER RISK

Elizabeth L. Wiley, MD

B enign breast disease, fibrocystic change, and fi-brocystic disease are interchangeable terms that include a wide range of morphologic entities found in the noncancerous breast. One reason clinicians need to be familiar with these entities is that some are associated with an increased risk of subsequent breast cancer, whereas others are not.

Overall, women diagnosed with benign breast disease have an increased risk of subsequently developing breast cancer compared with those who have not been so diagnosed.[1–7] Women participating in the National Surgical Adjuvant Breast and Bowel Project's breast cancer prevention trial with biopsy-proven benign breast disease had 2 to 2.5 times the risk of invasive breast cancer as women who had not been so biospied.[6] Table 4-1 summarizes these lesions and their associated risk of carcinoma.

Benign breast disease is common in the general population.[1,8–12] Care must be taken when reviewing these[1–12] and other studies to determine the risk of subsequent breast cancer associated with a particular form of benign breast disease, because the terminology used to describe various lesions is only now becoming standardized.[13,14] As a result, it has been difficult to compare studies seeking to establish the level of breast cancer risk seen with benign breast disease. Some benign breast lesions have been referred to by several names, and some names have been used to identify several different lesions. For example, the lesion of radial scar is also called complex sclerosing lesion, radial sclerosis, and sclerosing papilloma. However, sclerosing papilloma can also refer to a papilloma that has undergone fi brosis or scarring. Also, the term blunt duct adenosis, which ordinarily defines a small cluster of cysts with no epithelial hyperplasia formed by the termi-

nal ductules of the lobular unit,[13,15–17] has also been used to describe a cluster of microcysts having a variable epithelial component and pseudoangiomatous stromal hyperplasia.[18]

NORMAL MAMMARY HISTOLOGY

The breast is composed of 10 to 20 specialized apocrine sweat glands and a protective envelope of specialized stroma that facilitates the cyclic hypertrophy and regression of secretory glandular components. The mammary ducts contain the same epithelial components as apocrine sweat glands in the axillae and inguinal regions, although the mammary ducts are more elongated and branched. The ducts are lined by flattened cuboidal lining cells with tight cell–cell junctions and a specialized luminal membrane to conduct milk to the nipple region. The terminal duct lobular unit, which contains between 12 and 20 acinar buds in nonmenstruating women, is lined by milk-secreting acinar cells. Both the acinar buds and ducts have a layer of basal myoepithelial cells. Their contractile elements facilitate milk flow during lactation.

At menarche, the lobular unit undergoes cyclic growth and regression under the influence of both estrogen and progesterone. During the proliferative and early secretory phase of the menstrual cycle, estrogen stimulates acinar epithelial proliferation, and the buds elongate and branch several times. With progesterone stimulation in the secretory portion of the menstrual cycle, the acinar cells mature to secretory capability. With menstruation and the withdrawal of progesterone and estrogen, the epithelium of the lobular unit undergoes a wave of apoptosis and

TABLE 4-1 Breast Lesions and Their Associated Risk for Subsequent Invasive Breast Carcinoma

Lesions with high risk (6 to 10× or greater):	Ductal carcinoma in situ
	    (Ductal intraepithelial neoplasia 1c, 2, 3)
	Atypical ductal hyperplasia with family history
	    (Atypical intraductal hyperplasia, ductal intraepithelial
	        neoplasia 1b with family history)
	Lobular neoplasia, grade 3
	    (Lobular carcinoma in situ)
	Lobular neoplasia, grade 2, with ductal involvement
	    (Atypical lobular hyperplasia) with ductal involvement
	Epithelial hyperplasia with severe nuclear atypia, Black-Chabon
	    Score of 5[4]

Lesions with moderate risk (4–5×):	Atypical ductal hyperplasia
	    (Ductal intraepithelial neoplasia 1b [DIN1b]).
	Lobular neoplasia, grade 2
	    (Atypical lobular hyperplasia)

Lesions with mild risk (1.5–3×)	Florid duct hyperplasia
	    (Ductal intraepithelial neoplasia 1a [DIN1a])
	    (Intraductal hyperplasia)
	Lobular neoplasia, grade 1
	    (Lobular hyperplasia)
	Radial scars
	Intraductal papillomas without ADH
	Sclerosing adenosis without either ADH or LN
	Complex fibroadenoma
	Blunt duct adenosis[40]
	Epithelial hyperplasia with mild nuclear atypia, Black-Chabon
	    score 1–2[4]
	Cytologic atypia not otherwise specified[28]

Lesions with no elevated risk	Simple fibroadenoma Duct ectasia Metaplasias Simple adenosis Simple cysts Focal fibrosis

the acinar branches regress.[19] During pregnancy, regression does not occur, and secretory activity is initiated with prolonged progesterone exposure.

BENIGN BREAST DISEASE AND LEVEL OF BREAST CANCER RISK

Benign breast disease falls into two broad categories: architectural distortions and epithelial proliferations,

or, more specifically, epithelial hyperplasias. Architectural distortions are lesions such as adenosis, cysts, duct ectasia, fibroadenomas, fibrosis, or scars that disturb normal lobular architecture. Architectural distortions are clinically important because they present as radiologic imitators of breast cancer. The lesions may appear benign, as might a well-circumscribed ovoid fibroadenoma, or malignant, as might a spiculated radial scar. Most mammary epithelial proliferation is physiologic. All types of mammary epithelium undergo orderly proliferation and regression during the menstrual cycle.

Epithelial hyperplasia, however, is an abnormal increase in the number of epithelial cells in either ducts or lobular units. Cancer risk segregates toward lesions with hyperplasia. Multiple studies have shown that benign breast lesions with a component of epithelial hyperplasia have been shown to have an increased risk of cancer compared with lesions that do not have epithelial hyperplasia,[5,7–9,13,20–31] whereas most lesions with no additional risk lack a component of epithelial hyperplasia. Epithelial hyperplasia may occur alone or may occur in combination with an architectural distortion.

Most forms of mammary epithelial hyperplasia are combinations of either ductal and basal myoepithelial cells or lobular and myoepithelial cells. The histologic type of epithelial hyperplasia does not necessarily reflect the location of the hyperplasia (within a duct or lobular unit) or the amount of hyperplasia. For example, hyperplasia of lobular epithelial cells can be found in true ducts.

BREAST LESIONS NOT ASSOCIATED WITH INCREASED RISK OF BREAST CANCER

Cysts

Cysts are fluid-filled, nonproliferative lesions of the breast that frequently distort architecture. Cysts are thought to form as a result of duct blockage. If the blockage is at the level of terminal ducts leading to lobular units, the resultant lesion is a cluster of small cysts. For this reason, the same lesions may be called adenosis or microcysts.

Simple cysts have not been found to have an elevated risk of carcinoma.[7] Bodian and colleagues did find an increased risk of breast cancer in patients with cysts that were palpable and yielded fluid on cyst aspiration. This risk was higher for those who underwent multiple aspirations of cysts.[32] However, the patients in this study did not have surgical biopsies to exclude other lesions with an increased risk of carcinoma, such as hyperplasias, that may have cystic components.

Duct Ectasia

Duct ectasia is chronic dilatation of a large duct or ductal system. The affected duct or ductal tree is filled with secretory and/or inflammatory debris. The usual cause of duct ectasia is infection or inflammation of a duct with subsequent blockage. The intraluminal debris can become solidified, causing the formation of a sausage-shaped or branched mass. With resolution of the cause of inflammation and removal of the debris, macrocysts may be a residual lesion. Duct ectasia has no increased risk of carcinoma.[7]

Metaplasia

Epithelial metaplasia is a common finding in biopsies and autopsy studies of breast disease.[11,33] Metaplasia is the replacement of normal epithelial cells with another, benign type of epithelium. Although epithelial metaplasias of the breast do not always cause architectural distortions, metaplastic epithelium is frequently found in cysts and variants of adenosis.

Apocrine metaplasia is replacement of acinar or duct luminal cells with a cell that resembles the secretory cell of apocrine sweat glands. The cell is made up of a granular eosinophilic cytoplasm and secretes by breaking off small portions of cytoplasm into a lumen. Apocrine metaplasia is frequently found lining cysts of all sizes and in lobular units showing microcystic change or adenosis. Although apocrine metaplasia is a more frequent finding in patients with breast cancer than in random autopsy specimens of women without breast cancer,[34] it has not been found to be a marker for breast cancer risk when studied prospectively.[25]

Complex apocrine metaplasia or papillary apocrine metaplasia, which can present as a complex cyst, does not have an elevated cancer risk when present without other forms of epithelial hyperplasia.[35] Other metaplastic changes that can occur are clear cell metaplasia, lactational metaplasia, mucinous metaplasia, and squamous metaplasia.[15] As these later forms of metaplasia are less common, they have not been studied individually; as a group they do not have an elevated cancer risk.

Stromal Fibrosis

Stromal fibrosis refers to a mass lesion composed of connective tissue. It may be cellular and may engulf ducts and lobular units.[36] It may be clinically evident as a palpable mass or present as a mammographic lesion. Stromal fibrosis encompasses a variety of histologies including dense linear fibrosis that is identical to diabetic mastopathy, dense concentric collagenous rings around ducts and acini, and fibrosis that involves both the lobular units and interlobular stroma.[37] These lesions are also referred to as fibrosis of the breast,[38] focal fibrous disease,[39] and fibrous mastopathy.[40]

Pseudoangiomatous stromal hyperplasia is a form of fibrosis that is characterized by fibroblastic proliferation. Although it may present as a solitary mass lesion,[36] it frequently is associated with epithelial hyperplasia in the form of gynecomastia, gynecomastia-like hyperplasia, or blunt duct adenosis (BDA) as described by Shaaban and colleagues.[18]

Although fibrosis may present as a lesion necessitating biopsy or excision to exclude carcinoma, stromal fibrosis is not associated with an increased risk of breast cancer.

Adenosis

The term adenosis designates an alteration in lobular architecture. The simplest form, in which the lobule is slightly dilated and is lined by flattened epithelium, is usually what is referred to as simple adenosis or adenosis NOS.[16] However, the term may also be used for any alteration of the lobular unit, including lesions with components of epithelial hyperplasia and atypia.

Lesions of adenosis may or may not have microscopically visible secretions, but when present, the secretory material is not a prominent component. Many lesions of simple adenosis appear as a cluster of microcysts in which the epithelial lining may be low cuboidal or flattened epithelium with or without apocrine metaplasia (apocrine adenosis). The American Joint Committee on Cancer Staging System for Breast Cancer considers simple adenosis a lesion without elevated risk of carcinoma.[7]

LESIONS ASSOCIATED WITH ELEVATED RISK OF CARCINOMA

Epithelial Hyperplasia with Cytologic Atypia

Atypical epithelial hyperplasia is hyperplasia that has morphologic features similar to those of carcinoma in situ. Lesions of atypical hyperplasia occupy a position between benign hyperplasia and carcinoma in situ. The term atypical hyperplasia is used for two types of lesions. The term is sometimes used to designate epithelial proliferations in which there is cellular atypia, such as nuclear pleomorphism, aberrant mitoses, or abnormal chromatin patterns.[4,41,42] Atypical hyperplasia is also defined as a lesion with architectural features that mimic low grade ductal carcinoma in situ (DCIS). This form of atypical hyperplasia will be discussed in the sections on atypical ductal hyperplasia and lobular neoplasia.

Epithelial hyperplasia with cytologic atypia in benign breast disease is associated with increased risk of carcinoma. Black and Chabon developed a scoring system to assess cellular atypia.[43] Kreiger and Hiatt used this system to assess benign breast disease and found that risk of carcinoma increased directly with degree of atypia, rising from a rate ratio of 1.8 among women with Black-Chabon scores of 1 and 2 (95% confidence interval [CI] 1.5–2.2) to 7.2 among women with a Black-Chabon score of 5 (95% CI 1.8–28.9).[4] Even nuclear enlargement without other features of cytologic atypia appears to be associated with increased risk of carcinoma. Mommers and colleagues, using nuclear morphometry, found that women with nuclear enlargement above the 75th percentile had a 1.6 to 1.7 times elevated risk of carcinoma compared with patients with nuclear size below the 75th percentile.[44] Bodian and colleagues, in a long-term study of Haagensen's patients with biopsied benign breast disease, found that moderate to severe cytologic atypia in a lesion was associated with a risk of subsequent carcinoma 3.0 times that of normal populations.[41]

Ductal Hyperplasias

Ductal hyperplasia (DH) is the most common form of proliferative breast disease. Table 4-2 groups the various terms used to categorize ductal hyperplasia and associated risk of carcinoma. DH is hyperplasia of epithelium that resembles the luminal cells of mammary ducts.[4,23,24,45,46] Normally, ducts are lined by two layers of cells, basal contractile myoepithelial cells and low cuboidal cells with specialized luminal borders and tight cell–cell junctions to keep secretions within duct lumina. Because DH occurs not only in mammary ducts but also in metaplastic epithelium of expanded lobular units, it is important to remember that the term ductal hyperplasia does not refer exclusively to hyperplasia of epithelium in true ducts but also refers to hyperplasia of ductal-type epithelium regardless of location within the breast.

TABLE 4-2 Types of Ductal Hyperplasia

Type of Hyperplasia	Other Terms	Associated Risk of Cancer
Ductal hyperplasia, NOS	Usual, Simple	Normal population
Florid duct hyperplasia	Moderate, Severe, Ductal intraepithelial neoplasia 1a (DIN 1a), Epitheliosis, Papillomatosis	Slight increase (1.5–2×)
Atypical ductal hyperplasia	Ductal intraepithelial neoplasia 1b (DIN1b)	Moderate increase (3–5×)
Low grade duct carcinoma in situ (LG DCIS)	Grade 1 DCIS, Low grade intraductal carcinoma, Ductal intraepithelial neoplasia 1c (DIN 1c)	High risk (10×)

Adapted from Fitzgibbons PL et al.[45]

Ductal hyperplasias are grouped by architectural and cellular features. Ductal hyperplasias that increase the number of cells or the number of layers of cells without appearing to distort or distend the ductal contour are called mild, simple, usual, or hyperplasia NOS.[41] Simple DH also includes duct-like lumens lined with metaplastic pseudostratified tall columnar cells as well as those lined with multiple layers of flattened cells oriented concentrically around a lumen. Simple duct-type epithelial hyperplasia does not increase the risk of breast carcinoma.

Ductal hyperplasia that fills or plugs ducts and/or lobules with epithelial cells is associated with a slightly elevated risk of subsequent invasive carcinoma. This type of epithelial hyperplasia, which forms papillae, cellular plugs, bridges, microlumens, fenestrations, or sheets that fill, expand, or otherwise distort ductal lumens is called florid or severe-type ductal hyperplasia (FDH).[47] Other terms equivalent to FDH include intraductal hyperplasia, as in Tavassoli and Norris' 1990 study of breast cancer risk; Tavassoli's term ductal intraepithelial neoplasia DIN 1a;[48–50] and papillomatosis and epitheliosis.[24,41] FDH is always made up of hyperplasia of both duct-type luminal cells and basal myoepithelial cells.[51] Other cell types, including metaplastic apocrine cells, foam (histiocytes) cells, lymphocytes, and spindled myoepithelial cells, may also be present in FDH. FDH has morphologic features that resemble DCIS: epithelial bridges, plugs, papillae, microlumina, and fenestrations. However, the presence of both myoepithelial and luminal cell hyperplasia in lesions of FDH is indicative of its benignity. Compared with women without a history of breast disease, women with FDH have a 1.5 to 2.5 times or slightly elevated risk of subsequent invasive breast cancer.[23,48]

Atypical Ductal Hyperplasia

The term atypical ductal hyperplasia (ADH) is defined as the form of ductal hyperplasia that morphologically mimics low grade DCIS. ADH has been the subject of several papers attempting to set strict morphologic criteria for its diagnosis.[23,48,52,53] ADH has a more uniform population of epithelial cells when compared with typical forms of simple and florid hyperplasia.[23] ADH also lacks the cytologic atypia of lesions studied by Kreiger and colleagues[4] and Bodian and colleagues[41] and lacks the nuclear atypia and necrosis found in intermediate and high grade DCIS.[23,54] Lesions of ADH have predictable intraluminal structures and lack the streaming and spindling of cells found in true benign hyperplasia. Most lesions of atypical ductal hyperplasia are small. They will involve only a portion of a large duct or only a few small duct-like structures totaling less than 2 millimeters with a single population of cells. In contrast, low grade DCIS will totally replace the normal cells of a lobule or duct with a uniform clonal population and involve a larger area of breast tissue.[23]

Whereas FDH has normal to increased numbers of myoepithelial cells, ADH will have a reduced to nearly absent population of myoepithelial cells. Although immunohistochemical stains are not routinely employed to make a diagnosis of ADH, antibodies to various cell markers show a uniform pattern of estrogen and progesterone receptors and various types of cytokeratin.[49,55] This staining pattern is similar to that found in low grade DCIS.

The reduction of myoepithelial cells in ADH can also be demonstrated by special stains.[49]

Both Tavassoli[49,50] and Rosai[52] have proposed using the term intraepithelial neoplasia instead of ductal hyperplasia and carcinoma in situ to describe the duct-type epithelial proliferations that carry an elevated risk subsequent to invasive breast carcinoma. Tavassoli has formalized this proposal in papers and her textbook.[49,50,56] Ductal intraepithelial neoplasia grade 1b or DIN 1b is equivalent to ADH.[50] Some examples of columnar metaplasia of lobular units also have a single, clonal population of atypical cells resembling low grade micropapillary carcinoma and are regarded as a form of atypical ductal hyperplasia.[18,57]

Atypical ductal hyperplasia is found in 3 to 4% of women undergoing breast biopsy and is associated with a relative risk of invasive cancer 2.5 to 5 times that of normal, a level that is considered moderately elevated.[4,23,48,58,59] The absolute risk for invasive breast cancer after a diagnosis of ADH is about 10% for a period of 10 to 15 years after biopsy and then decreases towards average.[23,28] The risk of invasive cancer is higher (6.5 times) in perimenopausal women.[23] Overall, breast cancer risk for women with ADH is one-half the risk of developing invasive cancer after a diagnosis of DCIS. Women with low grade DCIS carry risk for invasive carcinoma in the same (ipsilateral) breast. In contrast, Connolly and Page and their colleagues found that the risk of subsequent cancer for women with ADH was bilateral,[23,60] whereas Tavassoli's study found greater risk in the ipsilateral breast.[48]

Family history of breast cancer further increases the risk of subsequent invasive carcinoma in women with ADH. Women diagnosed with ADH who had a first-degree relative with breast cancer had nearly a 10-fold risk for subsequent invasive breast cancer development, whereas those without a family history had only a 3-fold risk for subsequent cancer.[23,61,62] The use of low-dosage conjugated estrogen after menopause in women with ADH does not appear to further elevate risk beyond that seen with a diagnosis of ADH alone.[12]

Lobular Neoplasia

Hyperplasia of lobular-type epithelium has several names and descriptors. Stewart and Foot in 1941 used the term lobular carcinoma in situ (LCIS) to describe a lesion in which lobular units were filled and distended by a lobular cell.[63] Haagensen and

colleagues, in their large series of similar cases, named the process lobular neoplasia (LN).[64] Others found lobular neoplasia to be rare but involving both breasts in up to two-thirds of women so affected.[65–69] Because LN was found to be associated with invasive carcinoma, it was considered to be an early form of carcinoma, and many patients were subjected to mastectomy upon diagnosis.[70] Lesions with some but not all of the characteristics of LCIS were termed atypical lobular hyperplasia (ALH) and lobular hyperplasia (LH).[23] In 1992, Tavassoli proposed using Haagensen's term, lobular neoplasia, to encompass all lesions of lobular-type epithelial hyperplasia and to use a grading system to indicate the volume of disease or the severity of changes.[71] The terminology is gaining general acceptance, in part because it uses a uniform terminology for this disease process, which has been given different names depending on the volume of disease, and avoids the use of the term LCIS, which, for many women and their physicians, is indicative of carcinoma rather than a lesion associated with an increased risk of invasive breast cancer development.

Unlike ductal hyperplasias, which have cells displaying varying types of cytokeratin and cellular differentiation, LN is a single population of abnormal cells. The cells of lobular neoplasia have scant, rigid cytoplasm and small round, bland nuclei. LN cells exhibit loss of cell–cell adhesion and lack of luminal orientation, causing lesions of LN to resemble a bag of marbles in routine microscopic sections. LN cells lack immunoreactive expression of E-cadherin, a component of cell–cell junctions.[72] LN cells (and, incidentally, invasive lobular carcinoma) frequently contain intracytoplasmic lumens, complete with membrane border apparatus, with and without mucin.[73–75] There are atypical forms of LN cells with apocrine change, pleomorphic nuclei, or signet ring cell features.[42,76–78] Long-term studies differentiating risk associated with LN with cytologic atypia have not been published. LN cells frequently displace and/or replace duct-type epithelium in true mammary ducts.[79] Smaller lesions of lobular neoplasia retain a complement of myoepithelial cells, but larger lesions have either markedly reduced numbers or an absence of myoepithelial cells. Lobular neoplasia may involve other benign lesions of the breast including sclerosing adenosis and radial scars. Risk should be assessed according to the type of involvement of LN in these lesions.

There is significant variability in the classification of lesions of lobular neoplasia.[64,80–84] Lobular neoplasia is presently divided into at least two or, more commonly, three categories, depending on the volume or amount of disease and subsequent morphologic changes. The smallest form of lobular neoplasia is called grade 1 (LN1).[84,85] LN1 shows no distention of the lobular unit with partial to complete replacement by cells characteristic of lobular neoplasia.[71] Lobular neoplasia with only lesions of LN1 is focal disease. Page found that women diagnosed with LN1 carried a risk of subsequent invasive carcinoma 1.7 times that of the general population, a risk similar to that found associated with FDH.[79]

The fully developed form of lobular neoplasia is called lobular carcinoma in situ or lobular neoplasia, grade 3 (LN3). Page and colleagues defined lesions of fully developed LN as lesions in which the LN cells fill, distort, and distend at least one-half of the acini of a lobular unit and in which acinar lumina are obliterated.[85] A diagnosis of LN3, thus defined, is associated with an 8- to 11-fold increase in the risk of subsequent invasive carcinoma of the breast, and the risk appears to be bilateral.[23] Other published series on lobular neoplasia have demonstrated different associated risks of invasive carcinoma. However, this difference appears to be related to the relative incidence of LN3 compared with that of the intermediate lesion of LN (a.k.a. atypical lobular hyperplasia and lobular neoplasia, grade 2 [LN2]). The intermediate lesion of lobular neoplasia (LN2) is defined as LN cells filling and distending some or all acini of a lobular unit, but acinar outlines remain distinct, the acini are separate, and residual lumens may be present. A lobular unit with complete involvement by LN cells and only minimal distension also qualifies as LN2.[84] Page and colleagues found LN3 in only 0.51% of their study group of over 10,000 patients; the intermediate lesion of LN2 was found almost three times as frequently.[23] Tavassoli found similar proportions of LN2 and LN3 as Page.[84] Other published series on lobular neoplasia have demonstrated different proportions of LN2 and LN3 and associated risk of carcinoma. Rosen and colleagues' series had a reverse ratio of LN3 to LN2: 99 to 13.[67,86] Studies with higher incidences of LN3 have had generally lower relative risks of cancer than LN3 as defined by Page.[64,66,85,87]

Page found that women with the intermediate lesion of LN had a 4- to 5-fold increase in the risk of subsequent invasive carcinoma compared with women without LN. This risk is similar to that of ADH. Page also made a distinction between the fully developed lesions of LN3, intermediate lesions of LN2, and lesions of LN2 with ductal involvement. He found that women with ductal involvement by LN had a risk of developing invasive carcinoma that was intermediate between the risk associated with LN3 and LN2 without ductal involvement (6 to 7).[79] Page and colleagues have also found that LN2 with or without ductal involvement carries a proportionally greater risk of ipsilateral carcinoma. In women who had a diagnosis of only LN2, 77% of the subsequent invasive carcinomas arose in the ipsilateral breast.[88] LN is also more strongly associated with risk for premenopausal than postmenopausal carcinoma.[59]

Connolly and Schnitt have suggested that the fully formed and intermediate lesions of LN be combined, because (1) both lesions have a significant elevated risk of subsequent invasive carcinoma, (2) the same cell type causes both lesions, (3) they cannot be distinguished cytologically, (4) the lesions differ only in terms of qualifying volume, and (5) the two lesions are not uniformly diagnosed.[89] The risk of carcinoma for women with LN2 and LN3 is from 5 to 10 times that of women without LN, similar to that associated with ADH and ADH with family history.

ARCHITECTURAL DISTORTIONS ASSOCIATED WITH ELEVATED RISK OF CARCINOMA

Complex Fibroadenoma

Fibroadenomas are the most common tumor of the breast in young women, and, because they present as a palpable mass, they are frequently biopsied.[90,91] Fibroadenomas are tumors of both the epithelium and specialized stroma of the breast. Most have a dominant stromal component that is relatively acellular. The use of oral contraceptives at a young age is associated with an increased risk of developing fibroadenomas.[92] In situ carcinoma and invasive carcinoma may be present in fibroadenomas or in the parenchyma adjacent to fibroadenomas.[93–95] Up to 50% of fibroadenomas may contain other elements of benign breast disease, including apocrine metaplasia, ductal hyperplasia, sclerosing adenosis, and macrocysts.[96] Fibroadenomas that contain any of these elements are termed complex fibroadenomas; those that lack all of these features are termed simple fibroadenomas. Women who were found to have simple fibroadenomas with no proliferative disease in adjacent breast tissue did not have an elevated risk of subsequent breast cancer. However, women diagnosed with complex fibroadenomas and/or with proliferative disease in breast tissue adjacent to their fibroadenomas had an elevated risk of subsequent cancer between 2.6 and 3.9.[97,98] Fibroadenomas presenting in older women have a higher risk of associated invasive carcinoma,[33] and fibroadenomas with florid duct hyperplasia are associated with the same slightly elevated risk (1.5 to 2) of cancer as FDH occurring outside of a fibroadenoma. In one large study, women who were diagnosed with fibroadenomas that contained atypical hyperplasia but did not have atypical hyperplasia in adjacent breast tissue did not demonstrate an increased risk of breast cancer.[99] One explanation for this finding may be that the patients studied who had atypical hyperplasia had their lesions excised to clear margins, whereas most patients with fibroadenomas and proliferative disease in the adjacent stroma did not have the proliferative disease routinely excised.

Sclerosing Adenosis

Sclerosing adenosis (SA) is a lesion that shows distortion of the normal lobular unit. Although some consider sclerosing adenosis to be an involutional change following lactation or a regressive change related to age, others consider it to be a proliferative lesion.[17,41] SA is characterized by proliferation of small tubules or ductules that resemble a tangle of hair, seaweed, or spaghetti in three-dimensional reconstructions. In microscopic sections, the lesions appear as a cluster of small tubules and epithelial nests. Most lesions of sclerosing adenosis have a component of epithelial and/or myoepithelial proliferation.[100–102] Lesions radiologically, grossly, and microscopically may mimic invasive carcinoma.[103] Lesions without epithelial proliferation are readily recognized as benign lesions. SA with epithelial hyperplasia will mimic invasive cancer, and sometimes special stains are needed to identify markers of benign disease. Rarely, SA may contain atypical ductal hyperplasia, lobular neoplasia, or DCIS. Distinguishing such lesions from invasive carcinoma may require special studies, multiple microscopic sections, and/or consultation.

The risk of subsequent carcinoma after a diagnosis of SA appears to parallel the degree of epithelial hyperplasia and atypia. Overall, women with SA have a slightly elevated relative risk of developing subsequent carcinoma of 2.1 to 2.2.[41,103] Studies assessing risk have not separated SA with ductal hyperplasia from SA without hyperplasia. However, if lesions of SA with atypical hyperplasia are excluded, the relative risk of cancer associated with SA drops to 1.7 times normal population, the same as florid duct-type epithelial hyperplasia. Patients with SA with ADH have 5.3 times relative risk of cancer over normal. Those patients with LN complicating SA have a 7.6 relative risk of subsequent invasive cancer. These rates of relative risk are similar to the risks associated with ADH and LN2 or 3 alone.

Blunt Duct Adenosis

A recent study of Shaaban and colleagues suggests that a subtype of adenosis, blunt duct adenosis (BDA), is associated with a slightly elevated risk of subsequent invasive carcinoma (2.2), and the presence of calcifications in BDA raises risk further.[18] In Shaaban's study BDA was described as a cluster of microcysts having a variable epithelial component and pseudoangiomatous stromal hyperplasia.[18] This description does not match that of BDA as described by others.[13,15–17] However, some lesions are nearly identical to illustrations of gynecomastia-like hyperplasia[104,105] and columnar alteration of lobules.[57,106] As isolated entities, the long-term risk of subsequent breast cancer associated with gynecomastia-like hyperplasia and columnar alteration of lobules has not been studied.

Intraductal Papillomas

Papillomas are epithelial growths composed of a fibrovascular tree that is covered by an overlying component of epithelium. Papillomas are relatively uncommon tumors, but papillomas located in the subareolar region of the breast are a common cause of nipple discharge. The degree of risk of malignancy of these lesions has been debated.[107–111] Because young patients presenting with papillomas have a high incidence of concurrent breast cancer and breast cancer in first-degree relatives, Rosen and colleagues have proposed that multiple papillomas in a young woman be considered a marker of breast cancer in the patient's family.[112] More recently, Levshin and colleagues found an increased risk of carcinoma in women presenting with papillomas.[113] Krieger and colleagues also found, in a series of 2,731 women, that the presence of intraductal papillomas indicated an elevated risk of subsequent carcinoma 3.9 times that of the general population.[4]

Page and colleagues, in their study of 368 women with papillomas of a cohort of 5,966 patients, found that the risk of subsequent cancer was elevated compared with normal women.[114] Thirty-one patients developed breast cancer. Overall, papillomas elevated the risk of carcinoma in this group of patients between 2 and 3 times normal population. Of interest is that smaller papillomas without hyperplasia (< 3 mm) had a higher risk of subsequent carcinoma than larger papillomas; the smaller papillomas tended to be multiple and associated with proliferative disease outside the papilloma. However, both large and small papillomas had higher risks of cancer when florid hyperplasia (2.3 to 3.3 times) or atypical hyperplasia (4.4 to 6 times) was present.

Radial Scar

Radial scars are architectural lesions with variable components of epithelial hyperplasia.[115,116] They have been the subject of numerous radiologic studies because their mammographic appearance mimics breast cancer. Microscopically they are composed of a central nidus of fibrosis and elastosis with distorted epithelial nests. The peripheral portions of radial scars have variable amounts and types of epithelial hyperplasia and cysts. Nielsen and colleagues considered them risk lesions only if they contained atypical hyperplasia or LN.[117] Jacobs and colleagues, in their study of 1,396 women enrolled in the Nurses' Health Study, found that women with radial scars had twice the risk of carcinoma as women without radial scars and that the risk was bilateral. Among women without atypical hyperplasia, the relative risk was 3 times greater for those with radial scars than those without.[115]

Lesions with Unknown Risk

There are many breast lesions described that have not been the subject of large epidemiologic studies. Many are uncommon or rare lesions, making them the subject of small case studies. These include atypical cystic lobules,[118,119] lactational and clear cell changes,[120] fibroadenomas with stromal cellu-larity, collagenous spherulosis[121] and mucinous spherulosis,[122] microglandular adenosis,[123,124] apocrine adenosis,[17] and adenomas (apocrine adenoma, lactating adenoma, adenolipoma, ductal adenoma, pleomorphic adenoma).[125]

SECOND OPINIONS

Most pathology services have standard operating procedures that automatically obtain concurrence of more than one pathologist for a diagnosis of carcinoma or evaluation of a difficult case. Large services usually conduct formal reviews of all such diagnoses in regularly scheduled daily consensus conferences. Small services generally require simply the concurrence of a second, and perhaps more senior, pathologist. Regardless of the institution, attempts to obtain concurrence for a diagnosis of carcinoma are the norm and standard of care in the practice of pathology.

For this reason, it is not a violation of custom or a mark of disrespect for a surgeon, radiologist, or oncologist to ask that another pathologist review a case or to ask that the case be reviewed by an outside specialist. It is usually a simple matter to cut duplicate slides and forward the slides to a second location; the only exceptions would be when only minute amounts of tissue have been obtained or when only a minute amount of tissue contains the lesion in question.

Second opinions should be obtained when the pathologist is uncertain about the diagnosis, when there is internal disagreement between two or more pathologists in a group about the diagnosis, when the patient or physician requests a second opinion, or when the patient is transferred to the care of another physician or medical institution. It is usually an appropriate requirement at most institutions that such review be performed before the transferred patient undergoes any invasive procedure based on a pathologic diagnosis. Practice varies in assignment of institutional second opinions. The second opinion may be assigned by duty rotation or by specialty.

A patient who has obtained a second (or more) opinion concerning treatment of a breast lesion and finds that a subsequent pathologic review differs from the original may be uncertain as to the validity of either diagnosis. It is important for the patient's physician to know that lesions of proliferative breast disease are not uniformly diagnosed. Terminology is becoming standardized, and pathologists are beginning to reconcile differing applications of diagnostic terms. Some lesions by definition are difficult to diagnose, and pathologic agreement is difficult to obtain. ADH, a borderline lesion, is morphologically difficult to separate from both low grade carcinoma in situ and florid duct hyperplasia. By definition, ADH shares features of both. Rosai, using slides of proliferative disease and DCIS, found that experts in the field of breast pathology had different thresholds for the diagnosis of hyperplasia, florid hyperplasia, atypical hyperplasia, and carcinoma in situ.[52] Not one of his cases had uniformity of opinion. Even Schnitt and colleagues, who in their study used a training set of slides, Page's definitions of lesions, and slides with only the test lesion visible, found complete agreement by all six experts in only 58% of test lesions.[53] One test lesion in the study had the full spectrum of diagnoses rendered, from hyperplasia to DCIS.

In instances of two or more pathologic opinions, especially those in which a patient's treatment recommendations differ based on the varying diagnoses, a physician should contact the original pathologist concerning the second opinion and ask that the pathologist review the material in light of the additional diagnoses. The difference in opinion may be simply a difference in terminology or interpretation. The pathologist, on review, may agree with the second opinion and change the original report or may disagree with the second opinion and suggest referring the material to an expert for evaluation. In situations in which the original material is a small biopsy, such as a core or fine needle aspiration, and the diagnosis is atypical versus either a lesser hyperplasia or carcinoma, resolution can also frequently be obtained by excising the lesion in question to enable pathologic review of the entire lesion.

REFERENCES

1. Cole P, Elwood JM, Kaplan SD. Incidence rates and risk factors of benign breast neoplasms. Am J Epidemiol 1978;108:112–20.
2. Kelsey JL, Gammon MD. Epidemiology of breast cancer. Epidemiol Rev 1990;12:228–40.
3. La Vecchia C, Parazzini F, Franceschi S, Decarli A. Risk factors for benign breast disease and their relation with breast cancer risk. Pooled information from epidemiologic studies. Tumori 1985;71:167–78.
4. Krieger N, Hiatt RA. Risk of breast cancer after benign breast diseases. Variation by histologic type, degree of atypia, age at biopsy, and length of follow-up. Am J Epidemiol 1992;135:619–31.
5. Hutchinson WB, Thomas DB, Hamlin WB, et al. Risk of breast cancer in women with benign breast disease. J Natl Cancer Inst 1980;65:13–20.
6. Wang J, Costantino JP, Tan-Chui E, et al. Benign breast disease and the risk of subsequent invasive breast cancer: findings from the National Surgical Adjuvant Breast and Bowel Project's breast cancer prevention trial [abstract]. Breast Cancer Res Treat 2002;76:S36.
7. Fitzgibbons PL, Henson DE, Hutter RV, et al. Benign breast changes and the risk for subsequent breast cancer. Arch Pathol Lab Med 1998;122:1053–5.
8. Sarnelli R, Squartini F. Fibrocystic condition and "at risk" lesions in asymptomatic breasts: a morphologic study of postmenopausal women. Clin Exp Obstet Gynecol 1991;18:271–9.
9. Tavassoli FA, editor. General considerations. In: Pathology of the breast. 2nd ed. Stamford (CT): Appleton and Lange; 1999. p. 28–74.
10. Frantz VK, Pickeren JW, Melcher GW, Auchincloss H. Incidence of chronic cystic disease in so-called normal breasts. Cancer 1951;4:762–83.
11. Bartow SA, Pathak DR, Black WC, et al. Prevalence of benign, atypical, and malignant breast lesions in populations at different risk for breast cancer. A forensic autopsy study. Cancer 1987;60:2751–60.
12. Berkowitz GS, Kelsey JL, LiVolsi VA, et al. Exogenous hormone use and fibrocystic breast disease by histopathologic component. Int J Cancer 1984;34:443–9.
13. Cook MG, Rohan TE. The patho-epidemiology of benign proliferative epithelial disorders of the female breast. J Pathol 1985;146:1–15.
14. Bodian CA, Perzin KH, Lattes R, Hoffmann P. Reproducibility and validity of pathologic classifications of benign breast disease and implications for clinical applications. Cancer 1993;71:3908–13.
15. Tavassoli FA, editor. Benign lesions. In: Pathology of the breast. 2nd ed. Stamford (CT): Appleton and Lange; 1999, p. 115–205.
16. Page DL, Anderson TJ, editors. Adenosis. In: Diagnostic histopathology of the breast. New York: Churchill Livingstone; 1987. p. 51–61.
17. Rosen PP, Oberman HA, Rosai J, editors. Benign proliferative lesions. In: Atlas of tumor pathology: tumors of the mammary gland. Washington (DC): Armed Forces Institute of Pathology; 1993. p. 49–66.
18. Shaaban AM, Sloane JP, West CR, et al. Histopathologic types of benign breast lesions and risk of breast cancer. Am J Surg Pathol 2002;26:421–30.
19. Longacre TA, Bartow SA. A correlative morphologic study of human breast and endometrium in the menstrual cycle. Am J Surg Pathol 1986;10:382–93.

20. Morrow M. Pre-cancerous breast lesions: implications for breast cancer prevention trials. Int J Radiat Oncol Biol Phys 1992;23:1071–8.

21. London SJ, Connolly JL, Schnitt SJ, Coldits GA. A prospective study of benign breast disease and risk of breast cancer. JAMA 1992;267:941–4.

22. McDivitt RW, Stevens JA, Lee NC, et al. Histologic types of benign breast disease and the risk for breast cancer. Cancer 1992;69:1408–14.

23. Page DL, Dupont WD, Rogers LW, Rados MS. Atypical hyperplastic lesions of the female breast. A long-term follow-up study. Cancer 1985;55: 2698–708.

24. Page DL, Dupont WD. Anatomic markers of human premalignancy and risk of breast cancer. Cancer 1990;66:1326–35.

25. Page DL, Vander Zwaag R, Rogers LW, et al. Relation between component parts of fibrocystic disease complex and breast cancer. J Natl Cancer Inst 1978; 61:1055–63.

26. Ciatto S, Biggeri A, Del Turco MR, et al. Risk of breast cancer subsequent to proven gross cystic disease. Eur J Cancer 1990;26:555–7.

27. Dupont WD, Page DL. Risk factors for breast cancer in women with proliferative disease. N Engl J Med 1985;312:146–51.

28. Dupont WD, Page DL. Relative risk of breast cancer varies with time since diagnosis of atypical hyperplasias. Hum Pathol 1989;20:723–5.

29. Page DL. Cancer risk assessment in benign breast biopsies. Hum Pathol 1986;17:871–3.

30. Page DL, Dupont WD. Histopathologic risk factors for breast cancer in women with benign breast disease. Semin Surg Oncol 1988;4:213–7.

31. Page DL, Dupont WD. Indicators of increased breast cancer risk in humans. J Cell Biochem 1992;16G: 175–82.

32. Bodian CA, Lattes R, Perzin KH. The epidemiology of gross cystic disease of the breast confirmed by biopsy or by aspiration of cyst fluid. Cancer Detect Prev 1992;16:7–15.

33. Shabtai M, Saavedra-Malinger P, Shabtai EL, et al. Fibroadenoma of the breast; analysis of associated pathological entities different risk marker in different age groups for concurrent breast cancer. Isr Med Assoc J 2001;3:813–7.

34. Wellings SR, Alpers CE. Apocrine cystic metaplasia: sub gross pathology and prevalence in cancer associated versus random autopsy breasts. Hum Pathol 1987;18:381–6.

35. Page DL, Dupont WD, Jensen RA. Papillary apocrine change of the breast: associations with atypical hyperplasia and risk of breast cancer. Cancer Epidemiol Biomarkers Prev 1996;5:29–32.

36. Shah RN, Wiley EL, Vasquez LA. Fibrosis presenting as mass lesions of breast: morphologic, radiologic and immunohistochemical analysis of 50 cases. In: Proceedings of the 51st annual meeting of the Histochemical Society. J Histochem Cytochem 2000;48:1723–4.

37. Venta LA, Wiley EL, Gabriel H, Adler YT. Imaging features of focal fibrosis: assessing concordance of non-calcified breast lesions. AJR Am J Roentgenol 1999;173:309–16.

38. Vassar PS, Culling CF. Fibrosis of the breast. Arch Pathol 1959;67:128–33.

39. Rivera-Pomar JM, Vilanova JR, Burgos-Bretones JJ, Arocena G. Focal fibrous disease of breast. A common entity in young women. Virchows Arch 1980; 386:59–64.

40. Minkowitz S, Hedayati H, Hiller S, Gardner B. Fibrous mastopathy. Cancer 1973;32:913–6.

41. Bodian CA, Perzin KH, Lattes R, et al. Prognostic significance of benign proliferative breast disease. Cancer 1993;71:3896–907.

42. Sniege N, Wabgm J, Baker BA, et al. Clinical, histopathologic and biologic features of pleomorphic lobular (ductal-lobular) carcinoma in situ of the breast: a report of 24 cases. Mod Pathol 2002; 15:1044–50.

43. Black EM, Chabon AB. In situ carcinoma of the breast. Pathol Ann 1969;4:18–210.

44. Mommers ECM, Page DL, Dupont WD, et al. Prognostic value of morphometry in patients with normal breast tissue or usual ductal hyperplasia of the breast. Int J Cancer 2001;95:282–5.

45. Fitzgibbons PL, Henson DE, Hutter RV. Benign breast changes and the risk for subsequent breast cancer: an update of the 1985 consensus statement. Cancer Committee of the College of American Pathologists. Arch Pathol Lab Med 1998; 122:1053–5.

46. Jensen RA, Rice JR, Wellings SR. Preneoplastic lesions in the human breast. Science 1976;191: 295–7.

47. Rosen PP, Oberman HA, Rosai J, editors. Intraepithelial (preinvasive or in situ) carcinoma. In: Atlas of tumor pathology: tumors of the mammary gland. 3rd series, Fascicle 7. Washington (DC): Armed Forces Institute of Pathology; 1993. p. 119–55.

48. Tavassoli FA, Norris HJ. A comparison of the results of long-term follow-up for atypical intraductal hyperplasia and intraductal hyperplasia of the breast. Cancer 1990;65:518–29.

49. Tavassoli FA. Ductal intraepithelial neoplasia of the breast. Virchows Arch 2001;438:221–7.

50. Tavassoli FA. Ductal carcinoma in situ: introduction of the concept of ductal intraepithelial neoplasia. Mod Pathol 1998;11:140–54.

51. Moinfar F, Man YG, Liniger RA, et al. Use of keratin 34betaE12 as an adjunct in the diagnosis of mammary intraepithelial neoplasia-ductal type B benign and malignant intraductal proliferations. Am J Surg Pathol 1999;23:1048–58.

52. Rosai J. Borderline epithelial lesions of the breast. Am J Surg Pathol 1991;15:209–21.

53. Schnitt SJ, Connolly JL, Tavassoli FA, et al. Interobserver reproducibility in the diagnosis of ductal proliferative breast lesions using standardized criteria. Am J Surg Pathol 1992;16:1133–43.

54. Crissman JD, Visscher DW, Kubus J. Image cytophotometric DNA analysis of atypical hyperplasias and intraductal carcinomas of the breast. Arch Pathol Lab Med 1990;114:1249–53.

55. Raju U, Crissman JD, Zarbo RJ, Gottlieb C. Epitheliosis of the breast. An immunohistochemical characterization and comparison to malignant intraductal proliferations of the breast. Am J Surg Pathol 1990;14:939–47.

56. Tavassoli FA, editor. Pathology of the breast. 2nd ed. Stamford (CT): Appleton and Lange; 1999.

57. Fraser JL, Raza S, Chorny K, et al. Columnar alteration with prominent apical shouts and secretions: a spectrum of changes frequently present in breast biopsies performed for microcalcifications. Am J Surg Pathol 1998;22:1521–7.

58. Moskowitz M, Gartside P, Wirman JA, McLaughlin C. Proliferative disorders of the breast as risk factors for breast cancer in a self-selected screened population: pathologic markers. Radiology 1980; 134:289–91.

59. Marshall LM, Hunter DJ, Connolly JL, et al. Risk of breast cancer associated with atypical hyperplasia of lobular and ductal types. Cancer Epidemiol Biomarkers Prev 1997;6:297–301.

60. Connolly J, Schnitt S, London S, et al. Both atypical lobular hyperplasia (ALH) and atypical ductal hyperplasia (ADH) predict for bilateral breast cancer risk [abstract]. Lab Invest 1992;66:13.

61. Webb PM, Byrne C, Schnitt SJ, et al. Family history of breast cancer, age and benign breast disease. Int J Cancer 2002;100:375–8.

62. Khurana KK, Loosmann A, Numann PJ, Khan SA. Prophylactic mastectomy: pathologic findings in high-risk patients. Arch Pathol Lab Med 2000; 124:378–81.

63. Foote FW Jr, Stewart FW. Lobular carcinoma in situ. A rare form of mammary cancer. Am J Pathol 1941;17:491–6.

64. Haagensen CD, Lane N, Lattes R. Neoplastic proliferation of the epithelium of the mammary lobules: adenosis, lobular neoplasia and small cell carcinoma. Surg Clin North Am 1972;52:497–524.

65. Nielsen M, Thomsen JL, Primdahl S, et al. Breast cancer and atypia among young and middle-aged women: a study of 110 medicolegal autopsies. Br J Cancer 1987;56:814–9.

66. Wheeler JE, Enterline HT, Roseman JL, et al. Lobular carcinoma in situ of the breast: long term follow-up. Cancer 1974;34:554–63.

67. Rosen PP, Kosloff C, Lieberman PH, et al. Lobular carcinoma in situ of the breast. Detailed analysis of 99 patients with average follow-up of 24 years. Am J Surg Pathol 1978;2:225–51.

68. Sunshine JA, Moseley HS, Fletcher WS, Krippaehne WW. Breast carcinoma in situ. A retrospective review of 112 cases with minimum 10 year follow-up. Am J Surg 1985;150:44–51.

69. Urban JA. Biopsy of the normal breast in treating breast cancer. Surg Clin North Am 1969; 49:291–301.

70. Lishman SC, Lakhani SR. Atypical lobular hyperplasia and lobular carcinoma in situ: surgical and molecular pathology. Histopathology 1999;35: 195–200.

71. Tavassoli FA, editor. Lobular neoplasia. In: Pathology of the breast. Stamford (CT): Appleton and Lange; 1992. p. 263–91.

72. Goldstein NS, Bassi D, Watts JC, et al. E-Cadherin reactivity of 95 noninvasive ductal and lobular lesions of the breast. Am J Clin Pathol 2001;115:534–42.

73. Andersen JA, Vendelboe ML. Cytoplasmic globules in lobular carcinoma in situ. Diagnosis and prognosis. Am J of Surg Pathol 1981;5:251–5.

74. Gad A, Azzopardi JG. Lobular carcinoma of the breast: a special variant of mucin secreting carcinoma. J Clin Pathol 1975;28:711–6.

75. Battifora H. Intracytoplasmic lumina in breast carcinoma. A helpful histopathologic feature. Arch Pathol 1975;99:614–7.

76. Salhany KE, Page DL. Fine needle aspiration of mammary lobular carcinoma in situ and atypical lobular hyperplasia. Am J Clin Pathol 1989;92:22–6.

77. Anderson JA, Vendelboe ML. Cytoplasmic mucous globules in lobular carcinoma in situ. Am J Surg Pathol 1981;5:251–5.

78. Eusebi V, Pich A, Macchiorlatti E, et al. Morphofunctional differentiation in lobular carcinoma of the breast. Histopathology 1977;1:307–14.

79. Page DL, Dupont WD, Rogers LW. Ductal involvement by cells of atypical lobular hyperplasia in the breast: a long term follow-up study of cancer risk. Hum Pathol 1988;19:201–7.

80. Haagensen CD, Cann C, editors. Lobular neoplasia (lobular carcinoma in situ) In: Diseases of the breast. 3rd ed. Philadelphia: WB Saunders; 1986. p. 192–241.

81. Haagensen CD, Snyder RE, Lucas JC, et al. Clinical and pathologic correlation with mammographic findings in lobular carcinoma in situ. Cancer 1969; 23:826–39.

82. Page DL, Andersen TJ, editors. Epithelial hyperplasia and carcinoma in-situ In: Diagnostic histopathology of the breast. New York: Churchill Livingstone; 1987. p.120–92.

83. Rosen PP. Axillary lymph node mestastases in patients with occult non-invasive breast carcinoma. Cancer 1980;46:1298–306.

84. Tavassoli FA, editor. Lobular neoplasia (lobular carcinoma in situ). In: Pathology of the breast. 2nd ed. Stamford (CT): Appleton and Lange; 1999. p. 373–400.

85. Page DL, Kidd TE Jr, Dupont WD, et al. Lobular neoplasia of the breast: higher risk for subsequent invasive cancer predicted by more extensive disease. Hum Pathol 1991;22:1232–9.

86. Rosen PP. Lobular carcinoma in-situ: recent clinicopathologic studies at Memorial Hospital. Pathol Res Pract 1980;166:430–55.

87. Andersen JA. Lobular carcinoma in situ. A long-term follow-up in 52 cases. Acta Pathol Microbiol Scand 1974;82:519–33.

88. Page DL, Schuyler PA, Dupont WD, et al. Atypical lobular hyperplasia as a unilateral predictor of breast cancer risk: a retrospective cohort study. Lancet 2003;361:125–9.

89. Connolly JL, Schnitt SJ. Benign breast disease [editorial]. Cancer 1993;71:1187–9.

90. Farrow JH, Ashikari H. Breast lesions in young girls. Surg Clin North Am 1969;49:261–9.

91. Fechner RE. Fibroadenomas in patients receiving oral contraceptives: a clinical and pathologic study. Am J Clin Pathol 1970;53:857–64.

92. Yu H, Rohan TE, Cook MG, et al. Risk factors for fibroadenoma: a case-control study in Australia. Am J Epidemiol 1992;135:247–58.

93. Buzanowski-Konakry K, Harrison EG Jr, Payne WS. Lobular carcinoma arising in fibroadenoma of the breast. Cancer 1975;35:450–6.

94. Pick PW, Iossifides IA. Occurrence of breast carcinoma within a fibroadenoma. A review. Arch Pathol Lab Med 1984;108:590–4.

95. McDivitt RW, Stewart FW, Farrow JH. Breast carcinoma arising in solitary fibroadenomas. Surg Gynecol Obstet 1967;125:572–6.

96. Oberman HA, French AJ. Chronic fibrocystic disease of the breast. Surg Gynecol Obstet 1961;112: 647–52.

97. Dupont WD, Page DL, Parl FF, et al. Long-term risk of breast cancer in women with fibroadenoma. N Engl J Med 1994;331:10–5.

98. LiVolsi VA, Stadel BV, Kelsey JL, Holford TR. Fibroadenoma in oral contraceptive use. A histopathologic evaluation of epithelial atypia. Cancer 1979;44:1778–81.

99. Carter BA, Page DL, Schuyler P, et al. No elevation in long term breast carcinoma risk for women with fibroadenomas that contain atypical hyperplasia. Cancer 2001;92:30–6.

100. MacErlean DP, Nathan BE. Calcification in sclerosing adenosis simulating malignant breast calcification. Br J Radiol 1972;45:944–5.

101. Sandison AT. A study of surgically removed specimens of breast, with special reference to sclerosing adenosis. J Clin Pathol 1958;11:101–9.

102. McDivitt RW, Rubin GL, Stevens JA, et al. Benign breast disease histology and the risk of breast cancer [abstract]. Lab Invest 1988;50:62.

103. Jensen RA, Page DL, Dupont WD, Rogers LW. Invasive breast cancer risk in women with sclerosing adenosis. Cancer 1989;64:1977–83.

104. Umlas J. Gynecomastia-like lesions in the female breast. Arch Pathol Lab Med 2000;124:844–7.

105. Kang Y, Wile M, Schinella R. Gynecomastia-like changes of the female breast, a clinicopathologic study of 4 cases. Arch Pathol Lab Med 2001;125:506–9.

106. Goldstein NS, O'Maller BA. Cancerization of small ectatic duct of the breast by ductal carcinoma in situ cells with apocrine snouts: a lesion associated with tubular carcinoma. Am J Clin Pathol 1997; 107:561–6.

107. Hart D. Intracystic papillomatous tumors of the breast, benign and malignant. Arch Surg 1927;14:793–9.

108. Kraus FT, Neubecker RD. The differential diagnosis of papillary tumours of the breast. Cancer 1962; 15:444–55.

109. Buhl-Jorgensen SE, Fischermann K, Johansen H, Peterson B. Cancer risk in intraductal papilloma and papillomatosis. Surg Gynecol Obstet 1968;127:1307–12.

110. Carter D. Intraductal papillary tumors of the breast: a study of 78 cases. Cancer 1977;39:1689–92.

111. McDivitt RW, Holleb AI, Foote FWJ. Prior breast disease in patient treated for papillary carcinoma. Arch Pathol 1968;85:117–24.

112. Rosen PP, Lyngholm BL, Kinne DW, Beattie EJ. Juvenile papillomatosis of the breast and family history of breast carcinoma. Cancer 1982;49:2591–5.

113. Levshin V, Pikhut P, Yakovleva I, Lazarev I. Benign lesions and cancer of the breast. Eur J Cancer Prev 1998;7 Suppl 1:S37–40.

114. Page DL, Salhany KE, Jensen RA, Dupont WD. Subsequent breast carcinoma risk after biopsy with atypia in a breast papilloma. Cancer 1996;78:258–66.

115. Jacobs TW, Bryne C, Colditz G, et al. Radial scars in benign breast-biopsy specimens and the risk of breast cancer. N Engl J Med 1999;340:430–6.

116. Nielsen M, Jensen J, Andersen JA. An autopsy study of radial scar in the female breast. Histopathology 1985;9:287–95.

117. Nielsen M, Christensen L, Andersen J. Radial scars in women with breast cancer. Cancer 1987;59: 1019–25.

118. Oyama T, Iijima K, Takei H, et al. Atypical cystic lobule of the breast: an early stage of low-grade ductal carcinoma in-situ. Breast Cancer 2000;7:326–31.

119. Kussssama R, Fujimori M, Matsuyama I, et al. Clinicopatholgical characteristics of atypical cystic duct (ACD) of the breast: assessment of ACD as a precancerous lesion. Pathol Int 2000;50:793–800.

120. Tavassoli FA, Yeh IT. Lactational and clear cell changes of the breast in nonlactating, nonpregnant women. Am J Clin Pathol 1987;87:23–9.

121. Clement PB, Young RH, Azzopardi JG. Collagenous spherulosis of the breast. Am J Surg Pathol 1987;11:411–7.

122. Mooney EE, Kayani N, Tavassoli FA. Spherolosis of the breast. A spectrum of mucinous and collagenous lesions. Arch Pathol Lab Med 1999;123: 626–30.

123. Tavassoli FA, Norris HJ. Microglandular adenosis of the breast: a clinicopathologic study of 11 cases with ultrastructural observations. Am J Surg Pathol 1983;7:731–7.

124. Eusebi V, Foschini MP, Betts CM, et al. Microglandular adenosis, apocrine adenosis, and tubular carcinoma of the breast. An immunohistochemical comparison. Am J Surg Pathol 1993;17:99–109.

125. Hertel BF, Zaloudek C, Kempson RL. Breast adenomas. Cancer 1976;37:2891–905.

CHAPTER 5

LIFESTYLE, ENVIRONMENTAL FACTORS, AND BREAST CANCER RISK

Susan M. Gapstur, PhD, MPH

Breast cancer is the most commonly diagnosed cancer and the second most common cause of cancer mortality among women in the United States.[1] Over the last decade, breast cancer mortality rates have decreased, whereas incidence rates have remained relatively stable. However, it is estimated that in 2002, more than 200,000 women were diagnosed with and nearly 40,000 women died of breast cancer. The large number of women affected by breast cancer underscores the importance of research focusing on effective strategies for breast cancer prevention.

Findings from a large and diverse body of research have identified a number of breast cancer risk factors, though unfortunately most of these risk factors are not considered modifiable by lifestyle changes (Table 5-1).[2,3] For example, among the strongest known risk factors for breast cancer are a positive family history of breast cancer in one or more first-degree relatives, particularly if the relative was diagnosed at an early age; a personal history of atypical hyperplasia; and radiation exposure at < 40 years of age. These risk factors confer an approximately 200 to 400% increased risk.[3] Other established risk factors include a younger age at menarche, older age at menopause and first birth, nulliparity, and height, but these factors are also not readily modified. However, based on most of the research conducted to date, use of hormone replacement therapy (HRT), moderate alcohol intake, and postmenopausal overweight or obesity are recognized as established and modifiable breast cancer risk factors. In addition, physical activity, a

TABLE 5-1 Hormonal, Lifestyle, and Environmental Factors and Their Associations with Breast Cancer Risk.

Risk Factor	Modifiable	Direction of Association
Established		
Family history of breast cancer	No	+
Personal history of atypical hyperplasia	No	+
High-dose radiation exposure at age < 40 yrs	No	+
Younger age at menarche	No	+
Older age at menopause	No	+
Nulliparity	No	+
Older age at first birth	No	+
Height	No	+
Combined hormone replacement therapy	Yes	+
Moderate alcohol intake	Yes	+
Overweight/obesity (postmenopausal)	Yes	+
Overweight/obesity (premenopausal)	Yes	–
Probable		
Physical activity	Yes	–
Fruit and vegetable intake	Yes	–
Longer duration of lactation	Yes	–

+ = positive association; – = inverse association.

diet high in fruits and vegetables, and breastfeeding have been associated, albeit less consistently, with a lower risk. The majority of evidence does not support a meaningful relationship of other exposures such as oral contraceptive use, environmental pollutants, and cigarette smoking with breast cancer.

There are few data from randomized clinical trials of the effects of lifestyle modifications on breast cancer incidence and/or mortality specifically. Although the results of the Women's Health Initiative (WHI) clinical trial in postmenopausal women demonstrated a clear adverse effect of combined HRT (CHRT) on breast cancer incidence, the study of changes in dietary habits on chronic disease incidence in the WHI is ongoing.[4] This information will be particularly useful to help guide postmenopausal women who are concerned about reducing their risk of breast cancer. Regardless, several national organizations have proposed a number of recommendations for overall health promotion and disease prevention.

HORMONE REPLACEMENT THERAPY

Because of the well-established link between endogenous estrogen exposure and breast carcinogenesis, there has been long-standing interest in the role of HRT in breast cancer etiology. Indeed, results from at least 65 observational epidemiologic studies and five large reviews of the association of HRT and breast cancer have been reported.[5] Although some studies showed a higher risk associated with HRT use, other studies showed a lower risk or no differences in risk when compared to women who never used hormones. Some of the inconsistencies across studies can be attributed to small sample sizes, differences in methods of statistical analysis, which can affect the ability to detect relatively modest associations, and differences in risk according to duration and time since last use. To address these issues, the Collaborative Group on Hormonal Factors in Breast Cancer collected original data from 51 studies, including over 160,000 women with known age at menopause.[6] In that study, there was a 14% ($p < .0001$) higher risk of breast cancer associated with ever use of HRT. It is important to note that compared to women who never used HRT, there was no evidence of an association with breast cancer risk for women who

stopped using HRT 5 or more years before diagnosis, whereas the risk of breast cancer increased by 2.3% per year of use ($p = .0002$) among women who currently or recently used HRT. Inconsistencies in results across studies also could be due to variations in the type of HRT considered in analyses. In one of the largest population-based case-control studies conducted to date, the risk of breast cancer increased by 6% per 5 years of unopposed estrogen use ($p = .18$), but for combined estrogen plus progestin risk increased by 24% per 5 years of use ($p = .005$).[7] The hypothesis that the addition of progestin enhances the risk of breast cancer is supported by research in primates where combined therapy induced greater breast cell proliferation than unopposed estrogen.[8] Similarly, data from the Postmenopausal Estrogen/Progestin Intervention (PEPI) Trial [9] were used to study the effects of conjugated equine estrogen (CEE), CEE plus cyclic or continuous medroxyprogesterone acetete (MPA), and CEE plus micronized progesterone (MP) on changes in radiographic breast density—an established marker of breast cancer risk.[10] In that study, the percentage of women with increased breast density was more than 2-fold greater for those randomized to CEE plus MPA or MP (> 18%) compared to those randomized to CEE alone (8%) or placebo (2%).

The WHI clinical trial of HRT was designed to examine the overall risks and benefits of hormone use and focused specifically on the risk of breast cancer and potential benefit of coronary heart disease (CHD) primary prevention. Although the WHI study on the use of estrogen alone in women who have had a hysterectomy is still ongoing, the effects of CHRT among women with an intact uterus were recently published after stopping that arm of the trial early.[4] The results clearly showed increased relative risks (RR) of breast cancer (RR = 1.26), CHD events (RR = 1.29), stroke (RR = 1.41), and pulmonary embolism (RR = 2.13), and reduced relative risks of colorectal cancer (RR = 0.63) and hip fractures (RR = 0.66) for women randomized to CHRT, compared with the placebo group.

Based on the findings of both observational studies and clinical trials of HRT and chronic disease risk, the US Preventive Services Task Force has recommended against the routine use of estrogen plus progestin for the prevention of chronic diseases in postmenopausal women.[11] However, others have noted that for an individual woman, factors such as the known benefits of short-term treatment for menopausal symptoms (eg, vasomotor instability, urogenital atrophy, mood), and improved quality of life should also be considered when deciding whether to use CHRT.[12]

ALCOHOL

A wide and growing body of evidence indicates consistent adverse effects of alcohol intake in breast cancer etiology. A modest, positive association between alcohol consumption and risk of breast cancer has been noted in most epidemiologic studies conducted to date.[13] In 1998, Smith-Warner and colleagues published results of pooled analyses of data from seven cohort studies that included more than 322,000 women.[14] In that study, they found an independent, dose-response relationship of alcohol consumption with breast cancer risk. The RR estimates showed a 9% higher risk per 10 g of alcohol intake (approximately one drink). Among most studies, there does not appear to be any difference in the risk according to type of alcoholic beverage (ie, beer, wine, spirits) consumed, nor does there appear to be any difference in the association of alcohol and breast cancer risk for premenopausal women compared to postmenopausal women. Data from animal models also support a link between alcohol and mammary tumorigenesis.[15]

There are several plausible mechanisms underlying an association between alcohol and breast cancer risk. For example, results of observational and experimental studies indicate that alcohol is associated with increased serum and urinary estrogen concentrations and decreased serum hormone binding globulin (SHBG) levels.[16–19] In the only long-term alcohol feeding study of premenopausal women, Reichman and colleagues showed significant increases in plasma concentrations of dehydroepiandrosterone sulfate (7%), estrone (21%), and estradiol (28%) after 30 g of daily alcohol consumption for 3 months compared to basal levels.[18] A second potential mechanism involves acetaldehyde, the primary metabolite of ethanol, which is genotoxic and has been shown to inhibit deoxyribonucleic acid (DNA) repair both in vivo and in vitro.[13] The metabolism of ethanol also increases the production of reaction oxygen species, which

could contribute to breast carcinogenesis.[20,21] Of recent interest is the interaction between alcohol and some dietary micronutrients, particularly those involved in one-carbon metabolism, which plays a central role in DNA synthesis and methylation.[22] Several studies have shown that diets high in folate mitigate the higher risk of breast cancer associated with alcohol intake.[23–25]

In summary, moderate to high levels of alcohol intake (ie, ≥ 1 drink per day) is among the most consistently associated, modifiable factors associated with breast cancer risk. Thus, based on the current body of evidence, the World Cancer Research Fund and the American Institute of Cancer Research recommend that women who do not drink should not start, and those who do drink should limit their consumption to no more than 1 drink per day.[26]

OBESITY AND PHYSICAL ACTIVITY

A substantial body of evidence suggests important relationships between obesity and physical activity with breast cancer risk. In general, there appears to be a positive association between body mass index (BMI) and risk of breast cancer for postmenopausal women, whereas for premenopausal women there is an inverse association.[2,27] Using pooled data from seven prospective cohort studies, van den Brandt and colleagues found an RR of 0.54 (95% confidence interval (CI) 0.34–0.85) for premenopausal women with a BMI greater than 31 kg/m^2 compared to those with a BMI less than 21 kg/m^2, whereas for postmenopausal women, the RR for women with a BMI greater than 28 kg/m^2 was 1.26 (95% CI 1.09–1.46).[28] In addition, there is growing evidence of an independent relationship of weight gain during adulthood with higher risk of postmenopausal breast cancer risk, and weight loss appears to be associated with a lower risk.[29–32] Similarly, data from several epidemiologic studies support a positive association between central adiposity as measured by waist-to-hip ratio and waist circumference with risk of postmenopausal breast cancer.[27]

Physical activity is also one of the few modifiable lifestyle factors that might play an important role in breast cancer prevention.[33] Although results of epidemiologic studies are inconsistent, higher levels of physical activity appear to be associated with a modestly lower risk of breast cancer. In a re-view of epidemiologic studies on the relationship between physical activity and breast cancer risk, there was a 10 to 60% lower risk for women in the highest activity level compared to the lowest level among the 15 of 21 studies that showed an inverse association.[33] Subsequently, several other studies re-ported either a protective effect[34-38] or no associa-tion.[39-41] Inconsistencies across studies could be at-tributed, in part, to the well-recognized limitations of most survey methods in assessing the type (eg, recreational vs occupational), frequency, and dura-tion of physical activity, which could lead to mis-classification and attenuated associations.[42]

The biologic mechanisms underlying a protec-tive effect of physical activity and an adverse affect of obesity on breast carcinogenesis are not clearly understood, although several mechanisms have been proposed.[43,44] These include alterations in en-ergy balance, immune function, and reproductive function, including lifetime exposure to endoge-nous estrogens and other steroid hormones. An al-ternative, albeit related, mechanism links obesity and physical activity with breast carcinogenesis through their effects on insulin and insulin-like growth factor (IGF), biosynthesis, and metabo-lism.[45] Both insulin and IGF are potent breast ep-ithelial cell mitogens[46] and act synergistically with estrogen to stimulate breast cell proliferation.[47]

Despite the uncertainty in the specific mecha-nisms involved, interventions aimed at preventing and reducing obesity, and a sedentary lifestyle could have profound implications for disease pre-vention. In the United States, overweight (ie, BMI ≥ 25 kg/m^2) and obesity (BMI ≥ 30 kg/m^2) are ma-jor public health epidemics. Indeed, recent esti-mates indicate that nearly 62% of adult women are overweight, and 33% are obese.[48] In addition, more than 35% of American women do not engage in regular leisure time physical activity.[49] To reduce the risk of cancer, including breast cancer, the American Cancer Society (ACS) recommends maintaining a healthful weight throughout life and losing weight if currently overweight or obese.[50] This goal can be achieved through behavioral changes related to maintaining an appropriate en-ergy balance. Therefore, it is also recommended that all individuals should adopt a physically active lifestyle. In particular, adults should participate in at least 30 minutes of moderate activity on 5 or

more days per week, whereas children should par-ticipate in at least 60 minutes of moderate to vigor-ous activity on at least 5 days per week.

DIET

It has long been postulated that diet might play an important role in breast cancer etiology.[51] This hy-pothesis is supported, in part, by results of interna-tional comparisons showing correlations of per capita consumption of specific dietary factors (eg, fat) with breast cancer mortality or incidence[52] and migrant studies showing a higher incidence of breast cancer among descendants compared to those in the country of origin.[53] However, a num-ber of other factors, such as reproductive patterns, as well as levels of obesity and physical activity, could also account for these international variations in breast cancer rates.

Despite the cross-cultural observations, a con-sistent relationship between most dietary factors and breast cancer risk has not been established. For example, in a metaanalysis of 12 case-control stud-ies, there was a positive relationship between di-etary fat and breast cancer risk.[54] In contrast, there was no evidence of an association in pooled analy-ses of data from prospective cohort studies.[55,56] Al-though the specific source of inconsistencies across epidemiologic studies is controversial, there is some concern that any association of fat intake with breast cancer might be attributed to its relative con-tribution to total energy intake. Results of animal studies have shown both a positive association of dietary fat independent of total energy intake[57] and a strong positive association of total energy intake but no association of dietary fat with mammary tu-morigenesis.[58] Whether dietary fat intake during adolescence, which could influence onset of menar-che and growth, is associated with breast cancer risk has not been studied, although height — an indi-rect marker of energy exposure during childhood — has been consistently associated with an in-creased risk.[2,3]

In 1997, an international consensus panel on diet and cancer risk concluded that a diet rich in fruits and vegetables is "probably" associated with a reduced risk of breast cancer.[26] This conclusion is supported by studies examining the relationship of antioxidant nutrient intake, such as carotenoids, with risk. Moreover, there is also evidence from some, but not all, prospective studies that serum carotenoid concentrations may be inversely associated with breast cancer risk.[59–62] In a recent publication of two nested case-control studies, serum β-carotene, lycopene, and total carotenoid concentrations were significantly inversely associated with risk up to 15 years after the blood sample was collected in one cohort; similarly, nonsignificant inverse associations with total carotenoids and lycopene were observed for the other cohort.[59]

Diet is clearly a complex exposure, and disentangling the effects of specific foods and/or micro-/macronutrients on risk of disease is limited by methods of dietary assessment, which require accurate recall. In addition, several important issues remain unanswered regarding the effects of diet on breast cancer risk. For example, there is growing interest in the independent associations of foods with a high glycemic response (eg, refined carbohydrates) and hyperinsulinemia with risk of breast cancer.[45] Recently, positive associations between glycemic index, glycemic load, and specific high glycemic index foods and risk were reported from a large, multicenter case-control study conducted in Italy.[63] In addition, the role of specific phytochemicals, including isoflavones, indoles, and lignans, minerals such as calcium, animal proteins, and cooking methods requires further study as the evidence to date on these dietary factors is inconclusive.

A number of individual, family, community, and worksite randomized studies have demonstrated the efficacy of interventions focusing on improving dietary habits.[64] However, few studies evaluated the effect of a dietary intervention on disease prevention, and among those that have, most focused on the prevention of CHD. Although there are no published reports from well-designed clinical trials on the effects of dietary modifications for the primary or secondary prevention of breast cancer, at least three studies are ongoing.[65–67] When completed in 2005, the results of the WHI dietary-modification component will provide the strongest evidence on the role of a low fat and high fruit/vegetable diet for the primary prevention of breast cancer in postmenopausal women.[66] Unfortunately, there are no randomized trials currently underway evaluating long-term dietary changes earlier in life, or dietary and physical activity changes that affect level of obesity on the occurrence of breast cancer.

Regardless of the uncertainty of the specific role of diet in breast cancer etiology, a number of recommendations have been proposed that, if followed, could potentially reduce cancer risk.[26,50] For example, the guidelines described by the ACS include (1) eating five or more servings of a variety of vegetables and fruits each day; (2) choosing whole grains in preference to processed (refined) grains and sugars; (3) limiting consumption of red meats, especially those high in fat and those that are processed; and (4) choosing foods that help you maintain a healthful weight.[50]

OTHER EXPOSURES

As mentioned previously, considerable research has focused on the relationships of several other exposures to the risk of breast cancer. For example, it has long been recognized that exposure to moderate to high doses of ionizing radiation is an established cause of breast cancer.[2,68] Early studies of atomic bomb survivors from Nagasaki and Hiroshima, Japan, showed that this single, high-dose exposure was associated with a breast cancer risk.[69,70] In addition, although no longer a part of standard medical practice, infants who were treated with radiation for enlarged thymus[71] and females who underwent repeated fluoroscopic examinations during the treatment of tuberculosis[72] are also at high risk. Moreover, there is a very high incidence of breast cancer for females who received mantle irradiation for Hodgkin's disease.[73–75] There is consistent data showing that the risk of breast cancer increased with increasing doses of radiation. Regardless of the type of radiation exposure, the age at which breast cancer occurs among those exposed is similar to that of the general population. However, it is important to note that the risk of breast cancer associated with radiation exposure after age 40 years is lower than the risk associated with exposure before age 40 years.[72,74,76] Even atomic bomb survivors who were less than age 5 years at the time of the bombing had a 9-fold higher risk.[76] It has been proposed that the irradiation of immature breast tissue results in DNA alterations and increased susceptibility of breast tissue to the tumor-promoting effects of steroid hormones.[71] Clearly, ionizing radiation does not account for a large proportion of breast cancer in the population; however, the finding of a higher risk of breast cancer with younger age at exposure underscores the importance of research focusing on the effects of exposures during early life that could persist throughout life.

Although results of several studies support a benefit of breastfeeding with breast cancer, this relationship has been difficult to establish because of the confounding effects of other reproductive factors such as parity and age at first birth. The Collaborative Group on Hormonal Factors in Breast Cancer pooled data from 47 epidemiologic studies conducted across more than 10 countries where the average total months of breastfeeding ranged from approximately 2 (United States and France) to 66 (India).[77] The RR of breast cancer decreased by 4.3% ($p < .0001$) per 12 months of breastfeeding, and there was an additional 7% ($p < .0001$) reduction in risk for each birth. The authors conclude that in addition to the known benefit to the child, these data suggest potentially meaningful reductions in breast cancer incidence in developed countries if women breastfed longer.

The possible adverse health effects of oral contraceptives (OCs) have been of concern since they were first introduced in the 1960s. In 1986, the investigators of the Cancer and Steroid Hormone (CASH) Study, one of the earliest studies, reported no association (RR = 1.0; 95% CI 0.9–1.1) between OC use and risk of breast cancer.[78] Subsequently, in 1996, the Collaborative Group on Hormonal Factors in Breast Cancer published a pooled analysis of data from 54 epidemiologic studies in which they showed a modest, statistically significant (RR = 1.24; 95% CI 1.15–1.33) higher risk for women who reported current OC use compared with nonusers, whereas there was no association 10 years after stopping OCs.[79] Then, in 2002, Marchbanks and colleagues reported findings of the Women's Contraceptive and Reproductive Experiences (Women's CARE) study.[80] The Women's CARE study was a large population-based case-control study designed to assess the relationship of OC use and breast cancer risk among a diverse group of women who were reaching the age at which the incidence of breast cancer is highest and who could have started using OCs early in their reproductive years. Similar to the results of the CASH study, there was no association observed between OC use and breast cancer risk. In addition,

there was no difference in risk for women who currently or previously used OCs, for black or white women, for women with or without a family history of breast cancer, or according to age at initiation of use. To date, there are no data available on the long-term use of Norplant (Wyeth Pharmaceuticals, Madison NJ). Although there does not appear to be a meaningful adverse effect of OCs on breast cancer, data do indicate a possible higher risk of other events such as deep vein thrombosis, ischemic stroke, liver cancer,[81] and perhaps cervical cancer among women who test positive for the human papillomavirus.[82] In contrast, other research suggests a potential protective effect of OCs on endometrial and ovarian cancer.[83,84] Thus, it has been suggested that further research should focus on development of OCs that could reduce risk of all endocrine-related cancers without increasing the risk of cardiovascular events.[85]

Few environmental exposures are more contentious than that of the environmental pollutants such as organochlorines—a diverse class of synthetic environmental contaminants that includes the pesticide dichlorodiphenyl-trichloroethane (DDT) and the group of industrial chemicals polychlorinated biphenyls (PCBs). Although the use of DDT and PCBs was discontinued in the United States during the 1970s, the long-term health consequences of organochlorines has been of interest because these compounds are lipid soluble and accumulate in adipose tissue. Data from experimental studies showing both weak estrogenic or antiestrogenic effects support the metabolic action of organochlorines as endocrine disruptors.[86] Organochlorine exposure does not appear to induce mammary tumors in animal models, however, their contribution to human breast cancer development has been of particular concern.[87,88] Prior to 1993, few epidemiologic studies of the association of endogenous organocholorine exposure with breast cancer risk had been published, and all of these studies were limited to small sample sizes. In 1993, Wolff and colleagues published findings from a nested case-control study in which they observed a statistically significant dose-response relationship between serum levels of the major metabolite of DDT (ie, 1,1,dichloro-2,2 bis(p-chlorophenyl)ethylene, (DDE)) and breast cancer incidence, but only a marginal relationship with PCBs.[89] However, the cumulative results of over 30 subsequent reports do not support a meaningful association between endogenous organochlorine levels and breast cancer risk overall.[90,91] The lack of an association between serum DDT (or DDE) or PCB levels and breast cancer risk was most recently supported by findings from the Long Island Breast Cancer Study Project, which was specifically funded and designed to address environmental issues in breast cancer.[92] In a summary of the laboratory and epidemiologic evidence, Calle and colleagues concluded that, in general, organochlorine exposure is not believed to be causally related to breast cancer.[90] However, breast cancer advocates, as well a public health scientist, are calling for further research to determine whether certain subgroups of women in the population may be genetically susceptible to the effects of organochlorines, as well as other environmental exposures.[93]

The results from epidemiologic studies of the associations between cigarette smoking and breast cancer risk have been inconsistent, showing higher, lower, or no risk for smokers compared with non-smokers.[94,95] Moreover, the nature of this relationship remains unclear. It has been proposed that smoking could have antiestrogenic effects, although the evidence to support a protective effect of cigarette smoking is weak.[96] Alternatively, there is a wide body of evidence suggesting that in experimental models the carcinogens present in tobacco smoke induce mammary tumorigenesis and have been shown to form DNA adducts in breast epithelial cells, which could lead to genetic alterations involved in neoplastic transformations.[95] In addition, there may be certain subgroups of women that might be at an increased risk based, for example, on their genetic susceptibility to carcinogens found in tobacco smoke.[97] Regardless, for both public health and individual risk purposes, the adverse effects of cigarette smoking on the overall burden of health have long been recognized, and the recommendation to not start or to quit smoking remains appropriate.

SUMMARY AND CONCLUSION

As women continue to live longer, and the proportion and number of older adults increases, the overall risks and benefits of lifestyle factors on the chronic diseases associated with aging are of growing importance. In particular, concerns about breast cancer often compel women to evaluate their current habits and consider adopting a healthier lifestyle. Unfortunately, there are no known strategies that will prevent all breast cancers. However, as mentioned previously, the use of CHRT for chronic disease prevention is not recommended,[11] and overall lifestyle modifications such as minimizing alcohol intake, increasing physical activity, and preventing weight gain or reducing obesity are recommended for overall disease prevention.[26,50]

REFERENCES

1. Jemal A, Thomas A, Murray T, Thun M. Cancer statistics, 2002. CA Cancer J Clin 2002;52:23–47.
2. Hankinson SE, Hunter DJ. Breast cancer. In: Adami HO, Hunter DJ, Trichopoulos D, editors. Textbook of cancer epidemiology. New York: Oxford University Press; 2002. p. 301–39.
3. Kelsey JL. Breast cancer epidemiology: summary and future directions. Epidemiol Rev 1993;15:256–63.
4. Rossouw JE, Anderson GL, Prentice RL, et al. Risks and benefits of estrogen plus progestin in healthy postmenopausal women: principal results from the Women's Health Initiative randomized controlled trial. JAMA 2002;288:321–33.
5. Bush TL, Whiteman M, Flaws JA. Hormone replacement therapy and breast cancer: a qualitative review. Obstet Gynecol 2001;98:498–508.
6. Collaborative Group on Hormonal Factors in Breast Cancer. Breast cancer and hormone replacement therapy: collaborative reanalysis of data from 51 epidemiological studies of 52,705 women with breast cancer and 108,411 women without breast cancer. Lancet 1997;350:1047–59.
7. Ross RK, Paganini-Hill A, Wan PC, Pike MC. Effect of hormone replacement therapy on breast cancer risk: estrogen versus estrogen plus progestin. J Natl Cancer Inst 2000;92:328–32.
8. Cline JM, Soderqvist G, von Schoultz E, et al. Effects of hormone replacement therapy on the mammary gland of surgically postmenopausal cynomolgus macaques. Am J Obstet Gynecol 1996;174(1 Pt 1): 93–100.
9. Greendale GA, Reboussin BA, Sie A, et al. Effects of estrogen and estrogen-progestin on mammographic parenchymal density. Postmenopausal Estrogen/Progestin Interventions (PEPI) Investigators. Ann Intern Med 1999;130(4 Pt 1):262–9.
10. Boyd NF, Lockwood GA, Byng JW, et al. Mammographic densities and breast cancer risk. Cancer Epidemiol Biomarkers Prev 1998;7:1133–44.
11. U.S. Preventive Services Task Force. Hormone replacement therapy for primary prevention of chronic conditions: recommendations and rationale. Rockville (MD): The Task Force; 2002.

12. Batur P, Thacker HL, Moore HC. Discussing breast cancer and hormone replacement therapy with women. Cleve Clin J Med 2002;69:838,840,843–4.

13. Singletary KW, Gapstur SM. Alcohol and breast cancer: review of epidemiologic and experimental evidence and potential mechanisms. JAMA 2001; 286:2143–51.

14. Smith-Warner SA, Spiegelman D, Yaun SS, et al. Alcohol and breast cancer in women: a pooled analysis of cohort studies. JAMA 1998;279:535–40.

15. Singletary K. Ethanol and experimental breast cancer: a review. Alcohol Clin Exp Res 1997;21:334–9.

16. Muti P, Trevisan M, Micheli A, et al. Alcohol consumption and total estradiol in premenopausal women. Cancer Epidemiol Biomarkers Prev 1998; 7:189–93.

17. Ginsburg ES. Estrogen, alcohol and breast cancer risk. J Steroid Biochem Mol Biol 1999;69:299–306.

18. Reichman ME, Judd JT, Longcope C, et al. Effects of alcohol consumption on plasma and urinary hormone concentrations in premenopausal women. J Natl Cancer Inst 1993;85:722–7.

19. Dorgan JF, Reichman ME, Judd JT, et al. The relation of reported alcohol ingestion to plasma levels of estrogens and androgens in premenopausal women (Maryland, United States). Cancer Causes Control 1994;5:53–60.

20. Knecht KT, Bradford BU, Mason RP, Thurman RG. In vivo formation of a free radical metabolite of ethanol. Mol Pharmacol 1990;38:26 30.

21. Musarrat J, Arezina-Wilson J, Wani AA. Prognostic and aetiological relevance of 8-hydroxyguanosine in human breast carcinogenesis. Eur J Cancer 1996;32A:1209–14.

22. Herbert V. The role of vitamin B12 and folate in carcinogenesis. Adv Exp Med Biol 1986;206: 293–311.

23. Zhang S, Hunter DJ, Hankinson SE, et al. A prospective study of folate intake and the risk of breast cancer. JAMA 1999;281:1632–7.

24. Rohan TE, Jain MG, Howe GR, Miller AB. Dietary folate consumption and breast cancer risk. J Natl Cancer Inst 2000;92:266–9.

25. Sellers TA, Kushi LH, Cerhan JR, et al. Dietary folate intake, alcohol, and risk of breast cancer in a prospective study of postmenopausal women. Epidemiology 2001;12:420–8.

26. World Cancer Research Fund. Nutrition and the prevention of cancer: a global perspective. Washington (DC): American Institute for Cancer Research; 1997.

27. Friedenreich CM. Review of anthropometric factors and breast cancer risk. Eur J Cancer Prev 2001; 10:15–32.

28. van den Brandt PA, Spiegelman D, Yaun SS, et al. Pooled analysis of prospective cohort studies on height, weight, and breast cancer risk. Am J Epidemiol 2000;152:514–27.

29. Barnes-Josiah D, Potter JD, Sellers TA, Himes JH. Early body size and subsequent weight gain as predictors of breast cancer incidence (Iowa, United States). Cancer Causes Control 1995;6:112–8.

30. Huang Z, Hankinson SE, Colditz GA, et al. Dual effects of weight and weight gain on breast cancer risk. JAMA 1997;278:1407–11.

31. Trentham-Dietz A, Newcomb PA, Egan KM, et al. Weight change and risk of postmenopausal breast cancer (United States). Cancer Causes Control 2000;11:533–42.

32. Friedenreich CM, Courneya KS, Bryant HE. Case-control study of anthropometric measures and breast cancer risk. Int J Cancer 2002;99:445–52.

33. Friedenreich CM, Thune I, Brinton LA, Albanes D. Epidemiologic issues related to the association between physical activity and breast cancer. Cancer 1998;83(3 Suppl):600–10.

34. Gilliland FD, Li YF, Baumgartner K, et al. Physical activity and breast cancer risk in Hispanic and non-Hispanic white women. Am J Epidemiol 2001;154:442–50.

35. Dirx MJ, Voorrips LE, Goldbohm RA, van den Brandt PA. Baseline recreational physical activity, history of sports participation, and postmenopausal breast carcinoma risk in the Netherlands Cohort Study. Cancer 2001;92:1638–49.

36. Friedenreich CM, Bryant HE, Courneya KS. Case-control study of lifetime physical activity and breast cancer risk. Am J Epidemiol 2001;154: 336–47.

37. Moradi T, Nyren O, Zack M, et al. Breast cancer risk and lifetime leisure-time and occupational physical activity (Sweden). Cancer Causes Control 2000; 11:523–31.

38. Verloop J, Rookus MA, van der Kooy K, van Leeuwen FE. Physical activity and breast cancer risk in women aged 20–54 years. J Natl Cancer Inst 2000; 92:128–35.

39. Lee IM, Cook NR, Rexrode KM, Buring JE. Lifetime physical activity and risk of breast cancer. Br J Cancer 2001;85:962–5.

40. Luoto R, Latikka P, Pukkala E, et al. The effect of physical activity on breast cancer risk: a cohort study of 30,548 women. Eur J Epidemiol 2000; 16:973–80.

41. Rockhill B, Willett WC, Hunter DJ, et al. Physical activity and breast cancer risk in a cohort of young women. J Natl Cancer Inst 1998;90:1155–60.

42. Ainsworth BE, Sternfeld B, Slattery ML, et al. Physical activity and breast cancer: evaluation of physical activity assessment methods. Cancer 1998;83 (3 Suppl):611–20.

43. Bernstein L, Henderson BE, Hanisch R, et al. Physical exercise and reduced risk of breast cancer in young women. J Natl Cancer Inst 1994;86:1403-8.

44. Gammon MD, John EM, Britton JA. Recreational and occupational physical activities and risk of breast cancer. J Natl Cancer Inst 1998;90:100–17.

45. Kaaks R. Nutrition, hormones, and breast cancer: is insulin the missing link? Cancer Causes Control 1996;7:605–25.

46. Sachdev D, Yee D. The IGF system and breast cancer. Endocr Relat Cancer 2001;8:197–209.

47. Lai A, Sarcevic B, Prall OW, Sutherland RL. Insulin/insulin-like growth factor-I and estrogen cooperate to stimulate cyclin E-Cdk2 activation and cell cycle progression in MCF-7 breast cancer cells through differential regulation of cyclin E and p21(WAF1/Cip1). J Biol Chem 2001;276: 25823–33.

48. Flegal KM, Carroll MD, Ogden CL, Johnson CL. Prevalence and trends in obesity among US adults, 1999–2000. JAMA 2002;288:1723–7.

49. National Center for Health Statistics. Adults not engaging in leisure-time physical actvity by age and sex, United States, 2002: Figure 10 Health, United States, 2002: with chartbook on trends in the health of Americans. Hyattsville (MD): US Government Printing Office; 2002.

50. Byers T, Nestle M, McTiernan A, et al. American Cancer Society guidelines on nutrition and physical activity for cancer prevention: reducing the risk of cancer with healthy food choices and physical activity. CA Cancer J Clin 2002;52:92–119.

51. Wynder EL, Gori GB. Contribution of the environment to cancer incidence: an epidemiologic exercise. J Natl Cancer Inst 1977;58:825–32.

52. Armstrong B, Doll R. Environmental factors and cancer incidence and mortality in different countries, with special reference to dietary practices. Int J Cancer 1975;15:617–31.

53. McMichael AJ, Giles GG. Cancer in migrants to Australia: extending the descriptive epidemiological data. Cancer Res 1988;48:751–6.

54. Howe GR, Hirohata T, Hislop TG, et al. Dietary factors and risk of breast cancer: combined analysis of 12 case-control studies. J Natl Cancer Inst 1990; 82:561–9.

55. Hunter DJ, Spiegelman D, Adami HO, et al. Cohort studies of fat intake and the risk of breast cancer — a pooled analysis. N Engl J Med 1996;334: 356–61.

56. Smith-Warner SA, Spiegelman D, Adami HO, et al. Types of dietary fat and breast cancer: a pooled analysis of cohort studies. Int J Cancer 2001; 92:767–74.

57. Albanes D. Total calories, body weight, and tumor incidence in mice. Cancer Res 1987;47:1987–92.

58. Freedman LS, Schatzkin A. Sample size for studying intermediate endpoints within intervention trails or observational studies. Am J Epidemiol 1992; 136:1148–59.

59. Sato R, Helzlsouer KJ, Alberg AJ, et al. Prospective study of carotenoids, tocopherols, and retinoid concentrations and the risk of breast cancer. Cancer Epidemiol Biomarkers Prev 2002;11:451–7.

60. Toniolo P, Van Kappel AL, Akhmedkhanov A, et al. Serum carotenoids and breast cancer. Am J Epidemiol 2001;153:1142–7.

61. Comstock GW, Helzlsouer KJ, Bush TL. Prediagnostic serum levels of carotenoids and vitamin E as related to subsequent cancer in Washington County, Maryland. Am J Clin Nutr 1991;53(1 Suppl): 260S–4S.

62. Dorgan JF, Sowell A, Swanson CA, et al. Relationships of serum carotenoids, retinol, alpha-tocopherol, and selenium with breast cancer risk: results from a prospective study in Columbia, Missouri (United States). Cancer Causes Control 1998;9:89–97.

63. Augustin LS, Dal Maso L, La Vecchia C, et al. Dietary glycemic index and glycemic load, and breast cancer risk: a case-control study. Ann Oncol 2001;12: 1533–8.

64. Bowen DJ, Beresford SA. Dietary interventions to prevent disease. Annu Rev Public Health 2002;23: 255–86.

65. Pierce JP, Faerber S, Wright FA, et al. Feasibility of a randomized trial of a high-vegetable diet to prevent breast cancer recurrence. Nutr Cancer 1997; 28:282–8.

66. Design of the Women's Health Initiative clinical trial and observational study. The Women's Health Initiative Study Group. Control Clin Trials 1998;19: 61–109.

67. Cohen LA, Rose DP, Wynder EL. A rationale for dietary intervention in postmenopausal breast cancer patients: an update. Nutr Cancer 1993;19:1–10.

68. John EM, Kelsey JL. Radiation and other environmental exposures and breast cancer. Epidemiol Rev 1993;15:157–62.

69. McGregor H, Land CE, Choi K, et al. Breast cancer incidence among atomic bomb survivors, Hiroshima and Nagasaki, 1950–69. J Natl Cancer Inst 1977;59:799–811.

70. Tokunaga M, Norman JE Jr, Asano M, et al. Malignant breast tumors among atomic bomb survivors, Hiroshima and Nagasaki, 1950–74. J Natl Cancer Inst 1979;62:1347–59.

71. Hildreth NG, Shore RE, Dvoretsky PM. The risk of breast cancer after irradiation of the thymus in infancy. N Engl J Med 1989;321:1281–4.

72. Miller AB, Howe GR, Sherman GJ, et al. Mortality from breast cancer after irradiation during fluoroscopic examinations in patients being treated for tuberculosis. N Engl J Med 1989;321:1285–9.

73. Hancock SL, Tucker MA, Hoppe RT. Breast cancer after treatment of Hodgkin's disease. J Natl Cancer Inst 1993;85:25–31.

74. Aisenberg AC, Finkelstein DM, Doppke KP, et al. High risk of breast carcinoma after irradiation of young women with Hodgkin's disease. Cancer 1997;79:1203–10.

75. Bhatia S, Robison LL, Oberlin O, et al. Breast cancer and other second neoplasms after childhood Hodgkin's disease. N Engl J Med 1996;334: 745–51.

76. Tokunaga M, Land CE, Yamamoto T, et al. Incidence of female breast cancer among atomic bomb survivors, Hiroshima and Nagasaki, 1950–1980. Radiat Res 1987;112:243–72.

77. Breast cancer and breastfeeding: collaborative reanalysis of individual data from 47 epidemiological studies in 30 countries, including 50302 women with breast cancer and 96973 women without the disease. Lancet 2002;360(9328):187–95.

78. Oral-contraceptive use and the risk of breast cancer. The Cancer and Steroid Hormone Study of the Centers for Disease Control and the National Institute of Child Health and Human Development. N Engl J Med 1986;315:405–11.

79. Breast cancer and hormonal contraceptives: collaborative reanalysis of individual data on 53 297 women with breast cancer and 100 239 women without breast cancer from 54 epidemiological studies. Collaborative Group on Hormonal Factors in Breast Cancer. Lancet 1996;347(9017):1713–27.

80. Marchbanks PA, McDonald JA, Wilson HG, et al. Oral contraceptives and the risk of breast cancer. N Engl J Med 2002;346:2025–32.

81. Food and Drug Administration, Center for Drug Evaluation and Research. Guidance for industry: combined oral contraceptives-labeling for healthcare providers and patients. Draft guidance. 2000. Available at: http://www.fda.gov/cder/guidance/index/htm (accessed January 18, 2003).

82. Moreno V, Bosch FX, Munoz N, et al. Effect of oral contraceptives on risk of cervical cancer in women with human papillomavirus infection: the IARC multicentric case-control study. Lancet 2002;359 (9312):1085–92.

83. The Cancer and Steroid Hormone Study of the Centers for Disease Control and the National Institute of Child Health and Human Development. Combination oral contraceptive use and the risk of endometrial cancer. JAMA 1987;257:796–800.

84. The reduction in risk of ovarian cancer associated with oral-contraceptive use. N Engl J Med 1987; 316:650–5.

85. Davidson NE, Helzlsouer KJ. Good news about oral contraceptives. N Engl J Med 2002;346:2078–9.

86. US Environmental Protection Agency. Endocrine disruptor screening program: what are endocrine disruptors? Washington (DC): Office of Pesticide and Program and Toxic Substances; 2001.

87. World Health Organization/International Agency for Research on Cancer. DDT and associated compounds. IARC Monogr Eval Carcinog Risks Hum 1997;53:179–249.

88. World Health Organization/International Agency for Research on Cancer. Polychlorinated biphenyls. IARC Monogr Eval Carcinog Risks Hum 1998; 18:41–103.

89. Wolff MS, Toniolo PG, Lee EW, et al. Blood levels of organochlorine residues and risk of breast cancer. J Natl Cancer Inst 1993;85:648–52.

90. Calle EE, Frumkin H, Henley SJ, et al. Organochlorines and breast cancer risk. CA Cancer J Clin 2002;52:301–9.

91. Laden F, Collman G, Iwamoto K, et al. 1,1-Dichloro-2,2-bis(p-chlorophenyl)ethylene and polychlorinated biphenyls and breast cancer: combined analysis of five U.S. studies. J Natl Cancer Inst 2001;93: 768–76.

92. Gammon MD, Wolff MS, Neugut AI, et al. Environmental toxins and breast cancer on Long Island. II. Organochlorine compound levels in blood. Cancer Epidemiol Biomarkers Prev 2002;11: 686–97.

93. Twombly R. Long Island study finds no link between pollutants and breast cancer. J Natl Cancer Inst 2002; 94:1348–51.

94. Laden F, Hunter DJ. Environmental risk factors and female breast cancer. Annu Rev Public Health 1998;19:101–23.

95. Terry PD, Rohan TE. Cigarette smoking and the risk of breast cancer in women: a review of the literature. Cancer Epidemiol Biomarkers Prev 2002;11 (10 Pt 1):953–71.

96. Baron JA, La Vecchia C, Levi F. The antiestrogenic effect of cigarette smoking in women. Am J Obstet Gynecol 1990;162:502–14.

97. Ambrosone CB. Impact of genetics on the relationship between smoking and breast cancer risk. J Womens Cancer 2001;3:17–22.

BREAST CANCER RISK IN THE CONTEXT OF OVERALL HEALTH

Aarati Didwania, MD
Aparna Priyanath, MD, MPH

Clinicians who care for women at high-risk for breast cancer should be familiar with the issues surrounding their overall health. Risk assessment for breast cancer is helpful for identifying women at high risk and for providing recommendations for increased surveillance and/or chemoprevention. In the overall population, a woman's lifetime risk of developing breast cancer by age 85 is approximately 1 in 8. This means that, on average, for any group of eight women, breast cancer will develop in one of them at some time in her life, but not in the remaining seven. The woman in whom breast cancer develops has a 60% chance of surviving that cancer and of dying from another cause.[1] The risk of breast cancer for a woman in any given decade of her life never approaches 1 in 8. Breast cancer is uncommon at younger ages, so the risk in earlier decades is lower than in older ages. Older women are more likely to have breast cancer, but they are also more likely to have coexisting conditions such as cardiovascular disease. Women seeking risk assessment may be at low to slightly increased risk of breast cancer but may have significantly more risk of other conditions. Therefore, the clinical visit for breast cancer risk assessment provides an opportunity to address overall health maintenance and to put breast cancer risk in perspective to other conditions potentially more likely to lead to mortality and morbidity. Other major conditions affecting women include cardiovascular disease, with risk factors for this condition including hypertension, diabetes, and elevated cholesterol; lung cancer; colon cancer; cervical cancer; and osteoporosis.

Overall health care involves monitoring and preventing causes of major mortality and morbidity. Preventive care interventions are categorized as primary, secondary, or tertiary. Primary prevention aims to remove or reduce disease risk factors (eg, immunizations). Secondary prevention promotes early detection of a disease or its precursor state (eg, mammography or ductal lavage). Tertiary prevention limits the impact of established disease (eg, surgical removal of tumor).[2] The US Preventive Services Task Force defines several types of clinical preventive services involving primary and secondary prevention strategies for many common health conditions.[3] Healthcare providers counsel patients on healthy behaviors and advise patients about the importance of changing behaviors that have negative health consequences. Disease risk factors are those characteristics of an individual that increase his or her risk of disease; some, such as age and gender, are not modifiable, whereas others can potentially be changed. Recognizing and addressing the modifiable risk factors affecting a woman's overall health promotes general well-being. This chapter will provide information about the issues to consider for the overall health of a patient at high risk for developing breast cancer.

The major leading cause of death in women is from diseases of the heart, as shown in Table 6-1. Thus, women's health care must involve a comprehensive approach that assesses and prevents not only breast diseases but also attempts to modify risk factors leading to other causes of morbidity and mortality.

TABLE 6-1 Rank and Percent of Total Deaths for the 10 Leading Causes of Death in Women, All Races, All Ages: United States, 1999

Cause	Rank	Percent of Total Deaths
Diseases of the heart	1	30.7
Malignant neoplasm	2	21.7
Cerebrovascular diseases	3	8.5
Chronic lower respiratory diseases	4	5.1
Diabetes mellitus	5	3.1
Influenza and pneumonia	6	3.0
Accidents	7	2.8
Alzheimer's disease	8	2.6
Nephritis, nephrotic syndrome, and nephrosis	9	1.5
Septicemia	10	1.4
All other causes	11	19.7

Adapted from Anderson RN.[4]

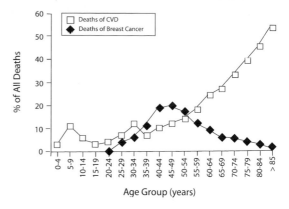

Figure 6-1 Actual risk of death from cardiovascular disease and breast cancer based on data from a cohort study of 1,000 women in the Ontario Cancer Registry.[1,6] Reproduced with permission from New England Journal of Medicine.[1] CVD = cardiovascular disease.

CARDIOVASCULAR DISEASE

Cardiovascular disease (CVD) includes three major areas: (1) coronary heart disease (CHD) manifested by myocardial infarction, angina pectoris, congestive heart failure, and coronary death; (2) cerebrovascular disease manifested by stroke and transient ischemic attack; and (3) peripheral vascular disease manifested by intermittent claudication. CHD has been recognized as the leading cause of death among middle-aged men, but it is an equally important cause of death and disability among women. As the leading cause of death in women, CHD significantly outweighs breast, lung, colon, and gynecologic cancers, lung disease, infections, diabetes mellitus, and suicide as a cause of death.[4] The American Heart Association (AHA) reported the latest statistics on heart disease and stroke. According to these data, CVD is the leading cause of death in US women, with more than 10 times as many women dying of CVD compared with breast cancer. In 1998, 503,927 women died of CVD and 41,737 women died of breast cancer.[5] Figure 6-1 demonstrates the actual risk of death from cardiovascular disease and breast cancer.[1,6]

A woman of age 50 has a 46% lifetime risk of developing CHD and a 31% risk of dying from this disease. In contrast, her risk of developing breast cancer is 10% and risk of dying from this disease is 3%.[7] For women, the mortality rate of cardiovascular disease is half that of men until the age of menopause. After the middle of the fifth decade, the rate of CHD in women increases significantly and approaches that of men by the eighth decade. Over the past two decades, the number of men dying of CVD has been steadily decreasing; however, in women, there has been no reduction in morbidity and mortality rates related to CVD. Figure 6-2 shows that the number of women dying of CVD has not been decreasing.[5,6]

Risk Factors for Cardiovascular Disease

Most of the risk factors for coronary heart disease and the strategies for preventing disease among men are also important for women. Atherosclerosis is responsible for almost all cases of coronary heart disease. The process begins with fatty streaks, progresses into plaques, and culminates in thrombotic occlusions and coronary events. A variety of factors are associated with an increased risk for atherosclerotic plaques in coronary arteries and other arterial beds.[8] Table 6-2 lists the primary cardiovascular risk factors in women according to the guidelines of the National Cholesterol Education Program (NCEP)[9] and a scientific statement from the AHA and American College of Cardiology (ACC).[10]

Elevated triglycerides, obesity, and a sedentary lifestyle, although not considered primary risk factors in the NCEP guidelines, are highly associ-

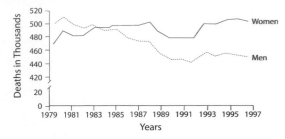

Figure 6-2 Cardiovascular disease mortality trends for women and men. Reproduced with permission from the American Journal of Cardiology.[6]

ated with coronary risk, and assessment is recommended by the AHA/ACC guidelines.[10]

These cardiovascular risk factors are higher among ethnic minority women than among white women.[11] The Third National Health and Nutrition Examination Survey of 1,762 black, 1,481 Mexican-American, and 2,023 white women found that cardiovascular risk factors were higher in black and Mexican-American women than white women of comparable socioeconomic status.[12] Modification and recognition of these risk factors will aid in the primary prevention of CHD.

Family History

Family history is a significant independent risk factor for CHD, particularly among younger individuals with a family history of premature disease. Family history was evaluated in a prospective study from the Physician's Health Study of 22,071 men followed for 13 years and the Women's Health Study

TABLE 6-2 Primary Cardiovascular Risk Factors in Women

- Personal history of coronary heart disease (CHD)
- Age over 55
- Dyslipidemia: high LDL and/or low HDL
- Family history of premature CHD (first degree relative under age 55 or a female under age 65)
- Diabetes mellitus
- Smoking
- Hypertension
- Peripheral vascular disease

Adapted from Executive Summary of the Third Report of the National Cholesterol Education Program (NCEP).[9]
LDL = low density lipoprotein.
HDL = high density lipoprotein.
CHD = coronary heart disease.

TABLE 6-3 Relative Risk of Cardiovascular Disease Based on Family History Compared with No Parental History of a Myocardial Infarction

History	Men	Women
Maternal history	1.71	1.46
Paternal history	1.40	1.15
Maternal and paternal history	1.85	2.05

Adapted from Sesso HD et al.[13]

of 39,876 women followed for 6.2 years. Table 6-3 demonstrates the relative risk of cardiovascular disease based on family history from these studies.[13]

A case-control study from Italy predicts an increase in relative risk of myocardial infarction in men from 1.0 with no affected relatives to 2.0 with one affected parent to 3.4 with one affected sibling to 4.7 with two or more affected siblings to as high as 20 with two or more relatives with myocardial infarction before age 55.[14] This risk was multiplicative with that of other risk factors such as smoking or hyperlipidemia. Patients with a family history of myocardial infarction often have other contributory risk factors, such as hypertension, diabetes mellitus, or hypercholesterolemia. Recognition and aggressive modification of these risk factors may reduce mortality/morbidity in patients with family histories of coronary disease.

Dyslipidemia

The serum total cholesterol concentration is a clear risk factor for coronary heart disease. In the Multiple Risk Factor Intervention Trial of more than 350,000 middle-aged American men, the risk of CHD progressively increased with higher values for serum total cholesterol (Table 6-4).[15]

In general, lipid abnormalities associated with increased coronary risk include elevated LDL cholesterol, low HDL cholesterol, increased total-to-HDL cholesterol ratio, hypertriglyceridemia, increased lipoprotein (a) [Lp(a)], increased non-HDL cholesterol, and increased apolipoprotein B. The lipoprotein risk factors for CHD are somewhat different in women compared with men. Low HDL, rather than high LDL cholesterol, is more predictive of coronary risk in women.[16] Lipoprotein (a) is a determinant of CHD in premenopausal women and postmenopausal women under age 66.[17] The total cholesterol concentration appears to be associated with CHD only in premenopausal

TABLE 6-4 Relation between Plasma Cholesterol Concentration and Six-Year Coronary Heart Disease Risk in 361,662 Men Screened during the MRFIT Study

Mean Serum Cholesterol (mg/dL)	Relative Risk of CHD Mortality
153.2	1.00
175.0	1.05
187.1	1.31
197.6	1.33
207.5	1.72
216.1	1.84
225.9	2.20
237.7	2.33
253.4	2.88
289.5	4.13

Adapted from Stamler J et al.[15]

women or at very high levels (> 265 mg/dL) in older women.[17] It is, therefore, recommended that every woman over age 20 should have a fasting lipid profile (total cholesterol, LDL cholesterol, high density lipoprotein cholesterol, and triglyceride) measured once every 5 years; lipoprotein (a) and apolipoprotein B and A-1 levels should be measured if the standard profile is normal in women with CHD who are less than 60 years of age.[9]

Current practice is to treat women at high risk for CVD in the same fashion as men. Metaanalysis of the clinical studies that have included women have shown that lipid-altering medications have similar effects in women and men on both the lipid profiles and the reduction in CHD.[18] Table 6-5, reproduced from the Executive Summary of the

Third Report of the NCEP, defines the LDL cholesterol goals and cut points for therapeutic lifestyle changes and drug therapy in different risk categories.[9]

The major risk factors that modify LDL goals in Table 6-5 include cigarette smoking, hypertension (blood pressure ≥ 140/90 mmHg or on antihypertensive medication), low HDL cholesterol (< 40 mg/dL), family history of premature CHD, and age (men ≥ 45 years; women ≥ 55 years).[8] HDL cholesterol ≥ 60 mg/dL counts as a negative risk factor; its presence removes one risk factor from the total count. For persons with two or more risk factors, 10-year risk assessment is carried out with Framingham scoring to identify the LDL level at which to consider drug therapy.[9]

Therapeutic lifestyle changes to lower cholesterol levels include reduced intake of saturated fats and cholesterol, increased physical activity, and weight control. The dietary changes include reduction of saturated fats to < 7% of total calories and cholesterol to < 200 mg/day. Figure 6-3 demonstrates the steps taken in therapeutic lifestyle changes.[9] The population whose short-term or long-term risk for CHD is high will require LDL-lowering drugs in addition to lifestyle changes to reach the designated goal for LDL cholesterol. Secondary intervention trials aimed at regression of CHD have shown that women may have increased regression of coronary lesions and a similar improvement in survival with intensive lipid-lowering medications.[19] In the Scandinavian Simvastatin Survival Study, women who received simvastatin had equivalent reductions to men in serum total and LDL cholesterol, coronary heart disease mortality, major coronary events, and the need for revascularization.[20]

TABLE 6-5 LDL Cholesterol Goals and Cut Points for Therapeutic Lifestyle Changes and Drug Therapy in Different Risk Categories

Risk Category	LDL Goal (mg/dL)	LDL Level at Which to Initiate Therapeutic Lifestyle Changes (mg/dL)	LDL Level at Which to Consider Drug Therapy (mg/dL)
CHD or CHD risk equivalents (10-year risk > 20%)	< 100	≥ 100	≥ 130
2+ Risk factors (10-year risk ≤ 20%)	< 130	≥ 130	10-year risk 10–20%: > 130 10-year risk < 10%: ≥ 160
0–1 Risk factors	< 160	≥ 160	≥ 190

Adapted from Executive Summary of the Third Report of the National Cholesterol Education Program (NCEP).[9]

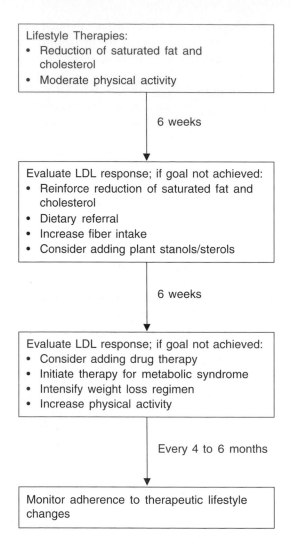

Lifestyle Therapies:
- Reduction of saturated fat and cholesterol
- Moderate physical activity

6 weeks

Evaluate LDL response; if goal not achieved:
- Reinforce reduction of saturated fat and cholesterol
- Dietary referral
- Increase fiber intake
- Consider adding plant stanols/sterols

6 weeks

Evaluate LDL response; if goal not achieved:
- Consider adding drug therapy
- Initiate therapy for metabolic syndrome
- Intensify weight loss regimen
- Increase physical activity

Every 4 to 6 months

Monitor adherence to therapeutic lifestyle changes

Figure 6-3 Model of steps in therapeutic lifestyle changes (TLC). Adapted from Executive Summary of the Third Report of the National Cholesterol Education Progam (NCEP).[9]

Hypertension

Hypertension and left ventricular hypertrophy are well-established risk factors for adverse cardiovascular outcomes, including CHD incidence, CHD mortality, stroke, congestive heart failure, and sudden death.[21,22] Systolic blood pressure is at least as powerful a coronary risk factor as diastolic blood pressure.[23] Additionally, isolated systolic hypertension is an established major hazard for CHD and stroke.[24] Postmenopausal women have a high prevalence of hypertension, and women above age 70 have a prevalence of hypertension between 70 and 80%.[25]

Compared with men, hypertension in elderly women is a stronger predictor of coronary risk and is more commonly seen in those with CHD.[26,27] In premenopausal women, the presence of hypertension is associated with up to a 10-fold increase in coronary mortality.[28] Data from the Framingham Heart Study found that recent and remote antecedent blood pressure (systolic, diastolic, and pulse pressure) predict cardiovascular risk incrementally over current blood pressure. This effect was seen in men and women, younger and older subjects.[29] In the Systolic Hypertension in the Elderly Program, women constituted 57% of the study population, and antihypertensive therapy resulted in a 25% reduction in CHD.[30]

These data suggest that effective prevention of CVD requires adequate blood pressure throughout life. Initial therapy in hypertensive women is similar to that in men. The recommendations of the Sixth Joint National Committee provide guidelines for therapy according to stratifications based on blood pressure level and presence or absence of other underlying conditions (Tables 6-6 and 6-7).[21]

Lifestyle modification involves weight reduction; reduction of sodium intake; consumption of fruits, vegetables, and low-fat dairy products; moderation of alcohol intake; and increased physical activity. Pharmacologic therapy is individually tailored based on comorbid conditions and degree of elevation. In general, major long-term trials have demonstrated the efficacy of beta-blockers and thiazide diuretics in reducing coronary artery disease and stroke. These agents should be considered as initial therapy in all patients who have not lowered their blood pressure with diet and exercise. Thiazide diuretics have a beneficial effect on calcium excretion and, therefore, may be appropriate for use in women who are at risk for osteoporosis. The recent Antihypertensive and Lipid-Lowering Treatment to Prevent Heart Attack Trial study shows that the thiazide-type diuretics are the drug of choice for first-step antihypertensive therapy. They are more effective than calcium channel blockers, angiotensin converting enzyme (ACE) inhibitors, and alpha-blockers in preventing one or more manifestations of CVD.[31] Additionally, in both men and women, an angiotensin II receptor blocker therapy is the preferred first-line agent in patients with electrocardiographic evidence of left ventricular hypertrophy.[32] The Heart Outcomes Prevention Evaluation (HOPE) trial demonstrated that ACE

TABLE 6-6 Components of Cardiovascular Risk Factors in Patients with Hypertension

Major Risk Factors	Target Organ Damage/Clinical Cardiovascular Disease
Smoking	Heart diseases:
Dyslipidemia	Left ventricular hypertrophy
Diabetes mellitus	Angina or prior myocardial infarction
Age older than 60 years	Prior coronary revascularization
Sex — men and postmenopausal women	Heart failure
Family history of cardiovascular disease:	Stroke or transient ischemic attack
Men under age 55	Nephropathy
Women under age 65	Peripheral arterial disease
	Retinopathy

Adapted from the sixth report of the Joint National Committee.[21]

inhibitors are warranted in many women with or at high risk for cardiovascular disease. In this study, patients were randomly assigned to ramipril or placebo. The primary endpoint was any cardiovascular event (ie, cardiovascular death, myocardial infarction, or stroke). In an analysis of the benefit in women, ramipril was associated with significant reductions in the primary endpoint and in cardiovascular mortality.[33]

Diabetes

Insulin resistance, hyperinsulinemia, and glucose intolerance are associated with atherosclerotic cardiovascular disease. In the Framingham Heart Study, diabetes was an independent predictor of cardiovascular disease.[34] Diabetes mellitus is a more powerful predictor of CHD risk and prognosis in women than in men.[35] This risk is in part due to diabetes being more commonly accompanied by other CVD risk factors in women.[36] Mortality rates for CHD are three to seven times higher among diabetic than nondiabetic women, as compared with rates that are two to four times higher among diabetic than nondiabetic men.[34, 37]

Although there is a dose-response relationship between the level of hyperglycemia and the incidence of coronary artery disease, studies have not clearly shown that tight control of type 2 diabetes

TABLE 6-7 Risk Stratification and Treatment of Hypertension in Adults

Blood Pressure Stage, mmHg	Risk Group A*	Risk Group B†	Risk Group C‡
High–normal 130–139/85–89	Lifestyle modification	Lifestyle modification	Drug therapy, if heart failure, diabetes or renal insufficiency; lifestyle modification
Stage 1 140–159/90–99	Lifestyle modification for up to 12 months	Lifestyle modification for up to 6 months; consider drugs as part of initial therapy in patients with multiple risk factors	Drug therapy and lifestyle modification
Stage 2 and 3	Drug therapy and lifestyle modification	Drug therapy and lifestyle modification	Drug therapy and lifestyle modification

Adapted from the sixth report of the Joint National Committee.[21]

*Risk group A: no risk factors, target organ damage, or clinical cardiovascular disease.

†Risk group B: at least one risk factor (not including diabetes), no target organ damage or clinical cardiovascular disease.

‡Risk group C: target organ damage and/or clinical cardiovascular disease and/or diabetes, with or without other risk factors.

reduces the risk of cardiovascular disease. However, secondary prevention trials have found that aggressive control of hypertension and hyperlipidemia does reduce the risk of reinfarction in women with diabetes.[38]

The elevation in cardiovascular risk is not limited to patients with diabetes, because there appears to be a graded rise in cardiovascular risk with increasing degrees of glucose intolerance not yet meeting the definition of overt diabetes. In a metaanalysis of 20 studies, there was a curvilinear increase in the risk for a cardiovascular event with increasing glucose intolerance.[39] Similarly, among survivors in the Framingham Heart Study, the hemoglobin A_{1c} concentration was significantly related to cardiovascular disease in women but not men. For each 1% increase in hemoglobin A_{1c}, the relative odds of CVD increased 1.39 (95% confidence interval [CI] 1.06–1.83).[36] In some patients, central obesity, hypertension, impaired glucose metabolism, and hyperlipidemia are clustered in the insulin resistance syndrome, which in women also overlaps with polycystic ovary syndrome. Both syndromes are associated with increased cardiovascular risk.

The clinical implication of these findings is that diabetic patients require prompt and early attention to risk management and early screening following American Diabetes Association (ADA) guidelines.

The ADA recommends that people be screened by measurement of fasting plasma glucose every 3 years beginning at age 45 years; screening should be considered at an earlier age or be carried out more frequently if diabetes risk factors are present.[41] Diabetes risk factors include

- Obesity (body mass index $\geq$ 27 kg/m^2)
- Family history of diabetes mellitus in a first-degree relative
- Habitual physical inactivity
- Belonging to a high risk ethnic or racial group (eg, black, Hispanic, Native American)
- History of delivering a baby weighing > 4.1 kg (9 lb) or of gestational diabetes mellitus
- Hypertension (blood pressure $\geq$ 140/90 mmHg)
- Dyslipidemia, defined as a serum high density lipoprotein cholesterol concentration < 35 mg/dL (0.9 mmol/L) and/or a serum triglyceride concentration > 250 mg/dL (2.8 mmol/L)
- Previously identified impaired glucose tolerance or impaired fasting glucose
- Polycystic ovary syndrome

The ADA provides dietary recommendations for type 2 diabetes with the emphasis on achieving glucose, lipid, and blood pressure goals. Mild caloric restriction is recommended to achieve mild to moderate weight loss. Food choices include 10 to 20% of calories from protein, < 10% of calories each from saturated and polyunsaturated fat, and the remainder of calories from monounsaturated fat and carbohydrates. Sugar is not specifically prohibited. If dietary and other lifestyle changes fail to achieve normal blood sugar, then control via oral hypoglycemic agents or insulin may be appropriate. Patients with diabetes must also be monitored for development of retinopathy, nephropathy, and neuropathy.[41] Tight glycemic control may prevent progression to retinopathy, nephropathy, neuropathy, and cardiac complications.

Obesity

Approximately 97 million adults in the United States are overweight or obese, a condition that has achieved epidemic proportions and has been cited as a key contributor to an estimated 300,000 deaths annually.[42] Obesity (defined as BMI $\geq$ 30 kg/m^2) has been recently reclassified as a major modifiable risk factor for CHD.[43] The epidemic proportions of overweight (BMI > 25.0 to 29.9 kg/m^2) and obesity in the United States reflect both dietary changes, with increased fat content and total caloric intake, and decreased energy expenditure due to a more sedentary lifestyle.

The association of obesity with diabetes, hypertension, and hyperlipidemia has been well documented.[44] In the Nurses' Health Study, body weight was directly related to mortality, with a relative risk of death from CHD of 4.1, and from all causes of 2.2 in women with a body mass index $\geq$ 32 compared to lean women with a BMI < 20.[45] Weight loss can cause significant improvement in the cardiovascular risk factors associated with overweight and obesity.[46] However, in the Behavioral Risk Factor Surveillance System survey, only 22% of men and 19% of women reported using the recommended combination of eating fewer calories and engaging in at least 150 minutes of leisure-time physical activity per week.[47] A multifaceted approach, which includes dietary modification, increased physical activity, behavioral therapy, and possible pharmacotherapy, is optimal for the management of obesity.

Hormonal Status

CHD is unusual in premenopausal women, particularly in the absence of other risk factors. The NCEP recognizes postmenopausal state as a risk factor for CHD, assigning it the same weight as male gender.[48] Surgical menopause, with or without hormone replacement therapy (HRT), carries an added risk of CHD, in excess of that noted for natural menopause.[49] Hormonal status is also an independent predictor of angiographic disease, improving both pre- and postexercise test estimates for the likelihood of CHD.[50] Despite these observations for a potential cardioprotective effect of estrogen, a protective effect of HRT for primary prevention was not confirmed in the Women's Health Initiative (WHI) nor for the secondary prevention in the Heart and Estrogen/progestin Replacement Study (HERS) trials. Estrogen-progestin replacement had no cardioprotective effect and may have produced harm.[51-53]

Tobacco

Cigarette smoking is an important and reversible risk factor for CHD. The incidence of myocardial infarction increases 6-fold in women and 3-fold in men who smoke at least 20 cigarettes per day compared with subjects who have never smoked. The risk increases with increasing tobacco consumption in both men and women and is higher in inhalers compared to noninhalers.[55] Smoking has been associated with one-half of all coronary events in women.[56] In contrast, the risk of recurrent infarction in a study of smokers who had a myocardial infarction fell by 50% within 1 year of smoking cessation and normalized to that of nonsmokers within 2 years.[57] The relative risk in women who had not smoked for 3 or more years was indistinguishable from that in women who had never smoked.[58] Encouraging smoking cessation will improve overall health and decrease cardiovascular events in all patient groups.

Additional Factors

Exercise. Exercise of even moderate degree has a protective effect against coronary heart disease and all-cause mortality.[58] In a retrospective study, men who engaged in moderately vigorous activity had a 23% lower risk of death than those who were less active. In addition to the amount of exercise, the degree of cardiovascular fitness, as determined by duration of exercise and maximal oxygen uptake on a treadmill, is also associated with a reduction in coronary heart disease risk and overall cardiovascular mortality.[59] The Nurses' Health Study of 72,488 women illustrated a graded benefit from exercise based upon energy expenditure group.[60] The Women's Health Study found that even light to moderate activity was associated with a lower risk of CHD.[61]

Diet. Diet also appears to play an important role in CHD risk factors. A diet rich in calories, saturated fat, and cholesterol contributes to other risk factors that predispose to CHD. The Nurses' Health Study evaluated 80,082 women who were free of CVD and hypercholesterolemia and noted that the risk of CHD increased by 17% for each 5% increase in energy intake from saturated fat and by 93% for each 2% increment in energy intake from trans-fatty acid. Additionally, the risk of CHD was reduced by 19% for each 5% increment of energy from monounsaturated fat and by 38% for each 5% increment in polyunsaturated fat. Women with a higher intake of fruits, vegetables, legumes, fish, poultry, and whole grains and lower intake of red and processed meats, sweets, fried foods, and refined grains had a significantly lower risk of CHD compared to those with the opposite dietary intake.[62,63] It was estimated that the risk of CHD would be reduced by 42% if 5% of energy from saturated fat were replaced with energy from unsaturated fat and by 53% if 2% of energy from trans fat was replaced by energy from unhydrogenated, unsaturated fat.

Alcohol. Alcohol intake above two drinks per day is associated with an increase in the incidence of hypertension. In comparison, mild to moderate alcohol intake may have a cardioprotective effect in men. In women, however, this issue is complicated by a potential increase in the risk of breast cancer associated with alcohol intake. A prospective study was conducted among 85,709 middle-aged women without a history of CVD.[64] Findings are described in Table 6-8.

Light to moderate drinking was associated with a decreased risk of death from cardiovascular disease. The benefit associated with light to moderate drinking was most apparent among women with risk factors for CHD and those 50 years of age or older. In a Nurses' Health Study report, the benefit of moderate drinking was most pronounced in women who also had a high intake of folate.[65]

Homocysteine. Elevated serum concentrations of homocysteine have been associated with an increased risk for CHD. One cause of hyperhomocystinemia is low intake of folate and vitamin B_6, which are cofactors for homocysteine metabolism. The Nurses' Health Study found a graded inverse association between higher intakes of folate and vitamin B_6 and CHD.[65] The lowest risk was seen in women with an intake of folate above 400 μg/day and an intake of vitamin B_6 above 3 mg/day.

Identification of Women with Coronary Heart Disease

The diagnosis of CHD presents a greater challenge in women compared with men. Gender differences in the clinical presentation of ischemic heart disease and diminished accuracy of diagnostic tools contribute to this difficulty.

Historically, chest pain has not been perceived to be of great prognostic value in women. The Framingham study indicated that women developed chest pain more often than men but it rarely progressed to infarction.[66] In the Coronary Artery Surgery Study, half of all women undergoing arteriography for suspected CHD did not have significant obstruction.[67] Probable angina had a 36% probability of angiographically defined disease, and classic angina had a 71% probability of disease.[68] Despite these limitations, the symptom of chest pain remains the most common initial manifestation of CHD in women. Chest pain and possible atypical symptoms of angina should be pursued in women, given the appropriate clinical context and based on the underlying probability of disease. The decision to perform further diagnostic testing should take into consideration stratification into low, intermediate, and high likelihood of disease based on the existence of minor and major determinants of CHD.[69]

TABLE 6-8 Relative Risk of Death in Drinkers Compared with Nondrinkers over a 12-Year Follow-up Period

Number of Drinks/Week	Relative Risk of Death
1–3	0.83
3–18	0.88
> 18	1.19

Adapted from Rosenberg L et al.[57]

Choosing and interpreting noninvasive imaging studies to characterize cardiovascular diseases poses a unique challenge in women. The lower prevalence of CHD compared to men, potential sex-based difference in the pathophysiology of coronary disease, altered referral patterns for women versus men, and features intrinsic to the testing procedure itself seem to influence gender difference in the presumed accuracy of various diagnostic tests.[70,71]

Therefore, the choice of procedures used to evaluate chest pain syndromes in women should involve gender. Electrocardiographic (ECG) stress testing in women has a lower sensitivity and specificity compared to men. This is thought to arise from both gender differences in the prevalence and extent of disease and because women are less likely to achieve an adequate heart rate response and more likely to have repolarization abnormalities.[72] Additionally, the specificity of ECG exercise testing in women can be reduced by use of HRT, which may induce a false-positive ST-segment depression.[73]

The sensitivity and specificity of pharmacologic or exercise treadmill testing is enhanced by adding imaging techniques. Myocardial perfusion imaging with thallium-201 has improved sensitivity over conventional treadmill testing. However, in women, breast tissue attenuation of radioactivity may lead to a false-positive test result.[74] Exercise echocardiography is currently the most valuable diagnostic tool in women. It is more specific than exercise electrocardiography and is considered a cost-effective approach to diagnosis of CHD in women.[75]

Prevention

In addition to screening and optimizing therapy for the risk factors of cardiovascular disease, attempts at reducing the morbidity and mortality associated with CVD involve pharmacologic prevention strategies. Identifying women at high risk for developing CVD via history and imaging studies will allow clinicians to optimize primary and secondary preventive measures.[76]

The risks and benefits of aspirin therapy for prevention of myocardial infarction in men are well known. The data suggest a 32% reduction in nonfatal myocardial infarction and 13% reduction in clinically important vascular events.[77] The Women's Health Study will provide the data necessary to assess the balance of benefits and risks of aspirin in primary prevention specifically for women.[78] For secondary prevention, a metaanalysis of randomized trials of aspirin demonstrated that among men and women with prior vascular disease, aspirin treatment reduced the risk of subsequent cardiovascular events by approximately 25%.[79] Low-dose aspirin increases risk for gastrointestinal bleeding and hemorrhagic stroke. Therefore, the benefits and risks of aspirin therapy, in light of a woman's comorbid conditions, must be weighed prior to initiating therapy.

Other pharmacologic management involves treatment with β-blockers. Beta blocker therapy is associated with a 21% reduction in mortality, a 30% decrease in sudden death, and a 25% reduction in reinfarction rate.[80] The Survival and Ventricular Enlargement study demonstrated that long-term therapy with an ACE inhibitor decreased mortality and morbidity among survivors of myocardial infarction with left ventricular dysfunction.[81] Additionally, the HOPE trial has demonstrated the benefit of ACE inhibitor therapy in high-risk patients with cardiovascular disease without a history of an acute event.[82] Antiarrhythmic drugs and calcium channel blockers have not demonstrated a reduction in mortality in randomized trials and are, therefore, not recommended as standard therapy during or after an acute myocardial infarction.[83]

As described earlier, epidemiologic data indicate that moderate alcohol intake has a protective effect on CHD. In a prospective study of 490,000 men and women in the United States, the rates of death from all cardiovascular diseases were 30 to 40% lower among men (relative risk [RR] 0.7; 95% CI 0.7– 0.8) and women (RR = 0.6; 95% CI 0.6–0.7) reporting at least one drink daily than among nondrinkers.[84]

A presumed protective effect of HRT for primary prevention was not confirmed in the HERS trials of secondary prevention. Estrogen-progestin replacement had no cardioprotective effect and may have produced harm.[51–53] Therefore, use of HRT for primary or secondary prevention of CVD is not recommended.

In women at high risk for cardiovascular disease, lifestyle modifications and therapeutic interventions addressing risk factors for primary prevention and secondary prevention measures are of utmost importance. Cardiovascular disease is the leading cause for mortality among women. Assessing women for other health conditions such as breast cancer is important and is made even more valuable when addressed in the context of a woman's overall health.

CANCER

Although breast cancer remains the foremost concern for women at high risk for breast cancer, other cancers surpass it in mortality (Figure 6-4).[85]

Lung Cancer

Lung cancer is the leading cause of cancer related deaths among men and women in the United States.[85] The American Cancer Society (ACS) estimates that it contributed 154,900 deaths in 2002, exceeding the combined mortality of breast, prostate, and colon cancers of 127,000.[85,86] Although this disease is by far the deadliest of all cancers, several studies have not demonstrated a benefit in mortality reduction with screening with periodic chest x-rays.[87] Smoking remains the biggest risk factor for lung cancer; thus smoking cessation remains the mainstay in prevention of lung cancer.

Colon Cancer

Colorectal cancer accounts for 148,000 cases and 57,000 deaths annually.[86] The incidence of colon cancer rises after the age of 40. Age is the biggest risk factor for sporadic colorectal cancers; however, most colon cancers arise from adenomatous polyps which progress in size and become dysplastic. Risk factors for colorectal cancer include family history in a first-degree relative, personal history of colorectal cancer or adenomatous polyps, or personal history of inflammatory bowel disease such as ulcerative colitis or Crohn's disease. Inherited syndromes include hereditary nonpolyposis colon cancer, familial adenomatous polyposis, Gardner's syndrome, and Turcot's syndrome. Some studies suggest a small association between *BRCA1* gene expression and colon cancers, with estimated lifetime risks of approximately 6%.[88] This association has not been confirmed in other studies.

In patients with adenomatous polyps, the progression to cancer may take 10 years; however, the natural history is not exactly known as most polyps are removed when found.[89] Two-thirds of polyps are adenomatous, and the remaining third are hyperplastic and are not thought to progress to

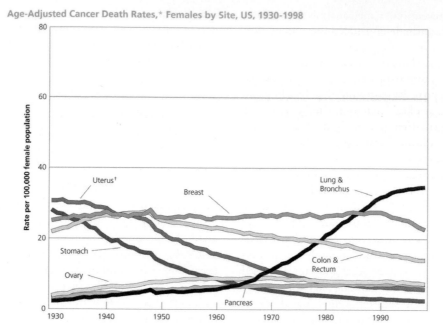

Figure 6-4 Age-adjusted cancer death rates in women, 1930–1998, US. †Uterus cancer death rates are for uterine cervix and uterine corpus combined.
Adapted from American Cancer Society.[85]

cancer. In families with a history of adenomatous polyps or colorectal cancer, age of onset, occurrence in a first-degree relative, and multiple relatives or multiple polyps/cancers in an individual prompt screening at an earlier age, as early as age 40. Once cancer is diagnosed, close surveillance for the detection and removal of new polyps can reduce mortality by 90%.[90]

Screening for colon cancer includes fecal occult blood testing (FOBT), sigmoidoscopy, colonoscopy, double contrast barium enema (DCBE), or a combination of these procedures. FOBT is the most frequently used test in average-risk individuals and utilizes guaiac-based tests to evaluate stool samples for occult blood. Randomized trials have shown a mortality reduction of 21% after 18 years of follow-up in patients who were screened biennially.[90] Incidence of colorectal cancer was reduced with annual or biennial screening after 18 years of follow-up.[91] A single stool specimen obtained on digital rectal examination will not suffice; rather, three specimens obtained on three consecutive stools are preferred. Recommendations for specific diets, for example avoidance of red meat, horseradish, turnips, vitamin C, and medications that may irri-

tate the gastric mucosa, such as aspirin and nonsteroidal antiinflammatory medications, will reduce the number of false-positive and false-negative results obtained on FOBT.

Sigmoidoscopy reaches the splenic flexure and can easily be performed in the office setting with minimal preparation by the patient. If adenomatous polyps are found on sigmoidoscopy, full colonoscopy should be advised due to increased risk of colon cancer in the proximal colon.[92,93] Polyps found on sigmoidoscopy that are greater than 1 cm in size should be excised during colonoscopy.

DCBE is a safe procedure that offers examination of the entire colon and rectum. Prior to colonoscopy, DCBE was in much greater use, however it has recently fallen out of favor. A recent study by investigators in the National Polyp Study Work Group found that it detected only 46% of adenomas greater than 1 cm and only 39% of all polyps when compared with colonoscopy.[94]

Colonoscopy is the preferred screening test by the American College of Gastroenterology.[95] The disadvantages of this procedure include expense and the need for adequate bowel preparation with a cathartic. The risk of perforation or major bleeding is about 1 per 1,000. Two studies performed in asymptomatic individuals demonstrated that a substantial number of patients were found to have advanced polyps or carcinoma located in the proximal colon. In the study by Imperiale and colleagues, 50 patients out of 2,000 screened had advanced proximal neoplasms; Lieberman and colleagues found similar results.[92,93] These studies did not examine the effect of screening with colonoscopy on long-term mortality.

The combination of yearly FOBT and sigmoidoscopy performed every 5 years has been shown to be the most cost-effective strategy when compared with annual FOBT, sigmoidoscopy every 5 years, DCBE every 5 to 10 years, or colonoscopy every 10 years.[96] The physician should counsel patients on the advantages and disadvantages of all of the options and assist patients in determining the optimal screening procedure, taking into consideration risk factors and patient preference.

Cervical Cancer

Cervical cancer accounts for 13,000 cases and 4,100 deaths annually.[85] Cervical cancer is a preventable disease due to a long preinvasive stage. Screening programs have dramatically reduced the incidence rates from 45 to 8 per 1,000 new cases per year.[86] Cervical cancer peaks at two points, between the ages of 35 to 39 and again at age 60 to 64.[86] Risk factors for cervical cancer are presented in Table 6-9.

Many groups, including the American College of Obstetricians and Gynecologists, the US Preventive Services Task Force (USPTF), the ACS, and others advocate annual PAP testing in sexually active women and beginning at age 18 for others.[85,97,98] Women with a subtotal hysterectomy, with an intact cervix, should be screened as mentioned above. Women with a total hysterectomy and a history of genital tract carcinoma or cervical dysplasia should continue yearly screening to examine vaginal epithelium. In women with hysterectomies for benign conditions, cytologic screening is not recommended by the USPTF; however, other groups such as the ACS recommend screening every 3 years unless the patient has risk factors. Frequency of PAP testing can be reduced in low-risk individuals and those who have had several normal PAP smears.

TABLE 6-9 Risk Factors for Cervical Cancer

Early age of first intercourse (< age 17)

Low socioeconomic status

Multiple sexual partners (greater than 2)

Tobacco use

History of sexually transmitted disease

History of lower genital tract neoplasia

Human papilloma virus infection (HPV)

Contraceptive hormones

HPV serotype 16 or 18

Radiation exposure

Immunosuppression (HIV infection, organ transplant, chronic steroid use)

Greater than 3 years since previous PAP smear

In 2001, the revised recommendations by the Bethesda System for standardization and classification of PAP smears were released (Table 6-10).[100] In women with abnormal results from PAP smears, such as atypical squamous cells of undetermined significance, referral to colposcopy can be done immediately for women who are noncompliant or who have risk factors for cervical cancer.[100] In otherwise lower risk populations, PAP smears can be repeated every 4 to 6 months until three consecutive tests are normal. If another smear during this period is abnormal, referral for colposcopy should be done. Alternatively, testing for human papillomavirus (HPV) can be performed, and, if positive, referral for colposcopy can be done at that time. For low-grade squamous intraepithelial lesion, high-grade squamous intraepithelial lesion, and atypical glandular cells, immediate referral for colposcopy and biopsy is recommended. The presence of glandular cells also warrants endometrial sampling to rule out endometrial neoplasia.[100]

In women who have human immunodeficiency virus (HIV), PAP smears should be obtained twice in the first year of diagnosis and, if normal, annually thereafter.[101,102] Screening for other sexually transmitted diseases such as HPV, gonorrhea, chlamydia, and herpes virus should be considered in individuals with HIV as often infections may coexist. A recent randomized controlled trial examined the use of an HPV-16 vaccine among young women infected with HPV-16, known to be associated with anogenital cancer. A significant reduction

TABLE 6-10 Bethesda Classification of Cervical Cytology

Specimen Adequacy
Satisfactory for evaluation (note presence/absence of endocervical zone)
Unsatisfactory for evaluation (specify reason)
Specimen processed and examined, but unsatisfactory for evaluation of epithelial abnormality because of (specify reason)
Specimen rejected/not processed (specify reason)

General Categorization (Optional)
Negative for intraepithelial lesion or malignancy
Epithelial cell abnormality

Interpretation/Result

Negative for Intraepithelial Lesion or Malignancy
Organisms (if present):
Trichomonas vaginalis, Candida sp., shift in flora suggestive of bacterial vaginosis, bacteria morphologically consistent with *Actinomyces* sp., cellular changes consistent with herpes simplex virus
Reactive cellular changes associated with inflammation (includes typical repair), radiation, intrauterine contraceptive device, atrophy

Epithelial Cell Abnormalities
Squamous cells
Atypical squamous cells (ASC)
of undetermined significance (ASC-US)
cannot exclude high-grade squamous intraepithelial lesion (ASC-H)
Low-grade squamous intraepithelial lesion (LSIL)
changes consistent with human papillomavirus/mild dysplasia/cervical intraepithelial neoplasia (CIN) 1
High-grade squamous intraepithelial lesion (HSIL)
encompassing: moderate and severe dysplasia, carcinoma in situ; CIN 2 and CIN 3
Squamous cell carcinoma
Glandular cells
Atypical glandular cells (AGC) (specify endocervical, endometrial, or not otherwise specified)
Atypical glandular cells, favor neoplastic (specify endocervical or not otherwise specified)
Endocervical adenocarcinoma in situ (AIS)
Adenocarcinoma
Other

Adapted from Solomon D et al.[99]

in the incidence of HPV-16 infection and HPV-16-related cervical intraepithelial neoplasia was found after a median of 17.4 months.[103] This vaccine is available only in clinical trials at present, but offers a promising intervention for the prevention of cervical neoplasia in the future.

MENOPAUSE

In women at high risk for breast cancer, the use of HRT for treatment of menopausal symptoms must receive careful consideration. It is well known that estrogen contributes to an increased risk of breast cancer development in animal models, observational studies, and randomized controlled trials. The WHI study was halted early due to the increased risk of breast cancer found among women who took both estrogen and progesterone.[53] For the menopausal woman, there are several alternatives that can be offered to the patient who is averse to participating in HRT. In this section, we will discuss issues related to atrophic vaginitis, urinary incontinence, and sexual health. Management of hot flashes will be discussed separately in Chapter 15.

An estimated 10 to 40% of postmenopausal women experience symptoms of atrophic vaginitis.[104] The vaginal epithelium undergoes changes in response to the reduced level of circulating estrogen throughout a woman's life. After menopause, the circulating estradiol levels reduce dramatically leading to changes including proliferation of connective tissue, fragmentation of elastin, and hyalinization of collagen.[105] These changes can also affect the urinary tract epithelium, as this is also estrogen-dependent tissue. Patients' complaints include vaginal dryness, dyspareunia, burning, and itching. Patients may also complain of increased frequency of urination, urethral discomfort, dysuria, and urinary incontinence. Sexual dysfunction may also result.

On physical examination, atrophic epithelium appears pale and smooth. Friability may be present which may not become obvious until the speculum has been introduced. A reduction in elasticity of the external vulvar area, dryness, and thinning of pubic hair may also be noted. Reduction in the depth of the vaginal cavity may be observed causing discomfort with the pelvic exam.[105] In some women, stenosis of the cervical introitus may be observed, preventing advancement of the cytobrush for Papanicolaou's staining.

HRT is the treatment of choice for atrophic vaginitis. After the results from the WHI were published in July 2002, clinicians and patients were faced with the dilemma of prescribing long-term estrogen replacement.[51] For women who would like to consider alternatives to HRT, several options are available. First, moisturizers such as Replens® (Lil Drug Store Products, Cedar Rapids, IA) or lubricants such as KY Jelly® (Johnson & Johnson, United States) can be offered for symptoms of dyspareunia or vaginal dryness. In women who do not find enough relief with nonestrogen compounds,

local vaginal estrogen therapy with estrogen cream, estradiol tablets (Vagifem®, Pharmacia & Upjohn Company, Kalamazoo, MI), and slow-release vaginal rings (Estring®, Pharmacia & Upjohn Company, Kalamazoo, MI) have been shown to be effective in the treatment of vulvovaginal symptoms. Estring provides consistent local effects of estrogen with lower systemic absorption than estrogen creams.[106] In a Swedish study, treatment with Estring did not significantly increase endometrial thickness or uterine diameter compared to no treatment after 6 months of therapy.[107] Estring involves the insertion of a silastic ring that delivers 6 to 9 μg of estradiol to the vagina. The ring can be changed by the physician or patient once every 3 months. Vagifem, containing 25 μg of estradiol, can be inserted twice weekly with minimal endometrial effects.[108] Vaginal estrogen creams are also an alternative; however, prescription of a progestin should be considered with long-term use exceeding a few months to avoid endometrial hyperplasia. A standard dose of 1 gram of vaginal Estrace cream contains approximately 100 μg of estradiol.

Urinary Incontinence

Urinary incontinence is a troublesome and embarrassing disorder which many postmenopausal women experience. Urinary incontinence is classified into several different categories (Table 6-11). Because there are multiple causes and contributing factors, a careful history and physical examination is essential. Physicians should inquire about frequency, timing, severity of episodes, precipitating factors, association with urge to urinate, and duration of symptoms. Voiding diaries, which include information about timing and urine volume, the presence of leakage, and quantitation of fluid intake and caffeine products, are very helpful. Use of medications such as diuretics or alpha-adrenergics, previous urogynecologic surgeries, and parity should also be elicited.[109] Physical examination should be performed by an individual trained in urogynecology and should include examination for anal sphincter tone, the presence of cystocele/rectocele, the presence of defects in support structures of the vaginal wall, pelvic masses, an assessment of the strength of the pelvic floor muscles, and neurologic dysfunction. Testing by the appropriately trained individual should include urinalysis, postvoid residual urine measurement, cotton swab test to assess

TABLE 6-11 Categories of Urinary Incontinence

	Presenting Symptoms	*Mechanism*	*Treatment*
Urge Incontinence	Abrupt urgency with leakage	Detrusor overactivity	Frequent voiding, behavioral biofeedback, oxybutynin, estrogen
Stress Incontinence	Leakage-associated coughing, laughing	Poor pelvic muscle support, failure of urethral closure, or urethral instability	Kegel exercises, pessary, estrogen, alpha-adrenergic agonists, surgery
Overflow Incontinence	Continuous urine leakage	Detrusor underactivity, outflow obstruction, or neurogenic	Intermittent catheterization, surgery

urethral hypermobility, and urodynamic studies to further differentiate the etiology of the urinary incontinence.[109] Treatment of incontinence will be based on identification of the etiology but can include strengthening of pelvic floor muscles with Kegel exercises, pessaries, estrogen therapy (local or systemic), oxybutynin, or surgery.

Estrogen deficiency has also been shown to contribute to frequent urinary tract infections (UTIs). Estrogen deprivation is postulated to increase the frequency of UTIs by increasing vaginal pH resulting from vaginal atrophy and decreased glycogen.[110] Subsequently, a decrease in lactobacilli and an increase in bacterial colonization by pathogenic flora predispose women to UTIs.[110] Estrogen deficiency will also affect the vaginal and clitoral tissues, causing a reduction in vaginal blood flow and a subsequent decrease in lubrication, increase in vaginal dryness, and dyspareunia. This can greatly affect the sexual response by delaying sexual arousal or causing a delayed or absent orgasm.[111]

OSTEOPOROSIS

Osteoporosis is a skeletal disorder characterized by compromised bone strength predisposing a person to increased risk of fracture.[112] Osteoporosis can result from bone loss and/or suboptimal bone growth during childhood or adolescence. Osteoporosis, as defined by the World Health Organization, is 2.5 standard deviations (T-score) below the mean value in young adults of the same sex and race. Risk factors for osteoporosis are presented in Table 6-12.

Screening for osteoporosis has become more frequent in recent years due to an increased awareness of the morbidity, mortality, and costs associated with fracture development. Fractures can result in chronic pain, interfere with activities of daily life, and affect psychological well-being. A recent large, prospective observational study, the National Osteoporosis Risk Assessment, screened 200,000 postmenopausal women using portable technologies that tested peripheral sites for bone density measurements.[113] Osteopenia, or bone mineral density (BMD) T-score range of −1.0 to −2.49, was found in approximately 40% of women, and osteoporosis was found in 7%. Osteoporosis was associated with a fracture rate 4 times that of normal BMD, and

TABLE 6-12 Risk Factors for Osteoporosis

Primary Causes	*Secondary Causes*
Female sex	Hypogonadism
Advanced age	Gastrointestinal diseases
White race	End-stage renal disease
Tobacco use	Medications (glucocorticoids, thyroid hormone, anticonvulsants)
Alcoholism	
Genetic disorders	
Previous history of fracture	Endocrine disorders (hyperthyroidism)
Estrogen deficiency (early menopause)	Connective tissue disorders
Low body weight/ low body mass index	Nutritional disorders
Family history of osteoporosis	

osteopenia was associated with a fracture rate 1.8 times that of normal BMD.[113] The financial consequences are enormous. In 1995, approximately $13.8 billion was spent in the United States for management of osteoporosis.[114]

Screening for osteoporosis should include measurement of bone mineral density. Plain radiographs are poorly sensitive in detecting osteopenia. Dual x-ray absorptiometry of the hip and spine is considered the "gold standard" for quantitative measurement of BMD.[115] Measurement of biochemical markers of bone turnover has not proven useful in screening.

Preventive recommendations should be provided for women of all ages. Peak bone mass occurs at the third decade of life, thus proper nutrition and caloric intake in adolescence and young adulthood is essential. Calcium (1,000 mg/day) supplementation may also be necessary in women who do not acquire enough from their diet. Regular physical exercise in the early years can contribute to higher peak bone mass; later in life, it can promote muscle mass and strength to protect the frail individual.

In women with documented osteopenia and osteoporosis, pharmacologic therapy should be considered. Prior to the results of the WHI, HRT was considered first-line treatment for osteoporosis. Women at high risk for breast cancer are usually averse to estrogen compounds. The development of selective estrogen receptor modulators (SERMs) has offered women who are worried about their breast cancer risk an alternative. These compounds offer the beneficial effects of estrogen on the bone and eliminate the effects on breast and endometrial lining. The US Food and Drug Administration has approved raloxifene for the prevention and treatment of osteoporosis. As described elsewhere, raloxifene has potential use in breast cancer reduction, although it has not been approved for this indication. Raloxifene has been shown to reduce the incidence of vertebral fractures; however, when compared with estrogen, it appeared less effective.[116,117] Similarly, tamoxifen, also a SERM, has demonstrated reduction in fracture rate, although it is not indicated for this.[118]

Bisphosphonates such as alendronate and risedronate are considered effective for women with documented osteoporosis. Bisphosphonates increase bone mass and reduce the incidence of vertebral fractures.[119] Caution must be advised to prevent side effects of esophagitis. Calcitonin should be reserved for patients who cannot tolerate other medications. Its analgesic actions provide a useful choice for relief of pain during the acute fracture setting.

IMMUNIZATIONS

Immunizations are an important part of general health maintenance and are often overlooked during an office visit. Table 6-13 presents indications for vaccines for healthy adults.

ALTERNATIVE/HERBAL THERAPIES

Physicians should inquire into the patient's use of alternative/herbal therapies. Trends from a national health survey indicate a substantial increase since 1990 in the use of alternative therapies such as herbal therapies and visits to alternative medicine practitioners.[120] Due to the paucity of research available, physicians face a significant challenge in offering guidance to patients seeking these therapies. The herbal therapies most often used by women include soy phytoestrogens, black cohosh, evening primrose oil, St. John's wort, valerian, gingko, and kava. A thorough inventory of herbal medication and alternative therapies in which the patient is participating is essential in order to avoid potential harmful interactions with other prescription medications.

CONCLUSION

Clinicians who care for women at high risk for breast cancer should be familiar with the issues surrounding their overall health. While considering the risk-stratification and risk-reduction options available for high-risk women, we must also consider competing risks for other diseases, such as the development of cardiovascular disease and other cancers. The effect of other health conditions on survival of women diagnosed with breast cancer has been studied longitudinally. Women with breast cancer and coexisting health conditions had an increased overall mortality rate compared with women without comorbidities.[121] Thus, implementing early detection programs for individuals

TABLE 6-13 Immunization Schedule for Healthy Adults

Indications	Contraindications
Influenza	Anaphylactic reaction to egg protein
Yearly dose recommended	
All persons age > 65	
Residents of chronic care facilities with chronic cardiopulmonary disorders, diabetes, renal dysfunction, or immunosuppression	
Healthcare workers for high-risk populations	
Pneumococcal vaccine	Pregnancy
Initial dose, repeat after 5 years	
All immunocompetent persons age > 65 years	
Institutionalized persons age ≥ 50 years	
Measles, Mumps, Rubella (MMR)	
Two doses in a lifetime required	
All persons born after 1956 without evidence of immunity or physician-documented illness	
Tetanus, Diphtheria	
All persons should undergo primary series of three vaccines if not done as a child.	
Booster Td should be provided every 10 years	
Hepatitis A	
Two doses at 0 and 6–12 months are recommended	
Persons living in or traveling to areas endemic with Hepatitis A	
Homosexual men	
Injection drug use	
Hepatitis B	
Three doses at 0, 1, and 6 months	
All young adults not previously immunized	
Homosexual men	
Injection drug use	
Multiple sexual partners	
Travel to areas endemic with Hepatitis B	
Varicella	
Two doses 4–8 weeks apart in healthy adults without varicella infection	

Adapted from United States Preventive Task Force.[97]

with multiple comorbidities may not provide a survival advantage. This issue is particularly relevant to older women who have a higher probability of dying from other causes. Although breast cancer mortality rates increase with advancing age, the number of extra incident cases found by screening in older women may exceed the number of prevented breast cancer deaths.[123] Therefore, when counseling women who are at high risk for breast cancer, it is important to provide an individualized assessment taking into consideration the personalized risk for developing breast cancer as well as the risk of morbidity and mortality from coexisting health conditions.

REFERENCES

1. Phillips KA, Glendon G, Knight JA. Putting the risk of breast cancer in perspective. N Engl J Med 1999;340:141–4.

2. U. S. Preventive Services Task Force. Guide to clinical preventive services. Baltimore: Williams & Wilkins; 1996.

3. Walsh JME, McPhee SJ. Prevention in the year 2002: some news, some issues. Prim Care Clin Office Pract 2002;29:727–49.

4. Anderson RN. National Vital Statistics Report, Washington DC; October 12, 2001. 2001;49(11): 14–49.

5. American Heart Association: 2002 Heart and Stroke Statistical Update. Available at: http://www.americanheartassociation.org/statistics/ (accessed December 13, 2002).

6. Lewis SJ. Cardiovascular disease in postmenopausal women: myths and reality. Am J Cardiol 2002;89: 5E–11E.

7. Schneck-Gustafsson K. Risk factors from cardiovascular disease in women: Bulletin of the World Health Federation [newsletter]. Geneva, Switzerland Heart Beat 2000;1–3.

8. Wilson PW. Established risk factors and coronary artery disease: the Framingham Study. Am J Hypertens 1994;7:7S–12S.

9. Executive Summary of the Third Report of the National Cholesterol Education Program (NCEP) Expert Panel on Detection, Evaluation, and Treatment of High Blood Cholesterol in Adults (Adult Treatment Panel III). JAMA 2001;285:2486.

10. Mosca L, Grundy SM, Judelson D, et al. Guide to preventive cardiology for women. J Am Coll Cardiol 1999;33:1751–5.

11. Winkleby MA, Kraemer HC, Ahn DK, et al. Ethnic and socioeconomic differences in cardiovascular risk factors: findings for women from the Third National Health and Nutritional Examination Survey, 1988–1994. JAMA 1998;280:356–62.

12. Grundy SM. Guidelines for cholesterol management: recommendations of the National Cholesterol Education Program's Adult Treatment Panel II. Heart Dis Stroke 1994;3:123.

13. Sesso HD, Lee IM, Gaziano JM, et al. Maternal and paternal history of myocardial infarction and risk of cardiovascular disease in men and women. Circulation 2001;104:393–8.

14. Roncaglioni MC, Santoro L, D'Avanzo B, et al. Role of family history in patients with myocardial infarction: an Italian case-control study. GISSI-EFRIM Investigators. Circulation 1992;85:2065–72.

15. Stamler J, Wentworth D, Neaton JD. Is relationship between serum cholesterol and risk of premature death from coronary heart disease continuous and graded? Findings in 356,222 primary screenees of the Multiple Risk Factor Intervention Trial (MR-FIT). JAMA 1986;256:2823–8.

16. Miller VT. Lipids, lipoproteins, women and cardiovascular disease. Atherosclerosis 1994;108:S73–S82.

17. Orth-Gomer K, Mittleman MA, Schenck-Gustafsson K, et al. Lipoprotein (a) as a determinant of coronary heart disease in young women. Circulation 1997;95:2:329–34.

18. Bengtsson C, Bjorkelund C, Lapidus L, Lissner L. Associations of serum lipid concentrations and obesity with mortality in women: 20 year follow-up of participants in prospective population study in Gothenburg, Sweden. BMJ 1993;307:1385.

19. Kane JP, Malloy MJ, Ports TA, et al. Regression of coronary atherosclerosis during treatment of familial hypercholesterolemia with combined drug regimens. JAMA 1990;264:3007.

20. Randomised trial of cholesterol lowering in 4444 patients with coronary heart diseases: the Scandinavian Simvastatin Survival Study (4S). Lancet 1994; 344:1383.

21. The sixth report of the Joint National Committee on prevention, detection, evaluation, and treatment of high blood pressure. Arch Intern Med 1997; 157:2413.

22. Brown DW, Giles WH, Croft JB. Left ventricular hypertrophy as a predictor of coronary heart disease mortality and the effect of hypertension. Am Heart J 2000;140:848.

23. Kannel WB, Gordon T, Schwartz MJ. Systolic versus diastolic blood pressure and risk of coronary heart disease: the Framingham Study. Am J Cardiol 1971;27:335.

24. Wilking SVB, Belanger AJ, Kannel WB, et al. Determinants of isolated systolic hypertension. JAMA 1998;260:3451–5.

25. Burt VL, Whelton P, Roccella EJ, et al. Prevalence of hypertension in the US adult population. Results from the Third National Health and Nutrition Examination Survey, 1988–1991. Hypertension 1995;25:305–13.

26. Rich-Edwards JW, Manson JE, Hennekens CH, et al. The primary prevention of coronary heart disease in women. N Engl J Med 1995;332:1758–66.

27. Sullivan AK, Holdrigh DR, Wright CA, et al. Chest pain in women: clinical, investigative, and prognostic features. BMJ 1994;308:883–6.

28. Cornoni-Huntley J, LaCroix AZ, Havlik RJ. Race and sex differentials in the impact of hypertension in the United States. The National Health and Nutrition Examination Survey I epidemiologic follow-up study. Arch Intern Med 1989;149:780–8.

29. Vassan RS, Massaro JM, Wilson PW, et al. Antecedent blood pressure and risk of cardiovascular disease: the Framingham heart study. Circulation 2002;105:48.

30. SHEP Cooperative Research Group. Prevention of stroke by anti-hypertensive drug treatment in older persons with isolated systolic hypertension: final results of the Systolic Hypertension in the Elderly Program. JAMA 1991;265:3255–64.

31. ALLHAT authors. Major outcomes in high risk hypertensive patients randomized to angiotensin-converting enzyme inhibitor or calcium channel blocker vs diuretic: the Antihypertensive and Lipid-Lowering Treatment to Prevent Heart Attack Trial (ALLHAT). JAMA 2002;288:2981–97.

32. Dahlof B, Devereux RB, Kjeldsen SE, et al. Cardiovascular morbidity and mortality in the Losartan Intervention for endpoint reduction in hypertension study (LIFE): a randomized trial against atenolol. Lancet 2002;359:995–1003.

33. Lonn E, Roccaforte R, Yi Q, et al. Effect of long-term therapy with ramipril in high-risk women. J Am Coll Cardiol 2002;40:693–702.

34. Kannel WB, McGee DL. Diabetes and cardiovascular disease: the Framingham Study. JAMA 1979;241: 2035–8.

35. Singer DE, Nathan DM, Anderson KM, et al. Association of HbA1c with prevalent cardiovascular disease in the original cohort of the Framingham Heart Study. Diabetes 1992;41:202–8.

36. Spelsberg A, Ridker PM, Manson JE. Carbohydrate metabolism, obesity and diabetes. In: Douglas PS, editor. Cardiovascular health and disease in women. Philadelphia (PA): WB Saunders; 1993. p. 191.

37. Manson JE, Colditz GA, Stampfer MJ, et al. A prospective study of maturity-onset diabetes mellitus and risk of coronary heart disease and stroke in women. Arch Intern Med 1991;151:1141–7.

38. Bedinghaus J, Leshan L, Diehr S. Coronary artery disease prevention: what's different for women? Am Fam Phys 2001;63:1393–400.

39. Coutinho M, Gerstein HC, Wang Y, et al. The relationship between glucose and incident cardiovascular events. A metaregression analysis of published data from 20 studies of 95,783 individuals followed for 12.4 years. Diabetes Care 1999;22: 233–40.

40. American Diabetes Association. Position statement: screening for diabetes. Diabetes Care 2001;24:S21.

41. The Diabetes Control and Complications Trial Research Group. The effect of intensive treatment of diabetes on the development and progression of long-term complications in insulin-dependent diabetes mellitus. N Engl J Med 1993;329:977.

42. McGinnis GM, Foege WH. Actual causes of death in the United States. JAMA 1993;270:2207–12.

43. Eckel RH, Krauss RM. American Heart Association call to action: obesity as a major risk factor for coronary heart disease. Circulation 1998;97:2099–100.

44. Mokdad AH, Ford ES, Bowman BA, et al. Prevalence of obesity, diabetes, and obesity-related health risk factors, 2001. JAMA 2003;289:76–9.

45. Manson JE, Willett WC, Stampfer MJ, et al. Body weight and mortality among women. N Engl J Med 1995;333:677–85.

46. Serdula MK, Mokdad AH, Williamson DF, et al. Prevalence of attempting weight loss and strategies for controlling weight. JAMA 1999;282: 1353–8.

47. Tuomilehto J, Lindstrom J, Eriksson JG, et al. Prevention of type 2 diabetes mellitus by changes in lifestyle among subjects with impaired glucose tolerance. N Engl J Med 2001;344:1343–50.

48. Grundy SM. Guidelines for cholesterol management: recommendations of the National Cholesterol Education Program's Adult Treatment Panel II. Heart Dis Stroke 1994;3:123–7.

49. Colditz GA, Willett WC, Stampfer MJ, et al. Menopause and the risk of coronary heart disease in women. N Engl J Med 1987;316:1105–10.

50. Morise AP, Dalal JN, Duval RD. Value of a simple measure of estrogen status for improving the diagnosis of coronary artery disease in women. Am J Med 1993;94:491–6.

51. Risks and benefits of estrogen plus progestin in healthy postmenopausal women: principal results from the Women's Health Initiative randomized controlled trial. JAMA 2002;288:321–3.

52. Hulley S, Grady D, Bush T, et al for the Heart and Estrogen/progestin Replacement Study (HERS) Research Group. Randomized trial of estrogen plus progestin for secondary prevention of coronary heart disease in postmenopausal women. JAMA 1998;280:605–13.

53. Grady D, Herrington D, Bittner V, et al. Cardiovascular disease outcomes during 6.8 years of hormone therapy: Heart and Estrogen/progestin Replacement Study follow-up (HERS II). JAMA 2002;288:49–57.

54. Prescott E, Hippe M, Schnohr P, et al. Smoking and the risk of myocardial infarction in women and men: longitudinal population study. BMJ 1998; 316:1043–7.

55. Willet WC, Green A, Stampfer MJ, et al. Relative and absolute excess risks of coronary heart disease among women who smoke cigarettes. N Engl J Med 1987;317:1303–9.

56. Wilhelmsson C, Vedin JA, Elmfeldt D, et al. Smoking and myocardial infarction. Lancet 1975;1:415–20.

57. Rosenberg L, Palmer JR, Shapiro S. Decline in the risk of myocardial infarction among women who stop smoking. N Engl J Med 1990;322:213–7.

58. Leon AS, Connett J, Jacobs DR, et al. Leisure-time physical activity levels and risk of coronary heart disease and death. The Multiple Risk Factor Intervention Trial. JAMA 1987;258:2388–95.

59. Laukkanen JA, Lakka TA, Rauramaa R, et al. Cardiovascular fitness as a predictor of mortality in men. Arch Intern Med 2001;161:825–31.

60. Manson JE, Hu FB, Rich-Edwards JW, et al. A prospective study of walking as compared with vigorous exercise in the prevention of coronary heart disease in women. N Engl J Med 1999; 341:650–8.

61. Lee IM, Rexrode KM, Cook NR, et al. Physical activity and coronary heart disease in women: is "no pain, no gain" passe? JAMA 2001;285:1447–54.

62. Hu FB, Stampfer MJ, Manson JE, et al. Dietary fat intake and the risk of coronary heart disease in women. N Engl J Med 1997;337:1491–9.

63. Fung TT, Willett WC, Stampfer MJ, et al. Dietary patterns and the risk of coronary heart disease in women. Arch Intern Med 2001;161:1857–62.

64. Fuchs CS, Stampfer MJ, Colditz GA, et al. Alcohol consumption and mortality among women. N Engl J Med 1995;332:1245–50.

65. Rimm EB, Willett WC, Hu FB, et al. Folate and vitamin B6 from diet and supplements in relation to risk of coronary heart disease among women. JAMA 1998;279:359–64.

66. Lerner DJ, Kannel WB. Patterns of coronary heart disease morbidity and mortality in the sexes: a 26-year follow-up of the Framingham population. Am Heart J 1986;316:1105–10.

67. Kennedy JW, Killip T, Fisher LD, et al. The clinical spectrum of coronary artery disease and its surgical and medical management. The Coronary Artery Surgery Study. Circulation 1982;66:16–23.

68. Wenger N. Coronary heart disease: diagnostic decision making. In: Douglas PS, editor. Cardiovascular health and disease in women. Philadelphia (PA): WB Saunders Co.; 1993. p. 28–36.

69. Douglas PS, Ginsburg GS. The evaluation of chest pain in women. N Engl J Med 1996;344:1311–5.

70. Douglas PS. Is noninvasive testing for coronary artery disease accurate? Circulation 1997;95:299–302.

71. Roger VL, Pellikka PA, Bell MR, et al. Sex and test verification bias. Impact on the diagnostic value of exercise echocardiography. Circulation 1997;95:405–10.

72. Cerqueira MD. Diagnostic testing strategies for coronary artery disease: special issues related to gender. Am J Cardiol 1995;75:52–60D.

73. Marmor A, Zeira M. Hormonal replacement therapy induces false-positive ST-segment depression in middle-aged women. Am J Noninvas Cardiol 1993;7:361–3.

74. Friedman T, Greene A, Iskandrian A, et al. Exercise thallium-201 myocardial scintigraphy in women: correlation with coronary angiography. Am J Cardiol 1982;49:1632–7.

75. Marwick TH, Anderson T, Williams MJ, et al. Exercise echocardiography is an accurate and cost-efficient technique for detection of coronary artery disease in women. J Am Coll Cardiol 1995;26:335–41.

76. Pearson TA, Blair SN, Daniels SR, et al. AHA guidelines for primary prevention of cardiovascular disease and stroke: 2002 update: consensus panel guide to comprehensive risk reduction for adult patients without coronary or other atherosclerotic vascular diseases. Circulation 2002;106:388–91.

77. The Medical Research Council's General Practice Research Framework: Thrombosis prevention trial: randomized trial of low intensity oral anticoagulation with warfarin and low-dose aspirin in the primary prevention of ischemic heart disease in men at increased risk. Lancet 1998;351:233–41.

78. Hennekens CH. Update on aspirin in the treatment and prevention of cardiovascular disease. Am Heart J 1999;137:S9–S13.

79. Antiplatelet Trialists' Collaboration. Collaborative overview of randomized trials of antipatelet therapy-I: prevention of death, myocardial infarction, and stroke by prolonged antiplatelet therapy in various categories of patients. BMJ 1994;308:81–106.

80. Yusuf S, Peto R, Lewis J, et al. Beta blockade during and after myocardial infarction: an overview of the randomized trials. Prog Cardiovasc Dis 1985;27:335–71.

81. Pfeffer MA, Braunwald E, Moye LA, et al, on behalf of the SAVE investigators. Effect of captopril on mortality and morbidity in patients with left ventricular dysfunction after myocardial infarction. N Engl J Med 1992;327:669–77.

82. Yusuf S, Sleight P, Pogue J, et al. Effects of an angiotensin-converting enzyme inhibitor, ramipril, on cardiovascular events in high-risk patients: the Heart Outcomes Prevention Evaluation (HOPE) Study Investigators. N Engl J Med 2000;342:145–53.

83. Hennekens CH, Albert CM, Godfried SL, et al. Adjunctive drug therapy of acute myocardial infaction — evidence from clinical trials. N Engl J Med 1996;335:1660–7.

84. Thun MJ, Peto R, Lopez AD, et al. Alcohol consumption and mortality among middle-aged and elderly US adults. N Engl J Med 1997;337:1705–14.

85. American Cancer Society. Cancer facts and figures 2002 Available at: http://www.cancer.org. (accessed January 6, 2003).

86. Jemal A, Thomas A, Murray T, Thun M. Cancer statistics, 2002. CA Cancer J Clin 2002;52:23–47.

87. Fontana RS, Sanderson DR, Woolner LB, et al. Screening for lung cancer. A critique of the Mayo Lung Project. Cancer 1991;67:1155–64.

88. Ford D, Easton DF, Bishop DT, et al. Risks of cancer in BRCA1-mutation carriers. Breast Cancer Linkage Consortium. Lancet 1994;343:692–5.

89. Eddy D. Screening for colorectal cancer. Ann Intern Med 1990;113:373–84.

90. Winawer SJ, Zauber AG, Ho MN, et al. Prevention of colorectal cancer by colonoscopic polypectomy. The National Polyp Study Work Group. N Engl J Med 1993;329:1977–81.

91. Mandel JS, Church TR, Bond JH, et al. The effect of fecal occult-blood screening on incidence of colorectal cancer. N Engl J Med 2000;343:1603–7.

92. Imperiale TF, Wagner DR, Lin CY, et al. Risk of advanced proximal neoplasm in asymptomatic adults according to the distal colorectal findings. N Engl J Med 2000;343:169–74.

93. Lieberman DA, Weiss DG, Bond JH, et al. Use of colonoscopy to screen asymptomatic adults for colorectal cancer. N Engl J Med 2000;343:162–8.

94. Winawer SJ, Stewart ET, Zauber AG, et al. A comparison of colonoscopy and double-contrast bar-

ium enema for surveillance after polypectomy. National Polyp Study Work Group. N Engl J Med 2000;342:1766–72.

95. Rex DK, Johnson DA, Lieberman DA, et al. Colorectal cancer prevention 2000: screening recommendations of the American College of Gastroenterology. American College of Gastroenterology. Am J Gastroenterol 2000;95:868–77.

96. Frazier AL, Colditz GA, Fuchs CS, Kuntz KM. Cost-effectiveness of screening for colorectal cancer in the general population. JAMA 2000;284:1954–61.

97. United States Preventive Task Force. Guide to clinical preventive services. 2nd ed. Baltimore (MD): Williams & Wilkins; 1997.

98. Committee on Gynecologic Practice. Recommendations on frequency of Pap test screening. ACOG Committee Opinion, Number 152,1995. Int J Gynaecol Obstet 1995;49:210–1.

99. Solomon D, Davey D, Kurman R, et al, for the Forum Group Members and the Bethesda 2001 workshop. The 2001 Bethesda system: terminology for reporting results of cervical cytology. JAMA 2002;287:2114–9.

100. Flowers LC, McCall MA. Diagnosis and management of cervical intraepithelial neoplasia. Obstet Gynecol Clin North Am 2001;28(4):667–84.

101. USPHS/IDSA Prevention of Opportunistic Infections Working Group. 1997 USPHS/IDSA guidelines for the prevention of opportunistic infections in persons infected with human immunodeficiency virus. MMWR Morb Mortal Wkly Rep 1997;46:RR12.

102. El-Sadr W, Oleske JM, Agins BD, et al. Evaluation and management of early HIV infection. Clinical practice guidelines no. 7. Rockville (MD): US Department of Health and Human Services; 1994. AHCPR publication No.: 94-0572.

103. Koutsky LA, Ault KA, Wheeler CM, et al for the Proof of Principle Study Investigators. A controlled trial of a human papillomavirus type 16 vaccine. N Engl J Med 2002;347:1645–51.

104. Mattsson LA, Cullbery G, Eriksson O, et al. Vaginal administration of low-dose ostradiol — effects on the endometrium and vaginal cytology. Maturitas 1989;11:217–22.

105. Bachmann GA, Nevadunsky NS. Diagnosis and treatment of atrophic vaginitis. Am Fam Physician 2000;3090–6

106. Pritchard KI. Hormone replacement in women with a history of breast cancer. Oncologist 2001;6:353–62.

107. Naesson T, Rodriguez-Macias K. Endometrial thickness and uterine diameter not affected by ultra-low doses of 17 B-estradiol in elderly women. Am J Obstet Gynecol 2002;186;944–7.

108. Mettler L, Olsen PG. Long-term treatment of atrophic vaginitis with low-dose oestradiol vaginal tablets. Maturitas 1991;14:23–31.

109. Flisser AJ, Blaivas JG. Evaluating incontinence in women. Urol Clin North Am 2002;29:515–26.

110. Leclair DM, Anandarajah G. Effects of estrogen deprivation. Vasomotor symptoms, urogenital atrophy, and psychobiologic effects. Clin Fam Pract 2002;4:27–39.

111. Berman JR, Berman LA, Werbin TJ, et al. Clinical evaluation of female sexual function: effects of age and estrogen status on subjective and physiologic sexual responses. Int J Impot Res 1999;11 Suppl 1:S31–8.

112. NIH Consensus Development Panel on Osteoporosis Prevention, Diagnosis, and Therapy. Osteoporosis prevention, diagnosis, and therapy. JAMA 2001; 285:785–95.

113. Siris ES, Miller PD, Barrett-Connor E, et al. Identification and fracture outcomes of undiagnosed low bone mineral density in postmenopausal women. Results form the National Osteoporosis Risk Assessment. JAMA 2001;286:2815–22.

114. Ray NF, Chan JK, Thamer M, Melton LJ. Medical expenditures for the treatment of osteoporosis fractures in the United States in 1995: report from the National Osteoporosis Foundation. J Bone Miner Res 1997;12:24–35.

115. Black DM, Cummings SR, Genant HK, et al. Axial and appendicular bone density predicts fractures in older women. J Bone Miner Res 1992;7:633–8.

116. Ettinger B, Black DM, Mitlak BH, et al. Reduction of vertebral fracture risk in postmenopausal women with osteoporosis treated with raloxifene. JAMA 1999;282:637–45.

117. Prestwood KM, Gunness M, Muchmore DB, et al. A comparison of the effects of raloxifene and estrogen on bone in postmenopausal women. J Clin Endocrinol Metab 2000;85:2197–202.

118. Black DM, Cummings SR, Karpf DB, et al. Randomised trial of effect of alendronate on risk of fracture in women with existing vertebral fractures. Lancet 1996;348:1535–41.

119. Fisher B, Costantino JP, Wickerham DL, et al. Tamoxifen for prevention of breast cancer: report of the National Surgical Adjuvant Breast and Bowel Project P-1 Study. J Natl Cancer Inst 1998;90:1371–88.

120. Eisenberg DM, Davis RB, Ettner SL, et al. Trends in alternative medicine use in the United States, 1990–1997: results of a follow-up national survey. JAMA 1998;280:1569–75.

121. Satariano WA, Raglan DR. The effect of comorbidity on 3-year survival of women with primary breast cancer. Ann Intern Med 1994;120:104–10.

Risk Management Strategies

CHAPTER 7

OUTCOME OF ROUTINE SURVEILLANCE OF THE HIGH-RISK WOMAN

Valerie L. Staradub, MD

Routine surveillance for breast cancer with annual screening mammography and clinical breast exams is considered the standard of care for all women of screening age. However, the details surrounding the initiation and frequency of screening as well as the efficacy of these screening tools have been the subject of ongoing debate. Even less clear is the role of routine surveillance for those at moderately elevated or frankly high risk for breast cancer based on general risk factors, family history, or genetic mutation. Studies have been done to characterize the utility of prophylactic mastectomy and tamoxifen in high-risk women, but few studies have examined what benefit, if any, a high-risk woman may expect from routine breast cancer surveillance, nor is there a wealth of data regarding exactly what screening protocol is most effective. In fact, the impact of current breast cancer surveillance strategies is likely to vary with the age and actual level of cancer risk of each individual patient. Yet the majority of high-risk women choose surveillance over medical or surgical risk-reducing measures.[1–4] This chapter will attempt to use both direct and indirect evidence to clarify some of these issues. Current information regarding the components of breast cancer surveillance and their contribution to the outcome of high-risk women will be reviewed. It is important to realize that "high risk" is a rather general term encompassing moderate elevations in breast cancer up to demonstrated genetic predisposition. Women at different risk tiers likely enjoy varied benefit from these surveillance practices.

COMPONENTS OF ROUTINE SURVEILLANCE FOR HIGH-RISK WOMEN

Breast cancer surveillance has traditionally included breast self-examination, clinical breast examination, and screening mammography. None of these modalities is sufficient to stand alone. In a recent study of women aged 50 or older not stratified by level of risk who were diagnosed with invasive breast cancer from a statewide registry from Wisconsin, 41% of tumors were detected mammographically, 48% were detected by the patient herself, and 11% were detected at clinical examination by a physician.[5] These percentages varied somewhat by tumor histology. For example, tubular cancers were far more likely to be identified mammographically than by physical examination, whereas lobular carcinomas were most commonly detected by patient or physician exam as interval cancers versus at mammographic screening. Each of these components, therefore, can be of benefit in the surveillance process. In addition, newer modalities such as magnetic resonance imaging (MRI) are being evaluated and may prove applicable in breast cancer surveillance for high-risk women. This section will review these individual components of breast cancer surveillance as well as their value in a high-risk population. Newer screening modalities such as ductal lavage, ductoscopy, and newer imaging modalities will be discussed in subsequent chapters.

Breast Self-Examination

Breast self-examination (BSE) has long been a controversial part of breast cancer screening. Clearly the goal of BSE is to promote the early detection of breast cancer, and it is a conceptually appealing option in that BSE has the potential to identify palpable breast cancer in the intervals between screening visits for breast imaging or clinical breast examination by a physician. Whether or not BSE actually plays an important role in breast cancer surveillance, however, has been the subject of some debate. If BSE is to be effective in reducing mortality, it must identify curable tumors at a smaller size or an earlier stage than would be detected without BSE. A case-control study nested within the Canadian National Breast Screening Study in the late 1990s demonstrated a reduction in mortality among the cohort correctly performing BSE for 2 or more years prior to diagnosis.[6] Beginning the practice of BSE within 1 year prior to diagnosis, however, provided no benefit. If BSE is to be effective in reducing mortality, it must be performed so as to identify tumors that are curable earlier than they would be detected without BSE. Women performing monthly BSE were more likely to find their tumors themselves than those who performed BSE less than monthly or not at all.[7] Additionally, regular BSE performers identified their tumors at a smaller size than nonperformers. Survival was significantly improved in the group that performed BSE than those who did not (5-yr overall survival 75% vs 57%, $p < .001$). Several other studies indicate a potential stage reduction and corresponding survival benefit from regular performance of BSE,[8,9] but these findings are far from uniform, with other studies demonstrating no difference.[10,11] These studies relied on women to report their own practices of BSE, however, and the woman who chooses to be diligent about monthly BSE is also likely to follow other healthy lifestyle guidelines, visit her physician regularly, and comply with recommendations for regular mammographic screening.

There have been two randomized, controlled trials of BSE, one in Shanghai[6] and one in Russia.[12,13] Neither is transmutable to the use of BSE as a part of a comprehensive routine surveillance program for women at risk for breast cancer, however, because mammography was not a component of screening in either country. The Russian study is planned to span 15 years and has yet to be completed. Interim analysis, however, revealed no significant difference in tumor stage or survival rates between the two groups.[14] Additionally, there were more physician visits for suspected pathology in the BSE group. The Shanghai study randomized 266,064 women to receive BSE instruction or no instruction.[15] The women in the BSE group also got scheduled supplementary instruction, reminders, and were required to perform BSE under supervision at least twice a year. The women in the control group, while not instructed in BSE, were not prevented from examining their breasts on their own. Mammographic screening was not available to these women, and regular breast exams by a clinician were not routine. During the follow-up period, there was no difference in the identification of cancer or in breast cancer mortality between the two groups; however, women in the BSE group did have significantly more benign breast biopsies than the control group.

In the Shanghai study as well as others, BSE resulted in an increase in the detection of benign processes by the patient (false positives).[13,15–17] False-positive BSE leads to an increase in clinic visits by the patient, interval diagnostic imaging, and biopsies. These have both an economic impact on the cost-effectiveness of surveillance programs and a psychological effect on the patient. It may be true that the false-positive rate of BSE is higher than the true-positive rate, which would make it an unsuitable method of screening.[17]

There has been no controlled randomized trial to assess the utility of BSE as an adjunctive part of a surveillance program. If BSE were responsible for the detection of interval cancers at a significant rate, it should have a favorable impact upon breast cancer mortality. However, a 1987 review by the US Preventive Services Task Force estimated that among studies reporting tumor stage by detection method, cancers detected by BSE were approximately equal to the number discovered incidentally by the patient.[17] In a recent set of clinical guidelines based on a broad literature review, Humphrey and colleagues conclude that there is insufficient evidence to promote the use of routine BSE.[16] Based on data from the Breast Cancer Detection Demonstration Project,[18] the task force estimated the overall sensitivity of BSE at 26%, whereas the sensitivity for mammography combined with clinical breast examination (CBE) by a health professional is approximately 75%. Interestingly, they reported a decline in BSE sensitivity with age, whereas the sensitivity of the combination of mammographic screening and CBE increased with age.[17]

It is important to note that no studies of the benefit of BSE have been performed specifically in the high-risk group. High-risk women have a greater likelihood of actually having a malignant mass to detect, which might impact the utility of BSE by increasing the true-positive rate of BSE findings. It has also been suggested that breast tumors in particularly high-risk women may grow more quickly than tumors in women of average risk, in which case there may be a larger cohort of tumors arising in the intervals between scheduled surveillance available to be detected by BSE.[19,20] For these reasons, studies of BSE done in women with standard risks of developing breast cancer may not be relevant to the high-risk woman.

Clinical Breast Examination

Clinical breast examination may be performed by a health practitioner either in a surveillance setting or in response to a symptom (often a mass) perceived by the patient. Its effectiveness as a surveillance tool depends mainly on the technique and experience of the examiner. There is significant variability in the literature regarding the accuracy of CBE (Table 7-1). In theory, CBE should be more accurate than BSE because most clinical examiners have felt a malignant breast mass, whereas few patients have.[21] The overall sensitivity of the CBE is 54%, with a range of 48 to 60%, and the specificity is reported as 94% (range 86 to 99%). There is a high false-positive and even higher false-negative rate associated with CBE. Breast size and texture can influence the accuracy of CBE. Of 752,081 CBEs performed by the National Breast and Cervical

TABLE 7-1 Utility of Clinical Breast Examination

Sensitivity	40–69%
Specificity	88–99%
Positive Predictive Value	4–50%

Adapted from Humphrey LL et al.[16]

Early Detection Program on 564,708 women over a 4-year period, 6.9% of CBEs were recorded as suspicious for cancer.[22] These included some exams performed for breast symptoms, often a self-detected mass. Among patients with an abnormal CBE and a normal or benign mammogram, the rate of cancer detection was 7.4 cancers per 1,000 exams, representing approximately 5% of the cancers diagnosed in this study. When the mammogram was suspicious and the CBE was normal, the cancer detection rate was over 5 times higher, at 42 cancers per 1,000 exams. However, when both CBE and mammography performed on the same day were abnormal, the rate of cancer detection was over 20 times higher. The sensitivity of CBE, similar to that of BSE,[17] decreased with age, whereas the specificity and positive predictive value rose with age (Table 7-2).[22] This study provides no information regarding the impact of CBE on reducing breast cancer mortality or stage at diagnosis, the main impetus of surveillance programs. Between 5.2 and 29% of breast cancers found by CBE are missed by imaging.[21] The mortality rate in this group of patients is higher than those in whom the cancer was detected by mammogram. It is hard to estimate the benefit from detection by CBE versus by subsequent mammogram or detection by the patient.

Screening with CBE alone was evaluated in the Canadian National Breast Screening Study.[23] The sensitivity for the first screening CBE was 71% in

TABLE 7-2 Accuracy of Clinical Breast Examination in Women at Standard Risk of Breast Cancer by Age at Evaluation

	Overall	< 40 yrs	40–49 yrs	50–59 yrs	60–69 yrs	≥ 70 yrs
Sensitivity	58.8	88.5	71.4	57.2	51.3	38.0
Specificity	93.4	86.0	91.6	95.1	96.0	96.8
PPV	4.3	1.4	3.6	6.1	7.4	7.0

Adapted from Bobo KJ et al.[22]

PPV = positive predictive value.

the women aged 40 to 49 years and 83% in the group aged 50 to 59 years. Interestingly, there was a demonstrable fluctuation in sensitivity between annual screenings. There was no difference between CBE performed by physicians and those performed by nurse examiners using a standard technique.

The higher the patient's risk of cancer, the greater the likelihood that a finding identified on CBE will be a malignant lesion (true positive). This has been demonstrated in studies showing that the positive predictive value of CBE is higher in older women than younger women in average risk groups.[18,23] CBE may be particularly useful in the subset of younger high-risk women, in whom mammography may be less sensitive (this discussion will be continued in the next section). At the Royal Marsden, 1,578 women with negative mammogram and CBE at the time of entry into the study were divided into a standard risk group (lifetime risk < 16%; $n = 1,500$) and a high-risk group (lifetime risk ≥ 16%; $n = 1,078$) and entered into a surveillance program.[24] Forty-five percent of the cancers detected in this study were palpable on CBE but not visible on mammogram. Specifically, in the high-risk group, 10 of the 19 cancers were detected by CBE only, as compared with 4 of 12 in the standard risk group. There was no distinction made, however, between true CBE and BSE performed by the patient, and a significant number of the palpable malignancies were detected by patients. Additionally, this study was not designed to evaluate for a survival benefit of using CBE in high-risk women. In general, however, detection of a tumor as soon as it is clinically apparent should increase the probability of breast conservation therapy as a possible surgical option, if not improve patient survival. Most screening programs incorporate CBE by a health professional as a regular part of breast cancer surveillance in high-risk women.

Routine Mammographic Screening

There has been much recent controversy regarding the utility of screening mammography, although most of these studies have focused on the general, non–risk-stratified population. There is no disagreement regarding the fact that mammograms detect breast tumors that are clinically occult.[25–27] The question is whether this provides benefit. Most frequently debated is survival benefit: Do mammograms save lives, especially in young women or women at particularly high risk for developing breast cancer?[16,25–27] A question that has received far less attention, however, is whether earlier detection by mammography increases the potential for breast-conserving therapy.

The accuracy of mammograms depends on technical features of the imaging, density of the breasts, and the expertise of the mammographer. There may be significant variability between radiologists in the interpretation of mammographic findings, particularly in the community where much of the general screening exams are done.[28] In the population at general risk, younger women, premenopausal women, and women with a family history of breast cancer have a higher likelihood of false-positive mammographic screening examinations.[16,28,29] Interestingly, the false-positive rate was higher in the 1990s than the 1980s.[28] The positive predictive value (PPV) of screening mammography was higher in the subsets of women with a family history of breast cancer in the age groups of 40 to 49 years and 50 to 59 years.[30] However, in women aged 30 to 39 years, 60 to 69 years, and 70+ years, a family history of breast cancer had no effect on the PPV of mammography. Screening mammography may have a greater impact in younger women with a family history of breast cancer because cancer is more prevalent in this group than in women of the same age with no family history.[1] Despite a better PPV and cost-effectiveness to screening women aged 40 to 49 years with a family history of breast cancer, an effect on mortality rates has not been demonstrated.[31] The significance of early detection of ductal carcinoma in situ (DCIS) in high-risk women is unknown. Not all DCIS becomes clinically relevant, however in theory this could reduce the incidence of invasive breast cancer and subsequent mortality.[20] This could become particularly important in the high-risk population. The lead time gained by detection of breast cancer by routine screening of high-risk women is likely to be under 1 year, therefore shorter screening intervals may be considered for women at very high risk.[20]

Interval cancers (cancers that become clinically apparent in the interval between mammographic screening examinations) may arise due to technical or interpretative errors. These are estimated to account for 10 to 36% of interval cancers identified.[32] True interval cancers arise when the most recent mammogram does not, in fact, demonstrate the tumor. This may be due to an inability to visualize a tumor on imaging because of masking by mammographic dense parenchyma, lobular histology, or the absence of microscopic and mammographic calcifications. Certainly, a subset of tumors appears to grow rapidly and achieve clinically detectable size in the interval between mammographic screens. Interval cancers have been reported to occur with a higher relative frequency in younger women.[17,32] In the 2 years after a negative screening mammogram, the ratio of interval cancers to screen-detected cancers was 1:2.5 in a group aged 50 to 64 years but only 1:0.75 in women aged 40 to 49 at entry into the DOM Screening Programme.[17] Of particular interest to the high-risk group, estrogen receptor (ER)-negative tumors are more likely to be detected in the screening interval.[32]

Breast Ultrasound

Breast ultrasound has been very useful as a tool in the evaluation of a palpable or mammographic breast lesion, but its utility as a screening tool has not been established.[33–36] Ultrasound is also well known to be a heavily operator-dependent study.[37] Conventional wisdom has been that screening breast ultrasound is not particularly useful for screening in addition to an established mammographic screening program in the general population.[36,38] However, studies using more refined indications and newer equipment have shown variable results. In 1,862 patients with negative mammogram and CBE with mammographically dense breast parenchyma, whole breast screening ultrasound detected cancer in six patients (0.3%).[39] The tumors identified included one DCIS and five Stage I cancers. Although this is a low detection rate, this was in fact a screening study involving women unselected for level of breast cancer risk, and the authors report a similar detection rate for screening mammography. Breast biopsy was recommended based on ultrasound findings in 3% of the patients, yielding a positive predictive value of 11.8%. A similar rate of cancer detection was seen with screening breast ultrasound in a study of 3,626 women with dense breasts again as a selection criterion.[40] The tumors identified by screening breast ultrasound were similar in size and nodal status to mammographically detected cancers and noted to be smaller than cancers identified by palpation. The addition of screening ultrasound to mammography

in women with dense breasts increased cancer detection by 17%. In a separate study of 11,130 asymptomatic women with dense breasts, 37% of the cancers identified with regular screening using all three modalities were seen only with whole breast ultrasound.[33] Of these, 70% were less than 1 cm in size and 89% were lymph node negative. The false-positive rate of ultrasonographic findings was 2.4%. These studies indicate that screening breast ultrasound is, therefore, capable of identifying tumors at an early stage.

Many authors do not recommend the use of screening ultrasound outside of a clinical trial; however, this remains controversial.[2,36–38,41] There has not been a particular proof of its benefit in reducing mortality or increasing rates of breast-conserving therapy.[37] Any benefit from screening breast ultrasound would likely be attained from restricting its use to women with breast parenchyma that is significantly dense, limiting the value of screening mammography. Although none of these studies have involved women at high risk for breast cancer, the proportion of younger women in this group would be higher than the general screened population.

Magnetic Resonance Imaging

Recent studies have begun to evaluate the role of MRI in the surveillance of the high-risk woman. MRI is an attractive option in the younger high-risk woman due to is its potential to evaluate breasts in which density may limit the sensitivity of a mammogram. MRI is quite sensitive in detecting invasive breast cancer.[42–45] The disadvantages of MRI as a screening tool, however, are the significant false-positive rates, with a specificity of 67 to 79%,[42] its questionable ability to detect DCIS,[44] and the high cost.[42,43] Spontaneous areas of enhancement may arise with the hormonal fluctuations of younger women, making MRI sometimes difficult to interpret and possibly necessitating a second MR study about 2 weeks after the initial study.[43] On the other hand, mammography certainly has a significant false-positive rate and itself leads to a nontrivial number of benign biopsies.

Of 109 women from the Netherlands at very high lifetime risk (> 25%) of developing breast cancer who had ≥ 50% dense fibroglandular tissue by mammogram receiving breast MRI, the MRI detected CBE- and mammographically-occult breast cancer in 3 patients (2.8%).[42] All three tumors were staged at T1N0. The breast MRI was falsely positive, however, in 6 women, and no tumor became evident in these women during the follow-up period. Suspicion raised by MRI, therefore, needs to be further evaluated before surgical therapy for breast cancer should be initiated. In Germany, MRI was compared to traditional mammogram and ultrasound in high-risk women with a mean age of 39 ± 9 years.[43] All 9 breast cancers were identified with MRI, and 4 patients had multicentric cancer prospectively identified so that the surgical procedure could be correctly altered. There were, however, 5 patients with false-positive MRI leading to biopsy and 19 additional patients with equivocal MRI findings, and short-term follow-up studies were recommended. This increases the cost of the screening program significantly, and findings such as this may limit the utility of MRI.

A Canadian study of 196 high-risk women, about half of whom had a known *BRCA1* or *-2* mutation, demonstrated six invasive cancers and one DCIS identified in the course of 33 biopsies for evaluation of abnormal CBE, mammogram, ultrasound, or MRI.[44] MRI identified all of the invasive carcinomas but did not demonstrate the DCIS, which was seen only on mammography. A total of 23 women had a suspicious MRI and underwent biopsy based on MRI findings. In 15 of these women, MRI was the only abnormal screening test. Cancer was identified in 6/23 women (26%). In 2 of the 6 women with cancer, MRI was the only ab-

normal screening test. Seventeen women had benign biopsies following an abnormal MRI. In the absence of MRI, 19 biopsies would have been performed leading to four cancers detected. The addition of MRI added 14 biopsies and the detection of two additional cancers. Clearly a reliable MRI biopsy system and more experience with the hormonal fluctuations in enhancement could increase the potential for MRI as a screening tool.

A more complete discussion of MRI as a screening modality for high-risk women can be found in Chapter 8 of this book.

CURRENT SURVEILLANCE RECOMMENDATIONS FOR THE HIGH-RISK WOMAN

Although the optimal surveillance plan for high-risk women remains in evolution, there is a basic screening protocol that is generally agreed upon (Table 7-3). Current recommendations for *BRCA1* and *-2* carriers include monthly BSE beginning at 18 to 21 years of age following careful instruction in the process and education regarding follow-up of identified abnormalities; CBE every 4 to 12 months (the standard recommendation is every 6 months) beginning at 25 to 35 years of age; and annual mammography beginning at age 25 to 35, with breast ultrasound as deemed necessary by the radiologist.[1,2,46–51] Monthly BSE may be omitted by

TABLE 7-3 Surveillance Recommendations for High-Risk Women

	BSE	CBE	Mammography	MRI
Slightly elevated risk	? Monthly*	Annually	Annually beginning at the age of 40	Not recommended
Moderately elevated risk	Monthly*	Every 6 months	Annually beginning at the age of 40 or 5–10 years earlier than the age at diagnosis of the youngest affected family member	In context of research protocol at this time
Very high risk (known mutation carriers)	Monthly*	Every 4–6 months	Annually beginning at the age of 25–35	In context of research protocol at this time

BSE = breast self-examination; CBE = clinical breast examination; MRI = magnetic resonance imaging.
*May be omitted if causes significant patient anxiety.

patient choice if this procedure produces significant anxiety.[47] At this time, screening MRI is considered investigational; therefore, it is recommended primarily in the context of a research protocol and should be used in conjunction with, rather than in place of, diagnostic mammography.[2,47]

Recommendations for women who are at moderately high risk for breast cancer based on their family history or as calculated by one of the various mathematical models are centered around the same tools as women at genetic risk. Monthly BSE is still recommended if the woman elects to do so, as is biennial CBE, both beginning in the patient's 20s or when elevated risk is identified. Annual mammographic imaging is recommended beginning 10 years before the age of the youngest affected relative or at the age of 40, whichever is earlier. In this population, mammographic screening rarely begins before age 35.[2,50]

Women at only slightly elevated risk for developing breast cancer are encouraged to follow the same surveillance guidelines as the general population.[51]

ADHERENCE TO BREAST CANCER SCREENING RECOMMENDATIONS

Screening protocols will have an impact only if they are properly followed. There have been several studies to determine to what extent women and their physicians adhere to these recommendations. Overall, many women at high risk for breast cancer do follow the recommended screening guidelines.[52–54] There is, however, significant variability in the vigilance of follow-up.[53,55,56] Women ranked family history of breast cancer their most important motivator for following a surveillance protocol.[56] Whereas perception of breast cancer risk does influence a woman's likelihood of ever having a mammogram, this does not necessarily translate to a high rate of compliance with recommendations for regular repeated screening.[55] A specific recommendation from a physician to have a mammogram is the best predictor of a woman's likelihood of following mammographic screening guidelines.[52,55] Other motivators to participate in a screening program include family history or a high perceived personal risk of developing cancer. Barriers to participation include anxiety regarding the procedure or the radiation involved, embarrassment, and concerns about the cost of the imaging procedure. Age, educational level, and marital status also influence the likelihood of initiating and continuing a screening program. These same variables affected the likelihood of a patient having had a recent clinical breast examination.

A study of women 35 years or older with at least one first-degree relative with breast cancer demonstrated that women whose relative was diagnosed within the past year were more likely to follow the screening guidelines than those whose relative was diagnosed more remotely.[53] Among women at high risk of developing breast cancer, factors that influenced the use of mammographic screening programs included age 40 years or older and positive gene mutation testing.[54] Regular CBE was also more frequently used in women with demonstrated gene mutations. The Framingham Offspring study evaluated mammography use in women with a family history of breast cancer.[57] Most of the women in this study used mammographic screening; however, the rates were higher in women with a first-degree relative with breast cancer. Use of CBE, however, did not differ with family history of breast cancer, nor did it change with the rate of mammographic screening; the two were used complementarily. Women who smoked, however, were noted to be less likely to have had a mammogram than those who did not.

The percentage of women following screening recommendations is higher in Australia than reported in the United States,[53,55,58] possibly because of insurance issues.[58] Out of 461 Australian women considered at high risk for breast cancer based on family history (most were considered to have a family history consistent with an inherited predisposition to breast cancer), 89% were compliant with mammographic screening guidelines, 90% received CBE as recommended, and 51% practiced regular BSE.[58] Women under the age of 40, however, were significantly less often compliant with recommendations than those 40 and above. Uptake of screening recommendations in this study was significantly higher than in the Australian population in general; however, the rate of practice of BSE was similar. Breast cancer anxiety and a woman's desire to take control of her own health matters may increase BSE practice; however, high levels of anxiety were not shown to inhibit practice of BSE among Australian women.[58]

Lerman and colleagues studied 216 women who were offered testing for *BRCA1* or *-2* carrier status based on a family history of genetic mutation.[4] Their behavior following the testing was evaluated at 1 year. Over the course of the year following the testing, 68% of the women who tested positive for a genetic mutation had a mammogram, as compared with 44% of the noncarriers and 54% of the women who had declined to be tested. These percentages were not much different than the percentage of women who underwent mammography in the year before testing (68% of carriers, 55% of noncarriers, and 67% of decliners). Younger noncarriers were not yet encouraged to obtain annual screening, so these numbers were felt to be appropriately lower. In women with a known mutation in the family, evidence of a personal mutation did not motivate these women to comply with annual screening recommendations.

Compliance with recommended surveillance procedures may also be influenced by the patient's emotional and psychosocial situation.[59] Factors may include fear, anxiety, and apprehension both about cancer risk and about the screening process as well as denial or depression regarding their risk status, all of which may lead to psychological distress. There is mixed data on whether anxiety regarding their breast cancer risk motivates women to get mammograms or acts as a barrier.[57]

OUTCOME OF CURRENT SURVEILLANCE STRATEGIES

Indirect Data

Information regarding careful surveillance programs for women at different tiers of breast cancer risk can be gleaned from the placebo arm of studies involving interventions in these women. In the National Surgical Breast and Bowel Program (NSABP) P-1 trial of tamoxifen for breast cancer prevention, high risk was defined as a Gail risk of at least 1.66% over the ensuing 5 years or lobular carcinoma in situ; these women were screened with CBE every 6 months and underwent annual mammographic imaging.[60] The placebo arm of this study included 6,707 women followed for a mean study time of 47.4 months. During follow-up, 244 cancers were identified in this group. There were 175 invasive cancers, giving a cumulative incidence through 69

months of 43.4 per 1,000 women, or an average annual rate of 2.68 per 1,000 women. Of these, 24 were found in the first year of follow-up, 46 in year two, 39 in year three, 31 in year four, 26 in year five, and 9 in year six. There were 69 cases of DCIS, for a 69 months' cumulative incidence of 15.9 per 1,000 women. Among the invasive tumors, ER-positive tumors were more common than ER-negative (5.02 per 1,000 women vs 1.20 per 1,000 women). The majority of the tumors identified were T1 (2 cm or less in size), and 36% were 1 cm or less in size. About two-thirds of the tumors in this group were node negative at diagnosis. There were a total of six breast cancer deaths in the 244 women diagnosed with breast cancer in the placebo group for a mortality rate of 2.5%. Clearly most of the tumors in this surveillance group were diagnosed in early stages; however, the stage at diagnosis was not stratified according to level or risk or by age. Women in this study ranged anywhere from mildly elevated risk to gene mutation carriers, and the ends of this spectrum clearly have different clinical concerns. A subset analysis of women in the P-1 trial demonstrated to be *BRCA* mutation carriers revealed that of the women in the placebo group who developed cancer, 3 had a *BRCA1* mutation and 8 carried a *BRCA2* mutation.[61] Of this group of 11 mutation carriers, 4 had an ER-positive tumor, 5 were ER-negative, and for the remaining 2, the ER status was unknown. This study reported the gene status of only those patients who developed invasive cancer and did not comment on the complement of genetic mutation carriers of the women in the surveillance (placebo) group who did not develop breast cancer. Incidence rates during the surveillance of these women could not be determined. In addition, size and nodal status were not reported in this analysis, therefore it is not possible to compare stage at diagnosis in these women at markedly high risk with the remainder of the study group.

It has been difficult to draw inferences regarding surveillance from the placebo arms of other studies of chemoprevention in women considered high risk. For example, the Italian prevention trial allowed the use of hormone replacement therapy (HRT), which is generally not advised for high-risk women in the United States.[62] However, this may be more practical, because certainly some high-risk women under surveillance will be using HRT whether or not they have been advised to discontinue use. In women using HRT during at least part of this trial, the cumulative incidence of breast cancer was 2.58% in the placebo group. There were no deaths from breast cancer as of this report. Most of the women who developed breast cancer in this study, however, had never used HRT. About half of the 3,566 women comprising the control group in the IBIS chemoprevention trial also used HRT at some time, including 39% during the trial period.[63] A report of preliminary results at a mean follow-up of 50 months (with about half of the women in the placebo group still receiving treatment and another quarter noncomplaint with the study requirements) identified 101 cancers with the majority as expected in women 50 years or older. Of these, 85% were invasive cancers, 59% were node negative, 63% were ER-positive, and 68% were T1 tumors. There were two breast cancer deaths in the placebo group at the time of this analysis. Clearly, in these three studies, surveillance, although not a means of prevention, seems to be effective in finding the majority of these tumors at a fairly early stage.

Control groups from studies of surgical interventions give us even less helpful information regarding the outcome of surveillance, because these trials cannot be randomized. Rebbeck and colleagues used a case-matched approach to examine the risk reduction for breast cancer in *BRCA1* patients following prophylactic oophorectomy at five large participating institutions.[64] The control group in this study consisted of 79 women with *BRCA1* mutations who had neither oophorectomy nor other risk-reducing interventions selected from the registries at the study sites and matched to the study participants. *BRCA2* mutation carriers were not included. The control group was followed for an average of 8.1 years after the time of the matched patient's oophorectomy. In the surveillance group, 30 of the 79 (38%) patients developed breast cancer during the follow-up period. The mean age for developing breast cancer was 43.4. Whereas fewer patients in the oophorectomy group developed cancer (23%), there was not a significant difference in the age of presentation from the surveillance group. Although this study evaluated women who fell in the highest known risk group, details about the size or nodal status of the cancers were not provided.

Women with one breast cancer are well known to be at somewhat elevated risk for developing a contralateral malignancy and tend to be under rather strict surveillance protocols, often with more frequent imaging and CBE than recommended for asymptomatic women. In a 9-year follow-up of women with DCIS, there was a 6.8% risk of developing a contralateral tumor, of which 3.1% were invasive.[65] In women randomized not to receive tamoxifen following unilateral invasive breast cancer, there was an 8% cumulative incidence of contralateral breast cancer at 10 years.[66] As in the oophorectomy study,[64] these contralateral tumors occurred less frequently in the intervention group, but the time from the initial diagnosis to the diagnosis of the contralateral tumor was no different.[66] Routine surveillance, then, appears to demonstrate tumors in high-risk women in a timely fashion and in general at a fairly low stage. A significant percentage, however, are node positive at the time of diagnosis.

Outcome Studies

There have been relatively few studies of the outcome of surveillance for high-risk women, considering that this is the strategy most often used in this group.[67,68] Among the published studies, most

TABLE 7-4 Surveillance Outcomes in High-Risk Women

	Sample Size (n)	Mean Follow-up (months)	Cancers (%)	Invasive (%)	Screen-Detected (%)	Interval Detected (%)	Node Negative
Brekelmans et al[69]	1,198	36.0	35	89	74	26	65
Macmillan[70]	8,783	12.4	103	81	81	19	61
Tilanus-Linthorst et al[71]	679	21.0	26	81	85	15	81
Kollias et al[72]	1,371	22	29	79	66	34	65
Chart and Franssen[73]	986	21.9	24	88	83	17	NR

NR = not reported.

suggest a benefit from organized screening of these women. The majority of cancers in high-risk women who are involved in surveillance protocols are screen detected and are node negative (Table 7-4). The rates of interval cancers and of nodal positivity, however, may be higher in women carrying a known *BRCA* mutation and high-risk women under the age of 40.[69] A retrospective national audit of the breast centers in the United Kingdom examined data regarding the surveillance of women under the age of 50 with significant family histories of breast cancer.[70] The women in this group had a breast cancer incidence over five times that of the general population, confirming that this study had captured a truly high-risk cohort. Yet the mean tumor size in this group was 17.2 mm, and for tumors detected at incident (routine interval) screens it was 13.9 mm. Interval tumors and tumors detected at prevalent initial screens were significantly larger, at 19.9 mm and 19.4 mm, respectively. Similarly, tumors detected at incident screens were more likely to be node negative (63%) than interval tumors (56%) and those identified at the prevalent screen (59%). It is fairly intuitive that tumors detected at incident screens would be more favorable than those detected at the prevalent screen. Interval tumors, however, remain a source of concern. They account for 15 to 34% of cancers identified by surveillance of high-risk women.[69–73] Additionally, interval cancers appear to be more frequent in mutation carriers than women at moderately elevated risk.[69] To qualify as an interval cancer, the tumor must appear in a woman who had had at least one negative screening evaluation, yet these tumors tended to be larger as well as more likely to be node positive.[71] It is unclear whether these are tumors missed at screening or if they represent a subset of cancers that grow particularly rapidly. In the latter case, it is possible that more frequent screening could lead to earlier detection.

As in the general population, a single screening modality is not sufficient for the surveillance of high-risk women. Including interval tumors, over half of cancers detected during the surveillance period were palpable, by either the patient or her clinician.[69,71] The percentage of tumors that were mammographically visible ranged from 62 to 81%,[69,71,72] and a minority of cancers were seen only on an MRI study.[69,71] Therefore BSE, CBE,

and imaging modalities are complementary and should be used together in a surveillance protocol. Physical examination is more useful in patients under the age of 50, who demonstrate more mammographically occult tumors.[71] The stage of cancers detected in this group is similar to that of high-risk patients over 50. However, patients in the surveillance group were more likely to have breast cancer detected as DCIS or Stage I than patients with a family history who present with breast symptoms. Mammography remains important in this younger group, however, because 38% of malignancies in the surveillance group were identified only by mammogram. Although both physical examination and mammographic screening made important contributions to cancer detection in younger women, physical exam did not significantly add to mammographic screening in the postmenopausal population.

Most of the surveillance outcome studies reported a benefit from screening,[70–73] although younger women and those with a known genetic mutation do not benefit as much as those at moderately increased risk.[69] Increasing the frequency of screening may or may not improve the outcome.

SUMMARY

The population of women at increased risk for developing breast cancer is a diverse one, and surveillance recommendations must be tailored to the level of risk for each individual patient. Breast self-examination, clinical breast examination, and breast imaging have all been used in screening these patients. When followed consistently, breast cancer surveillance seems to have a reasonable outcome in high-risk women, although more frequent screening may be indicated in women who are at very high risk. Even with careful surveillance, however, a significant percentage of women at high risk who are diagnosed with breast cancer will have node positive disease, and women making decisions regarding the management of their breast cancer risk should be clearly counseled to this effect. Efforts need to be made by the physician to ensure that high-risk women get referred for organized surveillance and that screening recommendations are followed, and that all of their risk-reducing options are carefully explained to them.

REFERENCES

1. Hartmann LC, Sellers TA, Schaid DJ, et al. Clinical options for women at high risk for breast cancer. Surg Clin North Am 1999;79:1189–2206.

2. Goodwin PJ. Management of familial breast cancer risk. Breast Cancer Res Treat 2000;62:19–33.

3. Stefanek M, Enger C, Benkendorf J, et al. Bilateral prophylactic mastectomy decision making: a vignette study. Prev Med 1999;29:216–21.

4. Lerman C, Hughes C, Croyle RT, et al. Prophylactic surgery decisions and surveillance practices one year following BRCA1/2 testing. Prev Med 2000; 31:75–80.

5. Newcomer LM, Newcomb PA, Trentham-Dietz A, et al. Detection method and breast carcinoma histology. Cancer 2002;95:470–7.

6. Harvey BJ, Miller AB, Baines CJ, Corey PN. Effect of breast self-examination techniques on the risk of death from breast cancer. CMAJ 1997;157: 1205–12.

7. Foster RS Jr, Costanza MC. Breast self-examination practices and breast cancer survival. Cancer 1984; 53:999–1005.

8. Greenwald P, Nasca PC, Lawrence CE, et al. Estimated effect of breast self-examination and routine physician examinations on breast-cancer mortality. N Engl J Med 1978;299:271–3.

9. Feldman JG, Carter AC, Nicastri AD, Hosat ST. Breast self-examination, relationship to stage of breast cancer at diagnosis. Cancer 1981;47:2740–5.

10. Auvinen A, Elovainio L, Hakama M. Breast self-examination and survival from breast cancer: a prospective follow-up study. Breast Cancer Res Treat 1996;38:161–8.

11. Philip J, Harris WG, Flaherty C, et al. Breast self-examination: clinical results from a population-based prospective study. Br J Cancer 1984;50: 7–12.

12. Semiglazov VF, Sagaidak VN, Moiseyenko VM, Mikhailov EA. Study of the role of breast self-examination in the reduction of mortality from breast cancer. The Russian Federation/World Health Organization Study. Eur J Cancer 1993; 29A:2039–46.

13. Semiglazov VF, Moiseyenko VM, Bavli JL, et al. The role of breast self-examination in early breast cancer detection (results of the 5-years USSR/WHO randomized study in Leningrad). Eur J Epidemiol 1992;8:498–502.

14. Semiglazov VF, Moiscyenko VM, Manikhas AG, et al. [Interim results of a prospective randomized study of self-examination for early detection of breast cancer (Russia/St.Petersburg/WHO)]. Vopr Onkol 1999;45:265–71.

15. Thomas DB, Gao DL, Ray RM, et al. Randomized trial of breast self-examination in Shanghai: final results. J Natl Cancer Inst 2002; 94:1445–57.

16. Humphrey LL, Helfand M, Chan BK, Woolf SH. Breast cancer screening: a summary of the evidence for the U.S. Preventive Services Task Force. Ann Intern Med 2002;137:347–60.

17. Brekelmans CT, Collette HJ, Collette C, et al. Breast cancer after a negative screen: follow-up of women participating in the DOM Screening Programme. Eur J Cancer 1992;28A:893–5.

18. Baker LH. Breast Cancer Detection Demonstration Project: five-year summary report. CA Cancer J Clin 1982;32:194–225.

19. Feig SA. Increased benefit from shorter screening mammography intervals for women ages 40-49 years. Cancer 1997;80:2035–9.

20. Lalloo F, Boggis CR, Evans DG, et al. Screening by mammography, women with a family history of breast cancer. Eur J Cancer 1998; 34:937–40.

21. Barton MB, Harris R, Fletcher SW. The rational clinical examination. Does this patient have breast cancer? The screening clinical breast examination: should it be done? How? JAMA 1999;282:1270–80.

22. Bobo JK, Lee NC, Thames SF. Findings from 752,081 clinical breast examinations reported to a national screening program from 1995 through 1998. J Natl Cancer Inst 2000;92:971–6.

23. Baines CJ, Miller AB, Bassett AA. Physical examination. Its role as a single screening modality in the Canadian National Breast Screening Study. Cancer 1989;63:1816–22.

24. Gui GP, Hogben RK, Walsh G, et al. The incidence of breast cancer from screening women according to predicted family history risk: does annual clinical examination add to mammography? Eur J Cancer 2001;37:1668–73.

25. Miller AB, To T, Baines CJ, Wall C. Canadian National Breast Screening Study-2: 13-year results of a randomized trial in women aged 50–59 years. J Natl Cancer Inst 2000;92:1490–9.

26. Kerlikowske K, Grady D, Rubin SM, et al. Efficacy of screening mammography. A meta-analysis. JAMA 1995;273:149–54.

27. Venta LA, Goodhartz LA. Age and interval for screening mammography: whom do you believe? Semin Surg Oncol 1996;12:281–9.

28. Elmore JG, Miglioretti DL, Reisch LM, et al. Screening mammograms by community radiologists: variability in false-positive rates. J Natl Cancer Inst 2002;94:1373–80.

29. Elmore JG, Barton MB, Moceri VM, et al. Ten-year risk of false positive screening mammograms and clinical breast examinations. N Engl J Med 1998; 338:1089–96.

30. Kerlikowske K, Grady D, Barclay J, et al. Positive predictive value of screening mammography by age and family history of breast cancer. JAMA 1993; 270:2444–50.

31. Neugut AI, Jacobson JS. The limitations of breast cancer screening for first-degree relatives of breast cancer patients. Am J Public Health 1995;85:832–4.

32. Porter PL, El Bastawissi AY, Mandelson MT, et al. Breast tumor characteristics as predictors of mammographic detection: comparison of interval- and

screen-detected cancers. J Natl Cancer Inst 1999; 91:2020–8.

33. Kolb TM, Lichy J, Newhouse JH. Comparison of the performance of screening mammography, physical examination, and breast US and evaluation of factors that influence them: an analysis of 27,825 patient evaluations. Radiology 2002;225:165–75.

34. Tardivon AA, Guinebretiere JM, Dromain C, Vanel D. Imaging and management of nonpalpable lesions of the breast. Eur J Radiol 2002;42:2–9.

35. Kaiser JS, Helvie MA, Blacklaw RL, Roubidoux MA. Palpable breast thickening: role of mammography and US in cancer detection. Radiology 2002;223: 839–44.

36. Flobbe K, Nelemans PJ, Kessels AG, et al. The role of ultrasonography as an adjunct to mammography in the detection of breast cancer. A systematic review. Eur J Cancer 2002;38:1044–50.

37. Gordon PB. Ultrasound for breast cancer screening and staging. Radiol Clin North Am 2002;40:431–41.

38. Kopans DB. Breast-cancer screening with ultrasonography. Lancet 1999;354:2096–7.

39. Kaplan SS. Clinical utility of bilateral whole-breast US in the evaluation of women with dense breast tissue. Radiology 2001;221:641–9.

40. Kolb TM, Lichy J, Newhouse JH. Occult cancer in women with dense breasts: detection with screening US — diagnostic yield and tumor characteristics. Radiology 1998;207:191–9.

41. Moon WK, Noh DY, Im JG. Multifocal, multicentric, and contralateral breast cancers: bilateral whole-breast US in the preoperative evaluation of patients. Radiology 2002;224:569–76.

42. Tilanus-Linthorst MM, Obdeijn IM, Bartels KC, et al. First experiences in screening women at high risk for breast cancer with MR imaging. Breast Cancer Res Treat 2000;63:53–60.

43. Kuhl CK, Schmutzler RK, Leutner CC, et al. Breast MR imaging screening in 192 women proved or suspected to be carriers of a breast cancer susceptibility gene: preliminary results. Radiology 2000; 215:267–79.

44. Warner E, Plewes DB, Shumak RS, et al. Comparison of breast magnetic resonance imaging, mammography, and ultrasound for surveillance of women at high risk for hereditary breast cancer. J Clin Oncol 2001;19:3524–31.

45. Kinkel K, Vlastos G. MR imaging: breast cancer staging and screening. Semin Surg Oncol 2001;20: 187–96.

46. Burke W, Daly M, Garber J, et al. Recommendations for follow-up care of individuals with an inherited predisposition to cancer. II. BRCA1 and BRCA2. Cancer Genetics Studies Consortium. JAMA 1997; 277:997–1003.

47. Eisinger F, Alby N, Bremond A, et al. Recommendations for medical management of hereditary breast and ovarian cancer: the French National Ad Hoc Committee. Ann Oncol 1998;9:939–50.

48. Vasen HF, Haites NE, Evans DG, et al. Current policies for surveillance and management in women at risk of breast and ovarian cancer: a survey among 16 European family cancer clinics. European Familial Breast Cancer Collaborative Group. Eur J Cancer 1998;34:1922–6.

49. Morrow M. Identification and management of the woman at increased risk for breast cancer development. Breast Cancer Res Treat 1994;31:53–60.

50. Hoskins KF, Stopfer JE, Calzone KA, et al. Assessment and counseling for women with a family history of breast cancer. A guide for clinicians. JAMA 1995;273:577–85.

51. Dershaw DD. Mammographic screening of the high-risk woman. Am J Surg 2000;180:288–9.

52. Lerman C, Rimer B, Trock B, et al. Factors associated with repeat adherence to breast cancer screening. Prev Med 1990;19:279–90.

53. Lerman C, Daly M, Sands C, et al. Mammography adherence and psychological distress among women at risk for breast cancer. J Natl Cancer Inst 1993;85:1074–80.

54. Peshkin BN, Schwartz MD, Isaacs C, et al. Utilization of breast cancer screening in a clinically based sample of women after BRCA1/2 testing. Cancer Epidemiol Biomarkers Prev 2002;11:1115–8.

55. Vogel VG, Graves DS, Vernon SW, et al. Mammographic screening of women with increased risk of breast cancer. Cancer 1990;66:1613–20.

56. Bondy ML, Vogel VG, Halabi S, Lustbader ED. Identification of women at increased risk for breast cancer in a population-based screening program. Cancer Epidemiol Biomarkers Prev 1992;1:143–7.

57. Murabito JM, Evans JC, Larson MG, et al. Family breast cancer history and mammography: Framingham Offspring Study. Am J Epidemiol 2001;154:916–23.

58. Meiser B, Butow P, Barratt A, et al. Breast cancer screening uptake in women at increased risk of developing hereditary breast cancer. Breast Cancer Res Treat 2000;59:101–11.

59. Lynch HT, Lynch J, Conway T, Severin M. Psychological aspects of monitoring high risk women for breast cancer. Cancer 1994;74:1184–92.

60. Fisher B, Costantino JP, Wickerham DL, et al. Tamoxifen for prevention of breast cancer: report of the National Surgical Adjuvant Breast and Bowel Project P-1 Study. J Natl Cancer Inst 1998;90:1371–88.

61. King MC, Wieand S, Hale K, et al. Tamoxifen and breast cancer incidence among women with inherited mutations in BRCA1 and BRCA2: National Surgical Adjuvant Breast and Bowel Project (NSABP-P1) Breast Cancer Prevention Trial. JAMA 2001;286:2251–6.

62. Veronesi U, Maisonneuve P, Sacchini V, et al. Tamoxifen for breast cancer among hysterectomised women. Lancet 2002;359:1122–4.

63. First results from the International Breast Cancer Intervention Study (IBIS-I): a randomised prevention trial. Lancet 2002;360:817–24.

64. Rebbeck TR, Levin AM, Eisen A, et al. Breast cancer risk after bilateral prophylactic oophorectomy in BRCA1 mutation carriers. J Natl Cancer Inst 1999; 91:1475–9.

65. Webber BL, Heise H, Neifeld JP, Costa J. Risk of subsequent contralateral breast carcinoma in a population of patients with in-situ breast carcinoma. Cancer 1981;47:2928–32.

66. Rutqvist LE, Cedermark B, Glas U, et al. Contralateral primary tumors in breast cancer patients in a randomized trial of adjuvant tamoxifen therapy. J Natl Cancer Inst 1991;83:1299–306.

67. Evans D, Lalloo F, Shenton A, et al. Uptake of screening and prevention in women at very high risk of breast cancer. Lancet 2001;358:889–90.

68. Lerman C, Narod S, Schulman K, et al. BRCA1 testing in families with hereditary breast-ovarian cancer. A prospective study of patient decision making and outcomes. JAMA 1996;275:1885–92.

69. Brekelmans CT, Seynaeve C, Bartels CC, et al. Effectiveness of breast cancer surveillance in BRCA1/2 gene mutation carriers and women with high familial risk. J Clin Oncol 2001;19:924–30.

70. Macmillan RD. Screening women with a family history of breast cancer — results from the British Familial Breast Cancer Group. Eur J Surg Oncol 2000;26:149–52.

71. Tilanus-Linthorst MM, Bartels CC, Obdeijn AI, Oudkerk M. Earlier detection of breast cancer by surveillance of women at familial risk. Eur J Cancer 2000;36:514–9.

72. Kollias J, Sibbering DM, Blamey RW, et al. Screening women aged less than 50 years with a family history of breast cancer. Eur J Cancer 1998;34:878–83.

73. Chart PL, Franssen E. Management of women at increased risk for breast cancer: preliminary results from a new program. CMAJ 1997;157:1235–42.

Newer Imaging Approaches to the High-Risk Woman

R. Edward Hendrick, PhD, FACR
Jean R. Paquelet, MD, FACR
Ellen B. Mendelson, MD, FACR

Whereas screen-film mammography (SFM) is the current standard for breast cancer screening, several new imaging modalities promise to improve breast cancer detection. New technologies proposed for breast cancer screening must equal or exceed the performance of screen-film mammography to find acceptance as a screening tool. As pointed out in a recent review of new technologies for breast cancer screening, a successful new screening modality must identify a higher fraction of early-stage cancers, identify cancers that are likely to progress to become lethal cancers, identify early changes before the appearance of true malignancies, or identify more of the cancers that are missed by SFM.[1] In addition, new technologies must meet the goals of an acceptable screening tool: they must be low risk, easy to perform, noninvasive, cost-effective, widely available, and acceptable to women being screened.[2] In screening for breast cancer, unless a new technology is 100% specific, it also should enable tissue sampling guided by the new technique.

Potential new technologies for screening high-risk women that have been taken to the level of clinical testing are listed in Table 8-1. As Table 8-1 shows, several new technologies other than SFM have been approved by the US Food and Drug Administration (FDA) for clinical use, but in most cases not explicitly for breast cancer screening. Some of these technologies have received FDA approval as diagnostic adjuncts to mammography. Only one of these new technologies, full-field digi-

tal mammography (FFDM), has successfully undergone the clinical testing that would justify its use in screening for breast cancer.

Obtaining FDA approval for screening requires applying the technology to an asymptomatic study population and comparing the performance of the new modality to that of SFM. The study group must include enough breast cancer cases and enough normal cases to compare its sensitivity and specificity to that of SFM. Although sensitivity to breast cancer is the major criterion for comparison, new modalities must keep recall rates adequately low (specificities adequately high) compared with SFM in testing on an asymptomatic study group. Of the new technologies listed, FFDM, breast ultrasound (US), breast magnetic resonance imaging (MRI), and breast scintimammography have received the most extensive testing to date. We will review the adequacy of these newer imaging modalities for screening high-risk women for breast cancer.

FULL-FIELD DIGITAL MAMMOGRAPHY

FFDM is a new technology that was recently approved by the FDA for breast cancer screening and diagnosis. Although digital mammography makes use of new image receptors that replace film and film cassettes, like conventional film-screen mammography, digital mammography still involves low-

TABLE 8-1 Current and Potential New Imaging Technologies for Breast Cancer Screening

Imaging Technology	Current Level of Evidence Supporting Use in Screening	FDA Approved for General Clinical Use	FDA Approved Specifically for Screening
Screen-film mammography (SFM)	Strong	Yes	Yes
Full-field digital mammography (FFDM)	Moderate	Yes	Yes
Ultrasound (US)	Moderate	Yes	No
Magnetic resonance imaging (MRI)	Moderate	Yes	No
Scintimammography	Weak	Yes	No
Positron emission tomography (PET)	Weak	Yes	No
Thermography	Strongly Negative	Yes	No
Computer-Aided Diagnosis or Detection (CAD) Technology			
CAD with SFM	Moderate	Yes	Yes
CAD with FFDM	Moderate	Yes	Yes
CAD with Breast MRI	Weak	No	No
CAD with Breast US	Weak	No	No

*Adapted from Nass SJ et al.[1]

dose x-ray exposure and parallel plate compression of the breast.

To obtain FDA approval, FFDM manufacturers had to demonstrate that their digital mammography systems were not significantly worse than SFM in terms of sensitivity, specificity, and receiver-operator characteristic (ROC) curve areas. The clinical studies by manufacturers to gain FDA approval were conducted primarily among smaller groups of women being examined by diagnostic mammography for work-up of mammographic or palpable findings.[3] It has been pointed out that a method of subject entry that includes suspicious findings on SFM can bias final results toward higher sensitivity for SFM and higher specificity for FFDM.[4] Moreover, the results have limited relevance to the performance of the modality as a screening tool, especially for determining specificity or recall rate in an asymptomatic population, where the prevalence of breast cancer is much lower.

The only completed and published study comparing FFDM to SFM for screening, although not performed exclusively in a high-risk group of screened women, was done on a single manufacturer's prototype system (Senographe 2000D digital mammography prototype, GE Medical Systems, Waukesha, WI) at two study sites.[5,6] The study re-

cruited asymptomatic women coming for their routine screening exams and obtained consent to add an FFDM screening exam to their routine SFM exam. A total of 6,736 women were recruited between August 1997 and June 2000. Results based on biopsy or 1-year follow-up indicated that FFDM had a significantly lower recall rate (11.8% vs 14.9%, $p < .001$) and significantly lower biopsy rate (14 vs 21 per 1,000 exams, $p < .001$) than SFM. However, FFDM had an insignificantly lower sensitivity (54% for FFDM vs 66% for SFM, based on a total of 50 cancers, $p > .1$) and insignificantly smaller ROC curve area (0.74 for FFDM vs 0.80 for SFM, $p = .18$) (Figures 8-1 and 8-2).[6] ROC curve area is an estimate of the probability that the radiologist will make the correct decision about breast cancer being present or absent, averaged over the entire study group.[7,8]

To date, three manufacturers have received FDA approval to market FFDM systems for screening and diagnostic mammography. As of January 2003, there were approximately 400 FFDM systems in clinical use in the United States, with an approximately equal number in use internationally.

Although the previous study is closed to enrollment, a larger study of similar design is now being conducted by the American College of Radiology

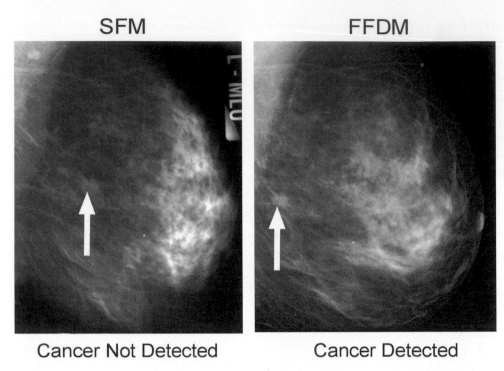

Figure 8-1 Example from the University of Colorado–University of Massachusetts screening study of digital versus screen-film mammography (SFM).[5,6] Screen-film mediolateral oblique (MLO) image is on the left; full-field digital mammography (FFDM) MLO image is on the right. The digital case was correctly interpreted as suspicious for cancer owing to the 1-cm spiculated lesion in the posterior aspect of the breast (*arrow*). The screen-film case was interpreted as negative, primarily owing to positioning differences, which made the lesion slightly less conspicuous and less spiculated in the screen-film MLO view (*arrow*). Images courtesy of Dr. John M. Lewin, University of Colorado Health Sciences Center, Denver, CO[6].

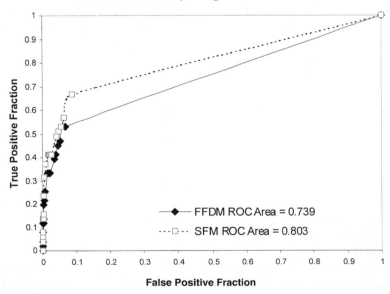

Figure 8-2 Receiver operating characteristic (ROC) curves for screen-film mammography (SFM) and full-field digital mammography (FFDM) in the final analysis of the University of Colorado–University of Massachusetts screening study. Adapted from Lewin JM et al.[6]

Imaging Network (ACRIN).[9] The digital mammographic imaging screening trial (DMIST) is a paired design to compare FFDM from four different manufacturers to SFM. Enrollment of 49,500 women receiving both digital and screen-film mammography is to be completed in October 2003, with 1-year follow-up of each case thereafter. This study is powered to detect a 0.06 difference in ROC curve areas with statistical significance, although it will be late 2004 before final results are available.

The main limitation to widespread use of digital mammography is the cost of the digital mammography system and required digital image archiving in comparison to SFM. Digital mammography systems cost $350,000 (US) to $500,000 (US), compared to approximately $100,000 (US) for a screen-film unit, cassettes, and film processor. Although digital mammography can eliminate the costs of film and film processing, it replaces that with the cost of electronic image archiving.

BREAST ULTRASOUND

Breast ultrasound (US) has become an important diagnostic adjunct to mammography. In the last decade, US used along with mammography has become the standard of care in characterizing breast masses. US provides differentiation between cysts and solid lesions in mammographically detected masses. US is a planar technique, where mammography is a projection (or summation) technique. The sensitivity of mammography is limited in dense breast tissue owing to the superposition of tissues and the similar x-ray attenuation of cancers and normal glandular tissues. US is a tomographic technique, complementary to mammography, by which masses may be depicted in thin slices, unobscured by overlying or underlying glandular tissues.

From the American College of Radiology's Standard for the Performance of the Breast Ultrasound Examination, the accepted indications for performing breast ultrasound are (1) identification and characterization of palpable and nonpalpable abnormalities and further evaluation of clinical and mammographic findings; (2) guidance of interventional procedures; (3) evaluation of problems associated with implants; and (4) treatment planning for radiation therapy.[10]

In addition to these targeted applications in problem solving, interest has increased in using US as an adjunctive screening examination for women with dense breast tissue, where the sensitivity of mammography for the detection of masses is limited. In the largest study to date on US screening (13,547 women), Kolb and colleagues found that mammography showed 98% of cancers in women with fatty breasts, but only 48% of cancers in women with dense breasts.[11] Therefore, in those women with radiographically dense breasts and high breast cancer risk, improved or additional methods of detection are needed.

Although positive results from individual studies of ultrasound screening for breast cancer have been published recently, no benefit was demonstrable for breast cancer screening with ultrasound in the 1980s.[12] Until the last several years, extensions of the applications of US have been resisted widely in the breast imaging community. For example, the 1998 version of the American College of Radiology's *Standard for the Performance of the Breast Ultrasound Examination* specifically enjoined against the use of ultrasound for breast cancer screening: "Although the efficacy of ultrasound as a screening study for occult masses is an area for research at the current time, ultrasound is not indicated as a screening study for masses or microcalcifications."[13] In its 2002 revision, the statement remained unchanged except for the significant deletion of the phrase "for masses" near the end of the sentence.[10] The change reflects the growing experience in clinical practice of performing survey ultrasound, particularly in women with dense fibroglandular tissue and a known or suspected focus of cancer in one breast.[14,15]

Reasons for concern about the use of US as a screening tool include its operator dependence, technical inadequacy, labor intensiveness, inconsistency in interpretation, incompletely proven diagnostic criteria for distinguishing benign from malignant solid masses, the relatively high rate of false positives, the unknown rate of false negatives, and overall inexperience with its use in breast imaging.[16,17] As US has become the imaging method of choice for guiding percutaneous biopsies of masses, and as major advances in ultrasound technology have been incorporated into systems in wide clinical use, ultrasound's applications in breast disease are being reevaluated.

In a 1995 study, Gordon and Goldenberg found 1,575 US-only solid masses in 12,706 women.[18] Forty-four cancers were found for a detection rate of 3.5 per 1,000 women screened (2.8% of solid masses were cancers), similar to the prevalence rate of mammographically detected breast cancers. Because the sensitivity of mammography for breast cancer is high in women with fatty breasts, Kolb and most other investigators have excluded women with fatty breasts from their studies. In 1998, Kolb and colleagues published US findings on 3,626 women with dense breasts and normal clinical and mammographic examinations.[11] Of 215 solid masses, Kolb found that 11 were malignant (3.0 per 1,000 women screened or 5.1% of solid masses were cancers). In 1999, Buchberger and colleagues reported on US screening of 6,113 asymptomatic women whose breasts were not fatty.[20] They found 23 cancers in 21 women (3.8 cancers per 1,000 women screened). Although the yield was low and another 353 incidental masses were aspirated or biopsied, the mean size of the cancers that both Buchberger and Kolb found was 0.9 cm. Kolb's 2002 update compared breast cancer detection rates of mammography, US, and physical examination in women with dense breasts. His results showed that US alone detected 37 of 145 cancers (26%), mammography alone detected 30 cancers (21%), and clinical examination alone detected 4 cancers (3%). Although Kolb's study design was criticized because he alone performed and interpreted all of the studies, most investigators to date report similar experiences of detecting mammographically occult, nonpalpable cancers with US (Figure 8-3).

Against the background of finding additional US-only cancers, screening sonography, along with other screening methods, has the drawbacks of false-positives and false-negatives. Follow-up studies and unnecessary procedures generated by false-positive US screens can cause increased anxiety, morbidity, and cost.

Effective use of US for screening requires established diagnostic criteria for solid masses. Stavros and colleagues found that uniformly echogenic masses, which are usually fat, are always benign. Circumscribed, macrolobulated, or oval masses, typically fibroadenomas, had a less than 2% likelihood of being malignant.[21] This 2% likelihood of malignancy was the same as that used by Sickles for his mammographic assessment of probably benign lesions.[22] Stavros found that irregularly shaped masses with angular or indistinct margins suggested malignancy. Many masses, however, fell into an indeterminate middle ground and were sampled. Although useful in interpretation, Stavros's criteria require multicenter revalidation using a lexicon of standardized descriptors for lesion characterization and reporting.[23] See Figure 8-4 for examples.

Although simple cysts may be diagnosed with nearly 100% accuracy if the lesions are anechoic, sharply defined, round or oval, and exhibit posterior acoustic enhancement,[24] small simple cysts only a few millimeters in diameter may be unclassifiable, and may demonstrate the low-level internal echoes that define the category of complicated cysts.[25] Complicated cysts and solid masses with benign ultrasound features are difficult to distinguish. Both are commonly encountered as incidental findings when whole-breast screening ultrasound is performed. The management of these masses has been inconsistent, varying from tissue sampling (fine needle aspiration or core biopsy) to short interval follow-up, the customary recommendation for lesions seen at mammography that are assessed as probably benign. In his 1998 screening study for breast cancer, Kolb noted that 27% of the women he scanned had cysts and another 3.6% had complicated cysts, all of which he assessed as benign or probably benign.[11] These lesions were without change, except for waxing and waning of cysts, on follow-up studies. Nevertheless, in several published studies, incidental findings on screening ultrasound prompted additional biopsies that were benign and accounted for up to 10% of the total number of biopsies.

Using standardized terminology, equipment, technique, and patient management approaches, a multicenter ACRIN trial comparing screening US to screening mammography will open in late 2003. The study group will consist of women with breasts at least 25% dense and at least a 25% lifetime risk of breast cancer, as determined by Gail or Claus Models. If the results of individual studies are corroborated in this multicenter effort, US breast cancer screening in a defined patient group, such as high-risk women, may be advocated.

Currently, in many breast imaging practices, the published and anecdotal diagnoses of additional invasive cancers in women with dense breasts and at

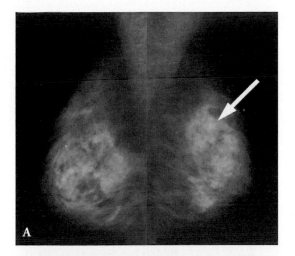

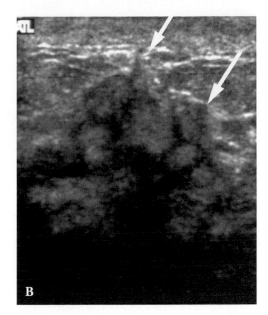

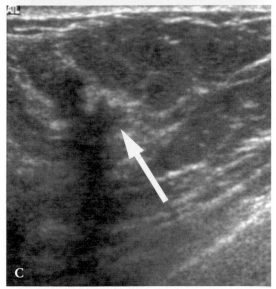

Figure 8-3 Ultrasound depicts bilateral invasive lobular carcinomas not seen mammographically. *A*, Bilateral mediolateral oblique views of the breasts show very dense breast tissue. No discrete masses can be identified; architectural distortion (*arrow*) is present in the left upper breast in an area of thickening perceived by the patient. *B*, Ultrasound (linear transducer, 12-5MHz) delineates large, hypoechoic area of cancer with spicules (*arrows*) and destruction of tissue planes in the left breast in the area of thickening. *C*, Right breast ultrasound image of smaller focus of nonpalpable invasive lobular carcinoma (*arrow*) in the upper breast, unsuspected clinically or mammographically.

least one known malignant lesion have led to survey sonography of remaining areas of the affected breast and the contralateral breast.

Operator dependence, inconsistency, false-positives that generate additional testing, and the labor-intensive nature of ultrasound remain as major impediments to the adoption of screening breast US. One answer to these problems was addressed by automated US systems developed in the late 1970s and 1980s in response to fears that radiation from mammography might cause breast cancer. These automated systems are now extinct, and the breast radiation doses from mammography are so low that radiation-induced cancers from mammography are

more of a psychological, than physical, concern. Automated US systems generated a large number of images, but the resolution was relatively high and, most importantly, the results were repeatable. This repeatability facilitates US follow-up of benign and probably-benign lesions, which is more difficult with handheld breast US as performed currently. The revival of automated systems is again being considered, particularly if the examinations can be correlated anatomically with mammographic positioning. Automated systems also may enable comparative studies of the efficacy of US and mammography or US and breast MRI for breast cancer screening.[26,27]

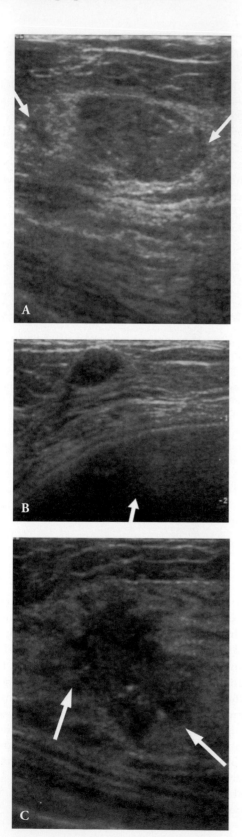

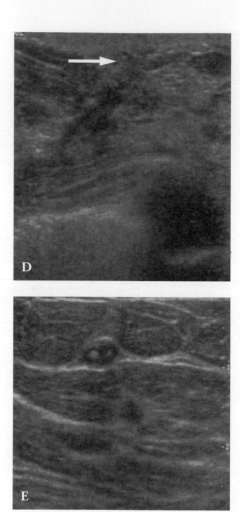

Figure 8-4 Solid breast lesions on ultrasound. *A*, Heterogeneous, oval, horizontally oriented mass (*arrows*) has circumscribed margin. Margin and shape characteristics are benign. Diagnosis: adenosis and fibrocystic change. *B*, Oval mass with microlobulated margin is a small, poorly differentiated invasive ductal carcinoma that simulates a fibroadenoma. Microlobulation suggests malignancy. Patient has a silicone implant (*arrow*). *C*, Infiltrating ductal carcinoma and ductal carcinoma in situ. Spiculated, hypoechoic, irregularly shaped mass (*arrows*) situated in echogenic fibroglandular breast tissue contains small, bright echogenic foci representing microcalcifications. *D*, Lumpectomy scar. Spiculated, irregularly shaped, vertically oriented lesion cannot be distinguished from carcinoma without clinical correlation. The scar extends to the skin (*arrow*). *E*, New small oval mass containing calcifications simulates a small fibroadenoma or papilloma; as a new finding seen mammographically in the fatty breast of an elderly woman, it was biopsied. Diagnosis: infiltrating ductal carcinoma.

BREAST MAGNETIC RESONANCE IMAGING

Over the past decade, MRI of the breast has become an important diagnostic adjunct to mammography and breast ultrasound for evaluation of breast cancer.[28-31] For example, in a series of 463 diagnostic patients imaged with breast MRI between January 1996 and December 1997, Fischer and colleagues found that contrast-enhanced breast MRI alone found multifocality in 30 of the 42 patients with multifocal breast cancer, multicentricity in 24 of 50 patients with multicentric breast cancer, and contralateral cancers in 15 of 19 cases of bilateral breast cancer.[38] Breast MRI correctly altered therapy in 66 patients (14.3%), while prompting biopsies in 16 patients (3.5%) with benign findings.

When used with an intravenous injection of an FDA-approved MR contrast agent, gadopentetate dimeglumine (Gd-DTPA), breast MRI has been shown to be sensitive to 83 to 100% of invasive breast cancers above a few millimeters in size.[28-30] A summary analysis of breast MRI cases obtained primarily from a diagnostic study population showed an overall sensitivity to breast cancer of 96%.[28]

The importance of using Gd-DTPA is illustrated in Figure 8-5, which shows one of 64 slices from a bilateral MR exam of a woman with a palpable le-

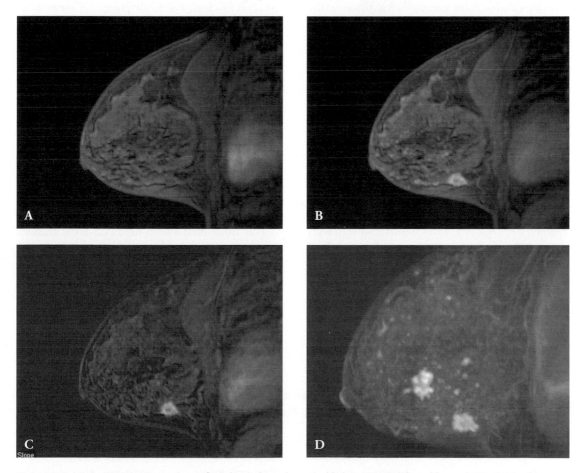

Figure 8-5 *A*, A precontrast scan (one of 64 slices) through a palpable lesion in a unilateral breast MRI. *B*, The first postcontrast scan through the same slice, where a spiculated lesion with rim enhancement becomes visible owing to the presence of gadopentetate dimeglumine (Gd-DTPA) selectively taken up by the lesion. *C*, A subtracted image (*B* minus *A*), which eliminates tissues not taking up Gd-DTPA. Subtracted images are used to construct maximum intensity projection (MIP) images of the entire breast (*D*). The MIP image shows the presence of a second lobulated and spiculated enhancing lesion, which was not palpable. Both enhancing lesions were determined by core biopsy and pathology to be invasive ductal carcinoma.

sion not visible on mammography. The first image (Figure 8-5*A*) was acquired before giving contrast agent. The second image (Figure 8-5*B*) was acquired approximately 2 minutes after injection of Gd-DTPA. Figure 8-5*C* is a subtracted image, where precontrast images are subtracted from postcontrast images. Use of Gd-DTPA not only makes the lesion visible, but provides additional details of lesion morphology, including irregular margins and rim enhancement, both adding to the suspicion of malignancy. Figure 8-5*D* is a maximum-intensity projection through the entire breast, showing a second lesion with rapid, focal enhancement and irregular margins. At histology, both lesions were determined to be invasive ductal carcinoma. Both were indistinguishable from normal breast tissue in the precontrast images but were highly suspicious based on morphology after administration of Gd-DTPA.

The high sensitivity of contrast-enhanced breast MRI to breast cancer in diagnostic studies suggests that breast MRI might also be useful in screening for breast cancer, especially in women at high risk. This has been tested in only a few published studies on high-risk women to date, each study involving screening of a limited number of high-risk women (under 200) and a limited number of breast cancers (6 to 13). [28-30]

In a study of subjects recruited between March 1996 and October 1998, Kuhl and colleagues screened 192 high-risk, asymptomatic women with breast MRI, mammography, and breast ultrasound.[32] The median age was 38 years (range 18 to 65 years), and nine cancers were detected for a cancer detection rate of 4.7% among these high-risk women.

The breast MRI techniques used in this study were bilateral imaging at high field (1.5 tesla) with two-dimensional (planar) acquisitions in the transaxial plane with 4-mm-thick slices. One precontrast and nine postcontrast scans covering both breasts were taken after bolus injection of Gd-DTPA at the standard dose of 0.1 mmol per kilogram of body mass (a 150-lb woman has a mass of 68 kg and would receive a dose of 6.8 mmol, typically a 13.6 mL volume of Gd-DTPA, which has a typical concentration of 0.5 mol/liter). Fat suppression was not used in their study, but precontrast images were subtracted from postcontrast images to aid in identification of enhancing lesions.

Table 8-2 indicates the sensitivity, specificity, positive predictive value, negative predictive value, and diagnostic accuracy of the three imaging modalities tested on this high-risk study group. Of greatest interest is that breast MRI had a sensitivity of 100%, compared with 33% for both mammography and breast US in these high-risk women.[31] Breast MRI also had high specificity: 95%, versus 93% for mammography and 80% for breast US. This screening study was designed as a 5-year study, and results of the entire study period should be available soon.

Another study conducted by Warner and colleagues screened 196 high-risk women between November 1997 and May 2000 with breast MRI, mammography, US, and breast physical examination.[33] The study group age ranged from 26 to 59 years, with a mean age of 43.3 years.

This study used a high-field (1.5 tesla) scanner to obtain bilateral three-dimensional (volume) breast MR images. Image datasets were acquired every 90 seconds, once before and up to seven times after injection of Gd-DTPA at 0.1 mmol per kilogram of body mass. Additional unilateral contrast-enhanced imaging was done at higher temporal resolution (approximately every 20 seconds).

TABLE 8-2 Performance of Three Modalities in Screening High-Risk Women for Breast Cancer

Diagnostic Index	Mammography	Breast Ultrasound	Breast MRI
Sensitivity	33% (3 of 9)	33% (3 of 9)	100% (9 of 9)
Specificity	93% (89 of 96)	80% (77 of 96)	95% (91 of 96)
Positive predictive value	30% (3 of 10)	14% (3 of 22)	64% (9 of 14)
Negative predictive value	94% (89 of 95)	93% (77 of 83)	100% (91 of 91)
Diagnostic accuracy	88% (92 of 105)	76% (80 of 105)	95% (100 of 105)

Adapted from Kuhl CK et al.[32]

Six invasive breast cancers, all of which were node negative and less than 1 cm in diameter, and one noninvasive breast cancer were found in the study group, for an invasive cancer rate of 3.1% among high-risk women. Breast MRI detected all six invasive cancers, whereas breast ultrasound detected three, and mammography alone and clinical breast exam alone each detected two invasive cancers.[33] Table 8-3 summarizes the performance of each imaging modality in this study.

Again in this study, the sensitivity of breast MRI to invasive breast cancer was 100%, compared with a much lower sensitivity for other detection methods, although the study included only six cancer cases. The negative predictive value of breast MRI was 100%, with a reasonably high specificity (91%). This specificity was the result of 23 women being recommended for biopsy based on the breast MRI exam, with 17 false positives. Thus, the specificity for breast MRI was 173 true negatives out of 190 noncancer cases (91%).

In a third breast MRI study, Stoutjesdijk and colleagues reviewed the records of 179 high-risk women imaged between November 1994 and February 2001.[34] Seventy-five of these women received both MRI and mammography exams within 4 months of one another. ROC curves were constructed for both MRI and mammography.

Breast MRI was conducted on a 1.5 tesla scanner using 3-D bilateral imaging once before and five times after administration of Gd-DTPA at a rate of 0.2 mmol/kg body mass, double the normal dose. Scanning was performed in the axial or coronal plane with a temporal resolution of 80 to 88 seconds per acquisition.

Table 8-4 indicates the diagnostic accuracy of mammography and breast MRI in this study under two different assumptions: one assuming that ACR Breast Imaging Reporting and Data System (BI-RADS) categories 3, 4, and 5 were positive, another assuming that only BI-RADS categories 4 and 5 were positive, while lower BI-RADS assessment categories were considered negative. For the entire cohort of 179 women (13 cancers), the ROC curve areas were 0.74 for mammography and 0.99 for breast MRI; this difference was statistically significant (p = .02). For the 75 women who had both exams, the ROC curve areas were 0.70 for mammography and 0.98 for breast MRI, with the difference at the margin of statistical significance (p = .05).[34]

A fourth study added breast MRI to breast physical examination and mammography in screening high-risk women who had a breast density of greater than 50%.[33,34] Out of a total of 109 women screened, MRI detected breast cancers in three women, while incurring no false-negative cases. The three MRI-detected breast cancers were occult to mammography and physical examination. MRI correctly designated four high-risk cases as benign, while incurring six false-positive cases. Although not comparing MRI to other modalities, this study suggests that triaging high-risk women to different screening modalities depending on risk status and breast density may have merit.

There were some important common elements to these breast MRI studies. All studies were conducted at high field (1.5 tesla). Higher field strength provides higher signal-to-noise ratios for the same spatial parameters, making images more reliable for detecting enhancing cancers. Higher field strength, which results in more uniform magnetic fields, also permits the use of fat suppression, which reduces spurious signals in subtracted images.

TABLE 8-3 Performance of Four Modalities in Screening High-Risk Women for Breast Cancer

Diagnostic Index	CBE	Mammography	Breast Ultrasound	Breast MRI
Sensitivity	33% (2 of 6)	33% (2 of 6)	60% (3 of 5)*	100% (6 of 6)
Specificity	99.5%	99.5%	93%	91%
Positive predictive value	66%	66%	19%	26%
Negative predictive value	97%	97%	99%	100%

Adapted from Warner E et al.[33]

*One cancer case was not imaged by ultrasound screening and is excluded from the total number of cancers for this modality.

CBE = clinical breast examination; MRI = magnetic resonance imaging.

TABLE 8-4 Performance of Mammography
and Breast MRI in a Retrospective Evaluation of High-Risk Women

Diagnostic Index	Mammography (3–5 positive)	Breast MRI (3–5 positive)	Mammography (4 or 5 positive)	Breast MRI (4 or 5 positive)
Sensitivity	42%	100%	42%	92%
Specificity	96%	93%	99%	98%
Positive predictive value	33%	43%	63%	71%
Negative predictive value	97%	100%	97%	99.6%

Adapted from Stoutjesdijk MJ et al.[34]

All studies employed bilateral imaging. Bilateral imaging is essential for screening, as it allows imaging of both breasts with a single injection of contrast agent. Bilateral imaging is also important in diagnostic evaluation, as MRI evaluations of the asymptomatic, mammographically normal contralateral breast in women with a known breast cancer have found bilateral breast cancer in approximately 5% of women.[37,38]

All mammography and breast MRI studies were interpreted using some variation of the ACR BI-RADS, even though the BI-RADS for breast MRI is still in draft form.[22] BI-RADS uses standardized diagnostic categories: 1 = normal, 2 = benign findings, 3 = probably benign, 4 = suspicious for breast cancer, 5 = highly suspicious for breast cancer. BI-RADS also uses specific language to describe breast findings that correlate with the likelihood of malignancy.

Three of the breast MRI screening studies made use of previous results from Kuhl and colleagues, which revealed that in premenopausal women, false-positive findings from contrast-enhanced breast MRI varied during the subject's menstrual cycle.[39] In that study, spurious enhancement of normal breast tissues was highest in the first and fourth week, lower in the third week, and lowest in the second week after menses. Thus, in all three studies, premenopausal subjects were imaged only during the second week of their menstrual cycle.

All studies were performed with adequate temporal resolution to include dynamic assessment of contrast agent uptake. Readers in all three studies used a combination of lesion morphology and dynamic information to help separate benign from malignant enhancing breast lesions.[38] Morphologic criteria that provide the greatest specificity for separating benign from malignant lesions include the shape and margins of contrast-enhancing lesions. Round, oval, or lobular shapes are typically benign, whereas linear, dendritic, or spiculated shapes are more typically malignant. Well-defined margins are typically benign, whereas ill-defined margins are more often malignant.

Contrast-enhancement features can increase specificity. Uniform enhancement is more typical of benign lesions, inhomogeneous enhancement is moderately suspicious, and rim enhancement is highly suspicious for malignancy. Rate of uptake of enhancing lesions provides weak separation of benign from malignant, with slowly enhancing lesions more likely to be benign, rapidly enhancing lesions (with signals increasing by 80% or more from pre- to early postcontrast images) more likely to be malignant. Applying enhancement rate alone with these criteria to separate benign from malignant, Kuhl and colleagues achieved a specificity of only 37%.[40]

Using the detailed shape of enhancement curves adds greater specificity (Figures 8-6 and 8-7). Benign lesions tend to have a continuous increase in contrast agent uptake and therefore continuous signal increase. In a study of 266 cases, 101 of which were cancers, Kuhl and colleagues found that only 6% of cases with continuous enhancement were malignant. Malignant lesions are more likely to take up contrast rapidly and then either maintain that enhancement, with signal staying constant (64% of lesions with plateau enhancement were malignant), or demonstrate a washout in contrast agent, decreasing in signal between 3 and 8 minutes after contrast agent administration (87% of lesions with rapid uptake and washout were malignant).[40] See Figure 8-7 for examples of malignant enhancement curves.

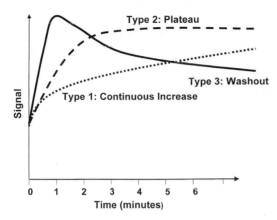

Figure 8-6 The time courses of contrast enhancement correlates with degree of suspicion. Type 1 curves (*dotted*) show continuous signal increase from pre- to postcontrast scans and have a relatively low probability of malignancy. Type 2 curves (*dashed*) show signal increase by at least 80% and then a plateau, reflecting an intermediate suspicion of malignancy. Type 3 curves (*solid*) increase by at least 80% from pre- to postcontrast within 3 minutes of injection and then wash out, indicating high suspicion of malignancy. Adapted from Kuhl CK, et al.[39]

Fischer and colleagues used their extensive data acquired on diagnostic subjects who underwent breast MRI to develop a quantitative approach to weighing each of the morphologic and contrast enhancement features to give the best separation between benign and malignant lesions.[38] Greatest weight was given to contrast-enhancement properties: amount of signal increase, curve shape, and non-uniform or rim enhancement patterns. Lesser weight was given to lesion shape and margins. Another study attempted to develop a decision-tree approach to determining which lesions are suspicious enough to justify biopsy based on MR findings alone, but this study used pulse sequences that captured only limited dynamic information.[40] The draft version of the ACR BI-RADS for breast MRI uses nomenclature for breast MRI reporting that accounts for imaging factors that help separate benign from malignant lesions, including all of the features listed above, without placing quantitative weighting factors on different lesion parameters.[22]

Because both details of contrast enhancement and detailed lesion morphology are important in separating benign from malignant lesions, new techniques in breast MR have focused on getting adequate temporal resolution (completing acquisi-

tion of images covering one or both breasts in less than 2 minutes) while getting high spatial resolution (having pixels that are 1 mm or less on a side and slices that are less than 2.5 mm thick). Because cancers typically achieve peak enhancement within about 2 minutes of giving contrast agent, a temporal resolution of 2 minutes or less is needed to determine the detailed shape of the enhancement curve. It is generally recognized that pulse sequences taking 4 minutes or more to acquire a set of images covering the entire breast may be highly sensitive to breast cancer but are inadequate to determine the detailed shape of enhancement curves and therefore may sacrifice specificity.

In the past, it has been a technical challenge to image the entire breast (and especially both breasts) rapidly enough to capture both detailed dynamic information and high spatial resolution. As a result, a decision had to be made by the radiologist to pursue either high spatial resolution or high temporal resolution breast MRI. The Rodeo sequence developed by Harms and colleagues obtained submillimeter spatial resolution on a single breast, with good fat suppression, but had the limitations of being a unilateral approach with 4- to 5-minute scan times.[42] Thus, Rodeo provided excellent morpho-

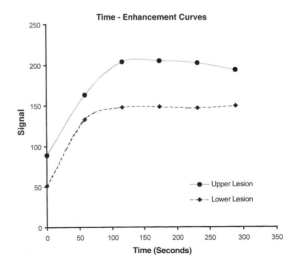

Figure 8-7 Time enhancement curves from the two lesions shown in Figure 8-5*D*. The upper lesion demonstrates signal increase by more than 100%, with a Type 3 enhancement curve. The lower lesion demonstrates more than 100% signal increase with a Type 2 enhancement curve. Both lesions were invasive ductal carcinoma at histologic diagnosis.

logic information and had high sensitivity, but lacked adequate temporal resolution to obtain detailed dynamic information about contrast uptake. Studies applying Rodeo to a diagnostic study group reported a specificity of only 37%.[42]

On the other hand, the screening studies described above performed bilateral imaging in times less than 2 minutes, but had thicker slices (3 to 6 mm) and larger in-plane pixel dimensions, limiting a detailed evaluation of lesion morphology.

New developments in MR gradient systems and pulse sequence techniques have made it possible to achieve both adequate temporal resolution and high spatial resolution simultaneously. For the past 2 years at Northwestern Memorial Hospital, we have used Siemens 1.5T MR Systems (Sonata or Symphony Quantum, Siemens Medical Systems, Iselin, NJ) to obtain high-resolution 3-D fat-suppressed bilateral breast scans in times short enough to obtain excellent dynamic information. These clinical techniques provide both high spatial resolution in three dimensions and detailed dynamic information. For example, 120 sagittal slices with 1 mm slice thickness through each breast in a bilateral acquisition, with 0.7 mm by 0.9 mm in-plane resolution, can be done in 74 seconds. This basic sequence is repeated once before contrast and four or five times after contrast agent administration with exactly the same spatial parameters and slice positions. Precontrast images are subtracted from each set of postcontrast images to highlight tissues enhancing with Gd-DTPA. This gives a clear depiction of vessels larger than 1 to 2 mm in diameter and of enhancing breast lesions larger than 2 to 3 mm in diameter. The nearly isotropic voxel sizes permit reconstruction of planar images in any orientation, along with viewing of the 3-D subtracted images collectively through the use of maximum-intensity projection. An example of a case of invasive lobular carcinoma is given in Figure 8-8.

Breast MRI has limitations, especially for screening. Current breast MRI exams require 45 minutes to 1 hour of scanner time, injection of Gd-DTPA, and careful interpretation of resulting images. A typical exam can generate several hundred to several thousand images, depending on scanning techniques. Interpretation of these images requires the use of an independent review console with functionality to page through images and the software necessary to evaluate the dynamics of contrast

agent uptake. Very few sites can afford the scanner time, personnel, and cost of the required equipment to perform high-quality breast MRI even for diagnostic evaluation. Even fewer sites are equipped to perform screening breast MRI.

We and others are addressing this issue by developing imaging protocols that achieve comparable results to those described above in a shorter total scan time. We can now complete the imaging for bilateral screening in less than 15 minutes of actual scan time, which shortens the total time required for a breast MRI screening exam to 30 minutes or less.

Another possible limitation of breast MRI is its performance in detecting ductal carcinoma in situ (DCIS). Breast MRI does not detect calcifications, the most common radiographic sign of DCIS. Some have hypothesized that breast MRI may be less sensitive to low-grade DCIS while being reasonably sensitive to poorly differentiated DCIS (R. Holland, private communication December 2002). In an analysis of missed breast cancers by contrast-enhanced breast MRI among diagnostic cases, DCIS was missed by breast MRI in 13 of 20 cases (65%), whereas invasive breast cancer was missed in only 28 of 334 cases (8.5%).[43]

Finally, screening high-risk women for breast cancer with contrast-enhanced breast MRI requires the ability to localize or obtain core tissue samples directed by the MR exam. A reasonable fraction (probably 50 to 85%) of suspicious lesions visible with contrast-enhanced MRI can be seen with second-look US.[44] US provides a simpler method to direct core biopsy tissue sampling. Even so, it is important that sites performing MR screening be able to direct biopsies by MRI. Several manufacturers have developed MR-compatible guidance and core biopsy systems, but cost, scanner time, and personnel capable of performing the procedure still limit the availability of this important link in the breast MR imaging chain (see Figure 8-8).

NUCLEAR MEDICINE

Sestamibi Scintimammography

^{99m}Tc Sestamibi is a radiopharmaceutical whose most common use is in evaluation of cardiac perfusion. In addition to its affinity for myocardial cells, sestamibi accumulates in several types of cancer cells, including breast cancer. In 1998, sestamibi

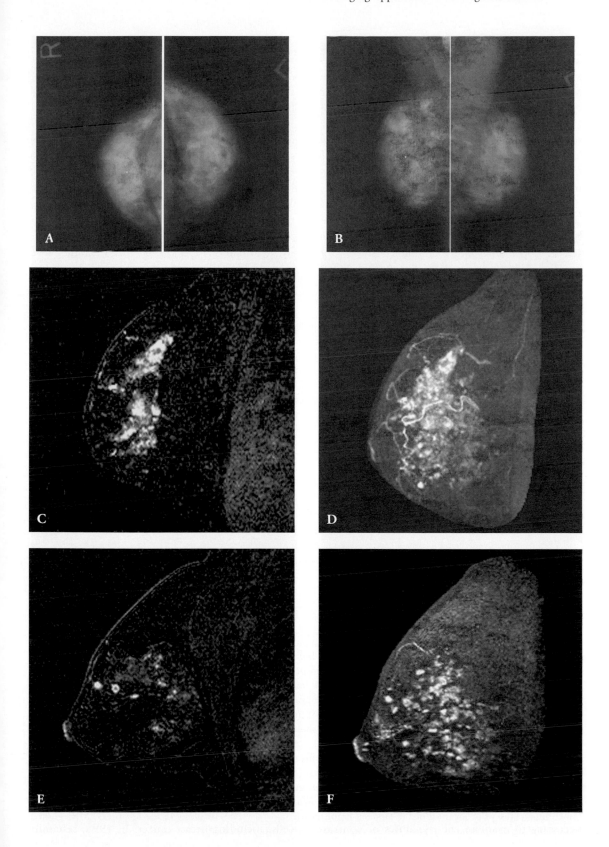

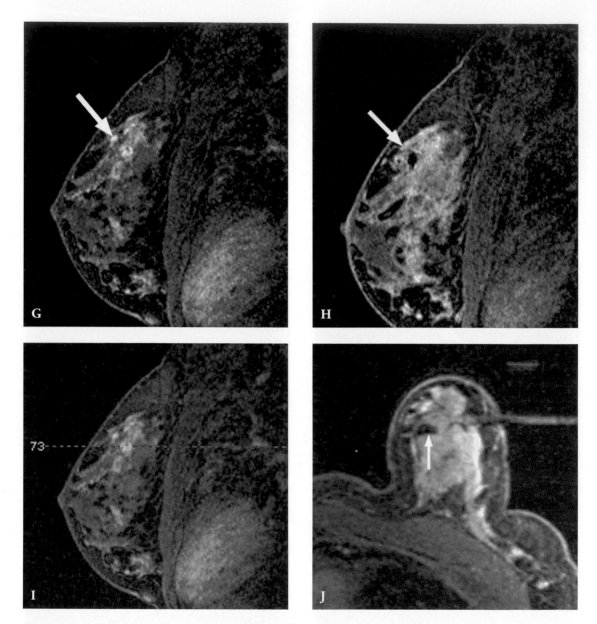

Figure 8-8 Craniocaudal (CC) (*A*) and mediolateral oblique (MLO) (*B*) mammograms of a 48-year-old woman diagnosed to have invasive lobular carcinoma of the right breast. *C*, One of 120 1-mm-thick subtracted postcontrast sagittal MR images through the right breast acquired immediately after injection shows significant uptake of Gd-DTPA in a large region of the breast. *D*, A subtracted MIP image of the entire right breast created from all 120 1-mm-thick slices, also in the sagittal projection, shows the extent of invasive lobular carcinoma. *E*, One of 120 1-mm thick subtracted postcontrast sagittal images of the left breast of the same woman, acquired immediately after contrast injection and simultaneously with the right breast images, showing several areas of focal enhancement. *F*, A subtracted MIP image of the entire left breast created from all 120 1-mm-thick slices, also in the sagittal projection, shows a number of areas of focal enhancement. *G*, MRI-guided breast biopsy was targeted to sample tissue from the lesion showing rim enhancement in the upper aspect of the breast (*arrow*). *H*, An MRI-compatible vacuum-biopsy was performed, leaving the tissue void as shown in this image (*arrow*). *I*, After tissue sampling, a metallic marking clip was placed, demonstrating a signal void artifact in an axial image (*J*), (*arrow*) which has been cross-referenced by the dashed line to the prior location of the targeted lesion in the sagittal view. Histology in the left breast MRI-guided tissue sampling demonstrated stromal fibrosis and proliferative fibrocystic change.

was approved by the FDA for use in breast imaging. Sestamibi is marketed under the name Miraluma (Dupont Pharmaceuticals, Wilmington, DE). Sestamibi scintimammography requires no patient preparation, except that the exam should be delayed several weeks after invasive breast procedures, because postoperative changes can cause false-positive results. The patient receives an intravenous bolus injection of 20 to 30 milliCuries (mCi) (740 to 1,100 megabecquerel [MBq] of sestamibi. Beginning 5 to 10 minutes postinjection, lateral views of each breast are acquired using a conventional gamma camera. These views take about 10 minutes each to acquire and are performed with the woman lying prone on an imaging table overlay so that the breast being imaged is pendent and the gamma camera head is in contact with the lateral breast. Some imagers also obtain a supine or prone anterior view, primarily to evaluate the axilla. In the anterior view, evaluation of the breast is limited owing to overlapping activity in the liver and heart.

Images are evaluated for focal areas of increased uptake that may represent breast cancer. Focal uptake of the radionuclide can be seen in axillary lymph node metastasis, but sensitivity of the technique for axillary spread is poor.[45] Other causes of increased uptake of the tracer are proliferative fibrocystic change and inflammation.

To date, there have been no published studies of the use of sestamibi in breast cancer screening. The published series detailing the sensitivity and specificity of sestamibi in breast cancer have all been performed on patients with palpable or mammographically detected breast abnormalities, or both (Figure 8–9). Table 8-5 summarizes the results of these studies.[45] The entry for Taillefer summarizes data from 20 previously conducted studies published between 1994 and 1998.[47] Other entries in Table 8-5 are individual studies of sestamibi applied to diagnostic study groups.[48–51] The results of these studies, performed in a diagnostic setting, suggest that sestamibi would be of limited utility as a primary or secondary breast cancer screening tool.

All but the most recent series of Khalkhali and colleagues[52] indicated sensitivities in the 81 to 89% range. In these studies, however, nearly 70% of subjects had palpable abnormalities. Khalkhali and colleagues reported a lower sensitivity of 71% and suggested that this lower sensitivity is due to their study population having fewer patients (45%) with palpable masses.[52] In all studies, sensitivity was higher for larger, palpable lesions than for smaller, nonpalpable ones.

The reported sestamibi series all demonstrate limited sensitivity of the technique for detection of small lesions. In these series, the reported sensitivity of the technique for detection of breast cancers in the range of 10 to 15 mm is about 55 to 60%.[53] Specificity of sestamibi for breast cancer in these diagnostic patients ranged from 52 to 89%. Specificity of the technique in a screening population is unknown.

The use of sestamibi in screening women at high risk for breast cancer would require stronger evidence that the technique is able to detect small, early-stage lesions, especially those not detected by physical examination or x-ray mammography. It has been suggested that development of dedicated high-resolution nuclear imaging cameras for scintimammography may allow detection of small lesions, but this has yet to be demonstrated. The cost of a sestamibi imaging study is high compared with x-ray mammography or breast US, making it less attractive for use in a screening setting. In addition, sestamibi scintimammography is limited by the lack of availability of localization and biopsy systems for use with scintigraphic guidance.

Positron Emission Tomography

The only FDA-approved radiopharmaceutical for breast imaging with positron emission tomography (PET) is the glucose analog 2-(^{18}F)-fluoro-2-deoxy-D-glucose (FDG). Its use in oncologic imaging is based on increased glucose metabolism in cancer cells compared with normal tissue. FDG is transported into the cell, like glucose, and is phosphorylated but cannot be further metabolized. Because it is a charged molecule, it cannot diffuse out of the cell and is trapped. When ^{18}F decays, it emits a positron, a positively charged antiparticle to the electron. When positrons and electrons interact, they annihilate one another and emit two 511 kiloelectron volt photons, which are emitted at 180 degrees relative to one another. The two photons arrive at two opposing detectors in the PET scanner, determining the line on which the interaction occurred. By making use of the slight time difference in arrival, the specific point of interaction along that line is determined. The PET scanner produces multiplanar tomographic images for evaluation.

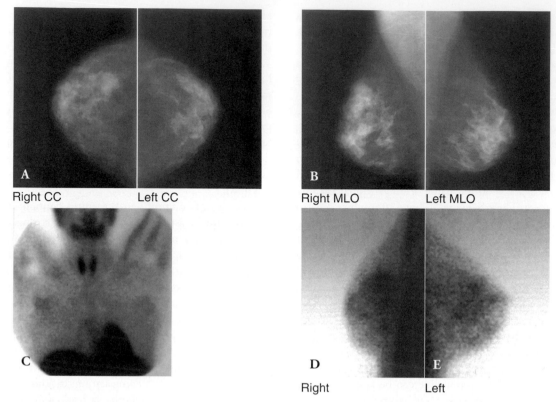

Figure 8-9 CC (*A*) and MLO (*B*) mammography of a 38-year-old woman with dense breasts. Sestamibi scans from the anterior view (*C*) demonstrate uptake in both breasts (right breast on left in *C*). Lateral sestamibi scan of right breast (*D*) shows large area of uptake that was subsequently determined by biopsy to be invasive lobular carcinoma. Lateral sestamibi scan of left breast (*E*) shows smaller regions of uptake that were subsequently determined by biopsy to be proliferative fibrocystic change.

In breast cancer, whole-body PET imaging is most often used in demonstrating local lymph nodes and distant metastases. There are also studies demonstrating FDG uptake in primary breast cancer. The first published study was by Wahl and colleagues, reporting 100% sensitivity for FDG in a group of 10 patients with breast cancer.[54] The average size of tumors in these women was greater then 5 cm. A more recent study by Palmedo and colleagues demonstrated 92% sensitivity and 86% specificity

TABLE 8-5 Diagnostic Accuracy of Sestamibi Scintimammography Applied to Breast Cancer Detection

Study	Number of Patients	Sensitivity	Specificity	PPV	NPV
Taillefer et al, 1999[47]*	2,009	85%	89%	89%	84%
Flanagan et al, 1998[48]	79	81%	81%	61%	92%
Cwikla et al, 1998[49]	70	89%	52%	84%	67%
Prats et al, 1999[50]	90	85%	79%	74%	88%
Buscombe et al, 2001[51]	353	89%	71%	79%	84%
Khalkhali et al, 2002[52]	558	71%	79%	70%	81%

PPV = positive predictive value. NPV = negative predictive value.

*Taillefer R[47] was a review of 20 previous studies published between 1994 and 1998.

for FDG-PET imaging of primary breast cancer in 20 women with a mean tumor size of 2.9 centimeters.[55] In other relatively small series of selected diagnostic patients, reported sensitivities of PET imaging of primary breast tumors were 80 to 96%, and reported specificities were 83 to 100%.[56-60]

One published paper has investigated the use of FDG-PET in cancer screening, not restricted to breast cancer.[61] In screening 1,148 asymptomatic women, one breast cancer was detected and four breast cancers were missed by FDG-PET. The number of breast cancer cases was small, but in addition to the low (20%) sensitivity, other factors suggest that FDG-PET is of limited value in screening for breast cancer. DCIS,[62] lobular carcinoma,[63] and well-differentiated tumors such as tubular carcinomas[64] have less FDG uptake than invasive ductal cancer, limiting their detectability with PET. The spatial resolution of currently available PET systems limits lesion detection to lesions larger than 1 cm in diameter. FDG and PET scanners are very expensive and their availability is limited, as is the availability of the cyclotron needed to produce the short-lived FDG radioisotope (its half-life is 110 minutes). Additionally, there is no commercially available system for biopsy under PET guidance. For all of these reasons, PET is unlikely to be adopted as a breast cancer screening tool.

COMPUTER-AIDED DIAGNOSIS

Over the last two decades, computer-aided detection and diagnosis (CAD) have been developed to aid radiologists in detecting lesions suspicious for breast cancer in mammograms.[65,66] We will briefly review the status of CAD for SFM, digital mammography, breast US, and breast MRI.

As of January 2003, the FDA had approved three commercial systems to aid radiologists in reviewing screening mammograms obtained on SFM systems. These systems digitize screen-film mammograms and apply sophisticated computer analysis to search each image independently for signs of suspicious breast lesions. Images of the breast are presented to the radiologist with markings of lesions deemed suspicious by the CAD system superimposed on lower-resolution images displayed on computer screens or printed paper. These markings are viewed after the radiologist has reviewed the original images on a viewbox or alternator. As of January 2003, approximately 500 CAD systems had been installed in the United States.

Several important clinical studies have been conducted to evaluate the effectiveness of commercial CAD systems in aiding radiologists in the performance of screening mammography.[67,68] Most have been done with the R2 ImageChecker CAD system (R2 Technology, Inc. Sunnyvale, CA).

For example, Warren Burhenne and colleagues analyzed the performance of film-based CAD by applying the R2 ImageChecker M1000 CAD system to 1,083 screen-detected cancers and to 286 prior mammograms (obtained 9 to 24 months prior to the diagnosis of cancer) that had evidence, from retrospective assessment by a radiologist, of the subsequently diagnosed breast cancer.[67] The CAD system correctly marked cancerous lesions in 906 of the 1,083 cases (84%), with correct markings in 400 of 406 cancers seen as microcalcifications (99%) and in 506 of 677 cancers seen as masses (75%). Among the 286 prior mammograms with cancers retrospectively assessed as visible, the CAD system correctly marked 171 cancers (60%). Compared with radiologists' independent assessment of the 286 prior mammograms, there were an estimated 89 additional cancers detected by the CAD system that would have been missed by the original radiologist's interpretation without CAD. This methodology assumes that the radiologist would have acted on all CAD-marked lesions that were cancer.

The CAD system placed an average of 4.1 marks per four-film case that did not correspond to the location of cancerous lesions. In a separate assessment of the effect of CAD on recall rate, however, historical data on 23,682 screening studies showed that 14 radiologists had a collective recall rate of 8.3% without CAD.[66] With CAD assistance in 14,817 different screening studies, the same 14 radiologists had a recall rate of 7.6%, indicating that the use of CAD did not significantly increase recall rates for screening interpretations.

In another large clinical series, Freer and Ulissey prospectively assessed the impact of a film-based CAD system (R2 ImageChecker M1000, Version 2.0) on 12,860 screening cases interpreted in a community-based breast center over a 12-month period.[68] Radiologists first interpreted each case without the use of CAD, then reevaluated each case with CAD. Without CAD, 830 women were recalled for evaluation of 863 findings.

CAD placed an average of 2.8 marks (1.2 microcalcification marks, 1.6 mass marks) per four-view exam. Radiologists reading with CAD recalled 986 women for evaluation of 1,026 findings. The use of CAD increased the number of recalled women (or lesions) by 19%, but increased the overall screening recall rate only slightly, from 6.5% to 7.7%, owing to the large number of negative cases. The use of CAD had no effect on biopsy positive predictive value, leaving it unchanged at 38%.

At the same time, CAD increased the number of cancers detected from 41 to 49, an increase of 19.5%, taking the overall detection rate from 3.2 cancers per 1,000 women screened to 3.8 cancers per 1,000 women screened. Seven of the eight additional cancers detected by CAD presented as clustered microcalcifications. The eight additional cancers found by CAD consisted of five cases of DCIS and three cases of Stage I invasive cancer, increasing the proportion of early cancers detected from 73% without CAD to 78% with CAD. These results indicate that film-based CAD systems can substantially improve the detection of early-stage malignancies in the typical screening practice with only a modest effect on recall rate.

Clinical Studies of CAD in Digital Mammography

Until recently, all studies have been performed using digitized screen-film mammography. Two recent clinical studies have reported preliminary results applying CAD to FFDM.[69,70]

A recent study by Baum and colleagues involved application of the R2 ImageChecker M1000 DM CAD system to 61 cases of histologically proven breast cancer imaged using the GE Senographe 2000D digital mammography system (Waukesha, WI).[69] The case set consisted of 14 cancers visible primarily as calcifications, 36 visible primarily as masses, and 12 containing both. Results of this study indicated that the digital CAD system had 89% sensitivity to breast cancers visible primarily as calcifications (95% confidence interval [CI] 70–98%), and had 81% sensitivity to cancers visible primarily as masses (95% CI 67–91%). The digital CAD system detected four of five BI-RADS category 3 cancers, 11 of 17 category 4 cancers, and 37 of 40 category 5 cancers. The BI-RADS categories were those assigned by the interpreting radiologist prior to the use of CAD. The CAD false-positive rate was an average of 0.35 false-positive calcification marks per film and 0.26 false-positive

mass marks per image, for a total CAD false-positive rate of 0.61 marks per image.

Another recent study by O'Shaughnessy and colleagues assessed the performance of the R2 ImageChecker in conjunction with images obtained on the GE Senographe 2000 FFDM system.[70] The case set included 90 biopsy-proven breast cancers (82 obtained from diagnostic studies, 8 from screening studies) and 71 normal cases, confirmed by 1-year follow-up. Of the 90 cancers, 67 were invasive cancer and 27 were DCIS. Thirty-four of the cancers were primarily visible by calcifications, and 56 were primarily masses. CAD analysis was considered correct if a lesion marker of the correct type (mass or calcification) was placed correctly on the lesion in either view (CC or MLO).

The digital CAD system correctly marked 33 of 34 microcalcification cancer cases (97% sensitivity for calcification-based cancers) and 47 of 56 mass cancer cases (84% sensitivity for mass-based cancers) for an overall sensitivity of 89% (80 of 90 cases correctly marked in at least one view). Among the 71 normal cases, the digital CAD system included an average of 0.55 marks per image (157 false-positive marks on 284 images). These digital CAD results are consistent with previous results based on the same CAD algorithms applied to digitized screen-film images.[67,68]

There are several inherent advantages to CAD used in conjunction with digital mammography. One is that the application of CAD is transparent to the user. The acquired images can be sent directly to the CAD processing system on every case without human intervention. The CAD algorithm is applied, generating a CAD overlay or new set of CAD-marked images that can then automatically be sent to the radiologist's review workstation for viewing. The second advantage of CAD with digital is that the CAD markers are displayed on the same softcopy display system used for image viewing. The radiologist simply pushes a button to display the CAD markers on the softcopy-displayed digital mammograms. Even when digital images are magnified or displayed in a grouped format, CAD markers can be turned on or off with the push of a single button. On the GE Senographe 2000D with the R2 digital CAD system, the user can "see through" the CAD markers by applying a digital magnification glass to the marked area.

Although CAD for digital mammography is still in an early stage of clinical application, its ease of use and promising clinical results suggest that there is great potential for improvement in diagnostic accuracy by combining these two new techniques.

CAD with Ultrasound and Breast MRI

With the potential use of US and breast MRI for screening, development is underway of CAD systems to aid breast US and breast MRI interpretations. Most CAD methods for these two modalities have focused on characterization of identified breast lesions.[70-74] Recently, however, new methods have been developed to aid in the detection of breast lesions on ultrasound.[73]

Eventually, CAD may play an important role in the interpretation of MRI scans in screening programs. One breast MRI computerized reading system that provides a color-coding of breast lesions based on enhancement curves has been FDA-approved for diagnostic use (CadStream, Confirma, Inc, Bellingham, WA). Similar display systems may be useful aids to the radiologist in detecting suspicious breast lesions and in accepting or dismissing areas of enhancement on breast MRI. Currently, most computerized analyses of enhancing breast lesions are focused on characterization of suspicious breast lesions.[73,74]

CONCLUSIONS

Whereas mammography is still the standard for breast cancer screening for asymptomatic, high-risk women, there is growing evidence that breast US and breast MRI may be useful for screening. The high sensitivity of breast MRI in studies that have been published to date suggests that this modality has great potential for screening high-risk women. What is less well established is the false-positive rate that would result if high-risk women were screened with these new modalities in addition to mammography. What may be approaching is a new method of triaging high-risk women to screening for breast cancer, where women with dense breasts are screened with US and breast MRI, while women with fatty breasts are screened with mammography alone or possibly mammography plus breast MRI. The effectiveness of these targeted, multimodality approaches to breast cancer screening is likely to be tested over the next decade.

REFERENCES

1. Nass SJ, Henderson IC, Lashof LJ, editors. Mammography and beyond: developing technologies for the early detection of breast cancer. Washington (DC): National Academy Press; 2001.
2. Obuchowski NA, Ruffin JG, Baker ME, Powell KA. Ten criteria for effective screening: their application to multislice CT screening for pulmonary and colorectal cancers. AJR Am J Roentgenol 2001; 176:1357–62.
3. Hendrick RE, Lewin JM, D'Orsi CJ, et al. Non-inferiority study of FFDM in an enriched diagnostic cohort: comparison with screen-film mammography in 625 women. In: Yaffe MJ, editor. IWDM 2000 5th International Workshop on Digital Mammography. Madison (WI): Medical Physics Publishing Co.; 2001. p. 475–81.
4. Lewin JM. Full-field digital mammography. A candid assessment. Diagn Imag 1999;21(9):40–5.
5. Lewin JM, Hendrick RE, D'Orsi CJ, et al. Comparison of full-field digital mammography to screen-film mammography for cancer detection: results of 4945 paired examinations. Radiology 2001; 218:873–80.
6. Lewin JM, D'Orsi CA, Hendrick RE, et al. Clinical comparison of full-field digital mammography and screen-film mammography for detection of breast cancer. AJR Am J Roentgenol 2002;179: 671–7.
7. Hanley JA, McNeil BJ. The meaning and use of the area under a receiver operating characteristic (ROC) curve. Radiology 1982;143:29–36.
8. Hanley JA, McNeil BJ. A method of comparing the areas under receiver operating characteristic curves derived from the same cases. Radiology 1983; 148:839–43.
9. Hillman BJ. Current clinical trials of the American College of Radiology Imaging Network. Radiology 2002;224:636–8.
10. Standard for the performance of breast ultrasound. Reston (VA): American College of Radiology; 2002.
11. Kolb TM, Lichy J, Newhouse JH. Occult cancer in women with dense breasts: detection with screening US – diagnostic yield and tumor characteristics. Radiology 1998;207:191–9.
12. Sickles EA, Filly RA, Callen PW. Breast cancer detection with sonography and mammography: comparison using state-of-the-art equipment. AJR Am J Roentgenol 1983;140:843–5.
13. Standard for the performance of breast ultrasound. Reston (VA): American College of Radiology;1998.
14. Berg WA, Gilbreath PL. Multicentric and multifocal cancer: whole-breast US in preoperative evaluation. Radiology 2000;214:56–66.

15. Berg W, Nguyen T, Gutierrez L, Ioffe O. Local extent of disease: preoperative evaluation of the breast cancer patient with mammography, ultrasound, and MRI. Radiology 2001;221:230.

16. Rahbar G, Sie AC, Hansen GC, et al. Benign vs. malignant solid masses: US differentiation. Radiology 1999;213:889–94.

17. Baker JA, Kornguth PJ, Soo MS, et al. Sonography of solid breast lesions: observer variability of lesion description and assessment. AJR Am J Roentgenol 1999;172:1621–5.

18. Gordon PB, Goldenberg SL. Malignant breast masses detected only by ultrasound: a retrospective review. Cancer 1995;76:626–30.

19. Kolb TM, Lichy J, Newhouse JH. Comparison of the performance of screening mammography, physical examination, and breast US and evaluation of factors that influence them: an analysis of 27,825 patient evaluations. Radiology 2002;225:165–75.

20. Buchberger W, DeKoekkoek-Doll P, Springer P, et al. Incidental findings on sonography of the breast: clinical significance and diagnostic workup. AJR Am J Roentgenol 1999;173:921–7.

21. Stavros AT, Thickman D, Rapp CL, et al. Solid breast nodules: use of ultrasonography to distinguish between benign and malignant lesions. Radiology 1995;196:123–34.

22. Sickles EA. Periodic mammographic follow-up of probably benign lesions: results in 3,184 consecutive cases. Radiology 1991;179:463–8.

23. Breast Imaging-Reporting and Data System (BI-RADS) 4th ed. Reston (VA): American College of Radiology; 2003. [In press]

24. Hilton SV, Leopold GR, Olson LK, Willson SA. Real-time breast sonography: application in 300 consecutive patients. AJR Am J Roentgenol 1986; 147:479–86.

25. Mendelson EB, Berg WA, Merritt CR. Toward a standardized breast imaging ultrasound lexicon, BI-RADS: ultrasound. Semin Roentgenol 2001;36: 217–25.

26. Gordon PB. Ultrasound for breast cancer screening and staging. Radiol Clin North Am 2002;40:431–41.

27. Kaplan SS. The utility of bilateral whole breast ultrasound in the evaluation of women with dense breast tissue. Radiology 2000;217:318.

28. Davis PL, McCarty KS Jr. Sensitivity of enhanced MRI for detection of breast cancer: new, multicentric, residual, and recurrent. Eur Radiol (Suppl) 1997;7:S289–98.

29. Orel SG, Schnall MD. MR imaging of the breast for the detection, diagnosis, and staging of breast cancer. Radiology 2001;220:13–30.

30. Heywang-Kobrunner SH, Dershaw DD, Schreer I. Diagnostic breast imaging. Stuttgart (NY): Thieme Publishing Co.; 2001.

31. Morris EA. Breast cancer imaging with MRI. Radiol Clin North Am 2002;40:443–66.

32. Kuhl CK, Schmutzler R, Leutner CC, et al. Breast MR screening in women proved or suspected to be carriers of a breast cancer susceptibility gene: preliminary results. Radiology 2000;215:267–76.

33. Warner E, Plewes DB, Shumak RS, et al. Comparison of breast magnetic resonance imaging, mammography and ultrasound for surveillance of women at high risk for hereditary breast cancer. J Clin Oncol 2001;19;3524–31.

34. Stoutjesdijk MJ, Boetes C, Jager GJ, et al. Magnetic resonance imaging and mammography in women with a hereditary risk of breast cancer. J Natl Cancer Inst 2001;93:1095–102.

35. Tilanus-Linthorst MM, Bartels CC, Obdeijn AI, Oudkerk M. Earlier detection of breast cancer by surveillance of women at familial risk. Eur J Cancer 2000;36:514–9.

36. Tilanus-Linthorst MM, Obdeijn AI, Bartels CC, et al. First experiences in screening women at high risk for breast cancer with MR imaging. Breast Cancer Res Treat 2000;63:53–60.

37. Liberman L, Morris EA, Kim CM, et al. MR imaging findings in the contralateral breast of women with recently diagnosed breast cancer. AJR Am J Roentgenol 2003;180:333–41.

38. Fischer U, Kopka L, Grabbe E. Breast carcinoma: effect of preoperative contrast-enhanced MR imaging on the therapeutic approach. Radiology 1999; 213;881–8.

39. Kuhl CK, Kreft BP, Bieling HB, et al. Dynamic breast MRI in premenopausal healthy volunteers: normal values of contrast enhancement and cycle phase dependency. Radiology 1997;203:137–44.

40. Kuhl CK, Mielcarek P, Klaschik S, et al. Are signal time course data useful for differential diagnosis of enhancing lesions in dynamic breast MR imaging? Radiology 1999;211:101–10.

41. Kinkel K, Helbich TH, Esserman LJ, et al. Dynamic high-resolution MR imaging of suspicious breast lesions: diagnostic criteria and interobserver variability. AJR Am J Roentgenol 2000;175:35–43.

42. Harms SE, Flamig DP, Hensley KL, et al. MR imaging of the breast with rotating delivery of excitation off-resonance: clinical experience with pathologic correlation. Radiology 1993;187: 493–501.

43. Teifke A, Hlawatsch A, Beier T, et al. Undetected malignancies of the breast: dynamic contrast-enhanced MR imaging at 1.0 T. Radiology 2002; 224:881–8.

44. Dhamanaskar KP, Muradali D, Kulkarni SR, et al. MRI-directed ultrasound: a cost effective method for diagnosis and intervention in breast imaging. Radiology 2002;225:653.

45. Yutani K, Shiba E, Kusuoka H, et al. Comparison of FDG-PET with MIBI SPECT in the detection of breast cancer and axillary lymph node metastasis. J Comput Assist Tomogr 2000;24:274–80.

46. Leung JWT. New modalities in breast imaging: digital mammography, positron emission tomography, and sestamibi scintimammography. Radiol Clin North Am 2002;40:467–82.

47. Taillefer R. The role of ^{99m}Tc sestamibi and other conventional radiopharmaceuticals in breast cancer diagnosis. Semin Nucl Med 1999;29:16–40.

48. Flanagan FL, Dehdashti F, Siegel BA. PET in breast cancer. Semin Nucl Med 1998;28:290–302.

49. Cwikla JB, Buscombe JR, Kelleher SM, et al. Comparison of accuracy of scintimammography and x-ray mammography in the diagnosis of primary breast cancer in patients selected for surgical biopsy. Clin Radiol 1998;53:274–80.

50. Prats E, Aisa F, Abós MD, et al. Mammography and ^{99m}Tc-MIBI scintimammography in suspected breast cancer. J Nucl Med 1999;40:296–301.

51. Buscombe JR, Cwikla JB, Holloway B, Hilson AJ. Prediction of the usefulness of combined mammography and scintimammography in suspected primary breast cancer using ROC curves. J Nucl Med 2001;42:3–8.

52. Khalkhali I, Baum JK, Villanueva-Meyer JV, et al. ^{99m}Tc Sestamibi breast imaging for the examination of patients with dense and fatty breasts: multicenter study. Radiology 2002;222:149–55.

53. Khalkhali I, Vargas H. The role of nuclear medicine in breast cancer detection: functional imaging. Radiol Clin North Am 2001;39:1053–68.

54. Wahl RL, Cody R, Hutchins GD, Mudgett E. Primary and metastatic breast carcinoma: initial clinical evaluation with PET with the radiolabelled glucose analog 2-(18F)-fluoro-deoxy-2-D-glucose (FDG). Radiology 1991;179:765–70.

55. Palmedo H, Bender H, Grunwald F, et al. Comparison of fluorine-18 fluorodeoxyglucose positron emission tomography and technetium-99m methoxyisobutylisonitrile scintimammography in the detection of breast tumours. Eur J Nucl Med 1997;24:1138–45.

56. Adler LP, Crowe JP, al-Kaisi ND, et al. Evaluation of breast masses and axillary lymph nodes with (F-18)2-deoxy-2-fluoro-D-glucose (FDG) PET. Radiology 1993;187:743–50.

57. Hoh K, Hawkins RA, Glaspy JA, et al. Cancer detection with whole-body PET using (F-18)fluoro-2-deoxy-D-glucose. J Comput Assist Tomogr 1993;17:582–9.

58. Nieweg OE, Kim EE, Wong WH, Broussard WF, et al. Positron emission tomography with fluorine-18-deoxyglucose in the detection and staging of breast cancer. Cancer 1993;71:3920–5.

59. Avril N, Dose J, Janicke F, et al. Metabolic characterization of breast tumors with positron emission tomography using F-18 fluorodeoxyglucose. J Clin Oncol 1996;14:1848–57.

60. Tse NY, Hoh CK, Hawkins RA, et al. The application of positron emission tomographic imaging with fluorodeoxyglucose to the evaluation of breast disease. Ann Surg 1992;216:27–34.

61. Yasuda S, Ide M, Fujii H, et al. Application of positron emission tomography imaging to cancer screening. Br J Cancer 2000;83:1607–11.

62. Avril N, Dose F, Bense S, et al. Metabolic characterization of breast tumors with positron emission tomography using F-18 flourodeoxyglucose. J Clin Oncol 1996;14:1848–57.

63. Avril A, Menzel M, Dose J, et al. Glucose metabolism of breast cancer assessed by 18R-FDG PET: histologic and immunohistochemical tissue analysis. J Nucl Med 2001;42:9–16.

64. Nieweg OE, Kim EE, Wong WH, et al. Positron emission tomography with fluorine-18-deoxyglucose in the detection and staging of breast cancer. Cancer 1993;71:3920–5.

65. Vyborny CJ, Giger ML, Nishikawa RM. Computer-aided detection and diagnosis of breast cancer. Radiol Clin North Am 2000;38:725–40.

66. Doi K. Computer-aided diagnosis and its potential impact on diagnostic radiology. In: Doi K, MacMahon H, Giger M, et al, editors. Computer-aided diagnosis in medical imaging. Amsterdam: Elsevier; 1999. p. 489–502.

67. Warren Burhenne LJ, Wood SA, D'Orsi CJ, et al. Potential contribution of computer-aided detection to the sensitivity of screening mammography. Radiology 2000;215:554–62.

68. Freer TW, Ulissey MJ. Screening mammography with computer-aided detection: prospective study of 12,860 patients in a community breast center. Radiology 2001;220:781–6.

69. Baum FT, Fischer U, Olbenauer S, et al. Computer-aided detection (CAD) in direct full-field digital mammography (FFDM): preliminary results. Radiology 2001;221:471.

70. O'Shaughnessy KF, Castellino RA, Muller S, Benali K. Computer aided detection (CAD) on 90 biopsy-proven breast cancer cases acquired on a full field digital mammography (FFDM) system. Radiology 2001;221:471.

71. Chen DR, Chang RF, Huang YL. Computer-aided diagnosis applied to US of solid breast nodules by using neural networks. Radiology 1999;213:407–12.

72. Horsch K, Giger ML, Venta LA, Vyborny CJ. Computerized diagnosis of breast lesions on ultrasound. Med Phys 2002;29:157–64.

73. Drukker K, Giger ML, Horsch K, et al. Computerized lesion detection on breast ultrasound. Med Phys 2002;29:1438–46.

74. Gilhuijs KGA, Giger ML, Bick U. Automated analysis of breast lesions in three dimensions using dynamic magnetic resonance imaging. Med Phys 1998;25:1647–54.

75. Penn AI, Bolinger L, Schnall MD, Loew MH. Discrimination of MR images of breast masses using fractal interpolation function models. Acad Radiol 1999;6:156–63.

ROLE OF BREAST EPITHELIAL SAMPLING TECHNIQUES IN HIGH-RISK WOMEN

Mehra Golshan, MD
Seema A. Khan, MD

Breast cancer risk assessment techniques available to the clinician for estimation of the probability of breast cancer occurrence in the individual have evolved significantly in the past decade or so, most importantly with the validation of the Gail Model in the Breast Cancer Prevention Trial of the National Surgical Adjuvant Breast and Bowel Project (NSABP).[1,2] However, it remains true that fewer than 30% of those who develop breast cancer can be identified as being at high risk using conventional risk factors,[3] and even though use of the Gail Model has led to very precise prediction of rates of breast cancer occurrence in groups of women,[2,4] the ability to identify individual women who will develop breast cancer remains poor.[5] The present paradigm for the development of breast cancer would suggest that in the breast, as in other epithelial organs, the etiologic pathways of malignancy converge in the causation of breast epithelial hyperplasia or intraepithelial neoplasia (IEN), which until recently has been identified only in women who developed signs or symptoms that required biopsy.[6] In such populations, the prevalence of atypical hyperplasia in an older series of open surgical biopsies is 3.5%[7] but is higher in series of core needle biopsies for mammographic findings, ranging from 4.3[8] to 9%.[9] Findings from autopsy studies suggest that the prevalence of occult atypical IEN is 12.5%[10] and could be as high 26%,[11] depending on the detail of the sampling. Among the known breast cancer risk factors, atypical hyperplasia carries the highest relative risk (other than

documented genetic susceptibility), and the effect of atypical hyperplasia compounds the risk level associated with a positive family history.[7,12]

The recent interest in techniques for the sampling of epithelium from clinically normal breasts is motivated by the expectation that an improved ability to identify occult IEN in normal breasts would lead to significant improvements in our ability to assess individual risk. Additionally, emerging data from the NSABP[13] and from our institution, Tchou and colleagues suggest that the acceptance of chemopreventive intervention by high-risk women is substantially greater in the presence of a diagnosis of atypical IEN, thus lending greater urgency to the development of valid methods of breast epithelial sampling in healthy high-risk women.[14] Finally, it is necessary to recognize that once the validity of a breast epithelial sampling technique is established, it would be logical to extend this to a standard-risk population, where, given the present imprecision of individual risk estimation, these techniques are likely to have the widest impact. Valid methods of breast epithelial sampling have another important application: the potential for the development of surrogate endpoints for the occurrence of malignancy, which are notably lacking in the field of breast cancer prevention at the moment.

The ideal method of breast epithelial sampling would be quick, inexpensive, provide sufficient cells for morphologic and biomarker evaluation in all women studied, and would provide reproducible results over time. Unfortunately, none of the current techniques (nipple fluid aspiration [NAF], the related technique of ductal lavage [DL], random fine needle aspiration [rFNA], and random core needle biopsy [rCNB]) possess all of these attributes. We will consider each of these methods in the following discussion.

NIPPLE ASPIRATION FLUID

Work in the 1950s by Brill and Koprowska established that the Papanicolaou technique for staining vaginal smears could be applied to breast secretions obtained from the nipple, and malignant cells could be recognized.[15] In 1958, Papanicolaou and colleagues reported on a series of 2,010 women, 917 of whom were without symptoms of breast disease. In these asymptomatic women, breast massage and a hand pump were used to elicit nipple fluid, and samples were obtained from 171 (18.5%) patients.[15] There was one instance of a Class III (suspicious for malignancy) report, which proved to be an intraductal papilloma on excision, and the authors classified this as a false-positive result. The only carcinoma diagnosed in this asymptomatic group as a result of nipple fluid aspiration was a comedo ductal carcinoma in situ (DCIS). The authors note that carcinoma was diagnosed on subsequent follow-up in 6 of 1,703 breasts from which fluid was not obtained; in 2 women, the carcinoma occurred in the non–fluid-yielding breast at an interval of 1.5 and 3.5 years, where the other breast had produced fluid with benign results. The remaining 4 carcinomas occurred in women who did not yield fluid bilaterally. These results cannot be compared with current practice because the rate of nipple fluid yield was less than 20%. Nevertheless, they serve as a reminder that the negative predictive value of a lack of nipple fluid is not known, and that women undergoing ductal lavage (see below) need to be counseled on this point prior to undergoing the procedure.

Based on the work of Papanicolaou and others, Sartorius and colleagues developed a breast pump device (Figure 9-1) designed to improve nipple fluid yield from asymptomatic women.[17] Of the 1,503 women studied, they reported being able to obtain fluid from 66% and cells sufficient for diagnosis from 55%. The relative frequency of atypia was sig-

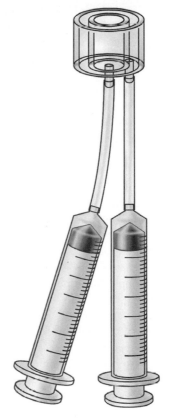

Figure 9-1 The Sartorius aspirator was applied to the nipple after breast massage while the subject compressed her breast gently. Negative suction was applied to the inner chamber for 10 seconds. If no fluid was seen, suction was applied to the outer chamber to obtain a better seal.

nificantly greater in 237 "high-risk" women than in 588 "standard-risk" women (40% vs 23%, $p = .01$). Based on nipple aspiration fluid (NAF) cytology, there were 27 suspected malignancies, of which 18 proved to be small cancers upon ductography-guided excision.[16] Around the same time, Buehring reported a 49% rate of fluid recovery from 1,744 "self-selected, mostly asymptomatic" women who were studied using the Sartorius breast pump to evaluate cytologic examination of nipple secretions as a screening tool for breast cancer. This investigator found that 36% of samples were satisfactory for diagnosis, and 2.8% had atypical findings.[18] The technique used in this study included manual expression and a negative pressure of 90 mm for a maximum of 45 seconds with the Sartorius aspirator. Cytology was prepared by Papanicolaou smears of the breast fluid on glass slides and immediate fixation with 95% ethanol. Seven women who underwent subsequent surgical biopsy for atypical cytology proved to have benign disease, and one was diagnosed with a DCIS. The follow-up period reported was only 1 year, and so the subsequent rate of carcinoma development is not known.

These early efforts revolved around attempts to use NAF as a cancer detection tool; the concept of epithelial sampling by nipple aspiration and possible relevance to breast cancer risk was pioneered by Wrensch and colleagues, who published a series of reports through the 1970s to the present characterizing nipple fluid yield and cytologic findings in healthy women. The impact of NAF cytologic findings on breast cancer risk was established in a landmark study by this group, in which 2,701 healthy standard-risk volunteers from the San Francisco Bay area underwent nipple fluid aspiration and were followed over the long term.[19] NAF could be obtained in 85% of subjects and was sufficient for cytologic diagnosis in 72% of the total. Twelve-year results on this cohort were reported at two levels: first, with the reference group being the women from whom NAF could not be obtained; and second, the ratio of observed to expected incidence rates, comparing the study population to the age-adjusted incidence of breast cancer in the San Francisco Bay area.

The first analysis showed that women with cytologic evidence of hyperplasia in their NAF developed breast cancer at 2.5-fold the rates seen in women who did not produce NAF (95% confidence interval [CI] 1.1–5.5), and for those whose epithelial samples had evidence of atypia, the relative risk (RR) was 4.9 (95% CI 1.7–13.9) compared with the same reference group (Figure 9-2). There appeared to be a further increase in risk for women who displayed atypia in NAF and also had a positive family history for breast cancer relative risk (RR = 6.0 when compared with atypia without a family history, 95% CI 1–30). Thus these results closely parallel those seen in studies of hyperplasia and atypical hyperplasia found in surgical biopsies.[7] However, it should be noted that the elevation in risk was significant only for women aged 25 to 54 (Table 9-1) and that older women had statistically nonsignificant elevations in risk.

The second analysis, comparing the study population to age-adjusted incidence rates in the San Francisco Bay area, showed that women who did not yield nipple fluid in this cohort had a lower

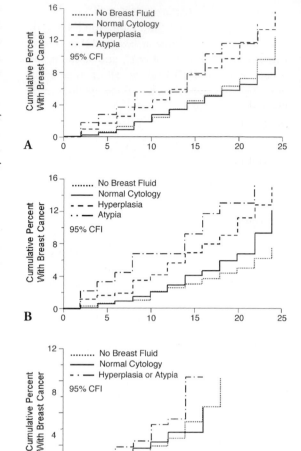

Figure 9-2 Breast cancer incidence rates in women undergoing NAF in two study cohorts from the University of California, San Francisco. *A*, Both study groups, 1973–99. *B*, Group 1, 1973–99. *C*, Group 2, 1981–99. CI = confidence interval.
Reproduced with permission from Wrensch MR et al.[19]

risk of developing breast cancer than the expected age-adjusted incidence in the San Francisco Bay area (observed/expected ratio 0.53). Those with unsatisfactory and normal specimens had an observed to expected ratio that approached unity; the ratio for women with NAF evidence of hyperplasia was 1.45, whereas those with atypical cells in NAF had a ratio of 2.86.

More recently, this group of investigators has published 20-year follow-up results on this original cohort and 9-year results on a second cohort of

TABLE 9-1 Breast Cancer Incidence Rates by Cytologic Diagnosis in Nipple Aspirates of Volunteer Women from the San Francisco Bay Area, 1973–91

Cytologic Diagnosis	Proportion with Breast Cancer	Percent with Breast Cancer	Adjusted Relative Risk	95% Confidence Interval
Age 25–54 years				
No NAF	1/178	0.6	1.0	—
Insufficient	8/168	4.8	6.7	0.8–53.4
Normal	41/1,031	4.0	6.4	0.9–46.3
Hyperplasia	16/281	5.7	9.5	1.3–71.7
Atypia	5/51	9.8	16.3	1.9–139.3
Age ≥ 55 years				
No NAF	8/144	5.6	1.0	—
Insufficient	7/132	5.3	0.8	0.3–2.2
Normal	15/224	6.7	1.0	0.4–2.3
Hyperplasia	2/41	4.9	0.7	0.1–3.3
Atypia	1/6	16.7	2.6	0.3–20.9

Adapted from Wrensch MR et al.[19]

healthy standard-risk women.[20] Failure to obtain NAF was substantially higher in the second cohort (59.6% vs 22.7% in the first study group), and the overall relative risk estimates for both study groups were lower, with substantially tighter confidence intervals: RR = 2.4 for women with hyperplasia (95% CI 1.6–3.7) and RR = 2.8 for those with atypical hyperplasia (95% CI 1.5–5.5). In the second study group, accrued between 1981 and 1991, the relative risk was 2.0 (95% CI 1.3–3.3) for the hyperplasia and atypical hyperplasia groups combined, because no cancers occurred in the 22 women with atypical hyperplasia, and a relative risk for this subset could not be computed. Thus, with longer follow-up, and a second validation cohort, the findings of increased risk for women with NAF cytology showing IEN hold up, but the relative risks are more modest, and it becomes apparent that even with the same group of experienced investigators, NAF yields can vary substantially.

The ability to obtain nipple aspirate fluid depends on several factors. A study of the epidemiology of nipple fluid secretion showed that NAF production was most frequent between the ages of 30 and 60, that women of European and African ancestry were more likely to produce fluid than those of Asian origin, and that increasing family income

was associated with increasing likelihood of nipple fluid production.[21] A history of an early menarche, of parity, and of lactation also predicted the presence of NAF, but the phase of the menstrual cycle did not appear to influence the success of nipple fluid aspiration. The use of postmenopausal hormone replacement therapy was also associated with a higher frequency of nipple fluid secretion, whereas oral contraceptive use (current or past) appeared to have no influence. Regular or frequent use of tranquilizers resulted in slightly higher rates of nipple secretion, but not markedly so. Finally, the presence of a positive family history of breast cancer had no influence on secretor status, but a history of "fibrocystic disease" was significantly associated with production of nipple fluid. The current high rates of obtaining nipple fluid (85 to 95%) involves the application of moist or dry heat to the breast, scrubbing of the nipple surface to dislodge keratin plugs, and use of an aspirator to elicit fluid with a modified breast pump (Figure 9-3).[22,23]

DUCTAL LAVAGE

DL is an extension of nipple fluid aspiration, designed to overcome the problems of scant cellularity

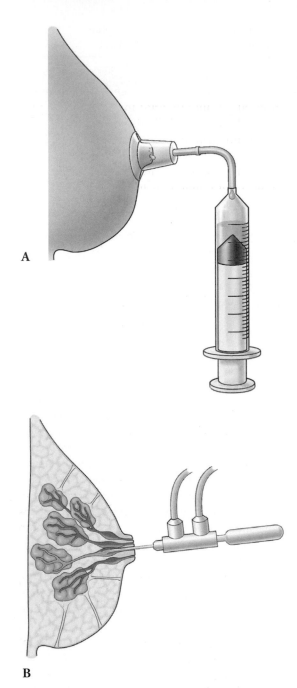

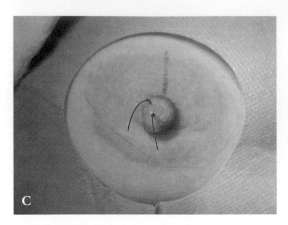

A

B

C

D

Figure 9-3 *A,* Following breast massage and nipple desquamation, the aspirator (Cytyc Health Corporation, Boxborough, MA) is applied to the nipple, the flat flange achieves an air seal on the areola, and negative pressure is applied using a 20-cc syringe, which can be followed by manual stripping of nipple ducts to elicit droplets of fluid. *B,* The duct lavage catheter (Cytyc Health Corporation, Boxborough, MA) is a single lumen catheter with a collection chamber leading to an inflow and an outflow tube. The catheter has an in-line dilator, which is withdrawn as the catheter is being seated in the duct. One to two cc of 1% lidocaine is instilled in the duct after introduction of the catheter, followed by several cycles of instillation of 2 to 3 cc of saline and breast massage. During the massage, a plume of cloudy fluid may be seen in the collection chamber. *C* and *D,* Nipple with prolene sutures in lavaged ducts and 8" × 8" nipple grid marked with duct location.

in NAF samples and to sample the entire ductal tree rather than cells in the proximal reaches of the ductal lumen.[22] The procedure involves application of a topical anesthetic or periareolar infiltration with lidocaine; the elicitation of nipple fluid as described above, cannulation of each fluid-yielding duct with a single lumen catheter (Cytyc Health Corporation, Boxborough, MA) (see Figure 9-3), and lavage with normal saline. The major technical difficulty encountered during duct cannulation is related to a tight nipple duct sphincter, which may require serial dilation with graded dilators. We have introduced an additional step of application of 2% nitroglycerine ointment to the nipple/areolar area for 30 minutes prior to beginning the procedure, and have since encountered fewer difficulties related to nipple sphincter spasm. This maneuver has also reduced the rate of duct perforation, which usually manifests itself as edema around or within the areola as the saline is being instilled, is often related to excessive pressure being used against a tight sphincter, and is the main technical cause of an insufficiently cellular DL sample. Once the catheter is seated, 1 to 2 cc of 1% lidocaine is instilled into the duct for intraductal anesthesia, intermittent breast massage is performed following the instillation of about 2 cc of saline, and this process is repeated 4 to 5 times, so that the total instilled volume is about 10 cc. The lavage effluent is fixed immediately in Cytolyte (Cytyc Health Corporation, Boxborough, MA) and centrifuged to recover a cell pellet that can be resuspended to allow slide preparation using either a cytospin technique or automated monolayer technology (ThinPrep, Cytyc, or Autocyte, Burlington, NC). The location of the fluid-yielding and cannulated ducts needs to be recorded on an 8" × 8" grid and can also be photographed after inserting a prolene suture into it, to facilitate recannulation at a later date if needed (see Figure 9-3).

The success rate of obtaining a cytologic diagnosis with DL was compared with that of NAF in a multicenter investigation sponsored and analyzed by the then manufacturer of the device (ProDuct Health, Inc., Menlo Park, CA)[22] where NAF was collected for analysis prior to cannulation of the fluid-yielding ducts (FYD) for lavage. The proportion of specimens inadequately cellular for diagnosis was much higher using NAF than DL (73% vs 22%), and the median number of cells obtained per duct was significantly higher with DL (13,500 vs 120). This cellularity rate for NAF is much lower than in studies where NAF was not followed by DL,[16,18,22] and raises the possibility that investigators who were focused on proceeding to the next step (ie, DL) did not collect the full volume of NAF available from a ductal orifice. The dramatic superiority of DL to NAF in terms of adequate cellularity for diagnosis reported in this study is therefore probably an overestimate, an important issue because the use of NAF is also dramatically less time intensive, less expensive, and better tolerated than DL. However, the greater abundance of epithelial cells in DL samples is undoubtedly a real finding and is important if biomarker studies are planned in addition to morphologic examination of ductal cells.

Ductal lavage cannot be performed in all women, because about 10 to 15% of subjects will not yield fluid from any of their nipple ducts; the fluid-yielding ducts cannot be cannulated in another 2 to 5%; and a further 15 to 20% will have acellular DL samples. Thus, of the starting population of women who present for DL, a cytologic diagnosis can be obtained in 60 to 65% (299/500, 59.8% in the multicenter DL study).[22] The results of this study in terms of procedural success rates and cytologic findings are presented in Table 9-2

TABLE 9-2 Procedural Success Rate and Cytologic Findings in Ductal Lavage Series Reported to December 2002

Series	Number	% with NAF	% Insufficient	% Benign	% Mild Atypia	% Marked Atypia
Dooley et al[21]	500	84	22	54	17	7
Francescatti and Woods*[23]	122	92	16	57.1	24.1	2.6
Woods and Ekbom[24]	160	?	19	72.4	26.3	2
Khan et al[25]	129	85	20	53	23	4

*Included women with nipple discharge.

along with those of several investigators who have reported their results in abstract form at national meetings.[24–26] In general, these results confirm the original findings, with the exception of epithelial cell yields, which in our hands have been somewhat lower, with a median of 5,000 cells per duct.[26]

Cytologic Processing and Evaluation of NAF and DL samples

Both NAF and DL samples are generally handled by immediate alcohol fixation (the sample can be added to tubes prefilled with the fixative). Slide preparation has been accomplished in the past by Millipore filtration, which may have some advantage in terms of cell recovery but is cumbersome and time-consuming and not compatible with studies of biomarkers. More recently, slide preparation is being performed by most groups using either cytospin technology or with liquid-based monolayer techniques (ThinPrep, Autocyte) followed by Papanicolaou staining. Histologically, the cell types contained in both spontaneous and induced secretion from the human mammary gland include duct epithelial cells, foam cells, macrophages, blood cells, and squamous epithelial cells. Cytologic evaluation of these samples requires some experience and should be performed by trained cytopathologists with an interest in breast cytology. A short, introductory, Web-based training program is available, developed by the manufacturer of the duct lavage catheter (<http://www.cytychealth.com>) for cytopathologists beginning to interpret duct lavage samples. However, the variability of interpretation among cytopathologists has not been established, and this may be considerable, particularly between the two most common diagnostic categories of "benign" and "mildly atypical." These important aspects of cytologic interpretation are an area of study at our institution and at others and will play a significant role in the wider adoption of NAF and DL sampling for risk stratification.

Applications of Ductal Lavage

Risk Assessment

Although direct data regarding the risk implications of atypical cytology in DL samples are lacking, improved risk stratification is the best established of the possible applications of DL. Evidence that the presence of cytologic atypia in random

samples of breast epithelium identifies a group of high-risk women is fairly robust. It is provided by two separate studies of healthy women who underwent breast epithelial sampling by different methods: the NAF data have already been discussed,[19,20] and random fine needle aspiration (rFNA) data[27] are discussed in detail below. The populations in these two studies differed in that women in the NAF study were not selected on the basis of risk status, whereas those in the rFNA study had a median 10-year probability of breast cancer development of 4% as determined by the Gail Model.[28] In both studies, women with cytologic atypia displayed a significantly higher incidence of breast cancer during the follow-up interval (20 years for NAF, and 3.75 years for rFNA). In both studies, the relative risk of breast cancer development in the presence of IEN was 2- to 5-fold that of the control population. Breast cancer incidence curves from these studies are shown in Figures 9-2 and 9-4 and are consistent with the studies of diagnostic breast biopsy samples which established the relevance of histologic atypical hyperplasia to breast cancer risk.[8] It seems reasonable to assume that atypical cells detected using ductal lavage are qualitatively similar to those seen in NAF samples, although there were a few instances in the multicenter NAF/DL study where atypical findings in NAF were not corroborated in DL samples from the same breasts.[21] Surprisingly, the incidence of cytologic atypia in DL samples was similar to the frequency of NAF detected atypia in the San Francisco study[19]: the DL detection rate for mild atypia was 17%, compared with 15% reported as hyper-

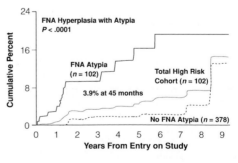

Figure 9-4 Short-term breast cancer incidence rates in high-risk women with and without evidence of atypical hyperplasia in random FNA samples. Reprinted with permission from Fabian CJ et al.[27]

plasia in NAF; and 6% of women in the DL study had severe atypia, compared with 2% reported as atypical hyperplasia in NAF in the San Francisco cohort, despite the fact that these populations were not comparable in terms of baseline risk.

Risk Assessment Questions

If one accepts that the presence of atypia in DL cytology samples is a valid marker of increased risk, the questions that emerge are

1. Which high-risk women should be advised to undergo ductal lavage?

   Investigators from several institutions agree that DL would add precision to the risk assessment of women already known to be at increased risk and might help these women to make decisions about the use of a risk-lowering intervention, specifically tamoxifen or participation in the Study of Tamoxifen and Raloxifene (STAR) trial.[29] A finding of atypical cytology in a woman who is already at increased risk but does not have a prior history of atypical hyperplasia on biopsy would elevate her estimated breast cancer risk, and this may convince her to undertake tamoxifen therapy. However, a woman who already carries a diagnosis of atypical hyperplasia or lobular carcinoma in situ (LCIS) is at sufficiently elevated risk that the use of tamoxifen would carry substantial benefit. If she then proceeds with lavage, it is not clear at present if her risk estimate is further elevated with a finding of atypical lavage cytology. Recent data from the NSABP presented at the 25th Annual Breast Cancer Symposium in San Antonio suggest that benign breast disease diagnosed in symptomatic women after they were randomized in the Breast Cancer Prevention Trial did produce a further elevation in risk.[30] These data were presented for all women who underwent benign breast biopsy after randomization, and women with preexisting IEN were not analyzed separately. If, on further analysis, this additional elevation applies equally to women who entered the study with a prior history of IEN and to those who were high risk because of other risk factors such as family or reproductive history, the indication of DL for further risk stratification of women with a history of IEN will be strengthened. At the moment, there are no data to suggest that two separate findings of atypia elevate risk above and beyond that conferred by a single episode, and therefore there is no evidence to support recommending DL for such women. Similarly, for women already at high risk on the basis of a diagnosis of contralateral breast cancer or a mutation in the *BRCA* genes, it is not clear whether cytologic atypia further alters risk, but a recent report regarding the prevalence of high-risk lesions in mutation carriers is of interest in this regard (see next page).

2. What proportion of women find DL results helpful in decision making regarding preventive intervention?

   For women whose risk estimate would be changed by a finding of lavage atypia, data regarding the decision-making value of this information are beginning to appear. In a study of women with DCIS at our institution who were offered tamoxifen for risk reduction, 72.8% accepted therapy.[31] In contrast, Port and colleagues reported that only 5% of women seen in a high-risk clinic accepted tamoxifen therapy.[32] However, an analysis of accrual patterns to the Breast Cancer Prevention Trial and the STAR trial show that 21% of all risk-eligible postmenopausal women were willing to enter the study and be randomized to tamoxifen or raloxifene, but the study participation rate in women with a history of atypical IEN was higher than in women without atypical IEN (36%).[14] Data from our institution show a similar trend for acceptance of prophylactic tamoxifen, in that the acceptance rate in 68 high-risk women who were offered tamoxifen because of a history of atypical IEN was 53%, compared with 29% of 65 women who were high risk for other reasons ($p = .008$).[14] These emerging data provide a strong incentive for women considering risk-reducing interventions to be encouraged to pursue breast epithelial sampling.

Women at increased risk because of genetic susceptibility related to a *BRCA* mutation are in a somewhat different category, because the prophylactic benefit of tamoxifen is not as certain, and the preventive intervention that many mutation carriers are considering is that of prophylactic mastectomy (see Chapter 16). Because the breast cancer risk of mutation carriers (particularly *BRCA1* carriers) is already very high, the value of atypical cytology in improving risk estimation remains to be proven. One could speculate that a mutation carrier with atypia of breast epithelium may be temporally closer to the appearance of a breast carcinoma than one without atypia, but again this needs to be established in a study setting. A recent report on the frequency of high-risk lesions in the breasts of *BRCA* carriers and women at high genetic risk supports this view.[33] Careful examination of prophylactic mastectomy specimens from women who had careful (and negative) physical and radiologic examinations prior to mastectomy showed an incidence of 37% and 39% for atypical lobular and ductal hyperplasia, respectively, and 25% and 15% for LCIS and DCIS, respectively. The relative odds of carrying occult high-risk lesions were 6.6 (p = .01) for women over 40 compared with those less than 40 years of age, and a history of oophorectomy substantially lowered these odds. Thus it seems likely that the presence of atypia in the breasts of this group of women may presage the development of malignancy and may have some decision-making value. Molecular markers of progression to malignancy (such as loss of the second *BRCA* allele) may also be useful in this setting, but there are no published data so far in this regard.

Women with a remote or recently diagnosed breast carcinoma are also candidates for tamoxifen chemoprevention, and again, there are no data at the moment to establish whether or not cytologic atypia further increases their risk of a new breast primary. However, for those who are unwilling to take tamoxifen for contralateral prophylaxis, information about the presence of occult atypia in the contralateral breast may persuade them of the benefits of tamoxifen therapy, and DL for prophylactic decision making may be reasonable in the setting of estrogen receptor (ER)-positive breast cancer. For women with ER-negative breast cancer, tamoxifen prophylaxis is of uncertain benefit because of the high concordance between ER status of a first and subsequent breast primary.[34]

Ductal Lavage for Serial Observation of Breast Epithelium

DL has a potential advantage over methods of random sampling of breast tissue in this area, because it may be possible to return to the same duct and observe changes in cellular morphology and molecular marker expression over time. There have been few published studies so far of molecular markers in breast epithelial cells obtained from DL, but it appears that it is feasible to examine these cells for markers such as deoxyribonucleic acid (DNA) methylation status of specific genes[35] and protein expression using immunohistochemistry.[36] This would provide a real opportunity to observe the effect of potential chemopreventive agents on breast epithelium and initiate meaningful phase II trials of such agents. The reliability and reproducibility of lavage findings is of particular importance in this setting, and early data from our institution are encouraging with regard to the ability to elicit fluid from the same duct after several months and recannulate the same orifice. In a pilot study where 42 high-risk women were randomized to dietary supplements of soy or casein, 40 returned for their postintervention lavage. The same ducts could be recannulated in 38 subjects (P. Gann, personal communication, October 2002). We are currently investigating the reproducibility of cytologic findings in women who return for DL after a several-months' interval, but preliminary data suggest at least some variability, particularly in the categories of benign and mild atypia. A further concern in the evaluation of chemopreventive agents with surrogate endpoints such as atypia and biomarker expression is the possibility that selective estrogen receptor modulator (SERM) drugs cause a decline in NAF yield over time; if this trend is observed with other potential agents, it will affect our ability to follow cellular changes using DL. Finally, the high cell yields of the multicenter study have not been reproduced, and we have observed a median of 5,000 cells per duct rather than the 13,500 originally reported by Dooley and colleagues.[22] Scant cellularity is therefore another concern in planning biomarker studies with DL samples, and the proportion of samples with sufficient cells to allow such investigation still needs to be defined.

Ductal Lavage as a Cancer Detection Tool

This potential application has generated significant interest and enthusiasm, fuelled partly by findings from the multicenter DL study, where 24% of 383 women who had successful lavage demonstrated atypical cytology (17% mildly atypical, and 7% markedly atypical). To date, 11 subjects with abnormal cytology have gone on to surgical evaluation, and 4 have been discovered to have DCIS lesions of various sizes.[22] The sizes varied from 0.2 to 6 cm; the grade ranged from high to intermediate.

One patient was followed over a period of time and then developed a DCIS lesion that matched the quadrant of the original lavage. However, the use of ductal lavage as a cancer detection tool is the most undeveloped of its possible applications, because of the lack of histopathologic correlation for the cytologic findings. The cytologic diagnostic categories currently recommended for the classification of cytologic findings are inadequately cellular (less than 10 epithelial cells), benign, mildly atypical, markedly atypical, and malignant. These categories were based on the consensus criteria for evaluation of breast fine needle aspiration (FNA) at the National Cancer Institute.[37] However, a finding of atypia in a diagnostic FNA sample of a focal lesion can cover a range of histopathologic findings and is usually interpreted by the clinician in the context of the clinical scenario (eg, the "triple test" of palpatory, radiologic, and cytologic findings). In a clinically normal breast, the context is the risk level of the patient. Additionally, the degree of variability between cytopathologists has not been defined. Early data from our institution in collaboration with the University of Florida Jacksonville (S. Masood) suggest that DL-detected mild atypia is a particularly troubling category, both in terms of reproducibility of cytologic diagnosis and of corresponding histologic findings.[38] Thus the concordance rate between two experienced cytopathologists who performed a blinded examination of 114 DL samples from our institution was 58%, with the categories of benign and mild atypia being responsible for most of the discrepancies.[39] Our data regarding the histologic correlates of mild atypia, acquired in two ongoing studies at the Lynn Sage Breast Center (see below) are similarly troubling, in that the histologic findings in ducts with mild atypia range from nonproliferative benign change and proliferative lesions to DCIS. Once the interpretation of these samples leaves the tiny realm of academic breast cytopathologists who are focused on the relevance of atypia to risk, and enters the wider world of clinical cytopathologists who interpret cytologic findings with the objective of ruling out malignancy, a potential exists for overdiagnosis and overtreatment.

Two ongoing studies at the Lynn Sage Breast Center at Northwestern may help to clarify some of these issues. In the first, women undergoing mastectomy have lavage of all fluid-yielding ducts in the operating room prior to mastectomy, followed by injection of the lavaged ducts with a colored gelatin once the breast has been removed, and serial subgross sectioning of the breast to allow precise correlation of histologic findings in the lavaged duct (dye-filled duct) with the cytologic findings in the DL sample (Figure 9-5).[40] The second study, to which we are recruiting women with mammographically detected microcalcifications that require core biopsy, addresses the spectrum of early disease. Participating women undergo DL prior to core biopsy, and a ductogram is performed through the DL catheter to assess if the fluid-producing, lavaged duct overlaps the area of calcifications. Preliminary results of these two studies are so far consistent and suggest that the diseased duct does not produce fluid in about half the cases, and that lack of fluid yield does not provide any assurance regarding the absence of significant pathology. In the mastectomy study, even when the cancer-bearing duct does yield fluid, DL cytologic findings are frequently benign or mildly atypical, and sensitivity of DL is approximately 40%.[40] The specificity of a finding of marked atypia appears high, however, and appears to be in the range of 90 to 100%. However, we have had a markedly atypical sample outside this study, in a woman who was found on ductoscopy to have a large benign papilloma. If these findings are confirmed, they would suggest that the sensitivity of DL for breast cancer detection is low, but the specificity may be substantially higher.

Clinical Management of DL Findings

This is an evolving area with many unanswered questions, but a reasonable algorithm is presented in Figure 9-6. A finding of inadequate material for diagnosis may be resolved with an early repeat DL, because a second attempt will yield adequate material for diagnosis in approximately 50% of cases. Benign cells on ductal lavage in high-risk women should lead to careful post-test counseling that the breast cancer risk estimate remains unchanged, and that routine breast care, including annual mammography, should continue. Given the lack of data regarding the negative predictive value of DL, and the expectation of many women that this is a method of early diagnosis of breast cancer, it is particularly important to remind women with benign findings on DL that the usual screening should continue, and breast cancer risk is not decreased. It

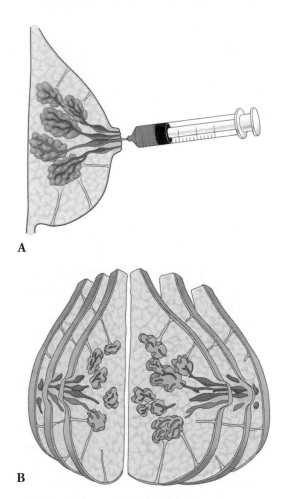

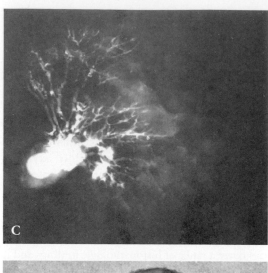

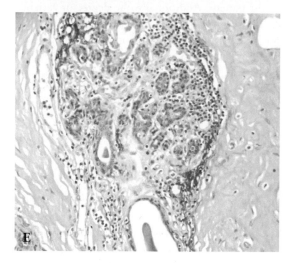

Figure 9-5 Study of cytology-histology correlation in women undergoing mastectomy: lavage was performed in the operating room prior to mastectomy, followed by ex-vivo instillation of a dye-gelatin-Omnipaque (Amersham Biosciences, Piscataway, NJ) mixture into the lavaged duct in the gross room. The specimen was x-rayed to confirm propagation of the dye-mixture along the ductal tree, chilled, and sliced at 3 to 5 mm intervals. The figure shows the study schema: *A*, Dye/Omnipaque injection into the lavaged duct. *B*, A cartoon of the scheme of serial sectioning of mastectomy specimen with gelatin-dye mixture seen traversing along ductal tree. *C*, Specimen radiograph follows to ensure that the dye has propagated along the ductal tree. *D*, Gross slices were photographed to record the distribution of dye-filled ducts in the breast. *E*, Dye dissemination down to the terminal duct lobular unit was frequently seen.

may be reasonable, in interested women, to repeat the DL procedure in the future, at an interval that may range from 2 to 3 years, although the benefits

of this in the risk assessment setting have not been defined, and the cancer detection value is similarly unproven. Antiestrogen therapy remains an option for high-risk women with benign DL findings and should be discussed again during postprocedure counseling.

Atypical cells can span a wide spectrum of histologic findings, from nonproliferative change to atypical hyperplasia, or carcinoma in situ. In the present model, a finding of mild atypia in a high-risk woman is presumed to be equivalent to a finding of IEN on surgical biopsy or random FNA.

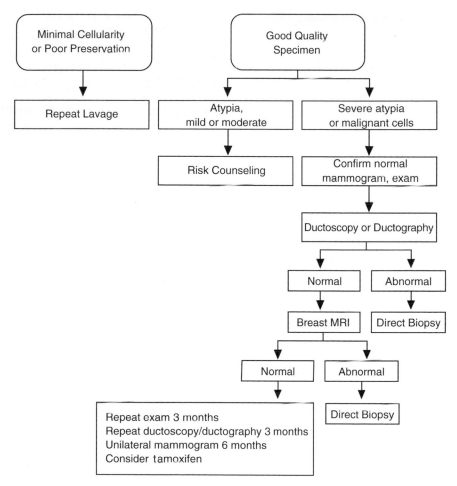

Figure 9-6 Algorithm for clinical management of women undergoing ductal lavage. Reproduced with permission from Morrow M, Vogel V, Ljung BM, O'Shaughnessy JA. Evaluation and management of the woman with an abnormal ductal lavage. J Am Coll Surg 2002;194:648–56.

Whether this can reasonably lead to a recalculation of breast cancer risk with the Gail Model, adding atypia where it was not present before, needs to be demonstrated. If this presumption is made, it will cause a significant elevation in the Gail Model risk estimate and may persuade a high-risk woman that the benefits of SERM therapy are worth the risks. Further diagnostic evaluation in a woman with mild atypia can be undertaken, but the yield is unknown. Prior to further (probably expensive and worrying) diagnostic intervention, it would be prudent to obtain a cytologic second opinion, particularly in the setting of mildly atypical lavage findings, because interobserver variability appears be greatest in this category. Another reasonable precaution to avoid excessive investigation of mild atypia would be to repeat the lavage in 6 months; if the second sample from the same duct is benign, this would provide reassurance, but in the face of progressing atypia, a search for a significant lesion may be warranted.

Marked atypia can more reliably be inserted in the Gail Model as an equivalent to atypical hyperplasia and should lead to renewed serious discussion of SERM therapy for risk reduction. However, a finding of marked atypia in a high-risk woman is also a reasonable indication for diagnostic investigation, because it has been associated with malignancy in about 30% of women who have undergone surgical resection reported to the voluntary Duct Lavage Tracking System (DLOTS) database being maintained by Cytyc Health Corporation.[41] This yield is equivalent to a Breast Imaging and Reporting Data System (BI-

RADS) 4 mammographic interpretation. Diagnostic options that are available to rule out malignancy include repeat mammography, ultrasonography to look for dilated ducts or intraluminal filling defects, ductography (which can be performed through the duct lavage catheter after a repeat lavage to confirm that the cannulated duct is indeed the one producing highly atypical cells), magnetic resonance imaging (MRI), and ductoscopy. The specific sequence of diagnostic procedures will be dictated by the institutional expertise. We have performed MRI in two cases of marked atypia on lavage, with no specific abnormalities identified. Ductoscopy has been more successful in our hands, and those findings are detailed below. If no lesion is found in the presence of marked DL atypia, we do not advocate blind surgical resection, because a single ductal tree can arborize very widely within the breast, and even resection of a large segment of breast tissue may not include a small peripheral lesion. The accuracy of instillation of lymphazurin through the ductal orifice and resection of the blue stained area has not been established in the setting of DL atypia, and because a fair proportion of markedly atypical samples are related to intraductal papillomata (6/21 in the DLOTS data), it would appear that the specificity of marked atypia on lavage is not sufficiently high to warrant resection of large segments of breast tissue in the hope of uncovering a tiny malignancy. Thus if the available combination of diagnostic tests has been exhausted, and a localizable lesion has not been discovered, we would advocate close observation of the patient and serious discussion regarding SERM therapy (ie, tamoxifen or participation in chemoprevention trials).

Frankly malignant cells on lavage are rare (about 1% of women) and should be handled along the lines outlined for markedly atypical lavage findings. If a search for a localizable lesion with the optimal means available does not yield a diagnosis, the main argument against a blind resection is the fact that malignant lavage cytology can be related to an intraductal papilloma. However, a diligent diagnostic investigation with state of the art techniques (MRI, ductoscopy, or ductography) is certainly warranted and should be repeated in 3 to 6 months if negative initially. Discussion with an anxious high-risk patient faced with the possibility of a nonlocalizable malignancy should clearly point out that a lesion may not be discovered if a blind resection is performed.

DUCTOSCOPY

Taking intraductal evaluation another step, endoscopic examination of mammary ducts for direct observation of intraductal lesions has evolved over the last 10 to 15 years to the point that it is currently available at about 40 US institutions. In 1991, Makita and colleagues reported successful duct endoscopy and endoscopic biopsy in 15 cases, using ductoscopes with a diameter of 1.25 mm.[42] They obtained two cytologically suspicious samples and performed resections of these ducts: one proved to contain a papilloma and the second a "borderline" malignancy. Subsequent work by Okazaki and colleagues in 1991 resulted in the development of silica fiberscopes with an outer diameter of 0.45 mm.[43] Further studies have shown that ductoscopy is feasible and provides good visualization of intraductal lesions, and that cytologic washings of adequate cellularity can be obtained.[44,45] The bulk of the data available so far involves ductoscopic evaluation of women with spontaneous nipple discharge and suggests that the sensitivity for detection of intraductal neoplasia is superior to that of ductography: of 70 women who underwent preoperative ductography in a series of 121, lesions were found in 76% by ductography and in 90% by ductoscopy.[45] The advantages of ductoscopy over traditional methods of evaluating spontaneous nipple discharge include avoiding surgery in women who have normal findings or limiting the area of resection.

Theoretically, endoscopic evaluation of the ductal lumen dovetails well with ductal lavage in that ductoscopy is not suitable as an initial step in intraductal sampling because it is significantly more expensive than ductal lavage ($3,000 [US] to $5,000 [US] per duct vs $1,000 [US] per duct), is more invasive, and requires greater expertise to perform. Nevertheless, in the woman with markedly atypical lavage findings, it has the potential of being the optimal second step, because it provides direct evidence of the presence of a lesion in a duct with atypical findings on lavage and allows localization of the lesion. Because intraductal neoplastic lesions, particularly papillomata but also DCIS, are not often visualized on MRI, either ductography or ductoscopy is a reasonable diagnostic modality for these women. Ductoscopy may have an advantage over ductography because of the possibility of greater sensitivity and the ability to obtain cytologic washings through the ductoscope (which can substitute for a confirmatory lavage). A present limitation of the rigid single-channel endoscopes in use in the United States (Acueity Inc., Palo Alto, CA) is that targeted biopsy of a visualized lesion is not possible at this time, although biopsy instruments are in the process of being developed. There are no published data so far regarding ductoscopic evaluation of women with atypical findings on ductal lavage; at our institution, we have encountered four women with markedly atypical lavage findings. Clinical data regarding these four women, and three additional women from Milwaukee, Wisconsin (J. Woods, personal communication, December 2002) are detailed in Table 9-3. Images are shown in Figure 9-7. Although extremely preliminary, these data support the notion that the presence of an identifiable focal abnormality in a woman with marked atypia on DL deserves diagnostic excision, but in the absence of such an abnormality, observation on tamoxifen therapy is a good option. We have also performed office ductoscopy on four high-risk women with mildly atypical DL findings and have not found any significant intraductal lesions other than occasional red patches (which usually represent duct hyperplasia) and wispy fronds of uncertain significance. The examination was incomplete in two of the five ducts examined in this group of patients because of duct perforations during the examination. In the future, improved flexible dilators may reduce this relatively high duct perforation rate in women who present only with aspirable nipple fluid rather than spontaneous or nonspontaneous nipple discharge.

In summary, ductoscopy is potentially a good follow-up intervention for women with atypical duct lavage findings, but experience is limited in most institutions so far, and improvements need to be made in the equipment before ductoscopy can be taken further.

RANDOM FINE NEEDLE ASPIRATION

In a different approach to breast epithelial sampling, several investigators have pursued rFNA of the

TABLE 9-3 Findings in Seven Women Undergoing Investigation of Markedly Atypical Lavage Cytology

Age (years)	DL Indication	MRI	Ductoscopy	Biopsy	Outcome
66	High risk	Negative	White nodular lesion	Grade 3 DCIS, 9 mm	DCIS excised, radiation, tamoxifen
60	High risk	Not done	Papillomatous lesion	Grade 2, 4 mm DCIS	DCIS excised, radiation, tamoxifen
45	High risk	Not done	Perforation	Planning mastectomy	Pending
36	High risk	Negative	Papilloma	Papilloma	On tamoxifen
60*	Contralateral cancer	Negative	Mild erythema	Mild atypia in ductoscopy washings	Disease-free 8 months on tamoxifen
64*	Contralateral cancer	Indeterminate enhancement	No lesion	US guided core of MRI lesions showed hyperplasia	Disease-free 15 months on tamoxifen
36*	Contralateral cancer	Negative	No lesion	Patient requested bilateral mastectomy	Mild ductal hyperplasia

*J. Woods, personal communication, December 2002.
All had normal physical examinations, mammography, and ultrasonography findings.
DCIS = ductal carcinoma in situ.
DL = ductal lavage.
MRI = magnetic resonance imaging.
US = ultrasound.

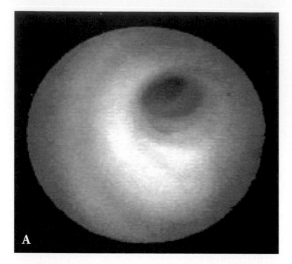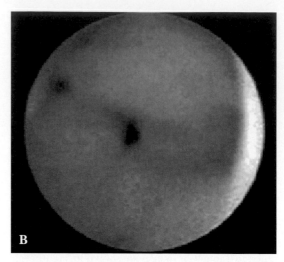

Figure 9-7 The normal duct is a shiny, smooth, white tube (*A*). The intraluminal lesion (*B*) proved to be ductal carcinoma in situ (DCIS) on excision.

breast in healthy, high-risk women. Conceptually, this is a different approach in that it assumes a field change in the high-risk breast which does not rely on reproducibility of location of sampling, but like the NAF and DL methods discussed above, the objective is to obtain a breast epithelial sample from the clinically normal breast in order to assess the presence of IEN and to develop markers of risk and surrogate markers for chemopreventive benefit. This idea was first tested in Utah in a group of women with clinically normal breasts and strong family histories (at least two affected first-degree relatives), a study that generated a series of reports in 1990 and 1991.[46–48] Aspiration was performed with a 1-inch, 22 gauge needle in four quadrants, 1 cm outside the areolar margin. Aspirates were rinsed into normal saline, and cells were retrieved by Millipore filtration (Millipore Corp., Bedford, MA) and subjected to Papanicolaou staining. In the largest report from this group of studies, 103 relatives and 31 controls were studied.[45] The procedure was well tolerated, although 12 women terminated the procedure before completion of sampling of all 8 quadrants owing to discomfort. Cytologic evidence of proliferative breast disease was present in 4 of 30 controls (13%) and in 27 of 77 women who were first-degree relatives of breast cancer cases (35%, *p* = .02). Pedigree analysis of this data set suggested that a model that included a genetic susceptibility for proliferative breast disease and an excess risk for breast cancer best explained the findings.

Subsequently, major work in this area has been reported from the University of Kansas by Fabian and colleagues, who have used the technique described above with some modifications.[27] Women were asked to stop nonsteroidal antiinflammatory agents and aspirin for 3 weeks prior to the procedure, buffered lidocaine was used for local anesthesia, and a 21-gauge needle attached to a 10-cc syringe was used to probe the breast deeply, making 8 to 10 passes, half in the upper outer quadrant and half through the upper inner quadrant. Cold packs were applied to the breast after aspiration, the breasts were firmly bound with gauze, and women were asked to wear a tight-fitting sports bra for several days. With these precautions, hematomas were rare, and the procedure was generally well tolerated. All rFNA passes from both breasts were pooled in 5 mL of tissue culture medium for processing, and results from the first rFNA procedure and a second one 6 to 12 months later were pooled. Breast cancer incidence rates in 486 high-risk women (median 5-year Gail Model estimate of 4%) followed for a median of 45 months showed that evidence of hyperplasia with atypia on random FNA equates with an increased short-term risk of breast cancer (see Figure 9-4). Hyperplasia with atypia was present in the initial fine needle aspirate in 21% of women and, along with the 10-year Gail risk above the median, was independently predictive of the probability of developing breast cancer. The proportion of women with atypical proliferation in this study was generally similar to that reported in rFNA samples from the normal breasts of a group of women with contralateral breast cancer, where the atypia rate was 16%.[49] Women with a 10-year Gail risk above 4% and hyperplasia with atypia on rFNA had a cumulative 3-year breast cancer incidence rate of 15%; those with Gail risk over 4% and no evidence of atypia had a 3-year breast cancer incidence of 4%; and those with Gail risk below 4% had no cancers detected in the first 3 years of follow-up. In contrast, the 20-year breast cancer incidence rate was 11% in Group 1 of the San Francisco NAF study, highlighting the difference in the starting risk and therefore the very different rates of cancer development in these two groups.

Cellular yield of rFNA is generally good, with a median of about 5,000 epithelial cells in the pooled samples, and sufficient material for morphologic and biomarker assessment is available in over 85% of women (B. Kimler, personal communication). Yield is related to age, with more abundant cellular material in women aged 30 to 60; women over age 60 have not been included in the Kansas City rFNA studies because of difficulty obtaining adequate cellular material.[27,50] This group has evaluated several putative molecular markers of risk; in earlier reports, those consistently associated with breast epithelial atypia in high-risk women include epidermal growth factor receptor, *p53* overexpression, and DNA aneuploidy.[49] Increased ER expression was not initially found to be associated with hyperplasia, but when the threshold for ER positivity was lowered, ER expression was included as part of their final three-test set (EGFR, ER, *p53*) and proved to be one of two parameters remaining independently significant ($p < .001$) in a multivariate model testing epidemiologic and molecular risk factors against epithelial atypia. The other parameter was any expression in a five-test set (EGFR, *p53*, ER, *HER2/NEU*, DNA ploidy).[27] When the outcome was cancer occurrence, however, only atypia and Gail risk remain significant.

These workers have taken random FNA to the next level, assessing the utility of new chemopreventive agents in short-term phase II/III studies that use surrogate endpoints related to cell morphology and biomarker expression in random FNA samples. Unfortunately, reversal of atypical cell morphology was not achieved with an investigational chemopreventive agent (a-difluoromethylornithine).[27,51] This is related at least in part to nonreproducibility in the finding of atypia in rFNA samples in the control

group, because the proportion of women with atypical cytology declined by 28% in both groups (only women with rFNA evidence of hyperplasia were eligible for the study).[51] Cell proliferation, another putative marker of chemopreventive efficacy, also did not change in the expected direction in this study, with pre- and postintervention values declining in the placebo rather than the treatment group. Changes in a number of other biomarkers were also not significantly different between intervention and placebo groups, and the authors postulate that this lack of difference is related to an inadequate dose of DFMO. An alternate explanation is that random sampling, which relies on the concept of a "field effect," may not lead to reproducible findings because field change may be patchy or discontinuous. In this regard, ductal lavage may have an advantage, because it is theoretically possible to sample the same duct over time. However, repeat sampling of the same duct relies on the continued presence of nipple fluid, a factor that may prove to be a barrier to the use of DL for serial observation of breast epithelium.

Random FNA does have several advantages over DL in the arena of repeat epithelial sampling. It is quick, inexpensive, may be performed with minimum morbidity, and is simple to learn. Random FNA can be performed in every eligible woman (as opposed to only NAF producers, as in DL) and yields a sufficient number of cells for diagnosis in about 85% of women. Both techniques are less applicable to older women because of declining cell yield. Because the operating concept for rFNA is field change, the question of diagnostic accuracy does not arise and has not posed a barrier to the use of the technique in risk stratification and prevention. The tolerability of both procedures appears reasonable, with study participants returning reliably for repeat rFNA and DL; an ongoing study chaired by C. Fabian is likely to provide valuable comparative information regarding this. However, the final utility of each of these approaches in chemoprevention studies remains to be demonstrated.

RANDOM CORE NEEDLE BIOPSY

With the availability of spring-loaded core needle biopsy devices, random core needle biopsy (rCNB) has become a possible approach to breast epithelial sampling. Although it has been successfully used for cancer diagnosis for over a decade, the reported experience in terms of sampling of normal breast epithelium is scant. According to one report of core samples obtained with 11-gauge, vacuum-assisted needles in 51 women undergoing stereotactically guided core needle biopsies of mammographic lesions, at least 2 normal tissue cores were obtained from 82% of the patients.[52] However, nonatrophic terminal duct lobular units (TDLUs) were present in 47% of patients, and the authors concluded that unless atrophic TDLUs are considered adequate for biomarker studies, core biopsies are unlikely to provide sufficient material for such studies. A subsequent study of 19 postmenopausal women who agreed to participate in a pilot study of letrozole as a preventive agent has shown more encouraging results.[52] The authors used ultrasound to locate glandular breast tissue and obtained 14 gauge core samples using a spring-loaded core biopsy device.[53] Up to seven cores were obtained from each subject through the same skin incision. On average, 3 of the 6 to 7 cores per subject contained epithelium, the rest being fatty. They were able to count 3,000 cells per case after Ki-67 labeling by combining a mean of 11 core-cut sections per subject. They did not find any significant difference in pre and post-treatment Ki-67 labeling indices.

An alternative approach for obtaining epithelial cells from core needle biopsy (CNB) samples was evaluated in a study of 114 women undergoing diagnostic CNB for mammographic lesions. A median of 8 cores (range 5 to 15) were obtained from each subject and placed in normal saline, then transferred to formaldehyde for fixation and pathologic processing. The saline rinse was used for flow-cytometric evaluation of the cellular material shed by the core samples while in saline, using cytokeratin staining to identify and count the epithelial cells.[54] The median number of cells obtained from benign lesions in this way was 6,641, a number very comparable to the yield of DL and rFNA. The possibility of random core biopsy for breast epithelial sampling is thus attracting attention and has the advantages of simplicity and possibly a better cell yield than rFNA, but reported experience is limited.

SUMMARY

The presence of atypical IEN appears to be a robust marker of increased breast cancer risk, whether it is discovered by surgical, core needle, fine needle, or intraductal sampling (NAF, lavage). In addition, the presence of breast epithelial atypia in both standard-risk and high-risk women appears to further increase breast cancer risk, and emerging data suggest that a diagnosis of epithelial atypia provides stronger motivation for women to accept risk-reducing medication than risk derived from other sources. Continued investigation of these areas, particularly refinements in breast epithelial sampling to achieve reproducibility of cytologic findings, will very likely yield more precise risk markers and lead to validated surrogate endpoints. These should result in substantial gains in the area of breast cancer risk stratification, toward the final goal of prevention strategies tailored to specific risk marker profiles of individual women.

REFERENCES

1. Costantino JP, Gail MH, Pee D, et al. Validation studies for models projecting the risk of invasive and total breast cancer incidence. J Natl Cancer Inst 1999;91:1541–8.
2. Fisher B, Costantino JP, Wickerham DL, et al. Tamoxifen for prevention of breast cancer: report of the National Surgical Adjuvant Breast and Bowel Project P-1 Study. J Natl Cancer Inst 1998;90:1371–88.
3. Seidman H, Stellman S, Mushinski MH. A different perspective on breast cancer risk factors: some implications of the nonattributable risk. CA Cancer J Clin 1982;32:301–13.
4. Hartmann LC, Schaid DJ, Woods JE, et al. Efficacy of bilateral prophylactic mastectomy in women with a family history of breast cancer [see comments]. N Engl J Med 1999;340:77–84.
5. Rockhill B, Spiegelman D, Byrne C, et al. Validation of the Gail et al. model of breast cancer risk prediction and implications for chemoprevention. J Natl Cancer Inst 2001;93:358–66.
6. O'Shaughnessy JA, Kelloff GJ, Gordon GB, et al. Treatment and prevention of intraepithelial neoplasia: an important target for accelerated new agent development: recommendations of the American Association for Cancer Research Task Force on the Treatment and Prevention of Intraepithelial Neoplasia. Clin Cancer Res 2002;8:314–46.
7. Dupont WD, Page DL. Risk factors for breast cancer in women with proliferative breast disease. N Engl J Med 1985;312:146–51.
8. Brown TA, Wall JW, Christensen ED, et al. Atypical hyperplasia in the era of stereotactic core needle biopsy. J Surg Oncol 1998;67:168–73.
9. Liberman L, Cohen MA, Dershaw DD, et al. Atypical ductal hyperplasia diagnosed at stereotaxic

core biopsy of breast lesions: an indication for surgical biopsy. AJR Am J Roentgenol 1995;64: 1111–3.

10. Bhathal PS, Brown RW, Lesueur GC, Russell IS. Frequency of benign and malignant breast lesions in 207 consecutive autopsies in Australian women. Br J Cancer 1985;51:271–8.

11. Nielsen M, Thomsen JL, Primdahl S, et al. Breast cancer and atypia among young and middle-aged women: a study of 110 medicolegal autopsies. Br J Cancer 1987;56:814–9.

12. Dupont WD, Page DL. Risk factors for breast cancer in women with proliferative breast disease. N Engl J Med 1985;312:146–51.

13. Vogel VG, Costantino JP, Wickerham DL, Cronin WM. Re: tamoxifen for prevention of breast cancer: report of the National Surgical Adjuvant Breast and Bowel Project P-1 Study. J Natl Cancer Inst 2002;94:1504.

14. Tchou J, Hou N, Rademaker A et al. Patient acceptance of tamoxifen as chemoprevention. Proc Am Soc Clin Oncol 2003;22:551.

15. Brill R, Koprowska I. Diagnosis of early carcinoma of the breast with the Papanicolaou technique. Am J Surg 1955;90:1016–9.

16. Papanicolaou GN, Holmquist DG, Bader GM, Falk EA. Exfoliative cytology of the human mammary gland and its value in the diagnosis of cancer and other diseases of the breast. Cancer 1958;11: 377–409.

17. Sartorius OW, Smith HS, Morris P, et al. Cytologic evaluation of breast fluid in the detection of breast disease. J Natl Cancer Inst 1977;59:1073–80.

18. Buehring GC. Screening for breast atypias using exfoliative cytology. Cancer 1979;43:1788–99.

19. Wrensch MR, Petrakis NL, King EB, et al. Breast cancer incidence in women with abnormal cytology in nipple aspirates of breast fluid. Am J Epidemiol 1992;135:130–41.

20. Wrensch MR, Petrakis NL, Miike R, et al. Breast cancer risk in women with abnormal cytology in nipple aspirates of breast fluid. J Natl Cancer Inst 2001;93:1791–8.

21. Petrakis NL, Ernster VL, Sacks ST, et al. Epidemiology of breast fluid secretion: association with breast cancer risk factors and cerumen type. J Natl Cancer Inst 1981;67:277–84.

22. Dooley WC, Ljung BM, Veronesi U, et al. Ductal lavage for detection of cellular atypia in women at high risk for breast cancer. J Natl Cancer Inst 2001;93:1624–32.

23. Sauter ER, Ross E, Daly M, et al. Nipple aspirate fluid: a promising non-invasive method to identify cellular markers of breast cancer risk. Br J Cancer 1997;76:494–501.

24. Francescatti D, Woods JH. Ductal lavage: the learning curve [abstract]. In: Proceedings of the Fourth Annual Lynn Sage Symposium; 2002; Chicago, IL. B6.

25. Woods JH, Ekbom GA. Managing high risk patients with ductal lavage [abstract]. In: Proceedings of the Fourth Annual Lynn Sage Symposium; 2002; Chicago, IL. B5.

26. Khan SA, Baird C, Ramakrishnan R, et al. Proportion of cytologically evaluable samples from duct lavage procedures [abstract]. In: Proceedings of the American Association of Cancer Research Frontiers in Cancer Research; Oct 14–18, 2002; Boston, MA.

27. Fabian CJ, Kimler BF, Zalles CM, et al. Short-term breast cancer prediction by random periareolar fine-needle aspiration cytology and the Gail risk model. J Natl Cancer Inst 2000;92:1217–27.

28. Gail MH, Brinton LA, Byar DP, et al. Projecting individualized probabilities of developing breast cancer for white females who are being examined annually [see comments]. J Natl Cancer Inst 1989; 81:1879–86.

29. O'Shaughnessy JA, Ljung BM, Dooley WC, et al. Ductal lavage and the clinical management of women at high risk for breast carcinoma: a commentary. Cancer 2002;94:292–8.

30. Wang J, Costantino JP, Tan-Chiu E, et al. Benign breast disease and risk of subsequent invasive breast cancer: findings from the National Surgical Adjuvant Breast and Bowel Project's Breast Cancer Prevention Trial [abstract]. Breast Cancer Res Treat 2002;76 Suppl 1:S36.

31. Lazarus L, Rademaker A, Acharya S, Morrow M. Acceptance of tamoxifen for risk reduction in patients with duct carcinoma in situ [abstract 188]. Proc Am Soc Clin Oncol 2002;21:481.

32. Port ER, Montgomery LL, Heerdt AS, Borgen PI. Patient reluctance toward tamoxifen use for breast cancer primary prevention. Ann Surg Oncol 2001; 8:580–5.

33. Hoogerbrugge N, Bult P, Widt-Levert LM, et al. High prevalence of premalignant lesions in prophylactically removed breasts from women at hereditary risk for breast cancer. J Clin Oncol 2003;21:41–5.

34. Swain S, Wilson J, Mamounas E, et al. Estrogen receptor (ER) status of primary breast cancer is predictive of ER status of contralateral breast cancer. Proc Am Soc Clin Oncol 2002;21:38a, 150.

35. Evron E, Dooley WC, Umbricht CB, et al. Detection of breast cancer cells in ductal lavage fluid by methylation-specific PCR. Lancet 2001;357:1335–6.

36. King BL, Crisi GM, Tsai SC, et al. Immunocytochemical analysis of breast cells obtained by ductal lavage. Cancer 2002;96:244–9.

37. The uniform approach to breast fine needle aspiration biopsy. A synopsis. Acta Cytol 1996;40:1120–6.

38. Masood S, Khan S, Nayar R. Atypia in ductal lavage: a follow up experience with ductography, ductoscopy and tissue biopsy [abstract]. Mod Pathol 2003;16(1):40A.

39. Nayar R, Ramakrishnan R, Baird C, et al. Breast ductal lavage (DL): cytologic findings in 114 samples [abstract]. Mod Pathol 2003;16(1):76A.

40. Khan SA, Rodriguez N, Baird C, et al. Ductal lavage findings in women with known breast cancer undergoing mastectomy. In: Proceedings of the San

Antonio Breast Cancer Symposium [abstract 25]. Breast Cancer Res Treat 2002;76:S35.

41. Dooley WC, Veronesi U, Phillips R, et al. Retrospective review of markedly atypical and malignant ductal lavage cytological results with histological correlation [abstract]. Soc Gynecol Oncol 2003; 215:156–261.

42. Makita M, Sakamoto G, Akiyama F, et al. Duct endoscopy and endoscopic biopsy in the evaluation of nipple discharge. Breast Cancer Res Treat 1991; 18:179–87.

43. Okazaki A, Okazaki M, Asaishi K, et al. Fiberoptic ductoscopy of the breast: a new diagnostic procedure for nipple discharge. J Clin Oncol 1991;21: 188–93.

44. Shen KW, Wu J, Lu JS, et al. Fiberoptic ductoscopy for patients with nipple discharge. Cancer 2000; 89:1512–9.

45. Dietz JR, Crowe JP, Grundfest S, et al. Directed duct excision by using mammary ductoscopy in patients with pathologic nipple discharge. Surgery 2002;132:582–7.

46. Skolnick MH, Cannon-Albright LA, Goldgar DE, et al. Inheritance of proliferative breast disease in breast cancer kindreds. Science 1990;250:1715–20.

47. Ward JH, Marshall CJ, Schumann GB, et al. Detection of proliferative breast disease by four-quadrant, fine-needle aspiration. J Natl Cancer Inst 1990;82:964–6.

48. Marshall CJ, Schumann GB, Ward JH, et al. Cytologic identification of clinically occult proliferative breast disease in women with a family history of breast cancer. Am J Clin Pathol 1991;95: 157–65.

49. Khan SA, Masood S, Miller L, Numann PJ. Random fine needle aspiration of the breast of women at increased breast cancer risk, and standard risk controls [abstract]. Breast J 1998;4:409–19.

50. Fabian CJ, Zalles C, Kamel S, et al. Breast cytology and biomarkers obtained by random fine needle aspiration: use in risk assessment and early chemoprevention trials. J Cell Biochem Suppl 1997;28-29:101–10.

51. Fabian CJ, Kimler BF, Brady DA, et al. A phase II breast cancer chemoprevention trial of oral alpha-difluoromethylornithine: breast tissue, imaging, and serum and urine biomarkers. Clin Cancer Res 2002;8:3105–17.

52. Mansoor S, Ip C, Stomper PC. Yield of terminal duct lobule units in normal breast stereotactic core biopsy specimens: implications for biomarker studies. Breast J 2000;6:220–4.

53. Harper-Wynne C, Ross G, Sacks N, et al. Effects of the aromatase inhibitor letrozole on normal breast epithelial cell proliferation and metabolic indices in postmenopausal women: a pilot study for breast cancer prevention. Cancer Epidemiol Biomarkers Prev 2002;11:614–21.

54. Stoler DL, Stewart CC, Stomper PC. Breast epithelium procurement from stereotactic core biopsy washings: flow cytometry-sorted cell count analysis. Clin Cancer Res 2002;8:428–32.

Chemoprevention

CHAPTER 10

BIOLOGIC BASIS FOR BREAST CANCER RISK REDUCTION WITH PHARMACOLOGIC AGENTS

V. Craig Jordan, OBE, PhD, DSc

Estrogen regulates physiology throughout a woman's body and controls reproduction. This knowledge, and advances in steroid endocrinology during the 1950s, led to the introduction of oral contraceptives as a logical approach to fertility control.[1] The actual mechanism of action is simple. Normally, ovarian steroids regulate the menstrual cycle in a precise sequence which simultaneously causes ovulation and prepares the uterus for the implantation of a fertilized egg. During the first half of the cycle, ovarian estrogen synthesis is regulated by a balance of negative and positive feedback mechanisms in the hypothalamo-pituitary axis (Figure 10-1). This regulates the pulsatile release of gonadotropins so ovarian stimulation is modulated. As a result, the maturing egg is primed for ovulation by an estrogen surge in midcycle. Simultaneously, unopposed ovarian estrogen causes growth of the uterus and proliferation in the endometrium. At the subcellular level, estrogen specifically causes synthesis of the progesterone receptor in the endometrium so that the uterus can convert from a proliferative to a secretory function after ovulation. The progesterone that prepares the uterus for implantation is made only in the corpus luteum under gonadotropin control, following ovulation. Thus, successful ovulation depends on a timed sequence of hormonal interactions. The prevention of ovulation by the continuous administration of low dose orally active synthetic estrogens and progestins completely disrupts the feedback mechanisms to the hypothalamo-pituitary axis, prevents normal ovarian steroid biosynthesis, and ultimately leads to the failure to advance the maturation of select eggs. Simply stated, constant daily levels of synthetic estrogens and progestins completely suppress gonadotropin secretion. No ovulation, no egg, no reproduction.

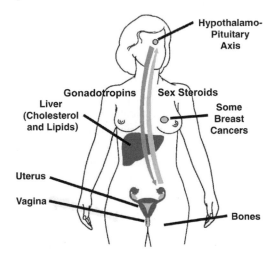

Figure 10-1 The location of estrogen target tissues around a woman's body. Estrogen receptors (ERs) in the hypothalamo-pituitary axis regulate the release of gonadotropins by both positive and negative feedback mechanisms. The gonadotropins, in turn, control the ovarian synthesis of estrogens and progestins that are essential to maintain the menstrual cycle and to reproduce. Estrogens cause proliferation in the uterine and vaginal epithelium through the ER. Additionally, breast cancer growth is supported through the ER in some breast cancers. The ERs located in liver and bone cells regulate the circulating levels of cholesterol and lipids, and bone density, respectively.

However, it is important to appreciate that although gonadotropins are suppressed by oral contraceptives, this is not the same as using a sustained release preparation of a gonadrotropin-releasing hormone superagonist such as goserelin (Zoladex, AstraZeneca, Wilmington, DE) to desensitize the pituitary gland completely. This form of medical oophorectomy results in complete suppression of ovarian steroidogenesis because no gonadotropins are released. Indeed, this approach to contraception has been proposed in young women to reduce the risk of breast cancer.[2,3] Oral contraceptives, on the other hand, substitute synthetic estrogens and progestins for the natural hormones but simultaneously switch off the normal function of the ovaries by feedback inhibition of gonadotropin release. Based on this knowledge, it is to be expected that women who take oral contraceptives for prolonged periods (5 to 10 years) would have a reduced incidence of ovarian cancer and, as might be anticipated, a reduced incidence of endometrial cancer.[4] In the case of endometrial cancer, women who have persistent annovulatory cycles or polycystic ovaries would now have progestin supplementation when they take oral contraceptives, and regular cyclical withdrawal bleeding would occur to counteract the impact of unopposed estrogen on the endometrium.

Applying the same physiologic principle from the uterus to the breast, premenopausal women who initially had high circulating levels of ovarian steroids would not be anticipated to have an increased or decreased risk of breast cancer by substituting exogenous synthetic steroids. There is believed to be no association between oral contraceptive use and breast cancer risk.[5]

Age is an important risk factor for the development of breast cancer. If the administration of oral contraceptives to younger women does not significantly enhance the process of promotion during carcinogenesis in women with normally high levels of sex steroids, the question could be asked whether the administration of estrogens or estrogens and progestins (as in hormone replacement therapy [HRT]) following menopause (ie, an environment with low levels of sex steroids) would have a deleterious effect on the incidence of endometrial cancer or breast cancer. The association between an increased risk of endometrial cancer and unopposed estrogen is well established. The small increase in endometrial cancer incidence is counter-acted by supplementation with a synthetic progestin to convert the endometrium from proliferative to secretory. Periodic cessation of HRT results in withdrawal bleeding and evacuation of malignant cells.

There is substantial epidemiologic evidence that combination HRT increases the risk of breast cancer in postmenopausal women.[6] Nevertheless, the Women's Health Initiative addressed the issue of the risks and benefits of HRT in a prospective clinical trial.[7] Overall, the benefits of HRT to reduce osteoporotic fractures and the risk of colon cancer were offset by increases in fatal thromboembolic events without a reduction in coronary heart disease. Additionally, the association of HRT with an elevated risk of breast cancer was confirmed.

The link between ovarian hormones and the growth and development of breast cancer has been known for more than a century, so it was only natural that clinical strategies to treat the disease should initially have focused on endocrine ablation (oophorectomy, adrenalectomy, and hypophysectomy) to restrict the production of steroid hormones.[8,9] However, it is the close collaboration between the laboratory and clinical research that has been the hallmark of the progress in endocrine therapy and chemoprevention.

BIOLOGIC BASIS FOR CURRENT CHEMOPREVENTION

Nearly a century ago, it was recognized that the inbreeding of mice produced strains with a high or low incidence of spontaneous mammary cancer. Spontaneous mammary cancer in mice is prevented by early oophorectomy,[10] but the finding that natural estrogens can enhance the incidence of mammary cancer in susceptible strains led Lacassagne to suggest in 1936 that if the "congestion" of estrogen in the breast was the cause of breast cancer, then an antagonist could be found to prevent the disease.[11] The definition of the estrogen receptor (ER) as the target,[12,13] and the application of both nonsteroidal antiestrogens[14,15] to block estrogen action and novel aromatase inhibitors[16] to prevent estrogen biosynthesis in postmenopausal women as strategies to treat breast cancer, together are the conceptual bases for current strategies to reduce the risk of breast cancer in either high- or low-risk populations.

SELECTIVE ESTROGEN RECEPTOR MODULATION

The idea that it is possible to target estrogen action selectively at tissue sites around the body originated in the laboratory during the 1980s and translated into clinical practice during the 1990s (Figure 10-2).[17,18]

In the 1970s, the development of nonsteroidal antiestrogens to treat breast cancer was based on the premise that estrogen-stimulated tumor growth could be blocked by simple nonsteroidal compounds binding to the ER.[14] Tamoxifen is the successful product of these research efforts.[15] However, the strategic development of the concept of long-term adjuvant tamoxifen treatment,[19,20] which resulted in the extension of clinical treatment from 1 to 5 years in both node-positive and node-negative breast cancer patients,[21,22] raised toxicologic concerns about the wisdom of using an antiestrogen to treat women with low risks for recurrence. Simply stated at the time, if estrogen was protective against coronary heart disease and osteoporosis, then an antiestrogen would control breast cancer recurrence but may predispose women to osteoporosis and coronary heart disease. If this was found to be true, then long-term antiestrogen therapy would be confined to ER-positive women with a high risk of breast cancer recurrence. Most importantly, the original concept to use estrogen antagonists to prevent breast cancer in high-risk women was unlikely to be acceptable if breast cancer was prevented in the short term, but osteoporosis and coronary heart disease both increased.[11] Indeed, these concerns were exacerbated throughout the 1990s; chemoprevention trials were underway, but the focus turned to the negative aspects of estrogen withdrawal on potential increases in dementia and Alzheimer's disease.

The nonsteroidal antiestrogen tamoxifen prevents the initiation and promotion of carcinogen-induced rat mammary carcinomas[23–25] and spontaneous mouse mammary carcinogenesis.[26] These data, along with the observation that tamoxifen reduces the incidence of contralateral breast cancer in patients receiving adjuvant therapy,[27] were initially used by clinical trialists to support the use of tamoxifen to prevent breast cancer in high-risk women.[28] There were, however, two clinical approaches to answer the questions about the safety of tamoxifen in well women. The primary goal of the Royal Marsden study initiated in the mid 1980s in the United Kingdom was to act as a vanguard for a broad international evaluation of the worth of tamoxifen as a chemopreventive in high-risk women. The women (approximately 2,000 to 3,000) were randomized to either treatment (20 mg tamoxifen daily for 8 years) or placebo, and an evaluation of bone density, gynecologic studies, lipid profiles, and general toxicities was built in as a safety evaluation.[29–31] The study was stated to be underpowered to answer the chemoprevention question.

An alternative strategy occurred in the United States, which led to the recognition of selective estrogen receptor modulation. The fact that tamoxifen was to be used strategically in women without cancer made a rigorous laboratory investigation mandatory. Although tamoxifen prevented rat mammary carcinogenesis,[20,23,32] paradoxically, the compound was found to have estrogen-like effects on bone in the rat that maintained bone density in oophorectomized animals.[33–35] Similarly, tamoxifen was an antiestrogen that prevented the growth of estrogen-stimulated ER-positive breast cancer cells in immunodeficient animals,[36,37] but again, paradoxically, caused the growth of endometrial cancers.[38] Thus the ER in two different human tumors, that is, breast and endometrial, was interpreting the tamoxifen ER complex as an inhibitory or stimula-

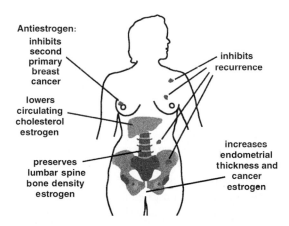

Figure 10-2 The target site specificity or selective estrogen receptor modulation of tamoxifen in the postmenopausal patient with breast cancer. The selective estrogen receptor modulator (SERM) tamoxifen has estrogen-like actions in bones, lowers circulating cholesterol, and increases the incidence of endometrial cancer. In contrast, tamoxifen is an estrogen antagonist in breast cancer.

tory signal in the same host.[38,39] Because it was already known from studies in the rat that tamoxifen lowered circulating cholesterol levels, one could predict that tamoxifen would have selective estrogenic and antiestrogenic effects around a woman's body.[40] A prospective clinical trial, organized at the University of Wisconsin in node-negative postmenopausal breast cancer patients, subsequently showed that tamoxifen could maintain bone density and reduce circulating cholesterol.[41,42] The idea thus emerged by 1992 that tamoxifen was unlikely to precipitate an excess of coronary heart disease and increase fractures if given to well women with a high risk of developing breast cancer.

The concept that tamoxifen was a selective estrogen/antiestrogen around the body was proven to be correct by the results of the chemoprevention trial published by Fisher and colleagues from the National Surgical Breast and Bowel Project (NASBP) P-1 trial in 1998.[43] These data show that, in women without breast cancer treated with tamoxifen, there is a nonstatistical decrease in fractures, an excess of endometrial cancer in postmenopausal women, but no increased risk of coronary heart disease.[43,44] Tamoxifen, the first clinically useful selective estrogen receptor modulator (SERM), is currently available for risk reduction in pre- and postmenopausal women with an elevated risk of breast cancer. Nevertheless, the concept of SERMs has subsequently been advanced with the goal of improving women's health in general.

A paradigm shift occurred in 1990 that catalyzed a refocusing of drug discovery by the pharmaceutical industry to exploit the emerging knowledge of SERM action. The new strategy for chemoprevention was stated simply:

"We have obtained valuable clinical information about this group of drugs that can be applied in other disease states. Research does not travel in straight lines, and observations in one field of science often become major discoveries in another. Important clues have been garnered about the effects of tamoxifen on bone and lipids so it is possible that derivatives could find targeted applications to retard osteoporosis or atherosclerosis. The ubiquitous application of novel compounds to prevent diseases associated with the progressive changes after menopause may, as a side effect, significantly retard the development

of breast cancer. The target population would be postmenopausal women in general, thereby avoiding the requirement to select a high-risk group to prevent breast cancer."[14]

The idea of using an analog of tamoxifen was based on the published knowledge that a chemical cousin of tamoxifen, keoxifene (LY156758),[45] a failed breast cancer treatment,[46] could prevent mammary tumors in rats[32] and preserve bone density in oophorectomized rats,[33] but had fewer estrogen-like actions in the rodent uterus, so there might be less likelihood of increases in endometrial cancer.[45]

Keoxifene was reinvented and repatented by Eli Lilly in 1992 as a SERM (now known as raloxifene) to prevent and treat osteoporosis but with breast and endometrial safety.[47–49] Based on the results of these pharmacologic studies, a whole range of new agents and SERMs is being developed.[50,51]

OPTIONS FOR SELECTIVE ESTROGEN RECEPTOR MODULATORS

Tamoxifen (Nolvadex, 20 mg daily, AstraZeneca), is available for risk reduction in pre- and postmenopausal women with an elevated risk for breast cancer. The recommended duration of treatment for the intervention is 5 years, but data from the overview analysis demonstrate that the beneficial actions of tamoxifen are maintained for at least a decade following the cessation of treatment.[52] The reason for the prolonged protective effect of tamoxifen is unclear, but laboratory evidence suggests that prolonged tamoxifen exposure may supersensitize the breast cancer cells to the apoptotic actions of physiologic estrogens (see "Exhaustive Endocrine Therapy," below).

Based on the clinical experience with breast cancer risk reduction during treatment for osteoporosis, raloxifene is being tested as a breast cancer preventive in high-risk postmenopausal women.[49] The Study of Tamoxifen and Raloxifene (STAR) will determine the relative efficacy of these two SERMs to reduce the incidence of breast cancer and determine their relative safety (Figure 10-3). Already, as of mid-2003, 15,000 high-risk postmenopausal volunteers have been recruited, and the goal of 19,000 women will be achieved in the next couple of years. Recruitment to the STAR trial remains a

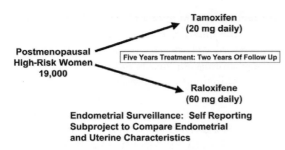

Figure 10-3 Study of Tamoxifen and Raloxifene (STAR) trial design. Nineteen thousand high-risk post-menopausal women are being randomized to 5-year treatment with either tamoxifen or raloxifene to determine whether long-term raloxifene therapy has increased or decreased ability to reduce the incidence of breast cancer. The trial will also compare the effects of the SERMs on fractures, coronary heart disease, and the incidence of endometrial cancer.

valuable option for the high-risk postmenopausal woman. Additionally, raloxifene causes a reduction in circulating cholesterol[53] and homocysteine,[54] and there are indications that raloxifene might cause a reduction in cardiovascular events.[55] As a result of these preliminary findings, the SERM is being evaluated in a prospective clinical trial called Raloxifene Use for the Heart (RUTH).[56] In light of the poor performance of HRT in reducing the risk of coronary heart disease in postmenopausal women, the anticipated results of the RUTH trial have now gained enhanced significance.[7]

Currently, raloxifene (Evista, 60 mg daily, Eli Lilly, Indianapolis, IN) is approved for the treatment and prevention of osteoporosis in postmenopausal women. Raloxifene is not to be used in the premenopausal woman primarily because of issues involving reproduction. However, the clinical question often arises whether it is appropriate to treat breast cancer patients with raloxifene to prevent osteoporosis after the recommended 5-year course of adjuvant tamoxifen treatment has stopped. The rationale has been stated to be that the beneficial effects of raloxifene to reduce the incidence of breast and endometrial cancer in well postmenopausal women could provide additional benefit and protection for the breast cancer patient.[49] There are, however, no clinical data to support this treatment strategy. In contrast, it is known that raloxifene is ineffective as an antitumor agent in breast cancer patients resistant to tamoxifen.[46] In other words, if occult breast or en-

dometrial cancer becomes resistant to tamoxifen during 5 years of adjuvant therapy, subsequent raloxifene treatment would enhance rather than retard tumor growth. This clinical scenario has been tested in the laboratory. Raloxifene has been shown to actively support the growth of tamoxifen-resistant breast and endometrial tumors implanted into athymic mice.[57] It is suggested that other nonendocrine methods be used to preserve bone density in woman who might become osteoporotic after stopping adjuvant tamoxifen treatment.

TOTAL ESTROGEN WITHDRAWAL

SERMs express estrogen-like actions at some target tissue sites; tamoxifen, in particular, has significant uterotropic activity in women and increases the risk of endometrial cancer. These clinical findings have encouraged the development of the third generation of aromatase inhibitors for the treatment and prevention of breast cancer.[16] The goal in the drug development program was to identify specific, nontoxic agents that would prevent the synthesis of nonessential estrogenic sex steroids in postmenopausal women. Complete inhibition of estrogen biosynthesis would potentially improve the response rate for breast cancer treatment and reduce the incidence of side effects such as blood clots and endometrial cancer.

The results of the recent Anastrozole versus Tamoxifen and the Combination (ATAC) trial demonstrate that an advance is being realized in adjuvant therapy.[58] Although the evaluation of efficacy and safety is perhaps premature, there are clear-cut indications that adjuvant anastrozole is superior to tamoxifen in reducing breast cancer recurrence rates at the current 3 years of treatment, and there are significant decreases in the incidence of endometrial cancer and blood clots in favor of anastrozole.

Most importantly, for the future strategies in chemoprevention, the use of anastrozole alone further reduces the known 50% reduction in the incidence of contralateral breast cancer produced by tamoxifen.[52,58] These encouraging data have resulted in a plan being initiated for the evaluation of anastrozole in postmenopausal women to test whether the side effects from total estrogen withdrawal will benefit significant numbers of women by reducing their risk for developing breast cancer. Clearly, there is a group of women who do not suffer significant menopausal symptoms or do not experience significant lifestyle problems owing to reduced vaginal secretions.[58] Obviously, because aromatase inhibitors increase the risk of fractures, the strategy is inappropriate for women with osteoporosis. Similarly, the development of osteoporosis needs to be carefully monitored in well postmenopausal women. Special attention to bones, with the introduction of additional therapeutic strategies to avoid osteoporosis, will be necessary. That being the case, the idea of testing whether a combination of a SERM to prevent osteoporosis and an aromatase inhibitor to prevent breast cancer selectively has recently occurred; the results are predictable, but nevertheless disappointing. Regrettably, there is no target site selectivity that can achieve the desired result. The aromatase inhibitor alone is more effective than tamoxifen in reducing primary breast cancer, but increases fractures because estrogen is denied to all sites that contain ER. A combination of an aromatase inhibitor, anastrozole, and a SERM, tamoxifen, is equivalent to tamoxifen alone in reducing primary (contralateral) breast cancer; the combination is inferior to anastrozole alone, but there are fewer fractures.[58] The mechanism is quite straightforward. In the estrogen-deprived woman during anastrozole treatment, the unoccupied ER cannot support tumor growth mechanisms because it cannot locate to the appropriate target genes. A SERM, coadministered with an aromatase inhibitor, would produce the biologic response at the relevant target tissue based on the intrinsic estrogenicity of the SERM–ER complex. In other words, the partially activated SERM–ER complex can locate and bind to estrogen-responsive genes. Bone will be maintained by the SERM–ER complex, but the estrogen-like action of the complex might also cause some *HER2/neu*-positive breast cancers to grow. Thus a combination of a SERM and an aromatase inhibitor would be expected to be only as good as a SERM alone. In other words, a comparison of nothing (the aromatase inhibitor) versus some activity (aromatase inhibitor plus SERM) is being made. The outcome of this simple principle is exemplified by the results of the ATAC trial: there are significant decreases in fractures in favor of tamoxifen-treated patients in the ATAC trial, but the combination of anastrozole and tamoxifen was no better than tamoxifen alone in the treatment and prevention of breast cancer.[58] Nevertheless, the question remains whether a new and improved SERM with fewer estrogen-like properties in the breast and uterus will be superior to aromatase inhibition in select women.

DRUG RESISTANCE AND MECHANISMS OF ACTION

The ER is a nuclear transcription factor that regulates estrogen-responsive genes through either classical or nontraditional (tethered) pathways. As a further tier of complexity, there are now known to be two types of ER: ERα is the receptor described in clinical medicine for the past 40 years[12–13]; the second, ERβ, was discovered in 1996 using screening techniques in the rat prostate.[59]

During the past 6 years there has been an enormous increase in the understanding of the subcellular actions of estrogen and SERMs. However, it is inappropriate to recapitulate all of the evidence here to support the current view of estrogen and SERM action at different target sites. The reader is referred to recent reviews of the refereed literature for the primary scientific sources.[50,51,60] Instead, a working model will be presented to act as a guide to estrogen and SERM action in target tissues and to understand the complexity of drug resistance to SERMs.

Estrogen action through the ER is modified by coactivator proteins that enhance the nuclear transcription of genes or corepressors that neutralize the activity of the unoccupied ER (Figure 10-4). In contrast, SERMs (tamoxifen or raloxifene) change the external surface of the SERM–ER complex compared with the estradiol–ER complex so that coactivators do not bind. Nevertheless, corepressors now bind to the SERM–ER complex. Simply stated, SERMs can block estrogen action by competing for the ligand binding domain of the ER, and then, by recruiting corepressors, prevent signal transduction of estrogen-responsive genes. As a result, that particular target site will have an antiestrogenic response.

In contrast, target sites that have both an increased level of coactivators from the family *SRC*, that is, *SRC1*, *-2*, and *-3*, plus an increase in cell surface signaling, appear to have an enhanced estrogenicity for tamoxifen rather than raloxifene.[61] The enhanced phosphorylation signals from cell surface receptor signaling, initiated by tyrosine kinases, increase both the

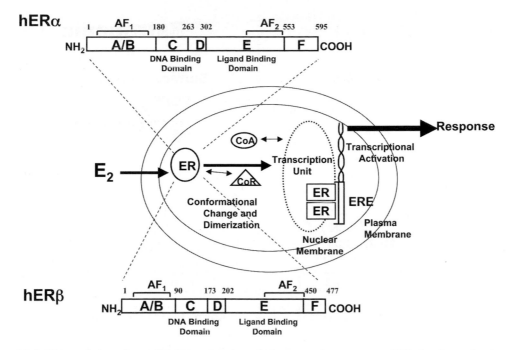

Figure 10-4 The regulation of estradiol (E_2) action through the two estrogen receptor (ER) signal transduction pathways. The respective ERα or ERβ proteins are activated and dimerize (homo- or hetero-) to form a transcription unit. This is located appropriately at an estrogen response element (ERE) in the promoter region of an estrogen responsive gene. The transcription unit is formed by coactivator (CoA) molecules but can be neutralized if antiestrogens are bound to the ER. The antiestrogen–ER complex does not bind CoA molecules but attracts corepressor molecules (CoR). SERM action might depend on the ratio of ERα to ERβ or the ratio of CoA to CoR molecules in different target sites.

phosphorylation status of the tamoxifen–ER complex (Figure 10-5) and phosphorylation of coactivators such as *SRC3* (*AIB1*).[62] The activated tamoxifen–ER and coactivator complexes now have the potential to initiate gene transcription and estrogen-like responses at select target sites such as the uterus. The fact that the raloxifene–ER complex is less estrogen-like probably results from the close interaction of the antiestrogenic side chain of raloxifene with amino acid 351 (aspartate) on the external surface of the raloxifene–ER complex.[63] It has been hypothesized that this interaction facilitates the binding of a corepressor at this site to prevent estrogen action.[64]

Drug resistance to SERMs can be viewed as an extension of the concepts of selective target site specificity. There are two forms of drug resistance to tamoxifen: intrinsic resistance and acquired resistance. Intrinsic resistance is illustrated by the fact that only half of the ER-positive breast cancers will respond to tamoxifen treatment initially. Recent studies by Osborne and colleagues have illustrated the impact of high *SRC3* and *HER2/neu* on the

initial effectiveness of tamoxifen as an adjuvant therapy.[65] A triumvirate, that is, three controlling factors of ER, *HER2/neu*, and high *SRC3*, is a potential predictive marker for the ineffectiveness of tamoxifen treatment. These data are also of importance during chemoprevention, as the same principle will be true for the effectiveness of preemptive tamoxifen treatment on subclinical disease, that is, microfoci of malignant breast cells that have not yet been detected. This, in part, could be the explanation for the low, but significant, incidence of ER-positive tumors noted in the early results from tamoxifen chemoprevention trials.[43]

Acquired resistance to tamoxifen (and cross-resistance with raloxifene) occurs during extended therapy.[57] This form of resistance is unique to SERMs and is characterized by SERM-stimulated growth. Initially, tamoxifen is effective as an antiestrogen in about half of ER-positive breast cancers, but then, probably through clonal selection, tamoxifen-stimulated tumors emerge. These tumors with acquired resistance to tamoxifen can be identified in

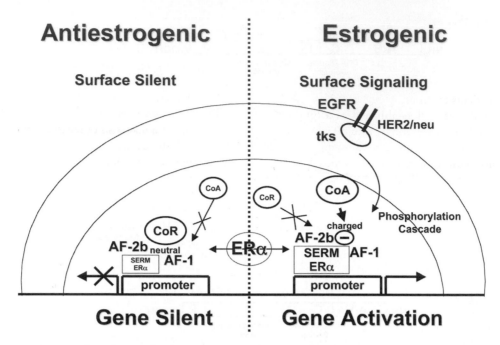

Figure 10-5 Integrated mechanism for the target site-specific action of SERMs in breast and uterine cancer. The two extremes of antiestrogenic or full estrogenic actions are shown. Estrogen-like actions could occur in cells expressing an excess of coactivators (CoAs) and/or a decrease in corepressors (CoRs). The charged surface of a tamoxifen ER complex at *AF-2b* (activating function) prevents CoR binding. The estrogenic action would be amplified by surface signaling with dimers of epidermal growth factor receptor (*EGFR*) and *HER2/neu* activating tyrosine kinases (tks). The phosphorylation cascade can activate *AF-1* on ERα directly or activate the excess of CoAs in high ER environment. Reduced levels of ER prevent the signal transduction pathway and promote antiestrogenic actions in a surface silent cell.

the clinic by a withdrawal of the drug resulting in decreased tumor growth rate.[68] Laboratory studies in vivo have replicated acquired tamoxifen drug resistance in breast cancer cell lines grown in athymic mice.[68] Interestingly enough, either tamoxifen or estrogen supports the growth of tamoxifen-stimulated tumors.[68,69] Clearly, the fact that either estrogen or tamoxifen will support the growth of tumors with acquired tamoxifen resistance is why aromatase inhibitors are effective as second-line therapies after tamoxifen treatment is stopped.[68] The patient is converted to an estrogen-free state.

CONSEQUENCES OF ANTIHORMONAL THERAPY IN TREATMENT AND CHEMOPREVENTION

The current target for the treatment and prevention of breast cancer is the ER.[18] The strategies to use the target have proved to be extraordinarily successful. During treatment, tamoxifen alone is estimated to have saved 400,000 lives, and chemoprevention studies demonstrate that the incidence in invasive and noninvasive (ductal carcinoma in situ [DCIS]) breast cancer can be cut by 50% in select populations. However, it is also important to consider the consequences of using long-term antihormonal therapies both on the patient and on the molecular biology of the emerging resistant tumor.

There is currently an intense debate about the appropriate strategy to use to prevent breast cancer in postmenopausal women.[70,71] The principal side effects observed with tamoxifen in postmenopausal women are an increase in blood clots and endometrial cancer.[43,72] By contrast, there is a lower incidence of blood clots and endometrial cancer noted when tamoxifen and the aromatase inhibitor anastrozole were compared in the ATAC trial.[58] However, as might be anticipated, there are fewer fractures in favor of the SERM compared with an aromatase inhibitor.[58] Thus, the debate that seeks to polarize the medical community into the "no estrogen at all" (aromatase inhibitor) approach versus the "is a balance best?" (SERM) approach should really be the answer to the question, "What is best for my patients on an individual basis?"

Tamoxifen is well established as a long-term therapy and chemopreventive, with 30 years of clinical experience. Nevertheless, there are clear-cut problems with recommending tamoxifen as a chemopreventive for all high-risk patients. Obese or inactive women, or women with a history of uterine dysfunction, blood clotting problems, and HRT use should probably avoid tamoxifen as a preventive.[73] These concerns, however, are confined to postmenopausal women. Conversely, postmenopausal women who are osteopenic or clearly osteoporotic should avoid chemoprevention clinical trials using aromatase inhibitors despite the possibility of taking bisphosphonates to avoid excessive further bone loss. It is clear that the physician has most of the information necessary to make a rational decision about what is best for the individual patient. The unknowns at present are the consequences of extended therapy with aromatase inhibitors on colon cancer risk (in light of the positive association between HRT and risk reduction),[7] exacerbated or accelerated dementia, discomfort during intercourse owing to no vaginal secretions, as well as alterations in the risk of osteoporosis and coronary heart disease. There is no doubt that the extensive clinical database on the use of tamoxifen for treatment was essential to protect women from the unforeseen consequences of using tamoxifen as a chemopreventive. There were few, if any, surprises for the clinical community. The same will undoubtedly be true for aromatase inhibitors once a 5- to 10-year treatment database is established. Also, it will be essential to establish whether raloxifene, in the STAR trial, is superior to tamoxifen as a SERM as it will clearly be the true comparator with aromatase inhibitors in future chemoprevention studies.

Despite the consequences of chemoprevention on a woman's physiology, there is no doubt that the risk for breast cancer can be reduced by antiestrogenic strategies. Tamoxifen has quantifiable actions on premalignant or microscopic subclinical lesions in the breast. Tamoxifen reduces the incidence of benign breast disease[74] and DCIS and reduces the transition from atypical hyperplasia to invasive

breast cancer by 80%.[43] These observations can all be used as evidence to support the view that early tamoxifen treatment prevents the progression of premalignant (or early malignant) breast epithelial cells to invasive breast cancer.

Nevertheless, there is also the possibility that subclinical disease is being treated by SERMs in women without a diagnosis of breast cancer. In this case, the majority of ER-positive breast cancers will be prevented from developing into a detectable tumor during the first few years of treatment. This concept is evidenced by the actions of tamoxifen,[43] raloxifene,[49,75] and anastrozole, which reduce the incidence of primary or contralateral breast cancer during very short treatment periods of less than 3 years.[58] However, although the antiestrogenic intervention will reduce incidence, there is still ample opportunity for clonal selection to occur during long-term treatment so that SERM-resistant (intrinsic and acquired) disease will develop (Figure 10-6).

In the case of acquired resistance, the SERM ultimately initiates the biochemical events that will cause SERM-stimulated cells to be cloned out and grow into a tumor. The response of the ER-positive cell to the SERM has recently been discussed in detail, but for the sake of completeness the general mechanism needs to be stated.[76] Estradiol-stimulated tumor growth functions primarily through a direct signal transduction mechanism via the nuclear ER. The E_2–ER complex initiates transcription-responsive genes. This finely tuned system in

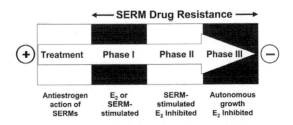

Figure 10-6 The evolution of breast cancer treatment and tamoxifen-induced drug resistance. The ER-positive tumor will eventually become stimulated by either tamoxifen or estrogen during Phase I drug resistance, but after about 5 years, Phase II resistance appears, in which estrogen alone now kills tumor cells. In the final phase of SERM resistance (Phase III), growth is autonomous and all ER-targeted therapies fail except estrogen. Finally, either the tumor burden becomes too great or the ER is lost and the chemotherapy is the only option remaining.

normal cells may be partially modulated by cell surface receptors (insulin growth factors [IGF] or epidermal growth factor [EGF]) that initiate phosphorylation cascades to impinge on the cell cycle machinery directly or via "cross talk." However, in the case of cancer cells, the *HER2/neu* oncogene, a cell surface receptor that is essentially unique to breast cancer, can be transcribed and dimerizes with other members of the cell surface receptor family (*erb 1, 3* and *4*) to dominate and ultimately subvert the actions of the nuclear ER. Not surprisingly, estrogen prevents the induction of *HER2/neu* messenger ribonucleic acid (mRNA) by sequestering coactivators, but antiestrogens do the opposite.[77] Coactivators necessary to synthesize the *HER2/neu* mRNA are released from the SERM–ER complex and induce mRNA for *HER2/neu* synthesis. The consequence of long-term SERM treatment is the development of surviving breast cancer cells that are *HER2/neu*-positive, ER-positive, and grow with SERM treatment. Additionally, SERMs consolidate the growth advantage of resistant breast cancer by enhancing the production of transforming growth factor β that encourages the synthesis of more coactivators which, in turn, enhance gene transcription. Thus, again, the triumvirate of ER, coactivators, and *HER2/neu* ultimately provides a growth advantage for the SERM-resistant cell.[76] It must, at this point, be stressed that chemoprevention will inhibit the progression of occult disease in the majority of women for many decades. Nevertheless, the ultimate development of SERM-resistant disease raises the question of a logical approach to treating breast cancer that occurs in women using tamoxifen or raloxifene for either breast cancer chemoprevention or prevention of osteoporosis, respectively.

PLAUSIBLE APPROACHES FOR TREATMENT OF ENDOCRINE REFRACTORY DISEASE

Patients who develop breast cancer during long-term SERM treatment may have either ER-positive or ER-negative disease.[43,49] ER-positive disease could be either SERM dependent (acquired resistance) or SERM independent (intrinsic resistance). Potential strategies for the treatment of SERM-resistant disease can be formulated based on the molecular biology of SERM action in breast cancer.

The potential targets in the signal transduction pathways of SERM-resistant tumors that subvert antiestrogen action are illustrated in Figure 10-7. The enhanced cell surface signaling through *HER2/neu* can potentially be blocked either by an antibody to *HER2/neu* or a tyrosine kinase (tk) inhibitor could be targeted to either the *HER2/neu* or EGFR tk. In either situation, the goal is to block the cell survival pathway, but any single-agent therapy must clearly be complemented with the appropriate combination cytoxic chemotherapy to provoke apoptosis. It must be stressed that this therapeutic approach following the termination of SERM treatment is hypothetical, although if the patient has amplified *HER2/neu* by fluorescent *in-situ* hybridization then this treatment approach would be appropriate.

In contrast, there is ample evidence, both from the laboratory and from clinical trials, that tamoxifen- (and presumably raloxifene) stimulated breast tumor growth is using the ER to initiate the growth mechanism. The ER, therefore, remains an effective target to treat breast cancer that develops during chemoprevention with tamoxifen or treatment for osteoporosis with raloxifene.

Tamoxifen-stimulated breast tumor growth is demonstrated clinically by a withdrawal response to tamoxifen.[66,67] However, it is also appropriate to use aromatase inhibitors to remove estrogen throughout the body that could enhance ER activation and tumor regrowth.[78–81] Alternatively, the ER could be destroyed by fulvestrant (Faslodex, AstraZeneca).[82] Recent studies demonstrate that anastrozole (Arimidex, AstraZeneca) and fulvestrant have equivalent effectiveness following the failure of tamoxifen therapy.[83,84] Although the majority of patients are nonresponsive to a second-line endocrine therapy, targeting the ER of select patients can result in long-term responses that can be maintained with few serious side effects.

EXHAUSTIVE ENDOCRINE THERAPY

The current trend for the application of long-term antihormonal approaches to prevent breast cancer (tamoxifen, raloxifene, and anastrozole) and the potentially indefinite use of raloxifene to prevent osteoporosis (or perhaps to prevent coronary heart disease depending on the results of the RUTH

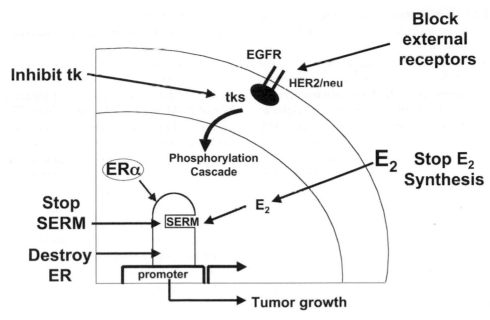

Figure 10-7 Treatment strategies that could potentially be applied to prevent the growth of SERM-resistant breast cancer. The use of an antibody to block cell surface receptors or a tyrosine kinase (tk) are currently investigational, but pure antiestrogen to destroy ER or an aromatase inhibitor to prevent estrogen synthesis are appropriate second-line therapies if tamoxifen-resistant disease occurs during chemoprevention.

trial) has mandated the close laboratory investigation of exhaustive endocrine treatment. The basic question being addressed is, "What will happen if occult breast cancer cells are exposed to SERMs or estrogen withdrawal for 5 to 10 years?" The findings have been quite surprising and hold enormous promise for further basic investigations with clinical applications in the future. It is perhaps inappropriate to provide all of the laboratory evidence that is currently emerging, but it is possible to summarize the advances being made to illustrate the dramatic change in our understanding of the evolution of endocrine resistance. Twenty years ago it was generally believed that exhaustive endocrine therapy would convert responsive ER-positive breast cancer cells to ER-negative cells through loss of a functional ER gene. The discovery of acquired tamoxifen resistance, which retained ER but in which the tumors grew in response to either tamoxifen or estrogen (now called Phase I resistance; see Figure 10-6), changed the historical view of resistance and accelerated the development of aromatase inhibitors and pure antiestrogens as new therapeutic agents to treat SERM-resistant disease.[38]

However, the reports of clinical and laboratory studies were observed only with several months of tamoxifen treatment and did not reflect the established treatment strategy with 5 years of adjuvant tamoxifen therapy. Laboratory studies of long-term tamoxifen treatment now demonstrate that more than 5 years of treatment paradoxically supersensitizes the tumor cells to undergo apoptosis in response to physiologic concentrations of estradiol (now called Phase II resistance; see Figure 10-6) when tamoxifen treatment stops.[85] Thus, a specific switch has occurred within the cells by the constant adaptation of breast cancer cells to the weak estrogen-like actions of SERMs. Clones of ER-positive cells emerge that grow in response to SERMs but now do not survive; they are killed when exposed to estrogen liganded to the ER. What is particularly interesting is that although the majority of tumors regress, those that regrow in the estrogen environment respond again to the antiestrogenic and antitumor actions of tamoxifen.[85] Finally, ER-positive tumors become refractory to all forms of endocrine therapy (Phase III; see Figure 10-6), but recent clinical studies indicate estrogen is still effective as a treatment.[86]

Clearly, it is important to determine the mechanism for the tumoricidal action of physiologic estrogen, because new clinical protocols could be devised to enhance tumor cell kill following adjuvant antihormone therapy. In other words, an appropriate "purge" with either synthetic or natural estrogens, or phytoestrogens could be used periodically to maintain a low tumor burden so that indefinite cycles of antihormonal therapy could turn breast cancer from an acute to a chronic, but manageable, disease.

Clues to the potential mechanism for the tumoricidal actions of estrogen have recently been reported using ER-positive breast cancer cells that have been maintained for years in an estrogen-free environment. Santen and colleagues noted that estrogen activates the apoptotic *fas/fas* ligand pathway in select MCF7 breast cancer cells in culture.[87] Similarly, studies in vivo and in vitro with SERM-resistant breast cancer cells show that estrogen not only activates the *fas/fas* ligand pathway with activated caspase 8 causing apoptosis, but also estrogen causes a decrease in survival pathways by completely depleting the phosphorylated *HER2/neu* cell surface receptor system and reducing the nuclear levels of the transcription factor NFkB. These molecular events are summarized in Figure 10-8.

There are several useful clinical application for the laboratory findings. As already mentioned, estrogen "purges" could be used to periodically reduce tumor burden and restore antihormone sensitivity. There is the possibility that dietary changes, with foods containing high levels of phytoestrogens, could be a viable option for delivering estrogen to appropriate patients. Alternatively, patients with advanced disease who have received exhaustive endocrine therapies could employ estrogen supplementation with standard chemotherapies to enhance apoptosis and reduce tumor survival mechanisms. Clearly, these new concepts provide new knowledge about the ability of the ER to remain a viable target that controls the life and death of the breast cancer cell. However, it is inappropriate at this stage to use these concepts in general practice. Only a series of controlled clinical trials will establish the safety and efficacy of low dose estrogen therapy following exhaustive antihormonal therapies. There is now a clearer understanding of the evolution of antihormonal drug resistance (summarized in Figure 10-6) that can be translated to clinical applications in the not too distant future.

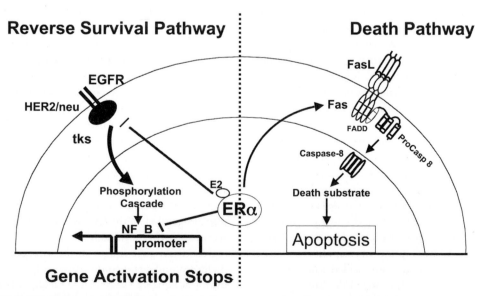

Figure 10-8 The proposed subcellular mechanism for estrogen-induced apoptosis of SERM-resistant (Phase II and III) breast cancer. The estradiol–ER complex collapses the cell survival pathway by blocking the synthesis of *HER2/neu* and decreasing the levels of the nuclear transcription factor NFkB. Simultaneously, there is an induction of the *Fas* receptor that becomes activated by the constitutively produced *Fas* ligand. Caspase 8 then initiates apoptosis.

FUTURE STRATEGIES FOR CHEMOPREVENTION

The past decade has seen important advances in the promise of the chemoprevention of breast cancer. New therapeutic strategies must, ultimately, be tested to achieve the goal. There are at least four possible strategies currently under consideration to advance chemoprevention using pharmacologic interventions. First is the consideration of all possible measures to avoid breast cancer development exclusively in those women with proven breast cancer susceptibility genes. Second is the established intervention with an antiestrogenic modality (tamoxifen) in select pre- and postmenopausal women with a high risk of developing breast cancer by the application of the Gail Model.[88] Third is the use of an aromatase inhibitor that specifically removes estrogen from all postmenopausal women. The goal is to reduce breast cancer risk completely but also to manage other diseases that might result from a no estrogen environment. Fourth, there is the application of multifunctional medicines (SERMs) that can reduce the risks for different diseases as beneficial side effects by treating osteoporosis and coronary heart disease or specifically targeting high-risk breast cancer populations.

Although much work has been accomplished taking ideas from the laboratory to the clinic, it is perhaps useful to restate the actual scientific principles that must be addressed to improve prospects for prevention in the future.[89] It is clear from animal studies that mammary tissue is the most sensitive to carcinogenic insults during the short period after puberty. If this is also true for humans, with the carcinogenic insult occurring early in the reproductive life of the woman, then breast cancer either progresses to manifest itself as premenopausal breast cancer or remains dormant for decades only to appear after menopause. Potential integrated strategies for intervention to address carcinogenesis are illustrated in Figure 10-9. Ideally, the discovery of a multifunctional contraceptive that desensitizes breast tissue would solve the problem of carcinogenesis, but this is unlikely to be advanced any time soon. Nevertheless, efforts to understand the protective effects of gonadotropins on mammary carcinogenesis are advancing rapidly with an understanding of gene regulation in sensitive and refractory mammary tissues. This is an extrapolation

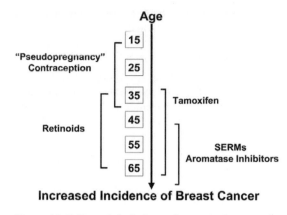

Figure 10-9 Potential windows of opportunity to apply prevention strategies.

of the known beneficial effects of early pregnancy. The administration of gonadotropins could be described as "pseudopregnancy." Future discoveries may translate to the clinic. However, the concern about interventions early in a woman's reproductive life has resulted in the majority of current strategies with antihormones focusing on the safer but later stages of the cancer continuum. Regrettably, efforts to use retinoids to enhance the chemoprevention armamentarium have proved to be disappointing.[90,91]

Clearly, it is time to rethink the strategic applications of chemoprevention. A focus on an extremely well-defined population where the intervention will provide greater benefits will avoid issues of side effects in low-risk populations. This strategy in the early stages of carcinogenesis would potentially also prevent ER-negative disease. A preemptive approach in very high-risk populations, coupled with a reinvigorated program of SERM research to identify superior medicines for postmenopausal populations, holds the greatest promise for a cost-effective public health policy for the prevention of breast cancer.

REFERENCES

1. Drill VA. History of the first oral contraceptive. J Toxicol Environ Health 1977;3:133–8.
2. Spicer DV, Shoupe D, Pike MC. GnRH agonists as contraceptive agents: predicted significantly reduced risk of breast cancer. Contraception 1991; 44:289–310.
3. Spicer DV, Pike MC, Pike A, et al. Pilot trial of a gonadotropin hormone agonist with replacement

hormones as a prototype contraceptive to prevent breast cancer. Contraception 1993;47:427–44.

4. Prentice RL, Thomas DB. On the epidemiology of oral contraceptives and disease. Adv Cancer Res 1987; 49:285–401.

5. Thomas DB. Oral contraceptives and breast cancer: review of the epidemiologic literature. Contraception 1991;43:597–642.

6. Collaborative-Group-on-Hormonal-Factors-in-Breast-Cancer. Breast cancer and hormone replacement therapy: collaborative reanalysis of data from 51 epidemiological studies of 52,705 women with breast cancer and 108,411 women without breast cancer. Lancet 1997;350:1047–59.

7. Writing Group for the Women's Health Initiative Investigators. Risks and benefits of estrogen plus progestin in healthy postmenopausal women: principal results from the Women's Health Initiative randomized controlled trial. JAMA 2002;288: 321–33.

8. Beatson GT. On the treatment of inoperable cases of carcinoma of the mamma: suggestions for a new method of treatment with illustrative cases. Lancet 1896;2:104–7.

9. Boyd S. On oophorectomy in cancer of the breast. BMJ 1900;ii:1161–7.

10. Lathrop AE, Loeb L. Further investigations on the origins of tumors in mice. III: on the part played by internal secretions in the spontaneous development of tumors. J Cancer Res 1916;1: 1–19.

11. Lacassagne A. Hormonal pathogenesis of adenocarcinoma of the breast. Am J Cancer 1936;27: 217–25.

12. Jensen EV, Jacobson HI. Basic guides to the mechanism of estrogen action. Recent Prog Horm Res 1962;18:387–414.

13. Jensen EV, Greene GL, Closs LE, et al. Receptors reconsidered: a 20-year perspective. Recent Prog Horm Res 1982;38:1–40.

14. Lerner LJ, Jordan VC. The development of antiestrogens for the treatment of breast cancer: Eighth Cain Memorial Award Lecture. Cancer Res 1990; 50:4177–89.

15. Jordan VC. Tamoxifen: a most unlikely pioneering medicine. Nat Rev Drug Discovery 2003;2: 205–13.

16. Goss PE, Strasser K. Aromatase inhibitors in the treatment and prevention of breast cancer. J Clin Oncol 2001;19:881–94.

17. Jordan VC. Selective estrogen receptor modulation: a personal perspective. Cancer Res 2001;61:5683–7.

18. Jensen EV, Jordan VC. The estrogen receptor: a model for molecular medicine. The Dorothy P. Landon AACR Prize for Translational Research. Clin Cancer Res 2003;9:1980–89.

19. Jordan VC, Dix CJ, Allen KE. The effectiveness of long term tamoxifen treatment in a laboratory model for adjuvant hormone therapy of breast cancer. In: Salmon SE, Jones SE, editors. Adju-

vant therapy of cancer. Vol 2. New York: Grune & Stratton, Inc.; 1979. p. 19–26.

20. Jordan VC. Laboratory studies to develop general principles for the adjuvant treatment of breast cancer with antiestrogens: problems and potential for future clinical applications. Breast Cancer Res Treat 1983;3(Suppl):S73–86.

21. Breast Cancer Trials Committee. Adjuvant tamoxifen in the management of operable breast cancer: the Scottish Trial. Report from the Breast Cancer Trials Committee, Scottish Cancer Trials Office (MRC), Edinburgh. Lancet 1987;2:171–5.

22. Fisher B, Costantino J, Redmond C, et al. A randomized clinical trial evaluating tamoxifen in the treatment of patients with node-negative breast cancer who have estrogen-receptor-positive tumors. N Engl J Med 1989;320:479–84.

23. Jordan VC. Effect of tamoxifen (ICI 46,474) on initiation and growth of DMBA-induced rat mammary carcinomata. Eur J Cancer 1976;12:419–24.

24. Jordan VC, Allen KE. Evaluation of the antitumour activity of the non-steroidal antioestrogen monohydroxytamoxifen in the DMBA-induced rat mammary carcinoma model. Eur J Cancer 1980; 16:239–51.

25. Jordan VC, Allen KE, Dix CJ. Pharmacology of tamoxifen in laboratory animals. Cancer Treat Rep 1980;64:745–59.

26. Jordan VC, Lababidi MK, Langan-Fahey S. Suppression of mouse mammary tumorigenesis by long-term tamoxifen therapy. J Natl Cancer Inst 1991; 83:492–6.

27. Cuzick J, Baum M. Tamoxifen and contralateral breast cancer [letter]. Lancet 1985;2:282.

28. Powles TJ, Hardy JR, Ashley SE, et al. A pilot trial to evaluate the acute toxicity and feasibility of tamoxifen for prevention of breast cancer. Br J Cancer 1989;60:126–31.

29. Powles TJ, Jones AL, Ashley SE, et al. The Royal Marsden Hospital pilot tamoxifen chemoprevention trial. Breast Cancer Res Treat 1994;31:73–82.

30. Powles TJ, Hickish T, Kanis JA, et al. Effect of tamoxifen on bone mineral density measured by dual-energy x-ray absorptiometry in healthy premenopausal and postmenopausal women. J Clin Oncol 1996;14:78–84.

31. Kedar RP, Bourne TH, Powles TJ, et al. Effects of tamoxifen on uterus and ovaries of postmenopausal women in a randomised breast cancer prevention trial [see comments]. Lancet 1994;343:1318–21.

32. Gottardis MM, Jordan VC. Antitumor actions of keoxifene and tamoxifen in the N-nitrosomethylurea-induced rat mammary carcinoma model. Cancer Res 1987;47:4020–4.

33. Jordan VC, Phelps E, Lindgren JU. Effects of antiestrogens on bone in castrated and intact female rats. Breast Cancer Res Treat 1987;10:31–5.

34. Turner RT, Wakley GK, Hannon KS, Bell NH. Tamoxifen prevents the skeletal effects of ovarian

hormone deficiency in rats. J Bone Miner Res 1987;2:449–56.

35. Turner RT, Wakley GK, Hannon KS, Bell NH. Tamoxifen inhibits osteoclast-mediated resorption of trabecular bone in ovarian hormone-deficient rats. Endocrinology 1988;122:1146–50.

36. Osborne CK, Hobbs K, Clark GM. Effect of estrogens and antiestrogens on growth of human breast cancer cells in athymic nude mice. Cancer Res 1985;45:584–90.

37. Gottardis MM, Robinson SP, Jordan VC. Estradiol-stimulated growth of MCF-7 tumors implanted in athymic mice: a model to study the tumoristatic action of tamoxifen. J Steroid Biochem 1988;30: 311–4.

38. Gottardis MM, Robinson SP, Satyaswaroop PG, Jordan VC. Contrasting actions of tamoxifen on endometrial and breast tumor growth in the athymic mouse. Cancer Res 1988;48:812–5.

39. Jordan VC, Robinson SP. Species-specific pharmacology of antiestrogens: role of metabolism. Fed Proc 1987;46:1870–4.

40. Harper MJ, Walpole AL. A new derivative of triphenylethylene: effect on implantation and mode of action in rats. J Reprod Fertil 1967;13:101–19.

41. Love RR, Mazess RB, Barden HS, et al. Effects of tamoxifen on bone mineral density in postmenopausal women with breast cancer [see comments]. N Engl J Med 1992;326:852–6.

42. Love RR, Wiebe DA, Newcomb PA, et al. Effects of tamoxifen on cardiovascular risk factors in postmenopausal women. Ann Intern Med 1991;115: 860–4.

43. Fisher B, Costantino JP, Wickerham DL, et al. Tamoxifen for prevention of breast cancer: report of the National Surgical Adjuvant Breast and Bowel Project P-1 Study. J Natl Cancer Inst 1998;90: 1371–88.

44. Reis SE, Costantino JP, Wickerham DL, et al. Cardiovascular effects of tamoxifen in women with and without heart disease: Breast Cancer Prevention Trial. National Surgical Adjuvant Breast and Bowel Project Breast Cancer Prevention Trial Investigators. J Natl Cancer Inst 2001;93:16–21.

45. Black LJ, Jones CD, Falcone JF. Antagonism of estrogen action with a new benzothiophene derived antiestrogen. Life Sci 1983;32:1031–6.

46. Buzdar AU, Marcus C, Holmes F, et al. Phase II evaluation of Ly156758 in metastatic breast cancer. Oncology 1988;45:344–5.

47. Delmas PD, Bjarnason NH, Mitlak BH, et al. Effects of raloxifene on bone mineral density, serum cholesterol concentrations, and uterine endometrium in postmenopausal women [see comments]. N Engl J Med 1997;337:1641–7.

48. Ettinger B, Black DM, Mitlak BH, et al. Reduction of vertebral fracture risk in postmenopausal women with osteoporosis treated with raloxifene: results from a 3-year randomized clinical trial. Multiple Outcomes of Raloxifene Evaluation

(MORE) Investigators [see comments]. JAMA 1999;282:637–45.

49. Cummings SR, Eckert S, Krueger KA, et al. The effect of raloxifene on risk of breast cancer in postmenopausal women: results from the MORE randomized trial. Multiple Outcomes of Raloxifene Evaluation. JAMA 1999;281:2189–97.

50. Jordan VC. Antiestrogens and selective estrogen receptor modulators as multifunctional medicines Part I: receptor interactions. J Med Chem 2003; 46:883–908.

51. Jordan VC. Antiestrogens and selective estrogen receptor modulators as multifunctional medicines Part II: clinical considerations and new agents. J Med Chem 2003;46:1082–111.

52. Early Breast Cancer Trialists' Collaborative Group (EBCTCG). Tamoxifen for early breast cancer: an overview of the randomised trials. Lancet 1998; 351:1451–67.

53. Walsh BW, Kuller LH, Wild RA, et al. Effects of raloxifene on serum lipids and coagulation factors in healthy postmenopausal women. JAMA 1998; 279:1445–51.

54. Walsh BW, Paul S, Wild RA, et al. The effects of hormone replacement therapy and raloxifene on C-reactive protein and homocysteine in healthy postmenopausal women: a randomized, controlled trial. J Clin Endocrinol Metab 2000;85:214–8.

55. Barrett-Connor E, Grady D, Sashegyi A, et al. Raloxifene and cardiovascular events in osteoporotic postmenopausal women. JAMA 2002;287:847–57.

56. Mosca L, Barrett-Connor E, Wenger NK, et al. Design and methods of the Raloxifene Use for The Heart (RUTH) study. Am J Cardiol 2001;88:392–5.

57. O'Regan RM, Gajdos C, Dardes RC, et al. Effects of raloxifene after tamoxifen on breast and endometrial tumor growth in athymic mice. J Natl Cancer Inst 2002;94:274–83.

58. The ATAC Trialist Group. Anastrozole alone or in combination with tamoxifen versus tamoxifen alone for adjuvant treatment of postmenopausal women with early breast cancer: first results of the ATAC randomized trial. Lancet 2002;359:2131–9.

59. Kuiper GG, Enmark E, Pelto-Huikko M, et al. Cloning of a novel receptor expressed in rat prostate and ovary. Proc Natl Acad Sci USA 1996;93:5925–30.

60. Pearce ST, Jordan VC. Alpha and beta estrogen receptors: are they important? Crit Rev Clin Oncol 2003 [In press]

61. Shang Y, Brown, M. Molecular determinants for the tissue specificity of SERMs. Science 2002;295: 2465–8.

62. Font de Mora J, Brown M. AIB1 is a conduit for kinase-mediated growth factor signaling to the estrogen receptor. Mol Cell Biol 2000;20.5041–7.

63. Liu H, Park WC, Bentrem DJ, et al. Structure-function relationships of the raloxifene-estrogen receptor-alpha complex for regulating transforming growth factor-alpha expression in breast cancer cells. J Biol Chem 2002;277:9189–98.

64. Yamamoto Y, Wada O, Suzawa M, et al. The tamoxifen-responsive estrogen receptor alpha mutant D351Y shows reduced tamoxifen-dependent interaction with corepressor complexes. J Biol Chem 2001;276:42684–91.

65. Osborne CK, Bardou V, Hopp TA, et al. Role of the estrogen receptor coactivator AIB1 (SRC3) and HER2/neu in tamoxifen resistance in breast cancer. J Natl Cancer Inst 2003;95:353–61.

66. Canney PA, Griffiths T, Latief TN, Priestman TJ. Clinical significance of tamoxifen withdrawal response. Lancet 1987;1:36.

67. Howell A, Dodwell DJ, Anderson H, Redford J. Response after withdrawal of tamoxifen and progestogens in advanced breast cancer [see comments]. Ann Oncol 1992;3:611–7.

68. Gottardis MM, Jordan VC. Development of tamoxifen-stimulated growth of MCF-7 tumors in athymic mice after long-term antiestrogen administration. Cancer Res 1988;48:5183–7.

69. MacGregor Schafer JI, Lee E-S, O'Regan RM, et al. Rapid development of tamoxifen stimulated mutant p53 tumors (T47D) in athymic mice. Clin Cancer Res 2000;6:4373–80.

70. Baum M. Has tamoxifen had its day? Breast Cancer Res 2002;4:213–7.

71. Jordan VC. A new day dawns: women without oestrogen or is a balance best? Breast Cancer Res 2002;4:218–21.

72. IBIS Investigators. First results from the International Breast Study: a randomized prevention trial. Lancet 2002;360:817–24.

73. Bernstein L, Deapen D, Cerhan JR, et al. Tamoxifen therapy for breast cancer and endometrial cancer risk. J Natl Cancer Inst 1999;91:1654–62.

74. Tan-Chiu E, Wang J, Costantino JP, et al. Effects of tamoxifen on benign breast disease in women at high risk for breast cancer. J Natl Cancer Inst 2003;95:302–7.

75. Cauley JA, Norton L, Lippman ME, et al. Continued breast cancer risk reduction in postmenopausal women treated with raloxifene: 4-year results from the MORE trial. Breast Cancer Res Treat 2001;65:125–34.

76. Jordan VC. Is tamoxifen the Rosetta Stone for breast cancer? J Natl Cancer Inst 2003;95:338–40.

77. Newman SP, Bates NP, Vernimmen D, et al. Cofactor competition between the ligand-bound oestrogen receptor and an intron 1 enhancer leads to oestrogen repression of ERBB2 expression in breast cancer. Oncogene 2000;19:490–7.

78. Dombernowsky P, Smith I, Falkson G, et al. Letrozole, a new oral aromatase inhibitor for advanced breast cancer: double-blind randomized trial showing a dose effect and improved efficacy and tolerability compared with megestrol acetate. J Clin Oncol 1998;16:453–61.

79. Kaufmann M, Bajetta E, Dirix LY, et al. Exemestane improves survival compared with megoestrol acetate in postmenopausal patients with advanced breast cancer who have failed on tamoxifen: results of a double-blind randomised phase III trial. Eur J Cancer 2000;36 Suppl 4:S86–7.

80. Nabholtz JM, Buzdar A, Pollak M, et al. Anastrozole is superior to tamoxifen as first-line therapy for advanced breast cancer in postmenopausal women: results of a North American multicenter randomized trial. Arimidex Study Group. J Clin Oncol 2000;18:3758–67.

81. Bonneterre J, Thurlimann B, Robertson JF, et al. Anastrozole versus tamoxifen as first-line therapy for advanced breast cancer in 668 postmenopausal women: results of the Tamoxifen or Arimidex Randomized Group Efficacy and Tolerability study. J Clin Oncol 2000;18:3748–57.

82. Wakeling AE, Dukes M, Bowler J. A potent specific pure antiestrogen with clinical potential. Cancer Res 1991;51:3867–73.

83. Osborne CK, Pippen J, Jones SE, et al. Double-blind, randomized trial comparing the efficacy and tolerability of fulvestrant versus anastrozole in postmenopausal women with advanced breast cancer progressing on prior endocrine therapy: results of a North American trial. J Clin Oncol 2002;20:3386–95.

84. Howell A, Robertson JFR, Quaresma Albano J, et al. Fulvestrant, formerly ICI 182,780, is as effective as anastrozole in postmenopausal women with advanced breast cancer progressing after prior endocrine treatment. J Clin Oncol 2002;20:3396–403.

85. Yao K, Lee ES, Bentrem DJ, et al. Antitumor action of physiological estradiol on tamoxifen-stimulated breast tumors grown in athymic mice [in process citation]. Clin Cancer Res 2000;6:2028–36.

86. Lonning PE, Taylor PD, Anker G, et al. High-dose estrogen treatment in postmenopausal breast cancer patients heavily exposed to endocrine therapy. Breast Cancer Res Treat 2001;67:111–6.

87. Song RX, Mor G, Naftolin F, et al. Effect of long-term estrogen deprivation on apoptotic responses of breast cancer cells to 17beta-estradiol. J Natl Cancer Inst 2001;93:1714–23.

88. Gail MH, Brinton LA, Byar DP, et al. Projecting individualized probabilities of developing breast cancer for white females who are being examined annually [see comments]. J Natl Cancer Inst 1989;81:1879–86.

89. Lewis J, Jordan VC. Biology of chemoprevention. In: Harris JR, Lippman ME, Morrow M, Osborne CK, editors. Diseases of the breast. Baltimore: Lippincott, Williams & Wilkins; 2003 [In press]

90. Moon RC. Vitamin A, retinoids and breast cancer. Adv Expt Med Biol 1994;364:101–7.

91. Veronesi U, DePalo G, Marubini E, et al. Randomized trial of fenretinide to prevent second breast malignancy in women with early breast cancer. J Natl Cancer Inst 1999;91:1847–56.

CHAPTER 11

TAMOXIFEN FOR CHEMOPREVENTION

D. Lawrence Wickerham, MD
Joseph P. Costantino, DrPH

It is estimated that 203,500 invasive breast cancers were diagnosed in the United States in 2002 and that an additional 54,300 women developed noninvasive breast cancer.[1] Despite improvements in both treatment and screening, 39,600 women are estimated to have died from the disease. Breast cancer continues to be a major health problem for women, and therefore the concept of prevention is an attractive addition to screening and treatment for this disease.

Although some breast cancer risk factors such as postmenopausal obesity and alcohol consumption may be modifiable, the greatest risk factors — gender, age, and family history — are not amenable to lifestyle modifications. Prophylactic mastectomy is another effective strategy for some women at high risk for the disease, but it is a drastic, irreversible choice.[2,3]

This chapter will focus on the chemoprevention of breast cancer, which has been described as pharmacologic intervention with specific nutrients or chemicals to suppress or reverse carcinogenesis and to prevent the development of invasive cancer.[4,5]

The selective estrogen receptor modulator tamoxifen is the chemopreventive agent with the largest clinical experience to date. This drug has been clearly demonstrated to reduce the risk of recurrence and the risk of dying from breast cancer.[6] Tamoxifen has also been shown to have an excellent, well-defined safety profile, with the added benefits that it helps maintain bone density in postmenopausal women and has a positive impact on lipid profiles.[7–11] The clinical trials in which tamoxifen was evaluated as a treatment for breast cancer have also demonstrated a substantial reduction in new primary cancers of the opposite breast that persists for up to 15 years.[6,12,13] It was these clinical observations, as well as a substantial amount of pre-clinical data, that led to the initial large randomized breast cancer prevention trials.[14–19]

TAMOXIFEN USE FOR THE REDUCTION OF BREAST CANCER RISK: FINDINGS FROM THE P-1 TRIAL

The majority of information defining the use of tamoxifen as a breast cancer risk reduction therapy comes from a clinical trial initiated by the National Surgical Adjuvant Breast and Bowel Project (NSABP), the Breast Cancer Prevention Trial (BCPT), also known as the NSABP P-1 trial.[20] In this study, more than 13,000 women were randomized in a double-blinded fashion to receive either 20 mg of tamoxifen or placebo for a duration of 5 years. To be eligible for participation in the trial, a woman had to be at high risk for the occurrence of breast cancer and to have had no history of invasive breast cancer or ductal carcinoma in situ. Being at high risk for breast cancer occurrence was defined as (1) being at least 60 years of age; (2) having a history of lobular carcinoma in situ (LCIS); or (3) having a 5-year projected breast cancer risk of at least 1.66% as determined by the modified Gail Model for breast cancer risk prediction.[21] Eligibility also required that a participant have no history of deep vein thrombosis or pulmonary embolism and no history of having taken hormone replacement therapy, oral contraceptives, or androgens for at least 3 months before randomization. In addition, the protocol required that trial participants not use these hormones during the course of the study.

The P-1 trial included a number of disease endpoints considered outcomes that were likely to be affected by treatment with tamoxifen. The primary endpoint of the trial was the incidence of invasive breast cancer. Several other endpoints were included in an effort to fully identify the potential benefits and detriments associated with the use of tamoxifen in relatively healthy women. Because therapy was randomized, double-blinded, and placebo-controlled, the trial design was maximized in terms of obtaining unbiased information about the efficacy of tamoxifen and the potential detrimental outcomes required to determine the therapeutic benefit/risk ratio. The specific secondary endpoints included the incidence of (1) all other invasive cancers; (2) noninvasive breast and endometrial cancers; (3) myocardial infarction, angioplasty, coronary artery bypass graft, new Q-wave on electrocardiogram, elevated serum enzymes indicative of infarction, and angina requiring hospitalization without surgery, as measures of heart disease; (4) hip, spine, and Colles' fractures, as measures of frac-

tures associated with osteoporosis; and (5) any death. In addition to a baseline assessment, the study required the systematic follow-up and evaluation of participants for the determination of the occurrence of study endpoints and quality of life measures at 3 months and at every 6 months thereafter. The reporting of the discharge diagnosis of all inpatient and outpatient visits was also required. The findings from the P-1 trial, including key beneficial and detrimental outcomes, are described below and summarized in Tables 11-1 and 11-2.

SUMMARY OF TAMOXIFEN EFFECTS

Breast Disease

The risk of breast disease was substantially reduced by treatment with tamoxifen. Compared to the rate in the placebo group, the incidence of invasive

TABLE 11-1 Summary of Disease Outcome Findings from the NSABP Breast Cancer Prevention Trial

Endpoint	Number of Events		Rate per 100 Women		RR	95% CI
	Placebo	Tamoxifen	Placebo	Tamoxifen		
Cancer						
Invasive breast cancer	175	89	6.76	3.43	0.51	0.39–0.66
Noninvasive breast cancer	69	35	2.68	1.35	0.50	0.33–0.77
Invasive endometrial cancer	15	36	0.91	2.30	2.53	1.35–4.97
Benign breast disease	1,014	750	42.13	30.16	0.72	0.65–0.79
Heart disease						
Myocardial infarction*	28	31	1.07	1.19	1.11	0.65–1.92
Severe angina†	14	13	0.53	0.50	0.93	0.40–2.14
Acute ischemic syndrome‡	20	27	0.77	1.03	1.36	0.73–2.55
Fractures						
Hip	22	12	0.84	0.46	0.55	0.25–1.15
Spine	31	23	1.18	0.88	0.74	0.41–1.32
Colles'	26	14	0.88	0.54	0.61	0.29–1.23
Vascular						
Deep vein thrombosis	22	35	.84	1.34	1.60	0.91–2.86
Pulmonary embolism	6	18	0.23	0.69	3.01	1.15–9.27
Stroke	24	38	0.92	1.45	1.59	0.93–2.77
Cataracts	507	574	21.72	24.82	1.14	1.01–1.29

*International classification of disease codes 410 to 411.

†Requiring angioplasty or coronary artery bypass graft.

‡New Q-wave on electrocardiogram without angina or elevation of serum enzymes or angina requiring hospitalization without surgery.

CI = confidence interval; RR = relative risk.

TABLE 11-2 Relative Risk of Depression Observed in the NSABP Breast Cancer Prevention Trial by Categories of Depression Risk Established at Baseline and Follow-up Time

Depression Risk Category	Period of Time of Follow-up					
	12 months		24 months		36 months	
	RR*	95 % CI	RR*	95 % CI	RR*	95 % CI
Low	1.02	0.86–1.02	0.96	0.80–1.13	0.86	0.71–1.03
Medium	0.99	0.81–1.22	1.04	0.82–1.30	1.01	0.79–1.29
High	0.62	0.41–0.92	0.83	0.54–1.28	1.00	0.64–1.57

CI = confidence interval; RR = relative risk.

*Relative risk, comparing tamoxifen to placebo for proportion scoring 16 or higher on the CES-D depression scale.

breast cancer was reduced 49%; 175 women were diagnosed with invasive breast cancer in the placebo group compared with 89 in the tamoxifen group. The relative risk (RR) comparing tamoxifen to placebo was 0.51, with 95% confidence intervals (CI) of 0.39–0.66. The rate of noninvasive breast cancer among those treated with tamoxifen was reduced by a magnitude similar to that seen for invasive breast cancer (50%); 69 women were diagnosed with noninvasive breast cancer in the placebo group compared with 35 in the tamoxifen group (RR = 0.50; 95% CI 0.33–0.77). The most notable feature of this effect of tamoxifen on breast cancer was that the drug reduced only the risk of estrogen-receptor (ER)-positive disease. There was a 69% reduction of the incidence of ER-positive disease (RR = 0.31; 95% CI 0.22–0.45), but there was no difference between treatment groups in terms of the incidence of ER-negative disease. In addition to reducing the risk of breast cancer, tamoxifen reduced the risk of benign breast disease by 28%; 1,014 women were diagnosed with benign breast disease in the placebo group compared with 750 in the tamoxifen group (RR = 0.72; 95% CI 0.65–0.79).[22] The cumulative incidence plots for these breast events are shown in Figure 11-1. As illustrated in these plots, the benefit of tamoxifen therapy in terms of reduced breast disease is evident within the first year of treatment, and the differential between the tamoxifen and placebo curves widens over the full length of follow-up.

Bone Fractures

Three specific sites of bone fracture were included in the BCPT as endpoints for markers of osteo-porotic fractures. These were fractures of the hip, fractures of the spine, and Colles' fractures. In total, there was a 45% reduction in the number of these fractures; there were 79 fractures in the placebo group and 49 in the tamoxifen group. For each site of fracture, the number of events in those who took tamoxifen was less than the number of events in those who took placebo. However, because the total number of events for each of the separate fracture sites is low, none of these individual site-specific risk reductions is statistically significant. The numbers of fractures in the placebo and tamoxifen groups, respectively, were hip fractures, 22 versus 12 (RR = 0.55; 95% CI 0.25–1.15); spine fractures, 31 versus 23 (RR = 0.74; 95% CI 0.41–1.32); and Colles' fractures, 26 versus 14 (RR = 0.61; 95% CI 0.29–1.23).

Heart Disease

The specific heart disease endpoints included in the P-1 trial were myocardial infarction, severe angina, and acute ischemic syndrome. Because tamoxifen treatment is known to reduce blood lipid levels, it was theorized that the risk of heart disease would be reduced in the tamoxifen group. However, no such effect of therapy was evident; there were 28 cases of myocardial infarction in the placebo group and 31 in the tamoxifen group (RR = 1.11; 95% CI 0.65–1.92). No statistically significant effect was evident for the other two heart disease endpoints included in the study; there were 14 cases of severe angina in the placebo group and 13 in the tamoxifen group (RR = 0.93; 95% CI 0.40–2.14), and 20 cases of acute ischemic syndrome in the placebo group compared with 27 in the tamoxifen

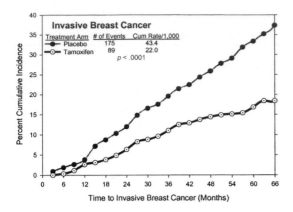

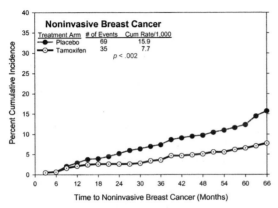

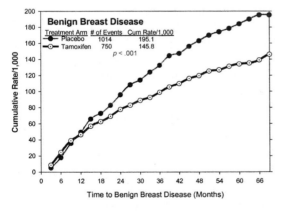

Figure 11-1 Cumulative incidence of breast disease among women in the NSABP Breast Cancer Prevention Trial (P-1).

history of heart disease at the time of randomization.[23] No significant differences between the treatment groups were seen for any of the three heart disease endpoints: combining all these endpoints, the RR was 0.96 (95% CI 0.63–1.46) for those without a history of heart disease and 1.39 (95% CI 0.73–2.67) for those with a history.

Outcomes Exhibiting a Detrimental Effect

Before the initiation of the P-1 trial, an association between therapy and an increase in the risk of two outcomes, endometrial cancer and thromboembolic events, had been well documented from the results of several breast cancer treatment trials. The elevation in risk seen in the P-1 trial for these outcomes was similar to that noted in the treatment trials. The RR for endometrial adenocarcinoma was 2.53 (95% CI 1.35–4.97), with 15 cases occurring in the placebo group compared with 36 in the tamoxifen group. This increased risk occurred predominantly among those who were age 50 or older at the time of randomization (Figure 11-2). There was no evidence to suggest that the endometrial cancer cases that occurred among women who received tamoxifen were any different in terms of pathology or pathogenicity from those that occurred among women who received placebo. The risk of uterine sarcoma also appears to be elevated among those receiving tamoxifen.[24] The most recent data from the P-1 trial indicate that four cases were reported among those receiving tamoxifen and one among those receiving placebo (RR = 3.98; 95% CI 0.39–195.94).

There is an increased risk of thromboembolic events associated with the use of tamoxifen. This risk is similar in magnitude to that seen with the use of estrogen replacement therapy. There was a 60% increase in the risk of deep-vein thrombosis noted in the P-1 trial (RR = 1.60; 95% CI 0.91–2.86), with 22 cases occurring in the placebo group and 35 in the tamoxifen group. The risk of pulmonary embolism for those taking tamoxifen was increased 3-fold (RR = 3.01; 95% CI 1.15–9.27), with 6 and 18 cases occurring in the placebo and tamoxifen groups, respectively. Although not statistically significant, there also appeared to be an increased risk of stroke of about 59% (RR = 1.59; 95% CI 0.93–2.77). There were 24 strokes among women in the placebo group and 38 in the tamoxifen group. As with endometrial cancer, the increased risk of

group (RR =1.36; 95% CI 0.73–2.55). To determine if there was a relationship between tamoxifen treatment and heart disease among those with a history of heart disease, subset analysis was performed based on a stratification of the BCPT population into those who did and did not report a

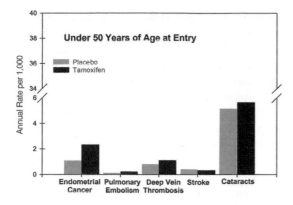

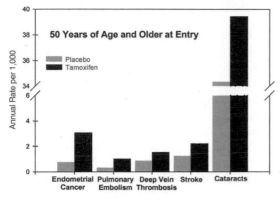

Figure 11-2 Comparison by age group of the incidence rates per 1,000 women for invasive breast cancer and detrimental outcomes experienced in the Breast Cancer Prevention (P-1) Trial.

thromboembolic events occurred predominantly among women 50 years of age or older at the time of randomization (see Figure 11-2). One theory to explain the association between tamoxifen and thromboembolic risk is that tamoxifen causes clotting among those who have mutations of genes associated with serum factors that increase the likelihood of clotting disorders such as factor V Leiden and prothrombin G20210A. However, an interaction of tamoxifen with these types of mutations is not evident. Although the risk of thromboembolic events does appear to be elevated among women who have these mutations, in the P-1 trial there was no difference in the magnitude of such risk between the placebo and tamoxifen groups.[25]

In an effort to examine the effect of tamoxifen on the eye, a group of 300 women participating in NSABP trial B-14 (tamoxifen vs placebo in node-negative, ER-positive invasive breast cancer) under-

went detailed ophthalmic examinations.[26] A significant increase in posterior subcapsular cataracts (OR = 4.03; p = .03) was identified in the women who received tamoxifen. In the P-1 trial, the incidence of cataracts was increased 14% (RR = 1.14; CI 1.01–1.29) in the tamoxifen group compared with that in the placebo group. As with the other detrimental outcomes associated with tamoxifen, the excess risk of this outcome occurred predominantly among older women (see Figure 11-2).

Quality of Life Measures

The quality of life measurements collected in the P-1 trial have been extensively evaluated.[27–29] There was no difference between tamoxifen and placebo groups in terms of scoring for depression scale (CES-D), summary scores for physical and mental assessments, or numerous subscales of physical and mental assessment including general health perception, physical functioning, vitality, bodily pain, mental health, social functioning, role-physical, and role-emotional. The lack of an association between depression and tamoxifen use illustrates the importance of a randomized, placebo-controlled trial as an unbiased method to assess the true nature and magnitude of possible side effects of treatment. Although there have been several reports of a possible association of tamoxifen with depression,[30–34] the data from the P-1 trial did not demonstrate such an effect. When stratified by level of depression risk based on conditions reported at baseline and by duration of follow-up, the relative risks of experiencing depression (a CES-D score of 16 or higher) were all very close to or less than 1, indicating no statistically significant difference between the tamoxifen and placebo groups (see Table 2). As with depression, weight gain had been anecdotally associated with tamoxifen. Again, the data from the P-1 trial failed to demonstrate such an effect; to the contrary, it was found that the proportion of women who reported weight loss during the first 3 years of treatment was greater in the tamoxifen group. The percent reporting weight loss was 44.9 and 42.0 for the tamoxifen and placebo groups, respectively.

Other self-reported symptoms were associated with tamoxifen use in the P-1 trial. The most common of such symptoms are vasomotor and gynecologic effects including hot flashes, night sweats, cold sweats, vaginal discharge, vaginal bleeding, and genital itching. These have been recognized as side effects from previous breast cancer treatment trials involving tamoxifen therapy. In the P-1 trial, the proportion of women ever reporting vasomotor symptoms was 19 to 45% higher among the women in the tamoxifen group than among women in the placebo group, depending on the specific symptom. The proportion of women ever reporting a specific gynecologic symptom was 3 to 60% higher among those in the tamoxifen group (Table 11-3). In addition to these symptoms, there were smaller increases in the tamoxifen group in reports of difficulty with bladder control and sexual functioning. Difficulty with bladder control was increased about 10%, and problems with sexual functioning were increased in the range of only 1 to 2%, depending on the nature of the specific problem and length of follow-up.[28,29]

WHO IS A CANDIDATE FOR TAMOXIFEN CHEMOPREVENTION TODAY?

The NSABP P-1 trial results are a huge first step in moving the concept of chemoprevention of breast cancer closer to clinical reality. However, two smaller European studies that also compared tamoxifen to placebo initially reported negative re-

TABLE 11-3 Proportion of Participants in the NSABP Breast Cancer Prevention Trial Reporting Symptoms at Least Once Within the First 36 Months of Follow-up

	Percent Reporting Symptom		Relative Risk*
Symptom	Placebo	Tamoxifen	
Vasomotor			
Cold sweats	14.77	21.40	1.45
Hot flashes	65.04	77.66	1.19
Night sweats	54.92	66.80	1.22
Gynecologic			
Genital itching	38.29	47.13	1.23
Vaginal discharge	34.13	54.77	1.60
Vaginal bleeding	21.26	21.96	1.03

*Relative risk, comparing tamoxifen to placebo for proportion with symptom.

sults.[35,36] Investigators have proposed a variety of reasons to explain these disparate findings, including insufficient power, poor compliance, and the use of hormonal replacement therapy in the European trials, a shorter follow-up period in the BCPT, and differences in patient selection among the trials.[37,38] The International Breast Cancer Intervention Study also compared tamoxifen and placebo in 7,144 women at increased risk for breast cancer. These women were identified using a newly developed and largely untested risk assessment tool.[39] The initial report demonstrated significantly fewer breast cancers in the tamoxifen-treated group (RR = 32%; 95% CI 8–50; p = .013).

The US Food and Drug Administration (FDA), after reviewing the findings from the P-1 trial as well as the initial reports of the two European studies, approved tamoxifen for risk reduction in women 35 years of age and older with a defined 5-year projected breast cancer risk of greater than or equal to 1.66%. The American Society of Clinical Oncology has issued two technology assessments of pharmacologic interventions for breast cancer risk reduction. Both reports indicated the Society's opinion that tamoxifen could be offered to reduce breast cancer risk outside clinical trials, despite a lack of overall health benefit or documented increases in survival.[40,41] Other published guidelines have proposed similar recommendations.[42,43] The US Preventative Services Task Force has also evaluated chemoprevention of breast cancer.[44] Although the task force recommended against the use of tamoxifen for primary prevention of breast cancer in women at low or average risk for the disease, they felt it appropriate to discuss chemoprevention with women at high risk for breast cancer and at low risk for the adverse affects of chemoprevention.

Many issues about the use of tamoxifen in breast cancer risk reduction are not yet resolved. Does this reduction in incidence represent true prevention or simply a delay in the clinical appearance of breast cancer? Women entering the P-1 trial were required to have a normal breast exam and a normal mammogram before entry to the study, but the subclinical period of breast cancer development is known to be quite long. Tamoxifen is a highly effective treatment for breast cancer, and the documentation of a tamoxifen benefit within the first year of follow-up suggests a treatment effect rather than true prevention. Investigators at the National Cancer

Institute (NCI) have modeled the data and feel that there is likely a combination of both treatment and prevention effects in the P-1 findings.[45] There is no demonstrated survival benefit to date in the tamoxifen prevention trials, although survival was not a primary endpoint of any of these studies. With the unblinding of the P-1 participants, more than 2,000 individuals in the placebo arm chose to receive tamoxifen or to be randomized into the NSABP's subsequent prevention trial, the Study of Tamoxifen and Raloxifene. As a result, meaningful survival data from the P-1 trial are unlikely to emerge. The European trials continue in a blinded fashion but are likely to be underpowered for survival endpoint. An observational study by Li and colleagues reported a tamoxifen-associated increase in receptor-negative breast cancers, suggesting a possible mechanism whereby tamoxifen use, despite reducing the incidence of breast cancer, could actually result in a survival detriment.[46] An accompanying editorial by Swain pointed out numerous flaws in this report; however, without a documented survival benefit from tamoxifen in the preventive setting, this will remain a concern.[47] The duration of tamoxifen therapy was selected to be 5 years based on the experience from the treatment setting showing that continued treatment beyond 5 years did not appear to add to the treatment effect or to further reduce the risk of contralateral breast cancer. The benefits achieved with 5 years of therapy appear to be durable and to persist for at least 15 years. However, longer or shorter duration of treatment in the prevention setting has not yet been evaluated. The daily 20 mg dose and schedule were also selected based on the treatment experience. Efforts are underway in Europe to evaluate the 10 mg dose, and intermittent dosing has also been considered.

For some clinicians, these unresolved issues will prevent their routine use of tamoxifen for chemoprevention until additional data are available. There were similar concerns when the initial reports of adjuvant chemotherapy were published. Bernard Fisher, MD, Chairman Emeritus of the NSABP, has pointed out that there are many women alive today because they chose to receive adjuvant chemotherapy for their breast cancer rather than waiting until all of the issues were resolved.

There are appropriate candidates for chemoprevention therapy today, and women interested in breast cancer chemoprevention should strongly consider entering ongoing clinical trials. That statement is more than a simple platitude. The advances in the treatment and now the prevention of breast cancer are the consequence of clinical trials and the women who have chosen to enter those trials. Several years ago, the Coalition of National Cancer Cooperative Groups commissioned a Harris poll that surveyed cancer patients, the family members of cancer patients, and the general public concerning their attitudes about cancer research. The poll identified that the single largest barrier to participation in clinical trials was not being offered the opportunity to enter a trial. Participation in clinical trials is particularly important for minority populations, who are frequently underrepresented in trials. Because the breast cancer incidence in the United States is lower in African-American women and in Hispanic women, fewer of these women will have a significantly elevated Gail score. Women from all walks of life who have an elevated Gail score should be encouraged to consider trial participation. Current breast cancer prevention trials can be identified on the NCI Web site, <http://www.cancer.gov/clinical_trials/>, or on the NSABP Web site, <http://www.breastcancerprevention.org/>.

For those women who are candidates for breast cancer chemoprevention and are not eligible for ongoing clinical trials or who choose not to enter those studies, tamoxifen remains a viable option. The FDA tamoxifen approval was for women with a 5-year projected breast cancer risk using the modified Gail score of 1.66% or greater. The 1.66% represents the average 5-year risk of a 60-year-old woman in the United States and translates into approximately a 10% lifetime risk. This level of risk was selected not for biologic purposes but was based on a statistical power calculation to determine the number of women needed for recruitment into the study. The average Gail score for the women who entered the trial was substantially higher, that is, 3.59%.

Due to the nature of the potential detrimental effects of tamoxifen, chemopreventive therapy with tamoxifen cannot be broadly applied to all populations at risk but rather to those who are likely to have a positive benefit/risk ratio from therapy. Using the best available community baseline data, and the data from P-1 trial, Gail and his colleagues developed a highly detailed method to identify such individuals.[48] Although this method is the best currently available, it is complex and cumbersome to use in the clinical setting. However, there are some easily identified groups of women in whom there is a high likelihood of tamoxifen benefit. The amount of absolute breast cancer risk reduction that can potentially be achieved by tamoxifen therapy increases directly with an individual's probability of developing a breast cancer. Therefore, the individuals most likely to achieve a positive benefit/risk ratio from tamoxifen therapy are those with high breast cancer risk, particularly if they are also at low risk for tamoxifen toxicity. Examples of such groups include

- Premenopausal women with an elevated Gail Model score. Premenopausal women under the age of 50 who have a 5-year Gail score ≥ 1.66% also have a substantially elevated lifetime risk of breast cancer. In the P-1 trial, there was no excess risk of the two major life-threatening tamoxifen toxicities, thromboembolic events and endometrial cancer, in premenopausal women. This lower risk of major toxicity combined with their higher breast cancer risks results in a better benefit/risk ratio, making such premenopausal women ideal candidates for tamoxifen use. The P-1 trial was restricted to women 35 years of age and older, and the FDA tamoxifen approval also incorporates that age restriction. It is important to remember that tamoxifen is a potential teratogen, and women must not be pregnant when they initiate therapy. Participants in the P-1 trial were required to avoid pregnancy and to use nonhormonal contraceptive strategies. This is an important issue in women receiving tamoxifen for both the treatment and prevention of breast cancer.
- Women with a biopsy-proven history of LCIS or atypical hyperplasia of the breast. Both LCIS and atypical hyperplasia are biopsy-proven risk factors that result in substantially increased 5-year Gail scores. In the P-1 trial, the annual breast cancer rate per 1,000 women in the placebo arm who had a history of LCIS at the time of entry was 12.99, and for those with a prior history of atypical hyperplasia it was 10.11. Both groups also showed substantial benefit from tamoxifen in P-1: LCIS (RR = 0.44; CI 0.16–1.06) and atypical hyperplasia (RR = 0.14; CI 0.03–0.47).
- Postmenopausal women with high Gail scores who have had a hysterectomy. Postmenopausal women who have had a hysterectomy, and thus have no risk of endometrial cancer, and who also have substantially elevated Gail Model scores are potential tamoxifen candidates. One of the barriers to the postmenopausal use of tamoxifen has been the recommendation to avoid concurrent hormonal replacement therapy. With the recent publication of the Women's Health Initiative results demonstrating no reduction in cardiovascular outcomes with hormonal replacement therapy and an expected increase in breast cancer risk, this barrier may be lessened.[49]
- Women with known *BRCA1* or *BRCA2* mutations. Data concerning the use of tamoxifen in women with known *BRCA1* or *BRCA2* inherited mutations are very limited, and definitive statements about effectiveness are not now possible. King and colleagues evaluated 288 breast cancer cases in the P-1 trial and identified only 19 women with inherited disease-predisposing *BRCA1* or *BRCA2* mutations.[50] Tamoxifen reduced the breast cancer incidence among *BRCA2* carriers by 62% (RR = 0.38; 95% CI 0.06–1.56), but a reduction was not noted in women with *BRCA1* mutations (RR = 1.67; 95% CI 0.32–10.70). Narod and colleagues published a matched case-control study that demonstrated significant protection against contralateral breast cancer in women with known *BRCA1* mutations who developed an invasive breast cancer and were treated with tamoxifen (OR = 0.38; 95% CI 0.19–0.74).[51] A lesser effect was noted in women with *BRCA2* mutations (OR = 0.63; 95% CI 0.20–1.50). Together, these papers suggest that women with *BRCA1* or *BRCA2* mutations who have or will develop ER-positive breast cancers are potential candidates for tamoxifen therapy. At the present time, it is not possible to determine which women with *BRCA1* and *BRCA2* mutations will develop ER-positive breast cancer.

PREEXISTING CONDITIONS THAT MAY LIMIT OR PRECLUDE THE USE OF TAMOXIFEN CHEMOPREVENTION

A variety of medical conditions may increase the risk of tamoxifen toxicity. The use of tamoxifen for such individuals with these conditions should be considered cautiously or avoided altogether.

Patients with a history of deep-vein thrombosis or pulmonary embolus are at higher risk for subsequent thromboembolic events, and such women were excluded from the P-1 trial. There are few data on the use of aspirin or other anticoagulants to reduce the risk of thromboembolic events in this setting, and because these are life-threatening toxicities, individuals with this history are currently not considered good candidates for tamoxifen. Similarly, individuals with a history of documented transient ischemic attacks or cerebral vascular accidents have a risk of subsequent events that may be increased with tamoxifen and therefore are not good candidates for tamoxifen therapy.

Women with current medical conditions that increase their risk for thromboembolic events should also avoid tamoxifen treatment. Such events include uncontrolled atrial fibrillation, uncontrolled diabetes mellitus, and uncontrolled hypertension. Once these conditions have stabilized, tamoxifen therapy could be considered. Similarly, should any of these conditions develop during the course of tamoxifen treatment, tamoxifen should be discontinued and reinstituted only when the problem is resolved.

A drug holiday should be considered in a variety of conditions including elective surgery or prolonged immobilization, both of which may increase the risk of thromboembolic events. Tamoxifen should be stopped in anticipation of the situation and restarted only after a return to full mobility.

CONCLUSION

The NSABP P-1 trial results as well as a metaanalysis of all four randomized tamoxifen chemoprevention trials demonstrate a significant effect of tamoxifen in reducing the risk of breast cancer.[52] These findings are in keeping with the experience in tamoxifen breast cancer treatment trials in which 5 years or less of tamoxifen therapy has resulted in a significant reduction in contralateral breast cancer incidence that persists for at least 15 years.

Tamoxifen use is associated with infrequent toxicities that may be serious or life-threatening. The best candidates for tamoxifen chemoprevention are those who are at high risk for breast cancer and at low risk for such toxicities. Methods to accurately identify these women are limited at best, but general categories of such individuals can be defined. They include

- Premenopausal women with an elevated 5-year projected breast cancer risk using the modified Gail Model
- Women with a biopsy-proven history of lobular carcinoma in situ or atypical hyperplasia of the breast
- Postmenopausal women with a high breast cancer risk and a previous hysterectomy
- Possibly, women with *BRCA1* or *BRCA2* mutations

Clinicians should evaluate all potential tamoxifen candidates for other medical conditions that may preclude tamoxifen use. Follow-up care should include not only yearly mammograms and gynecologic exams but also education concerning the signs and symptoms of uterine malignancy and thromboembolic disease. Tamoxifen compliance can be enhanced by discussing prospectively strategies and nonhormonal treatments to reduce menopausal symptoms, which are the most common side effect of tamoxifen.

The demonstration that tamoxifen is an effective method to prevent breast cancer is a huge step in the fight against breast cancer, but only a step. The next goal must be to identify more effective therapies that have even fewer toxicities. Several such studies are already underway or will start in the near future.

Efforts to more precisely identify women at risk for the development of breast cancer will allow current and future treatments to be directed at those individuals with the most to gain.

ACKNOWLEDGMENTS

NSABP P-1 study was funded by Public Health Service Grants from the National Cancer Institute (NCI-U10-CA-37377/69974).

The authors thank Barbara C. Good, PhD, for editorial assistance.

REFERENCES

1. Jemal A, Thomas A, Murray T, et al. Cancer statistics, 2002. CA Cancer J Clin 2002;52:23–47.
2. Hartmann LC, Schaid DJ, Woods JE, et al. Efficacy of bilateral prophylactic mastectomy in women

with a family history of breast cancer. N Engl J Med 1999;340:77–84.

3. Hartmann LC, Sellers TA, Schaid DJ, et al. Efficacy of bilateral prophylactic mastectomy in BRCA1 and BRCA2 gene mutation carriers. J Natl Cancer Inst 2001;93:1633–7.

4. Lotan R. Retinoids in cancer chemoprevention. FASEB J 1996;10:1031–9.

5. Mavne ST, Lippman SM. Retinoids and carotenoids. In: DeVita VT, Hellman S, Rosenberg SA, editors. Cancer principles & practice of oncology. 5th ed. Philadelphia (PA): Lippincott-Raven; 1997; p. 585–99.

6. Early Breast Cancer Trialists' Collaborative Group. Tamoxifen for early breast cancer. An overview of the randomised trials. Lancet 1998;351:1451–67.

7. Love RR, Mazess RB, Barden HS, et al. Effects of tamoxifen on bone mineral density in post-menopausal women with breast cancer. N Engl J Med 1992;326:852–6.

8. Kristensen B, Ejlertsen B, Dalgaard P, et al. Tamoxifen and bone metabolism in postmenopausal low-risk breast cancer patients: a randomized study. J Clin Oncol 1994;12:992–7.

9. Love RR, Wiebe DA, Feyzi JM, et al. Effects of tamoxifen on cardiovascular risk factors in post-menopausal women after 5 years of treatment. J Natl Cancer Inst 1994;86:1534–9.

10. Bruning PF, Bonfrer JM, Hart AA, et al. Tamoxifen, serum lipoproteins and cardiovascular risk. Br J Cancer 1988;58:497–9.

11. Saarto T, Blomquist C, Ehnholm C, et al. Antiatherogenic effects of adjuvant antiestrogens: a randomized trial comparing the effects of tamoxifen and toremifene on plasma lipid levels in post-menopausal women with node-positive breast cancer. J Clin Oncol 1996;14:429–33.

12. Early Breast Cancer Trialists' Collaborative Group. Systemic treatment of early breast cancer by hormonal, cytotoxic or immune therapy. 133 randomised trials involving 31,000 recurrences and 24,000 deaths among 75,000 women. Lancet 1992; 339:1–15.

13. Peto R. Tamoxifen as adjuvant breast cancer therapy. Presented at the NIH Consensus Development Conference on Adjuvant Therapy for Breast Cancer (2000). Available at: http://videocast.nih.gov.

14. Jordan VC. Antitumour activity of the antioestrogen ICI 46,474 (tamoxifen) in the dimethylbenzanthracene (DMBA)-induced rat mammary carcinoma model. J Steroid Biochem 1974;5:354.

15. Jordan VC. Effects of tamoxifen (ICI 46,474) on initiation and growth of DMBA-induced rat mammary carcinomata. Eur J Cancer 1976;12:419–24.

16. Jordan VC, Allen KE. Pharmacology of tamoxifen in laboratory animals. Cancer Treat Rep 1980;64: 745–59.

17. Jordan VC, Allen KE. Evaluation of the antitumour activity of the non-steroidal antioestrogen monohydroxytamoxifen in the DMBA-induced rat

mammary carcinoma model. Eur J Cancer 1980; 16:239–51.

18. Gottardis MM, Jordan VC. Antitumor actions of keoxifene and tamoxifen in the N-nitrosomethylurea-induced rat mammary carcinoma model. Cancer Res 1987;47:4020–4.

19. Jordan VC, Lababidi MK, Langan-Fahey S. Suppression of mouse mammary tumorigenesis by long-term tamoxifen therapy. J Natl Cancer Inst 1991; 83:492–6.

20. Fisher B, Costantino JP, Wickerham DL, et al. Tamoxifen for prevention of breast cancer: report of the National Surgical Adjuvant Breast and Bowel Project P-1 Study. J Natl Cancer Inst 1998;90: 1371–88.

21. Gail MH, Brinton LA, Byar DP, et al. Projecting individualized probabilities of developing breast cancer for white females who are being examined annually. J Natl Cancer Inst 1989;81:1879–86.

22. Tan-Chiu E, Wang J, Costantino JP, et al. Effects of tamoxifen on benign breast disease in women at high risk for breast cancer: findings from the National Surgical Adjuvant Breast and Bowel Project's Breast Cancer Prevention Trial (BCPT). J Natl Cancer Inst 2003;95:302–7.

23. Reis SE, Costantino JP, Wickerham DL, et al. Cardiovascular effects of tamoxifen in women with and without heart disease: breast cancer prevention trial. National Surgical Adjuvant Breast and Bowel Project Breast Cancer Prevention Trial Investigators. J Natl Cancer Inst 2001;93:16–21.

24. Wickerham DL, Fisher B, Wolmark N, et al. Association of tamoxifen and uterine sarcoma. J Clin Oncol 2002;20:2758–60.

25. Garber JE, Costantino JP, Wickerham DL, et al. Factor V Leiden and prothrombin G20210A mutations and risk of thromboembolic events in NSABP P-1, the Breast Cancer Prevention Trial [abstract]. In: Proceedings of the 25th Annual San Antonio Breast Cancer Symposium; December 2002; San Antonio.

26. Gorin MB, Day R, Costantino JP, et al. Long-term tamoxifen citrate use and potential ocular toxicity. Am J Ophthalmol 1998;125:493–501.

27. Ganz PA, Day R, Ware JE, et al. Base-line quality-of-life assessment in the National Surgical Adjuvant Breast and Bowel Project Breast Cancer Prevention Trial. J Natl Cancer Inst 1995;87:1372–82.

28. Day R, Ganz PA, Costantino JP, et al. Health-related quality of life and tamoxifen in breast cancer prevention: a report from the National Surgical Adjuvant Breast and Bowel Project P-1 study. J Clin Oncol 1999;17:2659–69.

29. Day R, Ganz PA, Costantino JP. Tamoxifen and depression: more evidence from the National Surgical Adjuvant Breast and Bowel Project's Breast Cancer Prevention (P-1) Randomized Study. J Natl Cancer Inst 2001;93:1615–23.

30. Anelli TF, Anelli A, Tran KN, et al. Tamoxifen administration is associated with a high rate of treat-

ment-limiting symptoms in male breast cancer patients. Cancer 1994;74:74–7.

31. Cathcart CK, Jones SE, Pumroy CS, et al. Clinical recognition and management of depression in node negative breast cancer patients treated with tamoxifen. Breast Cancer Res Treat 1993;27: 277–81.

32. Love RR, Cameron L, Connell BL, et al. Symptoms associated with tamoxifen treatment in postmenopausal women. Arch Intern Med 1991;151: 1842–7.

33. Pluss JL, DiBella NJ. Reversible central nervous system dysfunction due to tamoxifen in a patient with breast cancer. Ann Intern Med 1984;101: 652.

34. Shariff S, Cumming CE, Lees A, et al. Mood disorder in women with early breast cancer taking tamoxifen, an estradiol receptor antagonist. An expected or unexpected effect? Ann N Y Acad Sci 1995; 761:365–8.

35. Powles T, Eeles R, Ashley S, et al. Interim analysis of the incidence of breast cancer in the Royal Marsden Hospital tamoxifen randomised chemoprevention trial. Lancet 1998;352:98–101.

36. Veronesi U, Maisonneuve P, Costa A, et al. Prevention of breast cancer with tamoxifen: preliminary findings from the Italian randomised trial among hysterectomised women. Lancet 1998;352:93–7.

37. Pritchard KI. Is tamoxifen effective in prevention of breast cancer? Lancet 1998;352:80–1.

38. Costantino JP, Vogel VG. Results and implications of the Royal Marsden and other tamoxifen chemoprevention trials: an alternative view. Clin Breast Cancer 2001;2:41–6.

39. Cuzik J, Forbes J, Edwards R, et al. First results from the International Breast Cancer Intervention Study (IBIS-I): a randomised prevention trial. Lancet 2002;360:817–24.

40. Chlebowski RT, Collyar DE, Somerfield MR, et al. American Society of Clinical Oncology technology assessment on breast cancer risk reduction strategies: tamoxifen and raloxifene. J Clin Oncol 1999;17:1939–55.

41. Chlebowski RT, Col N, Winer EP, et al. American Society of Clinical Oncology technology assessment of pharmacologic interventions for breast cancer risk reduction including tamoxifen, raloxifene, and aromatase inhibition. J Clin Oncol 2002;20:3328–43.

42. NCCN Breast Cancer Risk Reduction Guideline: the complete library of NCCN Oncology Practice Guidelines [CD-ROM]. Rockledge (PA): National Comprehensive Cancer Network; 2001. Available at: http://www.nccn.org.

43. Levine M, Moutquin JM, Walton R, et al. Chemoprevention of breast cancer. A joint guideline from the Canadian Task Force on Preventive Health Care and the Canadian Breast Cancer Initiative's Steering Committee on Clinical Practice Guidelines for the Care and Treatment of Breast Cancer. CMAJ 2001;164:1681–90.

44. Chemoprevention of breast cancer: recommendations and rationale. Preventive Service Task Force. Ann Intern Med 2002;137:56–8.

45. Radmacher MD, Simons R. Estimation of tamoxifen's efficacy for preventing the formation and growth of breast tumors. J Natl Cancer Inst 2001;92: 48–53.

46. Li CI, Malone KE, Weiss NS, et al. Tamoxifen therapy for primary breast cancer and risk of contralateral breast cancer. J Natl Cancer Inst 2001; 93:1008–13.

47. Swain SM. Tamoxifen and contralateral breast cancer: the other side. J Natl Cancer Inst 2001;93: 963–5.

48. Gail MH, Costantino JP, Bryant J, et al. Weighing the risks and benefits of tamoxifen treatment for preventing breast cancer. J Natl Cancer Inst 1999; 91:1829–46.

49. Rossouw JE, Anderson GL, Prentice RL, et al. Risk and benefits of estrogen plus progestin in healthy postmenopausal women: principal results from the Women's Health Initiative randomized controlled trial. JAMA 2002;288:321–33.

50. King MC, Wieand S, Hale K, et al. Tamoxifen and breast cancer incidence among women with inherited mutations in BRCA1 and BRCA2: National Surgical Adjuvant Breast and Bowel Project (NSABP-P-1) Breast Cancer Prevention Trial. JAMA 2001;286:2251–6.

51. Narod SA, Brunet JS, Ghadirian P, et al. Tamoxifen and risk of contralateral breast cancer in BRCA1 and BRCA2 mutation carriers: a case-control study. Hereditary Breast Cancer Clinical Study Group. Lancet 2000;356:1876–81.

52. Cuzik J. Update on new studies in Europe [abstract]. Eur J Cancer 2002;38:520.

SERMs Other Than Tamoxifen for Chemoprevention

Ruth M. O'Regan, MD
William J. Gradishar, MD, FACP

Tamoxifen is an effective treatment for all stages of hormone receptor-positive breast cancer.[1] In addition, based on the National Surgical Adjuvant Breast and Bowel Project (NSABP) P-1 prevention trial, tamoxifen is approved for the prevention of breast cancer in high-risk women.[2] Tamoxifen is a selective estrogen receptor modulator or SERM, having antiestrogenic effects on certain tissues in the body, such as the breast and central nervous system, and estrogenic effects on other tissues, such as bone.[3] These mixed effects result in several beneficial effects, including the maintenance of bone density in postmenopausal women,[4] but result in unwanted toxicities, including an increased risk of endometrial cancer in postmenopausal women[1,2] and an increase in thromboembolic events.[2] Therefore, it is clear that tamoxifen is not an ideal SERM, and considerable ongoing preclinical and clinical research is evaluating newer SERMs, which may have a better toxicity profile compared with tamoxifen.

One such SERM is raloxifene, which was initially developed as a breast cancer treatment but did not have a clear advantage over tamoxifen in advanced breast cancer[5] and was subsequently developed as an osteoporosis treatment.[6] Raloxifene is currently approved for the prevention and treatment of osteoporosis in postmenopausal women. Review of the extensive osteoporosis databases that led to its approval as an osteoporosis preventive demonstrate that raloxifene, like tamoxifen, results in a reduction in breast cancer incidence compared with a population of untreated women.[7,8] Based on this finding, raloxifene is being compared with tamoxifen for the prevention of breast cancer in high-risk women, in the second NSABP prevention trial, the Study of Tamoxifen and Raloxifene (STAR) trial. This trial will determine whether one SERM is more effective than the other in preventing breast cancer, and whether raloxifene, like tamoxifen, will increase the risk of endometrial cancer in postmenopausal women.

Several other SERMs are in clinical development but are not as yet being examined clinically as chemopreventives. The aromatase inhibitor anastrozole has been compared with tamoxifen for the adjuvant treatment of early stage breast cancer. Preliminary results of the Arimidex, Tamoxifen, and Combination (ATAC) trial demonstrate that anastrozole is at least as effective, and likely more effective than tamoxifen, in preventing breast cancer recurrence.[9] Interestingly, with a median follow-up of 47 months (Buzdar San Antonio Breast Cancer Symposium 2002), anastrozole was associated with significantly fewer contralateral breast cancers compared with tamoxifen. One of the reasons that tamoxifen was chosen as an agent to examine for chemoprevention was the finding that it reduces the incidence of contralateral breast cancers by 50% (Figure 12-1) in patients whose first breast cancer was estrogen receptor (ER)-positive.[1] Clearly, the preliminary data from the ATAC trial on contralateral breast cancer is intriguing and suggests that anastrozole should be examined in the chemopreventive setting.

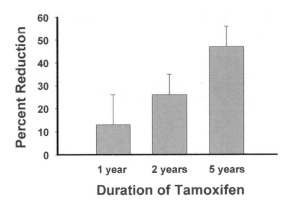

Figure 12-1 Incidence of contralateral breast cancer. Adapted from the Oxford Overview Analysis.[1]

TAMOXIFEN AS A CHEMOPREVENTIVE

Tamoxifen has been used extensively over the past 30 years in the treatment of advanced breast cancer and for the past 15 years in the adjuvant treatment of early stage breast cancer.[1] Based on preclinical data demonstrating that it prevented breast cancer in animals,[10–12] the fact that it reduces the risk of contralateral breast cancer in patients whose first breast cancer was ER-positive (see Figure 12-1),[1] and its well-documented safety profile in patients with early stage breast cancer,[1] tamoxifen was chosen as a possible preventive agent in women at high risk of developing breast cancer. In 1998, the first results of the NSABP P-1 prevention trial were published.[2] This trial randomized women at high risk of developing breast cancer, based on the Gail Model, which uses age, hormonal factors, and first-degree relative family history, to tamoxifen or placebo for 5 years.[13] The trial closed early, after accruing approximately 13,000 women, because of a significant reduction in breast cancer incidence in the tamoxifen-treated women. Overall, the rate of preinvasive breast cancer was reduced by 50% and the rate of invasive breast cancer by 49% in the women randomized to receive tamoxifen compared with the untreated women.[2] The benefits of tamoxifen were seen in all age groups of high-risk women (Figure 12-2).[2] As has been convincingly demonstrated in the advanced and adjuvant setting,[1] tamoxifen reduced the incidence only of ER-positive breast cancers.[2] Based on this large trial, tamoxifen was approved for the prevention of breast cancer in

high-risk women. However, there was considerable skepticism regarding the early results of the NSABP P-1 trial. Many felt that the trial did not prove that tamoxifen prevented breast cancer, and that tamoxifen may simply be treating occult breast cancers not detected at the time of study entry. Additionally, two other prevention trials published at the same time, a small pilot trial from the United Kingdom[14] and a small trial from Italy,[15] in which all women had had hysterectomies and were at low risk of developing breast cancer, failed to show any benefit for tamoxifen as a chemopreventive. Subsequently, however, tamoxifen was shown to reduce the incidence of benign breast disease, lending some credence to its value as a chemopreventive.[16]

Another question regarding tamoxifen's use as a chemopreventive relates to its value in breast cancer prevention in hereditary breast cancer. A small subset (approximately 6%) of women in the NSABP P-1 trial was found to be carriers of *BRCA1* or *BRCA2*.[17] Though no firm conclusions can be made owing to the small sample size, tamoxifen did not appear to reduce the incidence of breast cancer in *BRCA1* carriers, but the predicted reduction in *BRCA2* carriers was approximately 60%.[17] This observation likely relates to the fact that approximately 80% of breast cancers in *BRCA1* carriers are ER-negative, whereas over 80% are ER-positive in *BRCA2* carriers.[18] Despite the findings of NSABP P-1, there is evidence demonstrating that tamoxifen reduces the incidence of contralateral breast cancer in *BRCA1* carriers with primary breast cancer.[19] In addition, oophorectomy has been demonstrated to reduce the risk of primary breast cancer by 50%

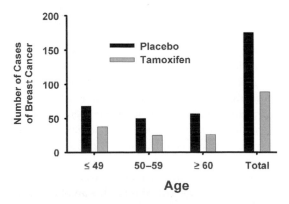

Figure 12-2 Breast cancer prevention with tamoxifen according to age in the NSABP P-1 trial.[2]

in *BRCA1* carriers.[20] Therefore, the potential value of tamoxifen as a chemopreventive, and of hormonal manipulation in general, in hereditary breast cancer remains unclear.

Another question surrounding the use of tamoxifen as a chemopreventive is the optimal duration of therapy. Five years of tamoxifen was used in the NSABP P-1 prevention trial based on data from the adjuvant breast cancer setting. Updated results of the NSABP B-14 trial, examining the outcomes of continuing tamoxifen beyond 5 years compared with stopping at 5 years, clearly demonstrate that continuing tamoxifen for longer than 5 years does not further reduce the risk of breast cancer recurrence and doubles the risk of endometrial cancer.[21] Another issue is the optimal age at which chemoprevention should be initiated in women at high risk of developing breast cancer.

DISADVANTAGES OF TAMOXIFEN AS A CHEMOPREVENTIVE

Tamoxifen is a SERM that has paradoxical estrogenic and antiestrogenic effects in various sites in a woman's body.[3] Some of these estrogenic effects are beneficial; for example, tamoxifen's effects on bones result in a maintenence of bone mineral density in postmenopausal women.[4] Unfortunately, likely owing to estrogenic effects on the endometrium, tamoxifen is associated with an increased risk of endometrial cancer.[1,2] Overall, this risk is seen only in postmenopausal women and is three to four times higher than the incidence in the general population.[2] To put this into perspective, the incidence of endometrial cancer in the general population is 1 in 1,000 women; therefore, on tamoxifen, the incidence increases to 3 to 4 in 1,000 women. Additionally, numerous trials have demonstrated that the endometrial cancers associated with tamoxifen are generally early stage and good grade cancers.[22] Most importantly, random endometrial biopsies[23] and uterine ultrasounds[24] have not been shown to be helpful in screening for endometrial cancer in woman on tamoxifen, but annual pelvic examination is essential.

Tamoxifen, again likely owing to its estrogenic effects, increases the risk of thromboembolic events, particularly in postmenopausal women.[1,2] The World Health Organization evaluated tamoxifen and stated that the benefits of tamoxifen outweighed the risks in women with early stage breast cancer.[25] However, these unwanted side effects are of greater concern in well women receiving tamoxifen for chemoprevention. Therefore, a number of agents are being examined preclinically and clinically as breast cancer preventives, in the hope of finding an agent as effective as tamoxifen but without the serious side effects.

RALOXIFENE, AN IDEAL SERM?

Raloxifene (Figure 12-3), formerly keoxifene, is another SERM, which was developed initially as a breast cancer treatment. However, trials examining raloxifene in metastatic breast cancer did not demonstrate a clear advantage over tamoxifen.[5,26] The first of these trials demonstrated no responses to raloxifene in 19 patients with heavily pretreated metastatic, tamoxifen-refractory breast cancer.[5] The second trial examined the use of high-dose raloxifene, 300 mg daily or 5 times the standard dose, as first-line treatment for advanced breast cancer.[26] A response rate of 30% was demonstrated, no better than what would have been expected with tamoxifen.[26] Following these disappointing results, the use of raloxifene as a breast cancer treatment was abandoned.

However, raloxifene is truly proof of the SERM principle. Like tamoxifen, raloxifene has been shown to maintain bone mineral density in ovariectomized rats[27,28] and at high doses has been shown to have similar effects to tamoxifen clinically on markers of bone turnover.[29] Based on these findings, raloxifene was evaluated in the management of osteoporosis. Postmenopausal women were randomized to raloxifene, at three different doses, or to placebo.[6] Raloxifene, at all doses examined, resulted in a significant increase in bone density compared with untreated women.[6] Based on these findings, raloxifene was approved at a dose of 60 mg/day for the prevention and treatment of osteoporosis in postmenopausal women. At a follow-up of 4 years, raloxifene resulted in a significant reduction in vertebral fractures compared with placebo-treated women.[30]

Raloxifene, like tamoxifen, has a beneficial effect on the lipid profile, reducing low density lipoprotein cholesterol.[6] However, retrospective evaluation of the Multiple Outcomes of Raloxifene Evaluation (MORE) trial, at a follow-up of 4 years, does not

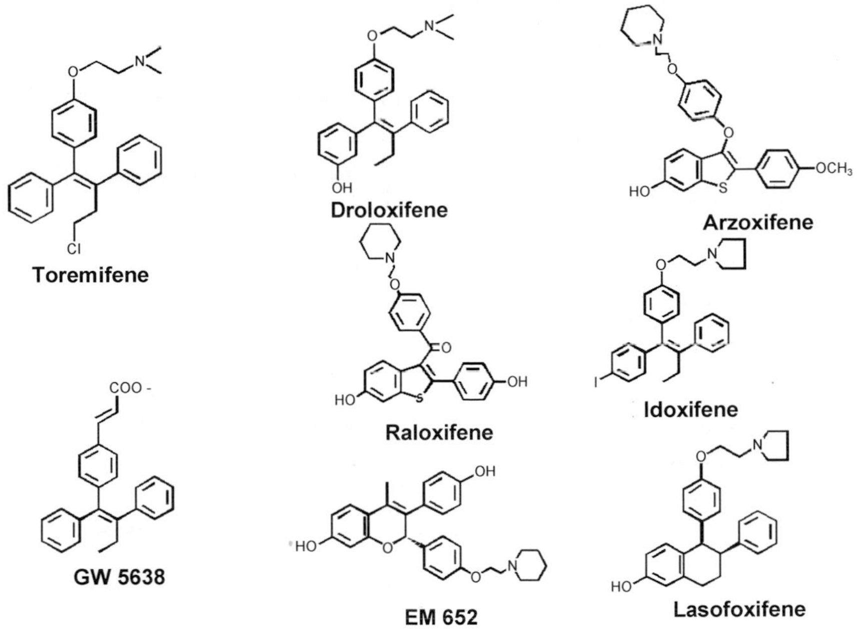

Figure 12-3 Structures of SERMs in preclinical or clinical development, compared with raloxifene.[32]

demonstrate a difference in cardiovascular or coronary events between the raloxifene- and placebo-treated women, taken as a whole.[31] Interestingly, there was a significant reduction in cardiovascular events in the subset of women with increased cardiovascular risk compared with the placebo-treated patients.[31] This issue is being examined prospectively in the Raloxifene Use for the Heart (RUTH) trial (Figure 12-4). This trial has accrued over 10,000 postmenopausal women with either known coronary heart disease or multiple risk factors for coronary heart disease, who were randomized to raloxifene 60 mg/day or to placebo.[32] The results of the RUTH trial will be particularly interesting in view of recent data demonstrating that hormone replacement therapy (HRT) does not appear to reduce the incidence of coronary heart disease.[33,34]

Like tamoxifen, raloxifene is associated with an increased incidence of thromboembolic events.[7] In the MORE trial, thromboembolic events were significantly more common in the raloxifene group compared with the placebo group (Figure 12-5A).[7] Overall, the rate of deep venous thrombosis was three times higher in patients receiving raloxifene compared with placebo.[7] However, although pulmonary emboli were also more common in the raloxifene group and one patient in this group died from a pulmonary embolus, the difference in incidence of pulmonary emboli was not significant compared with the placebo group.[7]

Similar to tamoxifen, treatment with raloxifene can result in hot flashes. In the MORE trial, there was a significant increase in hot flashes in the raloxifene-treated patients compared with the placebo group (Figure 12-5B).[7] Additionally, raloxifene treatment resulted in a significant increase in leg cramps, influenza-like syndromes, and peripheral edema compared with the placebo group in the MORE trial (Figure 12-5B).[7] Interestingly, however, a recent trial, which randomized over 1,000 women to combined HRT or to raloxifene, demonstrated that significantly more women in the raloxifene group were satisfied with their treatment, experienced improved quality of life, and better complied with treatment compared with the HRT group.[35]

To date, there are only preclinical data available on the effects of raloxifene on the endometrium. Raloxifene and its analogs have minor estrogenic effects on the rat uterus.[36] However, raloxifene does not appear to be completely devoid of estrogenic effects on the uterus, because estrogen-regulated genes are partially activated by the drug.[37] Clini-

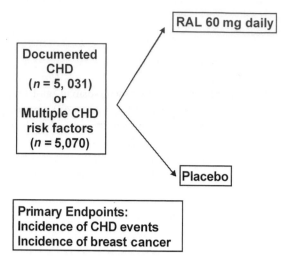

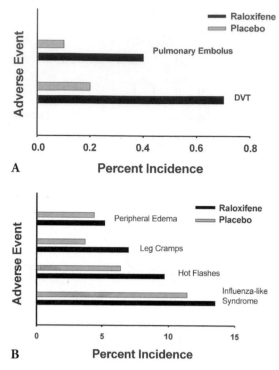

Figure 12-4 Schema and primary endpoints of the RUTH trial.[4]
CHD = coronary heart disease
RAL = raloxifene.

cally, raloxifene appears to have fewer estrogenic effects on the human uterus as compared with tamoxifen. Review of the osteoporosis trials demonstrate no difference in uterine thickness between women receiving raloxifene, compared with those receiving placebo.[6] Additionally, there was a trend to a reduced incidence of endometrial cancer in raloxifene-treated patients compared with placebo-treated patients in the osteoporosis trials.[7] In contrast, raloxifene has been shown to have similar effects to tamoxifen on the growth of human endometrial cancer in athymic mice.[38] In fact, raloxifene was less effective over a period of 3 months, compared with tamoxifen, in blocking the effects of postmenopausal estrogen on the growth of endometrial cancer in human athymic mice.[38]

Raloxifene as a Breast Cancer Preventive

Like tamoxifen, raloxifene has been demonstrated to prevent breast cancer in rat models. Raloxifene inhibits the growth of 7,12-dimethylbenz(a)anthracene (DMBA)-induced mammary carcinomata, and prevents the growth of N-nitrosomethylurea (NMU)-induced breast tumors in rats.[39–41] Clinically, two large osteoporosis databases have been examined retrospectively to determine if raloxifene can, like tamoxifen, prevent breast cancer in humans.[7,8] The MORE trial randomized 7,704 postmenopausal women with osteoporosis to ralox-

Figure 12-5 Thromboembolic events (*A*) and general adverse events (*B*) in the MORE trial in patients treated with raloxifene 60 mg/day compared with placebo. *P* values < .05 except for pulmonary emboli (*p* = .08). DVT = deep venous thrombosis.

ifene, at a dose of 60 or 120 mg/day or to placebo.[7] At 2 years, there was a highly significant reduction of 70% in the incidence of breast cancer in the raloxifene-treated patients compared with the placebo-treated patients (Figure 12-6).[7] In an updated report, at a follow-up of 4 years, raloxifene resulted in a 72% reduction in breast cancer compared with the placebo group.[42] As was demonstrated in the NSABP P-1 trial,[2] raloxifene was more effective in reducing the incidence of ER-positive breast tumors, resulting in an 84% reduction compared with the placebo group.[7] A second database analyzed all placebo-controlled trials using raloxifene and included over 10,000 women. At 3 years, there was a significant 54% reduction in the incidence of breast cancer in the raloxifene-treated patients compared with the placebo group (see Figure 12-6).[8] Like tamoxifen, raloxifene reduced the incidence only of ER-positive breast cancers.[8]

The MORE trial was further evaluated to determine the effectiveness of raloxifene in relation to

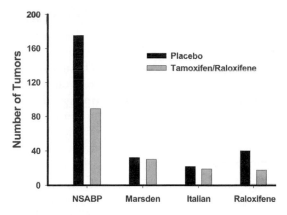

Figure 12-6 Breast cancer prevention with raloxifene[7,8] compared with NSABP P-1,[2] Royal Marsden PreventionTrial,[14] and the Italian Prevention Trial.[15]

lifetime estrogen exposure of the women. Breast cancer incidence was increased in women with the highest estradiol levels, with a 2.07-fold increase in breast cancer rate in women with the highest one-third estradiol levels.[43] Raloxifene significantly reduced the incidence of breast cancer in all subgroups, but was most effective in the one-third of women with the highest bone mineral density and in those with a family history (two markers of increased breast cancer risk), compared with the two-thirds with lower bone mineral density and a negative family history .[43]

Based on these findings, raloxifene is being evaluated prospectively as a breast cancer preventative. Incidence of invasive breast cancer is a co-primary endpoint of the RUTH trial (see Figure 12-4), mentioned earlier. The median 5-year risk of developing breast cancer in this trial is 1.4%, with approximately one-third of patients considered at high risk, with a 5-year risk of greater than 1.66%.[32]

The STAR trial (Figure 12-7) is the follow-up trial to the NSABP P-1 trial. This trial will randomize 19,000 postmenopausal women at high risk of developing breast cancer, based on the Gail Model, to 5 years of either tamoxifen or raloxifene. To date, over 100,000 women have been evaluated and almost 13,000 have been randomized.[44] The median age of the women randomized to date is 58 years.[44] The median 5-year risk of women randomized to date is 3.3%, of which 8.4% have a diagnosis of lobular carcinoma in situ (LCIS).[44] The primary endpoint of this trial is incidence of breast cancer. However, this trial should also determine whether the lack of estrogenic effects on the endometrium associated with raloxifene translates into no increase in the risk of endometrial cancer.

To date, there is little data on the use of raloxifene in premenopausal women. A small pilot trial treated 31 premenopausal (ages 23 to 47) women, at high risk of developing breast cancer based on the Gail Model, with raloxifene 60 mg/day.[45] An interim analysis[45] performed after 12 patients had received 12 months of raloxifene, demonstrated a small but significant reduction in bone mineral density of −1.74%, compared with baseline values, similar to that seen with tamoxifen.[46] Raloxifene was well tolerated, with menstrual irregularities, hot flashes, and mood lability being the most common side effects.[45] Ongoing trials will further evaluate raloxifene in premenopausal women.

In summary, although current preclinical[39–41] and available clinical data[7] suggest that raloxifene can prevent breast cancer, it should not be used for this indication until the results of the STAR trial and other ongoing trials are available. First, clinical data demonstrating that raloxifene reduces breast cancer incidence are available only from patients with osteoporosis, who may not be at especially high risk of developing breast cancer.[7] Second, although data to date suggest that raloxifene does not exhibit estrogenic effects on the endometrium and may not, therefore, be associated with an increase in endometrial cancer, there are no long-term data available to definitely address this issue.[6] Review of the tamoxifen breast cancer trials demonstrates that the increased incidence in endometrial cancer was not noted until the drug had been used for 15 years.[22] Clearly, all these issues will be addressed

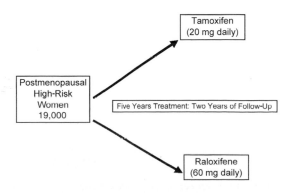

Figure 12-7 Schema of the STAR trial.

with the STAR trial and longer follow-up from other trials, but until this information becomes available, women at high risk of breast cancer should not be prescribed raloxifene for this indication and should continue to be treated with tamoxifen for chemoprevention.

CHEMOPREVENTION WITH OTHER SERMs

Despite the fact that raloxifene may be less estrogenic on the endometrium than tamoxifen and, therefore, may be less likely to increase the risk of endometrial cancer, it is not considered the ideal SERM for use as a chemopreventive in well women. The ideal SERM (Figure 12-8) will be an agent that acts as an antiestrogen on the breast and endometrium, thereby preventing breast and endometrial cancer, while acting as an estrogen on bones, maintaining bone mineral density, preventing coronary artery disease and thromboembolic disease, and reducing or abolishing hot flashes. Unfortunately, available evidence does not suggest that any of the current SERMs in preclinical and clinical development will be the ideal SERM.

Toremifene

Toremifene (Farneston) (see Figure 12-3) is a chlorinated derivative of tamoxifen which is approved in the United States as an alternative first-line agent for hormone-responsive, metastatic breast cancer. Toremifene has been extensively examined in clinical studies. Phase II studies demonstrated promising response rates, especially with high doses.[47–52] Toremifene has been compared with tamoxifen as first-line treatment for hormone-responsive, advanced breast cancer. One large study, in which patients with untreated advanced breast cancer were randomized to tamoxifen or toremifene, demonstrated no statistically significant difference between the two drugs with respect to response rate, median survival, or time to progression.[53] Toremifene has also been evaluated in patients with tamoxifen-refractory advanced breast cancer. In the largest trial, a response rate of only 5% was noted in patients with tamoxifen-refractory advanced breast cancer treated with toremifene 200 mg/day.[54] On the basis of these studies, toremifene, at a dose of 60 mg/day, is approved as an alternative first-line treatment for hormone-responsive breast cancer.

Toremifene has been compared with tamoxifen in the adjuvant setting. Postmenopausal women with node-positive early stage breast cancer were randomized to tamoxifen 20 mg/day or to toremifene 40 mg/day for 3 years (Figure 12-9A). The trial accrued 899 patients, and, at a median follow-up of 3.4 years, no differences in disease-free survival were seen between the two groups (see Figure 12-9B).[55] Additionally, there was no significant difference in hot flashes, thromboembolic events, or rate of contralateral breast cancer between the two agents.[55]

Toremifene acts as a partial estrogen agonist on the rat uterus[56] and, like tamoxifen, stimulates the growth of tamoxifen-stimulated endometrial tumors in athymic mice.[57] However, in the adjuvant trial, to date there has been no increase in the incidence of endometrial cancers in humans.[55] Additionally, a recent case-control study from the Finnish Cancer Registry demonstrated that tamoxifen significantly increased the risk of endometrial cancer by almost 3-fold, whereas there was no increase in endometrial cancers in toremifene-treated patients, although the number of toremifene-treated patients was small.[58] Toremifene has similar effects to tamoxifen on bones in postmenopausal women.[59] Additionally, toremifene decreases low density lipoprotein cholesterol, but, unlike tamoxifen, it increases high density lipoprotein cholesterol.[60]

Like tamoxifen and raloxifene, toremifene inhibits the growth of NMU-induced breast cancers in rats, both in terms of tumor numbers and in latency period of tumor development.[61] Toremifene has been compared with tamoxifen in the DMBA-induced rat

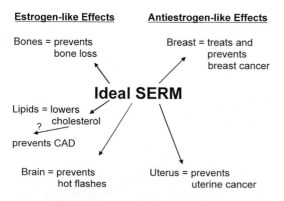

Figure 12-8 Properties of the ideal SERM. CAD = coronary artery disease.

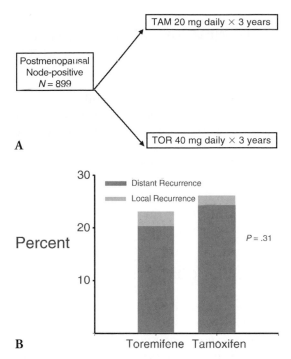

A

B

Figure 12-9 Schema (*A*) and results (*B*) of the adjuvant toremifene trial.[55]
TAM = tamoxifen; TOR = toremifene.

mammary tumor model.[62] Both agents prevented the development of DMBA-induced breast tumors when given by mouth from day 28 after carcinogen administration.[62] However, when the SERMs were stopped, the breast tumors regrew, suggesting that toremifene, like tamoxifen, has tumoristatic rather than tumoricidal effects in this tumor model.[62] These results suggest that toremifene would be a reasonable agent to evaluate as a chemopreventive in humans, particularly in view of the lack of endometrial cancers seen in the adjuvant trial.[55]

Droloxifene

Droloxifene (see Figure 12-3), or 3-hydroxytamoxifen, was initially evaluated as a breast cancer treatment but, like raloxifene, did not offer clear advantages over tamoxifen. Droloxifene maintains bone density in ovariectomized rats but is less potent than tamoxifen.[63] Droloxifene was developed as an osteoporosis preventative at one time, but its clinical development has now been abandoned. Like tamoxifen, droloxifene has partial estrogenic effects on the rat uterus.[64] Droloxifene, like tamoxifen, inhibits the growth of NMU-induced breast tumors

in rats.[65] Additionally, droloxifene is as effective as tamoxifen in inhibiting the growth of DMBA-induced breast tumors in rats.[66] Droloxifene may be examined in clinical trials in the future to determine how effective it is in preventing breast cancer.

Idoxifene

Idoxifene (see Figure 12-3), is another SERM that was evaluated in the treatment of metastatic breast cancer. Preclinical studies demonstrated that idoxifene, unlike tamoxifen, is not converted to 4-hydroxytamoxifen and is, therefore, a less potent antiestrogen.[67] In a small trial of patients with pretreated, metastatic breast cancer treated with idoxifene at three doses, an overall response rate of 14% was recorded.[68] Idoxifene, like raloxifene and droloxifene, does not appear to offer a clear advantage over tamoxifen as a breast cancer treatment. Like tamoxifen, idoxifene inhibits the growth of carcinogen-induced rat mammary carcinomata.[69] However, there are no plans to further develop idoxifene clinically either as a breast cancer preventive or as an osteoporosis agent.

Arzoxifene

Arzoxifene (LY 353.381.HCL) (see Figure 12-3) is another SERM, similar to raloxifene but with a longer half-life.[70] Arzoxifene is highly potent in preclinical studies and has improved bioavailabilty compared with raloxifene.[71] Like raloxifene, arzoxifene blocks the effects of estrogen on the growth of MCF-7 cells.[71,72] Like other SERMs, arzoxifene prevents tibial bone loss and preserves femoral neck strength in ovariectomized rats.[72] In preclinical studies, arzoxifene acts as an antiestrogen on the uterus and is more potent than tamoxifen in blocking the effects of estrogen on uterine weight in rats.[72] However, arzoxifene has similar effects to tamoxifen on the growth of tamoxifen-exposed human endometrial tumors in athymic mice.[73]

Arzoxifene has been evaluated as a treatment for tamoxifen-resistant advanced breast cancer. Response rates were low and arzoxifene does not appear to have clear advantages over tamoxifen.[74] A randomized trial between the two agents may be undertaken in the future.

Arzoxifene has recently been evaluated preclinically as a chemopreventive in the NMU rat model.[75] Arzoxifene was found to be more potent than raloxifene, but similar to tamoxifen in inhibiting the growth of NMU-induced breast cancers in rats.[75] In the future, arzoxifene may be examined as a chemopreventive in humans.

EM 652

EM 652 (see Figure 12-3), the active metabolite of EM 800, is another SERM, which was developed as a breast cancer treatment. Structurally, and at a molecular level, EM 652 appears similar to raloxifene.[76] Like the other SERMs, EM 652 is an antiestrogen on the breast and endometrium in preclinical studies.[77–79]

EM 652 has been evaluated in a phase III trial in which patients with tamoxifen-refractory advanced breast cancer were randomized to EM 652 or to the aromatase inhibitor anastrozole. This trial was closed early for unclear reasons, and further development of the agent has stopped. EM 652 inhibits the growth of DMBA-induced mammary cancers in rats and may be evaluated as a breast cancer preventive in humans in the future.[80]

Lasofoxifene

Lasofoxifene (CP 336,156) (see Figure 12-3) is being developed for the prevention of osteoporosis in postmenopausal women. Like other SERMs, lasofoxifene maintains bone mineral density in ovariectomized rats.[81] Long-term treatment with lasofoxifene completely prevents age-related bone loss and bone strength by inhibiting bone resorption and bone turnover.[82] Lasofoxifene reduces total cholesterol in rats, compared with untreated rats.[81,82] In preclinical studies, lasofoxifene acted as an antiestrogen on the uterus, having no effect on uterine wet weight in immature rats or causing uterine hypertrophy in mature rats and prevented bone loss in ovariectomized rats.[81] Lasofoxifene inhibits the growth of NMU-induced breast tumors in rats[83]: both tumor incidence and number are reduced, similar to tamoxifen-treated rats. There are no data as yet on the effects of CP 336,156 in humans. Prevention trials have been proposed.

GW 5638

GW 5638 (see Figure 12-3) is a triphenylethylene derivative of tamoxifen, with a novel carboxylic acid side chain, being developed as an osteoporosis agent.[84] At a molecular level, GW 7604, the active metabolite of GW 5638, interacts differently with the ER complex than estrogen or 4-hydroxytamox-

ifen, maintaining antiestrogenic properties.[84] Like the other SERMs, GW 5638 preserves bone density in ovariectomized rats, but, unlike tamoxifen, is antiestrogenic on the rat uterus.[84] GW 5638 is more effective than raloxifene in blocking the effects of postmenopausal estrogen on human endometrial cancer in athymic mice.[85] Unlike other SERMs, GW 5638 does not stimulate the growth of tamoxifen-resistant breast tumors in athymic mice and may find a role in the treatment of tamoxifen-refractory advanced breast cancer.[85] GW 5638 will be developed clinically as an osteoporosis agent but may prevent breast cancer as a beneficial side effect.

CONCLUSION

The results of the NSABP P-1 trial revolutionized the management of women at high risk of developing breast cancer. Unfortunately, the safety profile of tamoxifen does not make it the perfect option for use in well women. Based on current evidence, raloxifene may be a safer agent than tamoxifen on the endometrium and, in retrospective studies, seems at least as effective as tamoxifen in preventing breast cancer. This data forms the basis of the ongoing STAR trial. A number of other SERMs are in preclinical and clinical development, but available data do not suggest that any of these agents will offer significant advantages over tamoxifen or raloxifene. In contrast, preliminary data with the aromatase inhibitors suggest that these agents may be at least as effective as tamoxifen, with an improved safety profile. However, close attention will need to be paid to bone mineral density if the aromatase inhibitors are to be used in well women.

REFERENCES

1. Early Breast Cancer Trialists' Collaborative Group. Tamoxifen for early breast cancer: an overview of the randomized trials. Lancet 1998;351:1451–67.
2. Fisher B, Costantino JP, Wickerham DL, et al. Tamoxifen for prevention of breast cancer: report of the National Surgical Adjuvant Breast and Bowel Project P-1 Study. J Natl Cancer Inst 1998;90:1371–88.
3. Jordan VC, Morrow M. Tamoxifen, raloxifene and the prevention of breast cancer. Endocrine Rev 1999;20:253–78.

4. Love RR, Mazess RB, Barden HS, et al. Effects of tamoxifen on bone mineral density in postmenopausal women with breast cancer. N Engl J Med 1992;326:852–6.

5. Buzdar AU, Marcus C, Holmes F, et al. Phase II evaluation of LY 156,758 in metastatic breast cancer. Oncology 1988;45:344–5.

6. Delmas PD, Bjarnason NH, Mitlak BH, et al. Effects of raloxifene on bone mineral density, serum cholesterol concentrations, and uterine endometrium in postmenopausal women. N Engl J Med 1997; 337:1641–7.

7. Cummings SR, Eckert S, Krueger KA, et al. The effects of raloxifene on the risk of breast cancer in postmenopausal women: results from the MORE randomized trial. Multiple Outcomes of Raloxifene Evaluation. JAMA 1999;281:2189–97.

8. Cauley JA, Norton L, Lippman ME, et al. Continued breast cancer risk reduction in postmenopausal women treated with raloxifene. 4 year results from the MORE trial. Breast Cancer Res Treat 2001;65: 125–34.

9. ATAC Trialists' Group. Anastrozole alone or in combination with tamoxifen versus tamoxifen alone for adjuvant treatment of postmenopausal women with early breast cancer: first results of the ATAC randomized trial. Lancet 2002;359:2131–9.

10. Jordan VC. Antitumour activity of the antiestrogen ICI46,474 (tamoxifen) in the dimethylbenzanthracene (DMBA)-induced rat mammary carcinoma model. J Steroid Biochem. 1974;5:354.

11. Jordan VC. Effects of tamoxifen (ICI 46,474) on initiation and growth of DMBA-induced rat mammary carcinomata. Eur J Cancer. 1976;12:419–24.

12. Jordan VC, Allen KE. Evaluation of the antitumour activity of the nonsteroidal antioestrogen monohydroxytamoxifen in DMBA-induced rat mammary carcinoma model. Eur J Cancer 1980;16: 239–51.

13. Gail MH, Brinton LA, Byar DP, et al. Projecting individualized probabilities of developing breast cancer from white women who are being examined annually. J Natl Cancer Inst 1989;88: 1543–9.

14. Powles TJ, Eeles E, Ashley SE, et al. Interim analysis of the incident breast cancer in the Royal Marsden Hospital tamoxifen randomized prevention trial. Lancet 1998;362:98–101.

15. Veronesi U, Maissonneuve P, Costa A, et al. Prevention of breast cancer with tamoxifen: preliminary findings from the Italian randomized trial among hysterectomised women. Lancet 1998;352:93–7.

16. Tan-Chiu E, Costantino J, Wang J, et al. The effect of tamoxifen on benign breast disease. Findings from the NSABP Breast Cancer Prevention Trial [abstract 7]. Breast Cancer Res Treat 2001;69:210.

17. King MC, Wieand S, Hale K, et al. Tamoxifen and breast cancer incidence among young women with inherited mutations in BRCA1 and BRCA2: National Surgical Adjuvant Breast and Bowel Project (NSABP P-1) Breast Cancer Prevention Trial. JAMA 2001;286:2251–6.

18. Robson M, Gilewski T, Haas B, et al. BRCA-associated breast cancer in young women. J Clin Oncol 1998;16:2–9.

19. Narod SA, Brunet JS, Ghadirian P, et al. Tamoxifen and risk of contralateral breast cancer in BRCA1 and BRCA2 mutation carriers: a case-control study. Lancet 2000;356:1876–81.

20. Rebbeck TR, Lynch HT, Neuhausen SL, et al. Prophylactic oopherectomy in carriers of BRCA1 and BRCA2 mutations. New Engl J Med 2002;346: 1616–22.

21. Fisher B, Dignam J, Bryant J, Wolmark N. Five versus more than five years of tamoxifen for lymph node-negative breast cancer: updated findings of the National Surgical Adjuvant Breast and Bowel Project B-14 randomized trial. J Natl Cancer Inst 2001;93:684–90.

22. Assikis VJ, Neven P, Jordan VC, Vergote I. A realistic clinical perspective of tamoxifen and endometrial carcinogenesis. Eur J Cancer 1996;32A:1464–76.

23. Barakat RR, Gilewski TA, Almadrones L, et al. Effect of adjuvant tamoxifen on the endometrium in women with breast cancer: a prospective study using office endometrial biopsy. J Clin Oncol 2000; 18:3459–63.

24. Gerber B, Krause A, Muller H, et al. Effects of adjuvant tamoxifen on the endometrium in postmenopausal women with breast cancer: a prospective long-term study using transvaginal ultrasound. J Clin Oncol 2000;18:3464–70.

25. International Agency for Research in Cancer (IARC): tamoxifen. IARC Monographs 1996;66: 274–365.

26. Gradishar WJ, Glusman JE, Lu Y, et al. Effects of high dose raloxifene in selected patients with advanced breast cancer. Cancer 2000;88:2047–53.

27. Jordan VC, Phelps E, Lingren JU. Effects of antiestrogens on bone in castrated and intact female rats. Breast Cancer Res Treat 1987;10:31–5.

28. Black LJ, Sato M, Rowley ER, et al. Raloxifene (LY 139,481 HCL) prevents bone loss and reduces serum cholesterol without causing uterine hypertrophy in ovariectomized rats. J Clin Invest 1994; 93:63–9.

29. Draper MW, Flowers DE, Huster WJ, et al. Effects of raloxifene (LY 139,481 HCL) on biochemical markers of bone and lipid metabolism in healthy postmenopausal women. In: Christiansen C, Rii S, editors. Proceedings of the 4th International Symposium on Osteoporosis and Concensus Development Conference 1993; Aalborg, Denmark, Handelstrykkeriet: Aalborg ApS, Denmark. p. 119–21.

30. Delmas PD, Ensrud KE, Adachi JD, et al. Efficacy of raloxifene on vertebral fracture risk reduction in postmenopausal women with osteoporosis: four year results from a randomized clinical trial. Clin Endocrinol Metab 2002;87:3609–17.

31. Barrett-Connor E, Grady D, Sashegyi A, et al. Raloxifene and cardiovascular events in osteoporotic postmenopausal women. JAMA 2002;287:847–57.

32. Wenger NK, Barrett-Connor E, Collins P, et al. Baseline characteristics of participants in the Raloxifene Use for The Heart (RUTH) trial. Am J Cardiol 2002;:90:1204–10.

33. Grady D, Herrington D, Bittner V, et al. Cardiovascular disease outcomes during 6.8 years of hormone therapy: Heart and Estrogen/progestin Replacement Study follow-up (HERS II). JAMA 2002;288:49–57.

34. Rossouw JE, Anderson GL, Prentice RL, et al. Risks and benefits of estrogen plus progestin in healthy postmenopausal women: principal results from the Women's Health Initiative randomized controlled trial. JAMA 2002;288:312–33.

35. Voss S, Quail D, Dawson A, et al. A randomized, double-blind trial comparing raloxifene HCL and continuous combined hormone replacement therapy in postmenopausal women: effects on compliance and quality of life. BJOG 2002;109:874–85.

36. Jordan VC, Gosden B. Inhibition of the uterotropic activity of antiestrogens by the short acting antiestrogen LY 117018. Endocrinology 1983;113:463–8.

37. Jordan VC, Gosden B. Differential antiestrogen action on the immature rat uterus: a comparison of hydroxylated antiestrogens with high affinity for the estrogen receptor. J Steroid Biochem 1983;19:1249–58.

38. O'Regan RM, Gajdos C, Dardes RC, et al. Effects of raloxifene after tamoxifen on breast and endometrial cancer growth. J Natl Cancer Inst 2002;20:274–83.

39. Gottardis MM, Jordan VC. The antitumor actions of keoxifene (raloxifene) and tamoxifen in the N-nitromethylurea-induced rat mammary carcinoma model. Cancer Res 1987;47:4020–4.

40. Clemens JA, Bennett DR, Black LJ, et al. Effects of the new antiestrogen keoxifene LY 156758 on growth of carcinogen-induced mammary tumors and on LH and prolactin levels. Life Sci 1983;32:2869–75.

41. Anzano MA, Peer CW, Smith JM, et al. Chemoprevention of mammary carcinogenesis in the rat: combined use of raloxifene and 9-cis-retinoic acid. J Natl Cancer Inst 1996;88:123–5.

42. Cauley JA, Norton L, Lippman ME, et al. Continued breast cancer risk reduction in postmenopausal women treated with raloxifene: 4 year results from the MORE trial. Breast Cancer Res Treat 2001;65:125–34.

43. Lippman ME, Krueger KA, Eckert S, et al. Indicators of lifetime estrogen exposure: effect on breast cancer incidence and interaction with raloxifene therapy in the Multiple Outcomes of Raloxifene Evaluation study participants. J Clin Oncol 2001;15:3111–6.

44. Vogel VG, Costantino JP, Wickerham DL, et al. The study of tamoxifen and raloxifene: preliminary enrollment data from a randomized breast cancer risk reduction trial. Clin Breast Cancer 2002;3:153–9.

45. Zujewski J, Eng-Wong J, Reynolds J, et al. A phase 2 trial of raloxifene in premenopausal women at high risk for developing breast cancer [abstract 417]. Breast Cancer Res Treat 2002;76:S108.

46. Powles TJ, Hickish T, Kanis JA, et al. Effect of tamoxifen on bone mineral density measured by dual-energy x-ray absorptiometry in healthy premenopausal and postmenopausal women. J Clin Oncol 1996;14:78–84.

47. Valavaara R, Pyrhonen S, Heikkinen M, et al. Toremifene, a new antiestrogenic treatment of advanced breast cancer Phase II study. Eur J Cancer 1988;24:785–90.

48. Valavaara R, Pyrhonen S. Low-dose toremifene in the treatment of estrogen receptor-positive advanced breast cancer in postmenopausal women. Curr Ther Res 1989;46:966–73.

49. Valavaara R. Phase II experience with toremifene in the treatment of ER-positive breast cancer of postmenopausal women. Cancer Invest 1990;8:275–6.

50. Gunderson S. Toremifene, a new antiestrogenic compound in the treatment of advanced breast cancer. Phase II study. Eur J Cancer 1990;24A:785–90.

51. Hietanen T, Baltina D, Johansson R, et al. High dose toremifene (240 mg daily) is effective as first line hormonal treatment in advanced breast cancer – an ongoing phase II multicenter Finnish-Latvian cooperative study. Breast Cancer Res Treat 1990;16:37–40.

52. Modig H, Borgstrom M, Nilsson I, Westman G. Phase II clinical study of toremifene in patients with metastatic breast cancer. J Steroid Biochem 1990;36:235–6.

53. Hayes DF, Van Zyl JA, Hacking A, et al. Randomized comparison of tamoxifen and two separate doses of toremifene in postmenopausal patients with metastatic breast cancer. J Clin Oncol 1995;113:2556–66.

54. Vogel CL, Shemano I, Schoenfelder J, et al. Multicenter phase II efficacy trial of toremifene in tamoxifen refractory patients with advanced breast cancer. J Clin Oncol 1993;11:345–50.

55. Holli K, Valavaara R, Blanco G, et al. Safety and efficacy results of a randomized trial comparing adjuvant toremifene and tamoxifen in postmenopausal patients with node-positive breast cancer. Finnish Breast Cancer Group. J Clin Oncol 2000;18:3487–94.

56. Kangas L, Niemenen A-L, Blanco G, et al. A new triphenylethylene compound Fc-1157a II antitumor effects. Cancer Chemo Pharm 1986;17:109–13.

57. O'Regan RM, Cisneros A, England GM, et al. Growth characteristics of human endometrial cancer transplanted in athymic mice and treated with new antiestrogens, toremifene and ICI 182,780. J Natl Cancer Inst 1998;90:1552–8.

58. Pukkala E, Kyyronen P, Sankila R, Holli K. Tamoxifen and toremifene treatment of breast cancer and risk of subsequent endometrial cancer: a population based case-control study. Int J Cancer 2002; 100:337–41.

59. Saarto T, Blomquist C, Valimaki M, et al. Clodronate improves bone mineral density in postmenopausal breast cancer patients treated with adjuvant antiestrogens. Br J Cancer 1997;75:602–5.

60. Saarto T, Blomquist C, Ehnholm C, et al. Antiatherogenic effects of adjuvant antiestrogens: a randomized trial comparing the effects of tamoxifen and toremifene on plasma lipid levels in postmenopausal women with node-positive breast cancer. J Clin Oncol 1996;14:429–33.

61. Moon RC, Steele VE, Kelloff GJ, et al. Chemoprevention of MNU-induced mammary tumorigenesis by hormone response modifiers: toremifene, RU 16117, tamoxifen, aminoglutethimide and progesterone. Anticancer Res 1994;14:889–93.

62. Robinson SP, Mauel DA, Jordan VC. Antitumor actions of toremifene in the 7,12-dimethylbenzanthracene (DMBA)-induced rat mammary tumor model. Eur J Cancer Clin Oncol 1988;24: 1817–21.

63. Ke HZ, Simmons HA, Pirie CM, et al. Droloxifene, a new estrogen antagonist/agonist, prevents bone loss on ovariectomized rats. Endocrinology 1995; 136:2435–41.

64. Loser R, Seibel K, Roos W, Eppenberger U. In vivo and in vitro antiestrogenic action of 3-hydroxytamoxifen, tamoxifen and 4-hydroxytamoxifen. Eur J Cancer Clin Oncol 1985;21:900–85.

65. Winterfeld G, Hauff P, Gorlich M, et al. Investigations of droloxifene and other hormone manipulations on N-nitrosomethylurea-induced rat mammary tumours. J Cancer Res Clin Oncol 1992; 119:91–6.

66. Kawamura J, Mizota T, Kondo H, et al. Antitumor effects of droloxifene, a new antiestrogen drug, against 7,12-dimethylbenz(a)anthracene-induced mammary tumors in rats. Jpn J Pharmaco 1991; 57:215–24.

67. McCague R, Parr IB, Haynes BP. Metabolism of the 4 iodo derivative of tamoxifen by isolated rat hepatocytes. Demonstration that the iodine atom reduces metabolic conversion and identification of four metabolites. Biochem Pharm 1990;40: 2277–83.

68. Coombes RC, Haynes BP, Dowsett M, et al. Idoxifene: report of a phase I study in patients with metastatic disease. Cancer Res 1995;55:1070–4.

69. Chander SK, McCague R, Lugmani Y, et al. Pyrrolidino-4-iodotamoxifen and 4-iodotamoxifen, new analogues of the antiestrogen tamoxifen for the treatment of breast cancer. Cancer Res 1991; 51:5851–8.

70. Palkowitz AD, Glasebrook AL, Thrasher JK, et al. Discovery and synthesis of [6-hydroxy-3-[4-(1-piperidinyl)-ethoxy-phenoxy]-2-(4-hydroxyphenyl) benzo[b]thiophene: a novel, highly potent selective estrogen receptor modulator (SERM). J Med Chem 1997;40:1407–16.

71. Bryant HU, Glasebrook AL, Knadler MP, et al. LY 353,381.HCL: a highly potent, orally active selective estrogen receptor modulator [abstract]. In: Proceedings of The Endocrine Society 79th Annual Meeting; 1997. p. 3–446.

72. Sato M, Turner CH, Wang T, et al. LY 353,381.HCL: a novel raloxifene analog with improved SERM potency and efficacy in vivo. J Pharm Exper Ther 1998;287:1–7.

73. Dardes RC, Bentrem D, O'Regan RM, et al. Effects of the new selective estrogen receptor modulator LY 353381.HCL (Arzoxifene) on human endometrial cancer growth in athymic mice. Clin Cancer Res 2001;7:4149–55.

74. Munster PN, Buzdar A, Dhingra K, et al. Phase I trial of third-generation selective estrogen receptor modulator, LY 353381.HCL, in metastatic breast cancer. J Clin Oncol 2001;19:2002–9.

75. Suh N, Glasebrook AL, Palkowitz AD, et al. Arzoxifene, a new selective estrogen receptor modulator, for chemoprevention of experimental breast cancer. Cancer Res 2001;61:8412–5.

76. MacGregor Schafer JI, Liu H, Tonetti DA, Jordan VC. The interaction of raloxifene and the active metabolite of the antiestrogen EM-800 (SC 5705) with the human estrogen receptor (ER). Cancer Res 1999;59:4308–13.

77. Gutman M, Couillard S, Roy J, et al. Comparison of the effects of the EM-652 (SCH57068), tamoxifen, toremifene, droloxifene, idoxifene, GW5638 and raloxifene on the growth of human breast ZR-75-1 breast tumors in nude mice. Int J Cancer 2002;99:273–8.

78. Luo S, Sourla A, Labrie C, et al. Effect of twenty-four-week treatment with the antiestrogen EM-800 on estrogen-sensitive parameters in intact and ovariectomized mice. Endocrinology 1998;139: 2645–56.

79. Labrie F, Labrie C, Belanger A, et al. EM 652 (SCH57068), a pure SERM having complete antiestrogenic activity in the mammary gland and endometrium. J Steroid Biochem Mol Biol 2001; 79:213–25.

80. Luo S, Stojanovic M, Labrie C, Labrie F. Inhibitory effect of the novel antiestrogen EM-800 and medroxyprogesterone acetate on estrone-stimulated growth of dimethylbenz[a]anthracene-induced mammary carcinoma in rats. Int J Cancer 1997;3:580–6.

81. Ke HZ, Paralkar VM, Grasser WA, et al. Effects of CP 336,156, a new non-steroidal estrogen agonist/antagonist, on bone, serum cholesterol, uterus and body composition in rat models. Endocrinol 1998; 139:2068–76.

82. Ke HZ, Qi H, Chidsey-Frink KL, et al. Lasofoxifene (CP-336,156) protects against age-related changes in bone mass, bone strength, and total serum cho-

lesterol in intact aged male rats. J Bone Miner Res 2001;16:765–73.

83. Cohen LA, Pittman B, Wang CX, et al. LAS, a novel selective estrogen receptor modulator with chemopreventive and therapeutic activity in the N-nitroso-N-methylurea-induced rat mammary tumor model. Cancer Res 2001;61:8683–8.

84. Willson TM, Norris JD, Wagner BL, et al. Dissection of the molecular mechanism of action of GW 5638, a novel estrogen receptor ligand, provides insights into the role of estrogen receptor in bone. Endocrinology 1997;138:3901–11.

85. Dardes RC, O'Regan RM, Gajdos C, et al. Effects of a new clinically relevant antiestrogen (GW 5638) related to tamoxifen on breast and endometrial growth in vivo. Clin Cancer Res 2002;8: 1995–2001.

AROMATASE INHIBITORS FOR CHEMOPREVENTION

Paul E. Goss, MD, PhD, FRCPC, FRCP (UK)
Kathrin Strasser-Weippl, MD

Breast cancer is one of the most common cancers of women in the Western world. Approximately 170,000 new cases are reported annually in the United States, and there are about 1 million incident cases.[1] A modest impact on breast cancer mortality has been achieved by the implementation of improved screening techniques together with improved surgical, radiation, and systemic treatments.[2] In particular, adjuvant hormone therapy has reduced mortality significantly, but there is a substantial unmet medical need to either improve the outcome of patients already diagnosed with invasive breast cancer or, alternatively, to reduce the occurrence or progression of preinvasive breast lesions. Despite data implicating diet and other environmental risk factors, no lifestyle changes have yet been convincingly shown to significantly reduce the risk of breast cancer. The precise genetic steps required for epithelial cells to transform from normal to breast carcinoma are ill understood, but the estrogen receptor (ER) is increasingly expressed as normal epithelium undergoes changes to hyperplasia, hyperplasia with atypia, and then to ductal carcinoma in situ. Lifetime cumulative estrogen exposure is correlated with breast cancer risk, and the antiestrogen tamoxifen has been shown to reduce the incidence of both invasive cancer and preinvasive lesions. This proof of principle suggests that strategies inhibiting estrogen that build on the results seen with tamoxifen are a logical way forward. Aromatase (estrogen synthetase) inhibitors, which antagonize estrogen by blocking its synthesis from androgens, offer an alternate way of preventing the effects of estrogen and its metabolites on the breast. These inhibitors have already been shown to be superior to tamoxifen in advanced and early stage breast cancer both in terms of efficacy and with respect to toxicity.

In this chapter, the role of estrogen in the initiation and promotion of breast cancer is outlined. Specifically, the epidemiologic evidence for this, the preclinical models supporting it, and the molecular evidence for estrogen's role in the pathogenesis of breast cancer are described. The evidence that the aromatase inhibitors are superior to tamoxifen in terms of their efficacy in advanced breast cancer and in the neoadjuvant and adjuvant settings is outlined. Evidence that aromatase inhibitors reduce both the initiation and promotion of breast cancer in animal models is also given. Ongoing pilot trials and planned phase III chemoprevention trials are described in detail. A potential important difference in the therapeutic index between steroidal and nonsteroidal inhibitors is given, and the way in which that is being explored in ongoing and planned trials is described. Blocking other overexpressed growth factor pathways in conjunction with estrogen synthesis inhibition holds potential in breast cancer prevention. One example for this is the inhibition of the cyclooxygenase-2 (COX-2) pathway together with aromatase inhibition; two key trials employing this strategy are presented.

RATIONALE FOR ANTAGONIZING ESTROGEN IN BREAST CANCER PREVENTION

Epidemiologic Evidence

Epidemiologic studies point to an important role for estrogens in the development and growth of breast cancers. The almost 150-fold increased incidence of breast cancer in women compared with men reflects the relationship between female sex steroids and breast cancer. A number of clinical markers of excessive cumulative lifetime exposure to estrogens are linked to an individual's breast cancer risk. These include early menarche and late menopause,[3] high bone density,[4] and obesity in menopause,[5] which are all surrogates for exposure to estrogens. In addition, elevated levels of plasma estrogens are themselves directly associated with a raised risk of breast cancer[6–8]; it may well be that, in postmenopausal women, plasma estrogen levels are the most reliable intermediate biomarker of breast cancer risk. This is discussed in more detail below. In support of this finding, a correlation has been shown between high levels of urinary estrogens and the risk of breast cancer.[9] The relationship between exogenous estrogens and breast cancer risk has also been investigated in several large, epidemiologic studies. Three cohort studies and four case-control studies have overall shown that the use of hormone replacement therapy (HRT) in menopause increases the risk of breast cancer by one-third, although the results of the individual studies varied considerably.[10–16] The hormones used by the women in these studies ranged from pure estrogen replacement to combined estrogen-progestin therapy (with unspecified content of estrogen), and all regimens resulted in an increased breast cancer risk. However, it was reported that the increase in breast cancer risk in women using estrogen-progestin therapy is higher than in those using estrogen therapy alone.[11] Recently published data from the Women's Health Initiative (WHI), a prospective study in which 16,608 postmenopausal women were randomized to HRT versus placebo, confirmed this excess risk of breast cancer relative risk (RR = 1.29 after a median follow-up of 5.2 years).[17] Hysterectomized postmenopausal women in the WHI study receiving estrogen-only therapy versus placebo continue on study, and this arm of the trial will report in 2005. In one of the epidemiologic studies discussed above, the increase in risk was higher in women with a lower body mass index. This might mean that with a low amount of body fat, and thus lower levels of endogenous estrogens, the sensitivity to an increase in breast cancer risk caused by exogenous estrogens might be higher. The elevated breast cancer risk of women who have stopped taking HRT normalizes 5 years after cessation of therapy.[18] Longer follow-up of the WHI study will provide more information in this regard. The relationship between the use of oral contraceptives and breast cancer is less clear, because the studies addressing this issue have produced varying results. Several studies suggested a very slight increase in breast cancer risk with the use of oral contraceptives irrespective of the duration.[13,14,19] However, in a recently published population-based study including more than 9,000 women, breast cancer risk was not elevated in women currently using or having previously used oral contraceptives.[20] The findings did not differ according to duration of use, dose of estrogen used, race, or family history of breast cancer. In another study among *BRCA1* mutation carriers, an increase in breast cancer risk by one-third was seen in women who first used oral contraceptives before 1975, who used them before age 30, or who used them for 5 or more years. Oral contraceptives did not appear to be associated with risk of breast cancer in *BRCA2* carriers.[21] A summary of the available information on hormonally mediated indicators of elevated breast cancer risk is shown in Table 13-1.[22]

In addition to exogenous factors increasing breast cancer risk, epidemiologic studies have also identified certain dietary agents that decrease breast cancer risk in part via hormonal mechanisms. These primarily include flaxseed and soy, for which a high intake has been noted in geographic regions with a low breast cancer risk. For example, the mammalian lignans found in flaxseed inhibit aromatase and weakly antagonize estrogen binding to the ER as part of their putative anti-breast cancer mechanism of action.[23,24]

Epidemiologic studies have indicated that certain genetic polymorphisms of enzymes involved in estrogen synthesis and metabolism may also lead to an elevated breast cancer risk. For example, an increased risk of developing breast cancer for carriers of the *A1* variant of the aromatase gene was implied by two case-control studies.[25,26] In numerous other studies, correlations between certain polymorphisms of estrogen-catabolizing enzymes and breast cancer risk were demonstrated.[27–31] However, there is an equal number of studies which were unable to confirm these associations. It will take larger cohorts and the consideration of posttranscriptional influences on enzyme activity in order to clarify this important issue.

Evidence from Animal Studies

Another line of evidence linking estrogen to breast cancer comes from animal studies. Estrogen and its

TABLE 13-1 Hormonally-Mediated Indicators of Breast Cancer Risk

| Indicator | Risk Group | | Relative Risk* |
	Low	High	
Sex	Male	Female	150
Age	30–34 years	70–74 years	17.0
Age of menarche	> 14 years	< 12 years	1.5
Oral contraceptive use	Never	Ever	1.07–1.2
Age at first childbirth	< 20 years	≥ 30 years	1.9–3.5
Breastfeeding	≥ 16 months	Never	1.37
Parity	≥ 5	Nulliparity	1.4
Oophorectomy	Age < 35 years	No	3.0
Age at natural menopause	< 45 years	≥ 55 years	2.0
Estrogen therapy	Never	Current	1.2–1.4
Estrogen-progestin therapy	Never	Current	1.4
Obesity (BMI)† (postmenopausal)	< 22.9	> 30.7	1.6
Family history	No	Yes	2.6
Serum estradiol	Lowest quartile	Highest quartile	1.8–5.0
Breast density	None	≥ 75% density	6.0
Bone density	Lowest quartile	Highest quartile	2.7–3.5

Adapted from Clemons M and Goss PE.[22]
†Body mass index (kg/m²).
*Using low-risk group as reference.

metabolites induce breast cancer in several animal models. For example, in female ACI rats, tumors of the mammary gland develop rapidly on exposure to estrogen.[32] In several other animal models of tumorigenesis, the development or growth of tumors is enhanced by estrogen.[33] In the kidney of the male Syrian golden hamster, estrogen (E_2), estrone (E_1) and 2-hydroxycatechol estrogen (2-OHCE, an estrogen metabolite) are carcinogenic.[33–37] When 2-hydroxy- and 4-hydroxycatechol estrogens were compared, the 4-OH-metabolites were significantly more carcinogenic, leading to speculation that the specific pathway of estrogen metabolism might be important with respect to breast cancer risk. Interestingly, tumor formation is decreased in hamsters treated with estrogen plus inhibitors of its metabolism compared with hamsters exposed to estrogen alone.[38–40] This observation demonstrates a role for estrogen metabolites in carcinogenesis. In 2002, conjugated estrogens, estradiol, estrone, ethinyl estradiol, and mestranol were placed on the United States' list of probable cancer-causing substances be-cause of fulfilling the criteria for registration as human carcinogens.

Molecular Evidence

Important data on the molecular mechanisms of estrogen-induced carcinogenesis have been generated in the past few years. The classical paradigm was that estrogens manifest their effect on breast cancer via the estrogen receptor (ER). In this model, estrogen exposure of breast cells leads to deoxyribonucleic acid (DNA) synthesis and cell proliferation. Proliferating cells are susceptible to DNA damage, and with a high rate of proliferation, the time for DNA repair diminishes. Ultimately, the accumulating uncorrected genetic errors lead to a malignant phenotype.[41] In recent years, data have accumulated indicating two important new points. First, the metabolites of estrogen are at least as carcinogenic as the parent compounds. Second, receptor-mediated signal transduction is not the only pathway of carcinogenesis by estrogen and its metabolites.

The catechol metabolites of estrogen are signaling molecules which are able to bind to the ER and act in a proestrogenic way. As discussed above, their role in carcinogenesis has been extensively studied in the male Syrian hamster kidney and in the uterus of CD-1 mice.[33-37] In these models, the 2-OH and 4-OH catechol estrogens are able to induce malignant tumors in tissues expressing the ER. The fact that 4-OH catechols are much more potent carcinogens than the 2-OH catechols is important when discussing individual differences in estrogen metabolism and their implications for breast cancer risk. The catechol estrogens themselves give rise to genotoxic quinones, which can subsequently generate reactive oxygen species causing oxidative damage.[42,43] It has been shown in numerous studies that both estrogen and its catechol metabolites — apart from binding to the ER — cause multiple direct genotoxic effects such as aneuploidy,[44,45] structural chromosomal aberrations,[44-47] gene amplification,[48] and microsatellite instability.[49] Apart from nonspecific genetic damage, certain specific mutations triggered by estrogens have also now been confirmed.[50] As genetic lesions are known to cause cancer in humans, the genetic damage caused by estrogen metabolites might be an important step in the development of breast cancer.[51] Another line of evidence arguing for receptor-independent pathways of estrogen carcinogenesis comes from studies showing that ER-positive cells in the normal mammary gland are not the ones that proliferate in response to estrogen as measured by Ki67-positivity.[52,53] Furthermore, in ER-knockout mice, estrogen-induced mammary tumors develop independent of the ER.[54] Thus, tumors may be initiated by direct carcinogenic effects of estrogen and its metabolites and proliferate in response to receptor-mediated stimuli. Inhibition of estrogen synthesis with aromatase inhibitors and concomitant reduction in the levels of its metabolites may interfere with these cancer-causing effects.

Apart from circulating endogenous and exogenous estrogens, other tissue-related estrogenic factors have been implicated in the initiation of hormone-dependent breast cancer. The level of tissue expression of the aromatase enzyme, which is responsible for the synthesis of estrogens from androgens, might be important in this regard. It has been shown that aromatase expression and activity are higher in breast tumors than in peritumoral fat and

that peritumoral aromatase levels are higher in the quadrant where the tumor is located than in other quadrants of the breast.[55-59] In addition, there is increasing evidence indicating that this local estrogen production may play a major role in tumor proliferation.[60-63] The exact mechanisms involved in estrogen production within the breast are still ill-understood. There are tissue-specific promoters of the aromatase gene which are regulated by transcription factors, some of which have been demonstrated to be tumor related.[64] In addition, it is hypothesized that the aromatase gene may be constitutively activated in the breasts of certain women, causing an exaggerated and sustained estrogen stimulus on the breast and thereby acting as an oncogene to induce cancer.

CHEMOPREVENTION WITH TAMOXIFEN AS THE PROOF OF PRINCIPLE

Significant proof of principle that antagonizing estrogen in humans will lead to reduction in breast cancer incidence has been obtained from four large prospective placebo-controlled clinical trials in women at increased risk for breast cancer. These trials include the large National Surgical Adjuvant Breast and Bowel Project (NSABP) P-1 study,[65] the International Breast Intervention Study 1 (IBIS 1),[66] the Italian Breast Cancer Prevention Study,[67,68] and the Royal Marsden Hospital Breast Cancer Prevention Trial.[69] The metaanalysis of the data from these four studies, together with the Oxford overview metaanalysis of contralateral breast cancer reduction from adjuvant tamoxifen, reveals a net 38% reduction in invasive and preinvasive cancers.[70] In addition, a significant reduction in estrogen-related benign breast diseases — including adenosis, cysts, duct ectasia, fibrocystic disease, and atypical hyperplasia — and an overall reduction in the need for clinical biopsies were subsequently shown by the NSABP.[71] These proof-of-principle data imply that an interruption in the progression from preinvasive to invasive breast lesions is achievable through antiestrogenic means. Additional evidence for a steep dose-related curve of plasma estrogen levels with breast cancer risk has been obtained through the context of the multiple outcome raloxifene study in postmenopausal women

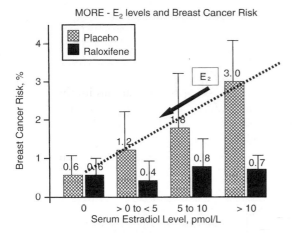

MORE - E$_2$ levels and Breast Cancer Risk

Figure 13-1 Reduction of breast cancer risk is dependent on endogenous estrogen levels in the MORE study. Adapted from Cummings SR et al.[72]

with osteoporosis.[72] As shown in Figure 13-1, reduction in the risk of breast cancer within the context of the study was seen most impressively in women with the highest quartile of postmenopausal serum estradiol levels. Taken together, this suggests that inhibiting aromatase and reducing postmenopausal serum and intrabreast estrogen levels may also result in a reduction in breast cancer risk. In the NSABP P-1 study and in the ongoing Study of Tamoxifen and Raloxifene (STAR) trial (tamoxifen versus raloxifene for 5 years in postmenopausal women), a Gail score (see Section One of this book) greater than 1.66 has been a principal study entry criterion. Increasingly, additional means of selecting postmenopausal women at high risk of breast cancer have been sought. Clinical markers of cumulative lifetime estrogen exposure have been identified as potential ways of achieving this, including elevated bone mineral density and plasma estrogen levels (as discussed above). In addition, breast density on screening mammography in healthy women has also been shown to be a marker of breast cancer risk and affords another potential selection tool for risk identification. These risk factors are discussed in greater detail in Section One of this book. The most definitive assessment of premalignant lesions comes from cyto- or histopathologic evaluation of breast cells. To this end, various techniques are being applied to characterize particular preinvasive lesions. These in-

clude fine needle aspiration targeted in a blind fashion in the upper outer quadrant of the breast, or to an area of breast density, or systematically in a periareolar fashion. In addition, nipple aspirate fluid has been obtained via ductal lavage of the breast. These and other means of surveillance in breast cancer risk management are delineated extensively in Section Two. As outlined below, they are also being used in ongoing breast cancer prevention pilot studies of aromatase inhibitors.

EFFICACY OF AROMATASE INHIBITORS IN BREAST CANCER

Mechanism of Action of Aromatase Inhibitors

Aromatase is the enzyme complex responsible for the last step in estrogen synthesis, the conversion of the androgens androstenedione and testosterone to the estrogens E$_1$ and E$_2$. Aromatase inhibitors can be classified in a number of different ways: first-, second-, and third-generation; steroidal and nonsteroidal; reversible (ionic binding) and irreversible ("suicide inhibitor," covalent binding).[73–75] The aromatase inhibitors in clinical use today include the third-generation nonsteroidal aromatase inhibitors anastrozole and letrozole and the third-generation steroidal aromatase inactivator exemestane. A diagram of the structures of the most important aromatase inhibitors is presented in Figure 13-2. All three of these inhibitors suppress estrogen levels profoundly in postmenopausal women.[76] In premenopausal women, there are less data, but early volunteer studies showed that estrogen levels were incompletely suppressed and, moreover, that a reflex rise in follicle-stimulating hormone and luteinizing hormone (FSH/LH) levels caused a hyperstimulation of the ovaries, producing abdominopelvic discomfort, fluid in the pouch of Douglas, and ovarian cysts. For this reason, monotherapy with aromatase inhibitors has not been advocated in premenopausal women. However, in combination with initial ovarian function suppression, the aromatase inhibitors are now being investigated in younger women.

The clinical significance of classifying the third-generation inhibitors is uncertain, but it is being addressed in studies that are currently being initiated. These are described in more detail below. With the traditional radioimmunoassays, it was dif-

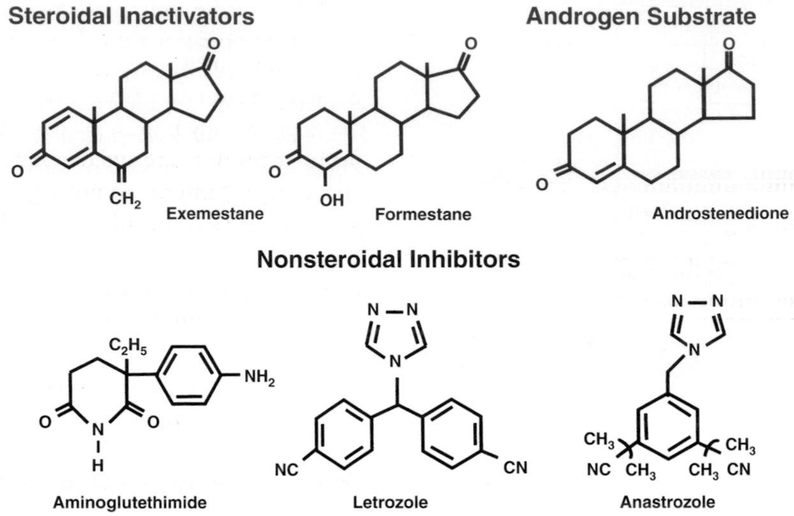

Steroidal Inactivators

Androgen Substrate

Exemestane

Formestane

Androstenedione

Nonsteroidal Inhibitors

Aminoglutethimide

Letrozole

Anastrozole

Figure 13-2 Structure of the most important aromatase inhibitors.

ficult to detect differences in the level of estrogen suppression between the inhibitors, but with more sensitive assays recently developed, small but possibly significant differences have been detected. Furthermore, having a steroidal structure (eg, exemestane) may impart to an inhibitor the potential to affect other steroid levels (eg, androgens) either directly by the parent compound or indirectly by its metabolites. This in turn could be relevant to the efficacy of chemoprevention of breast cancer and to important effects on other functions such as bone and lipid metabolism. Thus, dissimilarities between the two nonsteroidal third-generation reversible inhibitors letrozole and anastrozole and the recently approved steroidal third-generation irreversible inhibitor exemestane may afford different therapeutic indices and thus different clinical applications for these compounds.

Aromatase Inhibitors in Advanced Breast Cancer

In evaluating the potential of aromatase inhibitors as chemopreventives of breast cancer, their efficacy against established disease is of importance. Several years ago, all three third-generation inhibitors were approved for use in patients with advanced breast cancer when they were shown to be superior to megestrol acetate in women whose disease progressed on prior tamoxifen.[77] More recently, the results of two trials of anastrozole and one trial of letrozole compared with tamoxifen in the first-line

setting of metastatic breast cancer have been published, and preliminary results of a study comparing exemestane with tamoxifen are also available.[78–81] All three inhibitors are superior to tamoxifen in this setting, and anastrozole and letrozole are approved and being used widely for this indication in the clinic. In a neoadjuvant trial including 337 patients, letrozole was also found to be significantly better than tamoxifen in terms of clinical shrinkage of tumor and reduction in tumor size as measured by both ultrasound and mammography.[82] In all of these trials, the inhibitors also showed better toxicity profiles than tamoxifen, suggesting that they are well poised to be used in women with earlier stage breast cancer and possibly in well women for prevention.

Aromatase Inhibitors in the Adjuvant Setting

At least eight international adjuvant breast cancer trials are ongoing in postmenopausal women with receptor-positive breast cancer. The first-generation adjuvant trials are testing the aromatase inhibitors against tamoxifen. All of these studies will provide contralateral breast cancer incidence and thereby afford an initial view of the potential preventive effects of this class of agents. Several of these studies are shown in Figure 13-3. The first trial to report is the Arimidex versus Tamoxifen Alone or in Combination (ATAC) study; reduction in contralateral breast cancer incidence from tamoxifen, tamoxifen plus anastrozole, or anastrozole alone is shown in Figure 13-4.[83] An excess of clinical fractures and an

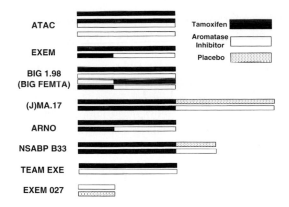

Figure 13-3 First-generation adjuvant trials with aromatase inhibitors.

ATAC = Arimidex versus Tamoxifen Alone or in Combination

Exem = Exemestane

BIG 1.98 (BIG FEMTA) = Breast International Group Femara-Tamoxifen

(J)MA.17 = National Cancer Institute of Canada Clinical Trials Group (Mammary)

ARNO = Arimidex-Nolvadex

NSBP B33 = National Surgical Adjuvant Breast and Bowel Project

TEAM EXE = Exemestane compared to Tamoxifen

EXEM 027 = Exemestane compared to Placebo

increase in musculoskeletal symptoms occurred in the anastrozole-treated arm of this study. Other known side effects of tamoxifen, including vaginal bleeding, endometrial cancer, and thromboem-

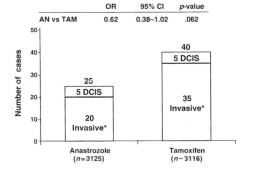

Figure 13-4 Adapted from ATAC Trialists' Group.[83] Disease-free survival in the ATAC trial.

DCIS = ductal carcinoma in situ.

bolism, were seen significantly less often in the anastrozole-treated patients. These data strongly suggest an equivalent or greater potential reduction in breast cancer risk from the aromatase inhibitor and a potentially important improvement in therapeutic index with the avoidance of very serious side effects. It is of interest to note that the combination arm in the ATAC trial of anastrozole plus tamoxifen is no more effective than tamoxifen alone. One putative explanation for why tamoxifen given concurrently with anastrozole would reduce the effectiveness of the anastrozole alone is the possibility of an enhanced estrogen agonist effect of tamoxifen in the presence of depleted ambient estrogen levels. This hypothesis was outlined by Morello and colleagues, and this phenomenon has been shown to possibly be less apparent for selective estrogen receptor modulators (SERM)s that are inherently less agonistic.[84] Newer generation SERMs may therefore perform better in combination with an aromatase inhibitor, and the opportunity to explore a total estrogen blockade, as initially conceived of for the combination arm of the ATAC trial, may yet be an achievable goal. Clinical trials employing alternative SERMS with aromatase inhibitors are thus underway in the metastatic setting.

The National Cancer Institute of Canada Clinical Trials Group Mammary.27 (NCIC CTG MA.27) study is a large North American adjuvant endocrine trial that was launched in the first quarter of 2003. It is the first head-to-head comparison of two aromatase inhibitors, anastrozole versus exemestane, in the adjuvant setting. Its goal is to show superior efficacy of the steroidal inhibitor as well as an improved profile on end-organ function such as bone and lipid metabolism. The rationale for the latter effects is outlined below. In addition, the value of adding a COX-2 inhibitor to anastrozole or exemestane will be evaluated in this trial. Celecoxib is an inhibitor of the COX-2 pathway and is an approved cancer prevention drug (for familial polyposis of the colon); it apparently synergizes significantly with exemestane in preclinical animal models.[85] Owing to its pleiotropic mechanisms of action and its inhibitory effect on receptor-negative breast cancer cells, in-vitro celecoxib may also achieve a reduction in ER-negative breast cancers, which disproportionately contribute to overall breast cancer mortality. The design of the MA.27 adjuvant trial is shown in Figure 13-5.

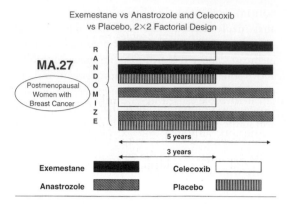

Figure 13-5 The National Cancer Institute of Canada Clinical Trials Group Mammary.27 (NCIC CTG MA.27) adjuvant study.

TOXICITY PROFILE OF AROMATASE INHIBITORS

The short-term common toxicity profiles of the third-generation inhibitors are similar, with the most common adverse events being nausea, vomiting, hot flashes, musculoskeletal discomfort, fatigue, and headaches. However, in the second-line metastatic breast cancer trials mentioned above, the aromatase inhibitors showed a superior toxicity profile compared with both megestrol acetate and aminoglutethimide. The available data from the first-line setting indicate at least equal short-term safety of the aromatase inhibitors compared with tamoxifen including symptoms of menopause and quality of life.

Although not statistically different in these trials, a trend in favour of the inhibitors for important toxicities such as thromboembolism was seen.[77] Although the aromatase inhibitors are often discussed together, there might be important differences in their side effect profiles, particularly between the steroidal and nonsteroidal inhibitors.

Anastrozole is the only agent for which results in the adjuvant setting have been presented. The toxicity data in comparison to tamoxifen, which were collected in the ATAC trial, are particularly important, as these patients were disease-free, "healthy" postmenopausal women.[83] Women taking anastrozole were at a significantly lower risk of developing endometrial cancer than those taking tamoxifen (p = .02). The nonstimulatory effect of anastrozole on the endometrium was also reflected by a significantly decreased rate of vaginal bleeding during the trial (4.5% vs 8.2%, $p < .0001$). In addition, both ischemic cerebrovascular and venous thromboembolic events (including deep vein thrombosis [DVT]) were rarer in the anastrozole group (1.0% vs 2.1% and 2.1% vs 3.5%, respectively, both p = .00006). By contrast, women taking anastrozole were more likely to suffer from musculoskeletal disorders (27.8% vs 21.3%, $p < .00001$), in particular fractures (5.9% vs 3.7%, $p < .0001$). In the ATAC trial, influences of either anastrozole or tamoxifen on the serum lipid profile have not been reported. In another small study, no influence of anastrozole on the lipid profile was seen.[86] The effects of letrozole and exemestane on organs other than the breast have not been as comprehensively studied to date. However, similar to anastrozole, letrozole has in several studies been shown to significantly increase parameters of bone resorption.[87] When letrozole was given to healthy women for 3 months, no influence was seen on their lipid profiles.[88] However, in another study including 20 women with breast cancer, letrozole significantly increased total and low density lipoproteins (LDL) cholesterol levels, as well as the atherogenic risk ratios total high density lipoproteins (HDL) and LDL/HDL cholesterol.[89] The effects of letrozole on bone metabolism and parameters of cardiovascular risk are being extensively studied in the ongoing adjuvant placebo-controlled NCIC CTG MA.17 trial (Figure 13-6).

The effect of exemestane on a marker of bone metabolism (excretion of pyridinoline) was studied in two preclinical studies of ovariectomized rats. In the first, control rats were oophorectomized (OVX), and treated animals received exemestane

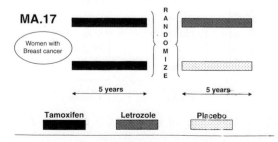

Figure 13-6 The NCIC CTG MA.17 adjuvant study.

100 mg/kg/week by intramuscular injection, the dose able to yield the optimal antitumor effect in tumor-bearing animals of the same breed.[90] Exemestane was able to prevent the increase in pyridinoline excretion compared with nonovariectomized rats by 96% ($p < .0001$ vs OVX control), and the profound reduction in BMD caused by oophorectomy was obviated in the exemestane-treated animals. A follow-up experiment of five groups of animals included two lower doses of exemestane, as well as a group treated with 17-hydroexemestane and another treated with the antitumor dose of letrozole (1 mg/kg) in this rat model.[91] The bone-sparing effects of all three doses of exemestane were demonstrated in a dose-dependent manner, and an equally positive effect of 17-hydroexemestane was demonstrated. Letrozole had no effect on bone metabolism in the castrated animals, which lack peripheral aromatase. In a follow-up study in postmenopausal women, bone biomarkers of formation and resorption were studied in groups of women given placebo, letrozole 2.5 mg/day, and exemestane 25 mg/day. In this experiment, exemestane-treated women appeared similar to placebo in terms of early markers of bone turnover, whereas letrozole increased bone resorption and reduced bone formation.[92]

This study therefore supported the notion that exemestane has a superior safety profile compared with the other third-generation inhibitors with regard to bone. Likewise, exemestane seems to have effects converse to the other aromatase inhibitors in terms of lipid metabolism. In a European Organisation for Research and Treatment of Cancer (EORTC) companion study, exemestane was compared with tamoxifen in breast cancer patients. After a treatment period of 24 weeks, exemestane had beneficial effects on triglycerides and a stabilizing effect on HDL and total cholesterol levels.[93] Similarly, in the two rat experiments cited above, exemestane improved the serum lipid profile in treated animals compared with either oophorectomy or letrozole treatment. Overall, it seems that being an androgenic steroid may make exemestane superior to the other inhibitors in terms of side effects caused by estrogen depletion of target tissues other than the breast.

Apart from the toxicities concerning endocrine-responsive tissues such as the endometrium, bone, and the lipid profile, the therapeutic index of aromatase inhibitors is influenced by their general tolerability. The side effect profiles reported from the metastatic studies may not be applicable in the preventive setting, and data from the adjuvant setting are available only on anastrozole.[83] In the ATAC trial, anastrozole caused significantly fewer vasomotor symptoms than tamoxifen as reported by the investigators, although in a parallel quality of life study by Fallowfield and colleagues this was not confirmed.[94] The incidence of cataracts, nausea/vomiting, fatigue, and mood disturbances was the same in both groups. In the case of exemestane and letrozole, data from studies in advanced breast cancer are all that are available at present to ascertain their tolerability. In a study in the first-line setting of metastatic breast cancer, exemestane induced fewer hot flashes and peripheral edema than tamoxifen. In terms of nausea and sweating, exemestane was also better tolerated than tamoxifen.[81] When letrozole was compared with tamoxifen in advanced breast cancer, the tolerability of the two agents was similar with respect to nausea and hot flashes.[80] The findings from the ATAC trial are important in that they provide the first data of relative toxicities of tamoxifen versus a third-generation aromatase inhibitor in healthy postmenopausal women. The weakness of these data, however, is that there was no placebo arm allowing a true estimation of the toxicities of the aromatase inhibitor.

CHEMOPREVENTION WITH AROMATASE INHIBITORS

Animal Models

Animal models that have been used to demonstrate the chemopreventive efficacy of aromatase inhibitors include the hormone-dependent carcinogen-induced N-methyl-nitrosourea (MNU) and 7,12-dimethyl-benz(a)anthracene (DMBA) rat mammary tumors.[95,96] To determine their chemopreventive effects, aromatase inhibitors have been given prior to or after carcinogen administration. Inhibition of tumor formation in these animals is viewed as a surrogate model for prevention of tumor initiation or promotion in humans.

The ability of aromatase inhibitors to block or reduce preneoplastic changes of the breast caused by aromatase overexpression has been studied in the recently developed aromatase-transgenic mouse model (int-5/aromatase).[62]

To date, chemoprevention with aromatase inhibitors has been tested only in these preclinical models. Inhibition of both the appearance of new tumors and their multiplicity has variably been shown with aminoglutethimide, fadrozole, vorozole, and letrozole in the MNU- and DMBA-carcinogen-induced mammary tumor models.[97,99]

Pilot Trial Designs

Based on the fundamental principles of considering novel agents, biomarkers, and cohorts for chemoprevention studies, a number of pilot trials with aromatase inhibitors have been launched. The eligibility criteria for these studies include a history of preinvasive breast cancer, elevated serum estrogen levels in postmenopausal women, and a prior history of receptor-positive breast cancer with increased density on subsequent screening mammography.

In some of these studies the primary endpoint of evaluation is a surrogate marker for the development of invasive breast cancer as discussed above, and in some cases it is also the primary inclusion criterion of the study. Examples of this are the breast density studies, in which breast density is used to select the cohort at risk, but reduction in breast density is also the primary endpoint because it is a putative intermediate marker of breast cancer risk reduction. Future chemoprevention pilot trials will use various combinations of the biomarkers discussed above as eligibility criteria and intermediate endpoints. If the predictive value of these surrogate markers for breast cancer occurrence can be confirmed with longer follow-up, definitive phase III trials may eventually use these surrogates as endpoints instead of breast cancer incidence. The most obvious example of this may be both the use of serum estrogen levels as a selection tool of risk and the reduction of estrogen levels as a definitive marker of breast cancer prevention.

Complex issues in chemoprevention such as optimal dose, duration, and scheduling are also of critical importance, and although some things are being learned from the ongoing adjuvant trials with aromatase inhibitors, further studies will be necessary to optimize these issues.

The Clinical Trials Group of the National Cancer Institute of Canada (NCIC-CTG) is currently conducting a double-blind, multicenter proof of principle prevention trial (MAP.1) in which letrozole is compared with placebo in 120 women. In this 1-year study, letrozole's ability to reduce mammographic density is being evaluated in postmenopausal women who are well but have breast density (> 25%) or who have had prior receptor-positive breast cancer and have breast density on follow-up mammography. The primary endpoint of this trial is reduction in mammographic density; additional endpoints include bone density, plasma lipid levels, and general toxicities. In selected women, serial core biopsies or fine needle aspiration biopsies are also being obtained from areas of density within the breast with a view to cytopathologic evaluation. In a similarly designed trial underway in North America, NCIC CTG MAP.2, exemestane is being compared with placebo in healthy postmenopausal women with moderate or high breast density. Other pilot chemoprevention trials of aromatase inhibitors in women with breast cancer risk factors are ongoing, including a study of letrozole in women with preinvasive breast lesions and two pilot trials studying the combination of the SERM raloxifene with letrozole and exemestane, respectively.

The most important goal of a chemoprevention study is to establish efficacy of the preventive agent against the primary endpoint and to study common toxicities. In pilot studies with aromatase inhibitors given to healthy women, it will be particularly important to carefully evaluate long-term end-organ effects such as bone metabolism, cardiovascular risk, and venous thromboembolism. The question of whether supportive care such as bisphosphonates or lipid-lowering agents should be added to aromatase inhibitors in chemoprevention will in part be based on the data provided by these studies. Menopausal quality of life, an important secondary endpoint in the ongoing adjuvant studies, will also be relevant in the chemopreventive setting. Apart from providing data on the efficacy and safety of the agents, these pilot trials will afford a sense of the feasibility of chemoprevention studies to conduct specific phase III trials.

Ongoing and Planned Phase III Clinical Prevention Trials

In Italy, a randomized phase III breast cancer prevention trial is underway in unaffected postmenopausal women who have known mutations for the *BRCA1* and *-2* genes. This trial randomizes women to exemestane versus placebo for a period of 3 years. The primary endpoint is incidence of breast cancer. Two adjuvant breast cancer trials in premenopausal women are being launched: the Suppression of Ovarian Function Trial (SOFT) and the Tamoxifen and Exemestane Trial (TEXT). These trials include ovarian blockade plus an aromatase inhibitor as part of their design. Along these lines, the possibility of including high-risk premenopausal women with *BRCA1* and/or *-2* mutations has been proposed. Following the results of the ATAC adjuvant breast cancer trial mentioned above and publication of the recent IBIS 1 study, the IBIS consortium is undertaking a randomized phase III study (IBIS 2) of anastrozole versus placebo in postmenopausal women at increased risk of breast cancer as defined by criteria similar to the IBIS 1 study.[66] Multiple secondary endpoints are being investigated within the confines of this trial, including disease-free status, overall and cause-specific mortality, as well as bone mineral density and other end-organ functions.

Based on the potential superiority of exemestane over the other third-generation inhibitors and the rationale for the use of celecoxib in breast cancer prevention, the NCIC CTG is launching a placebo-controlled trial of exemestane with or without celecoxib, NCIC CTG MAP-3, in postmenopausal women at increased risk of breast cancer. Its design is shown in Figure 13-7.

CONCLUSION

Chemoprevention of breast cancer is an important medical goal but will have to be achieved without compromising health in other ways, in particular with respect to bone and lipid metabolism and cardiovascular risk. Tamoxifen is approved by the US Food and Drug Administration for the short-term reduction of breast cancer incidence in women at high risk for breast cancer. The aromatase inhibitors appear to be superior in efficacy to tamoxifen both in terms of the treatment of metastatic breast cancer, in the neoadjuvant setting, and in the adjuvant setting in the ATAC trial. Common toxicities and serious but rare adverse effects of tamoxifen such as thromboembolism appear to be of less concern with the inhibitors. However, the effects on bone and lipid metabolism, cognitive function, and other estrogen-dependent organs need to be carefully evaluated. It is possible that even if negative effects are observed, they may be of such short duration and minimal scale that they are clinically irrelevant. Or it is conceivable that these effects can be obviated with concomitant supportive care. Finally, it is possible that at least one antiaromatase agent, exemestane, may exert positive effects on bone and other end organs, making it particularly attractive as a chemopreventive.

Ongoing efficacy, particularly contralateral breast cancer risk reduction, toxicity, and quality of life data, will be obtained from the ongoing adjuvant trials. Chemoprevention pilot trials, which are underway, will provide vital data in terms of toxicities, validity of intermediate endpoints, and feasibility of enrolling healthy women into large randomized clinical trials. Three ongoing or planned phase III trials will provide definitive evidence of breast cancer risk reduction. The introduction of an agent such as celecoxib, which is being investigated as a chemopreventive of many solid-tumor cancers, is of particular interest and may herald in an era of multiple solid-tumor reduction's for both women and men.

REFERENCES

1. Ries LAG, Kosary CL, Hankey BF, et al, editors. SEER cancer statistics review, 1973–1996: tables and graphs. Bethesda (MD): National Cancer Institute; 1999.
2. Chu KC, Tarone RE, Kessler LG, et al. Recent trends in U.S. breast cancer incidence, survival and mortality rates. J Natl Cancer Inst 1996;88:1571–9.
3. Pfaffenberger RS Jr, Kampert JB, Chang HG. Characteristics that predict risk of breast cancer before

Exemestane vs Placebo + / – Celecoxib, $n = 3 \times 1,700 = 5,100$

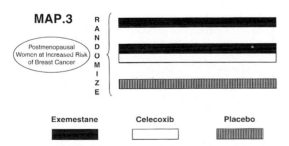

Figure 13-7 The National Cancer Institute of Canada Clinical Trials Group (NCIC CTG) MAP-3 chemoprevention study.

and after the menopause. Am J Epidemiol 1980; 112:258–68.

4. Zhang Y, Kiel DP, Kreger BE, et al. Bone mass and the risk of breast cancer among postmenopausal women. N Engl J Med 1997;336:611–7.

5. Magnusson C, Baron J, Persson I, et al. Body size in different periods of life and breast cancer risk in postmenopausal women. Int J Cancer 1998;76:29–34.

6. Toniolo PG, Levitz M, Zeleniuch-Jacquotte A, et al. A prospective study of endogenous estrogens and breast cancer in postmenopausal women. J Natl Cancer Inst 1995;87:190–7.

7. Thomas HV, Key TJ, Allen DS, et al. A prospective study of endogenous serum hormone concentrations and breast cancer risk in post-menopausal women on the island of Guernsey. Br J Cancer 1997;76:401–5.

8. The Endogenous Hormones and Breast Cancer Collaborative Group. Endogenous sex hormones and breast cancer in postmenopausal women: reanalysis of nine prospective studies. J Natl Cancer Inst 2002;94:606–16.

9. Adlercreutz H, Gorbach SL, Goldin BR, et al. Estrogen metabolism and excretion in Oriental and Caucasian women. J Natl Cancer Inst 1994;86:1076–82.

10. Schairer C, Lubin J, Troisi R, et al. Menopausal estrogen and estrogen-progestin replacement therapy and breast cancer risk. JAMA 2000;283:485–91.

11. Persson I, Weiderpass E, Bergkvist L, et al. Risks of breast and endometrial cancer after estrogen and estrogen-progestin replacement. Cancer Causes Control 1999;10:253–60.

12. Gapstur SM, Morrow M, Sellers TA. Hormone replacement therapy and risk of breast cancer with a favorable histology: results of the Iowa Women's Health Study. JAMA 1999;281:2091–7.

13. Brinton LA, Brogan DR, Coates RJ, et al. Breast cancer risk among women under 55 years of age by joint effects of usage of oral contraceptives and hormone replacement therapy. Menopause 1998; 5:145–51.

14. Titus-Ernstoff L, Longnecker MP, Newcomb PA, et al. Menstrual factors in relation to breast cancer risk. Cancer Epidemiol Biomarkers Prev 1998;7:783–9.

15. Henrich JB, Kornguth PJ, Viscoli CM, Horwitz RI. Postmenopausal estrogen use and invasive versus in situ breast cancer risk. J Clin Epidemiol 1998; 51:1277–83.

16. Magnusson C, Baron JA, Correia N, et al. Breast-cancer risk following long-term oestrogen- and oestrogen-progestin-replacement therapy. Int J Cancer 1999;81:339–44.

17. Writing Group for the Women's Health Initiative Investigators. Risks and benefits of estrogen plus progestin in healthy postmenopausal women: principal results from the Women's Health Initiative randomized controlled trial. JAMA 2002;288:321–33.

18. Colditz GA. Relationship between estrogen levels, use of hormone replacement therapy, and breast cancer. J Natl Cancer Inst 1998;90:814–23.

19. Rohan TE, Miller AB. A cohort study of oral contraceptive use and risk of benign breast disease. Int J Cancer 1999;82:191–6.

20. Marchbanks PA, McDonald JA, Wilson HG, et al. Oral contraceptives and the risk of breast cancer. N Engl J Med 2002;346:2025–32.

21. Narod SA, Dube MP, Klijn J, et al. Oral contraceptives and the risk of breast cancer in BRCA1 and BRCA2 mutation carriers. J Natl Cancer Inst 2002; 94:1773–9.

22. Clemons M, Goss PE. Estrogen and the risk of breast cancer. N Engl J Med 2001;344:276–85.

23. Adlercreutz H, Mousavi Y, Clark J, et al. Dietary phytoestrogens and cancer: in vitro and in vivo studies. J Steroid Biochem Mol Biol 1992;41:331–7.

24. Adlercreutz H, Bannwart C, Wahala K, et al. Inhibition of human aromatase by mammalian lignans and isoflavonoid phytoestrogens. J Steroid Biochem Mol Biol 1993;44:147–53.

25. Kristensen VN, Andersen TI, Lindblom A, et al. A rare CYP19 (aromatase) variant may increase the risk of breast cancer. Pharmacogenetics 1998;8:43–8.

26. Siegelmann-Danieli N, Buetow KH. Constitutional genetic variation at the human aromatase gene (Cyp19) and breast cancer risk. Br J Cancer 1999; 79:456–63.

27. Taioli E, Trachman J, Chen X, et al. A CYP1A1 restriction fragment length polymorphism is associated with breast cancer in African-American women. Cancer Res 1995;55:3757–8.

28. Ishibe N, Hankinson SE, Colditz GA, et al. Cigarette smoking, cytochrome P450 1A1 polymorphisms, and breast cancer risk in the Nurses' Health Study. Cancer Res 1998;58:667–71.

29. Feigelson HS, Coetzee GA, Kolonel LN, et al. A polymorphism in the CYP17 gene increases the risk of breast cancer. Cancer Res 1997;57:1063–5.

30. Lavigne JA, Helzlsouer KJ, Huang HY, et al. An association between the allele coding for a low activity variant of catechol-O-methyltransferase and the risk for breast cancer. Cancer Res 1997;57:5493–7.

31. Thompson PA, Shields PG, Freudenheim JL, et al. Genetic polymorphisms in catechol-O-methyltransferase, menopausal status, and breast cancer risk. Cancer Res 1998;58:2107–10.

32. Harvell DM, Strecker TE, Tochacek M, et al. Rat strain-specific actions of 17beta-estradiol in the mammary gland: correlation between estrogen-induced lobuloalveolar hyperplasia and susceptibility to estrogen-induced mammary cancers. Proc Natl Acad Sci USA 2000;97:2779–84.

33. Liehr JG, Fang WF, Sirbasku DA, Ari-Ulubelen A. Carcinogenicity of catechol estrogens in Syrian hamsters. J Steroid Biochem 1986;24:353–6.

34. Kirkman H. Hormone-related tumors in Syrian hamsters. Prog Exp Tumor Res 1972;16:201–40.

35. Li JJ, Li SA. Estrogen carcinogenesis in hamster tissues: role of metabolism. Fed Proc 1987;46:1858–63.

36. Kirkman H. Estrogen-induced tumors of the kidney. III. Growth characteristics in the Syrian hamster. Natl Cancer Inst Monogr 1959;1:1–57.

37. Newbold RR, Liehr JG. Induction of uterine adenocarcinoma in CD-1 mice by catechol estrogens. Cancer Res 2000;60:235–7.

38. Newbold RR, Bullock BC, McLachlan JA. Uterine adenocarcinoma in mice following developmental treatment with estrogens: a model for hormonal carcinogenesis. Cancer Res 1990;50:7677–81.

39. Liehr JG, Gladek A, Macatee T, et al. DAN adduct formation in liver and kidney of male Syrian hamsters treated with estrogen and/or α-naphtoflavone. Carcinogenesis 1991;21:385–9.

40. Liehr JG, Wheeler WJ. Inhibition of estrogen-induced renal carcinoma in Syrian hamsters by vitamin C. Cancer Res 1983;43:4638–42.

41. Feigelson HS, Henderson BE. Estrogens and breast cancer. Carcinogenesis 1996;17:2279–84.

42. Cavalieri EL, Stack DE, Devanesan PD, et al. Molecular origin of cancer: catechol estrogen-3,4-quinones as endogenous tumor initiators. Proc Natl Acad Sci USA 1997;94:10937–42.

43. Wang MY, Liehr JG. Induction by estrogens of lipid peroxidation and lipid peroxide-derived malonaldehyde-DNA adducts in male Syrian hamsters: role of lipid peroxidation in estrogen-induced kidney carcinogenesis. Carcinogenesis 1995;16:1941–5.

44. Banerjee SK, Banerjee S, Li SA, Li JJ. Induction of chromosome aberrations in Syrian hamster renal cortical cells by various estrogens. Mutat Res 1994;311:191–7.

45. Li JJ, Gonzalez A, Banerjee S, et al. Estrogen carcinogenesis in the hamster kidney: role of cytotoxicity and cell proliferation. Environ Health Perspect 1993;101 Suppl 5:259–64.

46. Tsutsui T, Barret JC. Neoplastic transformation of cultured mammalian cells by estrogens and estrogenlike chemicals. Environ Health Perspect 1997;105:619–24.

47. Tsutsui T, Tamura Y, Hagiwara M, et al. Induction of mammalian cell transformation and genotoxicity by 2-methoxyestradiol, an endogenous metabolite of estrogen. Carcinogenesis 2000;21:735–40.

48. Li JJ, Hou X, Banerjee SK, et al. Overexpression and amplification of c-myc in the Syrian hamster kidney during estrogen carcinogenesis: a probable critical role in neoplastic transformation. Cancer Res 1999;59:2340–6.

49. Russo J, Lareef MH, Tahin Q, et al. 17-β-estradiol is carcinogenic in human breast epithelial cells. J Steroid Biochem Mol Biol 2002;1656:1–17.

50. Kong LY, Szaniszlo P, Albrecht T, Liehr JG. Frequency and molecular analysis of hprt mutations induced by estradiol in Chinese hamster V79 cells. Int J Oncol 2000;17:1141–9.

51. Lengauer C, Kinzler KW, Vogelstein B. Genetic instabilities in human cancers. Nature 1998;396:643–9.

52. Clarke RB, Howell A, Potten CS, Anderson E. Dissociation between steroid receptor expression and cell proliferation in the human breast. Cancer Res 1997;57:4987–91.

53. Russo J, Ao X, Grill C, Russo IH. Pattern of distribution of cells positive for estrogen receptor alpha and progesterone receptor in relation to proliferating cells in the mammary gland. Breast Cancer Res Treat 1999;53:217–27.

54. Bocchinfuso WP, Hively WP, Couse JF, et al. A mouse mammary tumor virus-Wnt-1 transgene induces mammary gland hyperplasia and tumorigenesis in mice lacking estrogen receptor-alpha. Cancer Res 1999;59:1869–76.

55. Bulun SE, Price TM, Mahendroo MS, et al. A link between breast cancer and local estrogen biosynthesis suggested by quantification of breast adipose tissue aromatase cytochrome P450 transcripts using competitive polymerase chain reaction after reverse transcription. J Clin Endocr Metab 1993;77:1622–8.

56. Harada N. Aberrant expression of aromatase in breast cancer tissues. J Steroid Biochem Mol Biol 1997;61:175–84.

57. James VHT, McNeill JM, Lai LC, et al. Aromatase activity in normal breast and breast tumor tissues: in vivo and in vitro studies. Steroids 1987;50:269–79.

58. Miller WR, O'Neill J. The importance of local synthesis of estrogen within the breast. Steroids 1987;50:537–48.

59. Miller WR, Mullen P, Sourdaine P, et al. Regulation of aromatase activity within the breast. J Steroid Biochem Mol Biol 1997;61:193–202.

60. Brodie A, Lu Q, Liu Y, Long B. Aromatase inhibitors and their antitumor effects in model systems. Endocr Relat Cancer 1999;6:205–10.

61. Tekmal RR, Ramachandra N, Gubba S, et al. Overexpression of int-5/aromatase in mammary glands of transgenic mice results in the induction of hyperplasia and nuclear abnormalities. Cancer Res 1996;56:3180–5.

62. Tekmal RR, Kirma N, Gill K, et al. Aromatase overexpression and breast hyperplasia, an in vivo model – continued overexpression of aromatase is sufficient to maintain hyperplasia without circulating estrogens, and aromatase inhibitors abrogate these preneoplastic changes in mammary glands. Endocr Relat Cancer 1999;6:307–14.

63. Santner SJ, Pauley RJ, Tait L, et al. Aromatase activity and expression in breast cancer and benign breast tissue stromal cells. J Clin Endocr Metab 1997;82:200–8.

64. Jin T, Zhang X, Li H, Goss PE. Characterization of a novel silencer element in the human aromatase

gene PII promoter. Breast Cancer Res Treat 2000; 62:151–9.

65. Fisher B, Costantino J, Wickerham L, et al. Tamoxifen for prevention of breast cancer: report of the National Surgical Adjuvant Breast and Bowel Project P-1. J Natl Cancer Inst 1998;90: 1371–88.

66. Cuzick J, Forbes J, Edwards R, et al, writing committee for IBIS investigators. First results from the International Breast Cancer Intervention Study (IBIS-I): a randomised prevention trial. Lancet 2002;360(9336):817–24.

67. Veronesi U, Maisonneuve P, Costa A, et al. Prevention of breast cancer with tamoxifen: preliminary findings from the Italian randomised trial among hysterectomised women. Italian Tamoxifen Prevention Study. Lancet 1998;352:93–7.

68. Veronesi U, Maisonneuve P, Sacchini V, et al. Tamoxifen for breast cancer among hysterectomized women. Lancet 2002;359:1122–4.

69. Powles T, Eeles R, Ashley S, et al. Interim analysis of the incidence of breast cancer in the Royal Marsden Hospital tamoxifen randomised chemoprevention trial. Lancet 1998;352:98–101.

70. Cuzick J, Powles T, Veronesi U, et al. Overview of the main outcomes in breast-cancer prevention trials. Lancet 2003;361:296–300.

71. Tan-Chiu E, Costantino J, Wang J, et al. The effect of tamoxifen on benign breast disease. Findings from the National Surgical Adjuvant Breast and Bowel Project (NSABP) Breast Cancer Prevention Trial (BCPT) [abstract 7]. Breast Cancer Res Treat 2001;69:210.

72. Cummings SR, Duong T, Kenyon E, et al. Serum estradiol level and risk of breast cancer during treatment with raloxifene. The Multiple Outcomes of Raloxifene Evaluation (MORE) Trial. JAMA 2002;287:1528.

73. Brueggemeier RW. Aromatase inhibitors – mechanisms of steroidal inhibitors. Br Cancer Res Treat 1994;30:31–42.

74. Bossche HV, Moereels H, Koymans LMH. Aromatase inhibitors – mechanisms for non-steroidal inhibitors. Br Cancer Res Treat 1994;30:43–55.

75. Bhatnagar AS, Miller WR. Pharmacology of inhibitors of estrogen biosynthesis. In: Oettel M, Schillinger E, editors. Estrogens, antiestrogens II: pharmacology and clinical application of estrogens and antiestrogens. Vol 135/2. Berlin and Heidelberg: Springer; 1999. p. 223–30.

76. Boeddinghaus IM, Dowsett M. Comparative clinical pharmacology and pharmacokinetic interactions of aromatase inhibitors. J Steroid Biochem Mol Biol 2001;79:85–91.

77. Goss PE, Strasser K. Aromatase inhibitors in the treatment and prevention of breast cancer. J Clin Oncol 2001;19:881–94.

78. Nabholtz JM, Buzdar A, Pollak M. Anastrozole is superior to tamoxifen as first-line therapy for advanced breast cancer in postmenopausal women: results of a North American multicenter randomized trial. Arimidex Study Group. J Clin Oncol 2000;18:3758–67.

79. Bonneterre J, Buzdar A, Nabholtz JM, et al. Arimidex Writing Committee. Anastrozole is superior to tamoxifen as first-line therapy in hormone receptor positive advanced breast carcinoma. Investigators Committee Members. Cancer 2001;92: 2247–58.

80. Mouridsen H, Gershanovich M, Sun Y, et al. Superior efficacy of letrozole versus tamoxifen as first-line therapy for postmenopausal women with advanced breast cancer: results of a phase III study of the International Letrozole Breast Cancer Group. J Clin Oncol 2001;19:2596–606.

81. Dirix L, Piccart MJ, Lohrisch C, et al. Efficacy of and tolerance to exemestane (E) versus tamoxifen (T) in 1st line hormone therapy (HT) of postmenopausal metastatic breast cancer (MBC) patients (pts): a European Organisation for the Research and Treatment of Cancer (EORTC Breast Group) Phase II trial with Pharmacia and Upjohn [abstract 114]. Proc Am Soc Clin Oncol 2001; 20(Part 1):29a.

82. Eiermann W, Paepke S, Appfelstaedt J, et al. Preoperative treatment of postmenopausal breast cancer patients with letrozole: a randomized double-blind multicenter study. Ann Oncol 2001;12: 1527–32.

83. The ATAC Trialists' Group. Arimidex, tamoxifen alone or in combination. Anastrozole alone or in combination with tamoxifen versus tamoxifen alone for adjuvant treatment of postmenopausal women with early breast cancer: first results of the ATAC randomised trial. Lancet 2002;359(9324): 2131–9.

84. Morello KC, Wurz GT, DeGregorio MW. SERMs, current status and future trends. Crit Rev Oncol Hematol 2002;43:63–76.

85. Pesenti E, Masferrer JL, di Salle E. Effect of exemestane and celecoxib alone or in combination on DMBA-induced mammary carcinoma in rats [abstract 445]. Breast Cancer Res Treat 2001;69:288.

86. Dewar J, Nabholtz J-MA, Monneterre J, et al. The effect of anastrozole (Arimidex™) on serum lipids– data from a randomized comparison of anastrozole (AN) vs tamoxifen (TAM) in postmenopausal (PM) women with advanced breast cancer (ABC) [abstract 164]. Breast Cancer Res Treat 2000; 64:51.

87. Harper-Wynne C, Ross G, Sacks N, Dowsett M. A pilot prevention study of the aromatase inhibitor letrozole: effects on breast cell proliferation and bone/lipid indices in healthy postmenopausal women [abstract 136]. Breast Cancer Res Treat 2001;69:225.

88. Harper-Wynne C, Ross G, Sacks N, et al. Effects of the aromatase inhibitor letrozole on normal breast epithelial cell proliferation and metabolic indices in postmenopausal women: a pilot study for breast

cancer prevention. Cancer Epidemiol Biomarkers Prev 2002;11:614–21.

89. Elisaf MS, Bairaktari ET, Nicolaides C, et al. Effect of letrozole on the lipid profile in postmenopausal women with breast cancer. Eur J Cancer 2001;37: 1510–3.

90. Goss PE, Grynpas M, Qi S, Hu H. The effects of exemestane on bone and lipids in the ovariectomized rat [abstract 132]. Breast Cancer Res Treat 2001; 69:224.

91. Goss PE, Cheung AM, Lowery C, et al. Comparison of the effects of exemestane, 17-hydroexemestane and letrozole on bone and lipid metabolism in the ovariectomized rat [abstract 415]. Breast Cancer Res Treat 2002;76 Suppl 1:S107.

92. Goss P, Thomsen T, Banke-Bochita J, et al. A randomized, placebo-controlled, explorative study to investigate the effect of low estrogen plasma levels on markers of bone turnover in healthy postmenopausal women during the 12-week treatment with exemestane or letrozole [abstract 267]. Breast Cancer Res Treat 2002;76 Suppl 1:S76.

93. Lohrisch C, Paridaens R, Dirix LY. No adverse impact on serum lipids of the irreversible aromatase inactivator Aromasin® (exemestane [E]) in 1st line treatment of metastatic breast cancer (MBC): companion study to a European Organization of Research and Treatment of Cancer (Breast Group) Trial with Pharmacias' Upjohn [abstract 167]. Proc Am Soc Clin Oncol 2001;20(Part 1):43a.

94. Fallowfield L, on behalf of the ATAC Trialists' Group. Assessing the quality of life (QOL) of postmenopausal (PM) women randomized into the ATAC ('Arimidex', tamoxifen, alone or in combination) adjuvant breast cancer (BC) trial [abstract 159]. Proc Am Soc Clin Oncol 2002; 21:40a.

95. Moon RC, Steele VE, Kelloff GJ, et al. Chemoprevention of MNU-induced mammary tumorigenesis by hormone response modifiers: toremifene, RU 16117, tamoxifen, aminoglutethimide and progesterone. Anticancer Res 1994;14:889–94.

96. De Coster R, Van Ginckerl RF, Callens MJ, et al. Antitumoral and endocrine effects of (+)-vorozole in rats bearing dimethylbenzanthracene-induced mammary tumors. Cancer Res 1992;52:1240–4.

97. Lubet RA, Steele VE, Casebolt TL, et al. Chemopreventive effects of the aromatase inhibitors vorozole (R-83842) and 4-hydroxyandrostenedione in the methylnitrosourea (MNU)-induced mammary tumor model in Sprague-Dawley rats. Carcinogenesis 1994;15:2775–80.

98. Schieweck K, Bhatnagar AS, Matter A. CGS 16949A, a new nonsteroidal aromatase inhibitor: effects on hormone-dependent and -independent tumors in vivo. Cancer Res 1988;48:834–8.

99. Schieweck K, Bhatnagar AS, Batzl C, et al. Anti-tumor and endocrine effects of non-steroidal aromatase inhibitors on estrogen-dependent rat mammary tumors. J Steroid Biochem Mol Biol 1993;44:633–6.

QUALITY OF LIFE ISSUES WITH ENDOCRINE CHEMOPREVENTION

Stephanie R. Land, PhD
Patricia A. Ganz, MD

During the past two decades, there have been considerable advances in the methods for assessing patient outcomes associated with cancer treatments.[1,2] Broadly, this field has been referred to as quality of life (QOL) assessment, with its emphasis on collecting information directly from patients about their experiences with treatment. There are many definitions and conceptualizations of QOL, but in general, they involve the subjective assessment of well-being by the patient herself and focus on examination of multiple dimensions of health and well-being. The National Cancer Institute (NCI) defines quality of life as the "overall enjoyment of life... an individual's sense of well-being and ability to perform various tasks."[3] Cella and Bonomi have also provided the following definition: "Health-related quality of life refers to the extent to which one's usual or expected physical, emotional, and social well-being are affected by a medical condition or its treatment."[4]

To perform a scientific evaluation of QOL in the context of a clinical trial, researchers typically develop and administer a questionnaire that is completed by study participants at regularly scheduled visits during the course of the study. Often, the questionnaire combines psychometric QOL instruments with patient self-report symptom checklists. The QOL instruments tend to focus on the broader domains of functioning, which include physical functioning, emotional well-being, and social functioning. These instruments are scientifically evaluated prior to their use to assure reliability and validity with respect to the specific QOL domains they measure. Patient-administered symptom questionnaires are typically designed to capture the presence and severity that the patient attributes to the symptom. This contrasts somewhat with traditional reporting of side effects by health care providers ("observer reporting"), in which there is an effort to standardize the assessment of severity. Patient-administered questionnaires also provide an opportunity for patients to reveal symptoms of a personal nature, such as sexual function, which are not ordinarily reported by healthcare providers. Observer and patient symptom reporting thus tend to provide complementary and contrasting information. Analyses of QOL studies from cancer clinical trials often provide a description of both symptoms and QOL, and explore the relationship between the two.

The evaluation of QOL outcomes from the patient perspective is particularly salient in the setting of prevention, where individuals taking a chemopreventive treatment are in general healthy and asymptomatic.[5,6] Prevention contrasts with the treatment of patients with advanced cancer, who have clinical symptoms from the disease and are therefore willing to endure side effects for the potential of symptom relief and prolonged survival. If a preventive therapy produces serious side effects or impairs functioning, then compliance with the therapy is likely to be short-lived, and the benefits of prevention will not be achieved. In the prevention setting, information regarding QOL is especially important because healthy women must weigh the abstract benefit of risk reduction against any loss in quality of life associated with a preventive agent. This chapter provides readers with the

QOL information that is on one side of the equation, whereas other chapters in this volume address the risk reduction attributed to current endocrine chemopreventive therapies.

The next two sections focus on the endocrine agents that have been evaluated for breast cancer chemoprevention in randomized controlled trials. Tamoxifen citrate, the only endocrine chemopreventive agent for breast cancer approved by the US Food and Drug Administration, will receive particular attention. A detailed discussion will also be provided for a newer agent, raloxifene. If there had been no formal QOL studies of these agents, beliefs about their quality of life impact would be based largely on the observer-reported toxicity information gained from clinical trials. A major repository of this side-effect information is the Physician's Desk Reference (PDR).[7] To motivate the presentation of results from QOL studies, the description of the agents below includes a list of side effects that are attributed to tamoxifen and raloxifene in the PDR. Next, we provide the QOL information that is available from completed randomized phase III prevention trials of tamoxifen and raloxifene. We will focus our presentation on assessment of QOL using data from standardized self-report instruments, when available, as well as the self-reporting of symptoms that may impact QOL, such as vasomotor, urogenital, and sleep disturbances. The fourth section will discuss the endocrine agents that are currently being evaluated in phase II or III clinical trials for breast cancer prevention (or prevention of invasive cancer in patients who have been diagnosed with noninvasive breast cancer): anastrozole, exemestane, letrozole, gonadrotropin-releasing hormone (GnRH) analogs, and arzoxifene.

ENDOCRINE CHEMOPREVENTIVE AGENTS

Tamoxifen

Tamoxifen is a selective estrogen receptor modulator (SERM). It binds competitively with the estrogen receptor, thus inhibiting the growth of estrogen-dependent breast cancers. However, by reducing the activity of circulating estrogen in various target tissues, tamoxifen also causes the symptoms associated with menopausal estrogen deprivation. Because tamoxifen also has estrogen-agonist properties, it may also be associated with symptoms of estrogen excess, for example, vaginal discharge and bleeding.

In 2002, the PDR described the side effects from tamoxifen as "usually mild."[8] The PDR listed hot flashes, nausea, and vomiting as the most common side effects. Vaginal bleeding, vaginal discharge, menstrual irregularities, skin rash, bone pain, and diarrhea are listed as less common side effects. Distaste for food, vaginal itching, dizziness, lightheadedness, headache, mental depression, vaginal dryness, swelling of arms or legs, and hair thinning are listed as rare side effects. These lists are largely consistent with the beliefs about tamoxifen toxicity that were held several years earlier. For example, in a consent form developed in 1994 for a clinical protocol, the typical side effects associated with tamoxifen were listed as hot flashes, nausea, and vomiting.[9] The protocol listed vaginal bleeding or discharge, menstrual irregularities, elevated blood calcium levels, lowered platelet counts, lowered white blood cell counts, fluid retention, and rash as less frequent side effects. The list of rare side effects in the 1994 consent form was the same as in the 2002 PDR, except that vaginal dryness and swelling of arms or legs were not included in 1994, whereas loss of appetite, leg cramps, confusion, and fatigue were listed as additional rare side effects. The PDR in 2002 was not informed by the intervening publication of quality of life and symptom data for over 11,500 healthy subjects randomized to either tamoxifen or placebo in phase III tamoxifen chemoprevention trials. This chapter will summarize the information that was made available by those clinical trial participants and indicates the impact of side effects on quality of life.

Raloxifene

Raloxifene hydrochloride, the agent that is currently being evaluated as an alternative to tamoxifen for chemoprevention in postmenopausal women, is also a SERM. Unlike tamoxifen, however, it does not appear to cause endometrial stimulation and is therefore not expected to cause an increase in endometrial cancer. It is expected to cause vasomotor symptoms similar to tamoxifen, based on existing placebo-controlled trials in the treatment of osteoporosis, and has been associated with increased reports of leg cramps. The PDR listed the "more common" side effects as abdominal pain, arthritis, breast pain, bronchitis, chest pain, depression, diarrhea, dizziness, fever, flu symptoms, gas, gynecological problems, headache, hot flashes, increased cough, indigestion, infection, insomnia, joint pain, leg cramps, muscle ache, nasal inflammation, nausea, rash, sinusitis, sore throat, stomach and intestinal problems, sweating, swelling, tendon soreness, uterine discharge, urinary tract infection, vomiting, and weight gain.[8] The less common side effects were listed as decreased sense of touch, fainting, laryngitis, migraine, neuralgia, conjunctivitis, pneumonia, urinary disorders, varicose veins, and vaginal bleeding. In dramatic contrast, a cooperative group protocol written in 1999 stated that only hot flashes and leg cramps were believed to be associated with raloxifene.[10] This controversy regarding the side effects of raloxifene will, to some extent, be addressed by the data presented in the following section. Quality of life outcomes will frame the side effect information in the broader context of the patient experience.

COMPLETED PHASE III RANDOMIZED CONTROLLED TRIALS IN PRIMARY BREAST CANCER PREVENTION

Tamoxifen Trials

Methods

Trial design. Four randomized double-blind controlled trials have been performed to compare tamoxifen (20 mg/day) to placebo in primary prevention of breast cancer. From 1986 to 1996, the Royal Marsden Hospital (United Kingdom) Tamoxifen Chemoprevention Trial randomized 2,494 women who were deemed to be at a high risk for breast cancer (based on family history).[11] In 1992, three larger trials were launched. From 1992 to 1997, the Italian Tamoxifen Prevention Study enrolled 5,408 women who had had a hysterectomy for an indication other than cancer.[12–14] During the same years, the National Surgical Adjuvant Breast and Bowel Project (NSABP) Breast Cancer Prevention Trial (BCPT) randomized 13,388 subjects.[15] The participants were women whose 5-year probability of developing invasive breast cancer was at least 1.66% according to the Gail Model, that is, the risk for an average 60-year-old woman.[16] The International Breast Cancer Intervention Study (IBIS-I) closed in 2001 after randomizing 7,152 women to tamoxifen

or placebo for 5 years.[17] Subjects were required to be at high risk for breast cancer based on age, family history, and other factors.

The designs of the four trials have been compared elsewhere.[15,18–21] One difference was that the intended duration of treatment differed in the Royal Marsden trial, which required 8 years of therapy as compared with 5 years in the other trials. Participant populations differed mainly with respect to their family history of breast cancer: participants in the Royal Marsden trial were required to have a family history of breast cancer; whereas family history of breast cancer was not an eligibility criterion for the Italian trial; and in the BCPT and IBIS-I, this was only one of the risk factors considered for eligibility. Compliance to protocol therapy differed in the four studies, although specific comparisons have been controversial.[15,19,20,22]

Another difference among the studies that might impact toxicity and quality of life outcomes is the use of hormone replacement therapy (HRT), which was allowed in three of the trials and disallowed in the BCPT. In the Royal Marsden trial, 16% of subjects were on HRT at the time of randomization, and an additional 26% (641) of the women began to use HRT after randomization (336 in the tamoxifen group, 305 in the placebo group). HRT and tamoxifen were used concomitantly during 13% of the tamoxifen study period in the Royal Marsden trial.[23] Twenty-nine percent of women in the Italian study used HRT either at baseline or during the study (with similar numbers in each treatment group).[14] In IBIS-I, 40% of women used HRT at some time during active treatment.[17]

The four trials did not differ greatly with respect to the eligible age range: 30 to 70 years for the Royal Marsden study, 35 to 70 years for the Italian Tamoxifen Prevention Study and IBIS-I, and 35 years and older for the BCPT. However, the Italian and Royal Marsden Hospital studies accrued a younger population than the BCPT.

Quality of life and symptom evaluation. Formal QOL and symptom evaluations were conducted in the BCPT and in a sub-study of the Royal Marsden and IBIS-I trials. QOL and toxicity data are not available from the Italian study.

The BCPT participants were scheduled to complete the quality of life questionnaire at baseline, 3 months, and 6 months after the start of treatment, and every 6 months thereafter through 6 years. The study was unblinded in the spring of 1998, at which point 11,064 participants had been on the study for at least 3 years. The assessments of these 11,064 participants in the first 3 years were the basis of the primary BCPT quality of life report.[24] Reports regarding baseline compliance, depression and tamoxifen, and missing data issues are available elsewhere.[25–27]

The 104-item BCPT quality of life questionnaire included (1) the 20-item Center for Epidemiological Studies Depression Scale (CES-D), an epidemiologic measure designed to assess depressive symptomatology; (2) the Medical Outcomes Study (MOS) 36-item Short Form Health Status Survey (SF-36), a standardized measure of health status and quality of life; (3) a 43-item treatment-specific symptom checklist developed specifically for this trial; and (4) the 5-item MOS sexual functioning scale. Overall quality of life was assessed with the SF-36 Mental Component Summary (MCS) which is an aggregate of the Vitality, Social Functioning, Role-Emotional, and Mental Health subscales; and the SF-36 Physical Component Summary (PCS), an aggregate of the Physical Functioning, Role-Physical, Bodily Pain, and General Health subscales.

The Royal Marsden and IBIS-I trials did not include a self-administered quality of life evaluation, but 488 patients recruited from the two trials between 1992 and 1998 were also enrolled in a quality of life study (416 Royal Marsden Trial participants and 72 IBIS-I participants).[28] The baseline questionnaires included the Multidimensional Health Locus of Control, the Spielberger State/Trait Anxiety Inventory (STAI), the General Health Questionnaire 30 (GHQ-30), and a sexual activity questionnaire (SAQ).[29–33] Follow-up questionnaires included the STAI, GHQ-30, and SAQ instruments. The questionnaires were distributed by mail every 6 months for 5 years. The 48-month assessment also included a 42-item symptom checklist which was completed by approximately 360 patients (74%).

Results Related to Quality of Life and Symptoms

Psychological health. Tamoxifen does not appear to impact mental health. In the BCPT there was no difference between placebo and tamoxifen groups in terms of CES-D scores, the SF-36 Mental Component Summary, or the 5-item SF-36 Mental

Health subscale.[24,26] The BCPT CES-D results were robust to sensitivity analyses and other approaches to account for the effects of missing data.[27]

In the Royal Marsden/IBIS-I study, longitudinal measures of psychological morbidity (GHQ-30) and anxiety (STAI) slightly favored tamoxifen over placebo, with only marginal significance for the GHQ-30 and nonsignificance for the anxiety scores. Depression was also listed on the 48-month symptom checklist in the Royal Marsden/IBIS-I quality of life study. A greater proportion of placebo participants reported that depression was somewhat/quite a bit/very much of a problem since the start of the study (21.4% of placebo respondents versus 16.9% of tamoxifen respondents). Similar results were seen for the three other items on the symptom checklist that were related to mental health: mood swings, anxiety, and irritability.

Longitudinal data for several mental health-related measures in the BCPT and Royal Marsden/IBIS-I studies showed a decline initially after the start of therapy, followed by a partial return to baseline levels. Possible reasons for this phenomenon have been explored elsewhere, but it is noteworthy that this finding occurred equally in the two treatment arms and may reflect aspects of participating in a clinical trial as a high-risk woman.[27]

Sexual functioning. Tamoxifen did not impact sexual functioning to a clinically significant degree. The proportion of subjects in the BCPT who reported being sexually active declined throughout the study but was not significantly different between the two treatment groups (data not shown). However, there was some suggestive evidence of increased sexual difficulty among participants on tamoxifen in the BCPT. In two items of the MOS sexual functioning scale ("lack of sexual interest" and "unable to relax and enjoy sex"), a greater proportion of participants in the tamoxifen group reported a "definite" or "serious problem" at most of the assessment time points (adjusted for baseline differences). The differences were very slight, however, representing less than 1% of subjects (data not shown). In the Royal Marsden/IBIS-I study, results from the SAQ did not reveal a difference over time between treatment groups with respect to reduction in sexual activity, pleasure with sexual activity, vaginal dryness, or pain and discomfort during penetration.

Physical functioning and everyday symptoms. Tamoxifen and placebo groups also did not differ significantly in terms of the SF-36 Physical Component Summary. There was no difference in the time course of physical function: both groups experienced a subtle decline over the 36-month assessment period.

The aggregate number of symptoms reported by participants aged 35 to 49 years on the BCPT symptom checklist was slightly higher in the tamoxifen group than in the placebo group (with a mean difference of less than one symptom, one-sided $p = .0078$). This was consistent throughout most of the follow-up time frame that has been reported (3 to 36 months). There was no significant difference between treatment groups among older participants.

The largest odds ratio in the BCPT symptom checklist (in terms of the number of patients who reported experiencing the symptom) was seen for vaginal discharge, with the largest relative difference between tamoxifen and placebo groups occurring among the older participants. During the 3 years of assessments, the proportion of patients reporting hot flashes was elevated in the tamoxifen group at all time points, with the greatest relative increase seen among the younger participants (age 35 to 49 years). Nausea, diarrhea, headaches, and breast sensitivity/tenderness were all significantly reduced in the tamoxifen group as compared with the placebo group.

In the Royal Marsden/IBIS-I 48-month symptom checklist, the symptom that was most strongly associated with tamoxifen was cold sweats, followed by night sweats, vaginal discharge, and hot flashes. Three symptoms were significantly decreased among participants assigned to tamoxifen: low energy, breast sensitivity/tenderness, and blurring of vision.

Table 14-1 displays the percentage of patients experiencing each symptom as reported for the BCPT and Royal Marsden/IBIS-I trials. The table includes symptoms that were listed in the PDR or in the BCPT consent form (1994 amendment) or that were found to be treatment related in either study. Four symptoms (bone pain, swelling of arms and legs, distaste for food, and confusion) were listed in the PDR or the BCPT 1994 consent form but were not directly assessed in the studies and are therefore not included in the table. The BCPT

columns give the percentage of patients who reported experiencing the symptom on at least one questionnaire between the 3- and 36-month evaluations. The data in the Royal Marsden/IBIS-I columns give the percentage of patients who, on the 48-month symptom checklist, reported that the symptom had been at least "somewhat of a problem" since the start of the study. Odds ratios are presented rather than relative risks (as have been presented in past publications of BCPT data) in order to provide comparability between the BCPT results and the odds ratios presented by Fallowfield and colleagues.[28]

Additional information regarding symptoms in the Royal Marsden trial is available from the list of reasons given for early discontinuation of therapy (Table 14-2). Of the 877 women in the Royal Marsden trial who had prematurely stopped the study drug as of the time of the interim analysis, 56% stopped early because of toxicity (320 tamoxifen, 176 placebo). Presumably, these data reflect a greater severity of symptom discomfort than is reflected in the preceding summary. The differences in rates of withdrawing attributed to gynecological problems, hot flashes, and menstrual irregularity are consistent with patient-reported symptoms and suggest that these symptoms can be severe enough to impact patient care. These data also provide corroborating evidence that tamoxifen does not cause weight gain (consistent with self-report data from both the BCPT and Royal Marsden/IBIS-I studies, not shown) or headaches. In contrast with the QOL sub-study results, however, nausea and mood change were given as the cause of early discontinuation more often in the tamoxifen arm than in the placebo arm. The result for nausea did not reach statistical significance, however, and the result for mood change was based on only eight patients.

Raloxifene Trials

Methods

Design of trials. In the Multiple Outcomes of Raloxifene Evaluation (MORE) study, 7,705 postmenopausal women were randomized to receive either raloxifene at a dose of 120 mg/day, raloxifene at a dose of 60 mg/day, or placebo, for a treatment duration of 3 years.[34] Because the trial was primarily designed to evaluate the impact of raloxifene on osteoporosis fracture risk, participants were re-

TABLE 14-1 Rates of Patient-Reported Symptoms in
Phase III Placebo-Controlled Tamoxifen Trials.

Symptom	BCPT (reported the symptom on at least one assessment in first 36 months)			Royal Marsden/IBIS-I (at least somewhat of a problem from start of study to 48 months)		
	Tamoxifen (%)	Placebo (%)	Odds Ratio (95% CI)	Tamoxifen (%)	Placebo (%)	Odds Ratio (95% CI)
Symptoms listed in the PDR as common:						
Hot flashes	80	67	1.99 (1.83–2.18)	42	29	1.77 (1.14–2.74)
Vomiting	14	15	0.94 (0.84–1.04)	1	2	0.62 (0.10–3.77)
Nausea	37	40	0.88 (0.82–0.96)	5	8	0.71 (0.30–1.67)
Symptoms listed in the PDR as less common:						
Vaginal discharge	57	35	2.40 (2.22–2.59)	18	10	1.87 (1.01–3.48)
Menstrual irregularities				22	16	1.43 (0.81–2.51)
Skin rash				8	7	1.11 (0.51–2.41)
Vaginal bleeding	23	22	1.05 (0.95–1.14)	5	8	0.60 (0.25–1.42)
Diarrhea	43	50	0.77 (0.71–0.83)	8	9	0.90 (0.42–1.92)
Symptoms listed in the PDR as rare:						
Genital/vaginal itching	49	39	1.46 (1.35–1.57)	16	10	1.82 (0.97–3.44)
Vaginal dryness	52	50	1.07 (0.99–1.15)	22	29	0.68 (0.42–1.09)
Hair thinning				8	7	1.04 (0.48–2.29)
Dizziness	31	32	0.99 (0.91–1.07)			
Lightheadedness				17	23	0.67 (0.40–1.13)
Headache	80	83	0.83 (0.75–0.91)	24	30	0.77 (0.48–1.22)
Depression				17	21	0.75 (0.44–1.27)
Symptoms listed as less common or rare in the 1994 consent, but not listed in the 2002 PDR:						
Loss of appetite	29	27	1.09 (1.00–1.18)	1	2	0.64 (0.11–3.88)
Fluid retention*	59	60	0.98 (0.91–1.06)	18	22	0.76 (0.45–1.29)
Cramps/leg cramps†	34	35	0.95 (0.88–1.03)			
Fatigue/low energy‡				28	41	0.56 (0.36–0.87)
Not listed in 1994 consent or 2002 PDR:						
Night sweats	69	56	1.71 (1.58–1.85)	43	29	1.88 (1.21–2.92)
Cold sweats	22	15	1.58 (1.43–1.75)	10	3	3.59 (1.30–9.97)
Bladder control (laugh or cry/cough§)	54	48	1.28 (1.19–1.38)	27	28	0.96 (0.60–1.53)
Bladder control (other)	55	49	1.24 (1.15–1.34)	15	12	1.32 (0.71–2.45)
Pain in intercourse	29	25	1.24 (1.14–1.35)	12	12	1.08 (0.56–2.08)
Weight loss	46	43	1.14 (1.05–1.23)	2	4	0.40 (0.10–1.58)
Breast sensitivity/ tenderness	55	64	0.68 (0.63–0.74)	23	37	0.52 (0.32–0.82)
Blurred vision				11	22	0.41 (0.23–0.74)

*Results are shown for "swelling of hands and feet," the proxy for fluid retention used in the BCPT.
†The BCPT symptom checklist included "cramps," but the 1994 BCPT consent listed leg cramps.
‡This was listed as "low energy" in the Royal Marsden/IBIS-I study.
§The BCPT checklist included laugh and cry. The Royal Marsden/IBIS-I checklist included laugh and cough.
BCPT = Breast Cancer Prevention Trial.
IBIS-I = International Breast Cancer Intervention Study.
PDR = Physician's Desk Reference.

TABLE 14-2 Reasons for Early Discontinuation of Study Drug in Royal Marsden Trial

Reason Given for Premature Discontinuation of Study Drug	Tamoxifen (Number of Patients)	Placebo (Number of Patients)	p-value (Chi-squared Test)
Gynecological problems	69	18	< .0005
Hot flashes	51	13	< .0005
Menstrual irregularity	18	6	.01
Headaches	13	14	.8
Weight gain	6	12	.2
Nausea	12	6	.2
Mood change	8	1	.02
Other or unknown	143	106	.01

Adapted from Powles T et al.[11]

quired to have osteoporosis or previous vertebral fractures. Breast cancer incidence was a secondary outcome. Participants' mean age was 66.5 years. Participants who had been using systemic estrogen replacement therapy in the prior 6 months, or topical estrogen more often than 3 times per week, were not eligible. Estrogen replacement therapy during the trial was considered a protocol violation.

Additional quality of life information is available from two smaller studies. In a study at the Mayo Clinic, 143 postmenopausal osteoporosis patients were randomized to receive either raloxifene at a dose of 120 mg/day, raloxifene at a dose of 60 mg/day, or placebo, for a treatment duration of 1 year.[35] Women with clinically significant menopausal symptoms were excluded, as were women who had used HRT in the preceding 6 months. Another blinded placebo-controlled study sponsored by Eli Lilly and Company was designed to compare the effects of raloxifene and estrogen therapy on the endometrium.[36] In this study, 398 healthy postmenopausal women were randomized to receive either placebo, raloxifene given 60 mg/day, raloxifene given 150 mg/day, or estrogen therapy (0.625 mg/day), for a treatment duration of 12 months.

Assessment of Quality of Life and Symptoms

All women in the MORE study were questioned during each office visit about the adverse effects of treatment. In addition, a subset of women completed two osteoporosis-specific health-related quality of life questionnaires: the Osteoporosis Assessment Questionnaire and the quality of life questionnaire of the European Foundation for Osteoporosis. However, comparisons of the treatment groups in this sub-study were not available as of the date of this writing.

In the Mayo study, patients' moods were assessed with the Geriatric Depression Scale, administered at baseline and at 1, 6, and 12 months after the initiation of therapy. In the Eli Lilly study, quality of life was assessed with the Women's Health Questionnaire, administered at baseline and at 3-month intervals.[37,38]

Results Related to Quality of Life and Symptoms

In the MORE study, observer-reported rates of leg cramps, hot flashes, peripheral edema, and influenza-like syndromes were significantly higher for the raloxifene-treated participants as compared with those on placebo. The largest relative increase was seen for leg cramps (3.7, 7.0, and 6.9% in the placebo, 60 mg/day, and 120 mg/day groups, respectively). Hot flashes were increased from 6.4% in the placebo group to 9.7 and 11.6% for the 60 and 120 mg/day groups, respectively. Peripheral edema was increased from 4.4 to 5.2 and 6.5% for the raloxifene groups. Breast pain, which is listed in the current edition of the PDR as a "more common side effect" of raloxifene, was not different between the treatment groups (2.5% for the placebo group versus 2.4 and 2.7% for the raloxifene groups). Vaginal bleeding, which is listed in the PDR as a less common side effect, was also not different (3.1% for the placebo group versus 3.4 and 2.8% for the raloxifene groups).

In the Mayo Clinic study, there was no significant difference in mood between the treatment groups. In the Eli Lilly study, the overall score on the Women's Health Questionnaire did not change significantly in any treatment group from the start to the end of the 1 year of therapy.[37,38] Raloxifene also did not appear to cause a change in mean scores for six domains: depressed mood, somatic symptoms, memory/concentration, sexual behaviour, sleep disorders, and perceived attractiveness. It was associated with a marginally significant decrease in anxiety and fear as compared with placebo. The differences between placebo and raloxifene groups in terms of both vasomotor symptom disturbance and menstrual symptom disturbance appeared to be slight (and not significant).

CURRENT PHASE II-III TRIALS FOR BREAST CANCER PREVENTION WITH ENDOCRINE THERAPIES

There are currently several active studies of endocrine agents for breast cancer prevention. Because of the dramatic difference in the incidence of breast cancer in the MORE study (relative risk 0.24 for raloxifene versus placebo),[34] raloxifene is currently being compared with tamoxifen for chemoprevention in the NSABP Study of Tamoxifen and Raloxifene (STAR). STAR opened in 1999 and is expected to accrue 19,000 postmenopausal women who either have a history of lobular carcinoma in situ or who have a 5-year probability of developing invasive cancer of at least 1.66% (according to the Gail Model).[16] STAR includes a quality of life evaluation.

Another endocrine agent that is on the horizon of chemoprevention in postmenopausal women is the aromatase inhibitor anastrozole. IBIS-II-Prevention, a Phase III study under development in Europe, will compare anastrozole with placebo for primary prevention of breast cancer in high-risk postmenopausal women. In the adjuvant setting, anastrozole (one 1-mg tablet per day for 5 years) compared favorably to tamoxifen (one 20-mg tablet per day for 5 years) in the Arimidex, Tamoxifen Alone or in Combination (ATAC) Trial.[39] The trial enrolled 9,366 women in 21 countries between July 1996 and March 2000. The trial included a patient-completed quality of life sub-

study, which enrolled 1,105 randomized patients.[28] Quality of life was assessed with the Functional Assessment of Cancer Therapy – Breast (FACT-B) plus the FACT endocrine symptom subscale,[40] administered at baseline; at 3, 6, 12, 18, and 24 months; at suspected recurrence/withdrawal; and 1 month after recurrence.[4] There was no difference in overall quality of life (based on the FACT-B Trial Outcome Index, which is the sum of the physical, functional, and breast cancer-specific subscales) between the tamoxifen and anastrozole groups, nor between the combination and tamoxifen groups. There were also no significant differences in the endocrine symptom subscale. In terms of the number of patients who reported experiencing each symptom "very much" or "quite a bit," there was no significant difference between tamoxifen and anastrozole groups in hot flashes, cold sweats, night sweats, vaginal itching/irritation, vaginal bleeding/spotting, weight gain, lightheadedness/dizziness, vomiting, headaches, bloating, breast sensitivity/tenderness, mood swings, and irritability. The patients in the anastrozole arm did report significantly lower rates of vaginal discharge, whereas patients in the tamoxifen arm reported significantly lower rates of vaginal dryness, pain/discomfort with intercourse, lost interest in sex, and diarrhea.

Observer-reported toxicities in ATAC were not distinguishable between the tamoxifen only and tamoxifen plus anastrozole arms. Table 14-3 displays the percentage of patients who ever experienced each toxicity in each of the trial arms. Relative to tamoxifen given alone, patients receiving anastrozole were observed to experience significantly less vaginal bleeding, vaginal discharge, and hot flashes.

Two studies will also compare anastrozole with tamoxifen in postmenopausal women with ductal carcinoma in situ (DCIS). An NSABP study (Protocol B-35) opened in January 2003. Protocol B-35 includes a quality of life evaluation, primarily to confirm that tamoxifen and anastrozole are equivalent in terms of overall self-assessed mental and physical health, and to compare the rates of hot flashes between treatment groups. It is hypothesized that the self-reported disturbance owing to hot flashes will be greater in the anastrozole arm than in the tamoxifen arm, particularly among women under age 60. IBIS-II-DCIS, with a design that is similar to B-35, is still under development.

TABLE 14-3 Occurrence of Observer-Reported Symptoms in ATAC

	Anastrozole (n = 3,092)	Tamoxifen (n = 3,094)	Combination (n = 3,097)	p-value (A vs T)
Hot flashes	34.3%	39.7%	40.1%	< .0001
Nausea and vomiting	10.5%	10.2%	11.7%	.7
Fatigue/tiredness	15.6%	15.1%	14.0%	.5
Mood disturbances	15.5%	15.2%	15.6%	.7
Vaginal bleeding	4.5%	8.2%	7.7%	< .0001
Vaginal discharge	2.8%	11.4%	11.5%	< .0001

Adapted from The ATAC Trialists' Group.[39]

A = anastrozole; T = tamoxifen.

Another aromatase inhibitor, letrozole, is also under study in a phase II chemoprevention trial at the Dana Farber Cancer Center under the direction of Dr. Judy Garber. The WISE trial (Women at Increased Risk of Breast Cancer Based on Estradiol Level) uses elevated serum estradiol in postmenopausal women as the eligibility criterion, and in a 2:1 randomization assigns women to either letrozole for 12 months or placebo for 12 months, with safety, QOL, bone density, and adherence as the primary outcomes, and estradiol and mammographic densities as secondary endpoints. The QOL battery from the BCPT is being used in this study (J. Garber and P.A. Ganz, personal communication, January 2003). This pilot study should provide important data for the design of a larger prevention trial in this population of postmenopausal, high-risk patients.

An NCI-sponsored phase II study at the University of Kansas is testing the SERM arzoxifene (LY353381 hydrochloride) for primary breast cancer prevention in women age 18 and over who have fine needle aspiration cytologic evidence of hyperplasia and other risk factors for breast cancer. This study completed enrollment in December 2002. At Memorial Sloan-Kettering Cancer Center, the combination of the aromatase inactivator exemestane and raloxifene is being evaluated in a randomized phase II secondary breast cancer prevention study among women (age 18 and over) with a history of breast cancer (DCIS or invasive) who have no clinical evidence of disease at the time of enrollment. Both of these studies include a QOL evaluation.

In an alternative approach, breast cancer cells can be deprived of estrogen via chemical ovarian ablation with luteinizing hormone-releasing hormone agonists, also called gonadotropin-releasing hormone agonist analogs. However, these agents also appear to cause vasomotor symptoms and urogenital atrophy.[40] One such agent is goserelin. In a study conducted by the Royal Marsden Hospital, the combination of raloxifene and goserelin is being compared against observation alone for primary breast cancer prevention in women at high genetic risk of breast cancer. The study includes a quality of life evaluation. Lupron depot is a synthetic gonadotropin-releasing hormone GnRH which, has been previously studied by Spicer and Pike.[42] Recently, this approach has been used in a phase I-II trial of women who were carriers of hereditary susceptibility genes (BRCA1) using a newer GnRH formulation supplemented with estrogen and testosterone, with mammographic density as the endpoint.[42] QOL was assessed in this trial and the results of this pilot study should be available in the near future.

DISCUSSION

The BCPT and Royal Marsden/IBIS-I quality of life studies give us a clear picture of the quality of life implications of tamoxifen use in healthy women. Overall psychological and physical quality of life outcomes, measured by the SF-36 MCS and PCS in BCPT participants and the GHQ-30 in Royal Marsden/IBIS-I participants, was not diminished in the tamoxifen groups as compared with placebo groups. Sexual functioning was not diminished to any clinically significant degree. Mental health was not adversely affected. Patient-reported symptoms in the two studies also supported the same major conclusion, that tamoxifen causes vasomotor and menstrual symptoms. Minor differences did emerge from the patient-reported symptom summaries. Vaginal dryness and pain with intercourse appeared to be related to tamoxifen in the BCPT, but were not increased in the tamoxifen group in the Royal Marsden/IBIS-I study. This may be due to the use of HRT among patients in the Royal Marsden and IBIS-I studies.

In Table 14-1, the rates of patient-reported symptoms in the Royal Marsden/IBIS-I study are lower than the rates in the BCPT. This is not surprising for several reasons. First, the Royal Marsden/IBIS-I tallies were based on a higher threshold (at least "somewhat of a problem") than the BCPT, which tallied all patients who reported experiencing the symptom without regard for severity of disturbance. In addition, it should be noted that a varying but not insignificant number of participants in the Royal Marsden/IBIS-I trials were taking HRT during the trial. Third, the symptoms tallied for the Royal Marsden/IBIS-I study reflect the participants' recall from the start of the study to 48 months, whereas BCPT participants had up to seven opportunities to report each symptom. Therefore, it is not surprising that the rates in the BCPT columns are generally higher than the corresponding rates in the Royal Marsden/IBIS-I columns.

Although raloxifene has had only limited evaluation with patient-assessed QOL instruments, it was also not different from placebo in major QOL dimensions. It was associated with increases in hot flashes, leg cramps, and peripheral edema, but these symptoms were apparently not severe enough to impact patients' QOL. Considerably more information will soon be available when results are presented from the MORE trial QOL study, and when the STAR trial is completed and analyzed.

Anastrozole appears to be equivalent to tamoxifen in terms of overall QOL and to cause greater difficulty in sexual function as compared with tamoxifen. The results regarding vasomotor and menstrual symptoms were less clear. Vaginal discharge was decreased with anastrozole. Based on traditional adverse event reporting from the entire ATAC cohort, hot flashes and vaginal bleeding were also reduced in the anastrozole group. This was in dramatic contrast with the QOL sub-study, in which the odds ratios for these symptoms were

nearly 1.0.[28] Studies in advanced cancer were consistent with ATAC observer-report in terms of vaginal bleeding but were discordant with respect to hot flashes.[44,45] The Nabholtz and colleagues study found an increase in observer-reported hot flashes among patients on anastrozole as compared with tamoxifen (38.2% vs 27.5%),[44] but the Bonneterre and colleagues study found no difference (about 20% for both treatments).[45] If the hypothesis proposed in NSABP B-35 is correct, an important determinant of the effect of anastrozole is age: young postmenopausal women assigned to anastrozole will experience an increase in hot flashes relative to the same age group assigned to tamoxifen. The average age of women was 64 in the ATAC QOL substudy and 67 in the advanced disease trials. With a younger population expected to accrue to the B-35, an analysis by age group may clarify the differences with respect to hot flashes.

The quality of life and toxicity associated with preventive pharmacologic agents might also be compared against that of nonpharmacologic approaches to prevention, such as dietary and lifestyle approaches and risk-reduction mastectomy (RRM). Dietary and lifestyle approaches to breast cancer prevention include the consumption of soy and isoflavones, weight loss, and exercise.[46] The effects on quality of life of several weight loss and exercise programs have been found to be favorable, suggesting that these approaches can be undertaken with little or no decrement in quality of life.[47–49] A collective review of studies regarding risk-reduction mastectomy found that although the data are scarce (and randomized studies do not exist), there appear to be quality of life benefits associated with elective RRM.[50] Patients reported emotional benefits and high levels of satisfaction with their decision to undergo RRM.

There were striking differences between symptoms found to be associated with tamoxifen in double-blind prevention trials and the symptoms listed in the PDR. A number of problems that have been attributed to tamoxifen are merely common in aging women (eg, vaginal dryness and dizziness). Results for nausea, vomiting, and diarrhea are especially surprising because although they are listed in the PDR as common or less common side effects of tamoxifen, the evidence based on the BCPT and Royal Marsden/IBIS-I studies suggests no such effect, and possibly beneficial effects with respect to nausea and diarrhea. When the severity scores from the BCPT symptom checklist (maximum severity from months 3 to 36) were examined, the results were consistent: the placebo group reported higher or equal levels of nausea, vomiting, and diarrhea than participants in the tamoxifen group at each level of severity (data not shown). Meanwhile, night sweats and cold sweats, pain with intercourse, and bladder control all appear to be common problems that are increased with tamoxifen, and yet are not listed in the PDR.

Most importantly, the PDR fails to inform consumers and clinicians that despite some differences in symptoms between tamoxifen and placebo-treated groups, overall measures of quality of life, mental health, physical health, and sexual functioning were comparable in the two groups. Despite ample evidence that depression is not caused by tamoxifen, it remains listed as a rare side effect. The daunting list of symptoms and the omission of the broader quality of life results might be discouraging to some women who would otherwise be appropriate candidates for chemoprevention with tamoxifen.

In its recommendations regarding chemoprevention for breast cancer, the US Preventive Services Task Force concluded that "the balance of benefits and harms [of tamoxifen and raloxifene] may be favorable for some high-risk women but will depend on breast cancer risk, risk for potential harms, and individual patient preferences."[51] In the prevention setting, QOL will remain a strong determinant of patient preferences. As newer agents are tested and more chemoprevention options become available, it will be imperative to consider and compare the QOL implications of all choices.

ACKNOWLEDGMENTS

The authors would like to thank Maria Harper and Robert M. Gorman for editorial assistance, and Ginny Mehalik for secretarial assistance in the preparation of this chapter. Dr. Land was supported in part by Public Health Service grant U10-CA-69651 from the National Cancer Institute, National Institutes of Health, Department of Health and Human Services. Dr. Ganz was supported in part by an American Cancer Society Clinical Research Professorship.

REFERENCES

1. Cella DF. Methods and problems in measuring quality of life. Support Care Cancer 1995;3:11–22.
2. Ganz PA. Quality of life measures in cancer chemotherapy: methodology and implications. Pharmacoeconomics 1994;5:376–88.
3. National Cancer Institute Web site. Available at: http://www.cancer.gov (accessed May 8, 2003).
4. Cella DF, Bonomi AE. Measuring quality of life: 1995 update. Oncology (Huntington) 1995; 9(11 Suppl):47–60.
5. Ganz PA, Day R, Ware JE Jr, et al. Baseline quality-of-life assessment in the National Surgical Adjuvant Breast and Bowel Project Breast Cancer Prevention Trial. J Natl Cancer Inst 1995;87: 1372–82.
6. Moinpour CM, Lovato LC, Thompson IM, et al. Profile of men randomized to the prostate cancer prevention trial: baseline health-related quality of life, urinary and sexual functioning, and health behaviors. J Clin Oncol 2000;18:1942–53.
7. Physician's Desk Reference. 54th ed. Montvale (NJ): Medical Economics Staff, Inc; 2000.
8. Physician's Desk Reference online. Available at: http://www.pdrhealth.com/drug-info/index.html (accessed May 8, 2003).
9. NSABP Breast Cancer Prevention Trial Protocol amendment dated January 1994.
10. NSABP STAR Trial Protocol, version dated June 24, 1999.
11. Powles T, Eeles R, Ashley S, et al. Interim analysis of the incidence of breast cancer in the Royal Marsden Hospital tamoxifen randomised chemoprevention trial. Lancet 1998;352:98–101.
12. Veronesi U, Maisonneuve P, Costa A, et al. Prevention of breast cancer with tamoxifen: preliminary findings from the Italian randomised trial among hysterectomised women. Lancet 1998;352:93–7.
13. Decensi A, Bonanni B, Rotmensz N, et al. Update on tamoxifen to prevent breast cancer. The Italian tamoxifen prevention study. Eur J Cancer 2000;36: S49–S56.
14. Veronesi U, Maisonneuve P, Sacchini V, et al. Tamoxifen for breast cancer among hysterectomised women. Lancet 2002;359:1122–4.
15. Fisher B, Costantino JP, Wickerham DL, et al. Tamoxifen for prevention of breast cancer: report of the National Surgical Adjuvant Breast and Bowel Project P-1 study. J Natl Cancer Inst 1998;90: 1371–88.
16. Gail MH, Brinton LA, Dyar DP, et al. Projecting individual probabilities of developing breast cancer for white females who are being examined annually. J Natl Cancer Inst 1989;81:1879–86.
17. IBIS Investigators. First results from the International Breast Cancer Intervention Study (IBIS-I): a randomized prevention trial. Lancet 2002;360:817–24.

18. Pritchard KI. Is tamoxifen effective in prevention of breast cancer [comment]? Lancet 1998;352(9122):80–1.

19. Ross PJ, Powles TJ. Results and implications of the Royal Marsden and other tamoxifen chemoprevention trials. Clin Breast Cancer 2001;2:33–6.

20. Costantino JP, Vogel VG. Results and implications of the Royal Marsden and other tamoxifen chemoprevention trials: an alternative view. Clin Breast Cancer 2001;2:41-6.

21. Kinsinger LS, Harris R, Woolf SH, et al. Chemoprevention of breast cancer: a summary of the evidence for the U.S. Preventive Services Task Force. Ann Intern Med 2002;137:59–69.

22. Veronesi U, Maisonneuve P, Costa A, et al. Drop-outs in tamoxifen prevention trials. Lancet 1999;353:244.

23. Powles TJ. The Royal Marsden Hospital (RMH) trial: key points and remaining questions. Ann NY Acad Sci 2001;949:109–12.

24. Day R, Ganz PA, Costantino JP, et al. Health-related quality of life and tamoxifen in breast cancer prevention: a report from the National Surgical Adjuvant Breast and Bowel Project P-1 study. J Clin Oncol 1999;17:2659–69.

25. Ganz PA, Day R, Costantino J. Compliance with quality of life data collection in the National Surgical Adjuvant Breast and Bowel Project (NSABP) Breast Cancer Prevention Trial. Stat Med 1998;17:613–22.

26. Day R, Ganz PA, Costantino JP. Tamoxifen and depression: more evidence from the National Surgical Adjuvant Breast and Bowel Project's breast cancer prevention (P-1) randomized study. J Natl Cancer Inst 2001;93:1615–23.

27. Land S, Wieand HS, Day R, et al. Methodological issues in the analysis of quality of life data in clinical trials: illustrations from the National Surgical Adjuvant Breast and Bowel Project (NSABP) Breast Cancer Prevention Trial. In: Mesbah M, Cole B, Lee M, editors. Statistical design, measurement and analysis of health related quality of life. Klewer Academic Publishers; 2002. p. 71–85.

28. Fallowfield L, Fleissig A, Edwards R, et al. Tamoxifen for the prevention of breast cancer: psychosocial impact on women participating in two randomized controlled trials. J Clin Oncol 2001;19:1885–92.

29. O'Looney BA, Barrett PT. A psychometric investigation of the Multidimensional Health Locus of Control Questionnaire. Br J Clin Psychol. 1983; 22(Pt 3):217–218.

30. Spielberger CD, Gorsuch RL, Lusherie RE. STAI manual (Form Y). Palo Alto (CA): Consulting Psychologists Press; 1983.

31. Goldberg DP, Williams P. A user's guide to the General Health Questionnaire. London, England Windsor: NFER-Nelson; 1998.

32. Thirlaway K, Fallowfield L, Cuzick J. The Sexual Activity Questionnaire: a measure of women's sexual functioning. Qual Life Res 1996;5:81–90.

33. Stead ML, Crocombe WD, Fallowfield LJ. Sexual activity questionnaires in clinical trials: acceptability to patients with gynaecological disorders. Br J Obstet Gynaecol 1999;106:50–4.

34. Cummings SR, Eckert S, Krueger KA, et al. The effect of raloxifene on risk of breast cancer in postmenopausal women: results from the MORE randomized trial. JAMA 1999;281:2189–97.

35. Nickelsen T, Lufkin EG, Riggs BL, et al. Raloxifene hydrochloride, a selective estrogen receptor modulator: safety assessment of effects on cognitive function and mood in postmenopausal women. Psychoneuroendocrinology 1999;24:115–28.

36. Strickler R, Stovall DW, Merritt D, et al. Raloxifene and estrogen effects on quality of life in healthy postmenopausal women: a placebo-controlled randomized trial. Obstet Gynecol 2000;96:359–65.

37. Hunter M. The women's health questionnaire: a measure of mid-aged women's perceptions of their emotional and physical health. Health Psychol 1992;7:45–54.

38. Wiklund I, Berg G, Hammar M, et al. Long-term effect of transdermal hormonal therapy on aspects of quality of life in postmenopausal women. Maturitas 1992;14:225–36.

39. The ATAC (Arimidex, Tamoxifen Alone or in Combination) Trialists' Group. Anastrozole alone or in combination with tamoxifen versus tamoxifen alone for adjuvant treatment of postmenopausal women with early breast cancer: first results of the ATAC randomised trial. Lancet 2002;359:2131–9.

40. Cella DF, Tulsky DS, Gray G, et al. Functional assessment of cancer therapy scale: development and validation of the general measure. J Clin Oncol 1993;11:570–9.

41. Pritchard KI. Breast cancer prevention with selective estrogen receptor modulators: a perspective. Ann NY Acad Sci 2001;949:89–98.

42. Spicer DV, Ursin G, Parisky YR, et al. Changes in mammographic densities induced by a hormonal contraceptive designed to reduce breast cancer risk. J Natl Cancer Inst 1994;86:431–6.

43. Weitzel JN, Pike MC, Ursin G, et al. Proof of principle: mammographic density reduced by a gonadotropin-releasing hormone agonist (GnRHA)-based chemoprevention regimen for young women at high risk for breast cancer. Breast Cancer Res Treat 2002;(Suppl1):S107.

44. Nabholtz JM, Buzdar A, Pollock M, et al. Anastrozole is superior to tamoxifen as a first-line therapy for advanced breast cancer in post menopausal women: results of a North American multicenter randomized trial. J Clin Oncol 2000;18:3758–67.

45. Bonneterre J, Thurlimann B, Robertson JFR, et al. Anastrozole versus tamoxifen as first-line therapy for advanced breast cancer in 668 post menopausal women: efficacy and tolerability study. J Clin Oncol 2000;18:3748–57.

46. Greenwald P. Cancer prevention clinical trials. J Clin Oncol 2002;20 Suppl 18:S14–S22.

47. Gleason JA, Bourdet KL, Koehn K, et al. Cardiovascular risk reduction and dietary compliance with a home-delivered diet and lifestyle modification program. J Am Diet Assoc 2002;102:1445–51.

48. Kaukua J, Pekkarinen T, Sane T, Mustajoki P. Health-related quality of life in WHO class II-III obese men losing weight with very-low-energy diet and behaviour modification: a randomised clinical trial. Int J Obes Relat Metab Disord 2002;26:487–95.

49. Rejeski WJ, Focht BC, Messier SP, et al. Obese, older adults with knee osteoarthritis: weight loss, exercise, and quality of life. Health Psychol 2002;21:419–26.

50. Stefanek M, Hartmann L, Nelson W. Risk-reduction mastectomy: clinical issues and research needs. J Natl Cancer Inst 2001;93:1297–306.

51. United States Preventive Services Task Force. Chemoprevention of breast cancer: recommendations and rationale. Ann Intern Med 2002;137:56–8.

CHAPTER 15

IMPROVING QUALITY OF LIFE FOR WOMEN AT HIGH RISK FOR BREAST CANCER: SYMPTOM MANAGEMENT WITHOUT ESTROGEN

Tait D. Shanafelt, MD
Charles Loprinzi, MD

Breast cancer is the most common malignancy in US women and the second most common cause of cancer death.[1] Surgery, radiation, hormonal therapy, and chemotherapy have significantly improved the cure rate in women with early stage disease and can prolong survival in women with advanced disease. The 10-year survival for women diagnosed with early Stage I and II disease is now 60 to 88%, and many of these women will be long-term survivors.[2] Despite these benefits, curative and life-prolonging treatments can cause significant short- and long-term morbidity and often have deleterious effects on a woman's quality of life. Hot flashes, sexual dysfunction, osteoporosis, and cognitive dysfunction are common side effects of breast cancer treatment that profoundly affect quality of life. These sequelae may be caused by the physical disfiguration of surgery, hormonal changes owing to the induction of premature menopause, or the direct effects of cytotoxic chemotherapy.

Although estrogen therapy is often used to treat these problems in the general population, concerns about estrogen's potential to increase the risk of breast cancer in high-risk women or increase the risk of recurrence in breast cancer survivors have forced physicians to employ alternative treatments.

Furthermore, the results of the Women's Health Initiative (WHI) found that, whereas long-term hormone replacement therapy (HRT) had beneficial effects on women's bones, this was more than offset by an increased risk of venous thromboembolic disease, breast cancer, stroke, and coronary artery disease.[3] These results suggest that long-term combination therapy with estrogen and progesterone cannot be recommended to most women at this time. This chapter will provide an evidence-based review of the nonhormonal treatment options for breast cancer survivors. These therapies are also likely to be effective for symptomatic women with a high risk of breast cancer or women with a preference not to use hormonal therapies.

HOT FLASHES

Hot flashes are a common health problem for postmenopausal women.[4] Survivors of breast cancer are particularly vulnerable to hot flash symptoms as the sudden precipitation of menopause owing to chemotherapy can lead to the rapid and premature onset of severe hot flash symptoms.[5,6] Hot flashes are characterized by the sudden onset of intense warmth that begins in the chest and may progress to the neck and face. They are often accompanied by palpitations, anxiety, profuse sweating, and red blotching of the skin. Hot flash symptoms can lead to significant morbidity and affect a woman's social life, ability to work, sleep pattern, and general perception of health.[7-11]

Tamoxifen is the most commonly prescribed pharmacologic treatment for breast cancer and is associated with hot flashes in more than 50% of users.[12] Arimidex, a new aromatase inhibitor, also causes hot flashes. Tamoxifen-associated hot flashes gradually increase over the first several months of treatment and then tend to gradually resolve. Postmenopausal women with a history of significant hot flashes around the time of menopause are more likely to experience severe hot flashes with tamoxifen therapy.[12]

Dysfunction of central thermoregulatory centers owing to changes in estrogen levels are the postulated causes of hot flashes.[13] Perspiration and vasodilation, classic mechanisms of heat loss controlled by the hypothalamus, are activated during a hot flash.[13] In normal homeostasis, these mechanisms are activated to maintain core body temperature in a regulated range termed the "thermoregulatory zone." Recent studies have found that small changes in core body temperatures occur prior to hot flashes in up to 60% of hot flash episodes,[14] and women with hot flashes may have a thermoregulatory zone that is shifted downward and is more narrow than women without hot flashes.[15] Complex neuroendocrine pathways that involve norepinephrine, estrogen, testosterone, and endorphins govern regulation in the thermoregulatory nucleus and are possible sites where dysfunction may occur.[13,16,17] These studies suggest that subtle increases in temperature prior to a hot flash, coupled with a narrow homeostatic temperature zone, may trigger the heat loss mechanisms that lead to hot flash symptoms.

Hot flashes are effectively treated with HRT in most postmenopausal women.[18,19] Although subject to ongoing investigation, concern that HRT may promote breast cancer in high-risk women or breast cancer survivors precludes its use in many women at this time.[20-24] As noted above, the results of the WHI also suggest that long-term estrogen-based therapy cannot be recommended for most women at this time. Owing to this fact, many

women assume that hot flashes are an inevitable symptom of being a breast cancer survivor. It is important for oncologists and cancer nurses to inquire about hot flash symptoms and reassure women that effective nonhormonal treatments exist.

Treatment for an individual patient should begin with a careful history paying specific attention to the frequency and severity of hot flashes as well as how they impact the individual's function. Recording how hot flash symptoms impact the individual's work, sleep, and recreational activities allows the severity of symptoms to be classified. The aggressiveness of treatment interventions should match the severity of the symptoms. For individuals with mild symptoms that do not interfere with sleep or daily function, behavioral changes in conjunction with vitamin E (800 IU/day) represent a reasonable initial approach. A randomized, placebo-controlled, crossover trial in 120 women found a slight, statistically significant decrease in hot flash frequency with vitamin E therapy.[25] The low cost and minimal side effects of vitamin E make a trial of this agent reasonable despite its modest benefits. The effect of vitamin E may not be apparent for several weeks, and allowing an adequate trial may be necessary to assess its efficacy.

The most promising nonhormonal treatments for hot flashes are newer antidepressant agents. A double-blind, placebo-controlled trial in 191 breast cancer survivors randomized patients to placebo or to one of three venlafaxine doses (37.5, 75, or 150 mg/day).[26] After 4 weeks of treatment, placebo-treated patients had a 27% reduction in symptoms compared with 37, 61, and 61% in the three venlafaxine groups, respectively. For venlafaxine, we recommend a starting dose of 37.5 mg/day and titrating to a maximum dose of 75 mg/day after 1 week if optimal relief of symptoms is not achieved. Side effects observed with venlafaxine therapy include hypertension, dry mouth, decreased appetite, nausea, and constipation.

Selective serotonin reuptake inhibitors (SSRIs) have also been found to be effective for treating hot flashes. A double-blinded, randomized, placebo-controlled, crossover clinical trial also demonstrated that fluoxetine reduces hot flashes,[27] although the magnitude of efficacy did not appear to be as great in this trial compared with what was seen with venlafaxine.[26] No statistically significant toxicity, relative to placebo, was observed while patients were on the fluoxetine phase of this trial. A pilot study of open label paroxetine, another SSRI, suggests a similar degree of efficacy, although controlled studies are needed.[28] Four of 30 women in the paroxetine trial experienced somnolence, necessitating dose reduction in 2 patients and discontinuation of treatment in the other 2 patients.

In a small case series[29] and in pilot trials,[30] gabapentin appears to be a promising new therapy for relief of hot flashes in patients unable to use HRT. Side effects observed in the pilot trial included dizziness, nausea, somnolence, change in mood, fatigue, dry mouth, blurred vision, and indigestion but were present in only a small number of patients. The results of ongoing randomized trials to better determine its efficacy are eagerly anticipated. Although veralipride is an efficacious alternative to HRT for European women, it is not available in the United States and may cause dystonic reactions.[31–33] Clonidine, methyldopa, and belladonna for the treatment of hot flashes do not appear to be as useful as other agents owing to their modest efficacy and side effects.

For individuals with severe symptoms that are not responsive to nonhormonal agents, treatment with the progestational agents appears to be a reasonable alternative to treat hot flash symptoms. A double-blind, placebo-controlled, crossover trial in 97 breast cancer survivors and 66 men receiving androgen ablation treatment for prostate cancer found a 75 to 80% reduction in hot flashes with megesterol acetate compared with a 20 to 25% reduction in placebo-treated patients.[34] A starting dose of 40 mg/day may be tapered to 20 mg/day as tolerated after 1 month of treatment. Although minimal side effects were noted during the treatment period, 13% of women experienced withdrawal bleeding 1 to 4 weeks after discontinuing treatment. A 3-year follow-up of the patients in the above study suggests the benefit of megesterol acetate may be long lasting.[35] Another alternative progestational agent approach is to use medroxyprogesterone acetate. Three intramuscular doses of this drug (500 mg/dose) at fortnightly intervals appears to dramatically reduce hot flashes for a considerable time.[36] Although it is reasonable to believe that progesterone therapy is or, alternatively, is not safe in women with breast cancer, there are no long-term prospective data to establish either of these facts.

Patients treated for hot flashes should be followed regularly to monitor response and look for potential side effects of treatment. Comprehensive reviews of the pathogenesis and treatment of hot flashes in breast cancer survivors are available (Table 15-1).[37–39]

SEXUAL DYSFUNCTION

Sexual dysfunction occurs in up to 60% of breast cancer survivors and may be due to the effects of surgery, radiation, or chemotherapy.[40] Many women are hesitant to discuss sexual dysfunction with their healthcare providers.[40–42] Sexual dysfunction includes problems with desire (libido), lubrication, anorgasmy, dyspareunia, and satisfaction. In one study of breast cancer survivors, 64% of women reported decreased desire, 38% reported pain with intercourse, 44% anorgasmy, and 42% lubrication problems.[40] Overall, 96% of women reported at least one sexual problem. Sexual dysfunction may worsen over the first several years of treatment[43] but subsequently improve with longer follow-up.[44]

Speculation that the incidence and severity of sexual dysfunction correlates with the extent of surgery is not supported by the literature.[45–47] A prospective evaluation of 109 women during the first year after mastectomy or lumpectomy found no difference in sexual dysfunction or quality of life between groups.[45] Other studies with follow-up 4

TABLE 15-1   Treatment of Hot Flashes

- Classify severity
- Assess impact on sleep, work, recreation
- Nonhormonal treatments:
    a. Vitamin E 800 IU/d (for mild symptoms)
    b. Venlafaxine 37.5 to 75 mg/d
    c. SSRI (fluoxetine 20 mg/d; paroxetine 10 to 20 mg qd)
    d. Gabapentin 300 mg/d or 300 mg tid
- Progestational treatments:
    a. Megestrol acetate 20 to 40 mg PO bid
    b. Medroxyprogesterone acetate 500 mg IM q 2 w for 3 total doses
- Regular follow-up to assess the response to treatment and side effects of treatment

SSRI = selective serotonin reuptake inhibitors.

to 8 years after treatment also found no difference in sexual function between patients treated with mastectomy or breast-conservation surgery.[46,47]

The effect of mastectomy or breast-conservation surgery on feelings of sexuality may depend on patient age. Women younger than age 50 appear to have less psychological distress after lumpectomy,[47] and lumpectomy may also decrease body image problems.[42,45,48,49] The type of local treatment should be individualized after informed discussion with the patient.

Adjuvant chemotherapy appears to increase the risk of sexual dysfunction.[41,46,50–52] In one study of 67 women, patients who received chemotherapy were 5.7 times more likely to report vaginal dryness, 5.5 times more likely to report dyspareunia, 3 times more likely to report decreased libido, and 7.1 times more likely to report difficulty achieving an orgasm.[50] Similar to the effect of mastectomy, younger women appear to be at increased risk of sexual dysfunction after receiving chemotherapy.[41,53] Studies with longer follow-up (10 years), however, found no difference between women who had, versus those who had not, received adjuvant chemotherapy and suggest that the effect of chemotherapy on sexual function may decrease with time.[44]

In contrast to chemotherapy, hormonal therapy with tamoxifen does not appear to increase sexual dysfunction.[41,50,51,54] Ganz and colleagues surveyed 1,098 breast cancer survivors 1 to 5 years after treatment.[51] The 305 women who had been treated with tamoxifen did not report any increase in sexual dysfunction after controlling for the use of adjuvant chemotherapy. In another study, Mortimer and colleagues found no difference in sexual desire, sexual arousal, or the ability to achieve orgasm in 57 women treated with tamoxifen compared with a normative group of healthy women.[54]

It is important for oncologists to prepare women for a possible change in sexual function prior to treatment and to acknowledge the significance of sexual dysfunction.[41,55] Based on the above studies, a discussion regarding the potential of developing sexual dysfunction should be part of the informed consent process prior to chemotherapy.[55] This discussion prepares women for possible sexual difficulties and establishes the oncologist as a resource for problems that may arise.

Because many women are hesitant to report sexual dysfunction, healthcare providers should take the initiative to raise the topic for discussion.[56,57] Identifying the specific nature of the difficulty allows the clinician to distinguish between problems with aversion, arousal, desire, dyspareunia, or difficulty achieving orgasm.[42,58] Penson and colleagues provide suggestions for how providers can use the PLISSIT (*p*ermission, *l*imited *i*nformation, *s*pecific *s*uggestions, *i*ntensive *t*herapy) model to normalize patients' experiences and discuss sexual problems.[59]

Treatment of sexual dysfunction requires comprehensive assessment and intervention. A randomized trial found a significant decrease in sexual dysfunction in women randomized to a comprehensive assessment of menopausal symptoms by a nurse practitioner who screened for stress incontinence, hot flashes, and sexual dysfunction.[60] The study specifically targeted symptoms of vaginal dryness. If symptoms of sexual dysfunction were identified, recommendations for vaginal lubricants were provided along with individualized counseling and referral as indicated.

Vaginal dryness plays a significant, if not central, role in sexual dysfunction after chemotherapy.[42,52,60–63] Vaginal lubricants (Astroglide, Biofilm Inc, Vista, CA) and vaginal moisturizers (KY Jelly®, Johnson & Johnson, United States, Replens®, Lil' Drug Store Products, Inc [LDS], Cedar Rapids, IA) can be used to treat symptoms of dryness or inadequate lubrication and may indirectly improve other sexual problems as well.[42,60,62,64]

Pharmacologic treatment, other than vaginal lubricants, is limited. Depression should be identified and treated. Testosterone therapy has been shown to improve sexual desire and the frequency of sexual activity in women after surgical menopause or with sexual arousal disorders, and studies of testosterone in breast cancer survivors are currently in development.[65,66] The potential for testosterone to increase estrogen levels, and thereby theoretically increase the risk of breast cancer recurrence, should be acknowledged prior to recommending its use outside a clinical trial at this time.[67] Comprehensive reviews of sexual dysfunction in breast cancer survivors are available (Table 15-2).[42]

OSTEOPOROSIS

Osteoporosis is a skeletal disorder characterized by a decreased bone mass that renders bone more fragile and vulnerable to fracture. Estrogen and testosterone play important roles in regulation of bone

---

TABLE 15-2 Sexual Dysfunction

- Risk increased by:

  Chemotherapy (Note: tamoxifen and extent of surgery [lumpectomy vs mastectomy] do not appear to affect risk)

- Treatment:

  a. Comprehensive screen for symptoms

  b. Categorize problem: aversion, arousal, lubrication, desire, dyspareunia, anorgasmy

  c. Vaginal lubricants/moisturizers: Astroglide, KY Jelly, Replens

  d. Referral to psychiatrist or sex therapist as indicated

- On the horizon:

  Studies exploring the efficacy and safety of testosterone therapy for breast cancer survivors are underway

---

mineral density (BMD) and bone health.[68,69] At the time of menopause, women enter a 10-year period of accelerated bone loss responsible for a 20 to 30% loss of cancellous bone and a 5 to 10% loss of cortical bone. This decade is followed by an indefinite period of slower bone loss. In postmenopausal women, conversion of adrenal androgens to estrogen by the enzyme aromatase leads to continued low levels of circulating estrogen, which may play an important role in calcium homeostasis via effects on renal and gastrointestinal absorption of calcium.[70]

Multiple mechanisms are responsible for the increased risk of osteoporosis in breast cancer survivors. Women treated for breast cancer are at increased risk of osteoporosis and have a 5-fold increased risk of vertebral fracture compared with the general population.[71] Premature ovarian failure owing to chemotherapy,[72–74] estrogen-blocking therapies (eg, tamoxifen in premenopausal women, aromatase inhibitors),[75] and the direct effects of chemotherapy on bone[74,76–78] may all contribute to the increased risk of osteoporosis in breast cancer survivors. Fractures of the hip, vertebrae, and radius can result in pain, decreased mobility, and decreased independence and can profoundly impact quality of life.[79,80]

Sixty to 90% of premenopausal women treated with chemotherapy will experience ovarian failure in less than 1 year,[72,76] and these women are at an increased risk for developing osteoporosis.[77,81]

Chemotherapeutic agents, including cyclophosphamide, methotrexate, and doxorubicin have also been shown to have direct adverse effects on bone mineral density in animal models, which may compound chemotherapy-induced ovarian failure.[76–78] In addition to breast cancer treatments, risk factors for osteoporosis include a history of late menarche, early menopause, low body weight, decreased exercise level, decreased calcium intake, tobacco use, heavy alcohol consumption, Caucasian heritage, or a family history of bone fracture.

Tamoxifen has mixed agonist and antagonist effects on estrogen receptors and has different effects on BMD depending on the menopausal status of the patient at the time of treatment.[75,82–86] Powles and colleagues evaluated BMD in 179 pre- and postmenopausal women treated with either tamoxifen or placebo for chemoprevention of breast cancer.[75] Premenopausal women treated with tamoxifen experienced a 1.44% decrease in BMD per year over the 3-year study compared with placebo-treated premenopausal women. In contrast, postmenopausal women treated with tamoxifen experienced a comparable increase in BMD compared with postmenopausal women treated with placebo. Other investigators have reported a similar protective effect of tamoxifen in postmenopausal women.[82,84] Presumably, tamoxifen's partial antagonist effect blunts estrogenic activity on bone in premenopausal women with high circulating estrogen levels while the partial agonist activity confers a net benefit in postmenopausal women with minimal circulating estrogen. Aromatase inhibitors are another hormonal treatment that blocks the conversion of androgens to estrogen and may lead to problems with calcium homeostasis and BMD.

Prevention is the most important strategy to combat osteoporosis. It can be argued that all women who experience ovarian failure as a result of chemotherapy should undergo bone mineral density testing, and many experts advocate such testing for women who are postmenopausal at the time of diagnosis as well.[76,87,88] The World Health Organization criteria for the diagnosis of osteopenia by dual x-ray absorption (DXA) is a T score 1 to 2.5 standard deviations below the mean for healthy young adult women, whereas the criterion for osteoporosis is ≥ 2.5 standard deviations below the mean.[68]

Women with normal BMD, or meeting criteria for osteopenia on DEXA, should receive prophylactic treatment to prevent osteoporosis. Prophylaxis includes calcium (1,000 to 1,500 mg/day) and vitamin D (400 to 800 IU/day),[89–91] which have been shown to reduce hip and vertebral fracture by 43 and 32%, respectively.[89] Smoking cessation and maintaining weight-bearing physical activity should also be recommended to all women for osteoporosis prevention. The use of bisphosphonates (eg, alendronate or risedronate) for primary prevention is presently undergoing evaluation in breast cancer survivors without established osteoporosis.[73,74,81,92] Their use in standard clinical practice, however, cannot currently be recommended.[93]

Women with proven osteoporosis should be treated with the combination of a bisphosphonate (eg, alendronate 10 mg/day or 70 mg/week or risedronate 5 mg/day or 35 mg/week), calcium (1,500 to 2,000 mg/day), and vitamin D (800 IU/day).[94–97] These bisphosphonates appear to reduce the risk of fracture by 30 to 50%. Calcitonin (200 IU/day) is a less effective alternative for women who are unable to take a bisphosphonate.[98–101] Raloxifene is a selective estrogen receptor modulating agent (SERM) with US Food and Drug Administration approval for prevention and treatment of osteoporosis in postmenopausal women.[102–104] Its efficacy and safety for this indication in breast cancer survivors, especially those who have received 5 years of tamoxifen, remains to be determined. Trials evaluating its benefit for chemoprevention relative to tamoxifen are currently underway; these trials may also provide guidance for raloxifene's use to prevent and treat osteoporosis in women.

Of note, bisphosphonates are proven to be a beneficial treatment for women with bone metastases and may also be determined to have a role as an adjuvant treatment for prevention of bony metastasis in women with early stage breast cancer.[87,105,106] These topics are reviewed elsewhere (Table 15-3).[87,105,106]

COGNITIVE DYSFUNCTION

Cognitive dysfunction owing to chemotherapy or radiation was originally described in the 1980s[107–109] and has become increasingly appreciated as a potential side effect of cancer treatment.[110–114] Twenty to 40% of breast cancer survivors may experience cognitive changes[115] that may be a consequence of surgery,[116–118] radiation,[114]

TABLE 15-3 Osteoporsis

- Risk increased by:
  a. Chemotherapy: premature ovarian failure, direct effect on bone
  b. Tamoxifen in premenopausal women
  c. Steroids used as premedication or as an antiemetic
  d. Heparin
  e. Aromatase inhibitors
- Prevention:
  a. BMD testing for all women with chemotherapy-induced ovarian failure; consider for postmenopausal women and other breast cancer survivors as well
  b. Counseling: maintain weight-bearing activity level, smoking cessation
  c. Calcium 1,000 to 1,500 mg/d (total dose including diet)
  d. Vitamin D 400 to 800 IU/d
- Treatment:
  a. Calcium 1,500 to 2,000 mg/d (total dose including diet)
  b. Vitamin D 800 IU/d
  c. Alendronate 10 mg/d or 70 mg/w; or risedronate 5 mg/d or 35 mg/w; or calcitonin 200 IU/d
- On the horizon:
  a. Better identification of osteoporosis with screening and monitoring
  b. Evaluations of raloxifene and new bisphosphonates for prevention and treatment

BMD = bone mineral density.

or chemotherapy.[110–114] "Attention fatigue," "neurocognitive dysfunction," or "chemo brain" have all been used to refer to the constellation of short-term memory loss, decreased attention, and learning deficits that comprise cognitive dysfunction. Other symptoms associated with neurotoxicity include irritability, amotivation, slowed mental functioning, chronic fatigue, peripheral neuropathies, and motor incoordination.[119] In one early, cross-sectional trial evaluating 28 women treated with standard dose chemotherapy +/– tamoxifen, 75% of women showed mild to moderate clinical impairment in cognitive domains.[112]

Estrogen deficiency may play a role in the cognitive changes seen in breast cancer survivors. Menopausal women experience cognitive deficits in memory, learning, and attention that are similar to the symptoms observed in patients treated for breast cancer.[64,120–122] Reversal of these symptoms has been observed with HRT,[123–125] and some studies suggest that women who use estrogen may be at decreased risk for developing Alzheimer's.[126,127] Estrogen's effects on central nervous system blood flow and central cholinergic and serotonergic pathways have been proposed as mechanisms for estrogen's effects on neurologic health.

Neurotoxicity from chemotherapy has also been proposed as the cause of cognitive dysfunction after breast cancer treatment. The neurotoxicity of chemotherapy is suggested by documented white matter changes after high dose methotrexate, cytosine arabinoside, thiotepa, and cisplatin.[107,128] Free radicals and low oxygen tension have been implicated as a cause for chemotherapy-mediated neuronal damage.[129,130]

Adjuvant chemotherapy does appear to increase the risk of cognitive dysfunction in breast cancer survivors. An evaluation of the cognitive function of 104 high-risk Stage I breast cancer patients previously randomized to no adjuvant treatment, standard dose chemotherapy, or high dose chemotherapy, has been reported.[110] Cognitive impairment following treatment was found in 9, 17, and 32% of patients, respectively. Compared with the no-chemotherapy group, patients treated with high dose chemotherapy had an 8.2-fold higher risk of having cognitive dysfunction. No relationship was found between self-report of cognitive dysfunction and measured cognitive dysfunction, but a strong relationship was observed between self-reported cognitive dysfunction and psychological distress. Other investigators have also reported that women who received chemotherapy have decreased cognitive function.[111–114]

Tamoxifen does not appear to increase the risk of cognitive dysfunction. A retrospective study of 29 women randomized to tamoxifen or no treatment after prior chemotherapy compared subjects to 34 node-negative women who had not received chemotherapy.[111] Cognitive impairment was found in 28% of chemotherapy-treated patients versus 12% of controls ($p = .013$). Tamoxifen use after chemotherapy did not increase measured cognitive dysfunction over chemotherapy alone. Once again, self-report of cognitive dysfunction did not correlate with measured cognitive dysfunction but did correlate with psychiatric symptoms of anxiety and depression.

The cognitive sequelae of chemotherapy appear to develop during treatment and to persist once they develop. A recent study of cognitive dysfunction in breast cancer survivors evaluated 107 patients from one of three groups.[113] Group 1 patients were enrolled in active treatment with standard dose chemotherapy, group 2 patients were women 1 year from completion of standard dose chemotherapy, and group 3 patients were healthy controls. Approximately 50% of patients in groups 1 and 2 had moderate to severe cognitive impairment compared with 11% of controls.

The absence of baseline testing and retrospective study design are significant limitations of the above studies; confirmatory, prospective trials with a baseline assessment of cognitive dysfunction are underway.[131] An agenda for study design, measurements, and interventions in cognitive dysfunction has been proposed.[131,132]

The first step in evaluating cognitive changes is to exclude other treatable causes of dysfunction. Depression, anxiety, brain metastasis, medication side effects (analgesics, antiemetics), and treatment-related fatigue may all cause cognitive/neurologic symptoms that should be distinguished from treatment-related cognitive dysfunction.

Donepezil and *Ginkgo biloba* have been studied as treatments for dementia and Alzheimer's disease; in these situations, each of these drugs appears to maintain cognitive function better than does a placebo.[133,134] The role of these agents for treatment and prevention of cognitive dysfunction in breast cancer survivors is unknown and is the subject of ongoing investigation. In addition, erythropoietin is also undergoing prospective evaluation as an agent to prevent chemotherapy-induced cognitive dysfunction. Studies exploring the role of amifostine, a cysteine analog shown to protect normal tissues from the toxic effects of alkylating agents and cisplatin, do not show any decrease in neural toxicity.[135,136] Owing to the possibility that estrogen withdrawal contributes to cognitive dysfunction, some have speculated that HRT or SERMS may improve cognitive symptoms.[132] For reasons noted above, most physicians are hesitant to prescribe these hormonal therapies at the present time.

Thus, to date, a proven strategy to prevent cognitive dysfunction in breast cancer survivors has not been identified. Some investigators have recommended neuropsychiatric testing be a standard part of treatment for women undergoing chemotherapy to allow identification of women who may benefit from cognitive or vocational rehabilitation, but this is not currently considered to be standard practice.[131,132] Rather, the potential for chemotherapy to cause neurocognitive dysfunction needs to be factored into the decision of whether to employ adjunct cytotoxic chemotherapy in women with relatively low risks of developing recurrent breast cancer (Table 15-4).

TABLE 15-4 Cognitive Dysfunction

- Risk increased by:
  Chemotherapy (Note: tamoxifen does not appear to increase risk)

- Self-report of cognitive dysfunction:
  Associated with depression/anxiety: screen and diagnose

- Treatment:
  No proven therapy
  Vocational/cognitive rehabilitation

- On the horizon:
  Studies exploring role of donepezil, *Ginkgo biloba*, and erythropoietin for prevention of cognitive dysfunction are underway

SUMMARY

Advances in treatment for breast cancer have increased the number of breast cancer survivors, many of whom will live for years to decades after completing treatment. Efficacious nonestrogenic treatment options are available to treat menopausal symptoms and the common side effects of therapy. These treatments can improve the quality of life for breast cancer survivors and high-risk women with menopausal symptoms who desire to avoid hormonal therapies.

REFERENCES

1. Greenlee RT, Hill-Harmon MB, Murray T, Thun M. Cancer statistics, 2001. CA Cancer J Clin 2001; 51:15–36.
2. Bland KI, Menck HR, Scott-Conner CE, et al. The National Cancer Data Base 10-year survey of breast carcinoma treatment at hospitals in the United States. Cancer 1998;83:1262–73.
3. Risks and benefits of estrogen plus progestin in healthy postmenopausal women: principal results from the Women's Health Initiative randomized controlled trial. JAMA 2002;288:321–33.
4. McKinlay SM, Jefferys M. The menopausal syndrome. Br J Prev Soc Med 1974;28:108–15.
5. Berg G, Gottwall T, Hammar M, et al. Climacteric symptoms among women aged 60–62 in Linkoping, Sweden, in 1986. Maturitas 1988;10:193–9.
6. Carpenter JS, Andrykowski MA, Cordova M, et al. Hot flashes in postmenopausal women treated for breast carcinoma: prevalence, severity, correlates, management, and relation to quality of life. Cancer 1998;82:1682–91.
7. Roberts J, Chambers LF, Blake J, Webber C. Psychosocial adjustment in post-menopausal women. Can J Nurs Res 1992;24:29–46.
8. Daly E, Gray A, Barlow D, et al. Measuring the impact of menopausal symptoms on quality of life. BMJ 1993;307:836–40.
9. Greendale GA, Lee NP, Arriola ER. The menopause. Lancet 1999;353:571–80.
10. Finck G, Barton DL, Loprinzi CL, et al. Definitions of hot flashes in breast cancer survivors. J Pain Symptom Manage 1998;16:327–33.
11. Stein KD, Jacobsen PB, Hann DM, et al. Impact of hot flashes on quality of life among postmenopausal women being treated for breast cancer. J Pain Symptom Manage 2000;19:436–45.
12. Love RR, Cameron L, Connell BL, Leventhal H. Symptoms associated with tamoxifen treatment in postmenopausal women. Arch Intern Med 1991; 151:1842–7.
13. Casper RF, Yen SS. Neuroendocrinology of menopausal flushes: an hypothesis of flush mechanism. Clin Endocrinol (Oxf) 1985;22:293–312.
14. Freedman RR, Norton D, Woodward S, Cornelissen G. Core body temperature and circadian rhythm of hot flashes in menopausal women. J Clin Endocrinol Metab 1995;80:2354–8.
15. Freedman RR, Krell W. Reduced thermoregulatory null zone in postmenopausal women with hot flashes. Am J Obstet Gynecol 1999;181:66–70.
16. Rosenberg J, Larsen SH. Hypothesis: pathogenesis of postmenopausal hot flush. Med Hypotheses 1991; 35:349–50.
17. Kronenberg F, Downey JA. Thermoregulatory physiology of menopausal hot flashes: a review. Can J Physiol Pharmacol 1987;65:1312–24.
18. Koster A. Hormone replacement therapy: use patterns in 51-year-old Danish women. Maturitas 1990; 12:345–56.
19. Rabin DS, Cipparrone N, Linn ES, Moen M. Why menopausal women do not want to take hormone replacement therapy. Menopause 1999;6:61–7.
20. Loprinzi CL, Barton D. Estrogen deficiency: in search of symptom control and sexuality. J Natl Cancer Inst 2000;92:1028–9.

21. Vassilopoulou-Sellin R, Asmar L, Hortobagyi GN, et al. Estrogen replacement therapy after localized breast cancer: clinical outcome of 319 women followed prospectively. J Clin Oncol 1999;17:1482–7.

22. Yao K, Lee ES, Bentrem DJ, et al. Antitumor action of physiological estradiol on tamoxifen-stimulated breast tumors grown in athymic mice. Clin Cancer Res 2000;6:2028–36.

23. Col NF, Hirota LK, Orr RK, et al. Hormone replacement therapy after breast cancer: a systematic review and quantitative assessment of risk. J Clin Oncol 2001;19:2357–63.

24. O'Meara ES, Rossing MA, Daling JR, et al. Hormone replacement therapy after a diagnosis of breast cancer in relation to recurrence and mortality. J Natl Cancer Inst 2001;93:754–62.

25. Barton DL, Loprinzi CL, Quella SK, et al. Prospective evaluation of vitamin E for hot flashes in breast cancer survivors. J Clin Oncol 1998;16:495–500.

26. Loprinzi CL, Kugler JW, Sloan JA, et al. Venlafaxine in management of hot flashes in survivors of breast cancer: a randomised controlled trial. Lancet 2000;356:2059–63.

27. Loprinzi CL, Sloan JA, Perez EA, et al. Phase III evaluation of fluoxetine for treatment of hot flashes. J Clin Oncol 2002;20:1578–83.

28. Stearns V, Isaacs C, Rowland J, et al. A pilot trial assessing the efficacy of paroxetine hydrochloride (Paxil) in controlling hot flashes in breast cancer survivors. Ann Oncol 2000;11:17–22.

29. Guttuso TJ Jr. Gabapentin's effects on hot flashes and hypothermia. Neurology 2000;54:2161–3.

30. Loprinzi L, Barton DL, Sloan JA, et al. Pilot evaluation of gabapentin for treating hot flashes. Mayo Clin Proc 2002;77:1159–63.

31. David A, Don R, Tajchner G, Weissglas L. Veralipride: alternative antidopaminergic treatment for menopausal symptoms. Am J Obstet Gynecol 1988;158:1107–15.

32. Vercellini P, Vendola N, Colombo A, et al. Veralipride for hot flushes during gonadotropin-releasing hormone agonist treatment. Gynecol Obstet Invest 1992;34:102–4.

33. Wesel S, Bourguignon RP, Bosuma WB. Veralipride versus conjugated oestrogens: a double-blind study in the management of menopausal hot flushes. Curr Med Res Opin 1984;8:696–700.

34. Loprinzi CL, Michalak JC, Quella SK, et al. Megestrol acetate for the prevention of hot flashes. N Engl J Med 1994;331:347–52.

35. Quella SK, Loprinzi CL, Sloan JA, et al. Long term use of megestrol acetate by cancer survivors for the treatment of hot flashes. Cancer 1998;82:1784–8.

36. Barton D, Loprinzi C, Quella SK, et al. Depomedroxyprogesterone acetate for hot flashes. J Pain Symptom Manage 2002;24:603–7.

37. Shanafelt TD, Barton DL, Adjei AA, Loprinzi CL. Pathophysiology and treatment of hot flashes. Mayo Clin Proc 2002;77:1207–18.

38. Stearns V, Ullmer L, Lopez JF, et al. Hot flushes. Lancet 2002;360:1851–61.

39. Berendsen HH. The role of serotonin in hot flushes. Maturitas 2000;36:155–64.

40. Barni S, Mondin R. Sexual dysfunction in treated breast cancer patients. Ann Oncol 1997;8:149–53.

41. Ganz PA, Rowland JH, Desmond K, et al. Life after breast cancer: understanding women's health-related quality of life and sexual functioning. J Clin Oncol 1998;16:501–14.

42. Thors CL, Broeckel JA, Jacobsen PB. Sexual functioning in breast cancer survivors. Cancer Control 2001;8:442–8.

43. Ganz PA, Coscarelli A, Fred C, et al. Breast cancer survivors: psychosocial concerns and quality of life. Breast Cancer Res Treat 1996;38:183–99.

44. Joly F, Espie M, Marty M, et al. Long-term quality of life in premenopausal women with node-negative localized breast cancer treated with or without adjuvant chemotherapy. Br J Cancer 2000;83:577–82.

45. Ganz PA, Schag AC, Lee JJ, et al. Breast conservation versus mastectomy. Is there a difference in psychological adjustment or quality of life in the year after surgery? Cancer 1992;69:1729–38.

46. Schover LR, Yetman RJ, Tuason LJ, et al. Partial mastectomy and breast reconstruction. A comparison of their effects on psychosocial adjustment, body image, and sexuality. Cancer 1995;75:54–64.

47. Dorval M, Maunsell E, Deschenes L, Brisson J. Type of mastectomy and quality of life for long term breast carcinoma survivors. Cancer 1998;83:2130–8.

48. Kiebert GM, de Haes JC, van de Velde CJ. The impact of breast-conserving treatment and mastectomy on the quality of life of early-stage breast cancer patients: a review. J Clin Oncol 1991;9:1059–70.

49. Moyer A. Psychosocial outcomes of breast-conserving surgery versus mastectomy: a meta-analytic review. Health Psychol 1997;16:284–98.

50. Young-McCaughan S. Sexual functioning in women with breast cancer after treatment with adjuvant therapy. Cancer Nurs 1996;19:308–19.

51. Ganz PA, Rowland JH, Meyerowitz BE, Desmond KA. Impact of different adjuvant therapy strategies on quality of life in breast cancer survivors. Recent Results Cancer Res 1998;152:396–411.

52. Ganz PA, Desmond KA, Belin TR, et al. Predictors of sexual health in women after a breast cancer diagnosis. J Clin Oncol 1999;17:2371–80.

53. Lindley C, Vasa S, Sawyer WT, Winer EP. Quality of life and preferences for treatment following systemic adjuvant therapy for early-stage breast cancer. J Clin Oncol 1998;16:1380–7.

54. Mortimer JE, Boucher L, Baty J, et al. Effect of tamoxifen on sexual functioning in patients with breast cancer. J Clin Oncol 1999;17:1488–92.

55. Wilmoth MC, Ross JA. Women's perception. Breast cancer treatment and sexuality. Cancer Pract 1997;5:353–9.

56. Schover LR. The impact of breast cancer on sexuality, body image, and intimate relationships. CA Cancer J Clin 1991;41:112–20.

57. Anllo LM. Sexual life after breast cancer. J Sex Marital Ther 2000;26:241–8.

58. IV APATFoD. Diagnostic and statistical manual of mental disorders. 4th ed. Washington (DC): American Psychiatric Association; 1994.

59. Penson RT, Gallagher J, Gioiella ME, et al Sexuality and cancer: conversation comfort zone. Oncologist. First 2000;5:336–44.

60. Ganz PA, Greendale GA, Petersen L, et al. Managing menopausal symptoms in breast cancer survivors: results of a randomized controlled trial. J Natl Cancer Inst 2000;92:1054–64.

61. Nachtigall LE. Comparative study: Replens versus local estrogen in menopausal women. Fertil Steril 1994;61:178–80.

62. Loprinzi CL, Abu-Ghazaleh S, Sloan JA, et al. Phase III randomized double-blind study to evaluate the efficacy of a polycarbophil-based vaginal moisturizer in women with breast cancer. J Clin Oncol 1997;15:969–73.

63. Greendale GA, Reboussin BA, Hogan P, et al. Symptom relief and side effects of postmenopausal hormones: results from the Postmenopausal Estrogen/Progestin Interventions Trial. Obstet Gynecol 1998;92:982–8.

64. Phillips SM, Sherwin BB. Effects of estrogen on memory function in surgically menopausal women. Psychoneuroendocrinology 1992;17:485–95.

65. Davis SR, Tran J. Testosterone influences libido and well being in women. Trends Endocrinol Metab 2001;12:33–7.

66. Shifren JL, Braunstein GD, Simon JA, et al. Transdermal testosterone treatment in women with impaired sexual function after oophorectomy. N Engl J Med 2000;343:682–8.

67. Simon JA. Safety of estrogen/androgen regimens. J Reprod Med 2001;46:281–90.

68. Kanis JA, Melton LJ 3rd, Christiansen C, et al. The diagnosis of osteoporosis. J Bone Miner Res 1994; 9:1137–41.

69. Turner RT, Riggs BL, Spelsberg TC. Skeletal effects of estrogen. Endocr Rev 1994;15:275–300.

70. Prince RL. Counterpoint: estrogen effects on calcitropic hormones and calcium homeostasis. Endocr Rev 1994;15:301–9.

71. Kanis JA, McCloskey EV, Powles T, et al. A high incidence of vertebral fracture in women with breast cancer. Br J Cancer 1999;79:1179–81.

72. Bruning PF, Pit MJ, de Jong-Bakker M, et al. Bone mineral density after adjuvant chemotherapy for premenopausal breast cancer. Br J Cancer 1990; 61:308–10.

73. Delmas PD, Balena R, Confravreux E, et al. Bisphosphonate risedronate prevents bone loss in women with artificial menopause due to chemotherapy of breast cancer: a double-blind, placebo-controlled study. J Clin Oncol 1997;15:955–62.

74. Saarto T, Blomqvist C, Valimaki M, et al. Chemical castration induced by adjuvant cyclophosphamide, methotrexate, and fluorouracil chemotherapy causes rapid bone loss that is reduced by clodronate: a randomized study in premenopausal breast cancer patients. J Clin Oncol 1997;15: 1341–7.

75. Powles TJ, Hickish T, Kanis JA, et al. Effect of tamoxifen on bone mineral density measured by dual-energy x-ray absorptiometry in healthy premenopausal and postmenopausal women. J Clin Oncol 1996;14:78–84.

76. Pfeilschifter J, Diel IJ. Osteoporosis due to cancer treatment: pathogenesis and management. J Clin Oncol 2000;18:1570–93.

77. Friedlander G, Tross R, Doganis A, et al. Effects of chemotherapeutic agents on bone: 1. Short-term methotrexate and doxorubicin (Adriamycin) treatment in a rat model. J Bone Joint Surg 1984;66A: 602–7.

78. Wang TM, Shih C. Study of histomorphometric changes of the mandibular condyles in neonatal and juvenile rats after administration of cyclophosphamide. Acta Anat 1986;127:93–9.

79. Cooper C. The crippling consequences of fractures and their impact on quality of life. Am J Med 1997;103:12S–7S.

80. Leidig-Bruckner G, Minne HW, Schlaich C, et al. Clinical grading of spinal osteoporosis: quality of life components and spinal deformity in women with chronic low back pain and women with vertebral osteoporosis. J Bone Miner Res 1997;12: 663–75.

81. Powles TJ, McCloskey E, Paterson AH, et al. Oral clodronate and reduction in loss of bone mineral density in women with operable primary breast cancer. J Natl Cancer Inst 1998;90:704–8.

82. Grey AB, Stapleton JP, Evans MC, et al. The effect of the antiestrogen tamoxifen on bone mineral density in normal late postmenopausal women. Am J Med 1995;99:636–41.

83. Love RR, Mazess RB, Barden HS, et al. Effects of tamoxifen on bone mineral density in postmenopausal women with breast cancer. N Engl J Med 1992;326:852–6.

84. Resch A, Biber E, Seifert M, Resch H. Evidence that tamoxifen preserves bone density in late postmenopausal women with breast cancer. Acta Oncol 1998;37:661–4.

85. Love RR, Mazess RB, Tormey DC, et al. Bone mineral density in women with breast cancer treated with adjuvant tamoxifen for at least two years. Breast Cancer Res Treat 1988;12:297–302.

86. Fisher B, Costantino JP, Wickerham DL, et al. Tamoxifen for prevention of breast cancer: report of the National Surgical Adjuvant Breast and Bowel Project P-1 Study. J Natl Cancer Inst 1998;90: 1371–88.

87. Perez EA. Metastatic bone disease in breast cancer: the patient's perspective. Semin Oncol 2001;28:60–3.

88. Mincey BA, Moraghan TJ, Perez EA. Prevention and treatment of osteoporosis in women with breast cancer. Mayo Clin Proc 2000;75:821–9.

89. Chapuy MC, Arlot ME, Duboeuf F, et al. Vitamin D3 and calcium to prevent hip fractures in the elderly women. N Engl J Med 1992;327:1637–42.

90. Reid IR, Ames RW, Evans MC, et al. Long-term effects of calcium supplementation on bone loss and fractures in postmenopausal women: a randomized controlled trial. Am J Med 1995;98:331–5.

91. Dawson-Hughes B, Harris SS, Krall EA, Dallal GE. Effect of calcium and vitamin D supplementation on bone density in men and women 65 years of age or older. N Engl J Med 1997;337:670–6.

92. Saarto T, Blomqvist C, Valimaki M, et al. Clodronate improves bone mineral density in post-menopausal breast cancer patients treated with adjuvant anti-oestrogens. Br J Cancer 1997;75:602–5.

93. Hillner BE, Ingle JN, Berenson JR, et al. American Society of Clinical Oncology guideline on the role of bisphosphonates in breast cancer. American Society of Clinical Oncology Bisphosphonates Expert Panel. J Clin Oncol 2000;18:1378–91.

94. Liberman UA, Weiss SR, Broll J, et al. Effect of oral alendronate on bone mineral density and the incidence of fractures in postmenopausal osteoporosis. The Alendronate Phase III Osteoporosis Treatment Study Group. N Engl J Med 1995;333: 1437–43.

95. Black DM, Cummings SR, Karpf DB, et al. Randomised trial of effect of alendronate on risk of fracture in women with existing vertebral fractures. Fracture Intervention Trial Research Group. Lancet 1996;348:1535–41.

96. Cummings SR, Black DM, Thompson DE, et al. Effect of alendronate on risk of fracture in women with low bone density but without vertebral fractures: results from the Fracture Intervention Trial. JAMA 1998;280:2077–82.

97. Karpf DB, Shapiro DR, Seeman E, et al. Prevention of nonvertebral fractures by alendronate. A meta-analysis. Alendronate Osteoporosis Treatment Study Groups. JAMA 1997;277:1159–64.

98. Kapetanos G, Symeonides PP, Dimitriou C, et al. A double blind study of intranasal calcitonin for established postmenopausal osteoporosis. Acta Orthop Scand Suppl 1997;275:108–11.

99. Gallagher JC, Goldgar D. Treatment of post-menopausal osteoporosis with high doses of synthetic calcitriol. A randomized controlled study. Ann Intern Med 1990;113:649–55.

100. Calcitrol treatment is not effective in postmenopausal osteoporosis. Ann Intern Med 1989;110: 267–74.

101. Overgaard K, Hansen MA, Jensen SB, Christiansen C. Effect of salcatonin given intranasally on bone mass and fracture rates in established osteoporosis: a dose-response study. BMJ 1992;305:556–61.

102. Delmas PD, Bjarnason NH, Mitlak BH, et al. Effects of raloxifene on bone mineral density, serum cholesterol concentrations, and uterine endometrium in postmenopausal women. N Engl J Med 1997; 337:1641–7.

103. Chlebowski RT, Collyar DE, Somerfield MR, Pfister DG. American Society of Clinical Oncology technology assessment on breast cancer risk reduction strategies: tamoxifen and raloxifene. J Clin Oncol 1999;17:1939–55.

104. Ettinger B, Black DM, Mitlak BH, et al. Reduction of vertebral fracture risk in postmenopausal women with osteoporosis treated with raloxifene: results from a 3-year randomized clinical trial. Multiple Outcomes of Raloxifene Evaluation (MORE) Investigators. JAMA 1999;282:637–45.

105. Paterson AH. Adjuvant bisphosphonate therapy: the future. Semin Oncol 2001;28:81–5.

106. Diel IJ. Bisphosphonates in the prevention of bone metastases: current evidence. Semin Oncol 2001; 28:75–80.

107. Peterson LG, Popkin MK. Neuropsychiatric effects of chemotherapeutic agents for cancer. Psychosomatics 1980;21:141–53.

108. Silberfarb PM. Chemotherapy and cognitive defects in cancer patients. Annu Rev Med 1983;34:35–46.

109. Folstein MF, Fetting JH, Lobo A, et al. Cognitive assessment of cancer patients. Cancer 1984;53: 2250–7.

110. van Dam FS, Schagen SB, Muller MJ, et al. Impairment of cognitive function in women receiving adjuvant treatment for high-risk breast cancer: high-dose versus standard-dose chemotherapy. J Natl Cancer Inst 1998;90:210–8.

111. Schagen SB, van Dam FS, Muller MJ, et al. Cognitive deficits after postoperative adjuvant chemotherapy for breast carcinoma. Cancer 1999;85:640–50.

112. Wieneke M, Dienst E. Neuropsychological assessment of cognitive functioning following chemotherapy for breast cancer. Psychooncology 1995;4: 61–6.

113. Brezden CB, Phillips KA, Abdolell M, et al. Cognitive function in breast cancer patients receiving adjuvant chemotherapy. J Clin Oncol 2000;18: 2695–701.

114. Berglund G, Bolund C, Fornander T, et al. Late effects of adjuvant chemotherapy and postoperative radiotherapy on quality of life among breast cancer patients. Eur J Cancer 1991;27:1075–81.

115. Cimprich B. Symptom management: loss of concentration. Semin Oncol Nurs 1995;11:279–88.

116. Cimprich B. Development of an intervention to restore attention in cancer patients. Cancer Nurs 1993;16:83–92.

117. Cimprich B. Attentional fatigue following breast cancer surgery. Res Nurs Health 1992;15:199–207.

118. Cimprich B. Age and extent of surgery affect attention in women treated for breast cancer. Res Nurs Health 1998;21:229–38.

119. Ahles TA, Saykia AJ. Breast cancer chemotherapy- related cognitive dysfunction. Clin Breast Cancer 2002;3:S84–S90.

120. Kimura D, Hampson E. Cognitive pattern in men and women is influenced by fluctuations in sex hormones. Curr Dir Psychol Sci 1994;3:57–60.

121. Sherwin BB. Estrogenic effects on memory in women. Ann N Y Acad Sci 1994;743:213–31.

122. Jacobs DM, Tang MX, Stern Y, et al. Cognitive function in nondemented older women who took estrogen after menopause. Neurology 1998;50:368–73.

123. Henderson VW, Paganini-Hill A, Emanuel CK, et al. Estrogen replacement therapy in older women. Comparisons between Alzheimer's disease cases and nondemented control subjects. Arch Neurol 1994;51:896–900.

124. Robinson D, Friedman L, Marcus R, et al. Estrogen replacement therapy and memory in older women. J Am Geriatr Soc 1994;42:919–22.

125. Sherwin BB, Gelfand MM. Sex steroids and affect in the surgical menopause: a double-blind, cross-over study. Psychoneuroendocrinology 1985;10: 325–35.

126. Tang MX, Jacobs D, Stern Y, et al. Effect of oestrogen during menopause on risk and age at onset of Alzheimer's disease. Lancet 1996;348:429–32.

127. Paganini-Hill A, Henderson VW. Estrogen deficiency and risk of Alzheimer's disease in women. Am J Epidemiol 1994;140:256–61.

128. Lee YY, Nauert C, Glass JP. Treatment-related white matter changes in cancer patients. Cancer 1986; 57:1473–82.

129. Hammond C. Therapeutic options for menopausal health. Duke University Medical Center and MBK Associates; 1998.

130. Ganong W. Review of medical physiology. Norwalk (CT): Appleton & Lange; 1993.

131. Olin JJ. Cognitive function after systemic therapy for breast cancer. Oncology (Huntingt) 2001;15: 613–8, 621–4.

132. Bender CM, Paraska KK, Sereika SM, et al. Cognitive function and reproductive hormones in adjuvant therapy for breast cancer: a critical review. J Pain Symptom Manage 2001;21:407–24.

133. Le Bars PL, Katz MM, Berman N, et al. A placebo-controlled, double-blind, randomized trial of an extract of Ginkgo biloba for dementia. North American EGb Study Group. JAMA 1997;278:1327–32.

134. Rogers SL, Farlow MR, Doody RS, et al. A 24-week, double-blind, placebo-controlled trial of donepezil in patients with Alzheimer's disease. Donepezil Study Group. Neurology 1998;50:136–45.

135. Gelmon K, Eisenhauer E, Bryce C, et al. Randomized phase II study of high-dose paclitaxel with or without amifostine in patients with metastatic breast cancer. J Clin Oncol 1999;17:3038–47.

136. Gradishar WJ, Stephenson P, Glover DJ, et al. A Phase II trial of cisplatin plus WR-2721 (amifostine) for metastatic breast carcinoma: an Eastern Cooperative Oncology Group Study (E8188). Cancer 2001;92:2517–22.

Surgical Prevention

CHAPTER 16

PROPHYLACTIC MASTECTOMY AND OOPHORECTOMY

Faina Nakhlis, MD
Monica Morrow, MD

Until relatively recently, prophylactic mastectomy was the only option available for reduction of breast cancer risk, and the level of risk reduction with the procedure was uncertain. Today both prophylactic mastectomy and prophylactic bilateral oophorectomy are available as preventive strategies in women at high risk for breast cancer development. Prophylactic mastectomy is expected to remove the tissue at risk, whereas oophorectomy eliminates the source of estrogenic stimulation of the breast tissue, with the additional benefit of decreasing ovarian cancer risk in *BRCA1* and *BRCA2* mutation carriers. A number of criteria have been suggested to define the efficacy and feasibility of a prophylactic procedure.[1] These include effective prevention of the disease, easy identification of the population at risk, and cost-benefit analysis. The data on identification of high-risk women have been reviewed in detail in Chapters 2 through 5. In this chapter the available data pertaining to the efficacy and outcomes of prophylactic mastectomy and oophorectomy will be reviewed.

PROPHYLACTIC MASTECTOMY

Efficacy

Animal experiments assessing mammary cancer risk reduction after prophylactic mastectomy were not particularly promising. In Sprague-Dawley rats, prophylactic mastectomy 2 weeks after the administration of a mammary carcinogen did not reduce the incidence of mammary tumor development.[2] In a murine model of spontaneous mammary carcinoma, no decrease in tumor formation was seen following either a partial or a total prophylactic mastectomy compared with the nonsurgical group.[3]

Human studies of the efficacy of prophylactic mastectomy have been more promising, although methodologically limited, because there are no data from prospective randomized trials to clearly define the benefits of the procedure. Evidence of the efficacy of prophylactic mastectomy has been derived from retrospective reviews and cohort studies in women with and without a prior history of breast cancer.

Indirect evidence of the potential benefit of prophylactic mastectomy comes from studies of reduction mammoplasty. Baasch and colleagues examined the incidence of breast cancer in 1,240 Danish women undergoing reduction mammoplasty between 1943 and 1971.[4] Expected breast cancer incidence was determined from age and time interval specific rates for the Danish female population. Thirty-two cases of breast cancer were observed, whereas 52.6 were expected, a relative risk (RR) of 0.61 (95% confidence interval [CI] 0.42–0.86). The greatest risk reduction was observed in women who had 600 grams or more of tissue removed. Similar findings were reported by Boice and colleagues in a study of 31,910 Swedish women undergoing breast reduction.[5] Overall, 161 incident breast cancers occurred with a mean of 7.5 years of observation after reduction mammoplasty, compared with 223.9 expected (RR = 0.72; 95% CI 0.61–0.84). The reduction in risk was greatest in women having surgery after age 50. In a follow-up study, the amount of breast tissue removed was a significant predictor of risk, with those having greater than or equal to 1,600 grams of tissue removed from both breasts having a significantly lower risk (RR = 0.24; 95% CI 0.1–0.5) than those having less than 800 grams removed.[6]

Retrospective studies have addressed the benefit of prophylactic mastectomy in women with and without a prior history of breast cancer. McDonnell and colleagues reported on 745 patients, with both a personal and a family history of breast cancer, who underwent a contralateral prophylactic mastectomy at the Mayo Clinic between 1960 and 1993.[7] The Anderson contralateral breast cancer risk model, with adjustments for the use of tamoxifen and chemotherapy, was used to predict the rate of expected breast cancer.[8] This model is based on a cohort of 556 patients with a personal history of unilateral breast carcinoma and a family history of breast cancer in the patient's mother, sister, or a second-degree relative. Based on retrospective data, Anderson and Badzioch estimated that by 19 years after the diagnosis of breast cancer, the risk of a contralateral cancer was between 35 and 38% for women with a premenopausal diagnosis, and between 11 and 26% for those diagnosed postmenopausally.[8]

In the study of McDonnell and colleagues, subcutaneous mastectomy was performed in 40.5% of the patients, whereas the remainder had a total mastectomy. Breast reconstruction was performed on 63.9% of the patients.[7] At a median follow-up of 10 years, 6 breast cancers were observed in the premenopausal group compared with 106.2 predicted without prophylactic surgery (RR = 94.4; 95% CI 87.7–97.9). Among the postmenopausal patients, only 2 breast cancers were observed, whereas 50.3 were predicted (RR = 96; 95% CI 85.6–99.5). The median time to the development of breast cancer after prophylactic mastectomy was 2 years, with a range of 1 to 18 years. This relatively short interval suggests that unsampled cancer could have been present at the time of prophylactic surgery. Review of 2 of the 4 pathology specimens in those with early recurrence, which included additional sectioning, failed to reveal invasive or in situ carcinoma. Of the 8 women who developed breast cancer following prophylactic mastectomy, 4 had undergone a subcutaneous mastectomy, and residual breast tissue was identified in 2 of these women. Carcinoma developed lateral to the implant on the chest wall in 1 patient, and in an ipsilateral axillary node in the remaining patient. In the 4 women who had had a total mastectomy for prophylaxis, 3 out of 4 cancers were found in the ipsilateral axillary nodes, whereas only one occurred on the chest wall.

The results of this study indicate that in the patient with breast cancer and a family history of the disease, prophylactic mastectomy reduces the risk of subsequent breast cancer development. Whether the absolute benefit of prophylactic mastectomy is as great as that which is suggested is uncertain. The Anderson Model has not been prospectively validated, and it is not possible to determine the proportion of patients in this study with a family history suggestive of genetic mutation.[8] However, the risk of contralateral breast cancer in studies of unselected patient populations is substantially lower than that reported by Anderson and Badzioch.[8] Table 16-1 illustrates the incidence of second primary cancers in a variety of patient populations.[9–14]

TABLE 16-1   Incidence of Contralateral Breast Cancer After an Initial Cancer Diagnosis

Author	Population	Number of Patients	Rate of Contralateral Cancer	Follow-up
Mamounas et al[9]	NSABP trial participants	15,016	2.9% at 5 y	NS
Adami et al[10]	Swedish women, population based	1,351	5.1% lifetime risk	NS
Habel et al[11]	Ductal carcinoma in situ	1,929	4.1% (crude)	Mean 54 m
Broët et al[12]	Stage I to IIIa invasive cancer	4,748	4.1% at 5 y	Median 80 m
Healey et al[13]	Stage I and II invasive cancer with BCT	1,624	7.0% at 10 y	Median 95 m
Singletary et al[14]	Invasive and noninvasive cancer surgically treated at MD Anderson	4,554	3.1% (crude)	Median 6.1 y

NSABP = National Surgical Adjuvant Breast and Bowel Project; BCT = breast-conserving surgery and radiation; NS = not stated.

In these studies the rate of second cancers ranges from 0.4 to 1% per year and appears to be consistent over time. The use of tamoxifen treatment for the initial breast cancer clearly impacts the risk of a second primary tumor. Patients in the National Surgical Adjuvant Breast and Bowel Project (NSABP) trials in which tamoxifen was not used ($n = 8,244$) had a rate of contralateral breast cancer of 0.74 per year compared with 0.44 per year in women who received tamoxifen ($n = 6,772$).[9] Age at diagnosis was a significant predictor of risk in the three studies that examined this factor.[10,12,13] In the study of Adami and colleagues the relative risk of developing a second primary cancer was 9.9 (95% CI 3.8–25.8) for those diagnosed before age 50, compared with 1.9 (95% CI 1.1–3.2) for women diagnosed at an older age.[10] This translates to cumulative lifetime risks of 13.3 and 3.5%, respectively. Singletary and colleagues reported that second primary tumors were more likely to be noninvasive or node-negative than the initial carcinoma, presumably owing to the increased surveillance of patients known to be at increased risk.[14] Overall, the data provide little justification for the routine use of prophylactic mastectomy in women with a unilateral carcinoma, but suggest that in premenopausal women with a family history of breast cancer a discussion of the procedure may be appropriate. This is particularly true if mastectomy is necessary for the treatment of an initial cancer which appears to have a good prognosis (eg, extensive intraductal carcinoma associated with a small invasive cancer).

Several studies have examined the efficacy of prophylactic mastectomy in reducing risk in women without a prior cancer diagnosis. Pennisi and Capozzi reported the outcome of prophylactic subcutaneous mastectomy in 1,500 women treated by 165 plastic surgeons and reported to a voluntary registry.[15] Only 6 (0.6%) breast cancers developed after an average of 9 years of follow-up. Little is known about the actual risk status of the women undergoing surgery, but only 20% had a first-degree relative with breast cancer. In addition, 30% of the subjects were lost to follow-up. When the 510 women with demonstrated clinical or pathologic features indicating an increased breast cancer risk were studied, there was a 1.18% incidence of breast cancer.[16] However, because reporting was voluntary, a significant potential for selection bias exists even within this group.

A much more rigorous analysis of the efficacy of prophylactic mastectomy in a high-risk population was reported by Hartmann and colleagues.[17] In this retrospective review, 639 women with a family history of breast cancer who had undergone bilateral prophylactic mastectomy between 1960 and 1993 were identified. Follow-up data were obtained by telephone contact. Women were categorized as being at high risk for breast cancer if their family history was suggestive of an autosomal dominant predisposition to breast cancer. The criteria used for this determination are shown in Table 16-2. For the 214 women who met these criteria, the expected incidence of cancer was estimated using the age-specific breast cancer incidence and death rates among their sisters from the time of surgery to the end of follow-up. The remaining 425 women were designated as moderate risk, and the predicted incidence of breast cancer in this group was estimated using the Gail Model.[18] The probability of death in this group was determined using age-specific survival rates from the Surveillance, Epidemiology and End Results (SEER) program.

The median age at mastectomy in both the moderate and high-risk groups was 42 years, ranging from 18 to 79 years. The mean number of prior breast biopsies was 2.4 in the moderate risk group and 1.9 in the high-risk group. The median length of follow-up was 14 years (9,095 person-years),

TABLE 16-2 Criteria for Classification as High Risk

Two or more first-degree relatives with breast cancer

One first-degree relative and two or more second- or third-degree relatives with breast cancer

One first-degree relative with breast cancer diagnosed before 45 years of age plus one other relative with breast cancer

One first-degree relative with breast cancer and at least one relative with ovarian cancer

Two second-degree or third-degree relatives with breast cancer and at least one relative with ovarian cancer

One second- or third-degree relative with breast cancer and at least two relatives with ovarian cancer

Three or more second- or third-degree relatives with breast cancer

One first-degree relative with bilateral breast cancer

Adapted from Hartmann LC et al.[17]

with 2% of women lost to follow-up and 5% of women or next of kin refusing to fill out the questionnaire. A minimum of 2 years of follow-up was available for 99% of cases, and 95% were alive at the time of the analysis. The six women incidentally found to have breast cancer at the time of prophylactic mastectomy were excluded from the study.

Based on the Gail Model, 37.4 breast cancers were expected in the moderate-risk group, and 4 breast cancers were observed after prophylactic mastectomy, a risk reduction of 89.5% (95% CI 73–97; $p < .001$). A comparison of breast cancer incidence among 214 high-risk probands and their 403 sisters who had not had prophylactic mastectomy found that 3 women (1.4%) developed breast cancer after prophylactic surgery compared with 156 (38.7%) of their sisters who had not undergone surgery. The expected number of cancers in the women undergoing prophylactic surgery ranged from 30 to 52.9. This constitutes a risk reduction of 90 to 94% (95% CI 71–99), depending on the method of adjustment used for ascertainment bias. The estimated number of breast cancer deaths in the moderate risk group without surgery was calculated to be 10.4, and none occurred, a 100% reduction (95% CI 70–100). In the high-risk group, depending on the method used to calculate the expected rate of breast cancer–specific mortality, the reduction in the risk of death ranged from 81 to 94%.

The median time from prophylactic mastectomy to the development of breast cancer was 6 years, with a range of 2 to 25 years. All 7 of the cancers occurred in women who had undergone subcutaneous mastectomy, and 6 of the 7 were chest wall recurrences.

This study provides the best available estimate of the benefit of prophylactic mastectomy in a population with long-term follow-up, but it does have several limitations. First, as the authors noted in a subsequent publication, during the initial time period in which the prophylactic mastectomies were done, anyone with an affected close relative was considered to be at high risk for breast cancer development, which is now known not to be true.[19] This suggests that the predicted breast cancer risk in the high-risk women may have been overestimated. In addition, women who underwent prophylactic mastectomy had a median age of 42 years and were cancer free. Because 30 to 50% of *BRCA1*

and -*2* mutation carriers have developed cancer by this age, this suggests that many of the women in the high-risk group were not mutation carriers, although their sisters could have been.[20] The absence of a significant level of risk in many women is also suggested by the histologic review of the prophylactic mastectomy specimens. In 74.5% of cases, no proliferative changes were present, and only 1.5% had atypical hyperplasia identified. In contrast, Hoogerbrugge and colleagues found that 57% of high-risk women (66% documented mutation carriers) undergoing prophylactic mastectomy had atypical hyperplasia or in situ carcinoma present in their surgical specimen.[21]

Conversely, the benefit of prophylactic surgery may have been underestimated because the predominant surgical technique used was subcutaneous mastectomy. Among the 639 women who underwent bilateral prophylactic mastectomy, 575 had subcutaneous mastectomy. Seven breast cancers were observed in the prophylactic mastectomy group, and all of these occurred in women who had undergone subcutaneous mastectomy, suggesting superiority of total mastectomy to subcutaneous mastectomy as a prophylactic procedure, although this difference was not statistically significant owing to the small number of events. However, in spite of the methodologic problems inherent in its retrospective design, the study of Hartmann and colleagues provides useful information for counseling patients about the magnitude of risk reduction provided by prophylactic mastectomy.[17]

As genetic testing for *BRCA1* and *BRCA2* mutations has become more widespread, the question of the efficacy of prophylactic mastectomy in this population has attracted a great deal of attention. Because the predisposition mutations are present in all cells, and it is clear that even the most technically perfect prophylactic mastectomy leaves behind microscopic amounts of breast tissue, there was concern that prophylactic mastectomy might not provide a high level of risk reduction for women at risk on the basis of a genetic mutation. Several studies are now available that offer some reassurance about the efficacy of the procedure in gene carriers. Hartmann and colleagues revisited the study population at the Mayo Clinic, described above, in order to identify *BRCA1* or *BRCA2* mutation carriers among those who underwent prophylactic mastectomy.[22] Out of the 214 women in the high-risk group, 176 were recontacted and consented to be tested for the presence of a *BRCA1* or *BRCA2* mutation. Twenty-six mutation carriers were identified, 18 with known deleterious mutations and 8 with mutations of unclear clinical significance. There were no breast cancers detected in these 26 patients after a median follow-up of 13.4 years. Testing for *BRCA1* and *BRCA2* mutations was also attempted in the 3 patients who developed breast cancer after prophylactic mastectomy. One of the 3 women was tested and found not to have a mutation. The other 2 patients were deceased. However, in one case, the patient's mother, who had ovarian cancer, was tested, and no mutation was identified. Thus, her daughter was presumed to be mutation free. The authors analyzed breast cancer risk reduction from prophylactic mastectomy as if the remaining deceased, untested patient who developed breast cancer following prophylactic mastectomy was a mutation carrier, as well as if she was not. If this patient was presumed to be a mutation carrier, the observed risk reduction after prophylactic mastectomy in *BRCA1* or *BRCA2* mutation carriers was 89.5%, whereas if she was mutation free, the risk reduction reached 100%. Although the total number of *BRCA1* or *BRCA2* mutations identified was small, the substantial length of follow-up in this study supports the efficacy of prophylactic mastectomy as an acceptable preventive strategy for the carriers of these genetic mutations.

A recent study from the Netherlands addressed the efficacy of prophylactic mastectomy in a cohort of *BRCA1* or *BRCA2* mutation carriers followed prospectively.[23] In this group of 139 asymptomatic women, 76 underwent bilateral prophylactic mastectomy (performed as a total mastectomy) and 63 elected to undergo surveillance consisting of monthly breast self-exam, clinical breast exam biannually, and yearly mammography. The two groups of women had similar characteristics. The median age of women undergoing prophylactic mastectomy (35.8 years) was slightly lower than that of women opting for follow-up (39.9 years), but this difference was not statistically significant. The rate of premenopausal prophylactic oophorectomy was 58% in the surgery group compared with 38% in the surveillance group (p = .03). After a mean duration of follow-up of 2.9 years (219 woman-years) in the prophylactic surgery group, no breast cancers were observed (Figure 16-1). The mean follow-up was 3 years (190 woman-years) in the group undergoing regular surveillance, and 8 breast cancers developed during that interval. All of the cancers occurred in *BRCA1* mutation carriers, a yearly incidence of 2.5%. After adjustment for menopausal status, the reduction in cancer risk in the mastectomy group remained statistically significant. All 8 breast cancers in the surveillance group were of ductal histology, and although 6 tumors were 2 cm or less in size, 4 patients had node-positive disease, with one patient having 6 involved axillary lymph nodes.

This study indicates that bilateral prophylactic mastectomy in mutation carriers results in a signif-

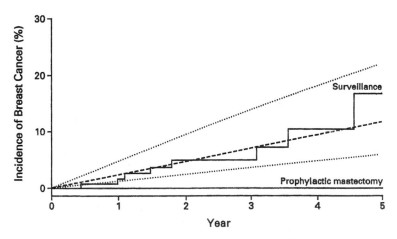

Figure 16-1 Actuarial estimate of breast cancer incidence in *BRCA1* or *BRCA2* mutation carriers following prophylactic mastectomy or during surveillance. The dotted lines indicate the 95% confidence intervals for the occurrence of cancer during surveillance.[23] Reproduced with permission from Meijers-Heijboer H et al.[23]

TABLE 16-3 Efficacy of Prophylactic Mastectomy in
Primary and Secondary Breast Cancer Risk Reduction

Author	Population	Number of Patients	Follow-up	Risk Reduction, % (95% CI)
McDonnell et al[7]	Breast cancer patients undergoing contralateral mastectomy	745	Median 10 y	94.9 (89.9–97.8)
Hartmann et al[17]	Women with a family history of breast cancer	639	Median 14 y	High risk: 92.0 (76.6–98.3) Moderate risk 89.5 (73–97)
Hartmann et al[22]	BRCA1 or BRCA2 mutation carriers	26	Median 13.4 y	89.5–100 (41.4–100)
Meijers-Heijboer et al[23]	BRCA1 or BRCA2 mutation carriers	139	Mean 3 y	100 (70–100)

icant reduction of breast cancer risk with short-term follow-up. However, the follow-up period of only 3 years is a limitation of the study, and the magnitude of risk reduction after longer follow-up remains to be determined. Additionally, the impact of the greater number of oophorectomies in the prophylactic mastectomy group on breast cancer incidence is difficult to quantify. In spite of these limitations, the results of this study, coupled with the data from Hartmann and colleagues,[22] indicate that prophylactic mastectomy is effective for both short- and long-term risk reduction in women with genetic predisposition mutations. The data on the efficacy of prophylactic mastectomy are summarized in Table 16-3.

Psychological Impact

Relatively little data on the psychological sequelae of prophylactic mastectomy are available to inform physicians or women at risk about noncancer outcomes of the procedure. Borgen and colleagues established a voluntary registry for women who had undergone bilateral prophylactic mastectomy by publicizing the registry in a variety of magazines.[24] The 370 respondents were invited to complete a mail-in questionnaire regarding their prophylactic surgery. The average age of the respondents at the time of surgery was 45.5 years, and the mean interval since surgery was 14.8 years. The population was 76% Caucasian. Only 5% of women reported regrets about having the surgery. Physician- rather than patient-initiated discussion of prophylactic surgery was the factor most strongly associated with

regrets about undergoing the procedure, with 7.5% of the 255 women who stated that their physician initiated the discussion of surgery reporting regret compared with 2% of those who introduced the topic themselves ($p < .05$). Age at the time of surgery, the use of breast reconstruction, the presence of a family history of breast cancer, and the use of preoperative psychological counseling did not correlate with regret about the procedure. As a follow-up to this study, 19 of the 21 women expressing significant regret after prophylactic mastectomy were contacted, and a structured telephone interview was conducted by a psychologist or psychiatrist.[25] Severe emotional trauma and a lack of postoperative psychological support, complications of surgery and reconstruction, dissatisfaction with the cosmetic outcome of the procedure, and phantom pain were the most common reasons for major regrets.

A more detailed study of overall psychological and social well-being and long-term satisfaction after prophylactic mastectomy was reported by Frost and colleagues.[26] They contacted 609 women who had undergone bilateral prophylactic mastectomy between 1960 and 1993 and were cancer free. Ninety-four percent ($n = 572$) completed the study questionnaire at a mean of 14.5 years after surgery. Seventy percent of the women surveyed reported being satisfied or very satisfied with the outcome of the procedure, 19% were dissatisfied or very dissatisfied, and 11% were neutral. Women cited physician advice (72%), a family history of breast cancer (68%), and nodular breasts (69%) as the three most common reasons that surgery was performed.

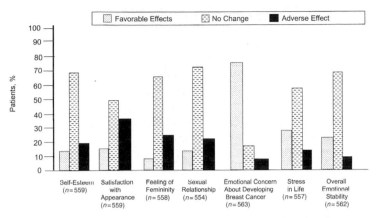

Figure 16-2 Psychological outcomes of prophylactic mastectomy. Reproduced with permission from Frost M H et al.[26]

Emotional concern about developing breast cancer was reported to be reduced after prophylactic mastectomy by 74%. Little change or a favorable impact on a variety of psychological outcomes was reported by the majority of respondents (Figure 16-2). Somewhat surprisingly, 64% reported no change or an improvement in their appearance. Favorable responses to the psychological questions were not associated with age at the time of surgery, level of breast cancer risk, length of follow-up, or simple versus subcutaneous mastectomy. The most common problems reported by those who were dissatisfied with the procedure were concerns about breast implants, adverse body image, and insufficient information or support.

Hatcher and colleagues conducted a prospective study of 143 women who were offered bilateral prophylactic mastectomy; 79 chose to have the surgery and 64 declined.[27] All participants had an initial interview shortly after they were offered surgery with follow-up interviews at 6 and 18 months. Psychological morbidity, as measured by a validated questionnaire, decreased significantly over time among those undergoing surgery and was unchanged in those declining surgery. Anxiety also declined significantly over time in those undergoing surgery. No significant differences in body image and sexual activity were reported before and after surgery.

This work, coupled with that of Frost and colleagues[26] and Borgen and colleagues,[24] would suggest that prophylactic mastectomy is an extremely well-tolerated procedure with minimal psychological morbidity. However, this conclusion ignores the fact that women who undergo surgery are self-selected and may have different baseline personality traits than those who refuse the procedure. It also does not address the acceptability of prophylactic mastectomy to the entire population of women at high risk for breast cancer development. In the study of Hatcher and colleagues, women who declined surgery were found to be significantly more prone to anxiety than those who accepted surgery.[27] In addition, those accepting surgery had significantly higher scores for using problem-focused coping than those who declined, whereas those who declined were more likely to use detachment as a coping mechanism. Only 10% of decliners felt that the development of breast cancer was inevitable, compared with 32% of those opting for surgery. Women undergoing surgery were also more likely to have had a previous breast biopsy (43% vs 19%; $p < .001$).

Stefanek and colleagues also examined factors associated with the decision to undergo prophylactic mastectomy using a group of 164 women at increased risk owing to a family history of breast cancer.[28] In this cohort, 58 were not interested in prophylactic mastectomy, 92 expressed interest but decided not to have the procedure, and 14 had prophylactic mastectomy. Age, number of affected first-degree relatives, Gail Model risk score, depression, and belief in the ability to prevent breast cancer or detect the disease early did not differ among groups. Women in the prophylactic mastectomy group had a significantly higher level of worry about breast cancer than those in the other groups. Although objective levels of breast cancer risk did not vary, women in the prophylactic mastectomy group felt that they had a significantly higher level of risk than those in the no-interest group (59.2% at 10 years vs 36.8%; $p < .05$). In all the groups, women estimated their level of risk to be 10 times higher than the level of risk predicted by the Gail Model, emphasizing the importance of quantitative risk assessment.

Choice of the Operative Approach

In the past, the majority of prophylactic procedures were subcutaneous mastectomies, done with or without reconstruction. This procedure is usually performed through an inframammary incision; it entails the removal of the majority of the breast tissue, whereas the nipple-areolar complex along with some underlying ductal tissue is preserved. The preservation of the nipple, in combination with the thicker skin flaps characteristic of subcutaneous mastectomy, is felt to offer an esthetic advantage over total mastectomy. However, subcutaneous mastectomy may leave a significant amount of breast tissue on the skin flaps or in the axilla.

Goldman and Goldwyn performed bilateral subcutaneous mastectomies on 6 female cadavers and then biopsied the tissue remaining in the area of the surgery.[29] In all 12 cases, residual breast tissue was present beneath the nipple-areolar complex. In 8 of the 12 cases, residual breast tissue was present in 2 or more additional areas. The absence of subcutaneous fat beneath the nipple-areolar complex mandates leaving behind some breast tissue with its blood supply to maintain the viability of the nipple and areola (Figure 16-3). In addition, it may be difficult to remove breast tissue to the level of the clavicle or in the axillary tail of Spence through an inframammary incision, particularly in women with large breasts (Figure 16-4). Multiple reports of breast cancer occurring after subcutaneous mastectomy have been published.[15,17,30,31]

Total mastectomy involves removal of all the apparent breast tissue including the nipple-areola complex. If mastectomy is being performed without reconstruction, a transverse elliptical incision, which incorporates the nipple-areolar complex and the excess skin of the breast, is used. When immediate breast reconstruction is to be performed, a skin-sparing approach is used with excision of the nipple-areolar complex only and incision of the medial and lateral breast skin to provide exposure

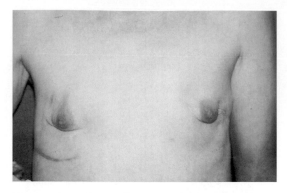

Figure 16-3 Chest wall appearance after bilateral prophylactic subcutaneous mastectomy without reconstruction. A significant amount of breast tissue is left behind to maintain viability of the nipple-areolar complex. A 0.5-cm cancer was present in the residual tissue in the right breast.

as needed (Figure 16-5). The skin flaps are raised superiorly to the inferior border of the clavicle, inferiorly to the superior aspect of the rectus sheath, medially to the lateral border of the sternum, and laterally to the latissimus dorsi muscle, as would be done in a therapeutic mastectomy. The thickness of the flaps will vary with the amount of subcutaneous fat but should be the same as would be used for a therapeutic mastectomy. The posterior extent of the surgery is the fascia of the pectoralis major muscle, which may be preserved in order to facilitate implant or tissue expander breast reconstruction. Careful attention is paid to the removal of the axillary tail of Spence. This is accomplished by following the latissimus dorsi muscle edge proximally until the axillary investing fascia is entered at the lateral aspect of the dissection. The medial portion of the tail of the breast is freed from the pectoralis major and minor muscles until the axillary investing fascia is entered medially. At this point the specimen is transected with care being taken to preserve the lowest branch of the intercostobrachial nerve. Although no formal attempt to perform an axillary dissection is made, a few of the low axillary nodes are often removed with this procedure.

Although total mastectomy offers a more complete removal of the breast tissue at risk than subcutaneous mastectomy, breast cancer following a total mastectomy has also been reported.[7] Careful attention to the creation of thin skin flaps, as would

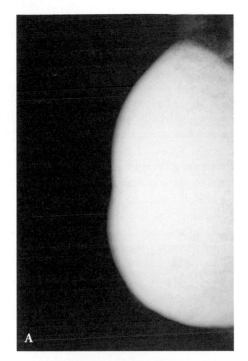

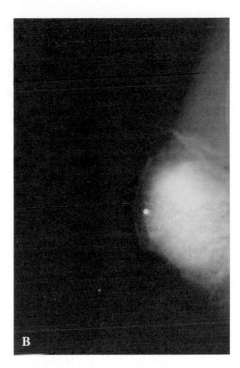

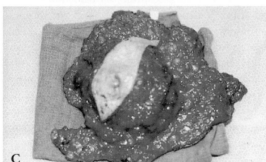

Figure 16-4 *A*, Mammographic appearance of subcutaneous mastectomy followed by implant reconstruction. *B*, Mammogram of the same breast on a special view where the implant is pushed back — a substantial amount of residual breast tissue is evident. *C*, Completion mastectomy in a patient who had previously undergone subcutaneous mastectomy with implant reconstruction. A large amount of residual breast tissue is evident at the periphery of the implant.

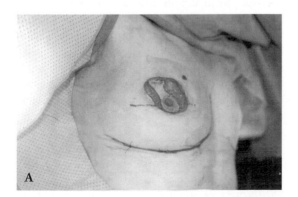

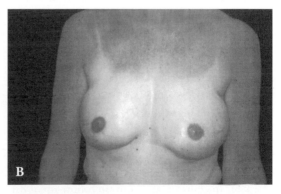

Figure 16-5 *A*, Incision used for a skin-sparing mastectomy. The dotted lines indicate extensions of the incision if needed for exposure. *B*, Final appearance of a woman who underwent bilateral prophylactic total mastectomy using a skin-sparing approach, with an immediate transverse myocutaneous rectus abdominus (TRAM) flap reconstruction.

be done for a therapeutic mastectomy, helps to minimize that risk. A study of biopsy of the skin flaps after bilateral prophylactic total mastectomy in 5 patients revealed that the most common sites of residual breast tissue were the lower skin flap (2 patients), the pectoralis fascia (1 patient), and the axilla (1 patient).[32]

PROPHYLACTIC OOPHORECTOMY

Exposure to ovarian hormones is a risk factor for the development of breast carcinoma.[33] Additionally, in women with *BRCA1* or *BRCA2* mutations there is an elevated level of risk for the development of both breast and ovarian carcinoma. In this section the efficacy of bilateral prophylactic oophorectomy for breast cancer risk reduction will be reviewed.

Early cessation of ovarian function, whether physiologic or secondary to surgery, is known to reduce breast cancer risk in the general population.[34] Because of the reproductive, psychological, and physiologic ramifications of bilateral oophorectomy in premenopausal women, this approach has not been adopted as a general risk-reduction strategy. In recent years, the utility of bilateral prophylactic oophorectomy for women at high risk owing to *BRCA1* and *BRCA2* mutations has been examined in several studies.

Rebbeck and colleagues performed a retrospective study of the efficacy of bilateral prophylactic oophorectomy in a cohort of known *BRCA1* mutation carriers with no personal history of breast or ovarian carcinoma.[35] This cohort of 43 women was assembled from five North American centers and was compared with an age-matched control group of 79 *BRCA1* mutation carriers without the diagnosis of breast or ovarian cancer who did not undergo prophylactic surgery. The mean age of the surgical subjects at the time of prophylactic oophorectomy was 39.4 years (range 22 to 63 years), whereas that of the control group at the time of the age-matched surgical subject's surgery was 35.3 years (range 17 to 65 years). After a mean follow-up of 9.6 years after oophorectomy, 10 breast cancers were identified in the surgical group (23.3%). In contrast, after a mean follow-up of 8.1 years, 30 breast cancers (38.0%) were diagnosed in the control group. In this study, bilateral prophylactic oophorectomy was associated with a statisti-

cally significant reduction in the risk of breast cancer development (RR = 0.53; 95% CI 0.33–0.84). Although the information regarding the menopausal status of all the surgical subjects was not available, 6 women in this cohort were older than 50 years of age at the time of prophylactic oophorectomy and were considered to be perimenopausal or postmenopausal (mean age at the time of surgery, 56.7 years; range, 52 to 63 years). If these 6 women along with their 10 age-matched controls were removed from the statistical analysis, the estimated relative risk of breast cancer development in the surgical group was found to be 0.57 (95% CI 0.36–0.92). In the small subset of women undergoing oophorectomy after 50 years of age (*n* = 6), no reduction in breast cancer incidence was observed. The benefit of oophorectomy in the subset of parous women was similar to that of the whole cohort (RR = 0.49; 95% CI 0.30–0.79).

This study also evaluated the effects of post-oophorectomy hormone replacement therapy (HRT) on the risk of breast cancer.[35] Information on hormone use was known or inferred for 32 of 43 surgical subjects (74%) and 67 of 79 controls (85%). Twenty-two of the 32 evaluable surgical subjects (69%) had any hormone exposure after the prophylactic oophorectomy, whereas only 4 of 67 controls (6%) had ever used hormones. The use of hormones following bilateral prophylactic oophorectomy had no significant effect on breast cancer risk reduction in a multivariate Cox model (*p* = .237).

This study was the first to examine the role of prophylactic oophorectomy in breast cancer risk reduction in *BRCA1* mutation carriers. In spite of a relatively small sample size, the findings indicate that bilateral prophylactic oophorectomy appears to play a protective role in individuals with *BRCA1* mutations, and the protective effects are evident only if the surgery is performed in women younger than 50 years of age. Although the study suggests that these beneficial effects are not negated by the use of postoperative HRT, this conclusion is based on limited data and requires verification.

In a larger follow-up study, Rebbeck and colleagues reported the outcome of bilateral oophorectomy in breast and ovarian cancer risk reduction in 551 *BRCA1* or *BRCA2* mutation carriers, identified from 11 North American and European registries of prophylactic oophorectomy.[36] The study included 259 women who had undergone prophylactic oophorectomy at a mean age of 42.0 years (range 21.2 to 74.8) and an age-matched control group of 292 women without any prophylactic surgical intervention (mean age 40.9 years at the time of surgical subjects oophorectomy, range 19.6 to 79.1). The surgical and the control groups were similar in their parity (p = .10) and in the distribution of BRCA1 and BRCA2 mutations (p = .49 and p = .82, respectively). However, the surgical subjects were much more likely to have received postoophorectomy HRT for the relief of menopausal symptoms (78.8% vs 21.8%, p < .001).

Two hundred and forty-one women (99 women in the surgical group and 142 women in the control group) were evaluated for breast cancer risk reduction. After a mean follow-up of 10.7 years, 21 women in the surgical group had developed breast cancer (21.2%) and 60 women in the control group were diagnosed with breast cancer at a mean follow-up of 11.9 years (42.3%). This is a 53% reduction in the risk of breast cancer development (RR = 0.47; 95% CI 0.29–0.77). There was a significant difference in patient age between the surgical subjects and the controls at the time of breast cancer diagnosis (52.5 years vs 46.7 years; p = .03). However, the difference in the mean length of time to diagnosis of breast cancer in the surgical versus the control group was not statistically significant (11.4 years vs 8.0 years; p = .09). This study also demonstrates a 96% reduction in the risk of ovarian cancer as a result of prophylactic oophorectomy.

This larger study confirms the beneficial effects of bilateral prophylactic oophorectomy on ovarian and breast cancer risk reduction in women with BRCA1 or BRCA2 mutations.[36] Rebbeck and colleagues recommend that prophylactic oophorectomy be performed once childbearing is completed and before the age of 50 and suggested that HRT can be safely prescribed until the age of 50 if needed to alleviate menopausal symptoms.[36] The authors appear to view the ovarian cancer risk reduction as the most compelling indication for prophylactic oophorectomy owing to the limitations of current screening techniques for ovarian cancer.

Further support for the benefit of oophorectomy in breast cancer risk reduction comes from the work of Narod and colleagues.[37] They studied 1,243 women with invasive cancer and a known BRCA1 and BRCA2 mutation. The 209 patients with bilateral cancer were matched to 384 unilateral disease controls. Premenopausal oophorectomy was associated with an odds ratio of 0.31 (95% CI 0.15–0.67) for the development of a contralateral breast cancer.

Kauff and colleagues conducted a prospective study of the benefits of prophylactic bilateral salpingo-oophorectomy in 170 BRCA1 or BRCA2 mutation carriers 35 years of age or older to address the role of this intervention in breast and ovarian cancer risk reduction.[38] Sixty-nine of 98 women in the prophylactic oophorectomy group (70%) had a personal history of breast cancer, and 45 women among the 72 controls had a prior diagnosis of breast cancer (62%; p = .32). At a mean follow-up of 24.2 months after surgery, 3 breast cancers had been diagnosed in the surgical group (3.1%) and 8 in the control group (11.1%), a risk reduction of 68% (p = .07). In a Cox proportional hazards model, the hazard ratio for breast cancer after surgery was reduced to 0.32 (95% CI 0.08–1.20), and that for breast or BRCA-related gynecologic cancer to 0.25 (95% CI 0.08–0.74). Five years after surgery, 94% of those undergoing oophorectomy were projected to be cancer free compared with 69% in the surveillance group (p = .006) (Figure 16-6). This study also quantified the complication rate of salpingo-oophorectomy. Four complications (5%) were observed including one bladder perforation, one uterine perforation, one early postoperative bowel obstruction, and one conversion of a laparoscopic procedure to a laparotomy which was followed by a wound infection. No complications occurred in the women who had a hysterectomy at the time of the salpingo-oophorectomy (n = 11) or in the 7 women whose uterine surgery status was unknown.

THE ROLE OF PROPHYLACTIC MASTECTOMY AND OOPHORECTOMY COMBINED

A number of decision analysis models have addressed the effects of prophylactic mastectomy and/or prophylactic oophorectomy on life-expectancy gains, as well as their impact on the quality of life of an individual at high risk for breast cancer development. In a study by Schrag and colleagues,[39] hypothetical cohorts of women with a BRCA1 or BRCA2 mutation were designed based on the Markov model.[40] The cohorts were defined

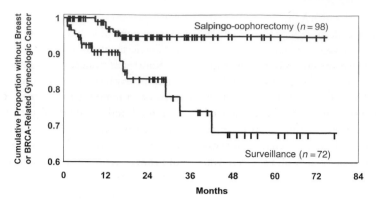

Figure 16-6 Actuarial estimates of the time to breast carcinoma or other *BRCA*-related gynecologic malignancies following prophylactic oophorectomy versus regular surveillance for breast or ovarian cancer. The actuarial mean times to the development of cancer are significantly different (p = .006), and the hazard ratio for cancer development is 0.25. Reproduced with permission from Kauff ND et al.[38]

according to their age and level of cancer risk and evaluated annually for the incidence of new breast and/or ovarian cancers and cancer mortality. Estimates of 85% breast cancer risk reduction from prophylactic mastectomy and 50% ovarian cancer risk reduction from prophylactic oophorectomy were chosen, and no reduction in breast cancer risk was attributed to prophylactic oophorectomy. In *BRCA1* and *BRCA2* mutation carriers, 80% of new breast cancers were assumed to be node-negative, and none to be associated with distant metastases. In contrast, in the general population 52% of breast cancers were assumed to be node-negative at the time of diagnosis, 43% to be node-positive, and 5% metastatic. The cohorts were divided into three hypothetical levels of risk: level A, 40% risk of breast cancer, 5% risk of ovarian cancer; level B, 60% risk of breast cancer, 20% risk of ovarian cancer; level C, 85% risk of breast cancer, 40% risk of ovarian cancer. Statistical analysis was also subdivided based on age at the time of prophylactic surgery (30, 40, 50, and 60 years). The authors calculated that a 30-year-old *BRCA1* or *BRCA2* mutation carrier would gain on average from 2.9 to 5.3 years of life expectancy from prophylactic mastectomy and between 0.3 and 1.7 years from prophylactic oophorectomy. The magnitude of gain in life expectancy was greater with increasing levels of risk and declined with age at the time of prophylactic surgery. Minimal benefit was noted for a 60-year-old mutation carrier undergoing prophylactic surgery.

A comprehensive evaluation of the life-expectancy gains, quality of life, and cost-effective-ness of prophylactic mastectomy and oophorectomy in high-risk patients was done by Grann and colleagues.[41] In this decision analysis, a Markov model was used to estimate the outcomes of four preventive strategies: prophylactic oophorectomy, prophylactic mastectomy, prophylactic oophorectomy and mastectomy, or surveillance, in *BRCA1* or *BRCA2* mutation carriers.

The main outcomes considered were good health, breast cancer, ovarian cancer, and death. The hypothetical cohort of 30-year-old *BRCA1* or *BRCA2* mutation carriers was followed for 50 years, and for every follow-up year with each preventive strategy, the risk of developing breast cancer, ovarian cancer, remaining well, or dying from any cause was calculated. Breast cancer risks of 40, 56, and 85% and ovarian cancer risks of 6, 16, and 63% were studied. The risk reduction from prophylactic mastectomy was assumed to be 90% and from oophorectomy 50%. Breast cancer risk was not altered by oophorectomy. In the hypothetical cohort undergoing surveillance, the incidence of node-negative breast cancer was presumed to be 80%. The quality of life results were expressed in quality-adjusted life-years (QALY).

This study found that among 30-year-old *BRCA1* and *BRCA2* mutation carriers the greatest benefit was derived from the combination of prophylactic mastectomy and oophorectomy in the women with high-penetrance mutation phenotypes. Life expectancy was estimated to be prolonged by 3.3 years in the low-risk and by 6.0 years in the high-risk women who had undergone both prophylactic procedures at 30 years of age. Mastectomy alone prolonged life by 2.8 to 3.4 years. In the cohort with the highest BRCA mutation penetrance, 1.9 QALY were gained by both prophylactic surgeries, and minimal or negative QALY in the lower risk groups. The increases in life expectancy in this study were very similar to those reported by Schrag and colleagues in spite of differences in the models used.[39,41] However, Grann and colleagues demonstrated that quality-adjusted survival gains were notably less than life-expectancy gains across all BRCA1 and BRCA2 mutation penetrance groups, emphasizing that surveillance or chemoprevention are rational alternatives to prophylactic surgery even in high-risk women.[41] An update to this decision analysis, which also included chemoprevention with tamoxifen as a management alternative, suggested that in BRCA1 and BRCA2 mutation carriers, chemoprevention, prophylactic surgery, or the combination may offer both survival and quality-adjusted survival benefits.[42] It also confirmed that the magnitude of benefit from preventive strategies diminishes with increasing age in a woman at risk.

Another decision analysis compared chemoprevention with tamoxifen or other hormonal agents with prophylactic bilateral mastectomy and oophorectomy.[43] In this model a simulated cohort of 30-year-old BRCA1 and BRCA2 mutation carriers was divided into groups to undergo prophylactic mastectomy; prophylactic oophorectomy; a combination of both procedures; or chemoprevention with tamoxifen, raloxifene, or oral contraceptives. The study results were consistent with the earlier study by Grann and colleagues, demonstrating a greater survival benefit from both prophylactic surgeries versus prophylactic mastectomy or prophylactic oophorectomy alone (4.3, 3.4, and 0.9 years, respectively).[41] Chemoprevention with tamoxifen and raloxifene resulted in survival gains of 1.6 and 2.2 years, respectively. However, chemoprevention offered better quality-adjusted survival compared to prophylactic surgery, even if the surgery was delayed until the age of 40 or 50.

Secondary breast cancer prevention in breast cancer patients who are BRCA1 or BRCA2 mutation carriers was examined in another decision analysis, involving prophylactic surgery alone or in combination with 5 years of tamoxifen.[44] In this study surveillance was compared with the following

seven prevention strategies: tamoxifen, contralateral mastectomy, prophylactic oophorectomy, prophylactic oophorectomy and contralateral mastectomy, contralateral mastectomy and tamoxifen, prophylactic oophorectomy and tamoxifen, or both surgeries and tamoxifen. The main outcome measure was total and incremental gain in life expectancy for each prevention strategy based on the level of penetrance of the BRCA mutation. The outcomes of primary cancer in these BRCA mutation carriers were assumed to be similar to those in women with sporadic breast cancer, and the stage and survival data were derived from the 1998 Oxford metaanalysis and the SEER data.[45] In this model, primary breast cancer mortality was presumed to be 12% at 10 years and 17% at 20 years for node-negative disease; for node-positive disease the presumed mortality was 26% at 10 years and 35% at 20 years. The model also assumed that there were no additional breast cancer–related deaths more than 20 years postdiagnosis. Cumulative contralateral breast cancer incidence was assumed to be 65% for high-penetrance, 43% for moderate-penetrance, and 24% for low-penetrance mutations. Ovarian cancer cumulative incidence was estimated to be 40, 16, and 6% for high-, moderate-, and low-penetrance mutations, respectively. The estimated contralateral breast cancer risk reduction in this model was 90% from prophylactic contralateral mastectomy, up to 50% from bilateral prophylactic oophorectomy and 47% from tamoxifen.

The statistical model showed the greatest benefit from secondary-cancer prevention strategies in breast cancer patients with high-penetrance BRCA1/2 mutations. The most effective preventive strategy in this study was prophylactic contralateral mastectomy combined with bilateral prophylactic oophorectomy and tamoxifen. The life expectancy gains for a 30-year-old with this approach were 4.4 years if the initial tumor was node-negative and 3.3 years for a node-positive tumor. Corresponding gains in life expectancy for a woman age 50 at diagnosis were 1.8 and 1.4 years, respectively.

This model demonstrates that there might be a select population of very young (age 30 years) high-risk breast cancer patients with high-penetrance BRCA1/2 mutations, who would benefit from a combination of surgical and pharmacologic strategies for secondary breast cancer prevention. However, our ability to identify individuals with high penetrance genes clinically is limited, making it more appropriate to discuss the range of potential benefit that could be expected from this strategy.

SELECTION FOR PROPHYLACTIC SURGERY

Provider Attitudes

There is no consensus on the level of risk that is sufficient to warrant a discussion of prophylactic mastectomy. Studies of physician attitudes toward the procedure show considerable variation on the basis of specialty. Houn and colleagues surveyed general surgeons (n = 219), plastic surgeons (n = 53), and gynecologists (n = 440) practicing in Maryland in 1992 regarding their attitudes toward prophylactic mastectomy.[46] The response rate was 51.8%, and the responding general surgeons were significantly older and more likely to be male than the respondents from other specialties. Only 44% of respondents agreed with the statement "Prophylactic mastectomy has a role in the management of high-risk women." But significant differences were noted by specialty, with 85% of plastic surgeons endorsing the statement compared with 38% of gynecologists and 47% of general surgeons. The mean threshold of risk at which surgeons stated they would recommend bilateral prophylactic mastectomy was 51% for general surgeons, 41% for plastic surgeons, and 54% for gynecologists (p = .008). Male respondents had a significantly lower threshold than female respondents (52% vs 58%; p = .005). These results were obtained prior to the widespread availability of *BRCA1* and *BRCA2* testing in clinical practice and before documentation

of the efficacy of prophylactic mastectomy. Prophylactic mastectomy was an acceptable management option for fewer than half of the physician respondents and only for women with risk levels consistent with genetic mutation. In a recent survey of physicians in France (47% female), only 236 of 700 respondents (33.7%) felt that prophylactic mastectomy should be performed in mutation carriers, and only 10.6% felt this was an acceptable intervention in women under 35 years of age.[47] In a 1998 survey in the United States, 12% of nurse practitioners (n = 143) and 33.7% of physicians (n = 296) said they would recommend prophylactic mastectomy to a woman testing positive for a *BRCA1* mutation.[48] General surgeons (50%) and oncologists (41%) were more likely than family practitioners (21%) or obstetrician-gynecologists (27%) to recommend the procedure. This may be due to the increased familiarity of surgeons and oncologists with cancer risk and prophylactic mastectomy in mutation carriers, or may be a reflection of fundamental differences in attitude among healthcare providers in different specialties. A survey of the National Society of Genetic Counselors Special Interest Group in Cancer in 1998 found that only 25% of this group would have a prophylactic mastectomy at age 35.[49] Respondents were 93% female, 88% were under age 50, and only 4% had an MD or PhD degree. The data on acceptability of prophylactic mastectomy to healthcare providers is summarized in Table 16-4.

Attitudes of Women at Risk

Although the high level of breast cancer risk in women with mutations of *BRCA1* and *BRCA2* seems to many healthcare providers to justify a dis-

TABLE 16-4 Acceptability of Prophylactic Mastectomy to Healthcare Providers

Author	Year	Group	Number	% Recommending Prophylactic Mastectomy
Houn et al[46]	1995	Maryland physicians	369	44*
Eisinger et al[47]	2000	French physicians	700	34
Geller et al[48]	1998	Maryland physicians	296	34
		Nurse practitioners	143	12
Matloff et al[49]	2000	Genetic counselors	163	25†

*Recommendation for women at increased risk for unspecified reasons. All other responses specific to *BRCA1* and *BRCA2* mutation carriers.

†Respondents were asked whether they would have prophylactic mastectomy, not whether they would recommend it to others.

TABLE 16-5 Acceptability of Prophylactic Surgery to Women at Increased Risk

Author, Year	Group	% Accepting	
		PM	PO
Geller et al,[48] 1998	US women < 50 years with first-degree relative with premenopausal breast cancer	5	—
Wagner et al,[50] 2000	Austrian *BRCA1* and *BRCA2* carriers	21	50
Lerman et al,[51] 1996	Unaffected American *BRCA1* and *BRCA2* carriers	17	33
Meijers-Heijboer et al,[52] 2000	Unaffected Dutch *BRCA1* and *BRCA2* carriers	51	64
Meiser et al,[53] 2000	Australian women attending familial cancer clinics	19	—
Eisinger et al,[54] 1998	French women attending cancer genetics clinics	11* (4)	27† (16)
Stefanek et al,[55] 1999	US women with affected first-degree relative	30	—
	US women, no family history of breast cancer	22	—

PM = prophylactic mastectomy; PO = prophylactic oophorectomy.

*Proportion accepting mastectomy plus oophorectomy. Number in parenthesis indicates number accepting mastectomy alone.

†Proportion accepting oophorectomy plus mastectomy. Number in parenthesis indicates number accepting oophorectomy alone.

cussion of prophylactic mastectomy, interest in prophylactic mastectomy among women with mutations is relatively low (Table 16-5).[48,50–55] Wagner and colleagues[50] and Lerman and colleagues[51] found that only 21 and 17% of proven mutation carriers would undergo prophylactic mastectomy. Wagner and colleagues, who studied mutation carriers with and without a prior personal history of breast cancer, found that acceptance of prophylactic mastectomy was higher in women with a personal history of breast cancer (29%) than in unaffected carriers (8%).[50] Two studies have examined the acceptability of prophylactic mastectomy in women attending cancer genetics clinics who were surveyed prior to their consultation.[53,54] Meiser and colleagues,[53] studying Australian women, found that their acceptance of prophylactic mastectomy (19%) was similar to that of proven gene carriers reported by Wagner and colleagues[50] and Lerman and colleagues.[51] Eisinger and colleagues found that only 4% of French women considered prophylactic mastectomy alone an acceptable option, although an additional 11% would consider mastectomy plus oophorectomy.[54] This is in marked contrast to the 51% of Dutch women with proven mutations who would undergo mastectomy, suggesting that cultural differences may be responsible for some of the variation in the use of prophylactic surgery.[52] Stefanek and colleagues found that the acceptance of prophylactic mastectomy was similar among women randomly selected from gynecologic office practices who had no family history of breast cancer and women at increased risk of breast cancer followed in specialty breast clinics, suggesting that the intervention is inherently unacceptable to a majority of women, regardless of their level of breast cancer risk.[55] In the four studies where women were questioned about both prophylactic mastectomy and oophorectomy, prophylactic oophorectomy was uniformly found to be the preferred intervention.[50–52,54] Between 27 and 64% of those questioned stated that they were willing to undergo oophorectomy.

Practical Considerations

Evaluation for prophylactic surgery begins with an assessment of the magnitude of risk and the factors responsible for risk. In women at increased risk owing to a family history suggestive of genetic predisposition, a referral for genetic counseling and a discussion of the merits of genetic testing (see Chapter 2) should be made prior to serious consideration of prophylactic surgery. Although the information discussed in the previous section suggests that a positive genetic test does not uniformly make prophylactic mastectomy an acceptable option, a negative test for an individual in a family of mutation carriers has the potential to prevent unnecessary surgery. In addition, clear benefit for prophylactic oophorectomy as a risk-reducing strategy has only been shown in mutation carriers, and this approach should be reserved for that group of women.[35–38]

An attempt to provide a numeric estimate of absolute risk in a defined time interval (5 years, 10 years, and lifetime) should be made. Although there are issues with applying Gail Model risk predictions to individuals, rather than populations (discussed in detail in Chapter 1), there is clear evidence that women at increased risk of breast cancer development substantially overestimate their level of risk, and this is a major factor in the decision to undergo prophylactic mastectomy.[27,28,55] The concept of relative risk is generally not well understood by those without formal statistical training and provides little useful information to a woman who is unaware of the baseline incidence of breast cancer in a population.

The risk of breast cancer development must also be distinguished from the risk of breast cancer death, which can conservatively be estimated as one-third of the risk of developing the disease. It is also useful to inform women that about 90% of Stage I cancers and 70% of Stage II and intraductal cancers can be treated with a breast-conserving approach rather than mastectomy.[56] The efficacy of current surveillance strategies for the detection of cancer (see Chapters 7 to 9) should be reviewed, and factors in an individual that might impact on surveillance (extremely nodular dense breasts) discussed. In this discussion it is important to emphasize that meticulous adherence to a surveillance program does not guarantee that cancer will be detected at a favorable stage. In the placebo arm of the NSABP P-1 study, only 28% of the 244 cancers detected were Stage 0, and only 38% of the invasive tumors were 1 cm or less in size, whereas 29% had nodal metastases.[57] This occurred in spite of protocol requirements for clinical breast exams at 6-month intervals and annual mammography. Alternative approaches to risk reduction including prophylactic oophorectomy (for gene carriers), tamoxifen, and participation in clinical research studies should be discussed. Competing risks owing to comorbid conditions should be assessed (see Chapter 6). In particular, for women with a diagnosis of unilateral breast carcinoma this will include an estimate of the risk of breast cancer mortality owing to the existing cancer, and for women with predisposition mutations, the risk of ovarian cancer occurrence and death.

The remainder of the consultation is devoted to a description of what the surgery involves, including a discussion of the anticipated hospital course and recovery period, side effects, and complications. It is important to clearly state that prophylactic mastectomy does not provide 100% protection against the development of breast cancer. The loss of sensation in the breast region secondary to surgery, which is present even after reconstruction, should also be discussed. Because reconstruction is an important component of this surgery, and problems with reconstruction contribute significantly to dissatisfaction after prophylactic mastectomy, consultation with a reconstructive surgeon should take place before a final decision about surgery is made.[24–26] Reconstruction is discussed in detail in Chapter 17.

Finally, the woman should be encouraged to express her particular concerns about both her level of risk and prophylactic surgery. For some women, fear of breast cancer death is the primary issue, whereas for others it is fear of disfigurement. Women are often motivated to seek risk counseling or information about prophylactic mastectomy after a breast cancer diagnosis or death in a family member or friend. This is a decision that should never be made in haste, and the large quantity of information that must be processed often requires multiple office visits. We also recommend psychological counseling as part of the decision-making process. Ultimately, the decision to undergo prophylactic mastectomy is made by a woman who finds her level of breast cancer risk to be unacceptable and feels that surgery is the risk-reduction strategy that best meets her needs.

REFERENCES

1. Lopez MJ, Porter KA. The current role of prophylactic mastectomy. Surg Clin North Am 1996;76: 231–42.
2. Wong JH, Jackson CF, Swanson JS, et al. Analysis of the risk reduction of prophylactic partial mastectomy in Sprague-Dawley rats with 7,12-dimethyl-benzanthracene-induced breast cancer. Surgery 1986;99:67–71.
3. Nelson H, Miller SH, Buck D, et al. Effectiveness of prophylactic mastectomy in the prevention of breast tumors in C3H mice. Plast Reconstr Surg 1989;83:662–9.
4 Baasch M, Nielsen SF, Engholm G, Lund K. Breast cancer incidence subsequent to surgical reduction of the female breast. Br J Cancer 1996;73:961–3.
5 Boice JD Jr, Persson I, Brinton LA, et al. Breast cancer following breast reduction surgery in Sweden. Plast Reconstr Surg 2000;106:755–62.

6. Briton LA, Persson I, Boice JD Jr, et al. Breast cancer risk in relation to amount of tissue removed during breast reduction operations in Sweden. Cancer 2001;91:478–83.

7. McDonnell SK, Schaid DJ, Myers JL, et al. Efficacy of contralateral prophylactic mastectomy in women with a personal and family history of breast cancer. J Clin Oncol 2001;19:3938–43.

8. Anderson DE, Badzioch MD. Bilaterality in familial breast cancer patients. Cancer 1985;56:2092–8.

9. Mamounas EP, Bryant J, Fisher B, et al. Primary breast cancer as a risk factor for subsequent contralateral breast cancer: NSABP experience from nine randomized adjuvant trials [abstract 15]. Breast Cancer Res Treat 1998;50:230.

10. Adami HO, Bergström R, Hansen J. Age at first primary as a determinant of the incidence of bilateral breast cancer. Cumulative and relative risks in a population based case-control study. Cancer 1985; 55:643–7.

11. Habel LA, Moe RE, Daling JR, et al. Risk of contralateral breast cancer among women with carcinoma in situ of the breast. Ann Surg 1997;225: 69–75.

12 Broët P, de la Rochefordière A, Scholl SM, et al. Contralateral breast cancer: annual incidence and risk parameters. J Clin Oncol 1995;13:1578–83.

13. Healey EA, Cook EF, Orav EJ, et al. Contralateral breast cancer: clinical characteristics and impact on prognosis. J Clin Oncol 1993;11:1545–52.

14. Singletary SE, Taylor SH, Guinee VF. Occurrence and prognosis of contralateral carcinoma of the breast. J Am Coll Surg 1994;178:390–6.

15. Pennisi VR, Capozzi A. Subcutaneous mastectomy data: final statistical analysis of 1500 patients. Aesthetic Plast Surg 1989;13:15–21.

16. Ziegler LD, Kroll SS. Primary breast cancer after prophylactic mastectomy. Am J Clin Oncol 1991;14: 451–4.

17. Hartmann LC, Schaid DJ, Woods JE, et al. Efficacy of bilateral prophylactic mastectomy in women with a family history of breast cancer. N Engl J Med 1999;340:77–84.

18. Gail MH, Brinton LA, Byar DP, et al. Projecting individualized probabilities of developing breast cancer for white females who are being examined annually. J Natl Cancer Inst 1989;81:1879–86.

19. Hartmann LC, Sellers TA, Schaid DJ, et al. Clinical options for women at high risk for breast cancer. Surg Clin North Am 1999;79:1189–206.

20. Ford D, Easton DF, Bishop DT, et al. Risks of cancer in BRCA mutation carriers. Lancet 1994;343: 692–5.

21. Hoogerbrugge N, Bult P, de Widt-Leveret LM, et al. High prevalence of premalignant lesions in prophylactically removed breasts from women at heredity risk for breast cancer. J Clin Oncol 2003; 21:41–5.

22. Hartmann LC, Sellers TA, Schaid DJ, et al. Efficacy of bilateral prophylactic mastectomy in BRCA1

and BRCA2 gene mutation carriers. J Natl Cancer Inst 2001;93:1633–7.

23. Meijers-Heijboer H, van Geel B, van Putten W, et al. Breast cancer after prophylactic bilateral mastectomy in women with a BRCA1 or BRCA2 mutation. N Engl J Med 2001;345:159–64.

24. Borgen PI, Hill ADK, Tran KN, et al. Patient regrets after bilateral prophylactic mastectomy. Ann Surg Oncol 1998;5:603–6.

25. Payne DK, Biggs C, Tran KN, et al. Women's regrets after bilateral prophylactic mastectomy. Ann Surg Oncol 2000;7:150–4.

26. Frost MH, Schaid DJ, Sellers TA, et al. Long-term satisfaction and psychological and social function following bilateral prophylactic mastectomy. JAMA 2000;284:319–24.

27. Hatcher MB, Fallowfield L, A'Hern R. The psychological impact of bilateral prophylactic mastectomy: prospective study using questionnaires and semistructured interviews. Br Med J 2001;322: 76–85.

28. Stefanek ME, Helzlsouer KJ, Wilcox PM, Houn F. Predictors of and satisfaction with bilateral prophylactic mastectomy. Prev Med 1995;24:412–9.

29. Goldman LD, Goldwyn RM. Some anatomical considerations of subcutaneous mastectomy. Plast Reconstr Surg 1973;51:501–05.

30. Goodnight JE, Quagliana JM, Morton DL. Failure of subcutaneous mastectomy to prevent the development of breast cancer. J Surg Oncol 1984;26: 198–201.

31. Eldar S, Meguid MM, Beatty JD. Cancer of the breast after prophylactic subcutaneous mastectomy. Am J Surg 1984;148:692–3.

32. Temple WJ, Lindsay RL, Magi E, Urbanski SJ. Technical considerations for prophylactic mastectomy in patients at high risk for breast cancer. Am J Surg 1991;161:413–5.

33. Key TJ, Pike MC. The role of oestrogens and progestagens in the epidemiology and prevention of breast cancer. Eur J Cancer Clin Oncol 1998;24:29–34.

34. Trichopoulous D, MacMahon B, Cole P. Menopause and breast cancer risk. J Natl Cancer Inst 1972; 48:605–13.

35. Rebbeck TR, Levin AM, Eisen A, et al. Breast cancer risk after bilateral prophylactic oophorectomy in BRCA1 mutation carriers. J Natl Cancer Inst 1999; 91:1475–9.

36. Rebbeck TR, Lynch HT, Neuhausen SL, et al. Prophylactic oophorectomy in carriers of BRCA1 or BRCA2 mutations. N Engl J Med 2002;346: 1616–22.

37. Narod SA, Brunet JS, Ghadirian P, et al. Tamoxifen and risk of contralateral breast cancer in BRCA 1 and BRCA 2 mutation carriers: a case-control study. Lancet 2000;356:1876–81.

38. Kauff ND, Satagopan JM, Robson ME, et al. Risk-reducing salpingo-oophorectomy in women with a BRCA1 or BRCA2 mutation. N Engl J Med 2002; 346:1609–15.

39. Schrag D, Kuntz KM, Garber JE, Weeks JC. Decision analysis - effects of prophylactic mastectomy and oophorectomy on life expectancy among women with BRCA1 or BRCA 2 mutations. N Engl J Med 1997;336:1465–71.

40. Sonnenberg FA, Beck JR. Markov models in medical decision making: a practical guide. Med Decis Making 1993;13:322–38.

41. Grann VR, Panageas KS, Whang W, et al. Decision analysis of prophylactic mastectomy and oophorectomy in BRCA1-positive or BRCA2-positive patients. J Clin Oncol 1998;16:979–85.

42. Grann VR, Jacobson JS, Thomason D, et al. Effect of prevention strategies on survival and quality-adjusted survival of women with BRCA1/2 mutations: an updated decision analysis. J Clin Oncol 2002;20:2520–9.

43. Grann VR, Jacobson JS, Whang W, et al. Prevention with tamoxifen or other hormones versus prophylactic surgery in BRCA1/2-positive women: a decision analysis. Cancer J Sci Am 2000;6:13–20.

44. Schrag D, Kuntz KM, Garber JE, Weeks JC. Life expectancy gains from cancer prevention strategies for women with breast cancer and BRCA1 or BRCA2 mutations. JAMA 2000;283:617–24.

45. Early Breast Cancer Trialists' Collaborative Group. Polychemotherapy for early breast cancer: an overview of the randomized trials. Lancet 1998; 352:930–42.

46. Houn F, Helzlsouer KJ, Friedman NB, Stefanek ME. The practice of prophylactic mastectomy: a survey of Maryland Surgeons. Am J Public Health 1995; 85:801–5.

47. Eisinger F, Julian-Reynier C, Sobel H, et al. Acceptability of prophylactic mastectomy in cancer-prone women. JAMA 2000;283:202–3.

48. Geller G, Bernhardt BA, Doksum T, et al. Decision-making about breast cancer susceptability testing: how similar are the attitudes of physicians, nurse practitioners, and at-risk women? J Clin Oncol 1998;16:2868–76.

49. Matloff ET, Shappell H, Brierley K, et al. What would you do? Specialists' perspectives on cancer genetic testing, prophylactic surgery, and insurance discrimination. J Clin Oncol 2000;18:2484–92.

50. Wagner TM, Möslinger R, Langbauer G, et al. Attitude towards prophylactic surgery and effects of genetic counseling in families with BRCA mutations. Austrian Hereditary Breast and Ovarian Cancer Group. Br J Cancer 2000;82:1249–53.

51. Lerman C, Narod S, Schulmam K, et al. BRCA 1 testing in families with heredity breast-ovarian cancer. A prospective study of patient decision making and outcomes. JAMA 1996;275:1885–92.

52. Meijers-Heijboer EJ, Verhoog LC, Brekelmans CT, et al. Presymptomatic DNA testing and prophylactic surgery in families with BRCA 1 or BRCA 2 mutation. Lancet 2000;355:2015–20.

53. Meiser B, Butow P, Friedlander M, et al. Intention to undergo prophylactic bilateral mastectomy in women at increased risk of developing breast cancer. J Clin Oncol 2000;18:2250–7.

54. Eisinger F, Julian-Reynier C, Stoppa-Lyonnet D, et al. Breast and ovarian cancer prone women and prophylactic surgery temptation. J Clin Oncol 1998; 16:2573–4.

55. Stefanek M, Enger C, Benkendorf J, et al. Bilateral prophylactic mastectomy decision making: a vignette study. Prev Med 1999;29:216–21.

56. Morrow M, Bucci C, Rademaker A. Medical contraindications are not a major factor in the underutilization of breast conserving therapy. J Am Coll Surg 1998;186:269–74.

57. Fisher B, Costantino JP, Wickerham DL, et al. Tamoxifen for prevention of breast cancer: report of the National Surgical Adjuvant Breast and Bowel Project P-1 Study. J Natl Cancer Inst 1998;90: 1371–88.

CHAPTER 17

BREAST RECONSTRUCTION

Neil A. Fine, MD, FACS
Robert M. Saltzmann, BA

In this era of multidisciplinary care and improved understanding of breast cancer risk, surgical approaches to prophylaxis are no longer considered methods of last resort. The identification of the *BRCA1* and *BRCA2* predisposition mutations marked a watershed in breast cancer risk assessment. We now have the ability to identify women at very high risk for developing breast and ovarian cancer. As growing numbers of high-risk women are confronted with the difficult and controversial decision to undergo bilateral or contralateral prophylactic mastectomy (PM), breast reconstruction is a major factor among the host of ancillary considerations they face. Technical refinements in reconstruction, especially in the area of autologous tissue flaps, continue to play an important part in our efforts to lessen the physical and psychological impact of PM. Indeed, the recent resurgence and reappraisal of PM, brought about by the marvelous progress made in the realm of breast cancer genetics, has clearly been aided by the availability and acceptance of breast reconstruction.

This chapter will explore the use of breast reconstruction in combination with PM, addressing relevant aspects of the complicated decision-making process involved in selecting the type and timing of reconstructive alternatives. We will review the myriad of current breast reconstruction procedures available to PM candidates, summarizing surgical techniques, benefits, drawbacks, and significant long-term risks of each, with an emphasis on the three most commonly encountered methods: expander/implant, transverse rectus abdominus myocutaneous (TRAM) flap (pedicled and free), and latissimus dorsi flap. This overview should provide a basic, working knowledge of breast reconstruction for those involved in the care of women facing the risks of breast cancer and the reconstructive repercussions of PM.

PREOPERATIVE CONSULTATION

Appropriate reconstructive measures have the potential to play an integral role in enhancing a patient's willingness to undergo, and ultimate satisfaction with, PM. At the same time, complications of reconstruction and dissatisfaction with the cosmetic outcome are major sources of regret about the entire experience of PM.[1-5] The preoperative conference sets the stage for patients to emerge satisfied with a reconstruction, which, admittedly, may yield unpredictable and/or suboptimal results. Key to establishing the foundations of satisfaction, the patient and her reconstructive surgeon must arrive at a mutual understanding of what constitutes a realistic and appropriate set of expectations, taking into account both specific desires and concerns of the patient as well as any predetermined surgical limitations.

Demographics

The majority of women who seek reconstructive measures are of higher socioeconomic status and better educated about the outcomes of mastectomy.[6] Women who choose reconstruction also tend to be younger and more sexually active, although one center has reported equal enthusiasm and use among older women, attributing their findings to increased patient education.[7-9] Attempts to further characterize a more specific and comprehensive demographic profile of women seeking reconstruction have been unsuccessful.[6]

In their detailed examination of bilateral prophylactic mastectomies performed at the Mayo Clinic, 1960 to 1993, Hartmann and colleagues reported that 94% of women elected to have reconstruction.[10] Given the Mayo Clinic's unique and extensive experience handling PM cases, this figure may best be interpreted as an approximation of the maximum proportion of women who would choose reconstruction if all such candidates were extensively educated about its benefits and drawbacks. The high percentage of breast reconstruction among bilateral PM patients underscores the belief that postmastectomy breast reconstruction may be an underused resource in breast cancer patients.[11]

Psychological Barriers

For the high-risk woman, PM is a traumatic event. Apprehensive candidates may find the availability of breast reconstruction reassuring, affording a chance to escape from a potentially destructive operation with scarring and cosmetic disfigurement that is less noticeable (or more easily concealable) than they may have feared. However, PM and breast reconstruction each involve an interplay of risks and benefits that every candidate must weigh carefully before making a final decision. Preoperative screening by the plastic surgeon should therefore comprise not only an assessment of surgical risk status, but also an evaluation of the patient's emotional and psychological suitability, including any preexisting issues with self-image, sexual identity, or other emotional instability.[12] As is the case in pre-PM counseling, women who demonstrate persistent difficulty interpreting or understanding information about the risks, complications, or prognosis of reconstruction may warrant further evaluation and/or referral to psychiatry.[2]

Given the weighty nature of the decision and a lack of immediacy to treat, a patient may have 6 to 8 months or more between genetic counseling and possible PM. With ample time to contemplate reconstruction, pressures to make a hasty decision are all but eliminated (assuming, of course, she has been counseled appropriately).[13] On the other hand, this also leaves a lot of time for vacillation. Like her counterpart with breast cancer, the very high-risk PM candidate may, at times, feel obligated to minimize the importance of reconstructive considerations.[14] This tendency to downplay the reconstructive aspect of her care is only natural when

juxtaposed with the potential for life-threatening oncologic concerns. What's more, prospective PM patients must cope with the added uncertainty of knowing that, without mastectomy, there is no guarantee they would ultimately develop a malignancy — and no guarantee that they will not develop breast cancer in the future, in spite of mastectomy. Once they've finally resolved to undergo PM, it is not uncommon for some women to struggle with feelings of selfishness or vanity when considering reconstruction.[15] Hence, without appropriate preoperative education and counseling, a subset of women considering PM run the risk of denying themselves the opportunity for postoperative reconstruction.

Ultimately, reconstruction is far from a panacea for the psychological sequelae of mastectomy. Among breast cancer survivors, long-term psychosocial outcomes and adjustment to mastectomy are not significantly different between those who have and those who have not had reconstruction.[16,17] As assessed by self-report questionnaire, bilateral PM patients also demonstrate similar postoperative mental health scores whether or not they receive reconstruction.[5] Notably, this data is derived from relatively small retrospective studies and should be interpreted with scrutiny. Results from large-scale prospective studies and metaanalyses are anticipated.

Expectations and Satisfaction

Once a woman has decided that she is interested in reconstruction, what can she reasonably hope to achieve? In general, women who choose reconstruction do so with sensible intentions. The most common psychosocial reasons for seeking postmastectomy reconstruction include the ability to wear a greater variety of clothes, the desire to maintain feelings of wholeness or "normalcy," or because of a personal sense that their femininity and body image would be damaged by mastectomy.[7,18,19] Evidently, women are incredibly self-motivated in desiring reconstruction, a finding that very often comes as a surprise to partners and husbands.[7]

Despite these practical motivations, the potential for some women to develop unrealistic expectations still exists. Reported dissatisfaction with PM is very often attributable to disappointment with unexpected aesthetic outcomes of reconstruction.[1-3] Frost and colleagues measured factors contributing to patient satisfaction after PM and found that fewer complications with implants was among the variables contributing to overall satisfaction.[1] In this study, the decision not to have reconstruction was a significant positive predictor of satisfaction. The authors surmise that women who choose methods to preserve their breasts, (such as reconstruction or breast conservation therapy (BCT), tend to be more concerned with body image and self-esteem and are, therefore, more likely to be dissatisfied with aesthetic outcomes.

Importantly, satisfaction with reconstructive outcome does not necessarily correlate with satisfaction concerning the mastectomy itself.[3,4] Rather, the relationship between breast reconstruction and general satisfaction with the mastectomy experience may be a function of the motives and expectations of the individual patient.[20] For example, cancer patients undergoing modified radical mastectomy (MRM) have very different incentives for, and expectations of, subsequent breast reconstruction than PM patients, and satisfaction scores between these two groups may differ accordingly.[21] Provided their new breasts are free of disease, most cancer patients are willing to overlook imperfections and tend to be quite happy with the results of reconstruction. Conversely, PM candidates who opt for reconstruction are not as forgiving of complications, asymmetry, or otherwise unsatisfactory cosmetic results in breasts that had previously been healthy.

There is also some evidence to suggest that physical activity level plays a role in patient satisfaction with reconstruction, at least among breast cancer survivors.[22,23] Whether this reflects the superior health status of physically active patients (leading to fewer surgical complications), enhanced psychosocial well-being, or some combination of both, has not been determined. The positive impact of physical activity likely holds true in PM patients as well, although this too has not been specifically demonstrated.

In the end, the plastic surgeon plays a vital role in helping to ensure patient satisfaction. He or she must be cognizant of patient expectations and correct misconceptions wherever apparent. In fostering satisfaction, preparing patients for the realities of breast reconstruction is critical, particularly the woman undergoing PM. It must be emphasized that the principal goal of PM is removal of the breast tissue, not cosmetic improvement. Patients should not expect to emerge from postmastectomy breast reconstruction with a more aesthetically pleasing breast mound than when they started. Even with a steadily growing armamentarium of available techniques, the art of breast reconstruction cannot reliably produce a breast that matches the native breast in aesthetics and can never match the native breast in sensation.

Risks and Benefits

An important part of the preoperation consult is ensuring that the patient fully understands the risks and benefits of the available types of breast reconstruction. Many long-term risks of reconstruction are incompletely understood and remain under investigation. Advising patients about what is not known is every bit as important as discussing what we do know about complication and failure rates.[24] Postoperatively, the variable and unpredictable nature of the healing process frequently interferes with bilateral symmetry and/or creates a breast mound that may lack the shape and texture of a natural breast. Additionally, mastectomy always obliterates sensory nerves to the breast, causing some degree of anesthesia, paresthesia, hypesthesia, or mastodynia in the reconstructed breast.[25] The sensation of the breast skin gradually will return along the periphery of the breast mound, but it may never return to the most central portion, and nipple sensation is invariably lost.

Patients considering implant reconstruction are often surprised to learn that multiple revisions are routinely required in order to achieve optimal cosmetic results. Another unavoidable drawback to implants is that several replacements are often needed over the course of a lifetime. When myocutaneous flaps are used, partial or total flap loss, fat necrosis, thrombosis, and donor site morbidity are the major concerns. The bilateral nature of PM magnifies (doubles) the surgery required for reconstruction. This doubling effect has little impact on implant reconstruction, but it significantly complicates donor site morbidity for autologous tissue flap breast reconstruction.[26]

It is impossible to overstate the importance of preoperative counseling in achieving patient satisfaction, not to mention establishing informed consent. Provided that patients are well informed, the cosmetic results of reconstruction may exceed their expectations.[12] Yet it is only within a context of reasonable expectations that reconstruction can hope to contribute to patient satisfaction.

Contralateral Prophylactic Mastectomy: Advantages of Bilateral Reconstruction

Reconstruction may be requested by a woman who is cancer-free and undergoing bilateral PM, or when a patient undergoing mastectomy for unilateral cancer opts for a contralateral PM. In either case, the plastic surgeon is faced with the need for bilateral reconstruction. Typically this will take place immediately following the bilateral mastectomies, as outlined in the following section. The nipple-areolar complex (NAC) is of particular significance in bilateral reconstruction. The NAC is the visual focal point of the breast and is pivotal in creating symmetry. By virtue of the fact that it is much easier to match two reconstructed nipples than it is to match a reconstructed nipple with a normal one, a bilateral procedure stands to significantly enhance the ultimate appearance and symmetry of the restored breast mounds.

A bilateral reconstruction can be lengthy and expensive, especially when autogenous free flaps are used. However, because symmetry is easier to achieve, the number of subsequent revisions is minimized. As a result, the net cost (through nipple reconstruction) is estimated to be only 5% more than that of unilateral reconstruction, which often necessitates multiple procedures to achieve optimal symmetry with the contralateral side.[27] Apart from implicit adjustments to accommodate the bilateral nature of the procedure, namely increased donor site morbidity and tranfusion risk for autologous flaps, the risk factors, complications, and fundamental challenges to bilateral reconstruction are generally no different than those encountered in unilateral operations.

Timing: Immediate versus Delayed

The timing of mastectomy does not readily dictate the most appropriate timing for subsequent reconstruction. Historically, most reconstructions were delayed secondary to early concerns about the psychological implications and medical safety of an immediate procedure. Prior to the 1970s, many plastic surgeons feared that patients would be unable to cope with the direct transition from their own breast to a reconstructed one.[28] To limit potential trauma, it was thought that patients should first acclimate themselves to the sight and feel of a mastectomy defect. A waiting period ranging from months to years would also ensure that the window

of highest risk for local recurrence had passed and that the patient had ample time to cope with the consequences of her cancer before taking on the additional mental burden of reconstruction.[18,29] The ensuing transition to a reconstructed breast would then be a more comfortable one.

Numerous studies have since shown this logic to be flawed.[9,15,30–33] It is now understood that immediate breast reconstruction (IBR) is not only safe, but actually offers psychological benefits in its own right. In particular, an immediate procedure spares the distress and sense of mutilation that women were found to have experienced with a delayed reconstruction, whereby the intervening period between mastectomy and reconstruction imposes an unavoidable daily reminder of their cancer (ie, the mastectomy site). We now appreciate that breasts acquired by immediate reconstruction are very rapidly experienced as part of the body and integrated into the patient's sense of self, whereas breasts created after a delay often take much longer to be fully assimilated into the body image.[15] The immediate approach also allows the patient to convalesce from both the reconstruction and the mastectomy concurrently.

The other concern prompting the use of delayed reconstruction was the idea that a prosthetic implant or autogenous flap might either compromise the detection of local recurrence or delay the administration of adjuvant therapy — or, that these might have reciprocal impacts on the reconstruction. Some even speculated that the reconstructive procedure itself might promote local recurrence, possibly via tumor seeding if a residual tumor was disturbed during the operation.[34,35]

To date, there is no convincing evidence that IBR interferes with adjuvant cancer treatment, impedes the detection of locally recurrent cancer, or in any way modifies cancer prognosis.[9,34–42] Studies also indicate that postoperative complication rates after IBR do not differ significantly from those after mastectomy alone or after delayed reconstruction.[30,43–45] Other than the rare implant infection secondary to chemotherapy-induced leukopenia, the use of postoperative chemotherapy is not associated with a significant increase in complication rate.[43] On the other hand, there is growing evidence that adjuvant radiotherapy does increase the incidence of postreconstruction complications, a subject that we will revisit below.

There are a number of important technical advantages of immediate over delayed reconstruction. The immediate postmastectomy setting allows the reconstructive surgeon to take advantage of malleable native breast skin prior to wound healing, facilitating the recreation of natural breast ptosis. For the patient who chooses implants, a major advantage of immediate over delayed reconstruction is the availability of extra skin following a skin-sparing or partial skin-sparing mastectomy. Having more skin at the time of expander placement means less expansion or stretching of the skin will be required to obtain the desired volume. The extra skin also helps with autologous tissue reconstruction by decreasing the size of the skin paddle that is inserted on the chest to replace the skin removed from the breast by the mastectomy. The increased operative time and complexity of immediate procedures remain potential drawbacks. Other technical and procedural advantages and disadvantages of IBR will be discussed in greater detail below, as they pertain to each individual reconstructive technique.

Finally, IBR may be more cost-efficient than delayed reconstruction. In 1993, Elkowitz and colleagues conducted a direct cost-benefit analysis and demonstrated measurable savings with immediate reconstruction, primarily attributable to the fact that a single consolidated procedure, albeit longer, obviates the expense of a second hospital admission and a second surgery.[46] In 1998, Khoo and colleagues at the M.D. Anderson Cancer Center in Houston determined that the cost of mastectomy followed by delayed reconstruction was 62% higher than that of mastectomy with IBR.[47] Still, at least one caveat to this finding is warranted: complications prompting secondary revisions or prolonging postoperative hospital stay can very quickly negate any such savings.

From 1983 to 1990, the use of immediate reconstruction grew from a small percentage of cases into the consensus method of choice. Backed by demonstrable psychosocial, cost-saving, and tissue-sparing advantages, IBR has since evolved into the standard for reconstruction timing in most practices.[8,11] Today, with improving operative techniques and better flap and prosthetic designs, contraindications to immediate reconstruction are few. Significant cardiopulmonary or major comorbid conditions remain contraindications to IBR.

When a delayed procedure is deemed appropriate, a delay of 3 to 6 months following mastectomy is usually sufficient to allow skin flaps to heal and regain some of their malleability and suppleness. Current trends continue to favor immediate procedures, but ultimately, the timing of reconstruction should be mutually agreeable to the patient, the oncologic surgeon, and the plastic surgeon.

Postmastectomy Radiation Therapy

Concerns about adjuvant chemotherapy and radiation are of less relevance to the high-risk, disease-free patient, but remain an issue for the woman undergoing contralateral PM. Preoperative radiation is a well-established risk factor for complications and remains a relative contraindication to breast reconstruction with implants.[48–53] Conversely, the relationship between postmastectomy radiotherapy (PMRT) and complication rates remains under investigation. Evidence from small case studies strongly suggests an association between adjuvant postmastectomy chest wall irradiation and an increased rate of fibrosis, capsular contracture, and implant failure.[54,55] Autogenous tissue flaps (eg, TRAM flaps) have consistently demonstrated greater, but not complete, resistance to radiation-induced damage than expander/implants and ultimately may render superior aesthetic results.[56–70]

Currently, PMRT is the most commonly cited reason for delaying reconstruction after therapeutic mastectomy.[55] Because it is often difficult to accurately identify those patients who will ultimately require PMRT, some surgeons have simply cited anticipated PMRT as an absolute contraindication to IBR, preferring to delay reconstruction until its completion.[71] Rather than forego the benefits of immediate reconstruction entirely, we have recommended an alternative solution, placement of a tissue expander, to patients considered likely to require PMRT.[72] As described below, tissue expansion is designed to be the first stage in a two-staged reconstruction. Hence, an expander can serve as a temporary solution, or intermediate step, during which chemotherapy, radiation, or both may be administered.[55] If and when they occur, radiation-related complications can be addressed with appropriate revisions at the time the expander is replaced by the final implant or autogenous tissue flap.

In addition to preserving the psychological and skin-sparing benefits of IBR, this scheme has the added benefit of extending the decision time available to ambivalent patients by separating the pressure-filled decision to proceed with mastectomy from the subsequent choice of a final method of reconstruction. It also affords her the opportunity to experience first-hand the feel of an implanted prosthetic device (ie, the expander), placing her in a more knowledgeable position to choose how to proceed in the second stage.

Weighing the Options

Once a woman has made the decision to undergo breast reconstruction and has considered its timing relative to the mastectomy, selection of the method of reconstruction must be addressed. At this point, women invariably want to know what the "best" procedure is. To answer this question, we must first define "best" and place it in proper context. Whereas the reduction of cancer morbidity and mortality is the logical standard used by surgical oncologists to measure the success of mastectomy, determining reconstructive success is not so straightforward. By convention, the measure of success in plastic surgery has arbitrarily been set using patient appearance in a photograph without clothing.[73] Although this is a quite reliable measure of cosmetic outcome, it is by no means the only way to gauge success and, in fact, may ignore other important factors in patient satisfaction.

Of the available procedures, TRAM tissue flaps from the abdomen have been widely promoted as the method producing the best cosmetic outcome, largely based upon assessment of the patient in photographs without clothing. However, to suggest that a TRAM flap is the "best" procedure for all women under all situations would be an inappropriate generalization. As discussed below, a TRAM flap procedure is invasive, adds considerable time to an already lengthy operation, leaves substantial scarring, and carries the risk of donor site (abdominal wall) morbidity. Although it is arguably true that a TRAM flap will produce the most natural-looking naked breast, many women are much more interested in achieving a satisfactory appearance in a bra or bathing suit, which, for some, can just as easily be accomplished using implants.

Our own patient survey data, in agreement with that of others, suggests that women undergoing expander/implant and TRAM or latissimus reconstruction ultimately express equal levels of satisfaction with their decision and willingness to repeat the same procedure in retrospect.[19,74,75] At the same time, those who choose expander/implant reconstructions do not share the same overall level of satisfaction as patients who receive autologous TRAM or latissimus reconstructions.[22,74] The distinction made here between satisfaction with one's decision and satisfaction with overall cosmetic outcome is often misunderstood — by physicians and patients alike.[2] In fact, there is nothing wrong with accepting the so-called suboptimal result of an implant in an effort to minimize scarring and more extensive surgery, provided that the risks involved and the likelihood of lower satisfaction scores are anticipated and understood as part of the decision-making process.

In short, what is best can only be defined in the context of each woman's individual goals, risk-benefit analysis, and body type. There is, unfortunately, no algorithm that best matches a woman with a reconstructive option, although ongoing outcome studies should greatly facilitate this process. At the Northwestern University Feinberg School of Medicine, our goal is to fully inform each patient of all available options and tailor the reconstruction to individual needs on a case-by-case basis. A table summarizing important points related to the three main types of reconstruction helps patients compare the available options (Table 17-1).

TYPES OF RECONSTRUCTION

In the wake of mastectomy, the individualized desires and circumstances of women vary widely. Likewise, there exists a diverse set of approaches to breast reconstruction to accommodate these needs. In the remainder of this chapter, we will summarize the operative techniques available to patients undergoing post-PM reconstruction, focusing on the three most common procedures: expander/implant, TRAM flap, and latissimus dorsi myocutaneous flap, along with their respective advantages and disadvantages. Less common autologous flap alternatives, including the deep inferior epigastric perforator (DIEP), gluteal, lateral transverse thigh, and deep circumflex iliac (Taylor-Rubens) flaps, and superficial inferior epigastric artery flaps, will also be described briefly for the sake of completeness.

In a planned IBR, close communication and collaboration between the oncologic breast and re-

TABLE 17-1 Procedure Comparison for Mastectomy Reconstruction

	Expander/Implant	Latissimus Back Tissue +/− implant	TRAM Abdominal Tissue
Initial surgery	Minimal	Moderate	Most involved
Secondary surgery in addition to the nipple	Always at least 2 operations	Sometimes	Least likely
Hospitalization	Minimal: currently 1–2 days	Moderate: currently 2–3 days	Longest stay: currently 3–4 days after surgery
Scars	No additional	On back	On lower abdomen
Shape and feel	No ptosis, firm, little motion, no change with weight fluctuation	Moderate to natural ptosis, less firm, more motion, little change with weight fluctuation	Natural ptosis, soft, normal motion, symmetric change with weight fluctuation
Opposite breast	Surgery often required to achieve optimal symmetry	Surgery for symmetry more optional	Surgery for symmetry almost always optional
Impact of radiation	Significant	Moderate	Least impact but can be significant
Bilateral mastectomy	Advantages magnified, disavantages minimized	Advantages unchanged, disadvantages somewhat magnified	Advantages unchanged, disadvantages magnified
Secondary gain	Flexibility with breast size in bilateral cases	None	Flat abdomen similar to an abdominoplasty
Back-to-work time on average	2 weeks	4 weeks	6–8 weeks

TRAM = transverse rectus abdominus myocutaneous.

constructive surgeons is essential.[9,76] For reasons of efficiency and quality, it is preferable for a general surgical team to perform the removal of the breast, after which a second team of plastic surgeons performs the subsequent reconstruction. Joint planning of incision placement optimizes aesthetic outcome without compromising oncologic results. In some autologous procedures (eg, TRAM), operative time can be minimized by harvesting the flap while the mastectomy takes place. Postoperative responsibilities are also shared, with the general surgeon continuing to monitor and make recommendations on the basis of oncologic factors, whereas the plastic surgeon assumes responsibility for ensuring proper wound healing and aesthetic satisfaction.

Subcutaneous and Total (Simple) Mastectomy

The subject of subcutaneous versus total mastectomy is discussed at length in Chapter 16. To review, no mastectomy is 100% prophylactic; neither subcutaneous nor total mastectomy leaves the breast completely devoid of residual tissue.[77] Thus far, studies have been unable to confirm a strict relationship between the proportion of breast tissue removed and the degree of prophylaxis conferred. Notwithstanding the paucity of evidence, total mastectomy is thought to confer a more complete degree of prophylaxis by virtue of its more complete removal of 95 to 98% of parenchymal tissue, including the NAC.[78] In contrast, by sparing the NAC and its underlying glandular tissue, subcutaneous mastectomy (SCM) can at best remove 90% of the breast parenchyma.[79] Consensus opinion is now heavily in favor of total mastectomy as the more appropriate method of prophylaxis, making subcutaneous techniques obsolete at many centers.[80]

The majority of existing literature in plastic surgery places reconstructive issues in the context of older SCM techniques, in large part because retrospective series have not yet caught up to current practice standards.[81–89] Admittedly, the more limited

SCM readily lends itself to superior reconstructive results, owing to decreased visible scarring along with a preserved NAC, obviating the need for nipple reconstruction. Fortunately, when combined with skin-sparing techniques, total mastectomy can and very often does permit aesthetically acceptable reconstructive results in the hands of an experienced surgeon. Skin-sparing techniques preserve a larger proportion of the original breast skin envelope and inframammary fold, facilitating the construction of a breast that more closely matches the color, size, and shape of the original mound. With ongoing improvements in nipple reconstruction techniques, the apparent cosmetic advantages of SCM are becoming progressively less relevant. The discussion of reconstructive techniques will be directed toward reconstruction in the setting of total mastectomy.

Staged Expander/Implant Reconstruction

By virtue of their simplicity, prosthetic implants are currently the most common method of postmastectomy breast reconstruction in the United States.[90] Implant procedures provide satisfactory results for most women and require the least amount of initial surgery compared with all other alternatives. Immediate insertion of bilateral expanders represents a small fraction of the surgical magnitude of more extensive tissue-based procedures, making implants especially appealing for post-PM reconstruction. Reconstruction with implants after bilateral PM is ideally suited for women with small- to moderately-sized breasts (A/B cup size of 300 cc volume or less). Even though implants do come in all sizes and there is no need to match a contralateral native breast, large implants, owing to the increased density of saline compared to glandular breast tissue and fat, place a greater strain on the remaining skin envelope and often feel heavy. Bilateral implant reconstruction offers women size flexibility. Because the expansion process occurs gradually in the postoperative period, women are free to choose a larger or smaller size for their final reconstruction (Figure 17-1).

Breast reconstruction had its beginnings in 1962 with the development of silicone gel implants for augmentation, but early single-stage procedures were fraught with problems. Prior to the advent of skin-sparing mastectomy techniques, tissue expansion, and flap enhancement, the residual skin envelope after a conventional mastectomy provided in-

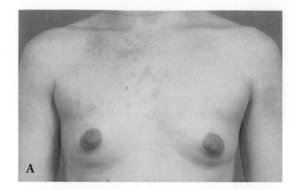

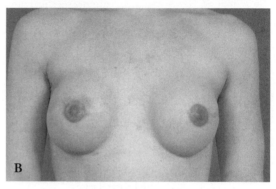

Figure 17-1 *A*, Preoperative view prior to bilateral prophylactic mastectomy. *B*, Postoperative view showing result of bilateral staged tissue expander/implant reconstruction.

sufficient coverage for most implants, particularly in women with larger breasts. Today, because complete skin closure is considered vital for cosmetic success, single-stage implant procedures (ie, those without preceding tissue expansion) are stringently reserved for women with small breasts and sufficient tissue coverage.

The introduction of anatomical tissue expansion by Radovan in the 1970s eliminated the need for supplemental coverage by a myocutaneous flap and the related issue of skin matching.[91] Since that time, skin-sparing techniques in mastectomy have also proven invaluable in facilitating implant reconstruction with matching skin. By expanding the existing skin envelope prior to insertion of the permanent implant (rather than relying on supplementary tissue from an autogenous flap), additional scars and donor-site morbidity are avoided. Tissue expansion is now the dominant method of implant reconstruction.

In light of the publicity resulting from the silicone controversy in the 1990s, the notion of a permanent prosthetic implant is undoubtedly familiar to most women. However, tissue expansion invokes a two-stage approach that may be foreign to those unfamiliar with contemporary techniques. A tissue expander is an inflatable implant made of textured silicone-based material that is contoured in shape and contains an integrated "port" to inject saline and "expand" the implant. In the immediate (first stage) procedure, the expander is placed in a submusculofascial pocket beneath the pectoralis major (described below), adding minimal time to the surgical procedure.

The expander is partially filled with saline at the time of its initial placement. The buried, integrated port of the expander is then used to serially inflate the expander with 50 to 200 cc of saline each week for 4 to 6 weeks. The expansions are performed in the outpatient setting and are generally well tolerated. The final number of injections is determined by the size requirements of the reconstruction. Other than infection, the only absolute contraindication to placement of an expander is the absence of viable skin flaps.[92] Owing to decreased skin flap vascularity, smoking and obesity are considered relative contraindications.[93] IBR with tissue expansion is associated with total, major and minor, complication rates of 23 to 45%, with absolute failures occurring in 3 to 25% of cases.[61,93–96] These rates are far from negligible, but they do not differ appreciably from those of mastectomy alone.[30]

After expansion is complete, an additional healing period of approximately 2 to 3 months is allotted, after which the temporary expander can be removed and exchanged with a permanent implant. Waiting 2 to 3 months after the final inflation allows the skin to take shape and soften, eventually resulting in a more ptotic breast mound.[97] Second-stage replacement with a permanent implant is a virtual necessity because textured expanders inevitably ripple and/or become palpably firm.[26] Fortunately, most subsequent procedures, including nipple reconstruction, can be completed under local anesthesia in the outpatient setting. To alleviate the need for two successive operations, adjustable expander/implants have also been developed for permanent use, although results have been less reliable.[98] Nipple-areolar reconstruction may be undertaken at the time of expander/implant exchange,

but this is usually postponed to a third stand-alone procedure. Accurate, symmetric placement of the NAC is too easily compromised with skin contraction and other skin changes if adequate time is not allotted for wound healing.

Despite noticeable cosmetic improvements with contoured and textured devices, prosthetic implants are inherently limited in their ability to mimic the curvature, projection, and ptosis of a natural breast.[97,99] Implants tend to appear artificially round, manifesting as fullness in the superior pole. Saline-filled implants and textured-surface expanders can develop a wavy, rippled appearance. In addition, implants are characteristically resistant to gravity, remaining upright and forward on the chest even when lying supine. A well-defined inframammary fold is likewise difficult to achieve. However, overfilling an expander to 150 to 200% of the volume of the intended cup size usually yields enough residual skin to recreate the inframammary fold and retain a moderate degree of ptosis after replacement with a smaller permanent implant (Figure 17-2).[100–102]

The most frequent, troublesome, and least predictable complication of implant reconstruction is contracture of the periprosthetic scar capsule, occurring in 15 to 20% of both delayed and immediate procedures.[9] Contraction of the scar pocket around the implant may cause rupture of the implant, painful tightness, wrinkling of the skin, hardening of the reconstructed breast mound, or an otherwise unsatisfactory breast morphology.[103] Capsular contracture is graded from I to IV on the

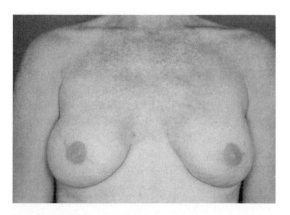

Figure 17-2 Bilateral implant reconstruction demonstrating natural droop or ptosis.

Baker scale, grade IV being most severe and noticeable on visual inspection.[104] Although a Baker III contracture is moderately firm and readily detectable, the result may still be considered acceptable in some individuals. Only class IV represents an unquestionably excessive contracture that demands revision. Although the incidence of Baker III and IV contracture's has declined with the use of textured-surface implants, the replacement of silicone gel by saline, and the shift toward two-stage expansion-based procedures, capsular contracture remains a serious concern.[102,105,106] A major benefit of tissue expansion is that the initial scar capsule can be incised by open capsulotomy or excised (capsulectomy) at the time of second stage replacement with the permanent implant. Nevertheless, fibrotic scar tissue invariably builds up again in the months and years that follow.

In the early days of implant reconstruction, the implant was placed directly beneath the skin. This led to unacceptably high rates of Baker III and IV capsular contracture, implant extrusion, flap necrosis, wound dehiscence, and infection.[107–109] Subcutaneous placement has therefore been abandoned in favor of submuscular placement beneath the pectoralis major. In order to accommodate the prosthesis, a continuous muscular pocket is created by dissection with the aid of electrocautery. Little and colleagues have described this pocket as a "living bra" or "muscle bra."[9,110] The pocket is bounded by the infraclavicular border (superiorly), the lateral sternal border (medially), a preoperatively designated lower inframammary mark (inferiorly), and the anterior axillary fold (laterally). In addition to the pectoralis major, the superior portion of the rectus abdominis fascia, the external oblique, and serratus anterior fascia may also be elevated to cover the inferolateral portion of the implant.[108]

The major drawback to retromuscular placement is that it further hampers the faithful reproduction of natural ptosis and teardrop shape, especially with a larger breast. Whereas the fullness of a natural breast is mostly contained within the lower pole, an implant becomes fixed above the inframammary fold, creating unnatural-looking fullness in the upper pole. The pocket is designed to place the expander in a low, medial position, 2 to 3 cm below the proposed inframammary fold. This placement is low enough to compensate for the effects of contracture and implant immobility, yet still high enough so as not to unnaturally invade the abdomen. Such low placement sometimes results in a loss of the inframammary fold, which can be recreated with internal suturing at the time of expander/implant exchange. Once an appropriately sized prosthesis is placed, muscle closure is completed such that there is no exposure of the prosthesis in the subcutaneous space near the incision — an outcome that may lead to exposure and loss of the expander if there is marginal necrosis of the mastectomy skin flaps.

Less prevalent complications with implants include infection, hematoma, extrusion, and deflation (iatrogenic or spontaneous). Spontaneous deflation of saline implants (estimated at 1% per year) is usually ascribed to excessive infolding of the implant wall.[111] This belief has led to the practice of overfilling implants beyond the manufacturer-recommended volume in order to reduce wall folds. Nevertheless, there remains considerable skepticism regarding the effectiveness of this technique in decreasing the incidence of deflation.[21]

Expander/implant reconstruction requires two operations by design, but three or more procedures are not uncommon over a lifetime. Any of the aforementioned complications may constitute implant failure, necessitating replacement with another implant and/or an autologous tissue flap. Several studies show that, for a variety of reasons, implants are replaced every 5 to 15 years on average.[112,113] Statistically, a *BRCA1*- or *BRCA2*-positive patient in her thirties who opts for implant reconstruction after bilateral prophylactic mastectomies may undergo as many as four to eight replacement procedures per breast during her lifetime.[113] Furthermore, implants have a tendency to shift unpredictably over time and with varying degrees on each side. This can lead to marked bilateral asymmetry and an overall poor degree of cosmesis, thereby negating the aforementioned benefits of bilateral reconstruction. Hence, although implants are less costly and less invasive than flap reconstructions in the short run, the aforementioned cost savings provided by an immediate, bilateral procedure may go unrealized in the long run.

Long-term monitoring of implant reconstruction for recurrence is straightforward. Mammography of the reconstructed breast is unnecessary. Palpation of residual breast tissue within the skin flap or pectoralis fascia — now situated directly beneath overlying skin, entirely anterior to the implant — is easily performed in self- or clinical examination. If palpable masses do arise, biopsy should be performed to obtain a diagnosis and plan future treatment.

Silicone

Only a handful of studies have examined reconstructive complication rates in the specific setting of PM. Contant and colleagues, at the University of Rotterdam, recently (2002) conducted a prospective review of women opting for PM and IBR.[114] During the 7-year study period, 1993–1999, 103 women underwent 193 PMs (90 bilateral, 13 unilateral) followed by IBR with silicone implants. The authors cite a 21% complication rate: 11% within the first 6 weeks postoperatively, and 10% over a median 3.5-year follow-up period, including 10 removed implants.

Interestingly, the reconstructions were all performed with silicone implants in a single-stage procedure at the time of mastectomy, a relatively unusual method by current US standards. Although 21% is not entirely unacceptable, it is typical for IBR with silicone gel-filled implants. The shift in the United States to two-stage expander/implant procedures using saline- rather than silicone gel-filled prosthetics has led to marked improvements in complication rates. In nonirradiated patients, the rate of significant complications in expander/implant reconstruction has been reported to be as low as 10% in selected series.[93,112] Refinements in autologous methods of reconstruction, described in the following sections, have led to even lower rates of major complication. Additional studies comparing the outcomes and complication rates of different reconstructive techniques in the setting of PM are needed.

Initially, the preference for silicone gel was almost universal, although saline was always used in a minority of cases. The consistency and viscosity of silicone gel bears a much closer resemblance to soft, native breast tissue and generates a more natural texture. Questions about a possible association between silicone gel implants and connective tissue (collagen) disease finally came to a head in 1992 with a $4.25 billion class action lawsuit and a moratorium announced by David Kessler, then commissioner of the US Food and Drug Administration (FDA).[115] In 1994, the FDA's ban on silicone gel implants was partially lifted for investigational purposes in breast reconstruction, but the negative media coverage of the early 1990s continues to have a reverberating influence on patients' perceptions regarding the risks involved. Saline implants have been the dominant implant type in the United States since the silicone moratorium.

To date, there has been no credible scientific evidence linking silicone exposure to systemic disease of any kind, connective tissue or otherwise.[116–118] Studies incited by the controversy have, however, helped to expose more legitimate cosmetic and medical dangers to silicone. In general, silicone gel implants behave much less predictably than saline. Silicone gel leakage, also known as "bleeding," is a virtual inevitability when implants are left in place for 10 years or more, whereas the low reported rate of spontaneous saline implant deflation is generally attributed to unit-to-unit variability (ie, a product deficiency). In fact, saline implant manufacturers in the United States continue to handle deflation complaints on a case-by-case basis.

Likewise, capsular contracture is more likely to occur when silicone implants are used. Thus, although a silicone gel-filled implant initially has a more natural feel, the majority will eventually develop hardness secondary to contracture.

At this point, the controversial choice between saline and silicone gel-filled implants is becoming a matter of renewed interest. The potential for silicone to be approved by the FDA and the introduction of new, shaped silicone implants has the potential to restore interest in their use. Some progress has been made in creating safer implant fills with properties more similar to those of silicone, but in the absence of preferable alternatives, saline has endured by default. Saline implants have a firmer texture, but long-term results are more reliable, and, given the choice, that seems to be the more important concern for most women.

Silicone gel-filled implants remain available for reconstruction, sanctioned by the FDA for investigational purposes only. Their use for augmentation purposes continues to be prohibited. Patients should exercise extreme caution and weigh the advantages and disadvantages carefully, in concert with their plastic surgeon, when considering silicone. Incidentally, implant shells continue to be made from a solid silicone polymer, the same form of silicone used in catheters and other internal devices. This form of silicone has never been linked to disease.

AUTOLOGOUS TISSUE

When combined with skin-sparing total mastectomy, immediate reconstruction with autologous tissue offers outstanding aesthetic results without interfering with cancer prophylaxis. Although expander/implants are currently the most common method of reconstructing the breast mound, the adverse publicity garnered by the 1990s silicone debacle has propelled a shift toward autologous tissue-based reconstruction. The safety and efficacy of myocutaneous tissue flap procedures, such as the TRAM and extended latissimus dorsi, continue to improve with experience. As plastic surgeons steadily gain proficiency with these techniques and, in turn, make them increasingly available to patients, a growing number of women are electing autologous methods of reconstruction.

Autologous reconstruction draws upon a flap of skin, subcutaneous tissue, and underlying muscle from another site on the patient's body to reconstruct the breast mound. The appeal of an autologous design is that, in using fatty tissue to replace glandular breast parenchyma, a more natural breast contour is created, both in shape and feel, while the cosmetic drawbacks of implant reconstruction are avoided. The lack of natural "feel" and unnatural appearance of a prosthetic implant may make it comparatively more difficult for a woman to fully integrate the restored breast into her composite sense of self. Implants can, at times, be reported to feel cold in cold temperatures, when there is inadequate blood flow in the skin flaps to warm the saline within the implant. A tissue flap, by contrast, creates a warm breast mound and may be more readily accepted into the woman's new sense of self-image. Autologous methods are also the most effective means of countering and salvaging complications with implants.

Prosthetic implant and autogenous tissue alternatives are not always mutually exclusive. Although tissue expansion can compensate for a relative deficiency in the skin envelope, closure of thin skin flaps around an implant or expander may be exceedingly tight, increasing the risk of vascular compromise and necrosis. Classical latissimus dorsi (LD) flaps were designed with this in mind, to provide additional tissue coverage for an underlying implant.[120] Occasionally the same may be done with a TRAM flap.[121]

Autologous flaps have the virtue of providing generous amounts of tissue in a single stage, availing both volume and skin coverage. This becomes an especially attractive option for the large-breasted woman because, unlike implant reconstruction, tissue flaps permit a faithful reproduction of natural breast ptosis. In addition, a tissue flap provides a mount upon which to recreate the nipple.

Tissue flaps rely on blood supply for successful transfer of tissue. There are two methods to achieve or maintain adequate blood flow: pedicled and free. In a pedicled design, the flap remains attached to its donor site along with the relevant blood supply (the vascular "pedicle"). Most or all of the underlying muscle is included in the flap harvest to ensure capture of the blood vessels. The flap is then tunneled subcutaneously to the breast where it is folded and shaped as necessary to recreate the breast mound. By contrast, a free flap is completely removed from the donor site and repositioned at the mastectomy defect. To accomplish this, microvascular dissection techniques are employed to more accurately isolate the donor flap blood vessels. This obviates the requirement for extensive muscle inclusion in the flap harvest, thereby minimizing functional morbidity at the donor site. The vessels are ligated and then anastomosed to the dissected vessels at the mastectomy defect.

Of course, the use of autologous tissue is not without limitations. First, all methods of tissue reconstruction significantly lengthen the duration of surgery. A patient undergoing a bilateral autologous procedure must be capable of tolerating 8 to 12 hours of general anesthesia. Second, to protect against necrosis, both pedicled and free flap techniques are exquisitely dependent upon the preservation and maintenance of the vascular pedicle. Hence, obesity and smoking, both risk factors for vascular compromise, are relative contraindications to autologous procedures. Fat and skin necrosis has been minimized through better flap design and surgical technique, but they remain key complications to monitor, especially because palpable nodularity often mimics malignancy. Third, once drains are removed, seromas may develop (in latissimus dorsi flaps especially, necessitating aspiration or drain replacement). A major cosmetic drawback to autogenous reconstruction is that the color and texture of flap skin derived from a distant donor site may be difficult to match with thoracic skin. Fortunately, skin-sparing techniques in mastectomy can help to minimize or even avoid this problem. This list is far from exhaustive; below, we shall consider other limitations and complications as they pertain to individual techniques.

A myriad of flap designs have been developed for breast reconstruction since the latissimus dorsi myocutaneous flap was first described for true breast reconstruction in 1977.[120] The TRAM flap is by far the most common, but enhanced microsurgical free flap techniques have now permitted the use of donor sites other than the back and abdomen, including the buttock, hip, and lateral thigh.

TRAM FLAP RECONSTRUCTION

Since its introduction by Hartrampf and colleagues in 1982, the TRAM flap has become the preeminent autogenous method of breast reconstruction.[122,123] The TRAM flap is composed of skin and fatty tissue harvested from the lower abdomen and transferred to the mastectomy defect — ideal for the woman at high risk of breast cancer who also happens to have an abundance of undesirable abdominal fat. TRAM flaps are such an attractive option because they are so multifaceted: (1) a large volume of well-perfused tissue is made available for autologous reconstruction; (2) the removal of unwanted abdominal tissue results in an abdominal contour similar to that of an elective abdominoplasty ("tummy tuck"); (3) a well-hidden scar is left behind; (4) the flap is uniquely capable of withstanding the effects of pre- or postoperative chest wall irradiation; and (5) they are versatile enough to create a variety of breast contours, all with excellent ptosis.[103,127] Recognizing that outcome assessment is highly patient-dependent and somewhat subjective, the outstanding cosmetic results of a TRAM flap are considered to be the gold standard in breast reconstruction (Figure 17-3).

Although a much more extensive procedure than implant reconstruction, IBR with TRAM flaps is now performed routinely at centers around the world, a testament to both its safety and its efficacy.[124] An immediate TRAM procedure offers significant technical, aesthetic, and economic advantages over a delayed procedure, without adversely affecting oncologic outcome or postoperative adjuvant therapy. If appropriately coordinated with the

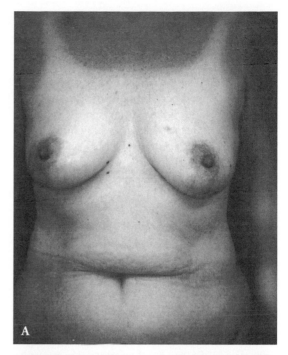

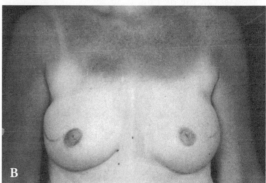

Figure 17-3 *A*, Preoperative view of a woman desiring to use excess abdominal tissue (TRAM flap) for reconstruction. *B*, Postoperative view of TRAM flap reconstruction.

general surgeon, the plastic surgeon can elevate the abdominal flap while the mastectomy takes place, thereby expediting operative time and minimizing blood loss. The general surgeon can also play a part in facilitating free TRAM reconstruction (described below) by exposing the recipient pedicle (typically the thoracodorsal vessels) during axillary dissection. Preservation of the inframammary fold and the use of skin-sparing techniques in the preceding mastectomy facilitate flap insetting and lead to a natural, symmetric reconstruction. The mastectomy specimen itself can be used as a template and expedites accurate volume replacement.

By contrast, delayed reconstruction involves the manipulation of residual breast skin that has had time to contract and possibly become fibrotic, necessitating the use of a much larger skin paddle from the abdominal donor site to compensate. Larger skin paddles, in turn, mean greater donor site morbidity and increased scarring. The net result is a less natural-looking, less cosmetically acceptable result.

Regardless of the precise surgical technique, of which there are a few, the TRAM flap harvest creates a defect in the abdominal wall, requiring reapproximation of the fascia to achieve donor site closure. Alone, fascial closure may not be sufficient to prevent hernia when a large amount of tissue is removed (as in a bilateral procedure), so prosthetic mesh is often used for reinforcement.[125] Like any reconstructive operation, the patient must accept a tradeoff. On the one hand, most women are quite pleased with the accessory cosmetic benefit of a concomitant abdominoplasty. On the other, the removal of muscle from the lower abdomen may cause functional limitations or predispose to abdominal wall hernia and bulging. Ultimately, most patients find that the tradeoff is worthwhile. In their assessment of abdominal wall morbidity, Mizgala and colleagues found that the vast majority of patients (93%) were happy with their decision to undergo a pedicled TRAM despite the fact that almost half (45.5%) noted some loss of abdominal strength.[126] A study by Kind and colleagues found that although a mechanical testing device could detect a decrease in muscle strength, neither women nor physical therapist could measure noticeable strength loss in unilateral TRAM flaps.[127] Bilateral TRAM flaps, as required for PM, demonstrated a more noticeable loss of strength.

In light of potential complications related to donor-site morbidity, careful patient selection is critical. The only absolute contraindication to TRAM reconstruction is prior division of the rectus abdominus perforating vessels, either through previous abdominoplasty or prior TRAM procedures. A TRAM flap, free or pedicled, is a one-time solution. Once abdominal tissue has been harvested, with or without the rectus muscles, the abdomen cannot be reused in subsequent salvage procedures.

More than likely, previous procedures would have disrupted the continuity of the perforating vessels to the skin and subcutaneous tissue of the proposed flap, making TRAM reconstruction impossible.[93] When contralateral PM is advised, women seeking bilateral reconstruction with TRAM flaps should make every attempt to schedule both mastectomies simultaneously. A patient who schedules sequential mastectomies and uses a TRAM flap to reconstruct the cancerous side will not be able to use a TRAM flap for delayed contralateral autologous reconstruction. The need to harvest from a second donor site (eg, the latissimus, the buttock, or lateral thigh) to reconstruct the opposite breast not only adds to overall morbidity but also impedes the achievement of bilateral symmetry.

A number of risk factors represent relative contraindications to a free or pedicled TRAM flap reconstruction. Methods now exist to quantify these risk factors by assigning a score value to each and then stratifying scores into a risk classification system.[128] Based on her score and risk classification, a patient's suitability for the procedure can be determined. In practice, however, most centers have been reluctant to adopt such exacting standards. The merits of the individual case and the experience level of the surgeon continue to play the most important role in determining whether TRAM reconstruction is advised.

Age and general health status are obviously of fundamental importance in evaluating a patient's ability to endure the length and invasiveness of a TRAM procedure. Underlying systemic disease (eg, diabetes, hypertension, chronic pulmonary disease, and collagen vascular disease) is a relevant concern and, depending on severity, may represent an absolute contraindication to TRAM reconstruction. Patients with chronic pulmonary diseases are especially likely to experience problems during rehabilitation. Excessive coughing and straining to breathe places undue stress on the anterior abdominal wall repair, inhibiting efficient wound healing. Moreover, when a tight fascial closure is required, the abdominal contents may be pushed up against the diaphragm, potentially impeding respiration. In the event this occurs, most healthy patients are able to adapt accordingly until healing and reexpansion of the abdominal fascia eases the tension. Conversely, the patient with preexisting pulmonary impairment may suffer.[128]

As previously mentioned, cigarette smoking, obesity, and perioperative irradiation also represent key risk factors. Chronic smoking will likely compromise flap microcirculation, promoting both necrosis and poor wound healing. Obesity is a known contributor to wound complications and infection in any surgical procedure, but may exacerbate complications with TRAM flaps in particular. At least one study has demonstrated a striking correlation between TRAM flap complication rates and the degree of patient obesity.[129] The "pot-belly" habitus, in which abdominal fat is deposited viscerally, deep to the peritoneum (as opposed to the more typical subcutaneous distribution), poses distinctive difficulties. Because transfer of the abdominal flap does not help redistribute any of this weight, fascial repair of an already weakened abdominal wall is subject to extreme stress postoperatively. TRAM flap breast reconstruction in these patients is relatively contraindicated and should only be considered after sufficient weight loss. The relationships between obesity and aesthetic outcomes in the breast and abdomen are somewhat less well defined.

At the opposite end of the spectrum, being too thin may also hinder a satisfactory outcome. A surprising amount of tissue can be obtained from a thin patient, but some women simply lack sufficient lower abdominal tissue to achieve an adequate breast volume. Attempting to compensate for this with a large flap harvest will inevitably create a widened scar and may cause excessive tension during closure in the already slender abdomen. Therefore, in the very slim patient, other donor sites may be more advisable than a TRAM flap. This is especially true for prophylactic mastectomy patients as all of these patients will be undergoing bilateral reconstruction. Bilateral reconstruction doubles the volume of tissue required, and a thin patient may be best served with an implant reconstruction solely on the basis of lack of available autologous tissue.

After judging the patient to be an appropriate candidate on medical grounds, the surgeon must also assess her psychological suitability for TRAM flap reconstruction. Namely, one must ascertain the patient's willingness to undergo, and ability to cope with, an extensive operative procedure as well as the difficult rehabilitation period that follows.[26] In our institution, the postoperative hospital stay is generally 3 to 5 days, depending upon the difficulty of the

individual case and the nature of the procedure, free or pedicled. Over the first 6 to 8 weeks postoperatively, abdominal wall function will recover enough to allow for resumption of daily activity. Full recovery takes place gradually over the ensuing year.[124]

As with any abdominoplasty, the patient should be made aware that her waist size will likely remain unchanged immediately after the operation. This is a somewhat paradoxical result given the large amount of skin and fat tissue that was just moved to the chest wall, but the typical course usually requires up to 6 to 8 months of healing and skin contraction before full improvement of the waistline is realized. The surgical scar may present issues of its own in wound healing, especially with respect to its visibility. Ideally, the donor-site defect should result in a low, thin scar without "dog ears."[124] Within limits, the scar may be adjusted at the patient's request to remain within the confines of contemporary bathing-suit fashions.

In addition to the associated risk of breast cancer, women with *BRCA1* and *BRCA2* mutations have a 15 to 60% lifetime risk of developing ovarian carcinoma.[115] In some cases, prophylactic bilateral salpingo-oophorectomy (BSO) may also be prudent. This presents a potential conflict in staging the procedure with immediate TRAM reconstruction as both require access to the abdominal wall. If the TRAM flap (pedicled or free) is raised first, a (third) gyn-oncology team can then perform the BSO via the incision in the now exposed posterior rectus sheath.[130] Procedural logistics, coordinating three surgical teams, represents the main obstacle for combined PM, TRAM reconstruction, and BSO.

As was the case with implants, postoperative mammography of the TRAM flap is not considered obligatory. Plagued by fat necrosis, microcalcification, scarring, and other subcutaneous firmness, such flap complications are just as likely to be mistaken for malignancy on imaging as they would be on palpation. On the other hand, because abdominal adipose tissue comprises the bulk of the flap, routine imaging is not as limited as it is with prosthetic implants, and it certainly does not obscure recurrence detection.[131]

Despite differences of opinion on the matter, there has been some attempt to continue routine surveillance postoperatively with both clinical breast examination and mammography. A 2002 study by Helvie and colleagues at the University of

Michigan purports that TRAM reconstruction does not interfere with detection of nonpalpable cancer recurrence, although primary cancer occurrence in women treated with PM was not found in this study.[40] Of 6 patients who underwent biopsy for Breast Imaging Reporting and Data System (BI-RADS) category 4 or 5 lesions, 4 (two-thirds) were found to be benign epidermoid cysts, fat necrosis, or fibrocystic change. Although this series is small, it supports the continued practice of monitoring TRAM flaps by clinical palpation rather than mammography. Greater experience and improved imaging techniques promise to one day permit the integration of mammography into postoperative monitoring. The ability to rapidly distinguish fat necrosis and other benign palpable nodularities from malignant change would dramatically hasten our efforts to relieve patient anxiety when they are discovered on self-examination.[113]

Pedicled TRAM

The conventional method of elevating a TRAM flap is to elevate the entire rectus abdominis muscle on one side, complete with its vascular pedicle, the superior epigastric vessels. Studies of abdominal blood flow have demonstrated that the abdominal wall skin is supplied by the periumbilical perforators (branches exiting the rectus muscle via perforations in the anterior rectus sheath, representing a confluence of the superior and inferior epigastric vessels).[132] These vessels should be incorporated into the flap design. Doing so substantially reduces the threat of partial skin flap necrosis and significantly minimizes fat necrosis.[43] Incorporating these vessels often leads to a final abdominal scar that is higher than would be expected in cosmetic abdominoplasty.

The patient is marked pre- or intraoperatively with a tapering transverse ellipse on the lower abdomen, including extensions of the design above the umbilicus to ensure that the superior perforating vessels are captured. The flap is subdivided into four zones, based upon blood flow and viability. Zone IV, which represents the distal 25% of the flap, is usually discarded because of its poor vascularity. Preoperative marking facilitates matching of the transverse flap to its ultimate position in the new breast, typically involving a rotation or twisting of the flap relative to its original position on the lower abdomen.

Techniques vary with respect to how much of the rectus abdominis should be raised. Our practice is to raise the entire rectus muscle, taking both the medial and lateral rows of perforators. The inferior epigastric vessels are also ligated at their origin from the external iliac vessels and transferred with the flap. In roughly 5% of cases, intraoperative examination reveals that flap perfusion via the superior epigastrics is less than ideal. Inclusion of the inferior epigastrics allows for an additional microvascular connection in the event this should occur. Such use of the inferior epigastric vessels to augment blood supply is called "supercharging."

After its elevation, the flap is passed through a subcutaneous tunnel and positioned into the mastectomy site. In bilateral reconstruction, the flaps may be transferred to the breast pockets from the ipsilateral or contralateral sides, depending upon the amount of lower abdominal tissue used and the degree of twisting that is required to position the pedicle into the chest. Passage of the flaps through the subcutaneous tunnel may create an unnatural epigastric bulging. The choice between ipsilateral and contralateral flap is usually made based on surgeon preference.

The main drawback to a pedicled flap is significant donor-site morbidity, including the surgical scar and the risk of subsequent hernia or bulging secondary to a weakened abdominal wall. Abdominal wall strength after bilateral TRAM procedures has been explored through overt functional assessment and subjective patient questionnaire.[133,134] Results suggest that bilateral pedicled flaps cause measurable deficit to abdominal-wall function and exercise ability, including the ability to flex and rotate the upper trunk, rise from a prone position, lift objects, or perform sit-ups. Evidence does not indicate any detrimental impact on pregnancy or childbirth.[126] Nonetheless, this operation is still relatively contraindicated in younger patients planning to become pregnant in the future.

Bilateral TRAM breast reconstruction requires a significant amount of tissue from the lower abdomen. When a patient requires bilateral reconstruction, as would be the case in a bilateral PM, we often use the free TRAM technique, which sacrifices much less of the rectus abdominis musculature and may yield a larger usable tissue volume. The advantage of increased blood flow to allow transfer of larger volumes of tissue is minimized in case of bilateral reconstruction because no tissue is taken across the midline. The lower abdominal tissue is split in the midline; one-half of the tissue is used for one breast and one-half is used for the other. In addition, when both rectus muscles have been raised in a pedicled fashion, closure of the remaining abdominal fascia may be excessively tight, necessitating prolene mesh for reinforcement. The free TRAM, discussed below, poses somewhat less risk to the patient's functional status and eases abdominal closure, but it does incur the added risk of total flap loss.

MICROSURGICAL FREE FLAP HARVEST

The free abdominoplasty flap was first introduced by Holmstrom in 1979.[135] Since then, the free superior gluteal, free TRAM, free inferior gluteal, lateral thigh, and deep circumflex iliac (Rubens) flaps have been described. Free flaps are based on the microsurgical dissection of the pedicle vasculature, conferring three major advantages over pedicled flap reconstruction:

1. A greater percentage of the underlying muscle is preserved, thereby minimizing donor site morbidity.
2. Free flaps alleviate the requirement for a subcutaneous tunnel, eliminating the risk of disrupting the inframammary fold or devascularizing the skin with excessive undermining.
3. With improved vascularity in the resultant breast, the incidence of fat necrosis and partial flap loss is markedly reduced — so much so, in fact, that cigarette smoking may not represent a significant contraindication.

Microvascular techniques are labor-intensive, requiring meticulous diligence and adding as much as 4 to 8 hours to operative time (relative to reconstruction with pedicled flaps). As the learning curve for these techniques is steep, free flaps are most commonly performed in larger, high-volume centers.

Free TRAM

It has been our practice to recommend free TRAM flaps when a TRAM reconstruction is requested after a bilateral mastectomy, as is the case in PM for breast cancer risk management.[43,93,136,137] Although bilateral pedicled TRAM is faster and technically simpler for the less-experienced surgeon, the free TRAM flap is uniquely suited for bilateral recon-

struction by virtue of improved blood supply and significantly less disruption to the abdominal musculature. Typically, only a small rectangular piece of the rectus muscle is sacrificed when a free TRAM flap is raised. This translates into lower incidences of herniation, functional impairment to the abdomen, fat necrosis, and partial flap loss.[136] The same can be said of the free TRAM's ability to withstand adjuvant radiotherapy, relative to the pedicled TRAM.[138] With appropriate application, free TRAM flaps carry a low 1 to 5% complication rate, well below those observed in conventional pedicle TRAM flaps.[113] These advantages are tempered by an increased risk of total flap loss, increased operative time, and a greater likelihood that blood transfusion will be necessary.

Whereas the blood supply of pedicled flaps is dominated by the superior epigastric vessels, free TRAM flaps are based upon the deep inferior epigastric arterial and venous system.[139] The superior epigastric vessels can be thought of as a secondary blood supply to the lower abdominal tissue, feeding the musculocutaneous perforators only indirectly. The deep inferior epigastrics are the primary blood supply to the lower abdomen and therefore provide more reliable and robust perfusion. This alleviates the need to include the perforating vessels in the flap and minimizes the amount of extraneous fascia that is harvested to do so.[27] Consequently, breast volumes of 15 to 20% greater magnitude can be created without increasing the extent of flap havest.[93]

Initially, a single flap is raised starting laterally and progressing medially. After microdissection of the inferior epigastric vessels is complete, the flap can be divided in two down the midline. The flap vessels are ligated and the two, now "free," flaps are then transferred directly to the chest without the need for subcutaneous tunneling. The general surgical team can facilitate this process by isolating recipient vessels in the chest and axilla during the mastectomy. Microanastomoses are then made between the inferior epigastrics and the blood supply of the chest. The vessels found in the axilla, especially the thoracodorsal, or subscapular are the most dependable recipients. The internal mammary, thoracoacromial, and lateral thoracic pedicles represent good secondary alternatives.

The most difficult aspect of a free TRAM is ensuring that the newly created microvasculature conduit is intact and provides adequate blood supply to the overlying skin and fat.[124] Whereas pedicled flaps are subject to partial flap loss, which may or may not be salvageable, free flaps are an all-or-none endeavor. Based on only a subset of the normal vascular supply, total flap loss secondary to thrombosis within the microvascular connection can render a free TRAM flap a total failure. Despite this risk, experience and rational preventive measures (eg, maintenance of optimal hydration, temperature, and blood pressure) have successfully kept total flap loss to a relative rarity (less than 1%).[93,101,113,140]

The isolated vessels of a free flap must be of sufficient caliber to protect against fat necrosis as well. Again, the free TRAM appears to confer some protection relative to conventional pedicled TRAM, even in smokers and obese patients who are at an increased baseline risk for fat necrosis. Using mammography to support their clinical findings, Kroll and colleagues at the M.D. Anderson Cancer Center showed a 2% incidence of fat necrosis in free TRAM follow-up, compared with 13% in pedicled TRAM flaps.[138] In addition, less fat necrosis ultimately means fewer false-positive findings on follow-up surveillance, reducing the number of unnecessary biopsies.

Once raised, the free TRAM allows much more latitude in reconstruction because almost 100% of the initial flap harvest can be used to achieve desired breast volume. Recall that a portion of the pedicled flap is discarded owing to inadequate blood supply/viability. Moreover, the larger free TRAM flap is almost completely devoid of the rectus musculature. Because less muscle has to be harvested, it is not surprising that recovery after a free TRAM tends to be faster than that following placement of a pedicled flap. Kroll and colleagues have demonstrated the functional consequences of this difference. Whereas 75% of patients are able to perform sit-ups after undergoing bilateral free TRAM reconstruction, only 26% of those with bilateral pedicled or bipedicled procedures were able to do so.[27,141]

In 1996, Kroll and colleagues compared the resource costs of free and conventional TRAM flap reconstructions.[142] Despite some inherent limitations, this series demonstrated that the cost of free TRAM reconstruction is only modestly higher than that of conventional TRAM. Specifically, there was a mere $727 (US) cost advantage to conventional TRAM flap (4.1% of the cost of mastectomy and conventional TRAM reconstruction), but this

difference was not statistically significant. Given all of its advantages, including improved patient outcomes, it can be argued that even a slight increase in costs is both fair and justified.

Bilateral free TRAM reconstruction provides long-term reliability compared with the somewhat less predictable long-term course of expander/implant reconstruction, but this long-term predictability comes at a substantial initial cost. The initial operation is significantly more extensive than other options and is the only type of reconstruction that carries a real risk for requiring blood transfusion. In the case of contralateral prophylactic mastectomy, the time constraints to treat the cancerous breast would not allow time for autologous blood donation. Patients undergoing bilateral PM with plans for bilateral free TRAM reconstruction should consider autologous blood donation. For many women, the opportunity to use excess abdominal tissue and flatten the abdomen confers a significant and tangible advantage to the TRAM procedure and may be the deciding factor in favor of TRAM flap reconstruction. Most importantly, the TRAM flap procedure provides a durable lifetime reconstruction that is natural in both form and texture. The free TRAM flap is undoubtedly one of the most successful, natural, and aesthetic options in the plastic surgeon's armamentarium.

Deep Inferior Epigastric Perforator Flap

To circumvent complications related to donor-site morbidity associated with a TRAM flap, the DIEP free flap has been developed.[143] The DIEP flap represents the latest evolution of the TRAM technique. It is a free flap composed of abdominal skin and subcutaneous tissue alone, sparing the rectus muscle entirely. This is accomplished by teasing the deep inferior epigastric vessels away from the rectus muscle. Almost no muscle or fascia is sacrificed, making abdominal closure simple and usually precluding the need for synthetic mesh reinforcement. This scenario is ideal for simultaneous bilateral breast reconstruction.

The disadvantage of DIEP flap reconstruction is that microvascular dissection of the perforators is significantly more tedious and time-consuming than a standard free TRAM flap, adding 5 hours or more to the operation. One witty surgeon describes this procedure as "nerve-wracking."[101] Theoretically, with an even more isolated blood supply, the likelihood of fat necrosis and total flap loss secondary to thrombosis is further increased. In practice, careful patient selection can minimize complication rates such that they are comparable to those of free TRAM.[144] Functional donor site morbidity is minimal, but some impairment of the oblique muscles has been noted during recovery.[145] The more limited muscle loss afforded by a DIEP procedure allows a faster recovery time and shorter hospital stay for most patients, making overall costs comparable to those of free TRAM as well.[146,147]

Despite its potential, the extensiveness of this procedure has kept its use relatively limited. Although initial recovery (the first week or two) is clearly improved, benefit beyond this time is unproven. To date, the theoretical advantages have not outweighed the increased surgical complexity. It will take a study demonstrating a more lasting and measurable improvement to overcome most surgeons' hesitation to offer this flap as a standard procedure.

Latissimus Dorsi Flap

After expander/implant and TRAM flaps, the LD myocutaneous flap is the third most prevalent method of reconstruction, although it is not necessarily a third choice by default. In its traditional form, the LD flap is used in combination with the pectoralis muscle to provide additional volume and skin coverage for an implant. This might, for example, allow a patient who wishes to avoid the time associated with serial expansion and second-stage implant exchange to gain desired breast volume and tissue coverage in a single stage. It also provides additional fullness to the inferolateral quadrant of the breast mound, where, as previously mentioned, volume is difficult to achieve with an implant alone.

When it was first introduced by Schneider and colleagues, and Muhlbauer and Olbrisch in 1977, the LD flap solved many of the problems related to inadequate skin coverage of implants, fueling its popularity and springboarding implants into mainstream practice.[148,149] After the emergence of skin-sparing techniques and the rapid adoption of the TRAM flap, LD flap reconstruction temporarily fell out of favor. For most patients, cosmetic results surpass those of expander/implant reconstruction alone, but do not quite compare to the TRAM.

Newer modifications of the standard latissimus flap have diminished our reliance on the implant's contribution to volume requirements. With better fatty tissue preservation in raising the latissimus muscle, less than 50% of the desired volume has to come from the implant. A greater proportion of native tissue thereby confers a more natural result.

Even in this modified form, the disadvantage of the standard LD flap is that it combines the risks of an autologous procedure (eg, longer surgery, donor site morbidity, flap necrosis) with those of an implant (eg, capsular contracture and deflation). In smaller breast mounds with lower volume requirements (ie, B or C cup size), an extended version of the LD flap has been designed for solitary use without an implant.[150] This exclusively autologous technique uses the latissimus muscle pedicle as an island upon which to carry a paddle of skin and subcutaneous fat to the mastectomy defect.[151] To compensate for the volume formerly furnished by the implant, the extended latissimus flap draws from five zones of fatty tissue: (1) fat underlying the cutaneous paddle; (2) fat on the latissimus muscle surface; (3) the scapular fat pad located above the superomedial border of the muscle; (4) an anterior zone of fat, deep to the muscle; and (5) the suprailiac fat pad, comprising "love handle" fat above the iliac crest, near the lower border of the latissimus.[152]

The extended latissimus bestows a shapely, ptotic breast and restores fullness to the anterior axillary fold and infraclavicular region. For the nonmicrosurgeon, this procedure is an excellent second-choice alternative for almost any patient who is unfit for a pedicled TRAM reconstruction but desires an autologous procedure. Other high-risk TRAM candidates, such as diabetics and smokers, do well with latissimus flaps because its superior vascularity is less susceptible to damage. Obese patients are ideal candidates because these patients are at high risk for abdominal wall morbidity in TRAM reconstruction but possess ample stores of extraneous back tissue for use in a latissimus flap. It is also useful in salvaging total or partial loss of a free TRAM flap or to replace flaps damaged by radiation.[151]

Despite these advantages, in the very thin patient who demonstrates less than 2 to 2.5 cm of back fat by a pinch test, use of an implant may be unavoidable. Thin patients often require implants of 100 to 200 cc (up to 25% of the reconstructed breast) to achieve desired volume. In all likelihood, many of these women would have needed an implant even had they chosen a TRAM flap.[151]

One of the biggest challenges to latissimus flap surgery, whether standard or extended, is that intraoperative repositioning of the patient is required to gain access to the back, axilla, and breast as needed. In order to facilitate the process, the patient is positioned on a beanbag in the lateral position, granting easy access to both the anterior chest (for mastectomy) and the back. A flap corresponding to the chest wall skin defect is marked and incised. A three-cornered "fleur-de-lis" skin paddle was the original design, but most surgeons today seem to prefer a crescent shape owing to its more favorable scar.[43,124,151] Since 1997, we have been using a modified version of the fleur-de-lis, taking an additional section of deepithelialized tissue perpendicular to the long axis.[93] This adds additional volume to the inferior pole of the breast and minimizes the dog-ear.

Another obstacle in shaping the breast with an LD flap is avoiding excessive lateral fullness at the axillae as the flaps are tunneled through. To circumvent this difficulty, the latissimus tendon is sectioned, the tunnel can be widened, and, if necessary, the flap may be sutured more firmly against the chest wall. In combination, these techniques are very effective at preventing inordinate bulging.[124] A second problem is that the latissimus muscle has a tendency to atrophy in the first 5 to 6 months following surgery, decreasing the size of the flap and increasing ptosis in the resultant breast. In anticipation of these changes, the rebuilt breast is deliberately designed to be 15 to 30% larger than desired breast volume and set higher on the chest.[152] Careful preservation of the thoracodorsal nerve helps to maintain muscle tone and volume.

If a sufficient skin envelope is available after skin-sparing total mastectomy, a completely deepithelialized flap may be used. The deepithelialized myocutaneous latissimus flap, originally described by Bohme in 1980, was, in fact, the first purely autologous method of reconstruction, predating the TRAM flap by 2 years.[151] The flap is buried completely within the preserved skin envelope to provide the needed breast volume. This also avoids any noticeable mismatch between dorsal (back) skin and the thinner, lighter, surrounding residual skin of the breast. This scenario is most likely in a patient who wants to reduce the size of her breasts.

Partial and total flap necrosis, the most critical complications in autologous breast reconstruction, are rare in autologous latissimus flaps (roughly 1% each).[152] Skin flap necrosis is typically not a problem when sufficient underlying tissue is incorporated into the harvest so as not to disturb the subcutaneous plexus. Functional loss to the back is also minimal; except in the case of extreme dependence on the latissimus (eg, mountain climbing), secondary muscles of the back and shoulder compensate quite well.

Dorsal seroma formation, a comparatively minor complication, is unequivocally the most troublesome drawback to autologous latissimus reconstruction, occurring in 79% of all cases and with even more regularity in obese patients.[152] Fortunately, seromas are relatively easy to manage with needle aspiration, repeated as necessary. The two biggest cosmetic shortcomings of LD muscle harvest are scarring and a visible contour deformity at the donor site. Most patients are accepting of the dorsal scar because this area is not scrutinized in a mirror on a daily basis. The scar can be placed horizontally to attempt coverage in the bra line or it can be placed obliquely to facilitate wearing a "V" back, depending on patient preferences. The dorsal contour depression comes as a natural consequence of transferring as much fat and subcutaneous tissue from the back as possible. The larger the volume of native tissue transferred from the back, the smaller the implant and the more natural the final result.

Without having to contend with severe functional morbidity, recovery after latissimus reconstruction is much more rapid than that of TRAM. Patients can expect to resume full athletic activity in as little as 3 to 4 months.[124] Again, postoperative recurrence monitoring is done in the clinical setting, by palpation rather than mammography. Ultimately, the latissimus dorsi flap is a simpler procedure, but the final result is not considered as natural-looking as TRAM, and the residual contour deformity is not nearly as acceptable a corollary as is abdominoplasty.

OTHER AUTOLOGOUS TECHNIQUES

Experience with microsurgical approaches in free TRAM reconstruction has not only led to refinements in the TRAM flap technique itself (eg, the DIEP flap) but has also paved the way for other free flap methods. The superior and inferior gluteal, lateral transverse thigh, and Taylor-Rubens peri-iliac free flaps all represent viable, though far less common, alternatives to the TRAM and extended latissimus techniques described above. All require extensive microvascular surgery and are usually restricted to those patients who, either by choice or by medical necessity, are not suitable candidates for TRAM or latissimus reconstruction. Bilateral simultaneous gluteal or Rubens free flaps are extremely long procedures. These techniques are significantly easier to execute when each breast is reconstructed separately.[27]

Gluteal Free Flaps

Of all autologous free flaps, gluteal flaps are by far the most technically challenging.[153,154] Nonetheless, even the thinnest of patients has sufficient gluteal tissue for breast reconstruction, making it an omnipresent if seldom-used alternative.[155] The gluteus maximus muscle is supplied by both the superior and inferior gluteal arteries. The superior or inferior portions of the muscle can be harvested independently for use as free flaps. Neither approach causes appreciable functional loss of the buttock, but between repositioning and a difficult dissection, both significantly prolong operative time, raising the likelihood of intra- and perioperative complications.

The superior gluteal flap, based on the superior gluteal artery, has notoriously frustrated surgeons. The vessel lies deep within the perisacral region, directly beneath the gluteus maximus, and is not easily exposed. Furthermore, the resultant vascular pedicle is short (1.5 to 2 cm), making microanastomosis with recipient axillary vessels exceedingly difficult. Because flap harvest can be so exhausting, bilateral reconstruction using superior gluteal free flaps is best approached in staged fashion, whereby one breast is reconstructed immediately and the contralateral breast is postponed to a second procedure. The introduction of the superior gluteal artery perforator flap has improved the pedicle length but does not lessen the tedious dissection and technical difficulty of the flap.

The longer, more easily dissected pedicle of the inferior gluteal flap solves many of the vascular problems, but donor site scarring and contour deformity represent major drawbacks.[101,155,156] The approach to the inferior pedicle can be made such that the scar is placed in the inferior gluteal crease, where it is easily concealed but is very uncomfortable. Second, the removal of 300 to 400 grams of fat from the buttock causes an unavoidable flattening that may be impossible to correct, similar but more notable than the dorsal defect of a latissimus flap. This might be wholly unacceptable were it not for the symmetry afforded by a bilateral procedure.[124]

Postoperative recovery is typically fast and uneventful with the notable exception of sciatica pain syndrome. Sciatica has been documented in some of the earliest patients to receive gluteal flap breast reconstruction, as a direct consequence of excessive tissue harvest, leaving the sciatic nerve without adequate padding. This was particularly the case for thinner patients, in whom residual tissue overlying the nerve can be scant. Ironically, these were some of the very patients who became candidates for the procedure because they lacked sufficient lower abdominal tissue for TRAM flap harvest.[124] Refinements in the technique have since minimized the amount of the gluteus muscle that is harvested, ensuring ample protective coverage of the sciatic nerve. Pain syndromes are now quite infrequent.

Lateral Transverse Thigh Flap

The lateral transverse thigh flap (LTTF) is the horizontal variant of the tensor fascia lata myocutaneous flap, taking advantage of skin and so-called "saddlebag" fat from the tensor fascia lata muscle to reconstruct the breast.[157] Blood supply is based on the lateral circumflex femoral vessels. It is ideal for non-TRAM, nonlatissimus candidates who desire immediate bilateral reconstruction, because flap harvest is relatively simple and does not require repositioning.

Dissatisfaction with this procedure stems from its residual effects. Conspicuous scarring on the lateral thigh over the greater trochanter is difficult to conceal with any bathing suit style. In addition, lateral contour depressions may be unavoidable and, as we saw with gluteal flaps, are moderated only by virtue of bilateral symmetry. Careful flap design and conservative tissue resection can help to minimize an "hourglass" appearance, but a smooth contour cannot always be achieved. Persistent donor site seromas are also problematic. Fortunately, the tensor muscle is small and is the only muscle interrupted by this procedure. As a result, no functional loss to the thigh is incurred, and recovery is generally uncomplicated. Some women are more accepting than others of the resultant cosmetic morbidity to this location. If a patient is willing to overlook donor site deformity, the LTTF represents an excellent autologous alternative to TRAM and extended latissimus flaps.

Taylor-Rubens Peri-Iliac Flap

The Rubens flap, as it is more commonly known, includes soft tissue and "love handle" fat above the posterior ileum on the lateral hip, reminiscent of the female figure depicted in Peter Paul Rubens' painting *The Three Graces* (hence the name).[43,158] It represents a non-bony modification of the deep circumflex iliac artery osteocutaneous flap first described by Taylor and colleagues in 1979.[159] In addition to patients who lack sufficient lower abdominal or back tissue, this option is ideally suited for patients who have had prior abdominoplasty or TRAM reconstruction because the donor incision represents a direct extension of the existing abdominoplasty incision.[43,124]

A small cuff of the internal and external obliques, as well as the transversalis muscle, must also accompany the flap to guarantee inclusion of perforating vessels and an intact flap perfusion. Surgical repair of the muscular defect requires fixation to the iliac crest, which has been known to elicit a transiently intense period of discomfort that usually abates after the first few days. Barring this pain, flank herniation secondary to disruption of the lateral abdominal wall is the most devastating complication. This flap produces much less contour deformity than the gluteal or lateral transverse thigh flaps — a distinct advantage. Recovery time is commensurate with that of the gluteal and lateral transverse thigh flaps as well. Although this technique is still under development and its usage remains limited, patient satisfaction has been resoundingly positive thus far.

Superficial Inferior Epigastric Artery Flap

This flap has the potential to be the ideal autologous flap for breast reconstruction, but variable anatomy and technical difficulties will limit the utility of this flap. This flap transfers the same abdominal tissue as the TRAM flap or DIEP flap, but it utilizes the superficial inferior epigastric artery and vein rather than the deep. This means the rectus sheath and rectus abdominus muscle are not cut or injured in any way. This completely eliminates the possibility of abdominal wall hernia or weakness. The main disadvantages of the flap are the variable anatomy of the superficial vessels and the technical requirement for microsurgical transfer (this flap must be transferred as a free flap). The superficial vessels will be large enough to use in a minority of patients only (less than 50%). Preoperative evaluation may be necessary to determine who may be a candidate for this procedure, and/or patients should be agreeable to a TRAM flap procedure if the superficial inferior epigastric vessels prove to be inadequate in the operating room. There are no published series using this flap, but as more experience is gained this flap will be a welcome, although limited, addition to breast reconstruction technique.

NIPPLE-AREOLAR RECONSTRUCTION

Reconstruction of the NAC represents the final stage or step in breast reconstruction. As the focal point of the breast, the NAC is pivotal in creating both symmetry and realism. In the absence of a nipple, the mound of reconstructed tissue does not seem to take on the form and contour of a true "breast." Yet, an asymmetrically placed NAC can just as easily detract from breast mounds that would otherwise exhibit perfect bilateral symmetry. Symmetric positioning, texture, and pigmentation therefore become the main objectives in nipple-areolar reconstruction.

Immediate nipple reconstruction, although possible, presents several limitations.[43,101] First, unless the breast mounds do not shift appreciably in size or position throughout the healing process, which is unlikely, there is no way to ensure that the NAC will ultimately be situated properly. Second, additional damage to the newly operated skin envelope demands sufficient perfusion to support the reconstructed nipple. Only well-vascularized autologous flaps, such as the free TRAM and extended LD flaps, can provide that level of sustenance, and even then the threat of skin contraction remains.

Accurate positioning is best accomplished when nipple reconstruction is delayed 2 to 3 months after the primary breast mound reconstruction. This allows postoperative edema and induration to resolve and also provides time for adjuvant treatments to be delivered. Conveniently, any revisions or refinements to breast shape and contour can also be performed in conjunction with second- or third-stage nipple reconstruction.

Older techniques to recreate nipple projection used free grafts derived from the contralateral nipple (in unilateral procedures, so-called nipple sharing), heterotopic reimplantation, or distant sites (the ear, labia minora, the groin, or toe pulp). In current practice, most of these methods have been supplanted by local skin flap techniques based on the new breast mound. Designs are many and include the skate flap, star (fishtail), Maltese cross, mushroom, and others.[101,160] Our preference has been to use a star flap, involving the elevation of a full-thickness flap with triangular wings, to create a projecting cylindrical nipple. This technique is simple to perform and produces a very realistic result.[43,93] For patients who have a circular skin paddle, from an autologous flap reconstruction following a skin-sparing mastectomy, an advancement flap technique can be used that maintains the circular orientation of the scar and skin paddle (Figure 17-4).

Reconstruction of the areola, formerly accomplished with skin grafts from areas of darker pigmentation, including the inner thigh, labia minora, and opposite areola (in a unilateral procedure), has now been outmoded by delayed intradermal tattooing techniques. Tattooing is more convenient, less invasive, and with skillful color matching produces an equally attractive result.[161] It is typically scheduled 4 to 8 weeks after reconstruction of the nipple itself. Because central sensory innervation of the breast mound is almost always decreased, techniques that use local flaps and tattooing are relatively painless.

SUMMARY

The barrage of difficult decisions facing the PM candidate can be daunting. In this chapter we have explored the process of breast reconstruction in its entirety, from initial patient consultation through nipple reconstruction, detailing the spectrum of options available and highlighting the salient facts that patients and physicians may need to know in order to demystify and guide decision making. Just as PM is not an absolute remedy to cancer recurrence, neither is reconstruction a panacea for its psychological and cosmetic aftermath. Neverthe-

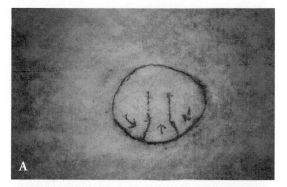
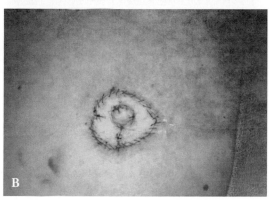

Figure 17-4 *A*, Nipple reconstruction; lines indicate incisions, arrows indicate direction of local flap movement to create the nipple projection and close the open area created by the construction of the nipple. *B*, Nipple reconstruction; scars have been limited to the circular areola and can be completely hidden by the tattoo used to provide color.

less, the woman at increased risk and opting for PM stands to reap significant benefits from reconstruction if matched to an appropriate reconstructive option. The method she ultimately chooses will depend on a complex interplay of factors, including her desires, expectations, and understanding and familiarity with potential drawbacks or complications. The essential challenge is to find a balance for each patient between less "surgery," with a faster recovery (implants), versus the durability and natural look and feel of more invasive autogenous tissue procedures (TRAM and latissimus). It is only through a thorough discussion of the pros and cons of each procedure, and a careful consideration of how those issues personally impact her, that a woman is able to make the "right" decision for her situation.

REFERENCES

1. Frost MH, Schaid DJ, Sellers TA, et al. Long-term satisfaction and psychological and social function following bilateral prophylactic mastectomy. JAMA 2000;284:319–24.

2. Payne DK, Biggs C, Tran K, et al. Women's regrets after bilateral prophylactic mastectomy. Ann Surg Oncol 2000;7:150–4.

3. Montgomery LL, Tran KN, Heelan MC, et al. Issues of regret in women with contralateral prophylactic mastectomies. Ann Surg Oncol 1999;6:546–52.

4. Stefanek ME, Helzlsouer KJ, Wilcox PM, Houn F. Predictors of and satisfaction with bilateral prophylactic mastectomy. Prev Med 1995;24:412–9.

5. Hopwood P, Lee A, Shenton A, et al. Clinical follow-up after bilateral risk reducing ('prophylactic') mastectomy: mental health and body image outcomes. Psychooncology 2000;9:462–72.

6. Noone RB, Frazier TG, Hayward CZ, Skiles MS. Patient acceptance of immediate reconstruction following mastectomy. Plast Reconstr Surg 1982;69:632–40.

7. Reaby LL. Reasons why women who have mastectomy decide to have or not have breast reconstruction. Plast Reconstr Surg 1998;101:1810–8.

8. Osteen RT, Cady B, Friedman M, et al. Patterns of care for younger women with breast cancer. J Natl Cancer Inst Monogr 1994;16:43–6.

9. Noone RB, Murphy JB, Spear SL, Little JW III. A 6-year experience with immediate reconstruction after mastectomy for cancer. Plast Reconstr Surg 1985;76:258–6.

10. Hartmann LC, Schaid DJ, Woods JE, et al. Efficacy of bilateral prophylactic mastectomy in women with a family history of breast cancer. N Engl J Med 1999;340:77–84.

11. Osteen RT. Reconstruction after mastectomy. Cancer 1995;76 Suppl 10:2070–4.

12. Romm S, Hutzler J, Berggren RB. Sexual identity and prophylactic mastectomy. Ann Plast Surg 1981;7:35–7.

13. Josephson U, Wickman M, Sandelin K. Initial experiences of women from hereditary breast cancer families after bilateral prophylactic mastectomy: a retrospective study. Eur J Surg Oncol 2000;26:351–6.

14. Morris RJ, Koshy CE, Zambacos GJ. Prophylactic mastectomy, oophorectomy, hysterectomy, and immediate transverse rectus abdominis muscle flap breast reconstruction in a BRCA-2-negative patient. Plast Reconstr Surg 2000;105:473.

15. Goin MK, Goin JM. Psychological reactions to prophylactic mastectomy synchronous with contralateral breast reconstruction. Plast Reconstr Surg 1982;70:355–9.

16. Baker C, Johnson N, Nelson J, et al. Perspective on reconstruction after mastectomy. Am J Surg 2002;183:562–5.

17. Rowland JH, Desmond KA, Meyerowitz BE, et al. Role of breast reconstructive surgery in physical and emotional outcomes among breast cancer survivors. J Natl Cancer Inst 2000;92:1422–9.

18. Schain WS, Wellisch DK, Pasnau RO, Landsverk J. The sooner the better: a study of psychological factors in women undergoing immediate versus delayed breast reconstruction. Am J Psychiatry 1985;142:40–6.

19. Tykkä E, Asko-Seljavaara S, Hietanen H. Patients' satisfaction with breast reconstruction and reduction mammaplasty. Scand J Plast Reconstr Hand Surg 2001;35:399–405.

20. Handel N, Silverstein MJ, Waisman E, Waisman J. Reasons why mastectomy patients do not have breast reconstruction. Plast Reconstr Surg 1990;86:1118–22.

21. Gutowski KA, Mesna GT, Cunningham BL. Saline-filled breast implants: a Plastic Surgery Educational Foundation multicenter outcomes study. Plast Reconstr Surg 1997;100:1019–27.

22. Alderman AK, Wilkins EG, Lowery JC, et al. Determinants of patient satisfaction in postmastectomy breast reconstruction. Plast Reconstr Surg 2000;106:769–76.

23. Segar ML, Katch VL, Roth RS, et al. The effect of aerobic exercise on self-esteem and depressive and anxiety symptoms among breast cancer survivors. Oncol Nurs Forum 1998;25:101–13.

24. Zuckerman DM. The need to improve informed consent for breast cancer patients. J Am Med Womens Assoc 2000;55:285–9.

25. Benediktsson KP, Perbeck L, Geigant E, Solders G. Touch sensibility in the breast after subcutaneous mastectomy and immediate reconstruction with a prosthesis. Br J Plast Surg 1997;50:443–9.

26. Bostwick J III. Prophylactic (risk-reducing) mastectomy and reconstruction. In: Bostwick J, editor. Plastic and reconstructive breast surgery. 2nd ed. St. Louis: Quality Medical Publishing, Inc.; 2000. p. 1337–97.

27. Kroll SS. Bilateral breast reconstruction. Clin Plast Surg 1998;2:251–9.

28. Goldsmith HS, Alday ES. Role of the surgeon and the rehabilitation of the breast cancer patient. Cancer 1971;28:1672–5.

29. Rosato FE, Horton CE, Maxwell GP. Postmastectomy breast reconstruction. Curr Probl Surg 1980;17:585–629.

30. Vinton AL, Traverso LW, Zehring RD. Immediate breast reconstruction following mastectomy is as safe as mastectomy alone. Arch Surg 1990;125:1303–8.

31. Wellisch DK, Schain WS, Noone RB, Little JW 3rd. Psychosocial correlates of immediate versus delayed reconstruction of the breast. Plast Reconstr Surg 1985;76:713–8.

32. Stevens LA, McGrath MH, Druss RG, et al. The psychological impact of immediate breast reconstruction for women with early breast cancer. Plast Reconstr Surg 1984;73:619–28.

33. Dean C, Chetty U, Forrest AP. Effects of immediate breast reconstruction on psychosocial morbidity after mastectomy. Lancet 1983;1:459–62.

34. Kaufman M, Schmidt R, Schmidt H. Rate of local recurrence and survival in patients with breast reconstruction following mastectomy. Geburtshilfe Frauenheilkunde 1988;48:524–7.

35. Georgiade GS, Riefkohl R, Cox E, et al. Long-term clinical outcome of immediate reconstruction after mastectomy. Plast Reconstr Surg 1985;76:415–20.

36. Sandelin K, Billgren AM, Wickman M. Management, morbidity, and oncologic aspects in 100 consecutive patients with immediate breast reconstruction. Ann Surg Oncol 1998;5:159–65.

37. Wickman M, Jurell G, Sandelin K. Immediate breast reconstruction: short-term experience in 75 consecutive cases. Scand J Plast Reconstr Surg Hand Surg 1995;29:153–9.

38. Frazier TG, Noone RB. An objective analysis of immediate simultaneous reconstruction in the treatment of primary carcinoma of the breast. Cancer 1985;55:1202–5.

39. Patel RT, Webster DJ, Mansel RE, Hughes LE. Is immediate postmastectomy reconstruction safe in the long-term? Eur J Surg Oncol 1993;19:372–5.

40. Helvie MA, Bailey JE, Roubidoux MA. Mammographic screening of TRAM flap breast reconstructions for detection of nonpalpable recurrent cancer. Radiology 2002;224:211–6.

41. Vandeweyer E, Hertens D, Nogaret JM, Deraemaecker R. Immediate breast reconstruction with saline-filled implants: no interference with the oncologic outcome? Plast Reconstr Surg 2001;107:1409–12.

42. Johnson CH, van Heerden JA, Donohue JH, et al. Oncological aspects of immediate breast reconstruction following mastectomy for malignancy. Arch Surg 1989;124:819–23.

43. Corral CJ, Mustoe TA. Controversy in breast reconstruction. Surg Clin North Am 1996;76:309–26.

44. O'Brien W, Hasselgren PO, Hummel RP, et al. Comparison of postoperative wound complications and early cancer recurrence between patients undergoing mastectomy with or without immediate breast reconstruction. Am J Surg 1993;166:1–5.

45. Trabulsy PP, Anthony JP, Mathes SJ. Changing trends in postmastectomy breast reconstruction: a 13-year experience. Plast Reconstr Surg 1993;93:1418–27.

46. Elkowitz A, Colen S, Slavin S, et al. Various methods for breast reconstruction after mastectomy: an economic comparison. Plast Reconstr Surg 1993;92:77–83.

47. Khoo A, Kroll SS, Reece GP, et al. A comparison of resource costs of immediate and delayed breast reconstruction. Plast Reconstr Surg 1998;101:964–8.

48. Collis N, Sharpe DT. Breast reconstruction by tissue expansion. A retrospective technical review of 197 two-stage delayed reconstructions following mastectomy for malignant breast disease in 189 patients. Br J Plast Surg 2000;53:37–41.

49. Forman DL, Chiu J, Restifo RJ, et al. Breast reconstruction in previously irradiated patients using tissue expanders and implants: a potentially unfavorable result. Ann Plast Surg 1998;40:360–3.

50. Krueger EA, Wilkins EG, Strawderman M, et al. Complications and patient satisfaction following expander/implant breast reconstruction with and without radiotherapy. Int J Radiat Oncol Biol Phys 2001;49:713–21.

51. Kroll SS, Schusterman MA, Reece GP, et al. Breast reconstruction with myocutaneous flaps in previously irradiated patients. Plast Reconstr Surg 1994;93:460–9.

52. Kuske RR, Schuster R, Klein E, et al. Radiotherapy and breast reconstruction: clinical results and dosimetry. Int J Radiat Oncol Biol Phys 1991;21:339–46.

53. Williams JK, Bostwick J III, Bried JT, et al. TRAM flap breast reconstruction after radiation treatment. Ann Surg 1995;221:756–64.

54. Recht A, Edge SB, Solin LJ, et al. Postmastectomy radiotherapy: clinical practice guidelines of the American Society of Clinical Oncology. J Clin Oncol 2001;19:1539–69.

55. Spear SL, Onyewu C. Staged breast reconstruction with saline-filled implants in the irradiated breast: recent trends and therapeutic implications. Plast Reconstr Surg 2000;105:930–42.

56. Hanks SH, Lyons JA, Crowe J, et al. The acute effects of postoperative radiation therapy on the transverse rectus abdominis myocutaneous flap used in immediate breast reconstruction. Int J Radiat Oncol Biol Phys 2000;47:1185–90.

57. Zimmerman RP, Mark RJ, Kim AI, et al. Radiation tolerance of transverse rectus abdominis myocutaneous-free flaps used in immediate breast reconstruction. Am J Clin Oncol 1998;21:381–4.

58. Hunt KK, Baldwin BJ, Strom EA, et al. Feasibility of postmastectomy radiation therapy after TRAM flap breast reconstruction. Ann Surg Oncol 1997 4:377–84.

59. Williams JK, Carlson GW, Bostwick J III, et al. The effects of radiation therapy after TRAM flap breast reconstruction. Plast Reconstr Surg 1997;100:1153–60.

60. Chawla AK, Kachnic LA, Taghian AG, et al. Radiotherapy and breast reconstruction: complications and cosmesis with TRAM versus tissue expander/implant. Int J Radiat Oncol Biol Phys 2002;54:520–6.

61. Castello JR, Garro L, Najera A, et al. Immediate breast reconstruction in two stages using anatomical tissue expansion. Scand J Plast Reconstr Hand Surg 2000;34:167–71.

62. Contant CM, van Geel AN, van der Holt B, et al. Morbidity of immediate breast reconstruction (IBR) after mastectomy by a subpectorally placed silicone prosthesis: the adverse effect of radiotherapy. Eur J Surg Oncol 2000;26:344–50.

63. Tran NV, Evans GR, Kroll SS, et al. Postoperative adjuvant irradiation: effects on transverse rectus abdominis muscle flap breast reconstruction. Plast Reconstr Surg 2000;106:313–7.

64. Vandeweyer E, Deraemaecker R. Radiation therapy after immediate breast reconstruction with implants. Plast Reconstr Surg 2000;106:56–8.

65. Kraemer O, Andersen M, Siim E. Breast reconstruction and tissue expansion in irradiated versus not irradiated women after mastectomy. Scand J Plast Reconstr Surg Hand Surg 1996;30:201–6.

66. Evans GR, Schusterman MA, Kroll SS, et al. Reconstruction and the irradiated breast: is there a role for implants? Plast Reconstr Surg 1995;96:1111–5.

67. Barreau-Pouhaer L, Le MG, Rietjens M, et al. Risk factors for failure of immediate breast reconstruction with prosthesis after total mastectomy for breast cancer. Cancer 1992;70:1145–51.

68. Spear SL, Majidian A. Immediate breast reconstruction in two stages using textured, integrated-valve tissue expanders and breast implants: a retrospective review of 171 consecutive breast reconstructions from 1989 to 1996. Plast Reconstr Surg 1998;101:53–63.

69. Ramon Y, Ullman Y, Moscona R, et al. Aesthetic results and patient satisfaction with immediate breast reconstruction using tissue expansion: a follow-up study. Plast Reconstr Surg 1997;99:686–91.

70. Von Smitten K, Sundell B. The impact of adjuvant radiotherapy and cytotoxic chemotherapy on the outcome of immediate breast reconstruction by tissue expansion after mastectomy for breast cancer. Eur J Surg Cancer 1992;18:119–23.

71. Tran NV, Chang DW, Gupta A, et al. Comparison of immediate and delayed free TRAM flap breast reconstruction in patients receiving postmastectomy radiation therapy. Plast Reconstr Surg 2001;108:78–82.

72. Marcus JR, Morrow M, Fine NA. The influence of expanding indications for postmastectomy irradiation on the technique of breast reconstruction. In: Plastic Surgical Forum XXIII. Proceedings of the 69th ASPRS Scientific Meeting; 2000 Oct 14–18; Los Angeles, CA. p. 417–8.

73. Kroll SS, Baldwin B. Comparison of outcomes using three different methods of breast reconstruction. Plast Reconstr Surg 1992;90:455–62.

74. Saulis A, Kshettry P, Mustoe TA, Fine NA. A restrospective analysis of patient satisfaction with breast reconstruction. [In preparation]

75. Tzafetta K, Ahmed O, Bahia H, et al. Evaluation of the factors related to postmastectomy breast reconstruction. Plast Reconstr Surg 2001;107:1694–701.

76. Beal JM, Conn J Jr. Prophylactic mastectomy and reconstruction. Ill Med J 1983;163:344–6.

77. Hicken NF. Mastectomy: a clinical pathologic study demonstrating why most mastectomies result in incomplete removal of the mammary gland. Arch Surg 1940;40:6–14.

78. Woods JE, Irons GB, Arnold PG. The case for submuscular implantation of prostheses in reconstructive breast surgery. Ann Plast Surg 1980;5:115–22.

79. Randall P, Dabb R, Loc N. "Apple coring" the nipple in subcutaneous mastectomy. Plast Reconstr Surg 1979;64:800–3.

80. Lopez MJ, Porter KA. The current role of prophylactic mastectomy. Surg Clin North Am 1996;76:231–42.

81. Eldar S, Meguid MM, Beatty JD. Cancer of the breast after prophylactic subcutaneous mastectomy. Am J Surg 1984;148:692–3.

82. Goldman LD, Goldwyn RM. Some anatomical considerations of subcutaneous mastectomy. Plast Reconstr Surg 1973;51:501–5.

83. Goodnight JE Jr, Quagliana JM, Morton DL. Failure of subcutaneous mastectomy to prevent the development of breast cancer. J Surg Oncol 1984;26:198–201.

84. Jarrett JR, Cutler RG, Teal DF. Aesthetic refinements in prophylactic subcutaneous mastectomy with submuscular reconstruction. Plast Reconstr Surg 1982;69:624–31.

85. Pennisi VR, Capozzi A. Subcutaneous mastectomy data: a final statistical analysis of 1500 patients. Aesthetic Plast Surg 1989;13:15–21.

86. Schuster DI, Lavine DM. Nine-year experience with subpectoral breast reconstruction after subcutaneous mastectomy in 98 patients utilizing saline-inflatable prostheses. Ann Plast Surg 1988;21:444–51.

87. Shons AR, Press BH. Subcutaneous mastectomy. Indications, technique, and applications. Arch Surg 1983;118:844–50.

88. Spira M. Subcutaneous mastectomy in the large ptotic breast. Plast Reconstr Surg 1977;59:200–5.

89. Horton CE, Adamson JE, Mladick RA, Carraway JH. Simple mastectomy with immediate reconstruction. Plast Reconstr Surg 1974;53:42–7.

90. ASPRS-Statistics. Arlington Heights (IL): National Clearing House of Plastic Surgery Statistics; 1998.

91. Radovan C. Breast reconstruction after mastectomy using the temporary expander. Plast Reconstr Surg 1982;69:195–208.

92. Fine NA, Mustoe TA, Fenner G. Breast reconstruction. In: Harris JR, editor. Diseases of the breast. 2nd ed. Philadelphia: Lippincott Williams & Wilkins; 2000. p. 561–75.

93. Mandrekas AD, Zambacos GJ, Katsantoni PN. Immediate and delayed breast reconstruction with permanent tissue expanders. Br J Plast Surg 1995;48:572–8.

94. Modena S, Benassuti C, Marchiori L, et al. Mastectomy and immediate breast reconstruction: oncological considerations and evaluation of two different methods relating to 88 cases. Eur J Surg Oncol 1995;21:36–41.

95. Dowden RV. Selection criteria for successful immediate breast reconstruction. Plast Reconstr Surg 1991;88:628–34.

96. Eberlein TJ, Crespo LD, Smith BL, et al. Prospective evaluation of immediate reconstruction after mastectomy. Ann Surg 1993;218:29–36.

97. Fan J, Raposio E, Wang J, Nordstrom RE. Development of the inframammary fold and ptosis in breast reconstruction with textured tissue expanders. Aesth Plast Surg 2002;26:219–22.

98. Gibney J. Use of a permanent tissue expander for breast reconstruction. Plast Reconstr Surg 1989; 84:607–17.

99. Hammond DC, Perry LC, Maxwell GP, Fisher J. Morphologic analysis of tissue-expander shape using a biomechanical model. Plast Reconstr Surg 1993;92:255–9.

100. Malata CM, McIntosh SA, Purushotham AD. Immediate breast reconstruction after mastectomy. Br J Surg 2000;87:1455–72.

101. Ward J, Cohen IK, Knaysi GA, Brown PW. Immediate breast reconstruction with tissue expansion. Plast Reconstr Surg 1987;80:559–66.

102. Woods JE, Mangan MA. Breast reconstruction with tissue expanders: obtaining an optimal result. Ann Plast Surg 1992;28:390–6.

103. Petit JY, Greco M. Quality control in prophylactic mastectomy for women at high risk of breast cancer. Eur J Cancer 2002;38:23–6.

104. Spear SL, Baker JL Jr. Classification of capsular contracture after prosthetic breast reconstruction. Plast Reconstr Surg 1995;96:1119–23.

105. Maxwell GP, Falcone PA. Eighty-four consecutive breast reconstructions using a textured silicone tissue expander. Plast Reconstr Surg 1992;89: 1022–34.

106. Wickman M, Jurell G. Low capsular contraction rate after primary and secondary breast reconstruction with a textured expander prosthesis. Plast Reconstr Surg 1997;99:692–7.

107. Mladick RA. Inflatable breast implants. Plast Reconstr Surg 1995;95:600.

108. Gruber RP, Kahn RA, Lash H, et al. Breast reconstruction following mastectomy: a comparison of submuscular and subcutaneous techniques. Plast Reconstr Surg 1981;67:312–7.

109. Jarrett JR. Prophylactic mastectomy. In: Marsh JL, editor. Current therapy in plastic and reconstructive surgery. Toronto: BC Decker Inc; 1989. p. 64–70.

110. Little JW III, Golembe EV, Fisher JB. The 'living bra' in immediate and delayed reconstruction of the breast following mastectomy for malignant and nonmalignant disease. Plast Reconstr Surg 1981; 68:392–403.

111. Spear SL, Majidian A. Immediate breast reconstruction in two stages using textured, integrated-valve tissue expanders and breast implants: a retrospective review of 171 consecutive breast reconstructions from 1989 to 1996. Plast Reconstr Surg 1998;101:53–63.

112. Hughes KS, Papa MZ, Whitney T, McLellan R. Prophylactic mastectomy and inherited predisposition to breast carcinoma. Cancer 1999;86: 2502–16.

113. Gabriel SE, Woods JE, O'Fallon WM, et al. Complications leading to surgery after breast implantation. N Engl J Med 1997;336:677–82.

114. Contant CM, Menke-Pluijmers MB, Seynaeve C, et al. Clinical experience of prophylactic mastectomy followed by immediate breast reconstruction in women at hereditary risk of breast cancer (HB(O)C) or a proven BRCA1 and BRCA2 germ-line mutation. Eur J Surg Oncol 2002;28:627–32.

115. Silverman BG, Brown SL, Bright RA, et al. Reported complications of silicone gel breast implants: an epidemiologic review. Ann Intern Med 1996;124: 744–56.

116. Schusterman MA, Kroll SS, Reece GP, et al. Incidence of autoimmune disease in patients after breast reconstruction with silicone gel implants versus autogenous tissue: a preliminary report. Ann Plast Surg 1993;31:1–6.

117. Gabriel SE, O'Fallon WM, Kurland LT, et al. Risk of connective-tissue disease and other disorders after breast implantation. N Engl J Med 1994;330: 1697–702.

118. Sanchez-Guerrero J, Coldiztz GA, Karlson EW, et al. Silicone breast implants and the risk of connective-tissue diseases and symptoms. N Engl J Med 1995;332:1666–70.

119. Fisher J, Hammond DC. The combination of expanders with autogenous tissue in breast reconstruction. Clin Plast Surg 1994;21:309–20.

120. Schneider WJ, Hill HL Jr, Brown E. Latissimus dorsi flap for breast reconstruction. Br J Plast Surg 1977;30:277.

121. Miller MJ, Rock CS, Robb GL. Aesthetic breast reconstruction using a combination of free transverse rectus abdominis musculocutaneous flaps and breast implants. Ann Plast Surg 1996;37: 258–64.

122. Hartrampf CR Jr, Scheflan M, Black PW. Breast reconstruction with a transverse abdominal island flap. Plast Reconstr Surg 1982;69:216–25.

123. Mustoe TA. Evolving concepts in breast reconstruction. In: Cameron JL, editor. Current surgical therapy. St. Louis: Mosby; 1998. p. 665–73.

124. Elliott LF. Options for donor sites for autogenous tissue breast reconstruction. Clin Plast Surg 1994;21: 177–89.

125. Zienowicz RJ, May JW. Hernia prevention and aesthetic contouring of the abdomen following TRAM flap breast reconstruction by use of polypropylene mesh. Plast Reconstr Surg 1995;96:1346–50.

126. Mizgala CL, Hartrampf CR, Bennett GK. Assessment of the abdominal wall after pedicled TRAM flap surgery: 5- to 7-year follow-up of 150 consecutive patients. Plast Reconstr Surg 1994;93:988–1002.

127. Kind GM, Rademaker AW, Mustoe TA. Abdominal-wall recovery following TRAM flap: a functional outcome study. Plast Reconstr Surg 1997;97:417–28.

128. Hartrampf CR Jr. The transverse abdominal island flap for breast reconstruction: a 7-year experience. Clin Plast Surg 1988;15:703–16.

129. Kroll SS, Netscher DT. Complications of TRAM flap breast reconstruction in obese patients. Plast Reconstr Surg 1989;84:886–92.

130. Spear SL, Pennanen M, Barter J, Burke JB. Prophylactic mastectomy, oophorectomy, hysterectomy,

and immediate transverse rectus abdominis muscle flap breast reconstruction in a BRCA-2-positive patient. Plast Reconstr Surg 1999;103:548–53.

131. Slavin SA, Love SM, Goldwyn RM. Recurrent breast cancer following immediate reconstruction with myocutaneous flaps. Plast Reconstr Surg 1994;93:1191–204.

132. Berrino P, Santi P. Hemodynamic analysis of the TRAM. Clin Plast Surg 1994;21:233–45.

133. Lejour M, Dome M. Abdominal wall function after rectus abdominis transfer. Plast Reconstr Surg 1991;87:1054–68.

134. Hartrampf CR Jr, Bennet GK. Autogenous tissue reconstruction in post mastectomy patients. Ann Surg 1987;205:508–19.

135. Holmstrom H. The free abdominoplasty flap and its use in breast reconstruction. An experimental study and clinical case report. Scand J Plast Reconstr Surg 1979;13:423–7.

136. Baldwin BJ, Schusterman MA, Miller MJ, et al. Bilateral breast reconstruction: conventional versus free TRAM. Plast Reconstr Surg 1994;93:1410–6.

137. Khouri RK, Ahn CY, Salzhauer MA, et al. Simultaneous bilateral breast reconstruction with the transverse rectus abdominus musculocutaneous free flap. Ann Surg 1997;226:25–34.

138. Kroll SS, Gherardini G, Martin JE, et al. Fat necrosis in free and pedicled TRAM flaps. Plast Reconstr Surg 1998;102:1502–7.

139. Boyd JB, Taylor GI, Corlett R. The vascular territories of the superior epigastric and the deep inferior epigastric systems. Plast Reconstr Surg 1984;73:1–16.

140. Schusterman MA, Kroll SS, Miller MJ, et al. The free transverse rectus abdominis musculocutaneous flap for breast reconstruction: one center's experience with 211 consecutive cases. Ann Plast Surg 1994;32:234–41.

141. Kroll SS, Schusterman MA, Reece GP, et al. Abdominal wall strength, bulging, and hernia after TRAM flap breast reconstruction. Plast Reconstr Surg 1995;96:616–9.

142. Kroll SS, Evans GR, Reece GP, et al. Comparison of resource costs of free and conventional TRAM flap breast reconstruction. Plast Reconstr Surg 1996;98:74–7.

143. Allen RJ, Treece P. Deep inferior epigastric perforator flap for breast reconstruction. Ann Plast Surg 1994;32:32–8.

144. Kroll SS. Fat necrosis in free transverse rectus abdominis myocutaneous and deep inferior epigastric perforator flaps. Plast Reconstr Surg 2000;106:576–83.

145. Hamdi M, Weiler-Mithoff EM, Webster MHC. Deep inferior epigastric perforator flap in breast reconstruction: experience with the first 50 flaps. Plast Reconstr Surg 1999;103:86–95.

146. Singletary SE. New approaches to surgery for breast cancer. Endocr Relat Cancer 2001;8:265–86.

147. Kaplan JL, Allen RJ. Cost-based comparison between perforator flaps and TRAM flaps for breast reconstruction. Plast Reconstr Surg 2000;105:943–8.

148. Schneider WJ, Hill HL Jr, Brown RG. Latissimus dorsi myocutaneous flap for breast reconstruction. Br J Plast Surg 1977;30:277–81.

149. Muhlbauer W, Olbrisch RR. The latissimus dorsi myocutaneous flap for breast reconstruction. Chir Plastica 1977;4:27–34.

150. Germann G, Steinau HU. Breast reconstruction with the extended latissimus dorsi flap. Plast Reconstr Surg 1996;97:519–26.

151. McCraw JB, Papp C, Edwards A, McMellin A. The autogenous latissimus breast reconstruction. Clin Plast Surg 1994;21:279–88.

152. Delay E, Gounot N, Bouillot A, Zlatoff P. Autologous latissimus breast reconstruction: a 3-year clinical experience with 100 patients. Plast Reconstr Surg 1998;102:1461–77.

153. Fine NA, Orgill DP, Pribaz JJ. Early clinical experience in endoscopic-assisted muscle flap harvest. Ann Plast Surg 1994;33:456–9.

154. Shaw WW. Breast reconstruction by superior gluteal microvascular free flaps without silicone implants. Plast Reconstr Surg 1983;72:490–501.

155. Paletta CE, Bostwick J III, Nahai F. The inferior gluteal free flap in breast reconstruction. Plast Reconstr Surg 1989;84:875–83.

156. LeQuang C. Two new free flaps proceeding from aesthetic surgery: the lateral mammary flap and the inferior gluteal flap. In: Transactions of the 7th International Congress of Plastic and Reconstructive Surgery; 1979, May; Rio de Janeiro, Brazil.

157. Elliott LF, Beegle PH, Hartrampf CR Jr. The lateral transverse thigh free flap: an alternative for autogenous-tissue breast reconstruction. Plast Reconstr Surg 1990;85:169–78.

158. Hartrampf CR Jr, Noel RT, Drazan L, et al. Ruben's fat pad for breast reconstruction: a peri-iliac soft tissue free flap. Plast Reconstr Surg 1994;93:402–7.

159. Taylor GI, Townsend P, Corlett R. Superiority of the deep circumflex iliac vessels as the supply for free groin flaps. Plast Reconstr Surg 1979;64:745–59.

160. Little JW III. Nipple-areola reconstruction. In: Spear SL, editor. Surgery of the breast: principles and art. Philadelphia: Lippincott-Raven; 1998. p. 661.

161. Wong RK, Banducci DR, Feldman S, et al. Prereconstruction tattooing eliminated the need for skin grafting in nipple areolar reconstruction. Plast Reconstr Surg 1993;92:547–9.

Practical Management Guidelines

CHAPTER 18

PRACTICAL MANAGEMENT GUIDELINES

1. Risk Evaluation: No Personal History of Cancer

2. Risk Evaluation: Nongenetic Factors

3. Risk Management Options: Nongenetic Risk

4. Risk Evaluation: Genetic/Familial Risk

5. Risk Management Options: Proven *BRCA1/2* Mutation Carrier

6. Evaluation for Ductal Lavage

7. Evaluation and Management after Ductal Lavage

8. Risk Evaluation of the Contralateral Breast: Past History of Breast Cancer

9. Risk Evaluation of the Contralateral Breast: Newly Diagnosed Breast Cancer

1. Risk Evaluation: No Personal History of Cancer

History
Age
Age menarche, menopause
Gravidity, parity, age 1st birth
HRT use: duration, type
Prior breast biopsy, diagnosis
Radiation exposure
Alcohol intake
Other major health problems

Physical Exam
Height and weight
Breast exam
    Degree of nodularity

Family History
Breast cancer
    Affected relative
    Age of onset
    Unilateral or bilateral
Ovarian cancer
    Affected relative
    Age of onset
Other cancers

Mammogram
BIRADS density
    Fatty
    Mixed
    Dense
    Extremely dense

Assessment of primary cause of risk → GENETIC/FAMILIAL

Assessment of primary cause of risk → OTHER

BIRADS = Breast Imaging Reporting and Data System; HRT = hormone replacement therapy.

2.   **Risk Evaluation: Nongenetic Factors**

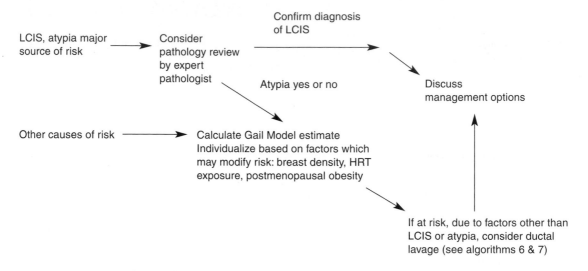

LCIS = lobular carcinoma in situ, HRT = hormone replacement therapy.

3.   **Risk Management Options: Nongenetic Risk**

Option	Risk Reduction	Favorable Candidates
Observation		
Monthly BSE; CBE twice per year; Annual mammogram	None; ~30% cancers diagnosed as DCIS; ~35% node positive	Limited risk elevation (Gail 5-year risk ≤ 2.5%); Older; Fatty/mixed density breasts; Major risks for other diseases
Tamoxifen		
	Overall: 49%; At risk due to atypia: 86%	Premenopausal women with Gail 5-year risk > 2%; Women at risk due to atypia or LCIS; Postmenopausal women with Gail risk > 3.0%, history of hysterectomy; Women with past history of ER-positive invasive or intraductal carcinoma not treated with endocrine therapy
Prophylactic Mastectomy		
	90%	Women with significant elevations in risk (Gail 5-year risk > 8%); Dense or extremely dense breasts; History of multiple biopsies; Severe anxiety regarding risk

BSE = breast self-examination; CBE = clinical breast examination; DCIS = ductal carcinoma in situ; ER = estrogen receptor; LCIS = lobular carcinoma in situ.

4.   Risk Evaluation: Genetic/Familial Risk

Personal History
Ovarlan or fallopian tube cancer
Breast cancer at < age 40 years
Ashkenazi ancestry,
    breast cancer at any age

→ Referral for genetic counseling

Models to estimate carrier probability
may be used prior to referral; see
Chapter 2

Family History
Breast and ovarian/fallopian tube cancer*
Male breast cancer
3 or more relatives with breast cancer*†
Early onset or bilateral breast cancer

→ Referral for genetic counseling

Models to estimate carrier
probability may be used prior to
referral; see Chapter 2

Family history not meeting criteria above

→ Estimate risk with Claus and
Gail Models; see algorithm 3
for management options

*History on same side of the family, maternal or paternal.
†Criteria for referral may be more liberal in those of Askenazi ancestry.

5.   Risk Management Options: Proven *BRCA1/2* Mutation Carrier

Option	Risk Reduction	Favorable Candidates
Observation		
Monthly BSE; Annual mammography beginning at ages 25–35; Consider MRI screening especially if dense breasts	None; High frequency of interval cancers in most reports	Young women who have not completed child bearing; Family history of later onset cancers
Tamoxifen	Uncertain; Perhaps more effective in *BRCA2* carriers due to higher rate of ER-positive disease	Carriers with a personal history of ER-positive cancer
Oophorectomy	Breast cancer: 50%; Ovarian cancer: 96%	Under age 50 years, completed child bearing; Family history of ovarian cancer
Prophylactic Mastectomy	90%	History of histologic or cytologic atypia; Dense breasts; Patient desire

BSE = breast self-examination; ER = estrogen receptor; MRI – magnetic resonance imaging.

6.   **Evaluation for Ductal Lavage**

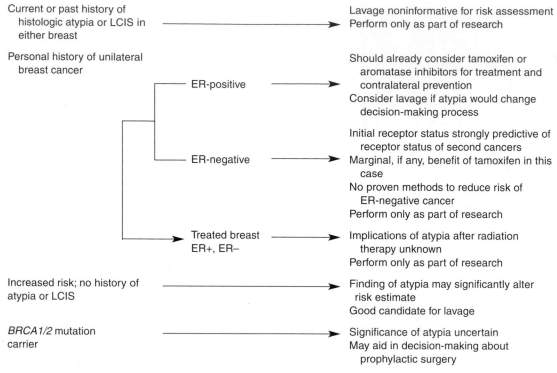

Current or past history of
histologic atypia or LCIS in   ———————————————▶   Lavage noninformative for risk assessment
either breast   Perform only as part of research

Personal history of unilateral
breast cancer   Should already consider tamoxifen or
                                                        aromatase inhibitors for treatment and
                        ER-positive   ————————▶   contralateral prevention
                                                     Consider lavage if atypia would change
                                                        decision-making process

                                                     Initial receptor status strongly predictive of
                                                        receptor status of second cancers
                        ER-negative   ————————▶   Marginal, if any, benefit of tamoxifen in this
                                                        case
                                                     No proven methods to reduce risk of
                                                        ER-negative cancer
                                                     Perform only as part of research

                        Treated breast ———————▶   Implications of atypia after radiation
                        ER+, ER–   therapy unknown
                                                     Perform only as part of research

Increased risk; no history of   ———————————————▶   Finding of atypia may significantly alter
atypia or LCIS   risk estimate
                                                     Good candidate for lavage

BRCA1/2 mutation   ———————————————▶   Significance of atypia uncertain
carrier   May aid in decision-making about
                                                        prophylactic surgery

ER = estrogen receptor; LCIS = lobular carcinoma in situ.

7.   **Evaluation and Management after Ductal Lavage**

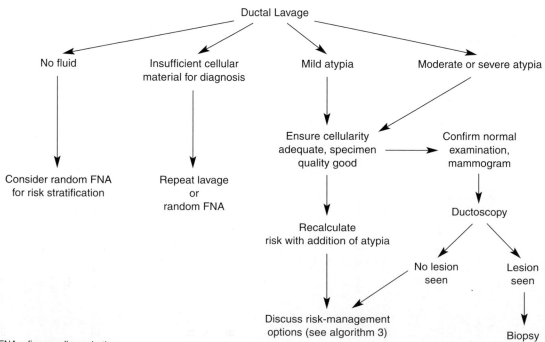

FNA = fine needle aspiration.

8.

Risk Evaluation of the Contralateral Breast: Past History of Breast Cancer

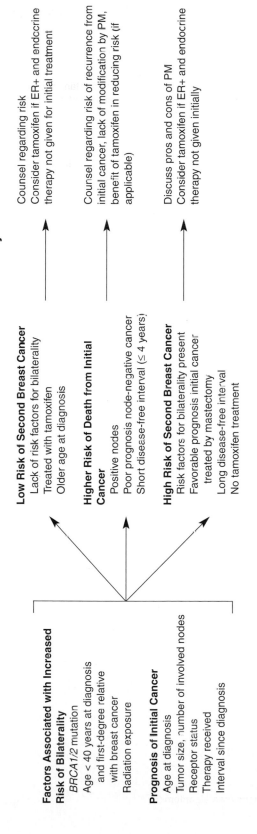

Factors Associated with Increased Risk of Bilaterality
BRCA1/2 mutation
Age < 40 years at diagnosis and first-degree relative with breast cancer
Radiation exposure

Prognosis of Initial Cancer
Age at diagnosis
Tumor size, number of involved nodes
Receptor status
Therapy received
Interval since diagnosis

Low Risk of Second Breast Cancer
Lack of risk factors for bilaterality
Treated with tamoxifen
Older age at diagnosis
→ Counsel regarding risk
Consider tamoxifen if ER+ and endocrine therapy not given for initial treatment

Higher Risk of Death from Initial Cancer
Positive nodes
Poor prognosis node-negative cancer
Short disease-free interval (≤ 4 years)
→ Counsel regarding risk of recurrence from initial cancer, lack of modification by PM, benefit of tamoxifen in reducing risk (if applicable)

High Risk of Second Breast Cancer
Risk factors for bilaterality present
Favorable prognosis initial cancer treated by mastectomy
Long disease-free interval
No tamoxifen treatment
→ Discuss pros and cons of PM
Consider tamoxifen if ER+ and endocrine therapy not given initially

ER = estrogen receptor; PM = prophylactic mastectomy.

9.

Risk Evaluation of the Contralateral Breast: Newly Diagnosed Breast Cancer

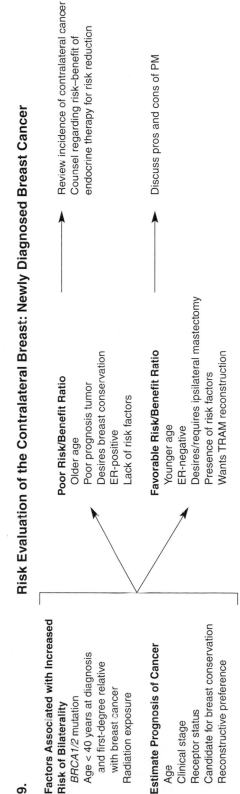

Factors Associated with Increased Risk of Bilaterality
BRCA1/2 mutation
Age < 40 years at diagnosis and first-degree relative with breast cancer
Radiation exposure

Estimate Prognosis of Cancer
Age
Clinical stage
Receptor status
Candidate for breast conservation
Reconstructive preference

Poor Risk/Benefit Ratio
Older age
Poor prognosis tumor
Desires breast conservation
ER-positive
Lack of risk factors
→ Review incidence of contralateral cancer
Counsel regarding risk–benefit of endocrine therapy for risk reduction

Favorable Risk/Benefit Ratio
Younger age
ER-negative
Desires/requires ipsilateral mastectomy
Presence of risk factors
Wants TRAM reconstruction
→ Discuss pros and cons of PM

ER = estrogen receptor; PM = prophylactic mastectomy; TRAM = transverse rectus abdominis myocutaneous flap.